COMMUNICATING IN BUSINESS

SECOND EDITION

ROBERT G. INSLEY

Kendall Hunt
publishing company

Book Team

Chairman and Chief Executive Officer   Mark C. Falb
President and Chief Operating Officer   Chad M. Chandlee
Vice President, Higher Education   David L. Tart
Director of Publishing Partnerships   Paul B. Carty
Senior Developmental Coordinator   Angela Willenbring
Vice President, Operations   Timothy J. Beitzel
Senior Permissions Editor   Caroline Kieler
Cover Designer   Jenifer Fensterman

Cover image © Shutterstock.com

Kendall Hunt
publishing company

www.kendallhunt.com
Send all inquiries to:
4050 Westmark Drive
Dubuque, IA 52004-1840

Copyright © 2014, 2017 by Kendall Hunt Publishing Company

ISBN 978-1-4652-9620-7

Printed in the United States of America

DEDICATION

Heartfelt thanks to Cheryl, Rachel, Laura, Katie, Alicia, Rob, Ronnie, Tim, Kathryne, Quinn, William, Henry, Caroline, Paula, and Lillian for your patience, support, and inspiration. You helped me turn a dream into a reality for which I am so grateful!

BRIEF CONTENTS

DETAILED CONTENTS

PART 6: EMPLOYMENT COMMUNICATION: THE JOB SEARCH PROCESS   539

CHAPTER 16: JOB SEARCH: PRE-INTERVIEW STEPS   541

PREFACE

BACKGROUND AND PHILOSOPHY

The vision for this book and accompanying website resources grew out of a perceived need for a comprehensive, introductory business communication textbook that would serve university, junior college, and community college students from a variety of disciplines, as well as corporate and government personnel. While the topic itself speaks most directly to business students and corporate and government personnel, the book offers a practical and valuable source for non-business majors who sense a need for some business training. For example, art majors and music majors who have ultimate responsibility for managing their careers will find the subject matter has practical application for them as well as for business majors and for corporate and government personnel. The content is presented in such a way that they will also be able to easily grasp the concepts presented here.

The number of ways organizational stakeholders communicate with each other is expanding rapidly which is evidenced by the popularity of social media, e-mail, texting, and wireless communication technologies. One result of this fluid environment is the challenge placed at the feet of business communication instructors and trainers to prepare students and employees to communicate effectively and efficiently in this ever-changing environment. This book is designed to assist instructors and trainers in meeting that objective.

This book is a culmination of the author's training in business communication, professional experiences, and strong desire to develop such a resource. While writing both the first and second editions of this book, the author drew from lessons learned during his graduate-level business communication training, undergraduate- and graduate-level teaching experiences, corporate and governmental consulting and training experiences, research efforts, and university and community service experiences.

ORGANIZATION OF THE TEXT

PART I: COMMUNICATION ESSENTIALS

Part I introduces several concepts important to students and organizations, alike. The chapter topics range from communicating in organizations and business etiquette to intercultural communication. Thus, Part I sets down several basic concepts essential to communicating effectively in organizations before it moves into more specific communication skill sets such as business communication technology, business writing, business presentations, and the like.

Chapter 1, *Communicating in Organizations*, provides a clear understanding of select aspects of organizational communications. This objective is accomplished through presentation of the following topics: the quality of communication in organizations, setting a strong communication base, evaluating communication, informal and formal communication, formal communication networks, and open communication environments.

Chapter 2, *Communicating Appropriately: Business Etiquette*, emphasizes the need for guidelines for how people should interact with each other in the business place. Specific business etiquette guidelines are presented. These objectives are accomplished through presentation of the following topics: introduction to business etiquette, business etiquette in the office, and business etiquette outside of the office.

Chapter 3, *Intercultural Communication*, emphasizes the importance of knowing how to communicate respectfully and effectively with people from other countries and cultures. This objective is accomplished through presentation of the following topics: global and domestic intercultural communication challenges, cultural considerations, language considerations, nonverbal considerations, and intercultural communication and international business sources.

PART II: BUSINESS COMMUNICATION TECHNOLOGY

Part II introduces readers to a wide range of timely communication technology concepts and issues. The chapter topics include communication technologies and social media. Thus, Part II sets down the communication technologies base before moving into more specific communication skill sets such as business writing, business presentations, communicating collaboratively, and the like.

Chapter 4, *Communication Technologies*, focuses on an overview of communication technologies and how to use them appropriately and effectively. These objectives are accomplished through presentation of the following topics: keeping up with technological developments, significant communication technology developments of the past, the Internet and World Wide Web, communicating via wireless technologies, using communication technologies effectively, and some cautious communication technology predictions. Communication technologies are also discussed in several other chapters. For example, communication technologies that pertain specifically to business reports are presented in the report writing chapter. Communication technologies pertaining to presentations are presented in the business presentations chapters.

There is even a separate chapter on writing electronically (e.g., texting, websites, social networking sites, etc.).

Chapter 5, *Social Media*, focuses on how social media platforms are currently being used in organizations with special focus on the more commonly-used platforms and how to write effective posts. These objectives are accomplished through presentation of the following topics: social media overview, the role of social media in organizations, social media writing suggestions, and social media netiquette.

PART III: BUSINESS WRITING

Part III introduces readers to the wide range of business messages and documents. Included here are chapter topics ranging from electronic writing and planning, drafting, and revising documents to business letters, memos, and reports. Thus, Part III addresses a specific business communication skill set—business writing skills.

Chapter 6, *Writing Electronically*, provides information pertaining to when and how to write electronic messages and documents. These objectives are accomplished through presentation of the following topics: electronic writing in organizations, writing effective e-mail messages, instant messages, text messages, websites, and choosing the right medium.

Chapter 7, *Planning & Drafting Business Documents*, provides information pertaining to the first two steps of the writing process—planning and drafting—as they pertain to business messages and documents. These objectives are accomplished through presentation of the following topics: how academic writing differs from business writing, stage one of the writing process (planning: defining your purpose, analyzing your audience, organizing your ideas, and choosing the best medium) and stage two of the writing process (drafting: getting started, moving past writer's block, drafting to support your purpose, types of supporting detail, drafting with your audience in mind, creating goodwill, drafting with organization in mind, building paragraphs, and managing the drafting process in organizations).

Chapter 8, *Revising Business Documents*, provides information about the third step of the writing process—revising—as it pertains to business messages and documents. This objective is accomplished through presentation of the following topics: stage three of the writing process (revising: revising for organization, revising for your audience--style and tone, proofreading, and managing the revision process in organizations).

Chapter 9, *Business Letters & Memos*, provides information pertaining to how to write effective business letters and memos. These objectives are accomplished through presentation of the following topics: written communication in organizations, the roles of letters and memos in organizations, impact of writing basics on letter and memo quality, business letters, business letter styles, business letter components, writing strategies, writing styles, and business memos.

Chapter 10, *Business Reports*, provides information pertaining to how to write effective business reports. This objective is accomplished through presentation of the following topics: description of business reports, the role of business reports in organizations, characteristics of business reports, research for report writing purposes, business report categories and types, the key components of formal business reports, report coherence, and electronic tools that support report development.

PART IV: BUSINESS PRESENTATIONS

Part IV introduces readers to the business presentation process. Included here are chapter topics ranging from developing business presentations to delivering business presentations. Thus, Part IV addresses another specific business communication skillset—business presentation skills.

Chapter 11, *Developing Business Presentations*, provides information pertaining to the stages and activities involved in planning, preparing, and practicing business presentations. These objectives are accomplished through presentation of the following topics: why business presentations are given, why you should develop good presentation skills, benefits of effective presentations, components of effective presentations, your feelings about giving presentations, planning business presentations, and preparing business presentations.

Chapter 12, *Delivering Business Presentations*, provides information pertaining to delivering presentations, question-and-answer sessions, and evaluating your presentations. These objectives are accomplished through presentation of the following topics: the final hours leading up to the presentation, presentation anxiety, delivering business presentations, conducting effective question-and-answer sessions, and evaluating your presentations.

PART V: COMMUNICATING COLLABORATIVELY

Part V introduces readers to concepts involving collaborative communication. Included here are chapter topics ranging from listening to communicating in business teams and communicating in business meetings.

Chapter 13, *Listening*, provides information ranging from the important role listening plays in organizations to the various aspects of listening. These objectives are accomplished through presentation of the following topics: the role of listening in organizations, the effects of good listening on individuals' careers, listening effectively when communicating electronically, the nature of listening, common barriers to effective listening, and recommended listening techniques.

Chapter 14, *Communicating in Business Teams*, provides information ranging from the role teams play in organizations to aspects of communicating effectively on teams. These objectives are accomplished through presentation of the following topics: the role of teams in organizations, team development, team member styles, team member roles, team leaders, effective communication in teams, writing teams, online collaborative writing tools, and virtual writing.

Chapter 15, *Communicating in Business Meetings*, provides information ranging from the role meetings play in organizations to aspects of communicating effectively in meetings. These objectives are accomplished through presentation of the following topics: the role of meetings in organizations, reasons for holding business meetings, business meeting approaches, obstacles to effective business meetings, business meeting agendas, and communicating effectively in business meetings.

PART VI: EMPLOYMENT COMMUNICATION: THE JOB SEARCH PROCESS

Part VI introduces readers to the seven-step job search process, with special emphasis on the communication aspects.

Chapter 16, *Job Search: Pre-Interview Steps*, provides information pertaining to steps 1–5 of the job search process—making the right career choice, locating job prospects, researching organizations and jobs, writing cover letters, and developing résumés. These objectives are accomplished through presentation of the following topics: step 1 (making the right career choice), step 2 (locating job prospects), step 3 (researching organizations and jobs, opportunities to persuade recruiters), step 4 (writing persuasive cover letters), and step 5 (developing effective résumés).

Chapter 17, *Job Search: Interviews & Beyond*, provides information pertaining to steps 6–7 of the job search process (interviewing and developing effective follow-up correspondence) and career management. These objectives are accomplished through presentation of the following topics: step 6—interviewing convincingly: interviewing goals, job candidates and recruiters, types of interviews, preparing for job interviews, job interviews on deck, job interviews on stage, and interviewing suggestions; step 7--developing effective follow-up correspondence, checking back with recruiters, reasons for rejection following job interviews, and managing your career.

STUDENT-ORIENTED TEXTBOOK FEATURES

A common body of features designed to facilitate student learning and to help instructors and trainers assess student performance are located in all the textbook chapters.

- **Learning Outcomes** inform students of desired outcomes and provide instructors with a base to make curriculum decisions and choose/develop performance assessment instruments.
- **Select Key Terms** are presented in *Wordles* (word clouds) on the first page of each chapter.
- **Benefits of Learning About (Chapter Title)** sections list benefits students will realize from learning the material.
- **Chapter Introductions** provide a clear overview for each chapter.
- **Practical Headings** inform students clearly of what they are about to read.
- **Bolded Key Terms** in the text signal students to pay special attention to them.
- **Running Glossaries** provide key concepts in side margins.
- **Section Summaries** highlight key points made in each section.
- **Figures** contain interesting and important information pertaining to chapter topics.
- **Illustrations and Photos** visually illustrate chapter concepts.
- **QR codes/URLs** within the chapters route students to additional information pertaining to chapter topics.
- **Website Icons** remind students of related student web content.
- **Sources** provide students ways (via websites, books, etc.) to locate additional information on a number of topics.
- **Glossary** lists key concepts.

STUDENT WEB CONTENT

Students have access to numerous resources and activities at the textbook website. These resources and activities are designed to enrich student learning and, in some instances, serve as performance assessment instruments. The Web access code is located on the inside front cover of the textbook. These resources and activities include:

- **Short Write-Ups** briefly outline the chapter contents.
- **Learning Outcomes** remind students of desired results.
- **Chapter Outlines** provide students with an overview of the chapter.
- **QR code/URL Titles** provide a convenient list of the articles and videos referenced in chapter margins, along with related URLs.
- **Interactive Exercises** engage students and test their retention and understanding of important course concepts via drag-and-drop and gaming exercises. A short assessment follows each exercise.
- **Preview Tests** briefly assess students' understanding of key concepts, leading them to areas in need of further study and leading instructors to areas in need of further coverage.

- **Chapter Assessment Tests** is an end-of-chapter activity for students designed to identify areas of strength and weakness as well as signal instructors to topics in need of further coverage.
- **YouTube Videos** provide an interesting way for students to reflect on and reinforce course topics and to learn and better retain information. Each video is followed by a short assessment.
- **Interactive Glossary** provides another way to review key terms via interactive flash cards.
- **Select Key Terms** are presented in an interesting way via *Wordles* (word clouds).
- **Power Point Slides** are available to print and take to class or to use for review purposes.
- **Writing Mechanics Rules and Guidelines** provide students with a source to consult when they have questions regarding grammar, punctuation, capitalization, number usage, abbreviations, and spelling.

INSTRUCTOR/TRAINER WEB CONTENT

Instructors and trainers have access to several resources at the online Instructor Resource Center. These include:

- **Sample Syllabi** for semester-long and quarter-long courses.
- **Questions Worth Reflecting On** provide a number of short-answer questions instructors and trainers can use at the start of classes and workshops to focus students' and employees' thoughts on the topic.
- **Self-Assessment Exercises** provide instructors with instruments that engage the students with the subject matter. These exercises could be assigned as homework, completed in class, or used to introduce topics.
- **Cases** provide a tool to engage the students with the topic. They are especially effective when completed in groups in class or used for class discussions.
- **Review Questions** are short-answer questions for instructors and trainers to use in classes and workshops or assign as homework.
- **Discussion Questions** typically require students to give more thought and prepare/give longer answers than review questions.
- **QR code/URL Titles** provide a convenient list articles and videos referenced in chapter margins, along with related URLs.
- **PowerPoint Slides** include abbreviated student versions, along with extensive instructor notes.
- **Additional Sample Business Letters** can be assigned, integrated into class activities, used as examples in class, or integrated into course exams.
- **Team Projects** provide sample projects, including detailed descriptions, forms, and assessment instruments.
- **Test Bank** provides instructors and trainers with a selection of short-answer questions, discussion questions, multiple-choice questions, and true/false questions for each chapter.

ACKNOWLEDGMENTS

I want to take this opportunity to thank the Kendall Hunt Publishing Company team that helped make this book a reality; especially Paul Carty, director of publishing partnerships; Angela Willenbring, senior editor; Sheri Hosek, senior production editor; Kara McArthur, copy editor; Anne Luty, project manager; Caroline Kieler, senior permissions editor; Jenifer Fensterman, cover designer; Kendra Klein, digital project manager; and Christina Neuwoehner, publishing solutions representative for all their support and encouragement. Special thanks to my wife Cheryl for her assistance developing textbook figures, locating textbook illustrations and photos, and developing significant portions of the student and instructor/trainer Web content. Added thanks to Katie Meador for reviewing websites and images throughout the book and Venkat Sai Gollapudi for his assistance with revising the student and instructor/trainer Web content. Couldn't have done it without you guys! In addition, many thanks to my early teachers and mentors Clara Hoffman, Denton Ricketts, Evelyn Knouse, and Nancy Compson for setting the educational foundation that made this book and so much more possible. Sincere thanks to my mentor and dear friend Larry Hartman who was the inspiration for this ongoing project. Last, but not least, heartfelt thanks to my family for their patience, support, and inspiration which was and continues to be so valued and appreciated.

–RGI

ABOUT THE AUTHOR

Robert Gayle Insley is coordinator for the business communication course offerings in the College of Business at the University of North Texas. He received his B.S. and M.S. degrees in Business Education from Bowling Green State University and his Ed.D. in Business Education, with a specialization in Business Communication, from Northern Illinois University. He was a high school business teacher and wrestling coach before working as a software quality reviewer for Zenith Data Systems. Next, he turned his attention to university teaching, research, and service. Robert is a senior faculty fellow in the *Next Generation* Course Redesign Program at the University of North Texas—a program that promotes engaged learning instructional strategies. He is also faculty advisor for the Alpha Nu chapter of Phi Chi Theta business and economics fraternity. He has won several university and college awards, including the university Honor Professor Award, College of Business Outstanding Teacher Awards, and the university Extraordinary Professional Service Award. He is a member of honor societies in business and business education.

Robert has over 30 years of experience teaching business communication courses and has taught organizational behavior, management concepts, and other business courses as well. He has served on several Doctoral dissertation committees and numerous university, college, and department committees. Over the years he has consulted and conducted training sessions for a number of corporations and governmental agencies, including the Ford Motor Company, UPS, Neiman Marcus, and Boeing Electronics.

Robert has conducted research on a variety of business communication topics, instructional pedagogies, engaged learning, communication technologies, university space management, and business ethics. He has had articles published in the *Journal of Business Communication, Business Communication Quarterly, The Bulletin of the Association for Business Communication, Journal of Business Ethics, Journal of International Technology and Information Management, Journal of Organizational Behavior Education, Journal of Business & Entrepreneurship, Journal of Computer Information Systems*, and elsewhere. Robert has written supplements for numerous business communication, organizational behavior, principles of management, introduction to business, and labor relations and negotiations textbooks. He has also given presentations and chaired/moderated sessions at numerous international and national professional conferences including the Association for Business Communication, Decision Sciences Institute, Comparative International Educational Society, American Educational Research Association, Society for Research in Higher Education, Sloan Consortium Blended Learning Conferences, and World Universities Forum Conference.

In addition, Robert has served on several of the public school district bond committees in his home town including chairing the technology and security subcommittee and has also served on several school district bond oversight committees and on ad hoc technology committees.

PART 1

BUSINESS COMMUNICATION ESSENTIALS

COMMUNICATING IN ORGANIZATIONS

1

LEARNING OUTCOMES

After reading this chapter, you should be able to:

1. Discuss how to set a strong communication base.

2. Describe the ways organizations, stakeholders, and others are affected by communication quality.

3. Discuss how to communicate effectively.

4. Discuss how to communicate efficiently.

5. Describe informal communication in organizations.

6. Discuss formal communication networks in organizations.

© Qvasimodo art/Shutterstock.com

BENEFITS OF LEARNING ABOUT COMMUNICATING IN ORGANIZATIONS

1. Organizations prefer to hire and retain individuals who are good communicators.

2. Organizations prefer to hire and retain individuals who understand the impact of good communication in the business place.

3. Good communication skills can contribute to your career growth, whereas poor communication skills can easily hinder your job stability and advancement potential.

4. Good communication skills can have positive effects on your personal life (e.g., fewer mistakes and misunderstandings, better relationships, etc.).

SELECT KEY TERMS

INTRODUCTION

The quality of communication in organizations affects organizations at large as well as their employees, customers and clients, investors, suppliers, economies at all levels, and societies. Businesspeople are encouraged to work continuously on improving their communication skills and to be ethical, congenial communicators. Furthermore, they should develop an assertive communication style, team communication skills, intercultural communication skills, and keep up with communication technology developments. In addition, they should have an appreciation for the role of informal communication as well as formal communication in organizations. Lastly, businesspeople are encouraged to have a strong understanding of formal communication networks in organizations as they pertain to downward communication, upward communication, horizontal communication, and diagonal communication.

The intent of this chapter is to provide you with a clear understanding of select aspects of organizational communications. This goal is realized through discussions regarding the following topics: the quality of communication in organizations, setting a strong base, evaluating communication, informal and formal communication, formal communication networks, and open communication environments. The information pertaining to the above-mentioned topics is reinforced by several student website resources including *Power-Point slides, preview tests, chapter assessment tests, YouTube videos, interactive exercises,* and the *interactive glossary.*

Before we go any farther, however, let's make sure we are clear on two terms that are used extensively throughout the book—communication and business.

Importance of Communication in an Organization http://www.managementstudyguide.com/importance-of-communication.htm

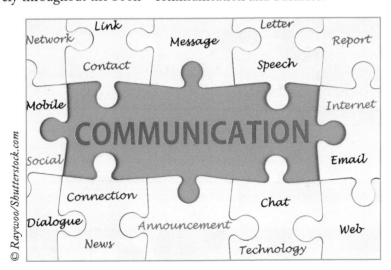

Communication is the process by which information is exchanged in writing, verbally, and/or nonverbally through a common system of language, gestures, symbols, or signals via traditional and electronic communication media. In the business place, communication is considered effective when it results in a common understanding between communication partners and the communication's intended results are achieved. The chances of realizing effective communication are improved when each communication partner attempts to understand the other. The common terms for this are *encoding* and *decoding*, where encoding is tied to message senders, and decoding to message receivers. Willingness to learn about your communication partners typically results in more effective word choice, tone, and media selection and in clearer understanding.

communication
The lifeblood of all organizations involving constant exchanges of information through traditional and electronic communication media.

Communicating Within
The Organization
http://www.bizmove.
com/skills/m8m.htm

Communication in organizations typically falls into one of three categories—written, verbal, and nonverbal. Written communication ranges from letters, memos, reports, and directives to e-mail messages, blogs, instant messages, text messages, and social media posts such as tweets. Verbal communication ranges from face-to-face conversations, presentations, and phone conversations to interviews, meetings, and video chats. Nonverbal communication ranges from use of body language, voice, and time to use of space and the physical environment. Nonverbal communication is typically categorized as shown in Figure 1-1.

FIGURE 1–1: NONVERBAL COMMUNICATION CATEGORIES

- **Kinesics.** The use of body language. Kinesics is considered unconscious language, thus honest language. Examples of kinesics include posture, gestures, head movements, facial expressions, eye movements, touch, and physical appearance. For example, to show respect and attentiveness during face-to-face conversations, American workers maintain eye contact with superiors, while in similar situations Japanese subordinates lower their eyes.
- **Paralanguage.** The use of voice. Paralanguage is also considered unconscious language, thus honest language. Examples of paralanguage are volume, pitch, rhythm, tone, intensity, yawning, throat clearing, grunting, laughing, crying, verbal fillers ("ah" and "um"), and pauses or periods of silence between utterances. For example, if an American businessperson speaks softly and quietly, some believe he or she possesses little self-confidence or is hiding something. Likewise, if an American businessperson speaks loudly, some believe he or she is boisterous, pushy, overconfident, or rude.
- **Chronemics.** The use of time. Message effectiveness is often affected by the promptness or delay in delivery or response. For example, when a worker responds both accurately and quickly to a directive from a supervisor, the worker's actions are typically viewed positively. To delay the response may be viewed as irresponsible or disrespectful behavior. American and Japanese businesspeople consider those arriving at business meetings late to be rude, while Latin American businesspeople purposely arrive late to meetings for fear of appearing too anxious to make a deal.
- **Proxemics.** The use of space. Proxemics addresses the distance people prefer to maintain between each other while conducting conversations. For example, North American businesspeople are uncomfortable when conversations are conducted at close quarters. They prefer to conduct face-to-face business conversations at a distance of approximately 30 inches (an arm's length), unlike their Venezuelan counterparts who prefer to maintain a distance of inches.
- **Environment.** The use of the physical environment. Environmental messages include office design, size, location, tidiness, temperature, colors, and furniture. For example, within American organizations, large, corner offices typically communicate higher status than do interior offices or cubicles. In addition, sitting areas make it possible for businesspeople to move out from behind their desks and conduct less formal conversations with visitors.

Other forms of nonverbal communication include objects, images, graphs, charts, photos, and videos. For example, the use of photos and videos in business for marketing purposes has grown along with the popularity of social media platforms such as *Instagram, Pinterest, Facebook,* and *YouTube.*

To avoid confusion before moving forward, let's clear up the meanings of two pairs of business terms that will be used interchangeably throughout this book. The first pair includes the terms *business* and *organization,* while the second pair includes the terms *customer* and *client.* The terms *business* and *organization* will be used interchangeably in reference to enterprises that provide goods and services to customers and clients whether for profit or not for profit. The terms *customer* and *client* will be used interchangeably in reference to purchasers of products and services.

THE QUALITY OF COMMUNICATION IN ORGANIZATIONS

The quality of communication within organizations typically has a ripple effect, both internally and externally. Unfortunately, this ripple effect is typically as far reaching when the communication quality is negative as when it is positive. In addition to the organizations themselves, others affected include employees, customers and clients, investors and suppliers, economies, and societies.

WAYS ORGANIZATIONS ARE AFFECTED

Communication in organizations involves constant exchanges of information through traditional means, ranging from face-to-face conversations and meetings to telephone conversations and reports as well as involving electronic means, ranging from e-mail messages, text messages, and instant messages to videoconferences, tweets, blogs, and social networks. Communication plays a vital role in organizations, being necessary for them to function. This essential role has led some to refer to communication as "the lifeblood of an organization."

© Igor Petrov/ Shutterstock.com

An organization's ability to achieve its goals depends, in large part, on how well its employees communicate. If its employees possess good communication skills, an organization can meet its goals more often. However, when employees' communication skills are poor, the organization's ability to achieve its goals is threatened. Employees who are good communicators support an organization's ability to achieve its goals by contributing to higher productivity and profits, improved stakeholder relations, and positive employee morale. These benefits, in turn, typically result in lower absenteeism and higher employee retention.

Wise organizational leaders promote effective communication throughout their organizations. They recruit, hire, retain, and promote good communicators. They also provide effective communication training when needed. And last, but not least, they themselves are good communicators who lead by example.

WAYS EMPLOYEES ARE AFFECTED

Wise businesspeople understand the benefits of effective communication as well as the negative ramifications of poor communications. Generally speaking, the higher an employee's position in an organization, the greater the amount of work time he or she spends communicating. While entry-level employees routinely spend approximately 25 percent of their work time communicating, top-level executives spend the vast majority their work time communicating.

Employees' ability to communicate affects them even before they are hired. How so? For example, your ability to communicate effectively with your professors and classmates affects the amount of knowledge and level of skills you acquire while earning your degree. In addition, your ability to communicate effectively affects the outcome of your networking efforts with fellow students, professors, and others. Furthermore, your chances of being invited to job interviews depend directly on the quality of the cover letters and résumés you develop. Finally, your ability to interview persuasively and write effective thank-you letters also increases your chances of receiving job offers.

Once on the job, an employee's ability to communicate effectively in a variety of communication settings is extremely important. Those who are good communicators cause fewer problems than their counterparts, which often results in increased job stability and career growth opportunities. In contrast, employees whose communication skills are poor to average cannot necessarily expect a high level of job stability, and employers often view them less favorably when making career advancement decisions.

WAYS CUSTOMERS AND CLIENTS ARE AFFECTED

Customers and clients are affected directly by the quality of communication they receive from organizations. If the communication they receive from an organization is effective, they frequently enjoy transactions that are free of misunderstandings, mistakes, and frustrations. As a result, the organization benefits from positive customer/client relations and public relations. If the quality of communication customers and clients receive from an organization is poor, they are often subjected to mistakes and frustrations. As a result, the organization may suffer from lost current and future business, not to mention poor public relations.

WAYS INVESTORS AND SUPPLIERS ARE AFFECTED

Investors and suppliers are affected directly by the quality of communication they receive from organizations. If the communication they receive from an organization is effective, they frequently enjoy transactions that are free of misunderstandings, mistakes, and frustrations. As a result, the organization benefits from positive investor/supplier relations and public relations. If the quality of communication customers receive from an organization is poor, the customers may be subjected to mistakes and frustrations. As a result, the organization may suffer from lost current and future business and poor public relations.

WAYS ECONOMIES ARE AFFECTED

When organizations succeed, due in part to effective communication, economies at all levels (local, state, regional, national, and international) typically benefit. For example, successful organizations generate a greater number of tax dollars for their communities. Successful organizations contribute to reduced unemployment rates as well. This, in turn, increases spending power, which leads to increased property values, among many other benefits.

These successes can even positively impact the economies of other countries, for example, with facilities located abroad and for those that conduct extensive trade. For example, if a prospering U.S.-based manufacturing company purchases a percentage of its component parts from a supplier in another country, that supplier and, in turn, the economies affected by it benefit from the success of the U.S.-based company.

WAYS SOCIETIES ARE AFFECTED

As indicated previously, a direct correlation exists between effective communication and organizational success, which, in turn, contributes to local, state, regional, national, and international economies. As economic benefits unfold, societies typically reap rewards. For example, when successful organizations pay taxes and make charitable donations, many societal needs can be met. For example, more monies can be routed to community services such as police and fire departments, parks departments, and social services. Furthermore, increased employment opportunities that typically accompany organizational success and growth decrease the drain on public support services and free up funds for use elsewhere.

Organizational success contributes to societies in other ways. For example, when employees' spending power increases, they typically contribute more and larger sums to charities. These funds, in turn, strengthen communities by improving their citizens' quality of life.

SUMMARY: SECTION 1— COMMUNICATION QUALITY AND ORGANIZATIONS

- Individuals' ability to communicate effectively affects their potential to learn, network, secure employment, and advance their careers.
- Organizations' ability to succeed and be profitable depends on their employees' ability and willingness to communicate effectively.
- Local, state, regional, national, and international economies benefit from the successes of organizations whose workforces are composed of good communicators.
- Societies benefit from the successes of organizations that have good communicators in their workforce.

SETTING A STRONG BASE: PRACTICAL SUGGESTIONS

While most of this book is devoted to discussions of specific communication techniques that will make you a stronger writer, listener, presenter, etc., let's first look at some practical suggestions to help you achieve and maintain your goal of being an effective communicator. These suggestions include: maintaining an appreciation for how challenging communicating effectively really is, working on improving your communication skills throughout your career, considering the impact of location on communication effectiveness, considering the impact of timing on communication effectiveness, analyzing your audience, being a congenial communicator, being an ethical communicator, choosing the best communication medium for the situation, choosing your most effective writing tool, developing an assertive communication style, developing effective team communication skills, developing effective intercultural communication skills, keeping up with communication technology developments, and using humor cautiously. Excellent communicators typically share most of these traits, whereas some, but not all, are noticeable in average-to-poor communicators.

MAINTAIN AN APPRECIATION FOR HOW CHALLENGING COMMUNICATING EFFECTIVELY REALLY IS

Good communicators understand that communicating effectively in any setting is a complex process with many obstacles and challenges. They view communication as a series of skillsets that they must learn, then practice and refine.

Effective communicators do not view communication simply as a series of commonsense activities. They do not believe that since they have been communicating in various forms since birth that no improvement is needed. Listening provides a perfect example of this point. We could easily dismiss the need to work on improving our listening skills by convincing ourselves that since we have been listening to others since birth, we need no improvement in that area. The truth is that effective listening is hard work that requires specific skills, knowledge of common barriers to listening, and the right attitude. It also requires continuous effort.

WORK TO IMPROVE YOUR COMMUNICATION SKILLS THROUGHOUT YOUR CAREER

© enciktep/Shutterstock.com

Good communicators understand that being an effective communicator with some degree of consistency is a career-long challenge that requires continuous practice and refinement. Communicators also understand the importance of identifying their specific communication strengths and weaknesses so that their efforts to improve are focused in the right direction. In turn, these communicators become even more skilled by working to overcome their communication weaknesses, while reinforcing their communication strengths. They also add communication skills to meet the constantly changing communication expectations of the domestic and global business communities. Keeping current with communication technologies is an excellent example of the latter point.

CONSIDER THE IMPACT OF LOCATION ON COMMUNICATION EFFECTIVENESS

Good communicators understand that effective business communication doesn't always take place in traditional workplace settings (e.g., an office, conference room, etc.). While some businesspeople communicate most effectively in such locations, others are able to communicate more creatively, effectively, and efficiently in nontraditional locations such as the beach or in a scenic mountain park.

You obviously won't always have a choice regarding where you communicate. However, when you do, consider communicating from the location where you can do your best job. First, determine the location or locations that best serve you. Then, enjoy the fact that today's mobile communication technologies make it possible for us to develop, transmit, receive, and respond to communication from a myriad of locations ranging from our parks and beaches to submarines and the space station.

CONSIDER THE IMPACT OF TIMING ON COMMUNICATION EFFECTIVENESS

Good communicators understand that timing plays a role in developing, transmitting, receiving, and responding to messages. Most of us are not the effective communicators we could be when we are tired or emotionally upset. Sometimes we need to get some rest or cool off before proceeding with the communication. For example, if you need to write an important letter and you are tired, wait until you are rested to write it if your schedule allows. Or, you receive an e-mail message that angers you. Instead of immediately writing a scathing response, cool off before responding.

In regard to timing, it is good to be in tune with that time of day or night when you develop your best documents and messages. Obviously, you won't always be able to capitalize on your most effective time, but sometimes you will. When these opportunities present themselves, use them to write those documents and messages that require best effort.

Good communication practice suggests that communication partners make efforts to understand each other. With this in mind, be careful not to get into a habit of forcing your communication partners into your schedule. For example, before calling them to discuss an important matter, consider the impact of timing on the effectiveness of the communication. If your communication partner is not a morning person, an 8 a.m. call will likely not be as productive as a call placed at 2 p.m. Or, if you schedule a meeting at 4:30 on a Friday afternoon, it is not going to be as productive as hoped for because most people's thoughts have shifted, in part, to the upcoming weekend.

ANALYZE YOUR AUDIENCE

Audience analysis suggests a willingness to get to know several factors about your communication partner. Audience analysis in organizations is more important today than ever before. The lightning speed of technological advances makes information instantaneous and the amount overwhelming. By analyzing your communication audiences, you will be better able to determine the appropriate words, strategy, and medium to use for each situation. In turn, with your analysis you should be able to minimize misunderstandings, while maximizing understanding. Figure 1-2 contains several audience analysis factors for you to explore.

audience analysis
Refers to both encoding and decoding.

BE A CONGENIAL COMMUNICATOR

Congeniality in this context means communication partners maintain friendly, pleasant relationships with each other during and after disagreements. Being a congenial communicator is important in organizations where it is imperative that stakeholders get along with each other.

FIGURE 1–2: AUDIENCE ANALYSIS FACTORS

- **Audience's Personal Qualities or Characteristics.** Individual or group, age, educational background, knowledge level.
- **Audience's Personal Barriers.** Biases, stereotypes, prejudices, and fears (e.g., computer fear).
- **Audience's Professional Qualities or Characteristics.** Job title, organizational position, degree of authority in the organization.
- **Audience's View of Communication Partner.** Previous communication with each other, degree of personal and professional respect for communication partner.
- **Audience's Expectations.** Message's format, length and degree of formality; communication media preferences and capabilities; what they hope to gain from the message.
- **Audience's Needs.** Degree of detail needed to promote common understanding, uses for the information, need for feedback, questions that might be asked.
- **Audience's Anticipated Reaction to Message.** Reaction to the message, degree of receptiveness to the message, time to be most or least receptive to the message, most effective message strategy, likelihood that desired action will be taken.
- **Audience's Communication Climate.** Open (trusting, informal, free flowing) or closed (rigid, formal), information overload, gender-related communication differences.

Of course, being a congenial communicator is easier said than done! Being congenial requires us to keep emotions in check and behave like a mature adult. Those who act otherwise run the risk of burning their bridges, implying they destroy relationships as a result of their actions.

Key to being a congenial communicator is your ability to control your emotions when a message or exchange is not to your liking or your communication partner is emotionally aggressive. If you anticipate a strong difference of opinion with your communication partner, focus on positive points in his or her message. When you anticipate an emotional reaction, enter the communication process when you can remain calm. If you find yourself in a situation where words become unexpectedly heated, remind yourself to remain calm and mature and be the professional you are paid to be. If these reminders do not keep you on the right track, walk away for a few minutes and return after you cool off and your communication partner has calmed down.

BE AN ETHICAL COMMUNICATOR

Ethics refers to suitable behavior. Being an ethical communicator implies that we will treat our communication partners honestly, openly, and fairly. Unethical communication typically leads to loss of trust and respect, which strike at the heart of effective communication.

While each of us has little to no control over the ethical behavior of our communication partners, we can at least attempt to be ethical communicators ourselves. Several suggestions regarding how to do so are presented in Figure 1-3.

FIGURE 1–3: COMMUNICATORS' ETHICAL RESPONSIBILITIES

- Treat communication partners with respect.
- Do not be manipulative.
- Do not use an abusive tone (e.g., aggressive, condescending, patronizing).
- Avoid taking advantage of communication partners whose command of the language or your company's jargon is not as good as yours.
- Communicate clearly and directly so your messages cannot be intentionally misinterpreted.
- Do not be a sexist communicator.
- Remove biases, prejudices, and stereotypes from your communication.

CHOOSE THE BEST COMMUNICATION MEDIUM FOR THE SITUATION

We are not all equally skilled and comfortable with all the communication media available today. However, you are strongly encouraged to make the best media choice for each communication situation even it is a medium with which you do not feel sufficiently skilled or comfortable. Be open to using communication media outside of your comfort zone when it is needed to enhance communication. For example: Some individuals like the ease of sending e-mail, but are uncomfortable when communicating orally. If such a person needs to communicate routine information and the message is brief, e-mail would be an effective medium. However, if the message is complex and/or controversial and has a number of discussion points, the more effective medium would be a face-to-face conversation. You are encouraged to be flexible when making communication media choices. Work toward becoming skilled and comfortable with a wide range of communication media.

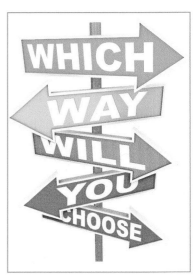

© iQoncept/Shutterstock.com

CHOOSE YOUR MOST EFFECTIVE WRITING TOOL

Some people do their best writing when they dictate their messages and documents. Others find they do their best writing on a keyboard. Some even prefer a manual keyboard to an electric or electronic keyboard. Still others do their best writing using a pen while others benefit most from dictating their messages and documents using speech recognition software such as *Dragon Natural Speaking*, *Speechnotes*, *Braina*, or a speech recognition app such as *Speechlogger*.

Do you know which writing tool supports your best writing? Is it a keyboard, a pen, speech recognition software, or a speech recognition app? If you are unsure, determine which one best supports your writing efforts and use it as often as possible.

DEVELOP AN ASSERTIVE COMMUNICATION STYLE

Communication styles typically range from aggressive to assertive to nonassertive. People who have an *aggressive communication style* are expressive, self-confident, and often take unfair advantage of others, whereas those who have a *nonassertive (passive) communication style* exhibit timid and self-denying behavior.[1] Neither style is consistently effective. For example, aggressive communicators rarely form lasting business relationships with their communication partners, and nonassertive communicators are rarely respected and are often taken advantage of.

In the business place, the *assertive communication style* is considered to be the most effective of the three styles. Individuals who have an assertive communication style are expressive and self-enhancing.[2] They are willing to express their interests and needs without being aggressive and without taking advantage of others. Assertive communicators develop their communication points carefully and logically. They are also tactful and courteous in their choice of words and how they deliver them. The same can be said about their visual nonverbal cues. In addition, when speaking with others in person, assertive speakers are careful not to invade their comfort zones. In other words, they do not step in overly close to their communication partners, which can cause discomfort and defensiveness. This cannot always be said of those exhibiting an aggressive communication style.

Assertive communicators are generally confident, feel good about themselves, and are respected by others. Because of their effective communication style, assertive communicators often get what they want and continuously increase the quality of their relationships with others.[3]

Understanding Your Communication Style
http://www.au.af.mil/au/awc/awcgate/sba/comm_style.htm

FIGURE 1-4: COMMUNICATION STYLES

	Description	Nonverbal Behavior Pattern	Verbal Behavior Pattern
Assertive	• Pushing hard without attacking • Permits others to influence outcome • Expressive and self-enhancing without intruding on others	• Good eye contact • Comfortable but firm posture • Strong, steady, audible voice • Facial expressions matched to message • Appropriately serious tone • Selective interruptions to ensure understanding	• Direct and unambiguous language • No attributions or evaluations of others' behavior • Use of "I" statements and cooperative "we" statements
Aggressive	• Taking advantage of others • Expressive and self-enhancing at others' expense	• Glaring eye contact • Moving or leaning too close • Threatening gestures (pointed finger, clenched fist) • Loud voice • Frequent interruptions	• Swear words and abusive language • Attributions and evaluations of others' behavior • Sexist or racist terms • Explicit threats or put-downs

FIGURE 1-4: COMMUNICATION STYLES

	Description	Nonverbal Behavior Pattern	Verbal Behavior Pattern
Nonassertive	• Encouraging others to take advantage of self • Inhibited • Self-denying	• Little eye contact • Downward glances • Slumped posture • Constantly shifting weight • Wringing hands • Weak or whiny voice	• Qualifiers ("maybe," "kind of") • Fillers ("uh,," "you know," "well") • Negatives ("It's not really that important," "I'm not sure")

Source: Kreitner and Kinicki, adapted in part from Waters.[4]

Figure 1-4 highlights the assertive, aggressive, and nonassertive (passive) communication styles, with special emphasis on related nonverbal and verbal patterns.

DEVELOP EFFECTIVE TEAM COMMUNICATION SKILLS

When asked to rank communication skills in terms of importance, U.S. organizations typically include *team communication skills* in the top five necessary skills. This should remind you that teamwork is commonplace in U.S. organizations.

To be successful, teamwork requires extensive communication. The types of communication activities found in teams typically include speaking, listening, collaborative writing, presenting, negotiating, and mastering nonverbal and interpersonal skills.

Here are some examples of effective team communication techniques.

- Encourage an open communication environment within the team (e.g., frequent communication, trust, respect, and empathy).
- Practice good listening techniques. Team problems often occur when team members all try simultaneously to get their points across while nobody listens.
- Ask the speaker to repeat or restate comments for clarification when needed, and encourage the same behavior in fellow team members. Make feedback an active, vital communication component.
- Practice effective collaborative writing and team presentation techniques.
- Practice good conflict resolution techniques. Members will disagree at times and occasionally get upset with each other. Learn to work through difficult situations and with difficult people.

DEVELOP EFFECTIVE INTERCULTURAL COMMUNICATION SKILLS

The ability to communicate effectively with people from an array of cultural backgrounds is important in today's business environment. Think about the ever-increasing volume of business that occurs among businesses around the globe. In addition, consider the vast cultural diversity that exists in the American workforce.

Figure 1-5 contains several techniques that will help you communicate effectively with businesspeople from other cultures.

FIGURE 1-5: COMMUNICATING WITH BUSINESSPEOPLE FROM OTHER CULTURES

- View and treat your communication partners as you prefer to be viewed and treated.
- Learn about their culture, their business practices, and their communication preferences.
- Respect your communication partners' customs even though they differ from yours.
- Ask your communication partners how you can communicate most effectively with them.
- Look for signs of confusion in your communication partners' facial expressions or voices as well as in their verbal requests for feedback.
- Use words that your communication partners will understand.
- Eliminate slang, profanity, and regional expressions that will lead to misunderstandings.
- Pronounce words clearly, and be careful not to let accents interfere with understanding.
- Know that nonverbal cues often mean different things in different cultures.
- Use communication media that is acceptable to your communication partners.
- Encourage your communication partners to seek feedback.
- Activate the feedback process when you suspect your communication partners are confused.
- Be patient with your communication partners. It may take them additional time to understand your messages.

Communicating with people from other cultures is not a choice for most of us, but a necessity. Instead of fighting it, embrace the challenge and enjoy broadening your understanding of people from other places and backgrounds. Through such interaction, we typically learn more about ourselves. For more information about communicating effectively with businesspeople from other cultures, explore the *International Association of Business Communicators* website at www.iabc.com.

KEEP UP WITH COMMUNICATION TECHNOLOGY DEVELOPMENTS

The pace at which communication technology has been and is being developed is staggering. The fast-paced development, however, does not eliminate the need to keep up. You need to remain current and competitive in today's marketplace.

© everything possible/Shutterstock.com

Most successful executives are familiar with communication technology. They typically know: (1) what communication technology exists and what is forthcoming; (2) how to use existing technology or, at minimum, to whom to turn for assistance; and (3) which technology best complements and enhances each communication situation.

If you are wondering how you will keep up, given the rapid rate of technological development, don't fret about it. Your reaction is normal. Decide you will move past those feelings of being overwhelmed and learn all you can. Be careful, however, not to give in to what could possibly be your single biggest obstacle—finding/making enough time to learn. Figure 1-6 lists a number of suggestions to help you keep up.

FIGURE 1–6: KEEPING UP WITH COMMUNICATION TECHNOLOGY DEVELOPMENTS

- You might prefer to keep up by attending workshops, attending community college or university classes, or taking Internet courses.
- Your preferred way of keeping up might be reading technology magazines, books, or research articles.
- You could attend local, regional, or national computer shows.
- Consider learning by teaching yourself through trial or error.

Your preferred method might take you to the website for the *Association for Business Communication* (http://businesscommunication.org/) where you will find a wealth of information and resource links regarding communication technology developments and other business communication topics.

USE HUMOR, BUT DO SO CAUTIOUSLY

Did you hear the joke about the duck and the bartender? Please avoid telling it or any other joke at the start of business presentations and during meetings. When using humor in the professional business place, avoid telling jokes. Instead, insert tasteful, humorous, on-topic references to situations and short stories that will not offend. The same goes in teams and job interviews, and when communicating with international business partners. While most people enjoy appropriate humor, they are typically turned off by offensive humor in professional settings. (And you never know what might be offensive to someone.)

From both a professional and a personal standpoint, having a sense of humor is healthy. Professionally, most people warm up to cheerful individuals, form trusting relationships with them more quickly, and are typically supportive of what they have to say. Personal benefits range from decreased stress to a more optimistic outlook on life. Just in case you have been experiencing a "humor drought," here are some suggestions for working humor into your life.

- Set a goal to laugh more frequently.
- Do not take yourself too seriously.
- Learn to relax; make it a priority.
- Be around people who laugh frequently.
- Make others laugh; you will end up laughing also.
- Read humorous books and cartoons.
- Watch humorous movies and television programs.
- Listen to humorous radio shows while commuting.
- Display humorous wall calendars and day calendars.
- Look for humor in tough situations.
- Start and end each day with laughter.

Humor is a good thing. It is healthy for you both personally and professionally. Just be careful to use on-topic, non-offensive humor in the business place.

Which of the above communication traits are already strong components of your communication make-up, and which are not? If your goal is to grow your communication skills beyond average, your first step is to identify the areas in need of improvement. Reflecting on the above communication traits is an excellent starting point!

SUMMARY: SECTION 2— ESTABLISHING A STRONG BASE

- Maintain an appropriate attitude regarding the challenges to effective communication.
- Work throughout your career to improve your communication skills.
- Consider the impact of location on communication effectiveness.
- Consider the impact of timing on communication effectiveness.
- Analyze your audience.
- Be a congenial communicator.
- Be an ethical communicator.
- Choose the best communication medium for the situation.
- Choose your most effective writing tool.
- Develop an assertive communication style.
- Develop effective team communication skills.
- Develop effective intercultural communication skills.
- Keep up with communication technology developments.
- Use humor, but do so cautiously.

Effective & Efficient Communication http://smallbusiness. chron.com/effective-efficient-communica-tion-56000.html

EVALUATING COMMUNICATION

Business communication is evaluated first and foremost on whether intended results are achieved. This suggests that the receiver not only understood the message, but also responded as desired. This occurs as a result of effective communication. Business communication is also evaluated in terms of the amount of time, effort, and resources required to achieve the desired response. When effective communication is achieved with a minimum of wasted time, effort, and resources, it is also considered efficient communication. A discussion regarding effective and efficient communication follows.

EFFECTIVE COMMUNICATION

Effective communication happens when a receiver understands a message as the sender intends it to be understood and when the receiver acts on it as the sender desires. Such an outcome depends on the quality of the audience analysis performed by the sender and even on the willingness of the receiver to understand the sender. For example, effective communication occurs when, after reading the job procedure, an employee performs the tasks as intended. Another example is a letter soliciting funds for a local charity that generates an outpouring of donations.

Several factors contribute to effective communication. Effective communication is clear and complete, and it occurs in settings where openness, trust, and honesty are encouraged. Respect among communication partners and receptiveness to each other's messages also contribute to effective communication.

© woaiss/Shutterstock.com

Effective Communication Methods in an Organization
http://smallbusiness.chron.com/effective-communication-methods-organization-2.html

Message clarity is an essential element of effective communication. Clarity emerges from words appropriate to each receiver's level of understanding. Clarity is promoted by providing sufficient detail and avoiding vague, abstract words. Clarity is further promoted when nonverbal messages are carefully developed and observed by communication partners as a means of reinforcing verbal messages. *Feedback*, in turn, is capable of resolving misunderstandings, including those resulting from contradictory nonverbal messages. Message clarity is also promoted when communication partners take into account cultural and language differences.

Tone refers to the sender's attitude toward the receiver and the message subject. Tone plays an important role in effective communication. Message tone should be positive and audience centered. It should be devoid of biases, stereotypes, accusations, sarcasm, and sexism, all of which threaten message acceptance and clarity and, in turn, communication effectiveness.

Other factors contributing to effective communication include active listening, accounting for gender-related communication differences, and taking care in channel (medium) selection. Sensitivity to timing when developing, delivering, and responding to messages is also important.

tone Refers to the sender's attitude toward the receiver and the message subject.

EFFICIENT COMMUNICATION

efficient communication Communication achieved with a minimum of wasted time and resources.

Efficient communication is effective communication that is achieved with a minimum of wasted time, effort, and resources. Today's highly competitive business environment requires communication be efficient as well as effective.

Efficient communication is developed and delivered in ways that minimize *wasted time*. For example, headings, graphic aids, and sectional introductions and summaries move readers through business reports more quickly and efficiently than documents lacking these features. Taking special care when developing the problem statements for formal business reports focuses writers' research efforts, which typically reduces the time required to collect, analyze, and interpret data for the readers.

Efficient communication is also characterized by minimal *wasted effort*. For example, a well-developed résumé helps a prospective employer readily identify a candidate's strengths. Eliminating unnecessary words and using lists where appropriate in business documents promotes efficiency. Using graphic (visual) aids in place of text to explain sets of facts or projections also promotes efficient communication.

© Rawpixel.com/Shutterstock.com

Finally, efficient communication suggests a minimum of *wasted resources*. This goal is accomplished when businesspeople reduce the cost of producing and transmitting messages. For example, using word processing to develop a letter is more efficient and less costly than using pen and paper. E-mail messages are transmitted more quickly and efficiently than express mail. Videoconferences are often less costly, thus more efficient, than face-to-face meetings that require participants to gather in one location.

SUMMARY: SECTION 3— EVALUATING COMMUNICATION

- Communication in businesses is evaluated on whether intended results are achieved.
- The best communication in businesses is effective and efficient.
- *Effective communication* occurs when receivers understand messages as senders intend them to be understood and they are acted on them as desired.
- *Efficient communication* is effective communication that is achieved with a minimum of wasted time, effort, and resources.

INFORMAL AND FORMAL COMMUNICATION

Communication in organizations is either *informal* or *formal*. *Informal communication* is unofficial communication, while *formal communication* is company-sanctioned communication intended to meet organizational goals and objectives. While the main focus of this book is business communication (e.g., business writing, listening, presentations, etc.) with the purpose of growing your individual skills, the following information on informal and formal communication gives you a glimpse into what is typically referred to as organizational communication.

INFORMAL COMMUNICATION

Informal communication is unofficial communication that occurs outside of official organizational channels. It may or may not address organizational concerns. Bull sessions and personal discussions during work breaks are examples of informal communication, as are gossip and discussions about nonwork-related topics, such as social activities and families.

Informal communication is an essential component of **organizational communication**. Employees, like most people, enjoy visiting with each other. Sometimes, they talk

informal communication Unofficial communication occurring outside of official organizational channels that may or may not address organizational concerns.

organizational communication All communication that takes place in organizations with both internal and external stakeholders.

© Mila Supinskaya/Shutterstock.com

Informal Communication Within Organizations http://www.grapevine-communications.co.uk/communications/communications.html

about good and bad things happening in their lives. Other times, they vent frustrations and concerns with fellow employees regarding work-related or personal matters. As a rule, it is unproductive for management to try to eliminate or control informal communication unless it interferes with worker productivity and the organization's ability to achieve its goals and objectives.

FORMAL COMMUNICATION

Formal communication is communication sanctioned by organizations and is intended to meet organizational goals and objectives. Formal communication occurs through official organizational channels, for example, business meetings, memos, manuals, and reports.

© Tyler Olson/Shutterstock.com

Three major functions are served by formal communication according to management theorists William G. Scott and Terrence R. Mitchell. They are *information*, *control*, and *emotive* (*motivational*).[5] Organizational communication typically involves one or a combination of these three functions.

The **information function** refers to communication initiated to gather, analyze, summarize, organize, and disperse information needed for decision making or for accomplishing organizational objectives and tasks. Financial statements, progress reports, surveys, and suggestion boxes are examples of written documents that serve the information function. The information function is served orally, for example, through meetings, presentations, quality circles, training sessions, and polling interviews.

The **control function** refers to communication initiated to control the behaviors of organization members as a means of realizing organizational goals. Specifically, the control function defines roles; clarifies duties, authority, and responsibilities; and explains organizational structure.[6] Examples of communication control vehicles are performance appraisal reports and interviews, policy manuals, and statements of organizational goals and objectives.

The **emotive (motivational) function** refers to communication that influences an organization's employees' feelings, emotions, and behavior, which increases acceptance of and commitment to organizational goals. This type of communication may take the form of written policies or memos that describe employee benefits, for example. Benefits may also be explained in meetings, brown-bag lunches with top-level executives, or CEO pep talks.

FORMAL COMMUNICATION NETWORKS

Company-sanctioned (formal) communication in most countries consists of the exchange of information necessary to accomplish organizational goals and objectives. In the process of meeting these goals and objectives, information moves in downward, upward, horizontal, and diagonal directions. The quantity, type, and importance of information flowing in each direction differ.

The emphasis on any one or any combination of the four directional flows varies among countries based on social, economic, political, and cultural preferences. For example, in Latin American countries most businesses run according to the patronage system, which results in greater emphasis on relational rather than linear communication. The outcome is a vertically structured system in which most communication flows in a downward direction. Downward communication also predominates in Nigerian organizations and countries comprising the former Soviet Union. On the other hand, managers in small North American organizations are concerned about horizontal communication, and managers in large North American organizations are most concerned about upward and downward communication.[7]

Advantages and Disadvantages of Formal Communication
http://thebusiness-communication.com/advantage-and-disadvantage-of-formal-communication/

DOWNWARD COMMUNICATION

Downward communication refers to messages and information sent from a source higher in the organization to person(s) lower in the organization. Downward communication clarifies, motivates, and influences employees' actions. Specifically, downward communications (1) give job instructions, (2) supply information about policies and methods, (3) provide feedback, (4) improve understanding of how jobs relate to other jobs, and (5) send information about the organization's goals and philosophies.[8]

downward communication
Messages and information sent from a source higher in the organization to someone lower in the organization.

The role of downward communication varies in organizations throughout the world due most often to customs and political rule. For example, downward communication in Jordanian, Saudi Arabian, and large and small public Indian organizations is formal and follows bureaucratic, structured channels. Downward communication in Nigeria is far less formal, as it is also in small private Indian organizations where personal interaction is commonplace.

Downward communication occurs in a variety of forms. Memorandums, letters, e-mails, company newsletters or newspapers, and electronic and cork bulletin board messages are written forms used extensively for downward communications in American businesses. Verbal forms popular in American organizations include meetings, face-to-face conversations, phone calls, presentations, videotapes, CDs, and increasingly, such media as closed-circuit television and videoconferences.

Memorandums are used extensively in downward communication in Nigeria where administrative assistants write, edit, and sign them for their bosses. Memos are also the dominant form of downward communication in large Indian organizations where individuals called *peons* deliver them.

Letters and memos are the predominate form of downward communication in Jordanian organizations. In small Jordanian organizations, written messages are delivered by carriers who perform this duty in addition to janitorial work. In Saudi Arabian businesses, face-to-face conversation is the preferred form of downward communication.

Downward communication is most effective when the information and messages are clear, complete, and audience centered. Downward communication is more effective when the tone is positive, respectful, and courteous. Aggressive, demanding, threatening, or condescending communications can negatively impact morale, attendance, employee retention, and productivity.

Anticipating concerns and explaining background and benefits help make downward communications effective. Workers will respond more favorably to a change in policy, for example, if they understand why it was developed and how it will affect them.

Encouraging open, two-way feedback also improves downward communication. Receivers should feel comfortable asking for clarification, and senders should be prepared to contact receivers to expand their explanations, especially when messages are complex or controversial.

Potential benefits of downward communication include "prevention/correction of employee errors, greater job satisfaction, and improved morale." On the other hand, potential problems of downward communication include "insufficient or unclear messages, message overload, and message distortion as it passes through one or more intermediaries."[9]

UPWARD COMMUNICATION

upward communication Messages and information sent from a source lower in the organization to someone higher in the organization.

Upward communication refers to messages and information sent from a source lower in the organization to a recipient higher in the organization. Upward communications are used mostly to interpret, motivate, and obtain information. Specifically, upward communication provides superiors with (1) feedback regarding employee attitudes and feelings; (2) new ideas and improvements; (3) feedback on how downward communication systems are working; (4) information about production and goals; (5) requests for supplies, assistance, or support; and (6) awareness of small problems before they become major ones.[10]

The role of upward organizational communication, like downward communication, varies throughout the world due predominantly to customs and political rule. For example,

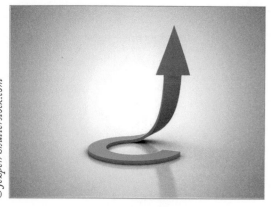
© Jezper/Shutterstock.com

upward communication in Mexican organizations and large public and private organizations in India is minimal. Upward communication in Mexican organizations tends to be filtered by others before reaching its final destination, as is the case in large public and private Indian organizations. Even then, subordinates generally communicate only what the superiors want to hear.

Upward communication is prevalent in U.S. organizations and in Nigerian organizations. In Nigeria, upward communication is typically in a brief written form, with a courteous tone using a direct writing style. Upward communication is less structured and less formal in Nigerian and small Indian organizations where superiors and subordinates are likely to call each other by their first names.

Upward communication in Saudi Arabian and Jordanian organizations typically follows the formal chain of command. In Jordanian businesses (especially small businesses), in cases of people-related problems, upward communication usually bypasses the chain of command and goes directly to the general manager or president of the business.

Upward communication occurs in many of the same forms as downward communication. For example, reports play a central role, as do memos, letters, and electronic bulletin board messages. Like downward communication, upward communication also occurs verbally in the form of meetings, face-to-face conversations, phone calls, presentations, and interactive videoconferences.

Face-to-face communication is the preferred form of upward communication in Saudi Arabian organizations. The majority of upward communication in Jordanian organizations also involves oral communication, with the exception of suggestions about work-related improvements, which are typically written. Most upward communication in large public and private Indian organizations occurs in the form of written reports.

Upward communication should be clear, concise, and thorough. Superiors typically make decisions based on information from upward communication. It should be objective and include supporting facts when available. In addition, the sender must be sensitive to tone. The tone of upward communication should not be aggressive, demanding, or threatening. Instead, it should be courteous, respectful, and cooperative. It should be formal when the receiver expects formality and persuasive when the situation requires persuasion.

Openness is an important component of upward communication. Messages sent up the organization should not gloss over bad news by limiting information to what senders think superiors want to hear. Superiors, in turn, should receive bad news objectively.

Benefits of upward communication include "prevention of new problems and solution of old ones, and increased acceptance of management decisions." Problems associated with upward communication include "superiors who may discourage, disregard or downplay [the] importance of subordinates' messages, and supervisors who may unfairly blame subordinates for unpleasant news."[11]

HORIZONTAL COMMUNICATION

Horizontal communication refers to messages and information sent among people and work groups on the same level of the organizational hierarchy. Horizontal communication usually (1) coordinates efforts among interdependent units and departments, (2) builds social support systems in organizations, and (3) serves as a primary way to share information.[12]

horizontal communication Messages and information among people and work groups on the same level of the organizational hierarchy.

©VLADGRIN/Shutterstock.com

The role of horizontal communication, like downward and upward communication, varies in organizations throughout the world. For example, in Mexico, horizontal communication is limited because communication is predominately vertical. Horizontal communication is also limited in the countries comprising the former Soviet Union.

In Saudi Arabian and U.S. organizations, horizontal communication is customary, far less structured than downward and upward communication, and relatively informal.

Horizontal communication is also relatively informal in Jordanian organizations and in large and small private Indian organizations.

Horizontal communication uses a wide array of communication formats, including memos, reports, informal notes, e-mails, voicemails, and bulletin board messages. However, horizontal communication relies more on oral communication, such as face-to-face conversations, phone calls, and meetings of committees, task forces, and quality circles. Such is the case in organizations in the United States, Jordan, Saudi Arabia, in large and small private organizations in India, and in entrepreneurial organizations in the countries comprising the former Soviet Union. Nigerian organizations, on the other hand, typically communicate horizontally in writing.

Horizontal communication is considered fast and efficient compared to the costs associated with the formal, vertical communication. Horizontal communication typically comprises the largest flow of information because of the amount of interaction that occurs in the routine conduct of business.

Like upward communication, horizontal communication should be clear and concise, yet thorough. It should also be sensitive to tone. A courteous, cooperative tone reinforces effective horizontal communication and promotes strong employee morale. An aggressive, demanding, or condescending tone has the opposite effect.

Benefits of horizontal communication include "increased cooperation among employees with different duties and greater understanding of [the] organization's mission." Problems associated with horizontal communication include "rivalry between employees from different areas, specialization [that] makes understanding difficult, information overload [that] discourages contacts, physical barriers [that] discourage contact, and lack of motivation."[13]

DIAGONAL COMMUNICATION

diagonal communication Messages and information among people in different departments and at different levels of the organizational hierarchy.

Diagonal communication refers to messages and information sent between people in different departments and at different levels of the organizational hierarchy. Like horizontal communication, diagonal communication is fast and efficient because of the reduced need to communicate through the formal, vertical communication chain. Diagonal communication (1) strengthens open communication and participative management, (2) facilitates interdepartmental coordination, and (3) saves time and money.[14]

© kentoh/Shutterstock.com

The role of diagonal communication varies in organizations throughout the world. In Mexican organizations, diagonal communication is limited because communication is predominately vertical. Diagonal communication is also limited in the countries of the former Soviet Union. This condition is changing, though, in entrepreneurial organizations where businesspeople are beginning to share information openly and are becoming aware of what each department does.

Diagonal communication is prevalent in American and Saudi Arabian organizations, but is more structured and formal than horizontal communication. This is especially true in large private Indian organizations where departments are usually distinctly different units, each having its own hierarchical structure. Diagonal communication in public Indian organizations is less common though, due to department rivalries.

The degree of formality associated with diagonal communication in Jordan varies by organizational size. For example, diagonal communication in large Jordanian organizations is formal, related to business matters, and dependent on personal relationships. In turn, diagonal communication in small Jordanian organizations is less formal than in large organizations and involves nonbusiness (personal) matters as well as business matters.

Diagonal communication occurs in many of the same forms as horizontal communication. For example, memos and reports play central roles, as do e-mails and voicemails. Like horizontal communication, diagonal communication also occurs verbally in the form of face-to-face conversations, telephone calls, and meetings.

Diagonal communication in Saudi Arabia and Jordan is typically written. Nigerian and Indian organizations also prefer diagonal communication to be in writing. North American organizations, on the other hand, readily communicate diagonally in writing and orally.

Like horizontal communication, diagonal communication should be clear, concise, and sensitive to tone. A courteous, cooperative tone reinforces effective diagonal communication and promotes strong morale.

OPEN COMMUNICATION ENVIRONMENTS

Organizations are encouraged to develop and maintain open communication environments. Open communication environments are characterized by frequent communication among employees no matter their job titles or status. Qualities such as trust, respect, and empathy play important roles in the communication process.

open communication environments Communication environments characterized by frequent communication among employees no matter their job titles and status, with trust, respect, and empathy being key components.

© Heather Lewis/Shutterstock.com

Communication effectiveness is promoted in open communication environments through its frequency and directness. Fear of ridicule or reprisal inhibits open communication. Typically, effective communication helps recipients become open to the communication needs and objectives of others. Open communication is typically more honest and more likely to inspire feedback and responsiveness among the communication partners.

© iQoncept/Shutterstock.com

Additional information and opportunities pertaining to business communication can be found at the *Association of Professional Communication Consultants* website: www.consulting-success.org.

SUMMARY: SECTION 4—
INFORMAL AND FORMAL COMMUNICATION

- Organizational communication refers to all communication that takes place in organizations with internal and external stakeholders.
- Formal communication is communication sanctioned by organizations and intended to meet organizational goals and objectives.
- The three major functions of formal communication are: information, control, and emotive (motivational).
- Informal communication is unofficial communication that occurs outside of official organizational channels and may or may not address organizational concerns.
- Downward communication refers to messages and information sent from sources higher in organizations.
- Upward communication refers to messages and information sent from sources lower in organizations.
- Horizontal communication refers to messages and information sent among people and work groups on the same level of the organizational hierarchy.
- Diagonal communication refers to messages and information sent among people in different departments and at different levels of the organizational hierarchy.
- Organizations should develop and maintain open communication environments.

Notes

1. Robert Kreitner and Angelo Kinicki, *Organizational Behavior*, 5th ed. (Boston: Irwin McGraw-Hill, 2000), 486.

2. Ibid.

3. P. H. Andrews and J. E. Baird Jr., *Communication for Business and the Professions*, 8th ed. (Long Grove, IL: Waveland Press) 158–59.

4. Kreitner and Kinicki, *Organizational Behavior*, 487 (adapted in part from J. A. Waters, "Managerial Assertiveness," *Business Horizons* v 25 n5 (1982): 24–29.

5. William G. Scott and Terrence R. Mitchell, *Organization Theory: A Structural Behavioral Analysis* (Homewood, IL: Irwin, 1979), 3.

6. James M. Higgins, *The Management Challenge* (New York: Macmillan, 1991), 535.

7. Larry R. Smeltzer and Gail L. Fann, "Comparison of Managerial Communication Patterns in Small, Entrepreneurial Organizations and Large, Mature Organizations," *Group & Organizational Studies* v14 n2 (1989): 198–215.

8. Jane Whitney Gibson and Richard M. Hodgetts, *Organizational Communication: A Managerial Perspective*, 2nd ed. (New York: HarperCollins, 1991), 219–21.

9. R. B. Adler and J. M. Elmhorst, *Communicating at Work: Principles and Practices for Business and the Professions*, 8th ed. (Boston: McGraw-Hill Higher Education, 2005), 15–19.

10. Ibid., 227.

11. Ibid., 15–19.

12. Ibid., 229.

13. Ibid., 15–19.

14. Ibid, 23.

COMMUNICATING APPROPRIATELY: BUSINESS ETIQUETTE

2

LEARNING OUTCOMES

After reading this chapter, you should be able to:

1. Describe the four major benefits of adhering to the rules and rituals of business etiquette.

2. Explain the difference between business etiquette and social etiquette.

3. Discuss the guiding principles of business etiquette.

4. Discuss the role of company culture on business etiquette.

5. Describe appropriate dress in today's business place.

6. Describe networking protocol.

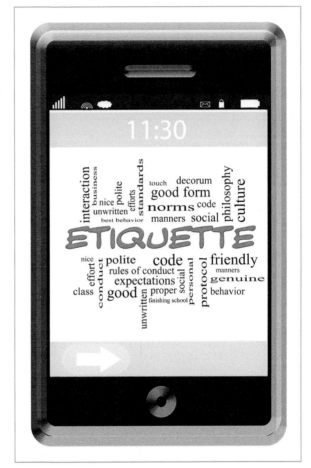

© Keith Bell/Shutterstock.com

BENEFITS OF LEARNING ABOUT BUSINESS ETIQUETTE

1. Knowing good business etiquette helps you present yourself with confidence and gives you the power to succeed in the workplace. Surviving in the highly competitive business climate of the 21st century includes outclassing the competition.

2. Understanding business etiquette helps you sharpen your business and sales strategies.

3. Mastering the often unspoken rules of business etiquette will allow you to avoid embarrassing yourself, your coworkers, your customers, and your clients in any business situation.

4. According to experts, to be a successful businessperson, you should possess three characteristics: competence in your field, confidence in your demeanor, and consideration for others (the #1 rule of business etiquette).

5. Mastering the fine points of how to make an impeccable impression—on the phone, in meetings, on sales calls, and at business functions—helps you climb the corporate ladder.

Select Key Terms

INTRODUCTION

Business etiquette refers to sets of suggested rules that guide how we interact with each other in the business place. Such rules vary somewhat among organizations as well as globally. Some of the benefits of adhering to business etiquette rules include improved employee morale, improved workplace quality of life, a sharper company image, and higher profits. With the popularity and proliferation of Internet-based electronic communication within organizations, netiquette, including social media etiquette, are increasingly important. Respect for others and courtesy, for obvious reasons, are central to good business etiquette.

The intent of this chapter is to impress upon you how employees are expected to act in the business place. This goal is realized through discussions regarding the impact of business etiquette, business etiquette in the office, and business etiquette when conducting business outside of the office. The information pertaining to the above-mentioned topics is reinforced by several student website resources including *PowerPoint slides, preview tests, chapter assessment tests, YouTube videos, interactive exercises,* and the *interactive glossary.*

THE IMPACT OF BUSINESS ETIQUETTE

Business etiquette is defined as "a set of rules that guide how we interact with each other in the business place. Such rules make is possible for us to communicate and interact in a civilized manner."[1] Without rules of civil conduct, work teams can become dysfunctional, business relationships can become strained, office morale can diminish, and productivity can decrease.[2]

The ability to communicate effectively and interact in a appropriate manner in today's diverse workplace is essential. Bad behavior in the professional workplace, in turn, can easily result in lawsuits and loss of business. Burgeoning litigation is one result of a workforce that is continuously adjusting to major changes in its composition.

One initiative that the business community is taking to avoid these hazards is to push for the return of etiquette and manners to the workplace. Many businesses have hired etiquette trainers to teach workshops on etiquette to their employees. Training in business etiquette is really behavioral training on consideration for others.[3] These businesses see considerable benefits in adhering to the rules and rituals of business etiquette. These benefits range from improved employee morale and lower employee turnover to higher productivity and improved public relations.

Knowing global business etiquette can also save you from many embarrassing situations when conducting business internationally. Besides, it provides a wonderful opportunity to learn about what others value and, in turn, show respect for your international business partners. Figure 2-1 contains some helpful global business etiquette reminders.

business etiquette Sets of proposed rules guiding how we interact with each other in the business place.

Importance of Business Etiquette
http://small-business.chron.com/importance-business-etiquette-2900.html

FIGURE 2-1: SAMPLE GLOBAL BUSINESS ETIQUETTE REMINDERS

While businesspeople around the world are similar in regard to some of their preferences, be careful not to assume they share all of your preferences. Here are some examples of some of our similarities and differences. Additional examples will be mentioned throughout the chapter.

- **Greetings.** Greetings are certainly commonplace. In many countries this involves a handshake. For example, in the United States a handshake is part of a standard greeting. The same is true in Guatemala when greeting a male. However, shaking hands with a Guatemalan woman is done only at her discretion.
- **Gift Giving.** While gift giving may be thought to be a simple process, there is plenty of room for offending your international business partner if you do not learn ahead of time what is acceptable and what is not. For example, recommended gifts for Hungarian business partners include alcohol and flowers. In contrast, you would not want to give your Malaysian counterpart alcohol as a gift since it is prohibited to practicing Muslims.
- **Punctuality.** Being punctual for all appointments, including meetings, is common in most countries. This is especially true in Germany and New Zealand. In contrast, punctuality is not strictly observed in Nicaragua. It is admired, however.
- **Dress.** While conservative, formal business dress (e.g., suit, tie, jacket, skirt, conservative dress) is the expectation in most countries, there are exceptions. For example, in Italy business attire should be elegant and fashionable. Furthermore, in Middle Eastern countries such as Kuwait, where modesty is highly valued, choose clothing that covers most of your body.

Practicing good business etiquette is a mainstay of professionalism. Some people believe that once they earn a college degree they are a professional. What determines if a person is a professional, instead, is how he or she conducts him or herself in professional working settings—not a college degree in hand. Thus, if we want to truly call ourselves professionals, we must walk the walk which involves being courteous, respectful, and civil with others in the workplace.

FIGURE 2–2: HAS SAYING THANK YOU BECOME A CLICHÉ?

This may sound like a silly question, but it is a question worth exploring. Saying thank you is a sign of courtesy, which is certainly an element of good business etiquette. However, there are many instances when these two simple words—thank you—go unmentioned. In such cases, others often form poor perceptions of us. They can easily perceive us as being ungrateful, rude, inconsiderate, entitled, unprofessional, etc. Such perceptions can, in turn, negatively influence a host of important decisions in the professional business place ranging from bonus and pay raise decisions to promotion decisions. Even though extending a thank you is such a logical thing to do, some people simply don't. For example, have you ever held a door for someone else behind you as you entered a building or room only to have them march through without saying thank you? Possibly this same thing has happened to you when you extended the common courtesy of holding an elevator door for another person to board only to be ignored. Or, someone e-mailed you asking you to do something for him or her which you then did but a thank you did not follow in any form be it an e-mail reply, a phone call, or a text message.

© karen roach/Shutterstock.com

Then, there is the matter of those who either believe they, and the rest of us for that matter, are too busy today to take the time to extend a thank you and/or believe "thank you" is cliché. Fortunately, I have not met a lot of people who share these viewpoints, but have met enough of them to get my attention. Where do you stand on such viewpoints? Hopefully you still believe in the need for and power of saying thank you. In the professional business world job stability and career growth are dependent, in large part, on good interpersonal skills (people skills), and your willingness to extend the two simple words "thank you" can go a long way in helping you achieve both.

Job Success: Business Etiquette
http://www.gcflearn-free.org/jobsuccess/4/print

This chapter covers the dos and don'ts of acceptable behavior in the workplace. First we will explore business etiquette in the office and then move on to business etiquette outside the office.

SUMMARY: SECTION 1— THE IMPACT OF BUSINESS ETIQUETTE

- Business etiquette is defined as a set of rules that allow us to communicate and interact in a civilized manner.
- Rudeness is on the rise, including in the workplace.
- Bad behavior in the workplace often results in lawsuits and loss of business.
- Some benefits of adhering to the rules and rituals of business etiquette include an increase in employee morale, an improved quality of life in the workplace, a sharper company image, and higher profits.
- Business etiquette expectations vary extensively around the globe. It is both necessary and respectful to learn and practice what your global business partners' value.

BUSINESS ETIQUETTE AT THE OFFICE

Business etiquette basics are simple, according to Hilka Klinkenberg, director of Etiquette International. The first general principle is the differences between business etiquette and social etiquette. Social etiquette is based on chivalry, a code based on the dated notion that women need protection. In contrast, business etiquette has its origins in the military code of etiquette, which is based on hierarchy and power. Business etiquette, then, is based on rank, or the pecking order, not on gender.

Business etiquette's first guiding principle is to treat people according to rank rather than gender. Men and women are peers in the workplace. If you are a man, you should hold open a door for a woman if you would hold it open for a man in the same circumstance.[4] The general rule is: Whoever reaches the door first, opens it. Whether you are a man or a woman, doors are held open for superiors, clients, and those who have their arms full of folders and packages. If it's a revolving door, you enter first to get it moving and then wait on the other side as your group files through.

FIGURE 2–3: HOLDING THE DOOR

Here are three general rules for holding doors:

1. Junior ranking people should open and hold doors for senior ranking people.
2. Doors should be opened and held for customers and clients.
3. Assistance should be offered to persons with a disability.[5]

Office Etiquette: Do You Know The Basics?
http://www.caree-realism.com/office-etiquette-basics/

Another instance of deciding who goes first is when exiting an elevator. Unless a woman happens to be your CEO or your client, whoever is closest to the door exits first, regardless of gender. A man who treats a woman in a chivalrous manner may be perceived as condescending. This perception can create a workplace climate of hostility. Many women believe that they cannot be perceived as equal if they are treated chivalrously.[6]

Professionals with disabilities should be treated with the same courtesy that you would afford any other business professional. When in doubt about how or whether to accommodate someone's physical needs, ask the person what he or she prefers rather than evade the situation. The main thing is to be yourself, and act as you would around anyone else.[7]

The second guiding principle of business etiquette is to always treat people with consideration and respect. This seems simple enough, but basic consideration of others seems to be lacking in today's workplace. The return of the Golden Rule to business means that you should treat everyone as you would like to be treated.[8]

MASTERING THE FINE ART OF INTRODUCTIONS

Introductions are a given in our business lives. The most important rule when making business introductions is to make them—even if you do not remember all the rules or all the names involved. The second most important rule is that business introductions are based on rank rather than gender. Therefore, you should always introduce the person of lesser rank to the person of greater rank, stating the name of the person of greater rank first, like this: "Ms. or Mr. Person of Greater Rank, I would like to introduce you to Ms. or Mr. Person of Lesser Rank."[9] Remember to look at each person as you say his or her name.

Remember that the person who outranks every person in your organization is the client. If a client is involved, always introduce the client first, even if the client holds a lesser position than the top executive in your firm.[10] Most executives prefer that the client be given the position of greatest importance in introductions.[11]

The best way to introduce two people is to make eye contact with the person who needs the information, not with the person whose name you are saying.[12] That way each person clearly hears the name of the other person.

One final tip when making introductions: Introduce people with thoughtful details, like this: "Ms. or Ms. Person of Greater Rank, meet Mr. or Ms. Person of Lesser Rank. Ms. Greater Rank is our executive vice president in charge of accounts. Mr. Lesser Rank is my colleague and works in the art department." By revealing a few details about each person, you will have helped to spark a short conversation between the two people when you leave them.

> **introductions** How people greet each other in the business place.

SHAKING HANDS

The basic component of the introduction is the handshake. Handshakes communicate friendliness and respect for the other person. In the business world, men and women in the United States should shake hands, rather than kiss or hug, as in some other countries. (For greeting people in other countries, see the discussion in chapter 3, Intercultural Communication.)

Shaking hands may seem elementary, but since you are judged by the quality of your handshake, the following list presents a few pointers to help you achieve that perfect "handshake."

© Rawpixel.com/Shutterstock.com

Top 10 Bad Business Handshakes video http://www.business. gov.au/news-and-up-dates/business-videos/ Pages/business-hand-shakes-video.aspx

- Keep fingers together and meet the web of your hand—the skin between the thumb and forefinger—with the web of the hand of other person.
- Shake hands firmly but without crushing the other person's hand. Usually a handshake lasts about three seconds and may be pumped once or twice from the elbow with a combined upward/downward movement of approximately 12 inches.
- Make eye contact with the other person throughout the introduction.
- Release after the handshake, even if the introduction continues.
- When someone extends a left hand—perhaps because the right is impaired—shake hands as best you can, maybe from the side of the hand.[13]
- Stand and shake hands when being introduced, no matter what the status of the person.
- Shake hands when meeting someone for the first time, when greeting someone you know, and for all good-byes.
- At cocktail parties, if you are drinking, keep your drink in your left hand to avoid a wet handshake.[14]

When being introduced to another person, remember to make eye contact with that person, shake hands, and repeat the person's name: "Hello, Ms. X" or "Nice to meet you, Ms. X." Repeating the person's name (1) helps you remember it and (2) gives the other person a chance to correct you if you are mispronouncing his or her name. In addition, never assume that you can use someone's first name. Always use their title—Mr./Ms./Dr./etc.—before their last name. If people want you to use their first name, they will tell you: "Please, call me Charles."[15] Your politeness and respect by using their last name will be appreciated. Once you have been introduced, say a few words, like, "It was nice to meet you," before walking away.

If you join a group of people who know each other well, no one may make the effort to introduce you. In a situation like this, wait for a pause in the conversation and introduce yourself.[16] If you are seated next to someone at a table and no one introduces you, introduce yourself briefly and make a comment. The person then may or may not choose to have a conversation with you.[17]

MAKING GROUP INTRODUCTIONS

When you must introduce one or more people to a group of five or more, state the name of the new person(s), and then ask the people in the group to introduce themselves. On the other hand, if you are dining at a restaurant and a group of people stops by your table to say hello, you do not need to introduce them to everyone at your table unless they stay for a while.

REMEMBERING NAMES

We have all forgotten someone's name during an introduction at one time or another. The embarrassment of forgetting a name can be so great that we paralyze our memories, which makes recalling the name almost impossible. If this happens to you, try one of the following techniques before you admit that you have gone totally blank.

Shake hands and introduce yourself to the other person, even if you believe the person remembers you: "Hello, I'm Jan Huff from PWC" or "Hello, I'm Jan Huff. Remember, I met you last year at the graphic artists' convention in San Francisco."[18] If this works, the person will respond with his or her full name. Giving your name first will spare him or her the embarrassment of not remembering your name. You would not want to prolong someone's embarrassment by making a joke of it, like "Ha, I knew you didn't remember me. I'll give you a hint: My name begins with S."

If you cannot remember the person's name, admit that you cannot remember by saying something self-deprecating like, "I cannot even remember my own name today; what was yours again?" or "I'm terrible with names. Could you please tell me yours again?" As long as you do not make it sound as though it is their fault for your forgetfulness—"You must not have made a very big impression on me because …"—then you will not offend anyone by asking. We have all been in that situation and know how it feels. To help improve your memory for names, look over the tips provided in Figure 2-4. You might find just the thing to help you remember.

FIGURE 2–4: SOME TRICKS FOR REMEMBERING NAMES

Use these hints to help you improve your memory for names:
- As you are introduced, concentrate on the name and the person rather than on yourself and what you will say next.
- Repeat the person's name when you say hello to them then keep repeating it in your mind.
- Imagine virtually writing the name on the person's forehead.
- Associate the name with something about the person's appearance or with a word that you associate with the name. For example, Ms. Green could remind you of green leaves or grass.
- Identify one or two standout features of the person such as their smile.

If you forget a person's name, go on with the introduction and admit that you have a terrible memory for names. Apologize but always perform the courtesy of making introductions.[19]

If you are introducing people and you go blank, say something like "I'm terrible with names. Would you all mind introducing yourselves?" Although this is not the best option for making introductions, it is definitely better than not making them at all.[20] The following list contains the most common mistakes in making introductions.
- Failing to introduce people.
- Remaining seated when meeting someone. Exceptions include when the other person is seated or when you are in a position that makes standing difficult. In that case, making an effort to rise is acceptable.
- Offering your fingers to someone rather than your hand.
- Failing to offer your hand in a business situation.[21]

LEARNING YOUR COMPANY'S CULTURE

Every company and organization has its culture. You have to be there to see, experience, and absorb it, but the faster you do, the greater your success will be.[22] The guiding rule for all employees in any workplace, no matter what their rank, is the Golden Rule: Always treat everyone with the same consideration and respect that you expect. In other words, remember to be polite and kind at all times. The following examples of polite behavior will improve your chances of successfully adapting to nearly any company culture.

- Make liberal use of words and phrases such as "Please," "Thank you," "I appreciate that," and "Excuse me."
- Make it a priority to always greet coworkers in the morning and say good bye when leaving for the evening.
- Smile, even when you do not feel like it.

These basic rules of consideration for others should be observed no matter what the level of formality at your workplace.

ADDRESSING OTHERS

Company culture dictates when you should use courtesy titles when addressing all other employees, regardless of rank. However, even if you work in an informal office where all employees, up and down the corporate ladder, call each other by their first names, when introducing your boss, peers, or subordinates to outsiders, use their full name or their title and last name as a courtesy. For example, if you were introducing your office receptionist to your client, you would say, "Meet Mr. Mahoney" or "Meet Mike Mahoney," not "Meet Mike." Of course, calling assistants "your boy" or "your girl" is definitely inappropriate.

INTERACTING WITH PEERS

Offices are made up of all types of people, people with whom you will spend more time than with your own family. While you do not want to be overly familiar with peers, you will soon find that it is hard to avoid getting pulled into the latest office gossip or argument. As you meet your coworkers, you will find that some people thrive on creating upset and contention, while others keep completely to themselves. Both extremes are dangerous. Learning to negotiate the thorny world of office politics is part of being successful in the workplace.

First, mastering the art of small talk is essential and an important part of building business relationships.[23] Whether you are waiting to use the copier, getting a cup of coffee, or waiting for a meeting to begin, chatting with coworkers is how you get to see their personalities and how they get to see yours. Being easy to talk to is something that is to your advantage in the workplace. Here are a few tips on making small talk.

- Avoid inflammatory, indiscreet, malicious, or derogatory topics.
- Be aware of the other person's receptiveness when you are initiating small talk. If the other person seems distracted or does not respond, take the hint and leave the chat for another time.[24]
- Whatever the subject, avoid dominating the conversation. Ask questions to get others involved. Listen carefully when others are talking, and respond with comments that show you are listening and that you have a genuine interest in others' opinions. Remember to ask people about themselves.
- When you are having a conversation, try not to let it drag on. Small talk should not get in the way of business.
- If you are talking in a hallway, move to the side to let others pass by. Also, be aware of the volume of your conversation and what effect it is having on those around you. If coworkers appear bothered or distracted by your conversation, move the conversation elsewhere.

- Keep up with what's going on in the outside world. This gives you more to talk about than the latest copy machine breakdown. On the other hand, avoid touchy subjects like religion or politics—if you know your coworker gets really heated about the subject—and personal issues such as people's weight, the state of marriage, and sexual topics.
- Be agreeable; be a good listener.
- To end small talk, leave on a positive note and only after you have made a closing statement. A comment like "Well, great talking to you, but I've got to get to that report now," makes a smooth transition back to work.
- If a coworker interrupts you at a bad time, make it clear that you're busy but that you'll touch base later. If you interrupt someone at a bad time, do not be offended if the person cannot stop to talk. Talk later when your coworker is available.

Second, be ready to deal with disagreements. Disagreements, even over minor details like keeping the coffee pot full, can balloon into full-fledged hostilities that divide offices, pitting coworkers against each other and forcing weaker coworkers to take sides. Needless to say, this kind of open hostility can taint the atmosphere of any office, making it uncomfortable to go to work each day. How should you handle this kind of situation when it happens to you?

If the situation is not integral to the work process, like keeping the coffee pot full or the printer loaded with paper, handle squabbles in private. Usually, you will find that a problem peer—the gossip, the victim, or the backstabber (see below for a discussion of these personality types)—is behind the hostilities and divisiveness. In these situations, try to be the mediator: Ferret out the facts that underlie the argument, be objective, and get to the heart of the problem. Listen carefully to all sides, then confront the parties involved with a compromise or solution. Others will quickly identify you as a truthful and trustworthy person who can cut through others' anger, petty jealousies, and frustrations. Your coworkers will open up and be truthful with you. If you do this a couple of times, you will quickly adopt the role of office mediator, a star employee in any office.

On the other hand, if the disagreement is integral to the work process—you favor one solution but someone else favors another—do not avoid confrontation; but avoid making it personal. Focus on the pros and cons of the argument. State your side calmly and objectively, and back it up with facts and figures. Avoid getting into a shouting match or name calling. If hostilities reach this level, it is best to call a truce and meet at another time after both parties have cooled off. If you win the argument, avoid gloating over it; if you lose, be gracious, rather than spiteful. For example, "John really knows his stuff" is more gracious than "John really knows his stuff, but he is still a jerk."

Another common office problem is gossip. Gossip is rampant in all offices. Whether it's called the grapevine, the dish, or the buzz, gossip happens wherever people spend lots of time together. Natural subjects for gossip include work-related topics, such as what is going to happen at the next meeting, who is being promoted and why, who is being fired, and in what direction management will choose to go next. Personal gossip is often malignant, whether intentional or not. Handling gossip and rumors, when they are directed toward you, is another matter.[25]

Anything you reveal about yourself, whether public or private, can make you the subject of office gossip. Refusing to reply to gossip or giving vague answers can be fodder for the gossip mill. When you believe you have become the subject of a potentially destructive rumor, try to uncover the source. Usually a close friend will name the source if you promise confidentiality. Then, in private, confront the person who started the rumor. Be concerned, not angry or confrontational: "Michael, I hear you told a couple of people that I'm looking for a new job and that I've been meeting with a headhunter. The truth is that I had lunch last week with my old college roommate, and he happens to work for an employment firm. But I am not looking for a job, and that story could really cause me a lot of trouble here."[26] Even if the gossiper denies everything, she or he will be stung by your direct approach and think twice before gossiping about you again.[27]

Gossiping cuts both ways. If you sit and listen to gossip and add a comment now and then, you are as much to blame as anyone. Gossiping can hurt your professional reputation. You never know who is friendly with whom, so remember that participating in gossip can backfire on you. Most important, remember that anything you reveal about your personal life, even in the strictest confidence, can and probably will make its way to someone else. Do not be surprised if your supervisor finds out about something that you thought you revealed strictly on the quiet and asks you about it, especially if for some reason the supervisor senses your work has lately been below par. The best way to handle gossip is to leave the room when people begin to gossip about someone else. You do not have to jump up and stalk out, simply say you have loads of work waiting and leave. You never know when one of your coworkers will end up being your supervisor, so it's best to treat everyone in a friendly, polite way and avoid gossiping as much as possible.

Every office has certain coworkers whom you should watch out for. These people are not usually innately hateful; however, they can make your life miserable if you do not know how to handle them.

backstabber
Someone who will turn on coworkers if it is to his or her benefit.

tattletale
Someone who willingly divulges something that should be held in confidence to another.

victim
Someone who is a pessimist and a chronic complainer.

- **The Backstabber.** The professional backstabbers are difficult to detect. They know their game well and always cover their tracks. These people may well be the most genuinely charming people you know; however, their charm masks a lack of human feeling. Backstabbers will turn on a coworker in an instant if it is to their benefit. The best way to deal with the backstabbers is to be friendly, watch your back, and scrupulously document all your office activities.
- **The Tattletale.** The tattletale is a less malicious version of the backstabber. This person loves a good story and will happily divulge any confidence to a willing listener. If you trace a rumor to its source, that source is often a tattletale. This person is not to be confused with the whistleblower, however, who reports genuine problems.[28]
- **The Victim.** The victim is the classic doomsayer and chronic complainer. This person blames management for his or her lack of advancement and trashes coworkers who have moved ahead. If the victim is a female, she may be quick to interpret innocent displays of friendliness from male coworkers as less than honorable.[29] The victim believes that management conspires against workers at all levels and disaster for all will occur any minute. The victim at his or her worst can taint the atmosphere of the entire office with groundless suspicions, accusations, and fears. The best way to combat the victim's statements is to counter them with provable facts that show these statements to be groundless.[30]

- **The Sycophant.** This person flatters anyone who can advance his or her career, especially the boss for whom this person cannot seem to do enough. In addition, agreeing with everything the boss says is this person's forte, at least whenever the boss is within hearing distance. While this person may be annoying, the sycophant's maneuvers are blatantly obvious and usually become the butt of office jokes rather than posing a threat to anyone.

sycophant
Someone who flatters anyone who can advance his or her career.

In most instances, coworkers want as much as you do to make the office a comfortable, pleasant place to work. Figure 2-5 contains several tips on how to be a star coworker as opposed to a problem one.

FIGURE 2–5: RULES TO WORK BY

Here are six rules to follow to be a model coworker.

1. Be friendly and helpful to newcomers and temps. Coworkers who are new to the office, especially temporary workers, often feel on the outside. Offering them a helping hand, showing them where supplies are kept or where the coffee is can ease their transitions and make them feel at home.
2. Remember to give credit where credit is due and to not hog all the credit, especially for team efforts.
3. Try not to be a know-it-all, especially around the boss.
4. Keep personal problems private unless you want to the entire office, including your supervisor, to know about them.
5. Accept responsibility. If it is your fault or partially your fault when something goes wrong, say so. Don't point fingers at others and blame them instead.
6. Stay away from gossip, and do not spread gossip yourself.
7. Being a top employee who moves easily up the corporate ladder means being an ethical employee. The tips in Figure 2-6 offer advice on taking workplace ethics seriously.

INTERACTING WITH SUBORDINATES

When dealing with employees in subordinate positions, avoid abusing your rank. If company culture dictates, use courtesy titles—Mr., Ms., or Mrs.—even if everyone calls everyone else by first names. If you are introducing an employee in a subordinate position to someone from outside your office, use the employee's courtesy title rather than his or her first name. Also, if your assistant is much older than you are, you should use a courtesy title to show respect until the person tells you that using his or her first name is fine. Remember to say, "Thank you," often and with sincerity.

FIGURE 2-6: THE ETHICS OF GOOD BUSINESS ETIQUETTE

Today, the extent to which an organization follows its own ethics policies can make or break how it is perceived by outsiders as well as by employees. When management sets high standards of behavior, it creates the perception that the organization maintains those standards and is a good corporate citizen. High ethical standards reflect the caliber of each person who works for that company. This is not only good for the organization's public perception, but for its internal perception as well. Employees who work in such an environment take pride in their company and in their work. They become more contented and productive.

The best ethics policies should be based on sound values rather than only on compliance with legal standards demanded by outside organizations, such as OSHA. While some cynics view corporate ethics policies as mere words, organizations are being forced to make their ethics policies more than just words on a page.[31]

Do your best to avoid pulling rank. Some employees pull rank on subordinates to get them to do work that they themselves should have done but did not. These rank pullers quickly become known as slackers. For instance, if the receptionist has the photocopying machine in his or her office and is in charge of keeping it running smoothly, do not assume that he or she must also be available to do your photocopying. In most offices, each person does his or her own copying. If you have a large job and are up against a deadline, politely asking for help from coworkers who are not busy at the moment is not out of line. However, when you habitually impose on subordinates to help you out, you are quickly labeled as an office shirker and someone to be avoided.

©Jiang Dao Hua/Shutterstock.com

Often you will find yourself in the position of needing last-minute help with a project. If you have freely given help to others in a pinch, if they can, they will usually help you out. When you are willing to help, others will be willing to return the favor.

INTERACTING WITH SUPERVISORS

Whatever name they go by (boss, supervisor, manager, executive), bosses have bosses, too; even the CEO must report to the board of directors, and entrepreneurs must report to lenders and to their market. Bosses are responsible for their performance to everyone above them in the hierarchy, and they are also responsible for your performance.[32] They, like everyone else in business, have ambitions and fears, hopes and insecurities; in short, they are human, too.[33]

Here are two simple rules to follow when dealing with your boss:

1. **Accept that the boss is in charge.** Show your respect for your boss's decisions by not grumbling or groveling when taking and carrying out orders.
2. **Do your job, and do it on time.** Before you begin to take on extra tasks to please your boss, master your job and do it well.[34] Doing your job well is important in building a good relationship with your boss. Remember that your boss's job is to get the work done in the most productive and profitable manner.[35] When you do your job well and complete it on time, you look good and you make your boss look good.

GETTING THE MOST OUT OF YOUR RELATIONSHIP WITH YOUR BOSS

Whether you like it or not, your boss is your superior. In that role, he or she deserves your respect, and it is your responsibility to get along with this person. Some people do not like to be in a subordinate role. They react either with extreme obsequiousness or masked hostility. Neither emotion will win you any points. Bosses do not want yes-types, nor do they want someone who will argue with their every decision or badmouth them behind their backs. In general, showing respect means "respecting the boss's intelligence and experience" while offering up your own ideas when needed.[36] Here are some tips on how to establish and keep a good relationship with your boss:

- **Respect rank.** Respecting your boss's rank means to use your boss's preferred courtesy title—Mr., Ms., Mrs., Dr.—until he or she tells you to do otherwise, and to respect your boss's privacy. If you need to meet with your boss, call ahead to set up a convenient time, and knock before you enter his or her office. Then wait a moment so that he or she can tell you to sit down if you're going to need more than a minute or so of his or her time. Avoid barging in without first knocking.
- **Offer ideas when appropriate.** Most bosses appreciate fresh ideas from the people they supervise.[37]
- **Do your homework.** Be prepared with your supporting documents before you meet with the boss. Have copies made ahead of time to show you are organized. Be clear and concise when presenting your ideas.
- **Be on the lookout for problems you can solve.** Supervisors like employees who show initiative.
- **Ask for help.** When you need help, do not hesitate to ask for it. It shows that you recognize the boss's knowledge and experience.
- **When you do not know, it is ok to say so.** Trying to make up answers, or answer questions about which you know nothing can get you in trouble and label you as untrustworthy. Instead, offer to find out, and make sure you get the answers in a timely manner.[38]

- **Be a team player.** Bosses like people who are part of a cohesive group and who are ultimately more productive than superstar individualists.[39]
- **Accept your boss's decisions.** Even when contrary to your ideas, graciously accept your boss's final decisions.
- **Accept criticism without hostility.** Learning to take criticism without taking it personally is difficult for many young people who have never been subjected to criticism. All supervisors will make both positive and negative judgments on your work, so it is best to develop a thick skin to profit from criticism. Rather than hear and react to criticism, listen and think.[40] This will enable you to learn and improve from it, rather than to look for hidden meanings: "Jeez, the boss hates me and my work. She thinks I'm stupid."
- **Be loyal.** Company politics can be brutal—reorganizations, mergers, layoffs—and your boss may be caught in the crossfire. Most etiquette manuals advise you to remain loyal to the person above you whatever the outcome, even if your boss gets fired or laid off. Loyalty is a scarce commodity in today's cutthroat workplace, and your willingness to support your boss in the face of company upsets will be noted by others.[41]

Finally, many of us forget that when we are having a one-on-one meeting with our supervisor, our body language reveals volumes about how we are feeling and how we are reacting. To become more aware of what your body language says about you and how to control it, especially around supervisors and managers, see Figure 2-7 for a crash course in body language basics.

FIGURE 2–7: BODY LANGUAGE BASICS

When dealing with coworkers and supervisors, be particularly mindful of what your body language says to them. Try not to send the following ambiguous signals:
- Folding your arms across your chest usually shows that you are either defensive or that you disagree. Sometimes people simply stand like this. If you typically cross your arms, try to be more aware of it, and keep your arms at your sides or rest them on the table at a meeting.
- The way you sit says a lot about you. Slouching may be interpreted as laziness or tiredness, leg crossing can be seen as defensive, and knee jiggling can show apprehension or insecurity.[42]
- Scratching the back of the neck or shrugging the shoulders may denote uncertainty.
- Covering one's mouth with the hand can say to some that you not being entirely truthful.
- Holding your boss's eyes a little too long may be interpreted as a sign of disrespect or as a challenge to authority. Staring at someone can look threatening or just plain strange.
- Fidgeting too much during a meeting—drumming your fingers, cracking your knuckles, rocking your leg back and forth—makes you look uninterested if not downright bored.
- Nodding is good—it can look like you are being attentive—unless you overdo it, in which case you can look like a brown-noser, especially if the nods are directed at your boss's every word.[43]

DEALING WITH DIFFICULT BOSSES

Difficult bosses are simply difficult people who have risen to a supervisory level. Difficult bosses are not tough bosses, the ones who have the ability to drive you to perform beyond your wildest expectations. Difficult bosses, in contrast, make life at the office a nightmare worthy of the best horror films. These bosses range from non-communicators to abusers. They may be control freaks, tantrum throwers, blamers, bigots, or abusers, but whatever they do, they are difficult and oblivious to the way their behavior affects their employees.[44] Beneath the surface, the difficult boss is simply an incompetent manager of people.

© PathDoc/Shutterstock.com

A non-confrontational meeting might help if you can both be specific about your complaints, and you can show that the problem is widespread and affects productivity.[45] If you can offer to help rather than blame your boss as being the root cause of the office's problems, you might be able to defuse your boss's immediate defensive reaction and even garner a willingness to adjust the nonproductive behavior in the future.[46] You could also go over or around your difficult boss to his or her supervisor or to human resources. However, if you take this route, keep the boss informed of your actions; do not do it behind his or her back. Emphasize that you are trying for positive change for everyone, including the boss.[47] Other than these tactics, you can try the following suggestions for dealing with a difficult boss.

- **The tantrum thrower.** This boss is out of control and erupts into screaming fits of rage for seemingly no reason. After these fits, he or she may feel genuinely sorry, but real abusers enjoy humiliating their employees when they least expect it, whether in private or in public. Three things may help you in dealing with the tantrum thrower: (1) document every detail of your boss's fits of rage; (2) set up a time for you and your coworkers to meet with your boss and confront the situation; and (3) if you have no other option, remember that you are not responsible for the boss's bad behavior, which is clearly out of control. Do not blame yourself.[48]

- **The blamer.** The blamer is difficult to spot because, unlike the tantrum thrower, he or she does not rant. Instead, he goes behind your back to assign blame to you when you are not present. The blamer acts from a defensive posture. He or she never accepts responsibility for his or her failures, blaming others instead. Low-level employees are particularly vulnerable to this kind of abuse as they are defenseless. Since the blamer always believes his or her own interpretation of events, the blamer cannot see your point of view. If you document your work and results carefully, performance reviews may present a chance for you to reveal his or her fabrications, since a solid paper trail and the testimony of others can refute a bad evaluation. If you can wait long enough, blamers will finally trap themselves in their lies and fabrications, or their superiors may finally grow tired of their constant refusal to accept responsibility.[49]

- **The bigot.** The bigot is a boss who makes demeaning remarks about people of different ethnicities, religions, nationalities, or sexual orientation. The bigot is detrimental to individuals in these groups because he or she often assigns them the less important work assignments, thereby granting him- or herself permission to pass over them

tantrum thrower
Someone who erupts into fits of rage for seemingly no reason.

blamer
Someone who goes behind another's back to assign blame to him or her when he or she is not present.

bigot
Someone who makes demeaning remarks about people of a different ethnicity, religion, nationality, gender, or sexual orientation.

when making promotion and merit raise decisions.[50] Bigots use their position to draw otherwise decent employees into silently supporting their unfair behaviors. Since federal and state laws forbid discrimination, the bigot is easy to foil these days. If employees document the bigot's words and actions, he or she will quickly be scrutinized by upper management. Today, companies are aware of their liability for their employees' words and actions. Employees with bigoted bosses should notify the boss's superiors immediately.[51]

TELEPHONE ETIQUETTE

Do not underestimate the power of the telephone as a vehicle to improve the public's perception of your organization. The way any employee, from entry level to the CEO, answers the phone, leaves voicemail messages, or engages in phone conversations reflects on the efficiency and client orientation of any business. Observe these essentials of impeccable **telephone etiquette**.

telephone etiquette
Guidelines for placing and answering telephone calls in the business place.

PLACING AND ANSWERING CALLS

Placing a phone call is second nature to most people. We just pick up the phone and place the call, right? It's not that simple if you are placing a business call. When placing a business call, get your thoughts in order before you place the call. Prepare for your call by having the information you need or want to impart in front of you on paper or screen. In addition, have your paper or electronic calendar nearby in case you need to look up dates. Finally, have a pen and notepad in front of you and be ready to take notes so you can refer to them later.[52] Avoid relying on your memory for facts, figures, and decisions that are mentioned during the phone conversation.

Keep in mind that unless you have a scheduled appointment to speak with the other person on the telephone, you are intruding into his or her day. When you begin your conversation, immediately ask if he or she is available for a short conversation or let the person know that you intend to make it quick.[53]

Remember that you may be the first contact a caller has had with your organization, so make a good impression. Be pleasant, polite, and efficient; inject interest in your tone; speak slowly and clearly; and show genuine enthusiasm without sounding ingenuous.

The polite greeting is usually some form of the following: "Good morning/afternoon. This is David Moyer at Handley Corporation. How may I help you?"[54] If you have caller ID, open by greeting the caller by name: "Hello, Mr. Moyer." Use the caller's courtesy title if you are unfamiliar with him or her; otherwise, use his or her first name. If the caller asks for you before you identify yourself, say, "This is he" or "This is David."[55]

If you are the receptionist, after you have identified the company, ask, "How can I direct your call?" Smile when you are speaking. A smile actually improves your tone of voice because when people are smiling, they typically sound alert and enthusiastic.[56]

When answering the phone avoid sounding abrupt or rude, mumbling, speaking in a disinterested monotone, failing to give your name or your company's name, or speaking so quickly that your name is garbled. Customers might hang up if they are put off by an inappropriate tone of voice or by an abrupt or rude reply to their questions.

SCREENING CALLS

If your calls are screened or if you screen calls for someone else, the tone and content of your explanation are important when establishing a good business relationship with the caller. The worst scenario is the caller who is asked, "What does your call concern?" then hears the ubiquitous you-are-now-on-hold music only to be told shortly that the person you wanted to speak with is unavailable. This caller feels as if he or she is being snubbed and that their call must not be important enough to warrant someone's attention. The question "What does your call concern?" if asked brusquely can also annoy the caller, who may resent having an assistant determine the worth of his or her call. While any language in this situation might provoke an annoyed reaction in the caller, a polite "May I ask what this call is in reference to?" or "Ms. Stein is in a meeting at the moment. May I have your name and company, and she'll return your call as soon as possible," or "Ms. Stein is unavailable at the moment. May I direct you to her voicemail?" may allay a caller's irritation at not getting through.

PLACING CALLERS ON HOLD

When you place a phone call, do you like to be placed on hold? I didn't think so. No one likes to be placed on hold. So, if at all possible, don't place callers on hold.

If you are forced to place callers on hold, however, do not say to them "May I place you on hold?" and then immediately switch them to hold before they have time to respond. Wait instead for callers to respond.

If the caller indicates that he or she is ok with being placed on hold, give an approximate length of time this will be. Even then, avoid leaving him or her holding for more than 20 seconds without giving him or her a progress update such as "I am sorry. Mr. Jackson is still on the other line." In addition, play some generally acceptable background music so the caller isn't left wondering if the call has been dropped. Don't substitute continuous-loop advertisements praising your company's exceptional products and customer service for background music. Such advertisements become very annoying for most!

A caller may instead prefer that you take a message, transfer him or her to voicemail, or call back later.[57] So ask him or her if he or she would prefer you take a message or transfer him or her to voicemail instead of continuing to hold. A basic courtesy such as making sure the caller's wishes are met shows that your company cares, and that can affect the way outsiders perceive your organization.[58]

Finally, avoid expressions such *"Please continue to hold. Your business is important to us"* which can easily be perceived as being hypocritical. After all, if a business truly values callers' business, they will extend the common courtesy of not placing them on hold.

LEAVING A VOICEMAIL MESSAGE

When you leave a voicemail message, be sure to include sufficient information (e.g., your name, date, time of day, where you can be reached, and a brief statement of the reason for your call). Speak clearly and more slowly than usual, especially when sharing your phone number and e-mail address. Phone numbers stated too quickly are often difficult for people to decipher and retain. Always try to respond to your phone messages within 24 hours. Doing so shows you are a courteous person.

TAKING A MESSAGE

When you take a message for someone, ask for the caller's complete name and the name of his or her company. Ask for the spelling of either or both if you are unsure, and read back the phone number and e-mail address to the caller.[59] The caller may give you a summary of the subject of the call. If so, get to the essence of the message so the message recipient will have an easy time following up. In addition, jot down the time and date of the call and add your initials to the written message to show who took the message in case the person wants to know more about who called.

WHILE YOU ARE TALKING

Remember that, while you are talking on the phone, the caller is registering the tone of your voice and word choice. Therefore, make an effort to sound both professional and personable.[60] As far as the tone of the conversation goes, take your lead from the other person on the call. If the person wants to talk business, do so. If person is chatty, go ahead and briefly discuss nonbusiness matters. This may lead to the discovery of common interests, which will help you develop a bond that will make your business relationship run more smoothly.[61]

If you are interrupted by another call and it is important that you speak to this caller, take the call but explain that you are in the middle of another conversation and will call back shortly. In any event, never leave your original caller on hold for more than 30 seconds. Generally speaking, it is rude to leave your original caller for another, so be sure the incoming call is urgent enough to do so. If you do, either ask your original caller to briefly hold or politely ask if you could call back shortly. Apologize and explain the reason for attending to the urgent interruption.[62] Otherwise, let the second call go to voicemail.

FIGURE 2-8: PHONE CALL GAFFES

Avoid the following telephone errors. They can make the person at the other end doubt your credibility.

- While on the phone, avoid doing other things at your desk such as texting, e-mailing, tweeting, or shuffling papers. If your phone partner suspects you are doing other things, he or she might think you are uninterested in the conversation.
- Do not chew gum or eat during phone conversations.
- Do not sneeze, cough, or blow your nose near the receiver. Excuse yourself and turn away.
- Always ask the caller's permission before putting him or her on the speakerphone.
- Always ask the caller's permission before putting him or her on hold.
- Do not answer calls while in meetings, training sessions, presentations, job interviews, conversing with others face-to-face or via a videoconference.
- Do not answer or place calls while on elevators.
- Do not answer or place phone calls while in restrooms.

ENDING THE CONVERSATION

Ending a business conversation can be tricky if you are dealing with a long-winded person. Wrap up the conversation with some indication of what you will do next. For example, "I'll get that report to you by Monday" or "I'll summarize the conclusions we reached in a memo and e-mail it to you tomorrow." Other things you can do to end a phone call include mentioning that you have an important meeting coming up or that you have pressing work. Of course, state your case politely, and end with a courteous, "Thank you for calling" or "I look forward to talking with you soon."[63]

CONFERENCE CALL ETIQUETTE

Conference calls are a fact of life in the workplace. The basics of conference call etiquette are simple. The person who sets up the call should set the agenda and be sure that everyone on the call receives a copy in advance of the call. This person should also make sure that everyone is connected before the business of the conference call begins and that everyone can be heard.

Other suggestions include making sure that you are in place when the call comes through, briefly saying "hello" to everyone when you are connected, speaking clearly and loudly enough so everyone can hear you, not interrupting while another person is speaking, refraining from making jokes in the background while someone is speaking, and signing off with a polite "Thanks everyone; it was good to talk to you" or something similar.[64] The person placing the call might also summarize what was accomplished and assign tasks if appropriate before signing off.

Etiquette that provides guidelines for acceptable behavior when communicating electronically is referred to as netiquette. Figure 2-9 contains a number of practical netiquette suggestions.

© Keith Bell/Shutterstock.com

FIGURE 2-9: ELECTRONIC DEVICES ETIQUETTE SUGGESTIONS

Avoid these errors when using electronic communication devices such as smartphones, cell phones, tablets, netbooks, and laptops.

- Smartphone and cell phone users should adhere to the following rule: Do not let your phone ring where it will disturb others, whether in meetings, theaters, restaurants, or any number of other settings. If you must take a call during a business meal or meeting, explain ahead of time to your guests or coworkers, put your phone on vibrate, and politely excuse yourself before you take the call outside.
- Be aware of the people around you when you are on a plane, train, bus, etc. If you talk business in close quarters, others around you cannot help but hear what you are saying. In addition, people nearby will be irritated with being subjected to your chatter. Keep business conversations private by making them in private locations.

- If you are making calls from a car, know the hazards of doing so. Inform the caller if others are in the car and will be privy to the conversation.[65]
- Do not allow your phone to ring during meetings, presentations, training sessions, etc.
- Do not request a pay raise or promotion via e-mail. Doing so is bad form.
- Do not resign from a job via e-mail or voicemail. Doing so is bad form.
- Do not reprimand employees via e-mail or voicemail.
- Do not participate in the following activities during meetings, presentations, training sessions, etc.: e-mailing, instant messaging, texting, blogging, tweeting.
- Do not check your voicemail messages during business conversations.[66]

SOCIAL MEDIA ETIQUETTE

The Remote Worker's Guide to Office Etiquette
http://lifehacker.com/the-remote-worker-s-guide-to-office-etiquette-1707166009

Nancy Flynn, author of the *Social Media Handbook*, sums up social media etiquette as follows. Adhere to the rules of social media etiquette. Be polite, polished, and professional. Write, post, and publish content that is 100 percent appropriate, civil, and compliant.[67] Figure 2-10 contains additional social media etiquette advice.

FIGURE 2-10: SOCIAL MEDIA ETIQUETTE

1. Fill out your online profiles completely with information about you and your business.
2. Use a different profile or account for your personal connections.
3. Create a section on your main profile detailing whom you are seeking to befriend and ask that visitors conform to that request.
4. Offer information of value.
5. Don't approach strangers and ask them to be friends with you so you can then try to sell them on your products or services.
6. Pick a screen name that represents you and your company well.
7. Do not send out requests for birthdays, invitations to play games, or other timewasters for those using the site.
8. Don't put anything on the Internet that you don't want your future bosses, current clients, or potential clients to read.
9. Check out the people who want to follow you or be your friend.
10. If someone does not want to be your friend, accept their decision gracefully.
11. Never post when you are overtired, jet lagged, intoxicated, angry, or upset. Otherwise you might be argumentative or inappropriate.
12. Compose your posts, updates, or tweets in a word processing document so you can check grammar and spelling before you send them.

Source: From Top 12 Rules of Social Media Etiquette by Lydia Ramsey. Copyright © 2010 by Lydia Ramsey. www.mannersthatsell.com. Reprinted by permission.

ELEVATOR ETIQUETTE

Using elevators is a fact of life in many office and apartment buildings. There are many elevator-related etiquette suggestions to keep in mind, ranging from allowing others to board first to holding the elevator doors open for others while you are exiting. When using elevators, there are plenty of opportunities to be courteous and helpful and, if you are not careful, plenty of opportunities to be rude and annoying.

While some people are comfortable using elevators, others are not. Some individuals avoid elevators altogether for a variety of reasons ranging from claustrophobia and sharing germs in close quarters to concerns about cables breaking and getting stuck in a malfunctioning elevator for an extended period of time. Whether a fellow passenger is mildly anxious about the ride or downright frightened, courteous behavior on your part will be appreciated. Here are some examples of good elevator etiquette that is typically appreciated by elevator passengers.

- Hold elevator doors open for others as they board.
- Offer to push the button for their desired floor.
- Wear a pleasant facial expression.
- Avoid staring at fellow passengers.
- If possible, keep out of fellow passengers' comfort zone (arm's length).
- Hold elevator doors open for others as you exit so the doors do not slam shut on them.
- Do not talk to others in elevators unless you know each other.

A little common sense, combined with basic respect for others, will go a long way toward reducing the anxiety some of your fellow passengers experience when riding on elevators. Unfortunately, everyone does not act accordingly. A CareerBuilder study of 3,800 workers nationwide provides us with a list of bad elevator-riding habits. These are listed in Figure 2-11 in rank order, starting with the most annoying behavior.

FIGURE 2–11: BAD ELEVATOR-RIDING HABITS

1. Talking on a cell phone.
2. Not holding the door open when others are running to get the elevator.
3. Standing too close to others when there is plenty of room in the elevator.
4. Squeezing into an already-crowded elevator.
5. Not stepping off the elevator to let others exit.
6. Holding the elevator doors open for an extended time while waiting for someone to get on.
7. Cutting in line to get on the elevator when other people have been waiting longer.
8. Taking the elevator to go up one or two floors instead of taking the stairs.
9. Pushing the wrong button, so the elevator stops at more floors.
10. Facing away from the elevator door, instead of toward the door like everyone else.

Source: From The Ups and Downs of Office Elevator Behavior by Susan Ricker. Copyright © 2012 by Career-Builder. Reprinted by permission.

On a related note, business employees are often judged on their interpersonal skills. With this in mind, in the world of elevator travel you can easily see plenty of opportunities to practice good interpersonal skills.

DRESS

Business dress is typically dictated by your profession and your corporate culture. Dress for men can range from the classic navy, black, or gray suits in conservative organizations to khakis, sports jackets, jeans, and golf-shirts in less formal organizations. Women have a wider range of clothing and styles from which to choose, but they should also observe the dress rules of their work environment. A general rule, men and women should dress conservatively during the first few weeks of a new job until they have had a chance to see and adapt to the office standard. Listed here are a few tips for dressing for success at the office. These should help keep you from making a major sartorial mistake.

- Although the navy, black, or gray suit is not as indispensable for men as it once was, you should have at least one well-tailored suit. You may find yourself wearing it for major presentations and meeting important clients. Be sure the weight of the fabric fits the season: cotton or gabardine for spring and summer; worsted wool for fall and winter.[68]
- For men, the tie is still the most important fashion accessory. While some believe in expressing their individuality with loud colors or wild designs, many fashion experts advise against quirky ties that may offend clients or customers.[69] As a compromise, keep a conservative tie in your office for a quick change if the situation dictates.
- If they work for a conservative organization, women should wear closed-toed pumps with no more than 1½-inch heels.
- Women should wear understated clothes. Your clothes should make you look authoritative and competent. Low-cut blouses, short skirts, or tight pants might be construed as alluring; an image you definitely do not want to project at work.

Any clothes that veer too far from the company standard could be considered as flippant or as showing contempt for standards. Neither will aid your career growth goals and could be cause for dismissal.

"I assume my reasons for abolishing Casual Fridays are clear to everyone in this room."

GROOMING

Men and women should pay careful attention to their grooming. Hair and fingernails should be clean and neat looking. For men, keep nose and ear hair clipped. Keep your breath fresh with a quick toothbrush touch-up after lunch and breath mints. Keep your shoes shined. Heels should not look worn down. Wear clothes that are clean and freshly pressed. Keep a spot remover in your desk for those unexpected accidents, and keep a lint removal brush nearby; especially if you have pets at home.

CUBICLE ETIQUETTE

Cubicles are small employee workspaces that are common-place in offices. Unlike offices with solid walls, a ceiling, and a door, cubicles have moveable partitions 4–5 feet high for walls, a ceiling too high to block out sounds, and no door. Furthermore, your cubicle may be bordered on three sides by other cubicles. Given the openness and closeness of cubicles, some cubicle etiquette suggestions are in order. These are presented in Figure 2-12.

As you can see, cubicle etiquette is grounded in respect for your coworkers. It really comes down to treating others as you would like to be treated. You will get along fine with your cubicle neighbors if you let your common sense and these suggestions guide your actions.

FIGURE 2–12: CUBICLE ETIQUETTE

- Do not stop by a coworker's cubicle uninvited. E-mail, text, or call him or her and arrange a time to visit.
- In your quest to personalize your cubicle, be sure it remains professional look-ing. Items such as small, framed pictures, desk accessories such as pen and business card holders, and small plants are advised.
- When speaking to others face-to-face or over the phone, keep your volume down for obvious reasons.
- Do not place calls on speaker phone.
- Do not eat noisy foods (e.g., chips, pretzels) in your cubicle. Doing so can easily distract fellow workers nearby.
- If you listen to music or the radio, use headphones.
- Do not subject your coworkers in neighboring cubicles to personal conversations.
- Be sensitive to the fact that coworkers can be distracted or harmed by (in the case of allergies) some smells (e.g., certain foods, hairspray, perfume).
- Do not make a habit of looking into coworkers' cubicles. Doing so is an invasion of their space. It is fine to smile and say hi as you walk by if the occupant is looking your way.

Source: Mindy Lockard, "Cubicle Etiquette: Sights, Sounds, and Smells."
http://www.forbes.com/sites/work-in-progress/2011/06/16/cubicle-etiquette-sights-sounds-and-smells/

RESTROOM ETIQUETTE

I suspect you are already familiar with what I will say about restroom etiquette. Hopefully, I will not insult your intelligence or offend you by sharing my thoughts. However, some basic reminders will not hurt.

As a general rule, when using the facilities, do not strike up conversations with people you do not know. Others often find that being drawn into such conversations is uncomfortable and awkward. Most of us visit restrooms for purposes other than conversation and prefer to get on with our business.

Do not participate in phone calls in restrooms. Doing so is considered to be in poor taste and unprofessional, speaks to a lack of modesty, and is discourteous to others using the facilities.

An age-old expression is "there is a time and a place for everything." Well, good etiquette suggests that when using the restroom, it is neither the time nor the place for conversations.

OFFICE PARTIES

A scene in the movie *Bridget Jones's Diary* captured the essence of an office holiday party gone bad. Bridget, complete with tinsel reindeer horns and a drink in her hand, slurs out a karaoke song at the office holiday party just as the boss walks in. According to etiquette gurus Peter and Peggy Post, such office parties are "virtually over and gone."[70] Today's office parties have grown up and are geared more toward building morale and providing employees a chance to form friendships rather than seeing who can drink the most alcohol. Even then, watch out for these office party pitfalls.

- Since drinking too much at work-related social functions can result in behaving in an unruly manner, limit your alcohol intake or do not drink alcoholic beverages at all. Otherwise, you may cause serious damage your reputation, credibility, and career hopes. An extreme drinking-related example resulted in tragedy at a holiday office party when an inebriated employee threw himself against a 22nd-floor, outer-glass wall to prove it was shatterproof. Unfortunately, it was not, and he fell to his death.
- As a concerned coworker or host, be a good colleague and watch out for fellow employees who are overindulging. Try to steer them away from the alcohol and, instead, toward the coffee pot. At least offer to drive them home (if you have not been drinking) or call a cab for them.[71]

When the party has ended, keep others' transportation needs in mind. If someone faces a commute with no designated driver, suggest a cab if no one can give the person a ride home.

BUSINESS ETIQUETTE OUTSIDE THE OFFICE

Whenever you conduct business outside the office, everything you do or say reflects not only on your professionalism and character, but also on the image and credibility of the organization you represent. The focus in this section is on interaction with clients and customers outside the office in areas ranging from networking and business card protocol to **dining etiquette**.

dining etiquette
Guidelines for conducting ourselves during business meals.

NETWORKING

Networking is about making business contacts. However, not all contacts are created equal. Hilka Klinkenberg, director of Etiquette International, recommends ways to make the most out of networking at industry and association events. These include mastering the art of the networking conversation and handing out business cards.

networking
Building a network of professional contacts for business purposes.

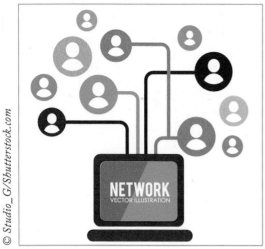

The key to successful networking is active networking, even when you are not looking for a job. If you are always networking and making connections, then when the time comes it will be more natural to mention that you are looking for a job. To maintain an active network, keep in touch with your connections, and help others out when you can. In addition to your natural network, take advantage of specific networking events.[72]

Employing the art of making conversation work for you at networking events begins with one simple rule: Never make a sales pitch at a networking function.[73] Doing so makes you appear pushy, desperate, and inexperienced, and it instantly turns the object of your pitch—the corporate client—against you. In fact, corporate members of organizations often complain of being so over hustled by consultants at industry events that the executives stay away to avoid the annoyance and stress of being barraged with unwanted solicitations.[74]

Rather than appear pushy, try the following ways to make the best of your networking time at any function.

Networking Etiquette: Small Talk and Mingling Skills
http://verilymag.com/2013/08/networking-etiquette-small-talk-and-mingling-skills

- Spend only 5–7 minutes with any one person, and never stretch it past 10. Once you have reached your goal with that contact or have reached a dead end, excuse yourself politely and move on. This gives the people with whom you talk a chance to meet other people.
- Listen more than you talk: Take the focus off yourself at networking functions by listening rather than doing all the talking. If you keep quiet and give the people you meet the opportunity to talk about themselves, they will appreciate your giving them that opportunity. Plus, you will have learned enough about that person to help you form a working relationship with that prospect in the future.[75]
- As you close a conversation with someone who you believe could be a quality contact, arrange to meet at a later date to discuss ideas you have that could be mutually beneficial.

BUSINESS CARD PROTOCOL

Your business card serves many purposes: (1) it invites a new acquaintance to get in touch with you; (2) it defines your position and responsibilities; and (3) it provides at least four ways for someone to reach you: your mailing address, your e-mail address, your phone number, and your fax number.[76] In addition, your business card can easily route others to additional information via a Quick Response Code (QR code). With the swipe of their smartphone over a QR code (optical label) on your business card, they will be able to digitally access information of your choosing that extends far beyond the basic contact information customarily included on business cards.

As a savvy businessperson, you should always have a few clean, unwrinkled business cards with you because you never know when you'll need them: at the baseball park, at dinner, or at a party. To keep them in pristine condition, buy a business-card holder at any office supply, department, or stationery store.[77]

Passing out business cards willy-nilly to anyone and everyone is not the approach to take unless you want them to wind up in the nearest dumpster or unless you want to hear from the person from whom you would least like to hear. One cardinal rule of offering your business card or asking for one is the rule of rank: If the person clearly outranks you, he or she should be the one to request your business card. Otherwise, be reasonably sure that you

FIGURE 2-13: CAPTURING BUSINESS CARD INFORMATION DIGITALLY

Imagine a scenario in which you get together in person for the first time with another businessperson. Early in this meeting you will likely decide to exchange business cards. This is a typical scenario in the business world. However, instead of cluttering your pockets, wallet, or top desk drawer with card-stock business cards, you decide to capture your business partner's business card information digitally. You can do this using a business card reader app such as *CamCard*. With *CamCard*, and similar apps, you simply snap a picture of your business partner's business card. From there, you can digitally store his or her business-card information.

© KPG_Payless/Shutterstock.com

This all sounds very practical. However, you are advised to consider varying cultural expectations pertaining to exchanging business cards. For example, Japanese businesspeople prefer exchanging traditional card-stock business cards. When a Japanese businessperson receives your business card, he or she will typically hold it with both hands while studying it and just might prefer you do the same. In contrast, simply snapping a photo of your Japanese business partner's business card may be perceived as being disrespectful and unprofessional. Furthermore, in several cultures the expectation is that the same information will be on both sides of the business card—in the business partner's native language on one side and in your language on the other side. In these cultures, you would hand the business card to your business partner with his or her native language facing up. Will such business card handling expectations fade away with the advent of business card reader apps such as *CamCard*? If so, it is doubtful it will happen soon. In the meantime, carry some card-stock business cards with you and be considerate of others' expectations pertaining to them.

If you do collect business cards the traditional way but want to store them digitally, you can do so easily with a business card scanner. Among the more highly rated of these are *WorldCard Pro* and *DSmobile*.

will be contacting a person in the future before you ask for his or her card and give yours in exchange. Remember that when you're given a card, you should take a moment to study it and perhaps even compliment the design before putting it into your wallet or datebook.[78] Finally, when you are attending a social event, offering your card privately to someone is fine; however, refrain from holding a business conversation at that time.[79]

BUSINESS DINING ETIQUETTE

Mealtimes have become one of the essentials of conducting business in a rapidly expanding global economy.[80] The business meal is one of the few places where all your social graces are on display, including your conversational abilities, your self-confidence, and your table manners.[81] How you use your knife and fork, put food in your mouth, and use your napkin are big parts of your professional and social image.[82] A lack of table manners is interpreted by others as a lack of polish and people skills, both essential in today's fast-paced and competitive business world. Luckily the rules of dining are not difficult to master, and knowing what to do and when to do it will relieve your nervousness and put you at ease in the most formal of business dining settings.

Dining/Business Etiquette
http://www.fresnostate.edu/studentaffairs/careers/students/preparation/etiquette.html

PROTOCOL FOR THE HOST

The host is an indispensable part of the business dinner. He or she is the person who makes every decision from where to have the meal and who to invite to paying the check and leaving the tip. One of the most important jobs of the host is to make everyone feel comfortable. This includes watching to make sure that all the guests are introduced to the other guests and that no one feels left out. Guests will fondly remember a host who pays careful attention to the smallest details and who is considerate of everyone.

The host picks the location of the meal and sets the time. The location should be convenient for the guests and should be a place where the host knows the guests will feel comfortable. Invitations are also the job of the host, who sets the time and contacts each guest to extend the invitation.[83]

Making reservations and picking a table that is out of the way and conducive to business are also the host's responsibilities. If you are the host, reconfirm your reservation the day before to make sure everything is set, and call the guests to confirm the date, time, and location. On the day of the meeting, as host, arrive at least 15 minutes early to check out the table and make arrangements to pay the check. Seat the other guests as they arrive, but refrain from ordering until the guest of honor arrives. If for some reason the guest of honor is more than 30 minutes late, you can either go ahead and order or leave a tip (for holding the table) and depart.[84]

SEATING ARRANGEMENTS

Seating arrangements are determined by rank and status. At formal affairs, place cards indicate where everyone is to sit. Tradition says that the guest of honor or a person of rank is seated to the host's right. Those lower in the business hierarchy are seated further down the table, reflecting where they fall in the pecking order.[85]

AT THE TABLE

Once seated, guests should wait for the host to unfold his or her napkin. Men should unfold the napkin and place it over one knee with the fold facing toward the knees. Women should also place the fold toward their knees, but they should put the napkin across their lap.[86] When you need to wipe your mouth, do so with the one edge of the folded napkin, dab the corners of your mouth, and then replace the napkin. Any food or stain will then be on the outer side of the napkin so that it will not soil your dress or pants.[87] If you need to leave the table, place your napkin either on the seat of your chair or to the left of your plate.[88]

TALKING BUSINESS

Guests should wait for the host to bring up business issues. For most formal dinners, only one or two business topics should be discussed. Save the serious negotiations for the office.

DECIPHERING THE FORMAL TABLE SETTING

A formal place setting can be daunting. However, every piece is set for a particular purpose and has a practical use. The silverware is placed in a logical progression from the outside in, and each piece corresponds to a particular food course. Sometimes the servers bring the necessary silverware as they serve the next course.[89] Usually, the forks are on left of the plate, and the knives and spoons on the right. The only fork you may find on the right is the seafood fork with its tiny tines.[90]

The only change in the fork arrangement occurs when you are eating in Europe or in a place that serves continental style with the salad coming after the entrée rather than before. In that case, the salad fork is the closest one to the plate.

The dessert fork and spoon usually appear above the dinner plate or on either side of the dessert plate, adjacent to it.[91] If there are also two forks to the left of your plate, the fork to the far left is for salad and the other for the entrée. If you are unsure what utensil to use next, watch the host. If you use the wrong utensil by mistake, do not panic, simply ask the server for another one before the next course.[92]

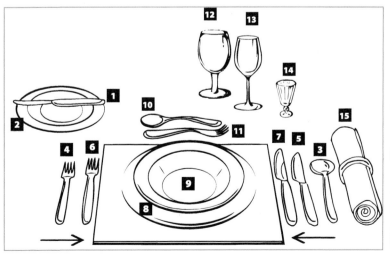

©Liza Dmitrieva/Shutterstock.com

GLASSES AND CUPS

Glasses and cups are always on the right and are arranged in the order they will be used. They are placed above the knife and the soup spoon with the water glass directly above the tip of the knife. Begin with the glass farthest to the right. Each glass is removed along with the course to which it was assigned.[93]

PLATES

The bread and butter plate is placed at the top of the setting to the left. Place your bread and the butter knife across the top of the bread and butter plate when you are not using it. You can use your bread and butter plate for bread and butter as well as for small pieces of paper, like empty packets of sweetener. Before you are served the entrée, you will often find a service plate in front of you. It serves as a place to put the various courses that arrive before the entrée. As the pre-entrée courses are brought to the table, they are placed on the service plate. It is removed when the entrée comes.[94]

ETIQUETTE BY COURSE

After the host directs guests to their seats, move to the right side of your chair and then sit down.[95] Once seated, unfold and place your napkin on your knee or across your lap. After receiving the meal, pause a minute to give the guest of honor the opportunity to pray or to bow silently for a moment.

Bread. If you are the person sitting directly in front of the bread/roll basket or plate, the correct way to pass bread is to one's right, but not before first extending the bread to the person on one's left as a gesture of courtesy.[96]

Soup. Hold the soup spoon like a pencil, and dip the soup away from you in a horizontal movement. Move the bottom of the spoon across the back of the bowl to remove excess that might drip. When you sip from the side of the spoon, do not make noises.[97] Always rest your soup spoon on the plate beneath your bowl, never in the bowl. If you accidentally hit the handle, it could go flying!

Fish Course. Use the fish fork to flake the fish before eating it. The tines of the fish fork are for lifting the skeleton of the fish if it is served with bones.[98] To signal that you are finished with a course, rest the knife and fork side by side in the 10 and 4 o'clock position diagonally on your plate. Always place the cutting edge of the knife toward the center of the plate and the tines of the fork facing down. The handles should extend toward the lower right side of the plate.[99] Place your silverware in the resting position to indicate you are pausing to sip water or take a break.

Sorbet Course. This follows the fish course and is used to cleanse your palate. This course is always served immediately before the entrée.

Entrée. When cutting the entrée, always cut off only one or two bites at a time.

Dessert. As for the dessert course, hold the spoon in your right hand and the fork in your left to secure a difficult dessert, like frozen pie, while you spoon into it. Pie or cake should be eaten only with the dessert fork, while pudding or ice cream should be eaten with the dessert spoon.

FIGURE 2-14: THE 10 MOST COMMON BUSINESS DINING TABOOS

1. Chewing with your mouth open, or speaking with food in your mouth.
2. Putting used cutlery back on the table.
3. Holding the knife like a dagger and the fork overhanded like you are bowing a cello.
4. Ordering indecisively and finishing the meal well before or after everyone else.
5. Using a cell phone during the meal.
6. Putting keys, gloves, a purse, or similar object on the table.
7. Picking or poking at your teeth.
8. Flapping the napkin and putting it on the table before the end of the meal.
9. Slouching, squirming in, or tilting the chair.
10. Leaving lipstick smears.

Source: Mary Mitchell, The Complete Idiot's Guide to Business Etiquette (Indianapolis: Alpha Books, 2000).

DRINKING ALCOHOLIC BEVERAGES AT A BUSINESS DINNER

First, do not feel you have to drink alcoholic beverages because others are. You should feel comfortable sipping on a glass of ice tea, soda, or water if that is your wish. If you do decide to drink an alcoholic beverage, know your tolerance and do not overdo it. However, if you are dining in an international venue, you may find yourself having to break with this strict limit to appear sociable.

For tips on dining etiquette when you are overseas, see Figure 2-15.

FIGURE 2-15: INTERNATIONAL DINING TIPS

- Accept what is on your plate with thanks. It indicates your acceptance of the host, country, and company.
- Whether you are offered sheep's eyes in Saudi Arabia or bear's paw soup in China, take at least a few bites. It is often better not to ask what you are eating.
- In Italy, Spain, and Latin America, lunch is the biggest meal of the day and can often go to seven courses. Of course, you are expected to work afterward. To avoid being overstuffed and overtired for those afternoon meetings, eat only a small serving of everything.
- Except for Islamic and some other cultures, many hosts try to get visitors tipsy as a sign of their hospitality. Usually, saying you do not drink will not get you off the hook. A few sips must be taken, especially when the toasts begin, to avoid offending your hosts.

TOASTS

The host may choose to make a toast before the appetizer or before the dessert. For this, the host stands while the guest remains seated. He or she may hold a glass but should not drink to him- or herself. The guest may then rise to propose another toast. When a toast is proposed, sipping water is fine or raising an empty glass is acceptable if you do not drink.

When the meal is completed, the host places his or her napkin to the left of the plate. The guests should then follow suit. Never refold a napkin or place it on a plate or in a used glass.

TEXTING DURING A BUSINESS DINNER

Texting during a business dinner is considered to be an ill-mannered behavior. Family and friends may tolerate such behavior when out to dinner at a restaurant, but texting during business dinners is strongly discouraged.

LEAVING THE TABLE DURING A BUSINESS DINNER

If you must leave the table during a business dinner, for example to use the restroom, simply say "Excuse me" and then leave. Keep in mind, however, that it is really bad manners to leave the dinner table to place a call.[100]

THANK-YOU NOTES

A thank you addressed to the host thanking him or her for the dinner should be handwritten on fine stationery or an appropriate card and mailed to the host within 24 hours of the dinner. This not only shows that you are considerate but also affirms that you enjoyed the meal. It seals the business relationship.

© joharbu/Shutterstock.com

SUMMARY: SECTION 3—
BUSINESS ETIQUETTE OUTSIDE THE OFFICE

- Your conduct outside the office reflects on both your professionalism and the credibility of the organization for which you work.
- Master the art of networking conversation and handing out business cards.
- When you are given a business card, take a second to look at it and perhaps to compliment the design before putting it in your wallet or datebook.
- Business meals are commonplace, and a lack of table manners is interpreted by others as a lack of polish and people skills, both of which are essential in today's fast-paced, competitive business world.
- Dinner hosts should not only make the dinner arrangements but also be the one to initiate conversation regarding business issues.
- While the number of alcoholic beverages you drink at international business dinners may vary significantly, the general rule in the United States is to limit yourself to three drinks—one before dinner, one during dinner, and one after dinner if you choose to drink alcoholic beverages.

Business Etiquette Tips
http://www.business-managementdaily.com/glp/28411/Business-Etiquette.html

Notes

1. June Hines Moore, *The Etiquette Advantage* (Nashville: Broadman & Holman, 1998), 1.

2. Ibid., 11.

3. Ibid., 3.

4. Hilka Klinkenberg, "Manners Mom Never Taught You." accessed June 23, 2002, http://www.etiquetteinternational.com/Articles/MannersMomNeverTaughtYou.aspx

5. Ibid.

6. Peggy Post and Peter Post, *The Etiquette Advantage in Business* (New York: Harper Resource, 1999), 71.

7. Klinkenberg, "Manners," 1.

8. Ibid., "Manners," 2.

9. Moore, *Etiquette Advantage*, 104–05.

10. Ibid., 106.

11. Ibid.

12. Ibid., 105.

13. Hilka Klinkenberg, "Cocktail Party Panache," http://www.etiquetteinternational.com/Articles/CocktailPartyPanache.aspx.

14. Moore, *Etiquette Advantage*, 112.

15. Ibid., 109.

16. Ibid., 110.

17. Ibid.

18. Ibid., 111.

19. Ibid., 119.

20. Post and Post, *Etiquette Advantage*, 53.

21. Ibid., 54.

22. Ibid.

23. Ibid., 61.

24. Ibid., 63.

25. Ibid.

26. Ibid., 71.

27. Ibid., 65.

28. Ibid.

29. Ibid.

30. Ibid.

31. Ibid., 105.

32. Ibid., 106.

33. Ibid.

34. Ibid., 107.

35. Ibid., 108.

36. Ibid., 115.

37. Ibid., 107.

38. Per Haldbo, *Gold Nuggets Galore—How to Behave in Business* (Copenhagen: Copenhagen Business School Press, 2005), 63.

39. Post and Post, *Etiquette Advantage*, 117.

40. Ibid., 118.

41. Ibid.

42. Peggy Post and Peter Post, *Emily Post's The Etiquette Advantage in Business*, 2nd ed. (New York: Harper Resource, 2006), 216.

43. Ibid., 118.

44. Ibid., 116.

45. Ibid., 117.

46. Ibid., 119.

47. Ibid.

48. Ibid., 288.

49. Ibid., 289.

50. Moore, *Etiquette Advantage*, 46.

51. Ibid., 49.

52. Ibid., 48.

53. Beverly Langford, *The Etiquette Edge: The Unspoken Rules for Business Success*, (New York: AMACOM Books, 2005), 91.

54. Moore, *Etiquette Advantage*, 51.

55. Post and Post, 292.

56. Ibid., 294.

57. Ibid.

58. Ibid., 294.

59. Ibid., 294–95.

60. Ibid., 297.

61. Moore, *Etiquette Advantage*, 60.

62. Ibid., 61.

63. Post and Post, 150–51.

64. Post and Post, 75.

65. Hilka Klinkenberg, "Networking No-No's," http://www.etiquetteinternational.com/Articles/NetworkingNoNos.aspx.

66. Ibid., 2.

67. Nancy Flynn, *The Social Media Handbook: Policies and Best Practices to Effectively Manage Your Organization's Social Media Presence, Posts, and Potential Risks* (San Francisco: Pfeiffer, 2012), 327.

68. Klinkenberg, 2.

69. Post and Post, 226.

70. Ibid., 226.

71. Ibid., 227.

72. Ibid., 314.

73. Ibid., 122.

74. Moore, *Etiquette Advantage*, 122.

75. Post and Post, 391; Moore, 122.

76. Moore, *Etiquette Advantage*, 122.

77. Ibid., 125.

78. Ibid., 127.

79. Post and Post, 434.

80. Moore, *Etiquette Advantage*, 136.

81. Ibid.

82. Ibid., 133.

83. Ibid.

84. Ibid., 134.

85. Ibid.

86. Ibid.

87. Ibid.

88. Ibid., 135.

89. Ibid., 141.

90. Ibid., 143.

91. Ibid., 144.

92. Ibid., 147.

93. Ibid.

94. Ibid., 148.

95. Ibid., 19.

96. Eddy Wang, "Business Dinners: Meal etiquette still matters," *The Dallas Morning News,* July 26, 2015, 2D.

97. Moore, 136.

98. Ibid.

99. Post and Post, 185.

100. Eddy Wang, "Business Dinners: Meal etiquette still matters," *The Dallas Morning News,* July 26, 2015, 2D.

INTERCULTURAL COMMUNICATION

LEARNING OUTCOMES

After reading this chapter, you should be able to:

1. Explain why the ability to communicate effectively with intercultural business partners is increasingly important to businesspeople.

2. Describe the role of intercultural communication in the U.S. workforce.

3. Discuss several ways to form strong relationships with international business partners.

4. Explain why learning your international business partner's native language is important.

5. Discuss written, verbal, and nonverbal communication guidelines as they pertain to intercultural communication.

© Anton Balazh/Shutterstock.com

BENEFITS OF LEARNING ABOUT INTERCULTURAL COMMUNICATION

1. You will increase your chances of receiving job offers and achieving your desired career goals if you can communicate effectively with people from other cultures.

2. You will appreciate the value the business community places on your ability to communicate effectively with people from other cultures.

3. You will gain a greater understanding of your own culture and of your own communication behaviors.

4. You will gain a greater level of respect for, understanding of, and empathy for people of other cultures.

5. You will learn how to obtain information regarding how to communicate with people from other countries and cultures, as well as how to conduct business in other countries.

SELECT KEY TERMS

Low-Context Cultures

Domestic Intercultural

Regiocentric Approach Dialect
Ethnocentric Approach

Translators

Accent Multinational Organization

Global Intercultural High-Context Cultures

Communication Interpreters

Global Approach

Polycentric Approach

INTRODUCTION

The Internet, electronic communication technologies, and rapid transportation have contributed greatly to growth in international business. Wise businesspeople understand their own culture as well as their international business partners' cultures. Furthermore, they respect others' cultures, are open-minded and flexible, and learn all they can about others' countries and cultures. In addition, they take into consideration that some cultures derive meaning primarily from the spoken and written word, whereas others derive meaning primarily from nonverbal and situational cues.

The intent of this chapter is to provide you with an appreciation for and information about intercultural communication. These goals are realized through discussions on the following topics: global and domestic intercultural communication challenges, cultural considerations, language considerations, nonverbal considerations, and intercultural communication and international business sources. The information pertaining to the above-mentioned topics is reinforced by several student website resources including *PowerPoint slides, preview tests, chapter assessment tests, YouTube videos, interactive exercises*, and the *interactive glossary*.

© Rawpixel.com/Shutterstock.com

GLOBAL INTERCULTURAL COMMUNICATION CHALLENGES

Ever-growing numbers of people from around the globe interact daily with each other for business and personal reasons thanks, in large part, to the Internet. Interactions among people of different countries and cultures are certainly not new. People all over the world have interacted with each other in various ways and for varying purposes practically since the beginning of humankind. For example, for thousands of years sailboats facilitated trade within regions and between continents. The ancient Romans are credited with building an elaborate network of stone and concrete roads and bridges connecting lands within and outside of the Roman Empire. These roads and bridges contributed to growth in international trade.

© Alan Uster/Shutterstock.com

While conducting global business is not a new activity, the rate at which it occurs is new. Today we are witnessing a steady increase in global business activity. The ease and speed with which global transactions are facilitated and communication is conducted have multiplied. Given these circumstances, we hear "The world is shrinking" voiced more frequently than ever before.

This increased size is being fueled by growing large-market economies (e.g., China, India), increased global trade, and the proliferation of affordable information and communication technologies, to name a few of the drivers. In addition, transportation improvements speed the rate at which goods move from point to point.

Three trends that have made great contributions to increased global business in the past few years are the privatization of companies formerly owned by governments, more porous national borders, and the growing sophistication of information (communication) technology. For example, trade agreements of recent years, such as the North American Free Trade Agreement (NAFTA), the Asia-Pacific Economic Cooperation (APEC), and the European Union (EU), have opened up many borders to free trade. Finally, the astounding rate of growth and increased sophistication in information technology has stimulated international business tremendously. The advent of communication technologies ranging from e-mail, instant messaging, text messaging, and tweeting to teleconferencing, videoconferencing, and telepresence systems is rapidly eliminating distance and time barriers our predecessors endured.

Organizations that participate in global business do so in a number of ways. For example, some companies develop products or services in their home countries and then sell all or a portion of them abroad. Others, such as Boeing, use a similar approach, but also use a network of suppliers from other countries to achieve their goals. Then, there are **multinational organizations**, such as General Motors and Honda, that produce and sell products in several countries. As can be expected, multinational organizations also employ multicultural workforces, which present internal communication challenges. Currently, there are approximately 60,000 multinational organizations, which is approximately twice as many as existed in 1990.

Within multinational organizations, there are four approaches to assigning management positions—*ethnocentric, polycentric, regiocentric,* and *global.*[1] Each approach holds the potential to enhance or hinder the quality and frequency of communication that transpires among multinational organizations' stakeholders. Multinational organizations that take the **polycentric and regiocentric approaches** assign parent country nationals to top-level management positions and assign host-country nationals or regional-country nationals to mid-level management positions and below. Multinational organizations that take the **ethnocentric approach** assign parent country nationals to all key management positions at both the top and mid-management levels. They assign host-country nationals to only the lower level management positions. Multinational organizations that take the

multinational organization Company that produces and sells products and/or services in two or more countries

polycentric approach Multinational organizations that assign parent country nationals to top-level management positions and assign host country or regional country nationals to mid-level management positions and below.

FIGURE 3-1: ETHICAL CONSIDERATIONS

Managers have always been faced with ethical decisions and challenges. They should make decisions based on high standards of integrity. They should not cast aside ethical actions in their quest to grow their companies, increase profits, or enhance their own careers. In the early years of the 21st century, we witnessed the decline of large multinational companies such as WorldCom, Enron, and Arthur Andersen where select employees apparently set aside their ethical obligations in their quest to improve the state of their companies, their own personal net worth, or both.

Here are examples of techniques that support ethical intercultural business communication.

- Be honest with your communication partners.
- Respect your intercultural communication partners. Avoid communication and business decisions based on stereotypes.
- Respect intercultural business partners' communication media preferences.
- Avoid rushing intercultural business partners to make decisions.
- Avoid using vague words, jargon, and other specialized terms as a way to manipulate intercultural communication partners.
- Avoid speaking quickly during conversations, meetings, and presentations as a way to manipulate intercultural communication partners.
- Include important details from messages, conversations, and presentations as a means of assisting intercultural communication partners.
- Do not "doctor" financial records so the resulting records mislead intercultural business partners and potential investors.
- Interpret and present statistics ethically.
- Avoid misleading and false advertising.
- Do not bribe politicians or others.

regiocentric approach Multinational organizations that assign parent country nationals to top-level management positions and assign host country or regional country nationals to mid-level management positions and below.

ethnocentric approach Multinational organizations that assign parent country nationals to all key management positions at both the top- and mid-management levels.

global approach Multinational organizations that make all management position assignments based on who is best qualified for the position, regardless of whether they are a parent country national, a host country national, or other.

global approach fill all management positions based on who is best qualified for the position regardless of whether they are a parent-country national or a host-country national.

The approach that holds the greatest potential to hindering communication is the ethnocentric approach because it is rooted in **ethnocentrism**, which is "the belief that one's native country, culture, language, and modes of behavior are superior to all others."[2]

DOMESTIC INTERCULTURAL COMMUNICATION CHALLENGES

In addition to the communication challenges inherent in global business, there are communication challenges in the U.S. business place directly related to the intercultural differences among domestic employees, customers, and other stakeholders. The U.S. workplace is one of pronounced cultural diversity. People from all corners of the globe reside and work in the United States. Some were born here and others are naturalized citizens. Still others are immigrants who have not obtained U.S. citizenship. Some immigrants hold work visas, while others are working in the United States illegally. No matter their status, each contributes to the great patchwork of diversity we find in the American workplace.

Overcoming Obstacles in Intercultural Communication
http://www.afs.org/blog/icl/?p=4881

The United States has a long history of cultural diversity in both the workplace and in its citizenry at large. This cultural diversity continues to expand. By the year 2020 more than one half of new entrants to the U.S. workforce will be minorities, with the greatest participation being that of Hispanics, African-Americans, and Asians.[3]

Gender differences often impede communication, even among people from similar cultural backgrounds. Such differences are more pronounced when communication partners have different cultural backgrounds. Gender-related communication challenges in the U.S. workplace will continue to grow as the percentage of women in the U.S. workforce increases. Women currently comprise slightly less than 50 percent of the U.S. workforce.

SUMMARY: SECTION 1— INTERCULTURAL COMMUNICATION— GLOBAL AND DOMESTIC CHALLENGES

- An ever-growing number of people from around the globe interact with each other daily for business and personal reasons.
- Three trends that have made the greatest contributions to increased global business in the past few years are the privatization of companies formerly owned by governments, more porous borders, and the growing sophistication of information (communication) technology.
- Within multicultural organizations, the effectiveness of intercultural communication depends on whether management positions are assigned using the *ethnocentric*, *polycentric*, *regiocentric*, or *global* approach.
- The cultural diversity of the U.S. workforce offers many intercultural communication challenges to U.S. businesspeople.

culture
A complex of language, customs, behavior, and arts that express the identity of a people.

CULTURAL CONSIDERATIONS

Before discussing the role of culture in intercultural communication, let's make sure we are clear about the meaning of the word culture. **Culture** is "a complex of language, customs, behavior, and arts that express the identity of a people."[4]

© Login/Shutterstock.com

Our cultural differences often affect our ability to communicate successfully with others. For example, Saudi businesspeople do not share their American counterparts' desire to "get down to business" in meetings. Saudi businessmen are typically relaxed in meetings, do not hurry, place and receive phone calls, and allow business contacts and others to roam in and out of the meeting room. Such actions often distract, frustrate, and upset American businesspeople who prefer shorter, more structured business meetings free of distractions. An excellent source for information about cultural differences and much more is Gerard Bannon and John Mattock's book *Cross-Cultural Communication: The Essential Guide to International Business.*[5] Another good source is the International Association of Business Communicators (IABC) website. You can visit the IABC online at www.iabc.com.

FIGURE 3-2: CHOOSING GIFTS FOR INTERNATIONAL BUSINESS PARTNERS

Even preferences regarding gift giving can vary significantly from country to country. For example, some international business partners may prefer a bottle of good whiskey over a nice pen set that bears your company's name and/or logo. Others prefer a box of good chocolates and some prefer an item representing the region in which you live. If you are from New Mexico or Arizona, they would like a nice print of a desert scene or some regional jewelry or pottery.

However, something as simple as a gift of flowers can cause problems when not carefully chosen. For example, in some countries carnations and/or purple flowers signify death, whereas red roses signify romantic interest.

Who would have thought that something as basic as gift giving could be so different and complex? The best advice regarding choosing gifts for your international business partners is to first learn what they prefer as well as be very aware of what you should definitely not give them.

COMMUNICATING IN LOW-CONTEXT AND HIGH-CONTEXT CULTURES

A popular way to view cultural differences involves categorizing them as either low-context cultures or high-context cultures. **Low-context cultures** derive meaning primarily from spoken and written words, whereas **high-context cultures** derive meaning primarily from nonverbal and situational cues.[6] Examples of low-context cultures include Germany, Switzerland, Scandinavia, the United Kingdom (UK or England), and Italy. Examples of high-context cultures include China, Korea, Japan, Vietnam, Saudi Arabia, Greece, and Spain.[7] Such cultural preferences are most pronounced and provide fewer communication challenges in countries such as Germany, Italy, China, and Spain where populations are relatively homogeneous.

However, in countries such as the United States and Canada where populations are heterogeneous and low- and high-context cultural preferences are intermingled, effective communication is challenging. For example, "African Americans, Asian Americans, and Native Americans tend to be higher-context communicators than Americans of European descent."[8] English-speaking Canadians are typically low-context communicators, except the French-speaking Canadians, who favor high-context communication.[9] Businesspeople who do not share the same cultural context preferences must make serious attempts at understanding each other's differences and preferences and adjust their own communication preferences and styles to achieve effective communication.

In her journal article, "Cross-Cultural Communication for Managers," Mary Munter summarized communication expert Edward Hall's work on low-context and high-context cultures. Munter discussed four similar, yet different characteristics of low-context and high-context cultures. The four characteristics include initial interaction between participants, what participants value, how agreement is reached, and negotiation preferences.[10]

Initial Interaction between Participants Participants from low-context cultures prefer to get down to business almost immediately, whereas participants from high-context

low-context cultures Societies that derive meaning primarily from spoken and written words.

high-context cultures Societies that derive meaning primarily from nonverbal and situational cues.

Cultural Differences –
High Context versus Low
Context
http://thearticulate-
ceo.typepad.com/
my-blog/2011/08/
cultural-differences-
high-context-versus-
low-context.html

© Mila Supinskaya/Shutterstock.com

cultures prefer to take the time to establish social trust first. For example, U.S. businesspeople prefer to get down to business with their foreign counterparts at the initial contact. In contrast, Saudi businesspeople prefer to become familiar and gain trust with foreign counterparts before formal business transactions occur.

What Participants Value Participants from low-context cultures value expertise and performance, whereas participants from high-context cultures value personal relations and goodwill. For example, U.S. businesspeople place a higher value on their foreign business counterpart's expertise and performance history than on establishing a strong relationship. In contrast, Spanish businesspeople find trust, rapport, and compatibility to be essential qualities that must be established before conducting business.[11]

How Agreement Is Reached Participants from low-context cultures reach agreement by specific, legalistic contracts, whereas participants from high-context cultures reach agreement by general trust. For example, U.S. businesspeople reduce agreements to detailed written contracts; similar agreements are often made in Korea on the basis of someone's word or on a handshake.

Negotiation Preferences Participants from low-context cultures prefer that negotiations move forward as efficiently as possible, whereas participants from high-context cultures prefer slow and ritualistic negotiations. For example, U.S. businesspeople prefer to move through negotiations quickly and they push to ensure a successful outcome. They view time as money and refuse to be wasteful. In contrast, Mexican businesspeople prefer to seek a mutually beneficial business agreement and do not appreciate a pushy business counterpart. They expect the "process to be an enjoyable give-and-take that is as much a test of social skills as a debate over business details."[12]

Common sense reminds us that the better we understand the cultures of our international business partners, the greater the chance that we will form strong business relationships and create win-win situations for all parties. The following tips suggest several ways to meet these objectives.

- Analyze and understand your own culture and subcultures before attempting to do so with others' cultures.
- Reflect on your perceptions of your foreign business partners' country, culture, and subcultures. Be careful not to stereotype your foreign business partners or criticize their way of life.
- Learn how people from other countries and cultures perceive your country, culture, and subcultures and the reasons supporting their perceptions.
- Develop the ability to be open to, understanding of, and accepting of other cultures and subcultures. Develop empathy and respect for other cultures.
- Be flexible, and allow yourself to modify your habits and attitudes.
- Learn all you can about your foreign business partners' culture and country. Learn about customs, traditions, beliefs, religion(s), educational system, politics, social

customs, holidays, recreational activities, history, geography, climate, and notable figures in their literature, music, sports, media, and politics.

Cultures vary greatly in regard to nonverbal cues and how they are interpreted. Figure 3-3 reminds us of the role of nonverbal communication in other countries.

FIGURE 3–3: CULTURAL DIFFERENCES AND NONVERBAL COMMUNICATION

Effective communicators in today's global business environment appreciate cultural differences and their impact on nonverbal communication. They strive to understand the basis of nonverbal messages by learning about the religions, history, and social and business customs of the people of other cultures. In addition, they learn to use nonverbal cues that reinforce effective communication and avoid those that threaten it. For example, American businesspeople visiting Saudi Arabia should greet their hosts with handshakes and warm smiles and Americans must avoid showing the soles of their shoes during conversations. American businesspeople visiting Japan should greet their hosts by bowing and smiling warmly and hand the host a business card printed in English on one side and in Japanese on the other, with the Japanese side up.

No matter how cultural differences are defined or categorized, they have the potential to affect our ability to communicate effectively. Understanding others based on low- and high-context cultural preferences is a good starting point. However, there is much more that needs to be learned about cultural differences. A willingness to learn about numerous communication differences and preferences as they apply to various cultures is necessary to support effective intercultural communication. As a way to assist you in this endeavor, information about a host of language considerations—including verbal and written communication as well as nonverbal considerations ranging from personal space and time preferences to body language—are discussed next.

SUMMARY: SECTION 2— CULTURAL CONSIDERATIONS

- Cultural differences play a significant role in intercultural communication.
- Low-context cultures derive meaning primarily from spoken and written words; high-context cultures derive meaning primarily from nonverbal and situational cues.
- The four characteristics of low-context and high-context cultures are the differences between their initial interaction between participants, what participants value, how agreement is reached, and negotiation preferences.
- Wise businesspeople understand their own culture as well as those of their international business partners, they respect others' cultures, they are open-minded and flexible, and they learn all they can about their foreign business partners' culture and country.

LANGUAGE CONSIDERATIONS

For a moment, imagine the frustrations and misunderstandings when people from different cultures try to communicate with each other. Effective intercultural communication is challenging. In addition to the challenges related to understanding and respecting cultural, written, nonverbal, and verbal differences and expectations, languages, accents, and dialects present substantial hurdles.

That some people are low-context communicators and others are high-context communicators reminds us that we should not assume that everyone values and interprets language to the same degree. This suggests that becoming fluent in your foreign communication partner's native language or using competent interpreters and translators won't always result in effective intercultural communication. This would likely be the case when communicating with high-context communicators, such as Chinese and Japanese, who derive meaning primarily from nonverbal and situational cues rather than language. In contrast, low-context communicators, such as Germans and Italians, derive meaning primarily from spoken and written words—from language. None of the above is meant to diminish the importance of either language or nonverbal and situational cues. In general terms, it is best to give adequate preparation and attention to each, thus preparing yourself to meet the full range of intercultural communication needs.

YOUR OPTIONS

Beyond adjusting for low- and high-context communication preferences, what are your options? If your intercultural communication partner's language is different from your native language, in what language will you choose to do business, and what are the implications? You have three language-related options. You can: (1) stick with your native language, (2) rely on interpreters and translators, or (3) learn your intercultural communication partner's native language.[13] Before reading further, how would you rank each of the three options in terms of its potential impact on intercultural communication?

Option 1 Sticking with your native language in situations where your communication partner's native language is different is the least effective choice. Do not be careless or lazy and assume English is the standard international business language around the globe. Approximately 90 percent of the people on the planet do not speak English. While English is used for the majority of outgoing and incoming international communication in the United States, for the majority of foreign business partners, English is a second language.

If English is your native language and you choose to stick with English, adhere to the suggestions presented in the following sections that address communicating in writing and verbally with intercultural communication partners.

Option 2 Relying on interpreters and translators is a viable option in situations where your communication partner's native language is different than yours. Interpreters are people who serve as oral translators between people speaking different languages.

interpreters
People who serve as oral translators between people speaking different languages.

© Macrovector/Shutterstock.com

FIGURE 3–4: TECHNIQUES FOR USING INTERPRETERS EFFECTIVELY

- Brief the interpreter in advance about the subject.
- Speak clearly and slowly.
- Avoid little-known words.
- Explain the major idea in two or three ways, so the major idea is clear.
- Do not talk more than a minute or two before giving the interpreter a chance to speak.
- While talking, allow the interpreter time to make notes of what is being said.
- Do not lose confidence if the interpreter uses a dictionary.
- Give the interpreter permission to spend as much time as needed in clarifying points whose meanings are obscure.
- Do not interrupt the interpreter as he or she translates, as interrupting causes many misunderstandings.
- Avoid long sentences, double negatives, or negative wordings when a positive form could be used.
- Inject pauses in long responses.
- Avoid superfluous words.
- Provide clarification of specialized business and technical terminology.
- Try to be expressive and use gestures to support your verbal messages.
- During meetings, write out the main points discussed, so both parties can double check their understanding.
- After meetings, confirm in writing what has been agreed on.
- Take frequent breaks (e.g., every 30 minutes or so).
- Consider using two interpreters if interpreting is to last a whole day or into the evening, so when one tires the other can take over.
- Be understanding if the interpreter makes a mistake.
- Ask the interpreter for advice if there are problems.

Sources: Philip R. Harris and Robert T. Moran, Managing Cultural Differences, 3rd ed. (Houston: Gulf Publishing Company, 1991) 63–64; David A. Victor, International Business Communication. (New York: HarperCollins, 1992) 41–42.

The 6 Key Qualities Of A Good Interpreter http://www.thelanguagefactory.co.uk/6-key-qualities-good-interpreter/

translators
  People who
  translate written
  documents and
  messages from
  one language to
  another.

Translators are people who translate written documents and messages from one language to another. Using interpreters and translators is potentially less effective than you being fluent in your communication partner's native language. For example, meaning may be lost in the process of interpreting between two languages. Given such potential shortcomings, it is imperative that you select competent, reliable professionals. Look for interpreters and translators who are (1) extremely well versed in the native languages of both business partners; (2) reputable—check credentials, work history, etc.; (3) ethical and discrete; (4) familiar with the necessary regional dialect(s); and (5) familiar with the necessary business and technical terminology.[17]

In addition to selecting a competent, reliable translator, you are encouraged to personally review translated documents as a means of identifying overlooked mistakes that might lead to miscommunication or unsuccessful business relations. Here are several suggestions:

- Verify the spelling of your name and the name of other parties mentioned in the document.
- Check for inclusion of job and political titles.
- Verify the spelling of company names, brands, products, and trademarks.
- Translate your product name to see what it means in your business partner's language. For example, General Motors learned this lesson the hard way when they promoted the Chevy Nova in Spanish-speaking cultures. The Spanish translation for *nova* is won't go! This is hardly the message General Motors meant to communicate.
- Evaluate the overall appearance of the document. For example, make sure the message is centered on the page, the font style is legible, the type size is reasonable, and the document is free of smudges and other unprofessional marks.
- Look for appropriate use of diacritical marks (e.g., squiggles, dashes, dots) that serve as accent marks in a number of languages including German, French, and Spanish.
- Look for a number of errors such as misuse of capitalization, abbreviations, and numbers.
- Back-translate the document. After reviewing the translated document and making corrections, have a new translator translate the document back into the original language as a way to identify errors or discrepancies.[18]

Advances in communication technology have resulted in electronic tools and software capable of translating both oral and written messages and documents into many languages and dialects. Such advances add to a long list of developments that enable people from different cultures and countries to communicate with each other more easily and quickly. Telephones and Telex were exciting developments that altered international communication. Of course, the Internet has added additional ways (e.g., e-mail, social media) to communicate quickly and easily with international business partners and, in turn, has greatly reduced the need to send messages via air mail. In addition, technologies ranging from conference calls and Video Chat to Zoom and Go-To-Meeting have provided global business partners with efficient alternatives to face-to-face meetings.

FIGURE 3–5: TRANSLATION TECHNOLOGY

Mobile translation apps such as *Google Translate, iTranslate, Waygo, iHandy, Voice Translator,* and *Microsoft Translator* for smartwatches; palm-size electronic translators such as *Franklin Speaking Global EST-7014, Lingo Voyager 6, ECTACO Partner XL-1500 Multilingual,* and *Nyrius Global Talking*; and translation software that translates oral and written messages into a variety of languages aid global business partners and travelers in overcoming language barriers. With these technologies, you type, write, or dictate a desired word or phrase and the unit's digitized voice responds in the desired language with proper pronunciation and voice inflection.

In addition, translation software containing extensive vocabularies can quickly translate written documents including text files, blogs, e-mail, web pages, instant messages, and chats into a variety of languages. Sample programs include *Babylon, Power Translator, Promt, Personal Translator, Systran, IdiomaX, Cute Translator, Word Magic,* and *NeuroTran.*

© Aleksandra Gigowska/Shutterstock.com

Translation apps, palm-size electronic translators, and translation software programs provide businesspeople with relatively inexpensive, effective tools to help them better communicate with their culturally diverse stakeholders.

Unfortunately, all translation apps, electronic translator devices, and translation software programs are not 100 percent accurate all of the time. This seems to be more noticeable in the free and less expensive options. While mistranslations may not be of concern when translating for personal uses, they could easily cause problems in business settings.

Option 3 Learning your communication partner's native language holds the greatest potential for effective intercultural communication. Successful international managers say there is no adequate substitute for knowing the local language.[19] As you might expect, learning your communication partner's native language is no small challenge. With approximately 7,000 languages and 40,000 alternative language names and dialects used around the globe, it is unrealistic to expect that you will learn all of them. However, you are encouraged to learn the native languages of those with whom you do business frequently or with whom you hope to do business. If you are currently training for a business career, make it a point to learn one or more languages. If you are not sure which language(s) you should tackle, consider learning one or more of those that are most commonly spoken. These are listed in Figure 3-6.

The World's Most Spoken Languages And Where They Are Spoken http://www.iflscience. com/environment/ worlds-most-spoken-languages-and-where-they-are-spoken

FIGURE 3-6: MOST WIDELY SPOKEN LANGUAGES IN THE WORLD

Rank	Language
1	Mandarin
2	Spanish
3	English
4	Hindi/Urdu*
5	Arabic
6	Portuguese
7	Bengali
8	Russian
9	Japanese
10	Punjabi

*Hindi and Urdu are nearly indistinguishable. Hindi is the official language of India; Urdu is the official language of Pakistan. Source: The Ten Most Common Languages, http://www.alsintl.com/blog/most-common-languages/

Fortunately, you should not have to look too far to locate university and community college language classes. Some of these are offered in face-to-face settings, while others are offered remotely, in multiple settings for large classes. You might consider learning a language using an online program, an audio program, or a book.

THE ROLE OF DIALECTS AND ACCENTS

dialect
A regional form of a language.

A **dialect** is a form of a language spoken in a specific region of a country. There are an abundance of dialects, and each holds the potential to interfere with effective intercultural communication. In addition to the approximately 7,000 languages mentioned previously, approximately 40,000 alternate languages and dialects are spoken. Just imagine the challenge of communicating in India, the home of more than one billion people where over 400 languages and an estimated 2,000 dialects are spoken! If you are an English-speaking businessperson, you will be pleased to know that English is widely used among business-people and politicians in India.[20]

Dialects present additional challenges to intercultural communication. Learning others' languages is no easy task but it is encouraged. The same can be said about dialects. Do not stop with merely learning another language, learn the regional dialect of your foreign business partners.

An **accent** refers to different ways people pronounce words, which results from the speaker's pitch and emphasis on a certain syllable. Accents, whether regional or foreign, certainly add a wealth of flavors to verbal communication. While accents add a degree of interest to verbal exchanges, they can interfere with clear communication. For example, two English-speaking people, one from Calcutta, India and the other from Houston, Texas, could have trouble understanding each other's accents. The Indian's accent combined with a rapid rate of speech may interfere with pronunciation, understanding, and retention. Likewise, the Texan may have a drawl resulting in a much slower rate of speech and a drawing out of vowels that may result in pronunciation, comprehension, and clarity problems.

No one is suggesting that people eliminate their accents; although some individuals have done so in the interest of growing their business careers and controlling others' perceptions of them. You are encouraged to look at accents realistically. Basically, slow down or speed up your rate of speech if you believe such a move will benefit your listeners. Focus a portion of your efforts on pronouncing words in such a way that your audience will understand them, so they are not left guessing or constantly asking you to repeat yourself. Be sensitive to the potential effects of accents on intercultural communication.

accent
The prominence given in speech to a particular sound.

COMMUNICATING IN WRITING WITH INTERCULTURAL COMMUNICATION PARTNERS

Clear, effective writing is challenging even when the communication partners share the same native language and even more so when they don't share the same native language. What follows is a list of practical suggestions to keep in mind when writing to intercultural communication partners followed by more detailed coverage of the process.

Here are a number of suggestions to keep in mind when writing to intercultural communication partners.

- Before deciding to communicate in writing, determine if your intercultural communication partner, indeed, prefers being contacted in writing over being contacted verbally. If he or she does, identify the most appropriate writing medium for the situation (e.g., *hardcopy letter, e-mail, text message*).
- Invite feedback. In other words, be clear that it is ok for him or her to contact you if questions arise or clarification is needed.
- Adapt your writing style and tone to that of your readers.
- Use the most common words with their most common meanings.
- Use short words wherever possible.
- Strictly follow grammatical rules.
- Avoid idioms, slang, jargon, buzzwords, and clichés.
- Avoid sports expressions (e.g., *out in left field* and *he struck out*).

Five Top Tips: Global Business Writing
http://www.writing-skills.com/five-top-tips-global-business-writing/

- Avoid metaphors (e.g., *up the creek without a paddle*).
- Be literal.
- Avoid humor. Humor is personal and translates poorly.
- Use active verbs instead of passive verbs (e.g., *she received*, not *she was given*).
- Use two-word verbs sparingly (e.g., *continue*, not *go on* or *accelerate*, not *speed up*).
- Keep sentences and paragraphs short.
- Keep sentence structure simple.
- Use one-sentence paragraphs as emphasis tools.
- Avoid sexist language, and do not assume the words *he* and *him* refer to women as well as to men.
- Use politically correct terms and phrases.
- Limit letters, memos, and e-mail messages to a single page.
- Proofread carefully. Careless writing and overlooked errors leave foreign business partners with poor perceptions of writers and the organizations they represent.[21]

DRAFTING FOR INTERNATIONAL AUDIENCES

Since English is a widely used international language of business and technology, business writers should be aware of the guidelines for writing international messages in English. English is now used for well over 90 percent of incoming and outgoing international correspondence. To communicate effectively with an international audience, writers in U.S. organizations should know (1) how to make messages as clear as possible and (2) how to accommodate cultural differences in business communication. Careless use of language in correspondence and in business meetings and insensitivity to local customs are recognized as being the two most serious impediments to effective international communication.[22]

According to Nicole Barde, manager of Intel Corp.'s business practices network, when doing business outside the United States, be aware of the nuances of language. Some common U.S. words and phrases like *team collaboration* and *constructive confrontation* have negative connotations in Asian countries. Therefore, to meet their business goals, Intel professionals use different terms but keep the intent of the message the same.

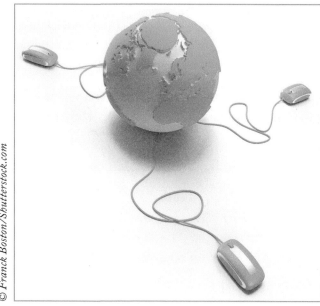

© Franck Boston/Shutterstock.com

BECOME FAMILIAR WITH INTERNATIONAL ENGLISH USAGE

International English is English for businesspeople who must deal with people whose native language is not English. International English is limited to 3,000–4,000 of the most common words in English. Helpful reference works include P. H. Collin, M. Lowi, and C. Weiland's *Beginner's Dictionary of American English Usage and International English Usage.*[23] However, variations in International English usage exist from country to country. For example, in Australia, *forestland* refers to grass, not trees. In the United Kingdom, *stocks* are called *shares,* time is quoted in military terms (e.g., *1 p.m.* is *13:00 hours,* but *1 a.m.* is *1 a.m.*), and a *tuxedo* is called a *dinner jacket.*[24]

Let's say you send a quick e-mail to a business associate in England asking her to buy 1,000 shares of a certain stock before 5 (meaning, of course, 5 p.m.). You also let her know that at your dinner meeting with her in London tomorrow night, you will be wearing a tuxedo. The quick e-mail could create misunderstandings that would be both costly and embarrassing. To avoid these kinds of costly errors, check your international messages for the five areas where mistakes are most often made.[25]

Be Literal and Avoid Humor Whatever message you send to an international audience, they will interpret it literally, so try to keep it clear. For example, if you indicate that your speaker will be using all the usual *bells and whistles* in his or her presentation, they may wonder why the speaker believes that bells and whistles are necessary. Or, if English is not your reader's first language, this sentence may really come as a surprise. *Forgive my delay in answering your letter of August 9. I must need a brain transplant.*

Remember that humor is a personal thing and does not translate well. Before using humor in international correspondence, ask yourself, "Is humor necessary for me to get my point across clearly?"

Avoid Idioms, Slang, Jargon, Buzzwords, and Clichés *Idioms* are words and expressions specific to American English, such as *back down* or *back off. Slang* is a specialized language created and used by particular people and groups, such as *ace in the hole* or *hard-nosed,* or *going postal. Jargon* and *buzzwords* are words specific to a particular profession, such as *bottom line, debug, blackball,* and *cutthroat competition. Clichés* are overused and often outdated expressions, such as *bite the bullet, bag of tricks,* and *per your request.* Before you send a business message abroad, delete the idioms, slang, jargon, and clichés, and replace them with standard English words that are easily translated. Here are some edited rewrites:

Translators' dictionaries rarely include technical jargon: The bug is agnogenic.

Revised: We do not know the cause of the software problem.

Slang presents big translation headaches: Be sure to let me eyeball the proposal before you kiss it goodbye.

Revised: Please allow me to look at the proposal before you sign it and return it.

Clichés are another translation problem: I see no need to beat a dead horse.

Revised: I see no need to take up more time on this issue. It is no longer of interest to either of us.

Use Short Words Use short, simple words to ease translation difficulties and to lessen the chance of misunderstandings.

Pretentious writing—using long, showy words to impress others—rarely impresses domestic audiences and only confuses international audiences. Language complexity only increases comprehension and translation difficulties. Edit your international correspondence for unnecessary inflated language. Substitute plain, basic terms such as the following.

Avoid	Use
Conjecture	Guess
Concerning	About
Conceptualize	Conceive of
Commence	Begin, start
Remuneration	Pay
Prioritize	Order
Maximize	Increase
Utilize	Use

While using short, simple words is a good idea when writing to audiences outside the United States, using contractions and acronyms to shorten words is not helpful. In most cases, these shortened forms are unfamiliar to your international readers. Instead use their longer equivalents.

Rather Than This	Use This
aren't	are not
don't	do not
hasn't	has not
there's	there is
Fax	Facsimile
Bike	Bicycle
Ad	Advertisement
ASCII	American Standard Code for Information Interchange
DOD	Department of Defense
SEC	Securities and Exchange Commission[26]

Use Short Sentences and Keep Sentence Structure Simple The same principle that applies to word length applies to sentences. Short sentences are easier to read and comprehend than long, complex sentences. Even though you would want to avoid writing a message using only short, choppy sentences for an English-speaking audience, a translated message is not read the same way. Choppiness and variety are not big concerns for an international reader. Understanding the message is the main concern. The following sentence is an example of a long sentence that can be shortened for clarity.

I am in receipt of your communication of September 7th in connection with our office's handling of the McDermott Manufacturing situation and despite the fact that our underwriting team is at this point in time managing and processing in excess of 300 active files I would like to point out that your request was accommodated well within the normal time parameters allowed for this type of business transaction and in addition was executed with extreme accuracy.

This wordy, complex sentence can be broken up into three short, simple sentences: I have your letter about McDermott Manufacturing, dated September 7. Currently, we have a backlog of 300 files. However, I am happy to tell you that your request was handled accurately and on schedule.

Shorter sentences reduce the risk of miscommunication. As a general rule, in international business correspondence, use short, simple sentences of 20 words or fewer.[27]

Conform to the Rules of Grammar: **Sentence Fragments** Edit your international correspondence carefully for sentence fragments. They are a translator's nightmare. "The suggestions for content and organization are standard. Most of them anyway." Rewrite that text to remove the fragment: "Most of the suggestions for content and organization are standard."

Dangling or Misplaced Modifiers Modifiers should be placed as close as possible to the word(s) they modify. When a modifier appears several words apart from the word(s) it describes, that is a *misplaced modifier*. When there is nothing for the modifier to modify in the sentence, it is a *dangling modifier*. Either one can cause real translation headaches.[28]

- **Edit for Misplaced Modifiers** I noticed your package getting onto the elevator. Thank you for sending it so promptly. (Was the package getting onto the elevator?)

Revise to place the modifier correctly: As I got onto the elevator, I noticed your package.

- **Edit for Dangling Modifiers** While requesting an extra shipment, the specialty cassettes were accidentally left out. (The specialty cassettes requested?)

Revise to include someone who could logically request the shipment: When I requested an extra shipment, I forgot to include the specialty cassettes.

RESPECT THE CUSTOMS OF YOUR READER'S COUNTRY BY ADAPTING YOUR WRITING STYLE AND TONE TO THEIRS

In the United States most business writers follow the conventions of the modern business style: direct organization (except in cases of bad news or special persuasive situations), conversational style, and "you-oriented" writing. In contrast, the tone and writing style of most international business correspondence is more formal and traditional. To build goodwill between you and your international contacts, be tactful and sensitive at all times. Keep cultural differences in mind to avoid sounding harsh or rude.[29]

The "you" or "reader" orientation does not work well when writing to a collectivist culture like Japan where it is improper for one person to be addressed or singled out. Use a "we-oriented" or "company-oriented" approach when addressing a Japanese audience.

The direct approach used by U.S. businesspeople when writing good news, routine requests, or inquiry letters may appear to be boastful or arrogant in another culture. In most countries, politeness is an important quality in business messages. Soften direct words such as *expect* or *require* to *would appreciate*.[30] Another way to show politeness is to include common phrases of the country or to include a compliment showing knowledge of the country's heritage to help the reader feel comfortable. For example, Japanese businesspeople always begin their letters, no matter what the subject, on a personal note with a statement about the season: "It is spring, and the cherry blossoms smile to the blue sky."[31] Germans are often direct with bad news. Latin Americans, in contrast, believe it is impolite to give bad news, so they avoid it completely. Japanese writers present negative news in a positive way to avoid causing the reader to lose face. A U.S. reader may feel this approach is deceitful rather than polite.[32]

In the United States, ending a negative message on a positive note is an important way to regain the reader's goodwill. However, the French do not consider this to be important and begin and end their letters very formally. "Please accept, dear Sir, this sincere expression of my best feelings," would be a typical ending for a French business letter. In addition, French writers express apologies and regret for any inconvenience caused, something U.S. writers do less frequently. German letters also have formal endings.[33]

As a writer, keep cultural differences in mind when you write business letters to people from another culture. Take the time to become familiar with the customs of the culture you are addressing, and moderate your writing style and tone to align with your knowledge of the person to whom you write.

COMMUNICATING VERBALLY WITH INTERCULTURAL COMMUNICATION PARTNERS

People from different cultures frequently communicate with each other verbally. They do so during face-to-face conversations, social gatherings, negotiations, phone conversations, business meetings (face-to-face, conference calls, and videoconferences), and business presentations. A number of guidelines for communicating effectively verbally with intercultural communication partners appear in the following two lists. The first list contains general guidelines for face-to-face conversations, social gatherings, negotiations, telephone conversations, and business meetings. The second list contains guidelines for presentations to international audiences. Some of these guidelines mirror those recommended when writing to intercultural business partners.

© Rawpixel/Shutterstock.com

The following list of verbal communication guidelines apply to face-to-face conversations, social gatherings, negotiations, telephone conversations, and business meetings with international communication partners.

- Before deciding to communicate verbally, determine if your intercultural communication partner, indeed, prefers verbal communication over written communication. If he or she does, identify the most appropriate verbal medium for the situation (e.g., *face-to-face conversation, phone call, Face Time, Skype, GoToMeeting*).
- Invite feedback. In other words, be clear that it is ok for him or her to ask questions and seek clarification if needed.
- Use the most common words with their most common meanings.
- Use short words wherever possible.
- Speak at a slower-than-normal rate. This will helps others to keep up, and it helps you with clear enunciation.
- Pronounce words precisely.
- Do not mumble or slur words.
- Control your accent.
- Speak with clear breaks between words.
- Avoid idioms, slang, jargon, buzzwords, and clichés.
- Avoid sports expressions (e.g., *out in left field* and *he struck out*).
- Avoid metaphors (e.g., *up the creek without a paddle*).
- Be literal.
- Avoid humor. Humor is personal. It translates poorly.
- Use active verbs instead of passive verbs.
- Use two-word verbs sparingly (e.g., use *continue* instead of *go on* and *accelerate* instead of *speed up*).
- Pause frequently for emphasis and to help your audience keep up with you.
- Avoid sexist language, and do not assume the words *he* and *him* refer to women as well as to men.
- Use politically correct terms and phrases.
- Avoid cursing.
- Avoid interrupting your communication partner when he or she is speaking.
- Show your communication partner that you are interested in his or her thoughts, ideas, and opinions by exhibiting excellent listening skills.
- Encourage and provide feedback.
- Promote clarity by repeating or restating important points.
- Paraphrase your communication partner's words, and encourage your communication partner to do the same with your words.
- Be patient with your communication partner.
- Following important verbal exchanges (meetings, face-to-face conversations, phone conversations, etc.), confirm what was said, agreed on, etc., in writing in your communication partner's native language.[34]

This next list contains verbal communication guidelines for business presentations given to international audiences. In addition to these suggestions, consider that most of the guidelines in the previous list also apply to business presentations and the subsequent question-and-answer sessions.

- Before beginning, tell your audience how long you will speak and your preferences regarding interruptions and questions.
- Before diving into your presentation, provide each audience member with a handout containing your basic outline for the presentation in your audience's native language.

Then, go through it briefly using a presentation software program (e.g., PowerPoint) or overhead transparencies.

- Meet your foreign audience's formality expectations (e.g., some prefer a conversational tone and some do not, some prefer visual aids be prepared in advance and for others it is not an issue, etc.).
- Talk to your audience instead of reading from a written or memorized script. You appear more interesting and dynamic, and thus, will better hold their attention.
- Make your points plainly, clearly, and one at a time.
- Use visual aids whenever possible.
- Use visual aids that are simple and clear in design and content.
- At the end, provide a detailed handout of your presentation in your audience's native language. Be sure to include your name and contact numbers, e-mail address, etc., so audience members can contact you if they need clarification.[35]

SUMMARY: SECTION 3— LANGUAGE CONSIDERATIONS

- The three language-related options for communicating with people whose native language is different than yours are: (1) stick with your own native language, (2) rely on interpreters and translators, or (3) learn your intercultural communication partner's native language.
- The most effective option is to learn your intercultural communication partner's native language.
- Accents interfere with intercultural communication.
- Communicating effectively in writing with intercultural communication partners is challenging; thus, you should practice the suggestions presented in this section.
- Communicating effectively during face-to-face conversations, social gatherings, negotiations, phone conversations, business meetings, and business presentations with intercultural business partners is challenging; thus, you should practice the suggestions presented in this section.

NONVERBAL CONSIDERATIONS

Nonverbal messages are those messages communicated without words. They comprise a large percentage of communication that occurs in domestic and global business places. Nonverbal messages are important components of communication in organizations abroad.

Nonverbal communication is valued, understood, and practiced differently from country to country and culture to culture based on traditions and preferences. The degree of value different cultures place on nonverbal communication was introduced earlier in the chapter through a discussion of low-context and high-context cultures and communicators. Recall that high-context communicators derive meaning primarily from nonverbal and situational cues. This preference is typical of Japanese, Koreans, Saudis, and Spaniards, to name a few. In turn, low-context communicators derive meaning primarily from the spoken and written word. This preference is typical of Germans, English people, and Italians, for example.

Nonverbal messages find their way into business communication no matter the country, culture, or context preference; however, the significance of nonverbal communication varies throughout the world. As a result, businesspeople around the globe are challenged to familiarize themselves with and respect these differences.

NONVERBAL COMMUNICATION CATEGORIES

Nonverbal messages are communicated in a variety of ways. Here we organize them into five categories:

1. *Kinesics* refers to the use of body language. Examples include posture, gestures, head movements, facial expressions, eye movements, touch, and physical appearance.
2. *Paralanguage* refers to the use of voice. Examples include volume, pitch, rhythm, tone, intensity, yawning, throat clearing, grunting, laughing, crying, nonfluencies (*ah* and *um*), and pauses.
3. *Chronemics* refers to the use of time. This reminds us that our attitudes about time and how we manage it often communicate messages to others. For example, U.S. businesspeople prefer to be on time for meetings, while Latin American businesspeople purposely arrive late because they do not want to appear too anxious to make a deal.
4. *Proxemics* refers to the use of space. This refers to matters of physical distance between individuals. Here we are reminded that people from varying cultures have different expectations regarding how much physical distance between business partners is appropriate.
5. *Environment* refers to the use of the physical environment. Examples include office design, size, location, tidiness, temperature, colors, plants, paintings, and furniture.

Several major forms of nonverbal messages are discussed in this chapter; however, it is not an all-inclusive list. The volume of information regarding intercultural nonverbal communication, combined with the scope of this book, limits our discussion of the topic.

Nonverbal Communication in Different Cultures http://www.brighthub-pm.com/monitoring-projects/85141-project-communication-tips-nonverbal-communication-in-different-cultures/

FIGURE 3–7: INTERCULTURAL NONVERBAL COMMUNICATION SOURCES

There are several good books you could go to as information sources regarding intercultural nonverbal communication.

- *Kiss, Bow, or Shake Hands* by Terri Morrison and Wayne A. Conaway (Avon, MA: Adams Media Corporation, 2006).
- *Kiss, Bow, or Shake Hands: Europe* by Terri Morrison and Wayne A. Conaway (Avon, MA: Adams Media, 2007).
- *Kiss, Bow, or Shake Hands: Latin America* by Terri Morrison and Wayne A. Conaway (Avon, MA: Adams Media, 2007).
- *Kiss, Bow, or Shake Hands: Asia* by Terri Morrison and Wayne A. Conaway (Avon, MA: Adams Media, 2007).
- *Kiss, Bow, or Shake Hands: Sales and Marketing*, by Terri Morrison and Wayne A. Conway (McGraw-Hill, 2012).
- *Gestures: The Do's and Taboos of Body Language Around the World* by Roger E. Axtell (New York: Wiley & Sons, 1998).

FIGURE 3-7: INTERCULTURAL NONVERBAL COMMUNICATION SOURCES

- *Do's and Taboos Around the World for Women in Business*, by Roger E. Axtell, Tami Briggs, Margaret Corcoran, and Mary Beth Lamb (New York: John Wiley & Sons, Inc., 1997).
- *Do's and Taboos of Humor Around the World*, by Roger E. Axtell (New York: John Wiley & Sons, Inc., 1997).
- *Understanding Arabs: A Contemporary Guide to Arab Society* by Margaret K. Nydell (Boston: Nicholas Brealey Pub, 2012).
- *Asian Business Customs & Manners* by Mary Murray Bosrock (New York: Meadowbrook, 2007).
- *The Travelers' Guide to Latin American Customs & Manners* by Elizabeth Devine and Nancy L. Braganti (New York: St. Martin's Griffin, 2000).

comfort zone
The amount of personal space businesspeople prefer to maintain between themselves and their communication partners.

Personal Space People of all cultures have a "comfort zone." **Comfort zone** refers to the amount of personal space businesspeople prefer to maintain between themselves and their communication partners. For example, U.S. and Canadian businesspeople are most comfortable when the personal distance is kept to approximately an arm's length.[36] When a communication partner steps in closer, U.S. and Canadian businesspeople perceive this action as an invasion of their space or even a sign of hostility or aggressiveness. The result is an uncomfortable feeling similar to sharing a crowded elevator. These uncomfortable feelings can be a distraction that compromises the quality of the communication.

U.S. businesspeople may also be distracted when their communication partner stands significantly farther than an arm's length away. They may believe their communication partner is distant or cold, does not care about what they are saying, cannot be trusted, or is trying to end the conversation prematurely by distancing him- or herself. Japanese businesspeople prefer to stand somewhat farther than an arm's length from their communication partners.[37] Hindu Indians typically stand 3–3½ feet apart.

Then, there are those cultures in which businesspeople prefer a shorter personal distance. Examples of these include most Latin American, southern European, and Middle Eastern countries.[38] For example, Venezuelan businesspeople prefer a distance of 4–6 inches—considerably closer than an arm's length!

There is an acknowledged connection between personal space preferences and high- and low-context cultures. As a general rule, people from high-context cultures (e.g., Chinese, Greek, Vietnamese) prefer less personal distance, whereas people from low-context cultures (e.g., Swiss, Germans, Scandinavians) prefer more personal distance.[37]

So, what should a person to do when communicating face-to-face with people of other cultures who define their comfort zone differently? First, learn what their preferred personal distance is. Then, adhere to their personal distance preference. Or, you might stand at a compromise distance. Of course, you might also ask your communication partners what they prefer. After all, they may be adjusting to your personal preferences.

Time How time and its use are viewed differs significantly among cultures. This can come as quite a surprise to uninformed U.S. businesspeople who subscribe to a philosophy that time is like money—it is spent, saved, or wasted.[40] For example, U.S. businesspeople adhere to tight time schedules, show up a few minutes early for meetings, and like appointments and meetings to start and stop on time. They also are susceptible to becoming impatient and frustrated when foreign business partners do not share the same view of time. In contrast, Kenyans rarely set ending times for meetings and are concerned with addressing all meeting matters as needed. Saudi businesspeople hold an opposite view of time than U.S. businesspeople and are likely to be frustrated by an U.S. businessperson's impatience.

Generally speaking, cultures have either a monochronic time preference or a polychronic time preference. **Monochronic time** refers to a preference for doing one thing at a time because time is limited, precise, segmented, and schedule driven.[41] Low-context cultures, such as Germany, Australia, and the Scandinavian countries, prefer to function on monochronic time. **Polychronic time** refers to a preference for doing more than one thing at a time because time is flexible and multidimensional.[42] High-context cultures, such as Mexico, France, Saudi Arabia, Portugal, Turkey, southern and western Asia, Africa, India, and the Caribbean prefer to function on polychronic time.

Do not be surprised if a business meeting in Saudi Arabia does not start on schedule or if it contains several interruptions, or if a presentation in Portugal lasts longer than anticipated. Along the same lines, be especially sensitive to how much time your foreign counterpart prefers to spend getting to know you before talking business. U.S. businesspeople prefer to keep this short, so they can get down to business. However, in some polychronic cultures, such as France, Mexico, and Middle Eastern countries, plan to spend several days or weeks getting comfortable with each other before getting down to business.

Familiarize yourself with the cultural and religious holidays of foreign business partners so you are not unnecessarily frustrated by times when it is more difficult to meet with you. For example, the Islamic holy month of Ramadan in Middle Eastern countries is a time when the general pace of everything slows considerably.[43] The same goes for popular vacation times when you are more likely to have difficulty talking or meeting with foreign business partners. For example, June, July, and August are popular vacation months in the United States, whereas January and February are popular in Australia.

Dress and Appearance Do not be too quick to judge the appearance and mode of dress of foreign counterparts negatively if they are different than yours. There is no one standard for business appearance and dress for men or women. The best advice is to adhere to the appearance and dress expectations of your culture and, in turn, be familiar with those in cultures in which you are conducting business.

U.S. businesspeople traditionally wore conservative business attire—dark suits, white shirts and blouses, and color-coordinated shoes and accessories. In recent years, many U.S. companies

have switched to dress policies that allow for casual dress (business casual)—slacks, casual shirts and blouses, no neckties. However, U.S. businesspeople are advised to dress in traditional business attire when meeting with external stakeholders and when meeting with foreign business partners, many of whom would view casual dress as a lack of professionalism.

The authors of *Kiss, Bow, or Shake Hands* share a wealth of information regarding global business dress expectations. For example, in Brazil, businessmen wear either three-piece or two-piece suits, with three-piece suits carrying an "executive" connotation. Brazilian businesswomen dress conservatively. In Malaysia, businesswomen wear skirts and long-sleeved blouses, and businessmen wear dark trousers and light-colored long- or short-sleeved shirts. In China, businessmen wear conservative suits, shirts, and ties, and businesswomen wear conservative suits, high-necked blouses, and low heels. South Korean and Danish businesspersons' dress is similar to U.S. businesspersons' dress, which is a combination of business dress and business casual. Mexican businesswomen wear either a dress or skirt and blouse, and Mexican businessmen wear conservative dark suits, white shirts, and ties. In New Zealand, businessmen wear dark suits, white shirts, and ties, and businesswomen wear a dress or skirt and blouse with a jacket. In Norway, businessmen wear ties for business appointments and often wear a sports jacket instead of a suit coat. Norwegian businesswomen wear dresses or pants. In Sri Lanka, businesswomen wear skirts and modest light blouses, and businessmen wear light shirts and pants. German businessmen wear conservative dark suits, sedate ties, and white shirts, and businesswomen wear equally conservative dark suits and white blouses.[44] You get the idea! Dress varies among cultures either as a result of tradition, religious reasons, or climate conditions.

Whether the preferred dress is traditional or business casual, personal grooming is important. Keeping one's hair well groomed, teeth brushed, and body clean is expected. In addition, whether it is American job recruiters or Colombian businesspeople, unpolished shoes are not appreciated. The person wearing unpolished shoes is often viewed as slovenly and unprofessional.

Then, there are issues pertaining to preferences regarding body piercings, tattoos, and jewelry. First, do not be surprised and distracted by them. Some cultures have a long history of body decorations while others do not. For example, U.S. businesspeople are advised to cover tattoos and remove piercing jewelry from their eyebrows, cheeks, noses, lips, and tongues when conducting business domestically and abroad. In Saudi Arabia, the law prohibits neck jewelry worn by men.

Finally, the general rule regarding make-up, perfume, and cologne is to be conservative. Too much or the wrong shade of make-up often distracts others, as does the relentless smell wafting from a communication partner who splashed on too much perfume or cologne.

Greetings   Greetings include a variety of forms of nonverbal communication. U.S. businesspeople typically greet others with a smile, a firm handshake, and a verbal greeting such as "hello" or "nice to meet you." In addition, it is common to exchange business cards. U.S. businesspeople typically have information printed in English on only one side of their business cards. When traveling abroad on business, you are advised to print the information on both sides of your business card—one side in your foreign business partner's native language and one side in English. When you present the business card to him or her, present the side in his or her native language. It is good practice to allow some time to study each other's business cards, as is traditional in Japan. It is not a good idea to simply shove cards in your pocket, briefcase, or wallet. In addition, use both hands when presenting and receiving business cards in Japan.

Not all businesspeople in all cultures shake hands when greeting each other. A handshake in Southern Europe and Central and South America is slightly longer and is accompanied by the left hand touching the other person's forearm, elbow, or lapel.[45] The traditional Indian greeting is the *namaste*, which involves holding the palms of your hands together just below your chin and nodding or bowing slightly; however, the handshake has become traditional in Westernized Indian cities. The greeting in Thailand, called the *wai*, is similar to the *namaste*. You will please Thais if you greet them with a *wai* instead of a handshake. South Korean businessmen typically greet others with a slight bow or nod and sometimes an accompanying handshake. The traditional greeting in Japan is the bow; however, Japanese businesspeople will often greet Westerners with a hand-shake. Middle Easterners shake hands, but prefer a gentle grip as a firm grip suggests aggressiveness. In Guatemala, businessmen shake hands, while businesswomen do so at their discretion. In Kenya, businesspeople shake hands and, when greeting those of higher status, grasp the right wrist with the left hand while shaking hands as a sign of respect. In Argentina businesspeople shake hands and nod when leaving each other as well as when they greet each other. The same is true in Brazil, Australia, and Italy. In Honduras, businessmen greet by shaking hands, and businesswomen pat each other on the right arm or shoulder. Then, there is the Latin *abrazo*, which is a hug.[46]

© Ljupco Smokovski/Shutterstock.com

In some cultures, gift giving is also a component of a greeting. For example, gifts of scotch, frozen steaks, and electronic toys for children of associates are often given at first business meetings in Japan. Ideally, they should be wrapped in rice paper. Gift giving is also common in Kuwait where gifts such as gold pens, finely made compasses, and business-card cases are popular. German businesspeople do not give or expect to receive gifts. If you feel compelled to give your German counterpart a gift, consider good quality pens, pocket calculators, or imported liquor. Russians are pleased to receive gifts, so you might consider baseball caps, picture or art books, perfume, American cigarettes, cameras, and watches. Gift giving is not expected in Saudi Arabia and is uncommon in Chile until a close rela-tionship has developed. Popular gifts in Taiwan include imported liquor, gold pens, maga-zine subscriptions, and items with small company logos on them as long as the items were not made in Taiwan!

Touching As it pertains to nonverbal business communication, touching includes placing one or more fingers or a hand on another person briefly, shaking hands, embracing (hugging), or kissing. Since handshakes were discussed in the previous section, they are not discussed again here.

Some cultures are open to touching, while it is routinely avoided in others, with the occasional exception of a handshake. Then there are countries that take the middle ground on the issue. Roger E. Axtell compiled a geographic measuring stick for touching. The geo-graphic regions and/or countries where touching is commonplace include Middle Eastern countries, Latin countries, Italy, Greece, Spain, Portugal, some Asian countries, and Rus-sia. The geographic regions and/or countries where the middle ground is taken regarding touching include China, France, India, and Ireland. The geographic regions and/or countries where touching is not preferred include Scandinavia, Estonia, the United States, Canada, Japan, England, Australia, and Northern European countries.[47]

Then, too, there is the issue of how often people touch. In his book *Nonverbal Communication for Business Success*, Ken Cooper reported the results of observing casual conversations at outdoor cafés in several countries. He reported 180 touch occurrences per hour in San Juan, Puerto Rico, 110 per hour in Paris, 2 per hour in Gainesville, Florida, and 0 per hour in London.[48]

Familiarize yourself with your foreign communication partners' feelings about touching and respect them. In countries where touching is prevalent, do not insult your hosts by acting surprised or backing away when they touch you. For example, Brazilian men typically hug when greeting, Russian men often kiss other men as a form of greeting, and in Middle Eastern countries, Korea, Indochina, Greece, and Italy, it is acceptable for two men to walk arm-in-arm or holding hands.[49]

Eye Contact In the United States, as well as in many Western cultures, some degree of direct eye contact is preferred. In these cultures, a lack of sufficient direct eye contact often takes on negative connotations. An individual avoiding direct eye contact might be seen as suspicious, unfriendly, insecure, untrustworthy, inattentive, or impersonal.[50]

Direct eye contact in Western cultures, however, does not mean that prolonged eye contact (staring) is appropriate! People in most cultures find staring to be rude, distracting, and uncomfortable. Even in Latin American cultures, where longer looking times are the norm, prolonged eye contact from an individual of lower status is considered disrespectful.[51] In contrast, Arabs give prolonged eye contact. As Edward Hall notes, in most cases "Arabs look each other in the eye when talking, with an intensity that makes most Americans highly uncomfortable."[52] Arabs believe "the eyes are the window to the soul and knowing a person's heart and soul is important in order to work well together."[53]

The Role of Eye Contact in Different Cultures http://blog.joytours. com/2012/12/20/the-role-of-eye-contact-in-different-cultures/

Direct eye contact is considered insulting in most Asian cultures. Vietnamese often look at the ground with their heads down as a show of respect, not avoidance. Edward T. Hall and Mildred Reed Hall observed that Japanese "are made uncomfortable by Americans who look at them directly; they choose to look down or at the corner of the room."[54] In addition, in Japan, looking subordinates in the eye is considered judgmental and punitive.

Learn the eye contact preferences of your foreign communication partners and adjust your cultural habits accordingly. Respect how uncomfortable direct eye contact is to people in several cultures and adjust your style to make them comfortable. Anticipate and expect prolonged, intense eye contact from Arabs. Respect their reasons for doing so and get on with building a strong business relationship.

Body Language Body language, also called *gestures*, differs considerably from one culture to another. Our differences are both many and interesting. Here are several examples. In most countries, when a person wiggles his or her nose it means he or she has an itch. A nose wiggle in Puerto Rico means *what's going on?* When a person nods her or his head up and down in the United States, it means yes; in Bulgaria, it means no. Italians and Latinos gesture with their hands more so than people in Western cultures. A quick tongue protrusion and retraction signifies embarrassment and self-castigation in modern South China, yet is offensive in the United States.[55] U.S. men consider backslapping to be acceptable, whereas Japanese men never engage in backslapping or in other forms of touching.

Belching after a meal is rude in most cultures; however, it is acceptable and even a compliment in China.[56] Patting a baby on the head in in Thailand is strongly discouraged as the head is considered to be a sacred part of the body where the spirit lives. In the United States doing so is viewed as a sign of affection. Arabs do not cross their legs while sitting because baring the bottom of one's feet is offensive. Americans do not share this belief, thus they routinely cross their legs. Pointing your index finger toward yourself insults the other person in Switzerland, the Netherlands, and Germany. In the United States some people summon others to come to them with one of their index fingers. However, in the Philippine Islands it is used to call dogs and is considered to be very rude. In Singapore and Japan it signifies death. The "hook 'em horns" sign (raised index and little finger) is frequently displayed by fans at the University of Texas athletic events to cheer on the Longhorns. The same sign is a good-luck gesture in Venezuela, represents a curse in parts of Africa, and signals to another in Italy that his or her spouse is being unfaithful.[57] In the United States an outstretched hand with palm facing outward means stop. In Greece it is considered to be offensive. Crossing the middle finger over the index finger is offensive in Vietnam, but means good luck in the United States. Throughout much of the world the "V" sign (raised and separated index and middle fingers) means victory or peace. In England, it means "Up Yours!" if the palm and fingers face inward.[58] The "A-OK" sign (thumb and forefinger curled into an O) is a friendly sign in the United States. It means "All right!" or "Good going." In Japan the same sign means money; in France it means zero or worthless; and in Australia, Brazil, and Islamic countries, it is an offensive gesture.[59]

These were but a few examples of how people around the world differ in terms of body language. While it would be difficult for any of us to learn all the differences and nuances for all cultures and countries, it is important that we learn about the body language preferences of our specific foreign communication partners and our own body language preferences. The best place to start is by understanding your own body language preferences. Roger E. Axtell presents a list of 20 gestures most commonly used by North Americans. You are encouraged to consider each not only in terms of how you perceive it, but also in terms of how your foreign communication partners perceive it. The list is presented in Figure 3-8.

FIGURE 3–8: THE INNOCENT ABROAD'S SHORT LIST OF GESTURES

1. Shaking hands
2. Making eye contact
3. Waving
4. Beckoning
5. Showing V for victory
6. Making the OK gesture
7. Showing the thumbs up gesture
8. Establishing space relationships
9. Touching
10. Kissing
11. Toasting

What do you think the one universal gesture is? According to Axtell, universal gesture is the smile, and he encourages us to do so freely and often![60]

Effective communicators in today's global business environment appreciate cultural differences and their effects on nonverbal communication. They strive to understand the basis of nonverbal cues by learning about religions, history, and social and business customs of people of other cultures with whom they interact. They learn to use nonverbal cues that reinforce effective communication and avoid those that threaten it.

SUMMARY: SECTION 4— NONVERBAL CONSIDERATIONS

- Nonverbal messages are significant components of intercultural communication.
- Nonverbal messages fall into one of the following categories: kinesics, paralanguage, chronemics, proxemics, or environment.
- Major intercultural nonverbal considerations include personal space, time, dress and appearance, greetings, touching, eye contact, and body language.

INTERCULTURAL COMMUNICATION AND INTERNATIONAL BUSINESS SOURCES

Anytime one sets out to learn about how to communicate effectively with people from other countries and cultures and how to conduct business abroad, there is much to learn first. Fortunately, a wealth of such information exists. The challenge quickly becomes knowing how to quickly and easily access the specific information you need. That is where the information presented in this section comes into play. Information sources discussed here are categorized as follows: journals, periodicals, books, databases, websites, YouTube videos, societies and associations, and other sources.

JOURNALS

There are a number of research journals that focus primarily on intercultural (cross-cultural) communication issues. Here is a sampling.

- *Journal of Intercultural Communication*
- *Journal of Management*
- *Bulletin for the Association of Business Communication*
- *Journal of Business Communication*
- *Journal of Business and Technical Communication*
- *American Business Review*
- *Business Horizons*
- *Applied Communication Research*
- *Harvard Business Review*

If you were to conduct a Web search to locate journal articles addressing intercultural communication issues, for example, you would find a wealth of sources including Neil Payne's article *Ten Tips for Cross Cultural Communication* at ezinearticles.com/?Ten-Tips-for-Cross-Cultural-Communication&id=2196. This article contains practical advice on topics ranging from avoiding slang and using humor cautiously to knowing appropriate topics of conversation. Another good example is Marcelle E. DuPraw and Marya Axner's article *Working on Common Cross-cultural Communication Challenges*, which describes six fundamental patterns of cultural differences, respecting our differences, and working together. This article also presents a list of helpful guidelines for multicultural collaboration. This article can be found at www.pbs.org/ampu/crosscult.html.

Then there are journals that frequently contain an international forum section or publish articles pertaining to international business issues. Examples include:

- *The International Executive*
- *International Journal of Intercultural Relations*
- *International Journal of Public Relations*
- *International Journal of Research and Marketing*
- *Foreign Language Annals*
- *Journal of International Studies*

Thanks to the widespread availability of the Internet, WiFi, and affordable computers and tablets, conducting searches for journal articles is fairly fast and painless.

PERIODICALS

Newsstand periodicals, such as *BusinessWeek*, *Fortune*, *Newsweek*, *Time*, and *The Wall Street Journal*, routinely include intercultural communication and international business articles. Most of these periodicals and related articles of interest can also be accessed over the Internet.

One of the major advantages periodicals have over books is the potential currency of the information. Given how rapidly economic and political conditions change in some countries and regions of the world, this is an important consideration.

BOOKS

Books offer yet another source of information relating to intercultural communication and international business. Fortunately there is no shortage of these books in the marketplace. Some are specialized, while others are more general. For example, some focus on specific regions of the world, while others have a global focus. Examples of these include:

- *Kiss, Bow, or Shake Hands: Europe* by Terri Morrison and Wayne A. Conaway (Avon, MA: Adams Media, 2007)
- *Kiss, Bow, or Shake Hands: Latin America* by Terri Morrison and Wayne A. Conaway (Avon, MA: Adams Media, 2007)
- *Kiss, Bow, or Shake Hands: Asia* by Terri Morrison and Wayne A. Conaway (Avon, MA: Adams Media, 2007)
- *Understanding Arabs: A Contemporary Guide to Arab Society* by Margaret K. Nydell (Boston: Nicholas Brealey Pub, 2012)

An excellent example of a book with a global focus is *Kiss, Bow, or Shake Hands* by Terri Morrison and Wayne A. Conaway (Avon, MA: Adams Media Corporation, 2006). This book presents intercultural information about 60 countries. Essentially, each chapter in this book speaks to a different country and the topics addressed are the same across all chapters. The topics addressed are varied, ranging from a country's history, language(s), and demographics to business practices, gestures, and gift giving.

There are also books that focus on specialty areas. Examples of these include:

- *Gestures: The Do's and Taboos of Body Language Around the World* by Roger E. Axtell (New York: Wiley & Sons, 1998)
- *Kiss, Bow, or Shake Hands: Sales and Marketing* by Terri Morrison and Wayne A. Conaway (New York: McGraw-Hill, 2012)
- *Asian Business Customs & Manners* by Mary Murray Bosrock (New York: Meadowbrook, 2007)
- *The Travelers' Guide to Latin American Customs & Manners* by Elizabeth Devine and Nancy L. Braganti (New York: St. Martin's Griffin, 2000)

A number of books focus on international business. Examples of these include:

- *Craighead's International Business, Travel, and Relocation Guide to 90 Countries* by Gale Group (Detroit: Gale Group, 2004)
- *The Europa World Year Book* (London: Routledge, 2012)
- *Mergent International Manual* (New York: Mergent, Inc., 2011)
- *The Statesman's Year-Book 2013: The Politics, Cultures and Economies of the World* by Barry Turner (Basingstoke: Palgrave MacMillan, 2012)

There is no shortage of book titles pertaining to intercultural communication and international business topics to choose from. Just keep in mind that such books can become dated as circumstances and customs change. Of course, this is not always the case, but it is certainly a consideration to keep in mind.

DATABASES

A number of databases contain information regarding intercultural communication and international business. A sampling of such databases is listed here.

- ABI/Inform
- Business Source Complete
- EconLit via Ebscohost
- Emerald FullText
- IMF Publications
- Lexis Nexis Academic
- PAIS
- Plunkett Research
- Preicast's PROMT
- World Newspapers.com (www.world-newspapers.com/)

Databases provide an efficient information-gathering option. We are fortunate to have databases so readily available, as well as the hardware necessary to access them. Gathering information has not always been so fast and efficient.

WEBSITES

As can be expected, a number of websites contain information on intercultural communication and international business topics. Here are some examples.

- **What's Up With Culture?** (www2.pacific.edu/sis/culture). A source the Peace Corps uses to prepare people before they travel abroad to work for the program.
- **International Business Etiquette, Manners, and Culture** (www.cyborlink.com/). Contains international business etiquette and manners suggestions.
- **World of Business Etiquette** (Florida Institute of Technology) (lib.fit.edu/library-displays/200604.php). Covers many topics, including introductions and greetings, dining, and gestures.
- **Going Global.com** (www.goinglobal.com/). Includes country profiles, cultural advice, career advice, job resources, employment trends, financial considerations, business and networking groups, CV and résumé advice, interviewing advice, and work permit and visa requirements for work abroad.
- **DoingBusiness.org** (World Bank) (www.doingbusiness.org/). Sponsored by the World Bank. Provides objective measures of individual countries' business regulations and their enforcement. Indicators cover topics such as starting a business, employing workers, paying taxes, getting credit, etc.
- **Import/Export Guide** (business.usa.gov/). Contents include getting started in exporting, how to obtain export financing, importing goods, trade agreements, business travel, and importing/exporting specific products.
- **Legal Research on International Law Issues Using the Internet** (www2.lib.uchicago.edu/~llou/forintlaw.html). Provides foreign and international law research guides.

As the Internet grows, anticipate even more such websites to become available. Locating information about intercultural communication and international business should not be a problem as long as you know how to conduct a search.

YOUTUBE VIDEOS

YouTube videos provide yet another source of information on intercultural communication and international business topics. Here are some examples.

- **Chinese Business Etiquette: Do's and Don'ts** (www.youtube.com/ watch?v=wY8JbFOsp5E&feature=bf_next&list=PLE38BB40F3E211F3F).
- **The Lowdown: Business Etiquette in Russia** (www.youtube.com/ watch?v=OtsRHObuqck&feature=bf_next&list=PLE38BB40F3E211F3F).
- **Chinese Business Etiquette: Formal Meetings** (www.youtube.com/ watch?v=hc6ppkNb-Aw&feature=bf_next&list=PLE38BB40F3E211F3F).

As I am sure you are aware, you will likely have to spend some time sorting through some YouTube videos that are not focused enough for your needs. This condition is not unique to YouTube videos. Such sorting and sifting is also typical when searching for information in journal articles, books, and databases. Do not be discouraged by the process. There is a wealth of good information on YouTube. You just need patience to locate it.

SOCIETIES AND ASSOCIATIONS

Societies and associations provide yet another source to turn to for information about intercultural communication and international business issues. Web searches provide an efficient way to identify societies and associations of interest to you. Here are some examples:

- Dutch-American Society
- Intercollegiate Turkish Students Society
- Finnish-American Society of the Midwest
- Greek-American Society
- Kiwanis Malaysia
- Malaysian Franchise Association
- India Association of North Texas
- Hispanic Business Association USA
- India Association of Indianapolis

An amazing number of such societies and associations exist. Fortunately, you will not have to access all of them! However, when you do need to learn more about how to communicate with people abroad or conduct business with them, it is good to have so much information so readily available to you.

OTHER SOURCES

Here are several other ways you can locate information regarding intercultural communication and international business topics.

- Visit the international studies office on your campus.
- Visit with foreign students in your classes.

- Contact campus foreign student organizations.
- Visit with foreign students who are members of campus organizations to which you both belong.
- Contact international trade resource centers.
- Contact a world trade center if one is located nearby.
- Join international trade associations.
- Conduct Web searches.

You now have an extensive arsenal of sources to turn to when you need information about intercultural communication and international business topics. Learning about others is both interesting and rewarding. The experience might even spur you to learn more about yourself. For example, people in Arab cultures do not shake hands with their left hand. This is not an issue with most Americans. If you are an American who just learned about this Arab preference, you might, in turn, reflect on why shaking hands with your left hand is not an issue. Our differences and similarities are typically rooted in such things as traditions, history, societal norms, and religious beliefs. Sometimes we act as we do simply because we are mirroring our elders and others around us without knowing the origins of our actions. Some exploration into these origins can be enlightening.

SUMMARY: SECTION 5— INTERCULTURAL COMMUNICATION AND INTERNATIONAL BUSINESS SOURCES

- Whenever one sets out to learn about how to communicate effectively with people from other countries and cultures and how to conduct business abroad, there is much to learn first.
- A wealth of information regarding intercultural communication and international business topics and issues exists.
- Knowing how to access information about intercultural communication and international business topics and issues is necessary to relate successfully with international communication partners.
- Sources that provide information on intercultural communication and international business topics and issues include journals, periodicals, books, databases, websites, YouTube videos, societies and associations, and numerous resources.

Notes

1. John B. Cullen, *Multinational Management* (Cincinnati: South-Western College Publishing, 1999), 413.

2. Robert Kreitner and Angelo Kinicki, *Organizational Behavior*, 5th ed. (Boston: Irwin McGraw-Hill, 2000), 109.

3. Ibid., 43–44.

4. H. Dan O'Hair, James S. O'Rourke IV, and Mary John O'Hair, *Business Communication* (Cincinnati: South-Western College Publishing, 2000), 138.

5. Gerard Bannon and John Mattock, *Cross-Cultural Communication: The Essential Guide to International Business*. (London; Sterling, VA: Kogan Page, 2003).

6. Kreitner and Kinicki, *Organizational Behavior*, 110–11.

7. Mary Munter, "Cross-Cultural Communication for Managers," *Business Horizon* (May-June 1993): 72.

8. Kreitner and Kinicki, *Organizational Behavior*, 111.

9. Phillip R. Harris and Robert T. Moran, *Managing Cultural Differences*, 3rd ed. (Houston: Gulf, 1991), 208.

10. Munter, "Cross-Cultural Communication," 111.

11. Peggy Kenna and Lacy Sonda, *Business Spain: A Practical Guide to Understanding Spanish Business Culture* (Chicago: NTC Publishing Group), 37.

12. C. Engholm and S. Grimes, *Doing Business in Mexico* (Paramus, NJ: Prentice Hall, 1997), 240.

13. Kreitner and Kinicki, *Organizational Behavior*, 115–116.

14. David A. Victor, *International Business Communication* (New York: HarperCollins, 1992), 41. Ibid., 42–44.

15. Kreitner and Kinicki, *Organizational Behavior*, 116.

16. Terri Morrison and Wayne A. Conaway, *Kiss, Bow, or Shake Hands* (Avon, MA: Adams Media, 2006), 167.

17. Cullen, *Multinational Management*, 93; D. I. Riddle and Z. D. Lanham, "Internationalizing Business English: 20 Propositions for Native English Speakers," *The Journal of Language for International Business* (1985); Sherron B. Kenton and Deborah Valentine, *Cross Talk: Communicating in a Multicultural Workplace* (Prentice Hall), 15–17.

18. P. H. Collin, M. Lowi, and C. Weiland, *Beginner's Dictionary of American English Usage and International English Usage*.

19. John Fontana, "E-Mail's Popularity Creating a Glut of Legal Issues," *Network World* no. 44, (October 30, 2000): 58–60.

20. Jan McDaniel, "E-etiquette: How to Write E-Mail That Brings Results," *Link-Up* 17, no. 1 (January/February 2000): 14–17.

21. Loretta Prencipe, "Seven Guides for Good Sense: Keep Your Meaning Clear When Managing Via E-Mail," *Info World* 23, no. 9 (February 26, 2001): 44–45.

22. David Stauffer, "Can I Apologize by E-Mail?" *Harvard Management Communication Newsletter* (1999, reprint no. C9911B): 3.

23. Ibid.

24. Mary A. DeVries, *Internationally Yours* (Boston: Houghton Mifflin, 1994), 52.

25. Ibid., 53–55.

26. Ibid., 49.

27. Ibid., 54–64.

28. Ibid., 167.

29. Ibid., 70–72.

30. Cullen, *Multinational Management*, 15–17, 93.

31. Phillip R. Harris and Robert T. Moran, *Managing Cultural Differences*, 3rd ed. (Houston: Gulf, 1990), 47; Sherron B. Kenton and Deborah Valentine, *Cross Talk: Communicating in a Multicultural Workplace* (Upper Saddle River, NJ: Prentice Hall, 1997), 14–15; Louis E. Boone and David L. Kurtz, *Contemporary Business*, 10th ed. (Harcourt College), 389.

32. L. Copeland and L. Griggs, *Going International: How to Make Friends and Deal Effectively in the Global Marketplace* (New York: Random House), 17.

33. Victor, *International Business Communication*, 212.

34. Ibid.

35. Edward T. Hall, *The Hidden Dimension* (Garden City, NY: Doubleday, 1990), 151.

36. Kreitner and Kinicki, *Organizational Behavior*, 114.

37. Ibid., 113.

38. Ibid.

39. Ibid.

40. Morrison, Conaway, and Borden *Kiss, Bow*, 134.

41. Roger E. Axtell, *Gestures: The Do's and Taboos of Body Language Around the World* (New York: Wiley & Sons, 1991), 24.

42. Morrison, Conaway, and Borden, *Kiss, Bow*, 152.

43. Axtell, *Gestures*, 43.

44. Ken Cooper, *Nonverbal Communication for Business* (New York: AMACOM, 1979), 164.

45. Cullen, *Multinational Management*, 95; Axtell, *Gestures*, 43.

46. Harris and Moran, *Managing Cultural Differences*, 44.

47. Ibid.

48. Hall, *The Hidden Dimension*, 151.

49. Harris and Moran, *Managing Cultural Differences*, 44.

50. C. H. Dodd, *Dynamics of Intercultural Communications* (Dubuque, IA: Brown, 1995), 265.

51. Edward T. Hall and Mildred Reed Hall, *Hidden Differences: Doing Business with the Japanese* (New York, NY: Doubleday Anchor Books, 1987), 122.

52. Harris and Moran, *Managing Cultural Differences*, 44.

53. "What's A-O.K. in the U.S.A. Is Lewd and Worthless Beyond," *New York Times*, August 18, 1996, taken from R. E. Axtell, *Gestures*, 53-54..

54. "What's A-OK".

55. Ibid.

56. Axtell, *Gestures*, 113.

PART 2

BUSINESS COMMUNICATION TECHNOLOGY

COMMUNICATION TECHNOLOGIES 4

LEARNING OUTCOMES

After reading this chapter, you should be able to:

1. Describe the importance of the terms *what, how,* and *when* as they apply to communication technologies.

2. Discuss the impact of the Internet on communication in the business place.

3. Discuss the impact of wireless communication technologies on the way people communicate in the business place.

4. Describe how to choose and effectively use communication technologies.

5. Describe several communication technology-related job, career, safety, and health concerns.

6. Describe assistive technologies that enable disabled individuals to communicate more easily and effectively in the business place.

© *agsandrew/Shutterstock.com*

BENEFITS OF LEARNING ABOUT COMMUNICATION TECHNOLOGIES

1. You will increase your chances of succeeding in business and achieving your desired career goals.

2. You will become familiar with significant communication technology developments of the past and see just how far we have come in a relatively short time.

3. You will understand the impact the Internet has had on communication in the business place.

4. You will understand the impact of wireless communication technologies on the way people communicate in the business place.

5. You will understand how to choose and use communication technologies.

6. You will have some sense of the communication technology developments to come.

SELECT KEY TERMS

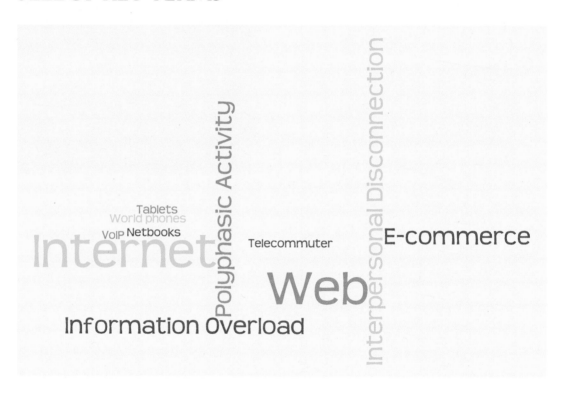

INTRODUCTION

You are strongly encouraged to know what communication technology exists and is forthcoming, how to use communication technologies effectively and efficiently, and when to use them. Each of these forms of knowledge will be critical to your success in the professional business world. The Internet, WiFi, and a host of wireless communication technologies have vastly changed the way much of the communication occurs in the business place. Be careful, however, not to get so comfortable with communicating electronically that you overlook the importance of face-to-face communication in a variety of domestic and international settings. Furthermore, don't feel the need to be connected to the technology all the time for work. It is healthy both physically and mentally to enjoy some downtime, which many would call vacations and weekends.

The intent of this chapter is to provide you with an overview of business communication technologies. This goal is realized through discussions regarding the following topics: keeping up with technological developments, significant communication technology developments of the past, the Internet and World Wide Web, communicating via wireless technologies, using communication technologies effectively, and some cautious communication technology predictions. The information pertaining to the above-mentioned topics is reinforced by several student website resources including *PowerPoint slides, preview tests, chapter assessment tests, YouTube videos, interactive exercises,* and the *interactive glossary*.

This chapter is not the only place we discuss business communication technologies in the book. Technologies related to specific communication topics are discussed in appropriate locations elsewhere in the book. For example, technologies that support teams' efforts, business meetings, business presentations, and other topics are discussed in the related chapters.

© everything possible/Shutterstock.com

KEEPING UP: WHAT, HOW, AND WHEN

It has been said there are only two certainties in life—death and taxes. While most would agree that death and taxes are inevitable, they are not the only certainties. Change is also an unavoidable certainty, as history reminds us. This is especially true of change in communication technologies. While recent changes in communication technologies do not constitute the first of their kind, the magnitude of recent changes, coupled with the rapid pace at which they are being introduced, poses a sizable challenge to organizations and employees. Furthermore, many of these technologies are changing the ways we communicate in the business place.

No matter the type or size of organization you work for, you need to keep up with communication technologies. Keeping up can be summed up in three words—*what, how,* and *when.*

WHAT

The term *what,* as used here, implies you should stay abreast of both current and projected communication technologies. You should consider reading specialized magazines, such as *Smartphone & Pocket PC, Smart Computing, PCWorld, or Pen Computing,* which covers mobile computing communication. These magazines and others like them focus exclusively on technological developments, issues, and trends. Another specialized technology magazine to consider is *PC Magazine,* a digital publication that can be accessed at www.pcmag.com. In addition, consider browsing periodicals such as *Fortune, BusinessWeek, and the Wall Street Journal* to locate articles about communication technology developments and trends. You can also visit money.cnn.com/technology/ to read about communication technology developments. Finally, you could take a communication technology workshop or class or attend a major electronics show such as the annual International Consumer Electronics Show.

HOW

Here the term *how* implies you should learn *how* to use both current and projected communication technologies. Your best bet is to either take a workshop or class or sit down with a friend or colleague who is willing to teach you. On the other hand, you might be the type of person who likes to teach yourself. This approach is a practical option for many.

WHEN

Here the term *when* pertains to two things. First, the term implies you will learn whichever specific communication technology is most appropriate for each communication situation you face. This information is presented later in the section titled "Choosing the Appropriate Communication Medium," where insights into how to make "when" choices are shared. An example would be making the decision to send an e-mail about a short, routine matter instead of conducting a videoconference. Second, the term *when* speaks to knowing when it is unwise to use electronic communication devices because doing so is considered unacceptable behavior as described in Figure 4-1.

FIGURE 4-1: AVOID USING COMMUNICATION TECHNOLOGIES WHEN …

Can you identify specific settings in schools and businesses where it is not in a student's or employee's best interest to be texting or browsing the Internet? No matter your response, it is in your best interest to know. Otherwise, you run the risk of compromising your learning potential and grades, ability to persuade faculty to write recommendation letters, employment stability, and ability to achieve desired career goals! Each of these represents a big price to pay for careless use of communication technologies.

Most college and university instructors discourage students from using electronic communication devices during class unless they are being used for specific, class-related purposes. For example, an instructor may want you to access information using your tablet or laptop, use your smartphone as a substitute device for a clicker, or work on a collaborative document from a wiki site during class. However, few instructors appreciate it when students use electronic devices for other purposes during class when they should, instead, be listening and joining in class discussions.

Even in organizations where there is a proliferation of communication technologies, there are settings in which using electronic devices such as smartphones, tablets, laptops, etc. is discouraged. For example, most managers justifiably do not want employees using such devices during presentations, meetings, and training sessions. One reason is the potential of distracting speakers, meeting chairpersons, trainers, and others seated nearby. Another reason involves missed opportunities and associated costs. Yet another reason has to do with lost knowledge. For example, when employees text or catch up on their e-mail during presentations, business meetings, or training sessions, they are not acquiring the information and ideas speakers, fellow meeting participants, and trainers are sharing. Finally, managers, presenters, etc. do not appreciate the rudeness and unprofessional nature of such actions. Inappropriate use of electronic communication devices can tarnish an employee's image in the eyes of his or her superiors and even tarnish his or her employer's image.

Make sure you know when and where at school and in the workplace it is appropriate to use electronic communication devices, and avoid using them in those settings where they should not be used. Unfortunately, many of today's communication technologies, such as smartphones and texting, are addictive for some. For example, seasoned employment recruiters routinely mention job candidates who answer their smartphones during job interviews. Wise job candidates control the desire to answer their phone when it rings during a job interview by leaving the phone in their car or at home.

Keeping up with current and projected communication technologies is important to businesspeople and organizations. In today's business environment neither individuals nor organizations can compete adequately if they do not keep up. This is not a new challenge for businesspeople or organizations. For example, around the time PCs were first developed

How Technology Changed How We Conduct Business http://money.howstuffworks.com/technology-changed-business.htm

in the late 1970s there were businesspeople who did not keep up with the new technology. Shortly thereafter some of these employees were replaced with others who were keeping up. Essentially it is no different today. Businesspeople who desire to remain marketable and useful need to keep up with current and projected communication technologies, and businesses that desire to be successful and grow need to do the same.

Just as ancient Rome's highways were important communication lines many centuries ago, the Internet and the associated communication technologies are important in today's organizations. It is essential to stay current with Internet-based communication technologies so one does not end up (as some would say) "as road kill on today's information superhighway."

Keeping up with communication technology developments is one of the major challenges you will face during your professional business career. Adopting an approach for "keeping up" that is rooted in the words *what, how,* and *when* will help you manage this challenge.

SUMMARY: SECTION 1— KEEPING UP: WHAT, HOW, AND WHEN

- Your willingness and ability to keep up with current and projected communication technology developments are critical to your career and to your organization's success.
- The term *what* implies you will stay abreast of both current and projected communication technologies.
- The term *how* implies you will learn how to use communication technologies effectively.
- The term *when* implies you will learn which specific communication technologies will be most appropriate for each communication situation you face.

SIGNIFICANT COMMUNICATION TECHNOLOGY DEVELOPMENTS OF THE PAST

Since so many of the communication technology developments of the past affect the ways people communicate in today's business place, it is useful to reflect on some advances that made a major impact. A brief historical look will leave you with a better appreciation for current communication technologies and a broader base from which to speculate on future developments.

Looking into the past reminds us that (1) communication technology development is not unique to our time, (2) many communication technologies currently in use are simply improved versions of past developments, and (3) people have a long history of searching for ways to improve on existing communication technologies and develop new communication technologies. Figure 4-2 provides a brief look at the major technological developments that have had profound effects on how we communicate today.

FIGURE 4-2: COMMUNICATION TECHNOLOGIES THAT LAID THE FOUNDATION

- **Printing Press.** Gutenberg's invention of moveable type in the 15th century made it possible to reproduce books, written documents, pictures, and images more quickly and accurately, thus leading the way to the mass distribution of information.

© Dja65/Shutterstock.com

- **Telegraph.** Prior to the invention of the telegraph in 1837, messages were transmitted in a variety of ways, including smoke, drum signals, and carrier pigeons. The first successful telegraph machine was patented by Samuel Morse in 1837 and became functional in 1844.

© Nolaluce/Shutterstock.com

- **Fax Machine.** The first commercial fax (facsimile) machine became available in 1865. However, fax machines did not achieve widespread use in most U.S. businesses until the 1980s when faster, less-expensive machines were introduced.

FIGURE 4–2: COMMUNICATION TECHNOLOGIES THAT LAID THE FOUNDATION

- **Telephone.** Alexander Graham Bell thought of the idea in 1874 and developed a working telephone in 1876. The first commercial line was installed in the United States in 1877 and 140 years later the telephone is the second most widely used communication medium in U.S. businesses.

© Chuck Rausin/Shutterstock.com

- **Typewriter.** The first successful typewriters were marketed in 1874. Electric typewriters were introduced in the 1920s, although they were not in widespread use until the 1940s. Electronic typewriters, with limited memory capacity and a few word processing features, appeared in 1971. Typewriters were the pre-PC workhorses.

© John Black/Shutterstock.com

FIGURE 4–2: COMMUNICATION TECHNOLOGIES THAT LAID THE FOUNDATION

- **Personal Computer.** PCs hit the market in the early 1980s and are still our computing workhorses. Before then, there were basically two types of computers in use in businesses—mainframes and minicomputers. Both of these were very expensive and, in the case of the mainframes, they were very large.

- **Internet.** In 1969, the first two remote computers were connected to create the nascent ARPAnet—the first computer network. This project was funded by the U.S. Defense Advanced Research Projects Agency (DARPA).[1] By the early 1970s, the main Internet-based business application was e-mail. Other early applications included posting and searching for information and file transfers. As time passed, companies developed LANs (local area networks) that gave employees access to e-mail, databases, and the Internet and to WANs (wide area networks) that allowed them to access company data and applications from remote locations.

Over the years, other technological developments have also impacted the way people communicate in the business place. Some of these technologies have since been retired to museums, storage closets, and landfills. However, others continue to play prominent roles in today's organizations. Can you identify which of the following technologies are still viable in today's business place: dictaphones, mimeograph machines, photocopiers, calculators, word processors, cell phones, voicemail, videoconferencing, scanners, personal digital assistants (PDAs), spreadsheets, desktop publishing?

SUMMARY: SECTION 2— SIGNIFICANT COMMUNICATION TECHNOLOGY DEVELOPMENTS

- While some of the significant communication technology developments are no longer commonplace, most still exist in various forms.
- Learning about past developments reminds us that humans have a long history of searching for new and improved communication tools and will continue to do so.
- The communication technology developments briefly mentioned in this section include moveable type, telegraph, telephone, fax machine, typewriter, personal computer (PC), and the Internet.

THE INTERNET AND WORLD WIDE WEB

Internet
A self-regulated network connecting millions of computer networks around the globe.

World Wide Web
(the Web) A collection of standards and protocols linking massive amounts of information on the Internet, thus enabling user access.

The **Internet** is a self-regulated network connecting millions of computer networks around the globe.[2] The Internet easily comprises the largest computer network in existence. Some people refer to the Internet as the Net, while others refer to it loosely as the **World Wide Web** or the Web. However, the Internet and the Web are not the same thing. The World Wide Web is a subset of the Internet. It is a collection of standards and protocols (rules) that link massive amounts of information located on the Internet across millions of discrete locations. The Internet was first introduced in 1969 and the World Wide Web in 1990.

© nasirkhan/Shutterstock.com

Information on the Web is available in a number of forms. Each web page can be a combination of text, pictures, illustrations, charts, graphs, and audio and video clips. It is common for web pages to contain **hyperlinks** (*links*), which are links to other web pages. Users simply click on the link and a *browser* retrieves the intended page.[3]

hyperlinks
Links to other web pages.

THE INTERNET'S IMPACT

The Internet has had profound effects on organizations as well as on governments and individuals. It is conceivable that the magnitude of the impact the Internet will ultimately have on U.S. organizations and society for that matter will exceed the combined impact the telegraph, railroad system, and Industrial Revolution had on the United States during the 19th century.

The Internet owes much of the credit for its rapid growth in popularity to a number of supporting developments in recent years ranging from affordable communication technology and WiFi to mobile devices such as smartphones and tablets. Of course, the early boost came from the introduction of the PC (personal computer) and the ensuing PC revolution which resulted in PCs being placed in great numbers in organizations, schools, libraries, and homes. Improvements to communication satellites and growth in their numbers supported Internet use, as did increased quality and use of fiber optic cables. Important support for Internet growth also came from the ability to digitize information of all forms ranging from text and photos to audio and video clips.

Finally, here is one more impact of the Internet worth noting. It sure has saved a lot of trees. In 2015 it was estimated that it would take 136 billion pieces of paper to print the content of the Internet. This would involve killing eight million trees and, if placed in a single stack, the paper print-out would stand 8,300 miles high.[4]

THE INTERNET AND ORGANIZATIONS

Most organizations use the Internet and a variety of other communication networks in an integrated manner to accomplish their objectives. Organizations have an interest in providing integrated networks that "enhance the ability of their employees to find, create, manage, and distribute information."[5] An organization, for instance, may access one or more intranets and extranets in addition to the Internet.

An **intranet** is a companywide computer network that facilitates internal communication, providing an efficient means of information distribution, collaboration, and access to databases. For example, intranets may contain information ranging from policy manuals and meeting minutes to job and project instructions. Intranets provide privacy and confidentiality through the use of *firewalls* that block outside Internet users from accessing internal information.[6] Intranets are popular in organizations for a number of reasons, including their speed and internal control over their structure and contents.

An **extranet** is a network that links the intranets of business partners via the Internet in such a way that the result is a private network.[7] For example, extranets provide electronic communication links among companies and select customers, suppliers, distributors, investors, and other strategic partners. They also provide efficient access to a number of professional associations. Just as intranets facilitate internal communication, extranets facilitate communication among a host of external business partners. In addition, extranets provide efficient, rapid access to vast amounts of external information in highly secured networks.

Internet
A companywide computer network serving as a LAN (local area network) and/or WAN (wide area network) developed with Internet technology.

extranet
A network linking the intranets of business partners via the Internet to create a virtually private network.

WAYS THE INTERNET ENHANCES COMMUNICATION

Several of the major ways businesses use the Internet that enhance communication are presented in Figure 4-3. While reading through the list, keep in mind that many of the uses are supported by intranets, extranets, and the Web as well.

FIGURE 4–3: COMMON WAYS BUSINESSES USE THE INTERNET TO ENHANCE COMMUNICATION

- Sending and receiving e-mail messages
- Sharing and retrieving information
- Conducting research
- Accessing databases
- Accessing computer programs
- Developing and transmitting newsletters, brochures, and other documents
- Social networking
- Building strong public relations
- Providing customer service
- Developing and transmitting policy and procedure manuals
- Designing, developing, and maintaining web pages
- Facilitating online discussion groups
- Supporting Internet telephones
- Enabling collaborative computing that lets people share information (e.g., through e-mail systems, collaborative software systems, videoconferencing, electronic white boards, electronic meeting systems, and computer-aided decision-making systems) without the traditional time and space constraints[8]
- Accessing specialized legal information and government regulations
- Providing online bulletin boards
- Providing and accessing distance learning training
- Buying, selling, trading, and tracking investments
- Posting job openings
- Maintaining résumé databases
- Recruiting employees
- Supporting a number of e-commerce functions such as e-marketing
- Access/use apps

Three of the uses mentioned in Figure 4-3 warrant a closer look, due to the impact that they are having: e-mail, research, and e-commerce.

E-mail   E-mail refers to electronically-generated messages and documents that are sent over the Internet, intranets, and extranets. E-mail is currently the most widely used communication medium in U.S. businesses.[9] Organizations use e-mail in a variety of ways. Some of the more common uses include coordinating work, sending attachments, keeping others informed, following up on earlier communication, sending the same message to many people simultaneously, and e-marketing.[10]

Organizations around the globe enjoy several benefits from e-mail. Included among these are:

- E-mail reduces the costs associated with distributing information to large numbers of employees or other stakeholders as well as the costs associated with paper preparation, duplication, and distribution.
- E-mail is a tool that supports and increases teamwork and collaboration because people can communicate easily and efficiently with others.
- E-mail, in conjunction with the Web, enhances research efforts.
- E-mail supports the mobility and flexibility benefits associated with mobile communication technologies such as laptops, cell phones, smartphones, and tablets.[11]

However, e-mail does pose some problems and challenges. Two of these that warrant mentioning are interpersonal disconnection and information overload.[12]

Interpersonal disconnection refers to a problem directly related to the use of e-mail in organizations. As employees send e-mails with greater frequency, they will likely engage in fewer face-to-face encounters, videoconferences, and phone conversations. The lack of nonverbal cues such as facial expressions and varying tones of voice has resulted in some employees feeling less connected to their fellow workers and organizations.[13] Employees may also feel less connected to clients and other stakeholders. Instant messaging, texting, blogging, and tweeting have all added to these problems. Furthermore, the overall quality of communication is compromised.

> **interpersonal disconnection** A potential problem directly related to the popularity of e-mail whereby users engage in fewer face-to-face and telephone conversations.

To encourage face-to-face communication, some companies now set aside a few "e-mail-free days" each month. Social interaction in the workplace is important to most people and, as can be expected, requires at least a minimal level of face-to-face and oral communication. To do otherwise potentially threatens employees' commitment and productivity levels as well as their overall job satisfaction. While there is no doubt that e-mail is a very popular and valuable business communication tool, we need to be careful not to use it to the extent that it creates interpersonal disconnection.

Information overload refers to situations in which businesspeople routinely receive more e-mail messages (or other communications) than they can effectively read, respond to, and act on. This situation is further exacerbated when employees go on vacation. For example, it is not uncommon for some employees to return from a vacation only to find hundreds of new e-mail messages waiting for them to process. To avoid such situations, some employees do not use all their allotted vacation time to relax. Some sort through and respond to incoming e-mail. Try not to take your e-mail on vacation with you. We all need downtime away from both the workplace and work tasks to rest, relax, and recharge our batteries. To do otherwise invites problems ranging from stress-related health problems to decreased productivity and burnout.

> **information overload** A situation in which people routinely receive more information and messages than they can effectively read, respond to, and act on.

In response to the problem of information overload, a variety of techniques are recommended to manage the problem. Several of these techniques are shared in chapter 6 in the section entitled *Managing High-Volume E-mail.*

Conducting Research If done correctly, conducting research on the Internet is cost efficient and time efficient. These efficiencies are especially evident when you contrast conducting research with today's electronic tools to a time not long ago when wading through hardcopy books, directories, journals, and magazines or squinting your eyes in an attempt to gather information from microfilm and microfiche were the norm.

Some of the same concerns researchers had in the past still exist in the Internet era, however. For example, researchers still need to question the validity of the information they acquire. Businesspeople and students, alike, face this challenge and are cautioned not to automatically assume that since information is posted on the Internet, it is credible. Your two best lines of defense for assuring the information you gather is valid are (1) gathering it from reliable Internet sources and (2) validating information you gather from the Internet through additional sources you know to be reliable, whether located on the Internet or elsewhere. For example, information posted on *Fortune* magazine's and the *Wall Street Journal's* websites can typically be relied on as being valid, whereas information posted on the websites of tabloids located near grocery store checkout stands may not be as reliable.

Be careful not to plagiarize. **Plagiarism** is the passing off as one's own the writings and ideas of others. Some of the common reasons some writers plagiarize are listed below:

- Some writers do not realize they are doing so.
- Some writers procrastinate during writing projects to the point of leaving themselves too little time to handle citations properly.
- Some writers think that if they located the information on the Internet, it is free and clear for the taking.
- Some writers are too lazy or careless to cite where needed.
- Some writers are simply unscrupulous.[14]

Be careful! Be especially careful not to plagiarize information found on the Internet. While it may be tempting to do so, especially when you are in a hurry, downloading information verbatim from online sources directly into your documents without citing these sources is plagiarism. Geraldine E. Hynes reminds us in her book *Surfing for Success in Business Communication* that writers should cite their sources when they (1) quote word-for-word, (2) closely paraphrase, or (3) repeat a series of phrases from documents posted on the Internet.[15]

E-commerce E-commerce (electronic commerce) refers to buying and selling products, services, and information over the Internet.[16] For example, many consumers log onto Amazon.com to buy books, music, and other items. When they do so, they are shopping in an e-commerce environment.

© Neirfy/Shutterstock.com

Another term that broadens the meaning of e-commerce is e-business. **E-business**, while addressing buying and selling activities, also implies servicing customers, collaborating with business partners, and conducting electronic transactions within an organization. The common thread that runs through all three of these functions is communication—electronic communication via the Internet.

plagiarism
The passing off as one's own the writings and ideas of others.

e-commerce
(electronic commerce) The transactions involved in buying and selling products, services, and information over the Internet.

e-business
A broader term for e-commerce that implies servicing customers, collaborating with business partners, and conducting electronic transactions within an organization as well as addressing buying and selling transactions.

While businesses developed around an e-commerce/e-business structure come and go like other forms of business, the concept holds great potential. Much of e-commerce success rests on the strength, diversity, and growth of the Internet. This is not to suggest that any time soon people will no longer shop in retail outlets and malls as they do today. Most people still like some face-to-face interaction with others, and many find the traditional approach to shopping to be a social outlet. Whatever the reasons, don't look for dot-com businesses to put retail outlets and malls out of business any time soon. E-commerce is growing in popularity. Every year greater numbers of people let their fingers do the shopping via the Internet.

Just how much impact this "e-structure" will have on businesses and customers is yet to be fully seen. Many believe it will have profound effects. Some even suggest e-commerce may result in a new industrial order. This point was made several years ago by former Vice President Al Gore when he said,

> We are on the verge of a revolution that is just as profound as the change in the economy that came with the Industrial Revolution. Soon electronic networks will allow people to transcend the barriers of time and distance and take advantage of global markets and business opportunities not even imaginable today, opening up a new world of economic possibility and progress.[17]

In many respects, Mr. Gore's predictions regarding the Internet were very accurate.

Current e-business growth is being fueled by a number of forces, including strong global competition, low-cost labor in many countries, the changing nature of the workforce, innovations and new technologies, and rapid decline in technology costs.[18] Benefits also stimulate growth. Some of the more noticeable benefits of e-commerce include the ability to expand into new markets, including global markets; reduced overhead; improved customer service; and reduced paper and transportation costs.[19] In summary, e-commerce is a new way to do business.

BARRIERS TO THE INTERNET

Despite the many applications and benefits the Internet offers, there are some barriers. Three in particular include restricted information flow, achieving sufficient broadband, and personal use by employees.

Restricted Information Flow This refers to governments that block access to many Internet sites and services within their borders. In his Cyberspace Independence Declaration, John Perry Barlow declared, "We are creating a world that all may enter without privilege or prejudice accorded by race, economic power, military force or station of birth."[19] However, Barlow's prediction still hasn't been fully realized. Some governments have learned how to regulate what information can be accessed by their businesspeople and citizens.[20] After all, the Internet is not owned and controlled by any one nation, organization, group, or individual. Each nation is left to determine how unfettered the information flow will be within its borders.

Achieving Sufficient Broadband *Broadband* refers to fast connections on the Internet. In the same vein, *bandwidth* refers to how fast Internet content can be delivered. Simply stated, there are still several areas in the world that do not have broadband access due to a combination of pricing, economic, and technical problems. On a positive note, the number of such areas is decreasing.

Non-work Use by Employees The Internet provides a nearly limitless source of websites, activities, information, chat capabilities, and social networking sites. Unfortunately, this wealth of activities, information, and distractions has contributed to major ethics and productivity problems in the U.S. workplace. The problem has to do with employees using the Internet for non-work purposes while at work. The problem has become prevalent enough that dismissing employees for inappropriate use of the Internet in the workplace is not unusual.

Just how common is this problem? Russ Warner, CEO of ContentWatch, reports that 64 percent of U.S. employees browse non-work related websites such as Facebook, LinkedIn, Google+, and Pinterest every day at work.[21] Among workers who browse non-work websites, those ages 18–35 do so most frequently with 73 percent reporting such activity. Respondents across all age ranges gave the following reasons for doing so: they don't feel challenged enough in their job, they work too many hours, the company doesn't give sufficient incentive to work harder, they're unsatisfied with their career, and they're just bored.[22] Shopping, conducting job searches, making travel arrangements, visiting social networking sites, downloading music, and viewing porn are among the more common reasons for visiting the Internet for non-work purposes, each of which can easily land an employee in the unemployment line!

While most employees keep personal Internet use to a minimum at work, others appear to be less committed to their workplace obligations. As can be expected, employees who use the Internet for non-work purposes contribute to lost productivity, which ultimately harms everyone in the company.[23]

Many businesses have responded to this problem by developing policies on inappropriate use of the Internet at work. Such policies typically pertain to misuse of company- and employee-owned electronic communication devices. Employees who own laptops, netbooks, tablets, and smartphones are expected to forgo using them for personal reasons while at work.

Other measures employers take to reduce the problem include blocking certain websites on employees' office computers, electronically monitoring employee use of the Internet, limiting employee access solely to an Intranet, and blocking employee access to the Internet entirely. Clear policies and measures reduce the instances of Internet misuse in the workplace. Clearly, such activity is greatly reduced when employees simply embrace their ethical responsibilities and work-related obligations to their employers.

SUMMARY: SECTION 3— THE INTERNET AND WORLD WIDE WEB

- The Internet is a self-regulated network connecting millions of computers worldwide.
- The Internet is popular throughout the world and has profoundly affected organizations, governments, and individuals.
- Intranets, extranets, and websites were developed using Internet technology.
- Businesses use the Internet in many ways to enhance communication efforts. Among them are sending and receiving e-mail, facilitating online discussion groups, providing distance learning, recruiting employees, and supporting e-commerce functions.
- Major barriers to full and equal access to the Internet include inadequate access in poor and rural areas of the United States, restricted information flow in many countries, limited broadband support, and misuse of the Internet by employees.

COMMUNICATING USING WIRELESS TECHNOLOGIES

© Tyler Olson/Shutterstock.com

It was not that long ago that most electronic communication tools depended on wires, cables, and modems to facilitate communication and information exchange. That was the age of the wired office. Given the right network configurations and electronic communication devices, combined with cloud computing, many of today's communication technologies function untethered. Businesspeople now conduct a large portion of their communication using wireless communication devices linked to personal area networks (PANs), local area networks (LANs), and wide area networks (WANs), and there are no indications that this trend will go away any time soon. It is much more likely that we will populate the world with billions more wireless electronic communication devices in the years to come.

Advances in communication technologies and network development, along with availability of WiFi and affordable technologies, enable businesspeople to perform many of their job responsibilities while moving from office to office, while traveling, and from their homes. From these varied sites, wireless technologies make it possible for them to send and receive text messages and e-mails; access social media sites; participate in conference calls and videoconferences; collaborate on group projects using group support systems (e.g., SharePoint, Google Docs, wikis, SkyDrive); share data files; and browse the Internet.

WIRELESS COMMUNICATION DEVICES

The most common devices with wireless communication capabilities that support uses such as those mentioned above include conventional and data-enabled cell phones, smartphones, laptops, netbooks, and tablets. Most of these devices have been standard business tools for a number of years, while others are relatively new entries. For example, **smartphones**, which merge cell phone and personal digital assistant (PDA) technologies, such as early models of the *BlackBerry*, are used extensively in today's businesses. Another example of a relatively new entrant is the **tablet.** These practical, affordable communication devices are another popular wireless communication tool in today's office. And just as the merging of cell phone and PDA technologies gave us smartphones, tablet and smartphone technologies have begun to merge, resulting in devices such as Samsung's Galaxy Note, which is a hybrid of a smartphone and tablet. Basically, this device has smartphone features and users can also write on the screen using a stylus. The current list of wireless communication devices has grown tremendously in a short time and will keep growing as people further embrace wireless, mobile technologies in the workplace and in their personal lives.

Five wireless communication devices that are making a noticeable impact on mobile communication: netbooks, tablets, cell phones, smartphones, and **Internet phones.**

Netbooks Netbook computers have been on the fringe of general laptop options, but now a new generation of netbooks is gaining market share. Netbooks are considerably smaller than normal laptops, with screen sizes that range from 5–13 inches and weigh as little as 2–3 pounds. **Netbooks** are highly portable devices whose main functions are to access e-mail, browse the Web, and use Web-based applications. Netbooks were originally

smartphones
Mobile phones offering advanced capabilities.

tablet
Relatively small touch pad computers with capabilities ranging from Internet access to standard PC functions.

Internet phones
Devices delivering voice communications over IP networks such as the Internet.

netbook
Small laptop whose main functions are to access e-mail, browse the Web, and use web-based applications.

© mozakim/Shutterstock.com

marketed as companion devices for laptop users who kept their data on the Web and mostly ran Web applications rather than software saved onto the computer itself. Now netbooks compete with laptops. Netbook popularity is driven partly by its low cost. An average netbook costs about $300. Thanks to technological advances, the lines between netbooks and laptops are becoming blurred. With increased processing power and additional features, some industry watchers suggest that netbooks are becoming little more than cheaper, smaller laptops.[24]

Tablets Tablets are also referred to as Tablet PCs, Webpads, and Touch Pads. There are a variety of tablets on the market, and the number keeps growing as more models are in various stages of development. Tablets are small touch pads with capabilities ranging from Internet access to standard PC functions. Users typically perform functions with their fingers or a stylus. They can also use a screen-based keyboard or attach a separate keyboard and mouse. Some tablets even respond to voice commands. Like several models of smartphones, tablets have a built-in camera and video recorder. Some models have a voice-activation feature. Most tablets have a 9-inch screen, are about 10x7½x½ inches in size, and weigh about one pound. Most of their surface is screen. Smaller tablets are also available. For example, Apple's Mini-iPad and Google's Android Tablet both have 7-inch screens. In contrast, Fuhu's nabi Big Tab HD 24 is the largest tablet with a 23.6 inch screen and weighs in at 10.5 pounds. It is designed predominately for children and families. Given that Apple received complaints about its first iPad weighing too much (roughly 1.5 pounds), the nabi Big Tab HD 24 is not necessarily intended to be a mobile tool—although the early portable PCs (luggables) that made their way onto the market in the early 1980s weighed closer to 40 pounds and businesspeople were happy to have them. Just imagine how much people would complain today about 40-pound portable communication devices!

© michaeljung/Shutterstock.com

Given tablets' low cost and wide range of features, some industry watchers suggest that tablets will eventually be the mobile electronic communication device of choice, eroding netbook and laptop sales. In 2015 tablets started outselling PCs, due in large part to their relatively-low cost, capabilities, features, and versatility.

Mobile Phones Long gone are the days when our ability to place and receive phone calls was limited to land line phones, pay phones, and costly long-distance charges. Today, mobile phones are very popular around the globe in and outside of the workplace. One might say that mobile phones are ubiquitous. For example, most Americans do not leave home without their mobile phones. And, if they do forget and leave their homes or offices without them, they're covered. While out and about, they buy a disposal mobile phone with airtime for a few dollars. However, disposable phones typically lack most of the features of conventional mobile phones.

Mobile phones are most frequently referred to as cell phones and smartphones, although many tablets also have phone capabilities. Tablets with phone capabilities include LG G Pad, Sony Xperia Z2, Samsung Galaxy Tab S, Apple iPad Air 2, Amazon Fire HDX 8.9, and Nvidia Shield Tablet.[25] Cell phones might simply be thought of as mobile phones with basic calling capabilities, whereas smartphones are cell phones with a host of features and capabilities that continue to increase with what seems to be the never-ending development of apps. Approximately 30 percent of Americans currently own one or more cell phones and approximately 66 percent own one or more smartphones. Cell phones and smartphones are popular communication devices due in great part to their mobility, small size, low cost, and ease of use.

Most smartphones have at least the basic functionality of PCs, making it possible for users to check and send text and e-mail messages, participate in IM exchanges, access social media, access company files, receive Internet faxes, and browse the Internet while engaged in a phone conversation. Smartphones also have scheduling and lists and notes features as well as GPS capability. Furthermore, smartphone digital and video cameras support Instagram, Pinterest, and YouTube needs. Last, but not least, Smartphones support a number of videoconferencing-related technologies including Video Chat, Snapchat, Skype, and FaceTime.

Mobile apps have vastly expanded mobile phone capabilities in recent years. At the current pace apps are developed, it is nearly impossible to keep up, although businesspeople are encouraged to do so with those that are applicable to business. Keeping up, in this regard, is most challenging given the rate new business apps are introduced. While there is not enough room in this book to address all of the current business apps, there is room to share what are considered to be several of the most useful business apps. These are presented in Figure 4-4. Possibly you are already familiar with most of them. If not, this is as good a time as any to get started.

FIGURE 4-4: USEFUL BUSINESS APPS FOR YOUR SMARTPHONE

Communication Apps
- MobileDay - conference caXll dialer app
- GoToMeeting - virtual meetings app

Enterprise Productivity/Internal Collaboration Apps
- Slack - team communication app
- Jira - issue and software tracking app
- Asana - e-mail-less project management app
- Trello - organizing app

Social Media Apps
- Snapseed - photo editing app for brands that are regular posters to social media sites
- Wordswag - Instagram word art and type over images app

Personal Productivity Apps
- Concur - expense reporting app
- Expensify - expense reports app
- Evernote - note-taking/collaboration app
- TheFreeDictionary – extensive dictionary app

Contact Management/Business Social Networks Apps
- LinkedIn - professional networking app

Mobile Payments/Wallet Apps
- Apple Pay - payment service app
- PayPal - payment service app

Mapping/GPS Apps
- Google Maps - map app

Travel Apps
- Uber - automobile transportation app
- Car2Go - car rental app
- Localeur - virtual tour guide app

News/Entertainment Apps
- HBO Go - entertainment app that is a good one for frequent business travelers
- Chromecast - entertainment app that is good for business travelers

Source: Aaron Strout, "Top 20 Most Useful Mobile Business Apps For 2015," April 30, 2015, http://marketingland.com/top-20-most-useful-mobile-business-apps-for-2015-126124.

Smartphones are typically larger than cell phones and come in a variety of sizes and shapes. Many models use touch-sensitive screens, while some even have slide-out keyboards. With the emergence of the iPhone, third-party development of applications, known as apps, have proliferated. Apps can be anything from games to driving directions to music lists. New apps are developed daily that help drive smartphone sales and, in turn, reduce the number of electronic devices people carry with them. GPS systems, digital cameras, video cameras, music players, voice recorders, PDAs, and electronic book readers are all examples of devices that have steadily been replaced by smartphones that have these features.

How To Charge On The Go jrossman@dallasnews-com

FIGURE 4–5: MOBILE PHONE CHALLENGES

- Concerned that others may hack your phone conversations while you are walking around your office, riding on the commuter train, or having coffee at a café?
- Knowing when and where it is appropriate to place and receive phone calls. Everywhere is not the answer. As a general rule, it is rude to place and respond to phone calls during face-to-face conversations, business meetings, presentations, business dinners, training sessions, and job interviews whether you are the recruiter or the job applicant.
- Being a courteous caller. Phone calls should be placed and received in a relatively quiet place where you are not disturbing others whether they are in the workplace cubicle next to yours, on the elevator, or next to you on a commuter train.
- Being aware of your surroundings while crossing streets. Unfortunately, some are so distracted by their mobile phone conversations, as well as texting, that they unknowingly step out in front of vehicles or fall through uncovered manholes. Death often results in these situations.
- Avoiding the urge to participate in phone conversations (and texting) while driving. Doing so is considered to be the equivalent of driving drunk and has resulted in numerous injuries and fatalities over the years. Possibly one day such driving safety concerns will be eliminated by smart cars that will essentially drive themselves. Imagine being able to put your car on auto pilot, pick up your smartphone, and talk or text without safety concerns.[26] For mobile phone safety tips, visit http://www.cellphonesafety.org/safer/tips.htm.
- Achieving seamless telephony for global travelers. This matter pertains to world phones.

World phones are cell phones with global roaming capabilities. The ideal world phone would enable a businessperson to place and receive wireless mobile phone calls to and from any location around the globe. Currently, world phone reception is available in some but not all global locations. However, the need to provide seamless telephony for global travelers exists, and progress continues in that direction.[27]

Internet Phones Internet phones are made possible, in part, due to Voice over Internet Protocol (VoIP), which refers to the delivery of voice communications over IP networks such as the Internet. These are also sometimes referred to as voice over broadband or Internet telephones. They are programs that allow people to talk to each other over the Internet. They are not really wireless communication devices like cell phones and smartphones;

world phones
Cell phones with global roaming capabilities.

however, they do enable communication over the Internet through wireless communication devices. The appeal of Internet telephones is the reduction or elimination of long-distance costs associated with conventional phone calls.

Without going into detail, the ability to communicate via Internet phones presumes that users have the appropriate software and hardware. These add-ons range from sound cards, speakers, and microphones to the software. The Internet phone is fairly new. It was introduced in 1995 by VocalTec. Despite some bugs in the technology, Internet phone use is growing, and market analysts predict that it has a bright future.[28]

Are you addicted to your mobile phone? If you find the term "addicted" to be a bit strong, how about replacing it with the term "deepening dependence" instead. The term addicted has such negative connotations for some. As discussed here, these two terms have similar meanings: the extremely anxious feelings many people suggest they would have if their mobile phone wasn't available or they couldn't use it with a relatively high degree of frequency. Recent Gallup polls concluded that almost half of American smartphone users "can't imagine" life without their device.[29]

FIGURE 4–6: IN THE EVENT OF A FIRE

In the event of a fire in your home, what would you save first? In a recent smartphone relationship survey, 53 percent of the respondents said that in the event of a fire, they would save their smartphones first. Really! This speaks to some level of addiction? Each of us just might want to pose this question to our loved ones, roommates, etc., just to see where we rank on the "save list" should a fire break out.

Source: Jae Yang & Veronica Bravo, "Rescuing smartphone," Motorola Smartphone Relationship Survey, USA Today, August 21, 2015, p. B1.

In addition, a study spanning Africa, China, and the United States that focused on the reasons behind digital distractions confirmed that addiction is one of the main reasons people text and the like in inappropriate settings.[30] If you are uncertain as to whether you are addicted to your mobile phone, so to speak, the following questions will likely help you arrive at an answer.

- Have you ever returned home to get your mobile phone after discovering you left home without it?
- Do you get noticeably stressed if your mobile phone battery is low? (When asked in a survey, 92 percent of Americans said they do.)
- Would you feel noticeably stressed if you did not have access to your mobile phone for several hours? Several days? (When asked in a survey, most Americans said they do. However, the length of time varies as could be expected.)

- What is the approximate number of times you check your mobile phone daily for phone and text messages? This is based on a 16-hour day. (Based on survey results, the typical American checks his or her mobile phone 103 times daily for phone and text messages which averages out to checking for them every seven minutes.)
- Are you using your mobile phone wisely (e.g., avoiding using it in inappropriate settings such as college classes, corporate training sessions, business meetings, etc.)?
- Are you using your mobile phone safely (e.g., avoiding using it while driving, crossing streets, etc.).

Your responses to the above questions should give you some sense of where you stand on the mobile phone addiction question. Hopefully you determined that you are not addicted. If you determined that you are, however, help is on the way. Figure 4-7 contains suggestions on how to beat the addiction or at least minimize it.

FIGURE 4-7: BEATING SMARTPHONE ADDICTIONS

- First, recognize the problem. Studies have linked smartphone dependence to stress anxiety and poor cognitive performance.
- Set short-term goals. Don't try to go cold-turkey for an extended period of time. Instead, wean yourself starting with a half-hour between stealing peeks. Then progressively increase the length of time between peeks.
- Spread the word. Tell your contacts what you are attempting to do. This will likely influence the frequency with which they contact you and expectations regarding how quickly and how often you will respond.
- Shut it down before bed. Reading on a bright screen in a dark room will not only delay sleep but can also cause less deep sleep and make you less alert the next day. In addition, reading on bright screens in dark places frequently has also been linked to detached retinas![31]

Smartwatches Smartwatches are a relatively new addition to the wearable communication technologies market, a market that has existed for several years. In fact, wearable computing and wearable technologies conferences are routinely held around the world and have been for a number of years. Some examples include WT (wearable technologies) Conferences, GizWorld Conferences, International Symposium on Wearable Computers (ISWC) conferences, and IDTechEx Wearable Conferences.

Smartwatches offer many of the same features as smartphones, but the availability of these varies among models. As can be expected, more expensive smartwatches often offer more features.

Businesspeople use smartwatches for a number of purposes ranging from checking e-mail and alerts to accessing business files. The hands-free nature of smartwatches is a very practical benefit.

On the downside, there are a number of drawbacks to smartwatches. For example, they are relatively expensive in contrast to netbooks, tablets, and smartphones. However, prices will eventually come down. In addition, early smartwatches were larger than most people preferred. This concern should diminish as smaller, voice-activated smartwatches hit the marketplace. Then too, there is the obvious concern about battery life. Screen size is another obvious drawback. For example, just how realistic is it to expect that most people will be able

Wearable Technology Conference http://wearablestech-con.com/

© wavebreakmedia/Shutterstock.com

to or even want to read e-mail messages and business documents on small 1.5- to 1.6-inch screens. There is another potential drawback that some might actually consider to be a benefit of smartwatches and that is the ability to easily check alerts and e-mails during meetings and training sessions. Most managers no more appreciate employees doing such things on smartwatches than on smartphones, tablets, and laptops during meetings and training sessions. Lastly, there are the potential drawbacks of never being disconnected that wearable technologies such as smartwatches pose. This point is made in the article "Never Offline."

Never Offline
http://time.
com/3326576/never-
offline/

© monicaodo/Shutterstock.com

Given the above-mentioned drawbacks, will smartwatches become widely used in the business world? Probably not if the drawbacks are not addressed. However, if manufacturers do address these concerns, ranging from cost and size to battery life, smartwatches just might become a popular mainstay.

© mindscanner/Shutterstock.com

THE IMPACT OF WIRELESS COMMUNICATION TECHNOLOGIES

Today's vast array of relatively low-cost, wireless communication technologies, combined with WiFi, has had a monumental impact on how communication occurs in the business place. Three ways organizations are impacted are presented below.

Working Away from the Office Possibly the most noticeable impact is the relatively new-found freedom businesspeople have experienced as a result of being freed from conventional, wired offices. For example, they no longer need to be tethered to stay in touch. Wireless communication devices have already and will continue to have a profound impact on how, where, when, and how frequently businesspeople communicate no matter the physical distance between business partners.

Wireless communication technologies are also playing a prominent role in transforming an ever-growing number of traditional U.S. office workers into telecommuters. **Telecommuters** refers to employees who perform some portion of their work away from the office while linked to it electronically. Before the advent of wireless communication technologies, telecommuters typically worked from their homes (or other fixed locations) using computers, fax machines, and telephones linked to their office through wired modems. Today's telecommuters who perform all or a significant portion of work from their homes are likely to use a combination of wired and wireless communication devices.

Telecommuting is increasingly popular with workers, businesses, and governments. The proliferation of communication technologies; potential cost savings related to buying, building, leasing, and maintaining office buildings; overcrowded streets and highways; deteriorating air quality; rising fuel and energy costs; and fear of terrorist attacks have together fueled telecommuting growth and popularity in the United States.[32] While employers see cost savings and potential benefits to the environment, most workers relish the idea of working in more relaxed and safer settings. Those who telecommute from their homes typically enjoy forgoing the expenses, hassles, and needed time associated with commuting and not needing to purchase as many expensive business clothes. Many also like the schedule flexibility typical of many telecommuting positions.

A set work schedule and a professional mindset are key to successful telecommuting for most people, whether the work is partially or fully performed from one's home. Without these, productivity typically suffers noticeably.

Even though today's communication technologies support telecommuting for many, it is not the right work structure for all employees. Those who do not adapt well to telecommuting are typically less productive and often eventually leave the company voluntarily due to dissatisfaction with their work environment. While businesses can relatively easily and inexpensively convert traditional workers into work-at-home telecommuters to "e-mobilize" their workforce, telecommuting will not bring out the best in all business employees. For example, some employees cannot be productive and meet deadlines without a structured schedule that involves traveling to and from an office during traditionally designated hours. Still others have difficulty separating work responsibilities from home and social distractions. In addition, it is common for some telecommuters to feel isolated because of the loss of daily contact with others, which leads to job burnout for some. For additional information on the challenges of working from home, visit http://www.glassdoor.com/blog/5-telecommuting/ and http://www.mnn.com/money/green-workplace/blogs/5-telecommuting-challenges-and-how-i-solved-them.

For obvious reasons, employers and employees need to be realistic about the extent to which telecommuter work is embraced. Survey instruments investigating the downsides and the benefits of telecommuting can be administered and followed up with interviews to determine an employee's suitability for telecommuter positions.

Once the decision is made to shift certain employees to telecommuter status, it is wise to closely monitor their productivity and job satisfaction for a while to determine if the change in job structure is working out as planned.

Just as telecommuting is not the right work structure for some employees, it does not support all job tasks. For example, work activities such as important meetings and presentations do not fit into the telecommuting work structure.

Telecommuter
An employee who performs some portion of his or her work away from the office while linked to the office electronically.

17 Tools For Remote Workers, Kevan Lee http://www.fastcompany.com/3038333/17-tools-for-remote-workers

Working Remotely? Here's How to Do it Right, Jessica Velasco http://www.success.com/article/working-remotely-heres-how-to-do-it-right

Moving Around the Office Untethered Just as wireless communication technology has made it possible for businesspeople to move around freely away from the office, it has opened the doors to mobile communication within the office. In wireless offices, workers are no longer tethered to desktop PCs, telephones, and defined office spaces such as cubicles. However, even in wireless offices, some closed-off spaces remain for status, quiet-time purposes, private meetings, conference calls, and videoconferences.

In wireless business environments, the trend is moving in the direction of working in common, open spaces rather than in isolated cubicles and offices. These large open spaces frequently look more like casual living rooms than traditional offices filled with desks and filing cabinets. Instead, these open spaces may be filled with comfortable furniture and flat-panel screens hanging from the walls.[33] This all sounds wonderful, but be careful not to settle into an exceptionally comfortable chair after a big lunch. You know what that will do to your productivity while you are napping!

Savings Associated with Wireless Offices The reduction or elimination of costs associated with setting up and maintaining wired offices is another way wireless communication technologies impact organizations. In the traditional wired office, much cost and effort went into running wires and cables to individual offices and cubicles to hook into an array of wired communication devices. Additional costs were incurred when employees were occasionally relocated within their buildings, requiring some rewiring. Wired offices also have the cost associated with hiring technical support personnel to maintain the systems.[34]

As popular and pervasive as wireless communication technologies are in the business place, it is wise to stay current. An excellent way to stay current is to routinely read magazines dedicated to wireless and mobile communication topics. Such magazines include *Wireless Business & Technology*, *Smartphone & Pocket PC*, and *Mobile Computing*. In addition, magazines and newspapers such as *Fortune, PC Magazine, BusinessWeek*, and the *Wall Street Journal* routinely include articles, editorials, and even extensive sections devoted to wireless communication technologies and processes. There are also a number of websites that contain information about wireless communication and wireless communication devices.

SUMMARY: SECTION 4—
GOING MOBILE: WIRELESS COMMUNICATION TECHNOLOGY

- The combination of smaller computer chips and a number of communication networks, such as PANs, LANs, and WANs, have led the way for a host of wireless electronic communication devices.
- Wireless electronic communication devices currently in use include cell phones, smartphones, world phones, Internet phones, laptops, notebooks, netbooks, and tablets.
- While cell phones and smartphones are ubiquitous, be mindful of their many courtesy and safety issues.
- Wireless communication devices play a prominent role in transforming an ever-growing number of U.S. office workers into telecommuters, as well as providing them with mobility within offices.

USING COMMUNICATION TECHNOLOGIES EFFECTIVELY

The sophistication and potential of the Internet combined with today's electronic communication technologies cannot be ignored. Their effects on the business place and elsewhere are numerous and are continuously changing how we work, play, relax, and interact with others. However, if we want to fully realize the potential benefits, we need to use these technologies effectively. Suggestions pertaining to how to use electronic communication technologies effectively are presented below.

CHOOSING THE APPROPRIATE COMMUNICATION MEDIUM

The importance of selecting the appropriate medium for each communication situation or setting was discussed at length. With all this talk about the Internet and electronic communication technologies further discussion of this topic is needed.

While electronic communication devices are the right media choice for some situations, they are not best for all situations. We need to be careful not to become so enamored with electronic communication technologies that we automatically choose them at the expense of effective communication.

The concept of information richness or media richness helps us make more effective communication media choices. **Information richness** refers to how robust a communication medium is. Some communication media are rich, some are lean, and the rest fall in between. The richest form of communication is face-to-face communication. It is considered the richest because most people find it to be the most natural way to communicate, and it contains the full range of nonverbal cues in addition to the spoken word. Immediate feedback is another benefit of face-to-face communication. Less robust media (e.g., text messages, e-mails, tweets) are lean and should be limited to messages regarding routine matters.

Given the rationale presented above, holoconferencing is the second richest communication medium followed, in descending order, by videoconferencing, Skype and video chat exchanges, phone conversations, conference calls, instant messaging, e-mailing, texting, tweeting, and blogging. **Holoconferences** are telepresence-based videoconferences in which screen images are replaced with 3-dimensional images of participants who are not physically present.

Be careful not to become so enamored with the convenience and cost- and time-saving benefits of electronic communications technologies that you skimp on face-to-face communication. Remind yourself that when a situation is important, complex, or controversial, there is no electronic substitute for face-to-face communication. Even videoconferencing falls short to face-to-face communication in terms of participant comfort level and relationship-building potential.

CONTROL COMMUNICATION TECHNOLOGY, RATHER THAN ALLOWING IT TO CONTROL YOU

As wonderful as the Internet and electronic communication devices are, they have their shortcomings and challenges. Recall the challenges pertaining to mobile phones and telecommuting that were discussed previously. Additional challenges are presented below.

information richness
Refers to how robust a communication medium is.

holoconferences
Telepresence-based videoconferences in which screen images are replaced with 3-dimensional images of participants who are not physically present.

Information Overload Challenges

Information overload results when individuals receive too many electronic messages to realistically process. This situation often results in the receiver becoming overwhelmed by the volume of information. Businesspeople must be sensitive to how many messages can be processed realistically given their daily demands on their time. Several techniques for managing e-mail volume are discussed in chapter 6 (Writing Electronically). In addition, we each need to search for and access information wisely in databases and on the Internet. The better we understand our purpose for gathering the information, the less likely we are to gather unneeded, excess information. In addition, the better we know how to navigate databases and the Internet, the less overwhelmed we are likely to become when conducting research.

Polyphasic Activity Challenges

Polyphasic activity refers to doing more than one thing at a time (e.g., multitasking). This is typical of humans. For example, carrying on conversations while walking or driving is polyphasic activity. Multitasking is a way of life in the workplace and for many people in their personal lives. What does this have to do with communication technologies? Today's communication technologies often make polyphasic activity a reality—a detrimental reality. For example, it is possible to participate in a conference call, check and respond to e-mail, and browse the Internet simultaneously. However, performing so many different activities simultaneously typically compromises the effectiveness of how each is handled. The point is that even though much of today's communication technology supports extensive polyphasic activity, we must be careful not to compromise the effectiveness of our efforts by overextending ourselves.

Balancing Work and Personal Life Challenges

Joan Greenbaum, author of *Windows for the Workplace: Computers, Jobs, and the Organization of Office Work in the Late 20th Century*, identified a growing technology-related problem. She suggested that because today's technology has empowered businesspeople to work anywhere at any time, many are working everywhere and all the time.[35] Some even feel guilty when they are not working most of the time. This is especially true of telecommuters who work extensively from their homes. The result is they are not getting away from their work, so they are not building in enough downtime to fulfill their personal needs and re-energize. Maintaining such a continuous work schedule for any serious length of time can easily result in negative outcomes ranging from increased feelings of stress and depression to medical problems such as ulcers and high blood pressure as well as job and career burnout. It is neither healthy nor logical for employees to be constantly connected to the workplace no matter whether employers require their employees to do so or employees voluntarily choose to do so. By 2015 the potential negative effects of such workplace actions led the German government to pass a law that restricts businesses from e-mailing employees after 6 p.m. on week nights and on weekends as a means of reducing worker stress.

So, what can you do to maintain your sanity and health as well as function effectively in work environments in which you are likely to overextend yourself? Consider scheduling set work times, and then do your best to stick to them. In turn, set aside time for personal matters, friends, and family and do as little work as possible during those times. In addition, do not allow yourself to be on call constantly. Furthermore, give yourself permission to disconnect from your electronic communication devices when you are not working. For example, do not get into the habit of checking your text messages, e-mails, voicemail, and various social media sites every waking hour of every day and night. Lastly, do not feel compelled to carry your laptop, tablet, smartphone, and/or smartwatch with you everywhere you go. It is healthy to disconnect periodically as described in Michael Harris's book *The End of Absence*.

The End of Absence
http://www.endofab-
sence.com/

Brevity, Tone, and Carelessness Challenges It is generally understood that we are expected to keep electronic messages and posts brief. Thus, we are encouraged to write relatively short e-mail messages, text messages, and social media posts as well as leave brief voicemails. The potential problem with this sweeping expectation is providing too little information to communicate our messages and posts adequately. To minimize this potential problem, have others read your messages and posts carefully to determine if clarity exists.

Improper tone is also a potential problem when developing electronic messages and posts. The tone-related problems include using a tone that is too informal or is less than tactful. For most of us, our early experiences with e-mail involved sending informal messages to family and friends. Furthermore, this informal tone was likely reinforced when we wrote text messages, tweets, and posts. The end result was very likely an informal writing style that worked well with your family and friends, but is too informal for most business e-mail messages. For some reason, many people do not state things as tactfully in electronic messages as they should. This is especially characteristic of e-mail, in which electronic alter egos have been known to take control in counterproductive ways.[36] Good advice when developing electronic messages that just might help you avoid tone issues is to assess your tone carefully before sending or posting.

Lastly, a careless writing style is typically looked upon unfavorably in the business world. However, when developing electronic messages for family and friends, many of us developed a careless writing style, a style that is frowned upon in the professional workplace. This means we should adhere to basic writing mechanics rules (e.g., grammar, punctuation, spelling) when developing electronic messages in business settings. To minimize this potential problem, before sending or posting, edit electronic messages and posts carefully with special focus on writing mechanics and accuracy.

Telephone Challenges There is probably no finer example of the potentially impersonal nature of electronic communication devices than what we are currently witnessing with the telephone. What started out in 1876 as such a simple, effective communication device has evolved into a device containing a host of features that present their own set of problems. Several of the more commonly mentioned telephone irritants are presented in Figure 4-8.

FIGURE 4–8: TELEPHONE IRRITANTS

- Not controlling background noise when using speaker phones.
- Automatically responding to call waiting calls when conversing with others.
- Not giving others your full attention during conference calls.
- Not giving a caller the choice to be placed on hold, and placing callers on hold for extended times (longer than one minute).
- Placing computer-generated calls and advertisements to people's offices, mobile phones, and homes.
- Subjecting callers to long, involved phone menus.
- Not providing callers with a telephone menu option to speak with a person.
- Placing telemarketing calls at dinnertime, during evenings, and on weekends and holidays.
- Placing and answering calls in inappropriate settings ranging from college classes and corporate training sessions to business meetings and job interviews.

Without exception, each of the telephone irritants mentioned in Figure 4-8 can be eliminated. The lesson in all this is that phone usage decisions should result in people treating others respectfully.

FIGURE 4–9: UNETHICAL USE OF THE TELEPHONE

Most people do not appreciate receiving unsolicited calls from telemarketers, fundraisers, and politicians during dinnertime, evenings, weekends, and holidays. In addition, most people do not appreciate receiving computer-generated calls making requests, advertising products and services, or endorsing politicians. Just because today's technology makes it possible for us to place unwanted calls so easily and inexpensively does not mean we should do it.

Technology Uses Challenges The issue here has to do with employees' perceptions about and proficiency with electronic communication technologies. Do you believe all business employees are comfortable and proficient with a wide range of electronic communication technologies? While most business employees adapt well to electronic communication technologies, some don't. In fact, some prefer a technology-free existence. Figure 4-10 reinforces these points through a list of 10 common "techno-types" that were identified by Dr. Francine Toder, emeritus faculty of California State University Sacramento. If you have not already thought about it, take this opportunity to identify which techno-type or combination thereof best describes you. Then, reflect on how your attitude toward technology will affect your career.

FIGURE 4–10: TECHNO-TYPES

- **The Imposter.** Imposters play around on computers, hoping that their lack of knowledge goes undetected.
- **The Challenger.** Challengers are angered by technology and afraid that it may be used against them.
- **The Resister.** Resisters prefer the simplicity of a tech-free existence. (Resisters are the most common techno-type!)
- **The Technophobe.** Technophobes are paranoid about technology.
- **The Procrastinator.** Procrastinators use technology for the easiest tasks and never go for the max.
- **The Addict.** Addicts eat, sleep, and drink technology.
- **The Driver.** Drivers use tech skills to outpace everyone.
- **The Player.** Players are grown-up gamers who live to play.
- **The Dreamer.** Dreamers harbor unrealistic expectations for technology.
- **The Hermit.** Hermits prefer electronic communication in lieu of face-to-face contact.

Source: From Tech Types *by Paula Felps. © 2000 by Paula Felps. Reprinted by permission.*

Are all business employees receptive to telecommuting and productive when placed in a telecommuting work environment that has them working out of a spare bedroom or converted garage in their home? Some structured, self-disciplined employees are satisfied, productive employees in telecommuting environments. In contrast, others do not adapt well to such environments.

It is important that managers keep employees' communication differences, preferences, strengths, and weaknesses in mind when making decisions regarding integrating electronic communication devices into the workplace and making telecommuting assignments. Bringing employees in on the decision-making process as it relates to technology choices and telecommuting shows them how they will potentially benefit personally from the proposed changes. Suffice it to say, e-mobilizing a company's workforce requires more thought and effort than simply distributing smartphones, laptops, netbooks, and tablets en masse.

Technology Over-Reliance Challenge Millennials (those born between 1982 and 2004) are now the largest segment of the American workforce, and it has been suggested that one of the biggest issues they are having in the workplace is over-reliance on electronic communication. When surveyed, 91% of millennials reported that they aspire to be leaders, and over half (58%) of those respondents indicated that they think the most important leadership skill is communication. Furthermore, 51% indicated that communication is one of their strongest skills. Given their reliance on electronic communication, are these millennials' overall communication skills as strong as they believe them to be? Or, is it possible that some of them, while having strong electronic communication skills, are lacking in other areas such as face-to-face communication, listening, and presentation skills, to name a few? All communication conducted in the business place cannot and should not done electronically. Thus, there is still a strong need for all business personnel of all ages to have strong communication skills whether they are communicating electronically or otherwise.[37]

Technology-Related Job Security and Career Concerns While most of today's communication technologies hold great potential for increased productivity, when misused they can lead to job loss and even threaten careers. Figure 4-11 contains a number of communication technology job security and career threats you are encouraged to keep in mind as you move through your working years.

FIGURE 4–11: TECHNOLOGY-RELATED JOB SECURITY AND CAREER THREATS

- Reduced productivity resulting from being connected too frequently (e.g., 24/7 connectivity).
- Job/career burnout from being connected too frequently (e.g., 24/7 connectivity).
- Job/career fallout from using communication technologies during business meetings, presentations, and training sessions (e.g., texting, tweeting, answering phone calls, browsing the Internet). The vast majority of U.S. managers discourage employees from doing so.
- Job/career fallout from using communication technologies for personal (non-work) reasons in the workplace (e.g., e-mailing friends, downloading music, browsing porn sites, e-shopping, and sexting which is on the rise among 20–26 year-olds in the United States).

Technology-Related Health and Safety Threats As mentioned previously, today's communication technologies hold great potential for increased productivity. However, today's communication technologies also pose health and safety threats when misused. Figure 4-12 contains several communication technology health and safety threats you are encouraged to keep in mind as you move through life. Each of us is vulnerable to these technology-related health and safety threats.

FIGURE 4–12: TECHNOLOGY-RELATED HEALTH AND SAFETY THREATS

- Vision impairment associated with viewing small screens with a fairly high degree of frequency. Hopefully you will be able to do most of your reading from good-sized monitors and even then increase the type size to ease eye strain. In addition, you are encouraged to take more frequent breaks than you would normally take to rest your eyes. Finally, consider purchasing a pair of glasses designed for small screens including e-books.
- Hearing loss associated with frequent use of mobile phone earpieces and ear buds.
- Carpal tunnel syndrome damage (repetitive motion nerve damage) associated with too much keyboarding—especially on small netbook keyboards and small mobile phone keypads. One relatively new entry to the list of carpal tunnel syndrome afflictions that you definitely do not want is "cellphone elbow." This can occur if you talk on a mobile phone for a long time while holding your neck crooked and your elbow bent.[38] Maybe it is time to buy a headset!
- Detached retinas resulting from using electronic communication devices such as mobile phones and tablets with a relatively high degree of frequency in dark settings. Turn on some lights!
- Stress-related health problems (e.g., high blood pressure) resulting from being on call 24/7, whether required to do so by your employer or exercising self-imposed behavior.
- Safety concerns associated with placing smartphone and cell phone calls, participating in phone conversations, texting, blogging, or tweeting while walking, jogging, running, and driving. You can Google the related injuries and fatalities statistics if you wish. The numbers are high and depressing as can be expected. Despite the related safety claims, voice-activated technology features in cars do not insure complete safety even after drivers end their calls. There is typically a transitional period (liminal space) of approximately 20-30 seconds following such calls during which drivers are still distracted before they once again focus their attention on driving.

Communication technologies are yours to use safely and effectively or to misuse at potentially high professional and personal costs. Here's hoping you use current and future communication technologies in ways that promote your career aspirations and your health and safety as well as that of others.

ASSISTIVE TECHNOLOGIES

assistive technologies Electronic devices enabling people with physical disabilities to communicate more easily and effectively.

Great strides have been made in the development of **assistive technologies** that enable people with a variety of disabilities to communicate more easily and effectively. Figure 4-13 contains some examples, but this is by no means an all-inclusive list of assistive technologies.

FIGURE 4-13: ASSISTIVE TECHNOLOGIES

- **Hearing.** For people who are either deaf or hearing challenged, TTY (text telephone) technology is helpful. Incoming calls are converted to text. Captioning capabilities on videos and similar technologies are also practical.

- **Speaking.** For people who are either deaf or speaking challenged, TTY (text telephone) technology is also helpful. For outgoing calls, they can keyboard their message, and their phone partner receives a computer-generated voice message.
- **Seeing.** For people who are blind or visually challenged, *JAWS* screen reading software converts text to voice. Apple's *VoiceOver* works in a similar way. There are also printers that print text in Braille.

Figure 4-13 provided you with a quick glimpse at assistive technologies. A more inclusive list of assistive technologies follows.

Alternative input devices allow individuals to control their computers through means other than a standard keyboard or pointing device. Examples include:

- **Alternative keyboards.** Featuring larger- or smaller-than-standard keys or keyboards, alternative key configurations, and keyboards for use with one hand.
- **Electronic pointing devices.** Used to control the cursor on the screen without the use of hands. Devices used include ultrasound, infrared beams, eye movements, nerve signals, or brain waves.
- **Sip-and-puff systems.** Activated by inhaling or exhaling.
- **Wands and sticks.** Worn on the head, held in the mouth, or strapped to the chin and used to press keys on the keyboard.
- **Joysticks.** Manipulated by hand, feet, chin, etc. and used to control the cursor on screen.
- **Trackballs.** Movable balls on top of a base that can be used to move the cursor on screen.
- **Touch screens.** Allow direct selection or activation of the computer by touching the screen, making it easier to select an option directly rather than through a mouse movement or keyboard. Touch screens are either built into the computer monitor or can be added onto a computer monitor.
- **Braille embossers.** Transfer computer generated text into embossed Braille output. Braille translation programs convert text scanned-in or generated via standard word processing programs into Braille, which can be printed on the embosser.

- **Keyboard filters.** Are typing aids such as word prediction utilities and add-on spelling checkers that reduce the required number of keystrokes. Keyboard filters enable users to quickly access the letters they need and to avoid inadvertently selecting keys they don't want.
- **Light signaler alerts.** Monitor computer sounds and alert the computer user with light signals. This is useful when a computer user cannot hear computer sounds or is not directly in front of the computer screen. As an example, a light can flash alerting the user when a new e-mail message has arrived or a computer command has completed.
- **On-screen keyboards.** Provide an image of a standard or modified keyboard on the computer screen that allows the user to select keys with a mouse, touch screen, trackball, joystick, switch, or electronic pointing device. On-screen keyboards often have a scanning option that highlights individual keys that can be selected by the user. On-screen keyboards are helpful for individuals who are not able to use a standard keyboard due to dexterity or mobility difficulties.
- **Reading tools and learning disabilities programs.** Include software and hardware designed to make text-based materials more accessible for people who have difficulty with reading. Options can include scanning, reformatting, navigating, or speaking text out loud. These programs are helpful for those who have difficulty seeing or manipulating conventional print materials; people who are developing new literacy skills or who are learning English as a foreign language; and people who comprehend better when they hear and see text highlighted simultaneously.
- **Refreshable Braille displays.** Provide tactile output of information represented on the computer screen. A Braille "cell" is composed of a series of dots. The pattern of the dots and various combinations of the cells are used in place of letters. Refreshable Braille displays mechanically lift small rounded plastic or metal pins as needed to form Braille characters. The user reads the Braille letters with his or her fingers, and then, after a line is read, can refresh the display to read the next line.
- **Screen enlargers, or screen magnifiers**. Work like a magnifying glass for the computer by enlarging a portion of the screen which can increase legibility and make it easier to see items on the computer. Some screen enlargers allow a person to zoom in and out on a particular area of the screen.
- **Screen readers.** Are used to verbalize, or "speak," everything on the screen including text, graphics, control buttons, and menus into a computerized voice that is spoken aloud. In essence, a screen reader transforms a graphic user interface (GUI) into an audio interface. Screen readers are essential for computer users who are blind.
- **Speech recognition or voice recognition programs.** Allow people to give commands and enter data using their voices rather than a mouse or keyboard. Voice recognition systems use a microphone attached to the computer, which can be used to create text documents such as letters or e-mail messages, browse the Internet, and navigate among applications and menus by voice.
- **Text-to-Speech (TTS) or speech synthesizers.** Receive information going to the screen in the form of letters, numbers, and punctuation marks, and then "speak" it out loud in a computerized voice. Using speech synthesizers allows computer users who are blind or who have learning difficulties to hear what they are typing and also provide a spoken voice for individuals who cannot communicate orally, but can communicate their thoughts through typing.

- **Talking and large-print word processors.** Are software programs that use speech synthesizers to provide auditory feedback of what is typed. Large-print word processors allow the user to view everything in large text without added screen enlargement.
- **TTY/TDD conversion modems.** Are connected between computers and telephones to allow an individual to type a message on a computer and send it to a TTY/TDD telephone or other Baudot equipped device.[39]

If you do not have a disability that impedes your ability to communicate easily and effectively with others, you have likely given little thought to assistive technologies like those mentioned in Figure 4-13. That is understandable. However, awareness of and familiarization with such technologies better positions you to help others by informing them of applicable technologies. For those with disabilities, such technologies have a profound and positive impact on their ability to communicate on the job as well as in their personal lives. Those who develop such technologies should be applauded!

SUMMARY: SECTION 5— USING COMMUNICATION TECHNOLOGY EFFECTIVELY

- Choose the best communication medium for the situation, which does not always mean an electronic communication device.
- Be sensitive to the negative effects of uncontrolled information overload and polyphasic activity.
- Strike a balance between work and personal life by scheduling non-work times and being willing to disconnect from your e-mail and cell phone for a time.
- Just because some electronic communication devices support brief messages, do not assume brevity is synonymous with clarity. Do not get careless with your tone and grammar when using electronic devices.
- When used improperly, telephone technology chases away customers and business partners.
- When possible, assign electronic communication devices to individuals best suited to use them effectively and productively.
- Use as needed and/or inform others of assistive technologies that enable people with a variety of disabilities to communicate more easily and effectively.

SOME CAUTIOUS COMMUNICATION TECHNOLOGY PREDICTIONS

Given the rapid rate at which communication technology developments occur, making predictions about what's to come is downright dicey business. As we all know, all predictions do not come to fruition. However, there are strong signs and trends supporting the communication technology predictions listed in this section.

You may laugh at the following prediction that was made several years ago because, in contrast to today's technology offerings, it sounds a bit silly. In a 1949 issue of *Popular Mechanics* magazine they predicted that "Computers of the future may weigh no more than 1.5 tons."[40] The sizes and weights of today's laptops, netbooks, and tablets certainly validated the 1949 prediction. In 1949 computers were mainframe computers that weighed thousands of pounds—often filling entire rooms. You can now see why people in 1949 longed for smaller, lighter computers.

It is important that people continue to make predictions and strive to turn them into reality. It is through this creative process and willingness to explore the unknown that improvements to existing technologies and development of new technologies occur. Imagine for a moment how different things would be in the workplace, our homes, and elsewhere if Alexander Graham Bell had not pursued the development of the telephone or Thomas Edison and others the development of the light bulb. The effect on organizations and elsewhere would be profound to say the least. So, the next time you read about or hear someone talk about research in the area of futuristic developments such as transporter systems and time travel, do not be too quick to think they are delusional and dismiss the possibilities. Instead, imagine the impact that such developments will have in the workplace and elsewhere. In other words, dare to dream!

Listed here are several communication technology predictions. Time alone will obviously tell for certain if they transpire. As an aside, no attempt was made to list these predictions in any perceived order of importance.

- The popularity of e-mail, texting, instant messaging, and numerous social media applications in the workplace, as well as in our personal lives, will continue.
- Social networking sites ranging from Facebook, LinkedIn, Instagram, Pinterest, and YouTube will increase in popularity and applications in and outside of the business world.
- Cloud computing will continue to grow at a fast pace. For example, between 2015 and 2018 International Data Corporation (IDC) projects that public cloud services revenue will double to $127 billion.[41]
- E-commerce sales will continue to grow in the United States and globally. While current U.S. e-commerce sales figures exceed $300 billion, they are projected to reach approximately $500 billion by 2019. Global e-commerce sales figures are approximately $2 trillion currently and are expected to reach approximately $2.5 trillion by 2019.
- The combined effects of the Internet and electronic communication developments will further global business interaction, much like e-mail, mobile phones, and social media have done thus far.
- Traditional single-function cell phones will continue to be replaced by smartphones and along with the smartphones will come more features and access to an even-larger number of apps.
- As smartphones and related service plans grow in popularity, more people will trade in, so to speak, their cell phones for smartphones. As mentioned earlier, cell phones can be thought of as essentially being mobile phones with basic calling capabilities, whereas smartphones also have extensive features.
- The number of landline phones will decrease as mobile phones meet the need.
- Despite the popularity of small-screened smartphones and tablets, large screen PC monitors have not gone away and appear to be gaining some traction. For example, Samsung offers a 29-inch ultra-wide curved screen LED monitor. While small screens are practical when on the go, large-screen monitors offer in-office users a more eye-friendly experience.
- With the steady demise of landlines and increased mobility within the business community, greater numbers of people will rely on external batteries to charge their

mobile phones and other electronic communication devices as needed. The *Power Castle 12000, Power Castle 13000,* and *Power Castle 14000* external batteries are well received and each weighs less than one pound.

- A greater number of multipurpose devices such as smartphones and tablets will be introduced.
- A greater number of established technologies will merge, giving way to new electronic communication devices, much as the combining of cell phone and PDA technologies led to the advent of smartphones.
- Tablets will continue to erode PC sales. Tablet sales surpassed PC sales in 2015. However, the PC is still considered to be workhorse in the office much like the typewriter was before PCs were invented.
- Handheld electronic devices that offer both smartphone and tablet features and capabilities may one day replace smartphones and tablets as we currently know them. Samsung's *Galaxy Note* is an example of one such device. The screen is larger than the typical smartphone, but smaller than a standard tablet screen.
- The number of apps for smartphones, tablets, and smartwatches will grow.
- The number of e-books will increase along with the number of e-book readers such as *Kindle Paperwhite, Kindle Fire HD, Kindle Touch, Kindle Fire Touch,* and *Nook Simple Touch.* **E-books** are books transmitted digitally and read on computers and e-readers. **E-readers** are electronic tablets designed for reading digitally transmitted e-books.

e-books
Books transmitted digitally and read on computers and e-readers.

e-readers
Electronic tablets designed for reading digitally transmitted e-books.

©*Sergy Nivens/Shutterstock.com*

- The number of college textbooks are available as e-books (including this textbook) will continue to grow.
- The number of public and private school systems that equip their students with e-book readers and e-books, in place of hardcopy textbooks, will continue to grow.
- Speech-recognition developments will lead to an even greater number of electronic communication devices that can be accessed orally, like most tablet users are currently able to do. *Dragon Dictate for Mac* and *Google Dragon* are examples of speech recognition software used with PCs, and *Bing Voice Search, Dragon Search*, and *Shoutout* are examples of speech recognition software used on mobile devices such as smartphones. Of course, these are just a few!
- Tablets and notebooks will eventually be activated by gestures.
- Interactive digital whiteboards called smartboards (e.g., Hitachi's StarBoard) will continue to grow in popularity in businesses and schools. **Smartboards** are large,

smartboards
Large, interactive, electronic screens containing practical applications for business meetings and presentations.

interactive, electronic screens containing practical applications for project teams, business meetings, presentations, and training sessions. They first became available in 1997.

© lucadp/Shutterstock.com

- Self-erasing paper may become more commonplace. This is paper on which you write, but in a few hours it is invisible, which is practical for privacy and security reasons.
- A greater number of electronic meeting technologies will offer alternatives for conducting business meetings. While conference call and videoconference technologies have made great inroads in the business world and are widely used, other technologies such as telepresence systems will grow in popularity. These systems actually place holograms (3-dimensional images) of your distant meeting partners in front of you in your geographic location.
- The continuous size reduction of transistors and computer chips will lead to smaller, yet more powerful electronic devices.
- More traditional tower-based desktop PCs in businesses will continue to be replaced with virtual desktops. Virtual desktops consist of a monitor, keyboard, and small connector box tied to a server.
- The number and quality of assistive devices (technologies) that help people with disabilities communicate more easily and effectively will continue to grow.
- Wireless communication devices will continue to e-mobilize growing numbers of office workers around the globe. In response, the number of traveling and home-based telecommuters will grow significantly.
- Greater numbers of business offices will adopt more open-environment working settings with fewer cubicles and traditional walled-in work spaces. Examples of technologies that should be prevalent in such settings include: smart glass that morphs into media screens, 3-D printers that produce small prototypes, subtitled conference calls, hologram tables, conference call suites with computer programs that translate languages instantaneously, and programs that will enable office workers to navigate computer screens with the flick of the wrist.[42]
- The number of people who are injured or killed by drivers of cars, buses, trains, planes, helicopters, boats, and other motorized vehicles while using mobile phones (e.g., smartphones) while driving will rise.[43]

- The number of cities, states, and countries in which citizens voluntarily reduce their use of mobile phones to place calls and text while driving will increase. You may believe this is wishful thinking; however, strong signs of this are appearing in Great Britain and Los Angeles, for example. In such places, participating in phone conversations and texting while driving are increasingly considered to be socially unacceptable behaviors.
- The number of countries, states, and municipalities outlawing drivers from placing cell phone calls, participating in cell phone conversations, and text messaging while driving will continue to rise.[44] Such bans first went into effect in the late 1990s.
- Digital pens will grow in popularity as their price drops. These pens record what you write and store it digitally. You can then download what you wrote. Most digital pens will also record your graphics and drawings. Some pens also have video and audio recording capabilities.
- Electronic pencils like the Apple Pencil that works in tandem with Apple's iPad Pro will likely grow in popularity. The Apple Pencil works like a regular pencil and supports the creation of art, animations, blueprints, and more.
- Virtual reality systems applications will increasingly fill entertainment voids as well as provide business applications ranging from making it possible for consumers to virtually test products before purchasing them to virtual mirrors in which consumers can see themselves in different clothing options without having to try them on.
- The number of wearable communication technologies will increase and be smaller (e.g., smartwatches, ear buds, headsets). Another example is Google's Glass which are glasses containing a computer. Through voice and touch the wearer can access the Web, place and receive calls, send and receive text messages, take photos, and access a host of other computer-based applications. Google is currently working on developing contact lenses with similar capabilities. Apple is working on developing wearable computers.[45]
- Telepathy—brain-to-brain communication—just might become a reality. According to Jerry Adler, researchers are breaching the boundaries of the mind, moving information in and out across space and time. Sounds like something out of a *Star Trek* movie, not a potential reality. Personally, I don't think others really want to know my every thought![46]
- Growing numbers of humanoid robots with modifiable personalities will be active members of our workforce that we will communicate with routinely.
- The number of jobs requiring creativity and complex human exchanges will increase as computers acquire some of the most advanced cognitive and physical human skills (e.g., humanoid robot plumbers, surgeons, robo-bosses, etc.). Many humans' ability to work may come down to what they can do better than computers.[47]
- The exponential growth in computing power will result in humans having the capability to create superhuman intelligence by 2045 which will result in the end of the human era shortly thereafter. Sounds like something out of a *Terminator* movie. You have heard of artificial intelligence, right? Experts in the field are currently warning us about the dangers of it and are making similar *Terminator* references about the real possibility of systems like Cyberdyne. Now how's that for an upbeat prediction to end on?![48]

Whether you personally find the above predictions to be far-fetched and unlikely to happen does not change the fact that, in our constantly changing, global marketplace, businesspeople and businesses need to stay abreast of electronic communication technologies if they want to remain competitive and viable. As mentioned at that beginning of this chapter, you need to know what communication technology is currently available, how to use it, and when to use it to keep up. Even that is not enough, however! You should be aware of projected technological developments—developments that will profoundly affect your career and the organizations you either work for or own and operate.

Keeping up with communication technology predictions is not all that easy unless you have a crystal ball. And, since most of us do not have a crystal ball to gaze into, you should consider, among other sources, reading about predictions and technology research and developments in *Technology Review* articles. *Technology Review* bills itself as "the authority on the future of technology." MIT has been publishing this magazine since 1899. (From 1899 until 1998 it was *The Technology Review*.) Other good sources for technology predictions and technology research and development updates are *Popular Mechanics* and *Popular Science*, magazines with long histories of making technology predictions.

SUMMARY: SECTION 6— WHAT'S NEXT? SOME CAUTIOUS PREDICTIONS

- The only thing certain about a prediction is that it will or will not produce the intended outcome.
- The popularity of the Internet and e-commerce will continue to grow, leading the way to further globalization.
- Social media will continue to fill several business needs.
- Combination devices and electronic tablets of all sorts will replace conventional PCs.
- Speech-recognition developments will change the way we interact with electronic communication devices and the Internet.
- Telepathy is close to a reality.
- Wireless communication devices, including wearable technology, will continue to e-mobilize office workers.
- Growth in computing power and the advent of humanoid robots could easily threaten job opportunities and even human identity as we know it.

Notes

1. Michael J. Miller, "Living History," *PC Magazine* 21, no. 5 (March 12, 2002): 153.
2. Efraim Turban, Jae Lee, David King, and H. Michael Chung, *Electronic Commerce: A Managerial Perspective* (Upper Saddle River, NJ: Prentice-Hall, 2000), 507.
3. John R. Levine, Carol Baroudi, and Margaret Levine Young, *The Internet for Dummies*, 4th ed. (Foster City, CA: IDG Books, 1997), 63.
4. "Work Number," *Southwest The Magazine* (June 2015): 45.

5. Internet World Stats: Usage and Population Statistics, Top 20 Internet Countries By Users, http://www.internetworldstats.com/top20.htm, 2012. Robert Kreitner and Angelo Kinicki, *Organizational Behavior*, 5th ed. (Boston: Irwin McGraw-Hill, 2000), 503.

6. Ibid.

7. Turban et al., *Electronic Commerce*, 507.

8. Kreitner and Kinicki, *Organizational Behavior*, 504.

9. Ibid., 483.

10. Doug Bedell, "From QWERTYUIOP, An E-mail Revolution," *The Dallas Morning News*, February 19, 2002.

11. Kreitner and Kinicki, *Organizational Behavior*, 504.

12. Paula Felps, "Hearing-Impaired Embrace Instant Messaging," *The Dallas Morning News*, February 20, 2001.

13. Ibid.

14. Kreitner and Kinicki, 505.

15. DeTienne, *Guide to Electronic Communication*, 14–19.

16. Turban et al., *Electronic Commerce*, 506.

17. Ibid., xxvii.

18. Robert Insley, "Managing Plagiarism: A Preventative Approach," *Business Communication Quarterly*, 74, no. 2, (June 2011): 184–85.

19. Ibid.

20. Jeremy A. Kaplan, Bruce Brown, and Marge Brown, "Pocket to Palm," *PC Magazine 20*, no. 1 (December 11, 2001), 143.

21. Cheryl Conner, "Employees Really Do Waste Time at Work," July 17, 2012, http://www.forbes.com/sites/cherylsnappconner/2012/07/17/employees-really-do-waste-time-at-work/.

22. Ibid.

23. Conrad H. Blickenstorfer, "Webpads," *Pen Computing 28*, no. 1 (Winter/Spring 2002): 72.

24. David Shier, "Siemens SIMpad SL4," *PocketPC* 5, no. 2 (May 2002): 17.

25. Xiomara Blanco, "Best tablets with cell service," March 14, 2012, Updated May 20, 2015, http://www.cnet.com/news/best-tablets-with-cell-service/.

26. Timothy Captain, "Wireless Messaging Services," *Laptop* 45, no. 3 (March 2002): 71.

27. Ibid.

28. Erica Ogg, "Time to Drop the Netbook Label," *CNN Technology* (August 20, 2009), http://w.cnn.com/2009/TECH/ptech/08/20/cnet.drop.netbook.label/index.html.

29. Katy Steinmetz, "Beat Your Smartphone Addiction," *Time*, July 27, 2015, 25.

30. Leida Chen, Ravi Nath, & Robert Insley, "Determinants of Digital Distraction. A Cross-Cultural Investigation of Students in Africa, China, and the U.S.," 23, Issue 3-4, (March 2014): 145.

31. Steinmetz, 25.

32. Ibid.

33. Jennifer M. George and Gareth R. Jones, *Understanding and Managing Organizational Behavior*, 3rd ed. (Upper Saddle River, NJ: Prentice-Hall, 2002), 289.

34. Tynan, "Technology in America—Office," 107.

35. Brickenstorfer, "Webpads," 72.

36. Ibid.

37. Rex Huppke, "Millennials want to lead; they just need a hand," *The Dallas Morning News*, July 26, 2015, 2D.

38. Nancy Churnin, "Call for Relief from Your Cell," *The Dallas Morning News*, September 29, 2009.

39. Microsoft Accessibility, "Types of Assistive Technology Products," https://www.microsoft.com/enable/at/types.aspx.

40. Andrew Hamilton, "Brains that Click," *Popular Mechanics* 91, no. 3 (1949).

41. "The Cloud Corp.," www.fortune.com/adsections , pp. S1, S3, & S6.

42. "Brave New Work: The Office of Tomorrow," *Fortune* 64, no. 1 (January 16, 2012): 49–54.

43. Ibid.

44. Nick Bilton, "Wearable Computers Are the Next Big Devices, Report Says," *The New York Times*, April 17, 2012.

45. Ibid.

46. Jerry Adler, "Mind Meld," *Smithsonian*, May 2015, 45–51.

47. Geoff Colvin, "In the Future Will There Be Any Work Left for People to Do?," *Fortune*, June 16, 2014, 193-202.

48. Lev Grossman, "sin.gu.lar.i.ty n: The moment when technological change becomes so rapid and profound, it represents a rupture in the fabric of human history," *Time*, February 21, 2011, 42-49.

SOCIAL MEDIA

LEARNING OUTCOMES

After reading this chapter, you should be able to:

1. Describe the most popular social media sites.

2. Describe how the nine most popular social media sites are used in organizations.

3. Describe various ways several popular types of social media are used in businesses.

4. Write effective social media content.

5. Discuss barriers to effective social media posts

6. Write effective social media policies.

7. Follow the rules of social media netiquette.

© Manczurov/Shutterstock.com

BENEFITS OF LEARNING ABOUT SOCIAL MEDIA

1. You will know how various social media platforms are currently being used in organizations.

2. You will be familiar with the major challenges social media pose along with several social media drawbacks.

3. You will know how write effective social media content for the most popular social media sites.

4. You will know how to write a professional bio for social media sites.

5. You will be familiar with a number of social media jobs.

6. You will understand the importance of social media netiquette when making social media content decisions and when writing the content.

SELECT KEY TERMS

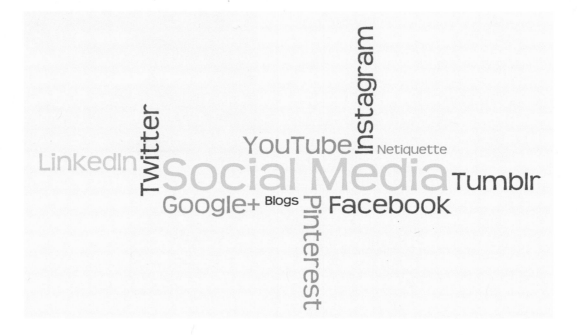

INTRODUCTION

Social networking is growing in popularity around the globe. According to global computer and telecommuting research company The Radicati Group, the number of social networking accounts is projected to grow to 5.2 billion by 2018.[1] Within organizations, social media platforms such as **Facebook**, **Twitter**, **LinkedIn**, and **Google+** are having profound effects on how needs are met and communication occurs. Social media is used in organizations for a host of purposes ranging from customer service, public relations, and marketing to acquiring customer feedback, increasing brand awareness, and locating job candidates. Effective writing is key to social media posts and while some writing suggestions pertain to all social media platforms, others are unique to specific platforms. Adhering to social media **netiquette** rules is also important when communicating with others via social media.

The intent of this chapter is to provide you with information regarding social media. This goal will be realized through discussions regarding the following topics: social media overview, the role of social media in organizations, social media writing suggestions, and social media netiquette. The information pertaining to the above-mentioned social-media topics is reinforced by several student website resources including *PowerPoint slides, preview tests, chapter assessment tests, writing mechanics rules and guidelines, YouTube videos, interactive exercises*, and the *interactive glossary*.

SOCIAL MEDIA OVERVIEW

What is **social media**? Hahn Nguyen did a nice job of capturing the essence of *social media* when she described it as the collective of online communications channels dedicated to community-based input, interaction, content sharing, and collaboration.[2]

© nasirkhan/Shutterstock.com

In short, social media makes it possible for individuals and organizations to form communities, communicate with each other, and produce and share content online. In addition, social media helps people increase their personal and professional networks and connect

social networking
The process of communicating with others via social media.

Facebook The most popular online social networking service and website.

Twitter An online social networking and microblogging service.

LinkedIn
An online business-oriented social networking service.

Google+
An online social networking and identity service.

netiquette
Rules about the proper and polite way to communicate with other people when using the Internet.

social media
Collective of online communication channels dedicated to community-based input, interaction, content sharing, and collaboration.

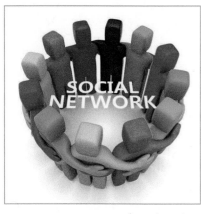

The High-Level Business Impact of Social Media http://smallbusiness.chron.com/highlevel-business-impact-social-media-38816.html

blogosphere
The universe of blogs.

with others who share their interests. Furthermore, social media helps individuals and organizations stay in touch with friends and stakeholders with whom they may otherwise have difficulties doing so. Communicating with others via social media is often referred to as *social networking*.

Social networking in organizations is often hosted on a number of popular social media platforms including *Facebook, Twitter, LinkedIn*, and *Google+*. Such sites typically require individuals and organizations to create a profile that typically includes demographic information, interests, preferences, pictures, and updates about current events or happenings. Most social media sites provide tools for users to create and facilitate content, upload pictures and videos, create blogs, review media, and share opinions and comments. Users can also group themselves depending on geographic location, interests, heritage, topics of interest, or professional and social associations. In turn, these groups facilitate communication and management of subgroups within larger social networks.

In organizations around the globe, social media is having profound effects on how needs are met and communication occurs. In addition, most organizations are actively searching for additional social media uses and opportunities.

Small businesses owners and operators, in growing numbers, are also discovering how social media sites can promote their businesses. While some small business owners write, blog, and post their own *Twitter* and *Facebook* entries, others simply do not have the time for it. This situation has fueled a number of support businesses that specialize in providing advertising and public relations services through social network sites including *3 Green Angels, Everywhere LLC, Red Square Agency Inc.*, and *ThinkInk LLC*.

As a means of maximizing social media's potential benefits, many organizations have developed social media strategies, policies, and codes of ethics. There is a difference between a policy and a code of ethics. For example, a blogging policy covers what a person can and cannot say for legal or company reasons; whereas a blogging code of ethics gives instructions on how to act in the **blogosphere**. The code of ethics works in tandem with blogging etiquette.[3] Figure 5-1 Contains a *Sample Corporate Blogging Policy* and a *Sample Blogger Code of Ethics.*

FIGURE 5–1: SAMPLE BLOGGING POLICY AND CODE OF ETHICS

Sample Corporate Blogging Policy:

1. Make it clear that the views expressed in the blog are yours alone and do not necessarily represent the views of your company.
2. Respect the company's confidentiality and proprietary information.
3. Ask your manager if you have any questions about what is appropriate to include in your blog.
4. Be respectful to the company, employees, customers, partners, and competitors.
5. Understand when the company asks that topics not be discussed for confidentiality or legal compliance reasons.
6. Ensure that your blogging activity does not interfere with your work commitments.

FIGURE 5–1: SAMPLE BLOGGING POLICY AND CODE OF ETHICS

Sample Blogger Code of Ethics:

1. I will tell the truth.
2. I will write deliberately and with accuracy.
3. I will acknowledge and correct mistakes promptly.
4. I will preserve the original post, using notations to show where I have made changes so as to maintain the integrity of my publishing.
5. I will never delete a post.
6. I will reply to e-mails and comments when appropriate and do so promptly.
7. I will strive for high quality with every post—including basic spellchecking.
8. I will stay on topic.
9. I will disagree with other opinions respectfully.
10. I will link to online references and original source materials directly.
11. I will disclose conflicts of interest.
12. I will keep private issues and topics private, since discussing private issues would jeopardize my personal and work relationships.

Source: Li, Charlene, "Blogging policy examples," Forrester, November 08, 2004 August 2007
<http://forrester.typepad.com/charleneli/2004/11/blogging_policy.html>.

Speed, convenience, low cost, and the ability to reach large numbers of people simultaneously are among the major reasons why social media has become an increasingly popular tool in organizations. Furthermore, affordable and easily accessible communication technologies such as smartphones, smartwatches, laptops, and electronic tablets, combined with widespread availability of WiFi and the Internet, have contributed to the growing popularity of social media in organizations. Thus, it should come as no surprise that the vast majority (90%) of businesses are using at least one type of social media.[4]

FIGURE 5–2: BENEFITS OF BUSINESS SOCIAL NETWORKING

1. **Return on Investment.** Private social media networks provide organizations with a return on investment for all their people. Such networks can reveal hidden gems; people who lack the nerve to talk aloud but have ideas and expertise to share. Social media networks can encourage and reward online contributions so that the hidden gems can reveal themselves through their contributions.
2. **Unlocked Information Silos.** Many large organizations develop **information silos,** which are departments that are self-contained. As a result, extensive connections across the organization do not happen. With private social media networks organizations can break down silos. They can let interaction, knowledge sharing, and collective problem solving become the normal communication pattern throughout the organization.

FIGURE 5–2: BENEFITS OF BUSINESS SOCIAL NETWORKING

3. **Improved Teamwork.** Sales is such a competitive occupation. Traditionally, compensation plans reward individual sales achievement. Cross-fertilization of successful strategies through the deployment of customer relations management (CRM) tools runs counter to this "all-for-one" sales mentality. A private social media network that encourages mentorship and rewards cooperative behavior can create winning sales teams that share strategies and compensate top sales-people for helping the "newbies." This represents a significant cultural shift for the normal sales organization. It means new compensation plans that acknowl-edge and reward both individual sales achievements and collective knowledge sharing contributions.

4. **Increased Customer Engagement.** The new business model is "customer web-centered." It has always been true that it is easier to sell to an existing customer than it is to recruit a new one. Hence the relationship with existing custom-ers is something that private social networking addresses. Through a private social media network, customers can be invited into online communities. These communities may include other customers with similar challenges. Communi-ties can become great listening posts for organizations to learn about common customer problems. They are also great places to do collective sales pitches.

5. **Better Employee Morale.** Private social media networks begin with individuals creating profiles, and these profiles can reveal great ways to discover hidden talents. We tend to pigeonhole people by job title but most of us are much more than our jobs. For example, I write music and do orchestration when I am not working with clients. People in the accounting department or in shipping may also enjoy music or play instruments. This type of discovery can pay huge dividends in improving morale within an organization. It can even impact the bottom line when you find out that someone is experimenting with open source software application develop-ment at home and has come up with a new widget or gadget that can be shared with others in the organization with similar interests, leading to who knows what.

Source: Rosen, Len. "Business Social Networking: Public and Private – There is a Place for Both," CMS Wire Aug 19. 2009. Sept 5, 2009. <http://www.cmswire.com/cms/enterprise-20/business-social-networking-public-and-private-there-is-a-place-for-both-005304.php>.

Despite the popularity of social media, businesspeople still need to determine which communication medium is most appropriate for each situation. Sometimes social media is the right choice, whereas other times it may be another communication medium such as face-to-face communication, e-mail, texting, a phone call, or a videoconference. Jim Blas-ingame, one of the world's foremost experts on small business and entrepreneurship, offers some practical advice to help you make good media choices. He encourages businesspeople to use the following two approaches when making communication media choices: (1) ask yourself which communication medium best suits the circumstance and (2) ask your cus-tomers and clients which communication medium they prefer.[5] Blasingame's advice mirrors some basic communication suggestions presented earlier in the book. In chapter 1 you were urged to reflect on the circumstances before selecting a medium. For example, messages about routine matters can typically be communicated effectively via e-mail, while messages involving important and/or controversial matters are best communicated face-to-face.

SOCIAL MEDIA CATEGORIES

The most common use of social media in businesses is to facilitate internal communication, followed by communication with customers, and then communication with external partners.[6] To facilitate internal communication, some organizations develop private social media networks to meet their needs. Some organizations hire others to develop their internal social media networks, while others use programs such as *Wall.fm* and *Ning* to do so. *Wall.fm* is an online service for building and hosting social media networks, and *Ning* is an online platform that can be used to create custom social media networks. In contrast, social media interaction with customers and other external partners typically occurs through public social media networks such as *Facebook, LinkedIn, Google+*, and others.

FIGURE 5-3: NETWORKING VIA SOCIAL MEDIA

Facebook, Twitter, and LinkedIn are great social media platforms for networking. According to Ashley Jones, owner of Skylight Creative Group, if interaction with these platforms is done correctly, organizations can gain lots of attention, fans, followers, and clients. Such is the case with social media. Here are several tips Ashley Jones offers for networking via social media.

- **Don't post something just to post it.** Make sure your content is relevant and/or interesting.
- **If you're using social media to network, stay professional.** Don't get too casual or personal.
- **Use the tools to their full potential.** Don't expect people to come to you if you are not engaging.
- **Don't spam.** This is self-explanatory.
- **Don't post too frequently.** Most people are already bombarded with updates, messages, etc.
- **Don't just post the same thing across different social media platforms.** If you are posting the same thing on several social media platforms, nobody will follow you on all of them.
- **Keep your content fresh.** Update at least once a week.
- **Follow up with connections.** Respond to posts, comments, and messages.

Networking should be a mutually beneficial experience, so if someone helps you, return the favor.

Source: Ricker, Susan. "How to network via social media." CareerBuilder. October 23, 2012.

MAJOR CHALLENGES SOCIAL MEDIA POSE

Despite the positive inroads social media has made into organizations, as can be expected, it also poses several challenges. Three of these challenges worth noting are described below.

1. **Honing traditional writing skills and acquiring new skills.** People read differently online than they do offline. Thus, adapting online copy to meet readers' needs is one of the challenges of writing for social media. Within this chapter, you will find specific writing suggestions that are applicable to all social media platforms as well as other writing suggestions that are applicable to specific social media platforms.

2. **Merging the basic writing process steps with the speed, convenience, and writing protocols associated with social media in ways that result in effective posts.** Much like e-mail and texting, social media encourages the development of short posts. As a result, some related problems are not uncommon. For example, in their quest to develop short posts, some writers ignore basic rules of grammar and punctuation and even get careless with spelling. In addition, some writers fall into the habit of not editing and revising their posts. Such carelessness can easily result in poorly written, confusing posts that contain too little detail to achieve clarity and/or leave readers with poor perceptions of their communication partners' writing abilities and professionalism. In turn, carelessly written posts can easily reflect poorly on the organization being represented. And if all that isn't enough to cause problems, such carelessly written posts can also damage writers' job stability and job growth potential.

3. **Being realistic about the importance of building relationships.** Strong relationships with stakeholders (e.g., colleagues, clients, suppliers) are crucial to long-term business success. Job stability and career growth are also influenced by relationships formed in the workplace. With this in mind, it is a good idea to remind ourselves that the most effective way to build strong relationships in the professional workplace is through face-to-face interaction. Herein lies the challenge! Be careful not to communicate so much on social media and other electronic media that you fail to build strong relationships with stakeholders due to insufficient face-to-face interaction. Otherwise, you might be eroding professional relationships and your chances of achieving the level of career growth you desire. As it pertains to building professional relationships, are there viable alternatives to face-to-face communication? While it is not a perfect substitute for face-to-face interaction, videoconferencing (e.g., *Skype*) is an alternative.

I trust you agree that the challenges described above are significant and should be taken seriously. Your task now is to benefit from your new-found awareness of them by keeping them in mind.

Seven Social Media Challenges and How to Turn Them Into Business Opportunities
http://blog.hootsuite. com/social-media- challenges-small- businesses-face/

SUMMARY: SECTION 1— SOCIAL MEDIA OVERVIEW

- Social media makes it possible for individuals and organizations to form communities, communicate with each other, and produce and share content online.
- Social media is having profound effects on how needs are met and communication occurs in organizations around the globe.
- Speed, convenience, low cost, and the ability to reach large numbers of people simultaneously are among the major reasons why social media has become an increasingly popular tool in organizations.
- The most common use of social media in businesses is to facilitate internal communication, followed by communication with customers, and then communication with external partners.
- Benefits of business social media networks include return on investment, unlocked information silos, improved teamwork, increased customer engagement, and better employee morale.

THE ROLE OF SOCIAL MEDIA IN ORGANIZATIONS

The vast majority of businesses worldwide use one or more types of social media. As mentioned previously, the most common use is to facilitate internal communication, followed by communication with customers and external partners in that order. Typical internal uses of social media include increasing knowledge sharing, building employee morale, improving collaboration and productivity within work groups, enhancing employee engagement, building communities (e.g., employees with common interests), and facilitating organizational culture changes.[7]

© Gil C/Shutterstock.com

Common external uses, also mentioned earlier, range from customer service, public relations, and marketing to acquiring customer feedback, increasing brand awareness, and locating job candidates. Marketing, in particular, is a very popular use of social media. Such marketing falls under the umbrella of *digital marketing* which includes marketing via social media, display ads, online searches, and e-mail. According to Forrester Research, it is projected that spending on digital marketing will reach $103 billion in 2019, which is nearly double the 2014 figure, and will soon surpass spending on television advertising.[8]

FIGURE 5–4: THE 15 MOST POPULAR SOCIAL MEDIA SITES

1. Facebook
2. Twitter
3. LinkedIn
4. Pinterest
5. Google+
6. Tumblr
7. Instagram
8. VK
9. Flickr
10. Vine
11. Meetup
12. Tagged
13. Ask.fm
14. MeetMe
15. ClassMates

Source: "Top 15 Most Popular Social Networking Sites," www.ebizmba.com/articles/social-networking-websites, *March, 2015*

Pinterest An online social curation and social networking service.

Tumblr An online microblogging platform and social networking website.

Instagram An online mobile social networking service that supports photo- and video-sharing.

MOST WIDELY-USED SOCIAL MEDIA SITES IN ORGANIZATIONS

Facebook, Twitter, LinkedIn, Pinterest, Google+, Tumblr, Instagram, YouTube, and *blogs* are currently among the most widely used social media sites for businesses. Brief descriptions of each, along with how they are used in businesses, follow.

© www.BillionPhotos.com/Shutterstock.com

- Facebook

  Facebook is an online social networking service that was founded in 2004 and is currently the most popular social media site with well over one billion active users worldwide. In addition to posting text-based messages, Facebook users can also post photos and videos. Facebook is used externally in businesses predominately as a customer service tool, a public relations tool, to identify target markets, to promote company websites, to screen job candidates, and to identify viable potential job candidates.

© Annette Shaff/Shutterstock.com

- Twitter

  Twitter is an online social networking and microblogging service that was founded in 2006. Twitter has over 300 hundred million active users worldwide and currently supports a large number of languages. Twitter enables users to send and read short, text-based messages (tweets). Twitter users can also post photos and videos. Twitter is used externally in businesses predominately as a customer service tool and a public relations tool. Twitter is also used to seek information from large numbers of people (*crowdsourcing*) and obtaining feedback. It is also used to increase brand awareness and monitor brand reputation. Twitter also offers businesses a powerful products and services feedback tool.

© tanuha2001/Shutterstock.com

- LinkedIn

  LinkedIn is an online business-oriented social networking service that was founded in 2002 and has several hundred million active users worldwide. LinkedIn is considered to be the world's largest professional network catering predominately to business professionals. LinkedIn is used externally in businesses predominately to identify business job candidates, for professional networking purposes, to feature business events (e.g., professional conferences), to increase branding/marketing presence in the marketplace, to build new relationships with potential customers, to increase company exposure, to promote their businesses, and to acquire customer feedback and insights.

© Evan Lorne/Shutterstock.com

How to Use LinkedIn for Business video
https://www.youtube.com/watch?v=yM5K0ytrDDA

- Pinterest

  Pinterest is a social networking service that was founded in 2010 and has several million active users worldwide. Pinterest provides a service whereby users can discover, collect, share, and store visual images. Pinterest is used in businesses predominately for advertising and conducting market research. Currently, approximately one-third of online adults use Pinterest, which reminds businesses of the growing popularity of photos and visual images.

© tanuha2001/Shutterstock.com

- Google+

  Google+ is a social networking and identity service that was founded in 2011 and has over a half billion active users worldwide. Google+ users can also post photos in addition to text-based messages. In many ways, Google+ is similar to Facebook. Google+ is used externally in businesses predominately as a customer service tool, for direct contact with customers, to identify target markets, and for internal and external communication.

© tanuha2001/Shutterstock.com

- Tumblr

  Tumblr is a microblogging platform and social networking website that was founded in 2007 and hosts several hundred million blogs worldwide. With Tumblr, users can post multimedia (e.g., videos, photos, music), links, and other content to a short-form blog. Tumblr is used in businesses predominately for implementing marketing campaigns, highlighting products and services, promoting brands, customer service, and creating blogs.

© 360b/Shutterstock.com

- Instagram

  Instagram is an online mobile social networking service that supports photo- and video-sharing. Users can also include comments and share feedback. Instagram was founded in 2010 and has several hundred million active users worldwide. Instagram is used in businesses predominately for marketing, advertising, conducting marketing research, and for internal purposes such as morale building. Currently, approximately one-third of online adults use Instagram which reminds businesses of the growing popularity of photos and video.

© tanuha2001/Shutterstock.com

Why Instagram Should Be Part of Every Business http://thenextweb. com/socialme- dia/2015/06/04/why- instagram-should-be- part-of-every-business/

- YouTube

YouTube is a free online mobile social networking service that supports video-sharing. YouTube was founded in 2005. The popularity of YouTube videos is typically measured by the number of times each video is viewed as well as subscriber status. YouTube is used in businesses in a number of ways both externally and internally. YouTube is currently used in businesses predominately for product and services advertising, retail promotion, direct sales, product support, recruiting, posting bulletins, internal training, and employee communications. [9]

© Your Design/Shutterstock.com

- Blogs

Blog is short for "web log," a type of user-generated website that acts as a communication and networking medium for the masses. It is a type of self-publishing via the Internet done through easy-to-use Internet applications and websites. Blogs are built for flexibility and designed to be short and frequently updated, unlike long essays or prose. Although blogs have been championed by social networks for personal use, they have made a significant impact on the business world, the journalism world, and in academia where they are being used in the classroom. All these blogs that the public has access to reside in the *blogosphere*, which is the universe of blogs. The blog was independently invented in 1997. Blogs are used in businesses predominately for marketing, tracking customer/client satisfaction, brand building, and as a customer service and public relations tool.

© nasirkhan/Shutterstock.com

The main type of business blog is the *corporate blog*, which is often used as an e-newsletter, viral marketing campaign, and open channel between businesses and consumers. The most popular types of blogs are *external blogs* and *internal blogs*. External blogs can be seen by anyone with an Internet connection, whereas internal blogs can be seen only by organizational employees and designated stakeholders.

EXTERNAL BLOGS

One of the biggest distinctions in external corporate blogs is who writes them. According to Chris Anderson, author of *The Longest Tail: Why the Future is Selling Less of More*, the best business blogs are not written by top managers or marketers, but by mid-level employees.[10] They are often more entertaining, more honest, and are less likely to repeat everything in the latest ad campaign or mission statement. They can also be more informative about the inner workings of the company. Consulting company Accenture directs new recruits to its Careers page, which displays blogs written by employees in various departments so that recruits can get a taste of the day-to-day activities of a new management consultant. Or, they can read the rants of a recruiter so they know what not to do.

One big draw of external blogs for companies is the feedback they receive from consumers. Because bloggers comment on blog posts and the relative anonymity of the Internet, consumers are less reluctant to tell companies exactly what they think. This can be invaluable information that was formerly only available through expensive polls and surveys. It is also instant or sometimes pre-emptive. Bloggers can tell a company what they think of a product before it hits store shelves, for example. That is the real key to successful blogs; a conversational style that solicits and receives feedback.

INTERNAL BLOGS

Internal blogs are used by companies so that only employees or a select group of people can see a particular blog. These are usually password protected, and sometimes are on a local intranet. Internal blogs are a good starting place for companies that are testing the waters of blogging. They can be used as testing grounds for speed, content, frequency, and authorship before a company enters the blogosphere. Although they can be a warm up for external blogs, internal blogs also have a place internally once a company is comfortable with the medium. Sample ways internal blogs are used in organizations are presented in Figure 5-5 below.

Internal blogs are great for acting as time-ordered business records that have many uses. They are also great for project members or leaders who can track projects and ideas without adding an extra archiving step. New project members can easily get an overview of the project and how it is developing. Possibly the most valuable use is for legal discrepancies. If a decision or action was subject to questions, the business would have clear and thorough documentation.

There is even a term that captures the essence of blogging effectiveness. The term is **hedonometer**. It refers to a computerized sensor that surveys the Web to measure the collective happiness of millions of bloggers.

hedonometer
A computerized sensor that surveys the Web to measure the collective happiness of millions of bloggers.

FIGURE 5–5: WHAT TO DO WITH YOUR INTERNAL BLOG

Communications and technology expert Shel Holtz provides us with the following list of ways you can use an internal blog:

- **Alerts.** Don't you hate getting those e-mails that let you know when the server's going to be down? People who need to know can subscribe to [the] list server status Weblog. Instead of having to send out those e-mails, IT can simply request that employees subscribe to their blog.
- **Projects.** Companies have terrible institutional memories when it comes to projects. Anybody who needs to delve into a project's records to find out how a decision was reached a year ago is probably out of luck. Project teams can set up a group blog to maintain an ongoing record of decisions and actions. Project leaders can also maintain a blog to announce to the rest of the company the current status of the project.
- **Departmental.** Departments can maintain blogs to let the rest of the company know of current offerings or achievements. Imagine the marketing department being able to submit a simple post to its own blog announcing the availability of new marketing brochures or other collateral material.
- **News.** Employees can contribute industry or company news to a group blog or cover news they have learned in their own personal blogs.
- **Brainstorming.** Employees in a department or on a team can brainstorm about strategy, process, and other topics over blogs.
- **Customers.** Employees can share the substance of customer visits or phone calls. When sharing such information with fellow employees, remain professional; even when the customer was difficult.
- **Personal Blogs.** Even though it sounds like a timewaster, a personal blog can prove valuable in the organization. Consider an engineer who reads a lot and attends meetings of his professional association. He updates his blog with summaries of the articles he's read in journals (with links to the journal's website) and notes he took at the meeting. Employees who find value in this information will read the blog; those who don't care—anybody who isn't an engineer, perhaps—aren't missing anything if they don't. And if he posts a few articles that have nothing to do with work, well who said work can never be fun?
- **CEO Blogs.** What a great way for the CEO to get closer to employees. Imagine a new CEO hosting a blog called "My First Hundred Days" in which she writes about her experiences daily and lets employees comment in order to help her get acclimated.

Source: Weil, Debbie. The Corporate Blogging Book: Absolutely Everything You Need To Know About Blogging to Get It Right. *New York, NY: Penguin Group, 2006.*

SOCIAL MEDIA DRAWBACKS

While the social media platforms described previously provide businesses with numerous benefits, there are potential drawbacks to specific social media platforms that should be kept in mind. For example, with *Facebook* negative comments about products and services are potentially viewed by large numbers of current and potential customers and clients which can, in turn, can have negative effects on sales and public relations. Similar observations can be made about *Google+*, *Tumblr*, and *Instagram*. "Manning the phones" so to speak with *Twitter* is potentially very costly when one considers the time needed to support all those back-and-forth tweets. Then, there are those *LinkedIn* users who compromise the networking potential *LinkedIn* offers when they do not join groups and associations and actively participate in discussions taking place within them. There are even potential drawbacks with *Pinterest*. For example, since the vast majority of *Pinterest* users are female, this can create a drawback for businesses that are not targeting female audiences exclusively. *Pinterest* is aware of this and is taking measures to increase the number of male users. Thus far they are making good headway in reaching this goal.

Here, we are reminded that there is a place for common sense measures when our goal is to eliminate, or at least minimize, social media hacking.

Disadvantages of Social Media http://www.theresearchpedia.com/research-articles/disadvantages-of-social-media

---

FIGURE 5–6: SOCIAL MEDIA COMMON SENSE SECURITY REMINDERS

We all know that one of the potential perils of posting information on the Internet is cyber theft. In short, some individuals or organizations will attempt to access information that you did not intend for them to access. Furthermore, some individuals and organizations have become very skilled at hacking into such information. With all this in mind, here are four common sense security reminders that just might reduce or eliminate the damage hackers can cause.

- Be aware that your information can be hacked. Don't be naive or unaware. By being aware, you will be much more likely to take measures to minimize the potential occurrence and/or damage.
- Reset passwords often using those that cannot easily identified. Then, keep them private!
- Keep antivirus software updated.
- Don't post/transmit information you don't want the wrong people and organizations to acquire (e.g., sensitive legal documents).

© Ivan Lukyanchuk/Shutterstock.com

There are also some potential drawbacks that span all social media platforms to varying degrees. For example, social media users are generally encouraged to develop and post brief messages/content. *Twitter* with its 140-character message limit is a good example. In the quest for brevity, which is so pronounced with social media, clarity can be easily compromised when too little is said to communicate clearly. Then too, there are potential health concerns associated with social media use. For example, excessive use of the technologies used to communicate on social media can result in health issues ranging from repetitive motion nerve damage (*carpal tunnel syndrome*) and vision deterioration to detached retinas and chronic shoulder and lower neck pain. If nothing else, common sense should remind us that spending significant amounts of time looking at small screens and composing on small keypads will eventually lead to health issues that could have been avoided. Furthermore, there are potential safety issues associated with social media use. For example, excessive use of the technologies used to communicate on social media can result in safety issues ranging from driving-related accidents (e.g., *tweeting while driving*) to pedestrian-related accidents (e.g., *unknowingly stepping out in front of oncoming traffic while tweeting*).

The good news is that most of the above-mentioned drawbacks can be eliminated or at least controlled. Awareness of their existence and potential damaging effects is a good starting point for all of us. For me, the most important among them are the potential health and safety issues.

FIGURE 5–7: ONLINE INCIVILITY: SOCIAL MEDIA'S DARK SIDE

Unfortunately some customers and clients use social media platforms to express disrespectful, rude, and/or malicious thoughts about organizations, products, services, and/or personnel. While organizations need to be open to feedback and can benefit greatly from feedback they receive via social media, less-than-civil feedback can be annoying, frustrating, and challenging to deal with. Organizations are challenged to identify which of these posts they should respond to and how they should respond. For example, in his book *BIFF: Quick Responses to High Conflict People*, Bill Eddy recommends responses that are *brief, informative, friendly,* and *firm*. It is imperative that organizations address these issues in their social media policies and codes of ethics.[11]

There have also been instances of employees who post inappropriate material on social media platforms. What should employees avoid posting? According to the National Labor Relations Board, they should not put up posts that damage a company, disparage its products or services, reveal trade secrets, or reveal financial information. Furthermore, they should not post information about clients or customers. In addition, employees should not put up posts that are racist, homophobic, sexist, or discriminate against a religion. As a means of reducing such instances, companies are encouraged to develop written social media policies that spell out what employees can and cannot post along with specific examples.

In regard to the issue of online incivility, Andrea Weckerle's book *Civility in the Digital Age: How Companies and People Can Triumph Over Haters, Trolls, Bullies, and Other Jerks* is a timely source you should consider reading before going to work in the professional workplace. This book focuses exclusively on disrespectful, rude, and/or malicious posts directed at organizations and how they should be handled.

Source: "What workers can, can't say on social media," The Associated Press – The Dallas Morning News, 4/5/15, 4D.

SOCIAL MEDIA WRITING SUGGESTIONS

The majority of this section is devoted to specific social media writing suggestions. Some of these suggestions are applicable to all social media, while others are specific to each of the nine social media platforms highlighted in this chapter (*Facebook, Twitter, LinkedIn, Pinterest, Google+, Tumblr, Instagram, YouTube,* and *blogs*). In addition, some coverage is also devoted to the following writing suggestions: writing professional bios for social media sites, writing social media policy, writing basics, and barriers to effective writing for social media sites.

Before presenting specific writing suggestions, however, it's a good idea to remind ourselves of the basic challenge business writers face whether they are writing for social media or other media. They are challenged to write effective messages and posts that their readers will interpret as they wanted them to be interpreted and, in turn, they will act upon their messages and posts as desired. By writing clear, professional-quality social media posts, business writers reduce the risk of confusing and frustrating their readers as well as negatively influencing their readers' perceptions of their businesses. Thus, when writing for social media, business writers need to devote sufficient time to developing their posts so the result is clear, professional-quality communication.

Figure 5-8 contains writing suggestions pertaining to all social media platforms. Following Figure 5-8, you will find writing suggestions that pertain specifically to each of the major social media sites highlighted in this chapter. These include *Facebook, Twitter, LinkedIn, Pinterest, Google+, Tumblr, Instagram, YouTube,* and *blogs.*

FIGURE 5–8: WRITING SUGGESTIONS PERTAINING TO ALL SOCIAL MEDIA PLATFORMS

- Craft posts that others will find valuable enough to share with friends and colleagues.
- Craft posts that center on your audiences' questions and concerns.
- Write strong, clear headlines.
- Write longer posts—at least long enough to achieve clarity.
- Write longer posts that include long-tail keywords to increase search queries.
- Consider writing longer posts as a means of increasing backlinks.
- Build in time between draft writing and editing blog posts to improve the quality of the posts.
- Include images (e.g., photos, graphics) in longer posts to keep readers' attention.
- Avoid repetition, unless you are using the technique for emphasis purposes.
- Put share buttons at the bottom of every post and page to make it easy for readers to share.

Source: Bennette, Cari. "10 Writing Tips for Great Social Media Posts," Socialmouths, 10/14/14, http://socialmouths.com/blog/2014/10/14/10-writing-tips-great-social-media-posts/

WRITING SUGGESTIONS SPECIFIC TO FACEBOOK, TWITTER, LINKEDIN, PINTEREST, GOOGLE+, TUMBLR, INSTAGRAM, YOUTUBE, AND BLOGS

You are encouraged to keep the following writing suggestions in mind when communicating via each of the social media platforms listed below.

Facebook Writing Suggestions

- Be natural and avoid boring posts.
- Be topical, timely, and relevant.
- Write posts that appeal to your target audience (e.g., talk about topics they are interested in).
- Be visual by including photos, videos, links, etc.
- Keep posts relatively short—80 characters or fewer is encouraged.
- Bring emotions into Facebook posts.
- Ask questions to engage readers.
- Post inspirational quotes. They are popular attention getters.
- Post full links (URLs) when posting to an external website.
- Be yourself so readers feel like you are talking to them directly.
- Include a call for action to encourage readers to become invested in you, your brand, or your event.[12 &13]

Twitter Writing Suggestions

- Start with a headline that is clear, catchy, and relevant.
- Be personable and conversational.
- Tweet links containing timely, relevant information.

- Use acronyms cautiously. Don't assume everyone understands what they mean just because you do. When in doubt, spell them out.
- Use abbreviations cautiously. Don't assume everyone understands what they mean just because you do. When in doubt, spell them out.
- Don't abuse basic writing rules (e.g., grammar, using all lowercase letters, etc.). Doing otherwise looks unprofessional.
- Spell words properly. Misspelled words reflect poorly on you and the organization you represent.
- Don't use emoticons and emojis because they look unprofessional. Emoticons are representations of facial expressions (e.g., smiley faces), whereas emojis are like emoticons in that they include facial expressions but also include common objects (e.g., cars), animals, places, etc.
- Don't be too quick to post a tweet. Write it and then let it sit for a while. Come back to it and do some editing. Then post it.
- Use hashtags that are related to your event or industry. Don't compromise your credibility by using hashtags that aren't related to your message.[14, 15, 16, & 17]

emoticons representations of facial expressions (e.g., smiley faces).

emojis like emoticons in that they include facial expressions but also include common objects (e.g., cars).

FIGURE 5–9: SIX SECRETS TO ONLINE SUCCESS WITH TWITTER

1. **Immediacy.** Real-time flow of comments and adaptability to mobile handsets makes tweeting more immediate than blogging.
2. **Brevity.** Limiting messages to 140 characters makes them easier to produce and easier to digest.
3. **Pull and Push.** The ability of users to choose whose tweets they follow makes it less random than e-mail.
4. **Searchability.** Messages can be searched, making the content more accessible than the comments on a social network.
5. **Mixing the Public and the Personal.** A user's personal contacts are on equal footing with public figures' contacts.
6. **Retweeting.** By copying and retransmitting messages, users can turn the network into a giant echo chamber.

Source: Waters, Richard. "Sweet to Tweet." Financial Times. February 27, 2009.

LinkedIn Writing Suggestions

- Write for your target audience—the *LinkedIn* demographic.
- Don't post too frequently. Schaffer recommends doing so on a weekly basis.
- Include visuals when and where appropriate.
- Include short, clear, professional headlines.
- Keep your posts in the 30-to-1000 word range.
- Tell a story. Don't just list facts and figures.
- Don't just cut and paste your résumé and cover letter.
- Don't exaggerate or knowingly make false statements about your work experiences, skills, and accomplishments.
- Optimize your LinkedIn profile.
- Include a company page.[18, 19, & 20]

LinkedIn Invitation Writing Suggestions

- Tell the person you want to connect with how you know or know of him or her.
- Personalize your invitation to connect in some way.
- Find something in common with your potential connection.
- Be enthusiastic.
- Be honest.
- Read your potential connection's profile and then reference something in it.[21]

LinkedIn Profile Writing Suggestions

- Include a professionally taken headshot (photograph) so you are portrayed in the best light.
- Develop a strong headline that will get you noticed.
- Include experiences that contain keywords that others are using to find someone like you.
- Customize your URL so you are able to add it to your e-mail signature, résumé, cover letter, letterhead, business cards, and marketing literature.
- Write an engaging, interesting, impressive summary.
- Customize the design of your profile's background.[22 & 23]

LinkedIn Summary Writing Suggestions

- Do not leave your summary section blank!
- Before writing, know what you want your summary to communicate.
- Before writing, know what you want your readers to do.
- Before writing, identify needed content and then gather it together. This would include lists of your most important accomplishments, values and passions, workplace strengths, qualities and skills that differentiate you from others, and honors and awards.
- Break up your summary with graphics, headers, etc.
- Use all 2000 characters you have available to you.
- Include your contact information![24, 25, & 26]

Pinterest Writing Suggestions

- Write longer descriptions that are at least 300 characters long.
- Include a link that further describes a product or service.
- Include the product or service price.
- Include hashtags and keywords that will increase your exposure.
- Include a short call to action.
- Mention those Pinterest users whose work you shared.
- Include appropriate, tasteful humor when the opportunity arises.
- Write clear, persuasive comments.
- Include your business information.
- Complete your profile.
- Keep your business-related boards separate from your personal-interest boards.
- Pin images that are applicable.
- Use various types of content throughout your boards.
- Spread your content out over several boards so followers can more quickly pinpoint content that interests them.[27, 28, & 29]

Google+ Writing Suggestions

- *Google+* posts are mini-blogs so don't make them too short. Kennedy recommends they be one-to-three paragraphs long.
- Use boldface and italicizing features to help your readers move around in and through your posts more easily.
- Include keywords and hashtags so you can be more easily found.
- Include visually appealing images to keep readers' interest and support your goals.
- Start with a headline that is clear, catchy, and relevant.
- Use acronyms cautiously. Don't assume everyone understands what they mean just because you do. When in doubt, spell them out.
- Use abbreviations cautiously. Don't assume everyone understands what they mean just because you do. When in doubt, spell them out.
- Don't abuse basic writing rules (e.g., grammar, using all lowercase letters). Doing otherwise looks unprofessional.
- Spell words properly. Misspelled words reflect poorly on you and the organization you represent.
- Don't use emoticons (e.g., smiley faces). They look unprofessional.
- Don't be too quick to post. Write a post and then let it sit for a while. Come back to it and do some editing. Then post it.
- Create a *Google+* page where you can provide information about your business and services. Link this page to your company website.[30 & 31]

Tumblr Writing Suggestions

- Choose a blog name that describes the theme of your blog.
- Choose or develop a theme that enhances and supports your purpose.
- Write blogs that target specific niches.
- Write blogs that serve a specific purpose.
- Know your target audience.
- Use a conversational tone.
- Link keywords in your blog to related pages on your company website.
- Pace yourself realistically by determining how much you will post and how often so you can settle into a regular, practical rhythm that you can maintain for the long-term.
- Craft your posts carefully so they are professional and engaging.
- Include images to assist in grabbing and keeping your readers' interest.
- Include keywords and hashtags so you can be more easily found.
- Start with a headline that is clear, catchy, and relevant.
- Use acronyms cautiously. Don't assume everyone understands what they mean just because you do. When in doubt, spell them out.
- Use abbreviations cautiously. Don't assume everyone understands what they mean just because you do. When in doubt, spell them out.
- Don't abuse basic writing rules (e.g., grammar, using all lowercase letters). Doing otherwise looks unprofessional.
- Spell words properly. Misspelled words reflect poorly on you and the organization you represent.
- Don't use emoticons (e.g., smiley faces). They look unprofessional.

- Don't be too quick to post. Write a post and then let it sit for a while. Come back to it and do some editing. Then post it.
- Provide contact information for your company.[32 & 33]

Instagram Writing Suggestions

- Edit your captions before posting.
- Edit your comments before posting.
- Include hashtags and keywords that will increase your exposure.
- Include a short call to action.
- Write clear, persuasive posts.
- Include your business information.
- Keep your posts about your brand.
- Run giveaways and promotions.
- Respond to other users' comments.[34, 35, & 36]

YouTube Writing Suggestions

Here are some suggestions pertaining to writing YouTube descriptions.

- Write short (concise) descriptions. YouTube has a 5000 character limit on descriptions, but do your best to write no more than two short paragraphs.
- Write compelling descriptions. Otherwise, people may look no further.
- YouTube descriptions should be searchable. Keywords are critical to this! Consider using Google's *AdWords* keywords tool if you need help with finding the right keywords.
- Use links extensively. They provide ways to promote your other videos as well as drive traffic to your other social media sites.
- Use timestamps. These work well with longer step-by-step videos and when you have a special announcement at a certain part of the video.
- Give credit where credit is due. If it is not already in your video, in your description you should mention individuals you collaborated with or who otherwise helped you with your video (e.g., director, cinematographer, make-up, etc.).[37]

Blog Writing Suggestions

- Know what you want to write about.
- Be narrow in focus.
- Be broad and complex enough that you do not run out of things to say.
- Keep content fresh.
- Keep writing style entertaining and conversational.
- Take risks on controversial topics if you want to increase the number of links to your post.
- Establish the appropriate tone. If it is too dry, they won't read it. If it is too informal, it might affect your organization's professional image.
- Update posts frequently. Updating corporate blogs once a week is recommended.

Blog Writing Suggestions: Don'ts

- Do not defame or discuss your colleagues and their behavior.
- Do not write anything defamatory.

- Do not write personal blogs on company time.
- Identify your blog as a personal blog and state that the views are your own.
- Do not reveal confidential information.
- Do not reveal trade secrets.[38]

WRITING PROFESSIONAL BIOS FOR SOCIAL MEDIA SITES

When writing bios for social media sites, keep them relatively short—essentially a few sentences. Here are some suggested ways to write a professional bio.

- Show, don't tell: "What have I done" > "Who I am". Essentially, don't just tell the reader you possess some desired quality such as leadership. Instead, give a good example of when you demonstrated that quality—a situation in which you were a good leader.
- Tailor your keywords to the specific audience you are targeting.
- Keep your language current. Avoid using overused words and phrases such as clichés.
- Answer one question for the reader: "What's in it for me?"
- Focus on the knowledge, skills, and experiences you bring as a means of gaining and keeping readers' attention.
- Update your bio frequently; preferably every quarter or so.[39]

WRITING SOCIAL MEDIA POLICY

© phoenixman/Shutterstock.com

Familiarity with social media policies increases the odds that employees will use social media effectively. Furthermore, well-written social media policies serve as models for the clear writing that employers expect from their employees. Nancy Flynn, author of *The Social Media Handbook*, offers a number of practical tips for writing effective social media policies. These are presented below.

- **Use Clear and Specific Language.** Avoid using language that is open to interpretation by employees.

- **Include Content Rules.** Here are some examples:

    - No illegal content.
    - No harassment or discrimination based on race, religion, age, etc.
    - No disclosure of confidential company, executive, or employee data.
    - No exposure of customers' personal financial data to outside parties.
    - No whining or complaining about the company, customers, or business.

- **Define Key Concepts and Terms.** Don't assume everyone understands the related terms and concepts. Just imagine the problems that could result from misunderstanding terms such as *confidential data* and *trade secret*, to name a few!
- **Use Plain English.** Here are some examples of how to do so. Avoid confusion, frustration, and misunderstandings by using short words in place of long words when you have the option to do so. Avoid including legal jargon and go easy on the use of technical terms. You can't always avoid using technical terms, but if you are not certain that others are familiar with them give a brief definition following the term. Then, there is the matter of abbreviations and acronyms. A good general rule regarding using abbreviations is don't. As for acronyms, spell them out the first time you use them in a social media policy followed by the acronym in parentheses. After that, just use the acronym.
- **Write With Accuracy.** Present accurate, reliable information.
- **Write Concisely.** Write social media policies that are short, simple, and straight to the point, all the while understanding that enough information must be included to achieve clarity.
- **Write Social Media Policies in Which Clarity is Evident.** Clarity, along with accuracy, are key components of well-written social media policies.
- **Adhere to Standard Writing Protocols.** Stick to standard writing protocols such as basic rules of grammar, punctuation, and spelling. It is difficult to embrace policies that are carelessly written!
- **Enhance Policy Readability by Using Effective Design Techniques.** Here are some examples:

    - Boldface headlines and subheads to emphasize important points.
    - Use bulleted or numbered lists.
    - Include a table of contents with lengthy policy documents.
    - Include a glossary containing social media, technology, and regulatory terms.[40]

Andrea Weckerle, author of *Civility in the Digital Age*, offers several additional tips for drafting robust and legal social media policies. She suggests that the following be incorporated into social media policies.

- An explanation for why a policy is created in the first place.
- An explanation for portions of a policy that may be controversial.
- What platforms the policy covers (e.g., company's social media channel, company's website).
- Which employees the policy covers (e.g., full-time, part-time).
- The importance for employees to avoid conflicts of interest and the appearance of conflict of interest.

- The importance of employees adhering to existing laws and to consider bringing legal questions or concerns to their supervisor and/or company's attorney.
- The importance for employees not to misuse their professional position for personal gain.
- Which employee actions will be frowned upon (e.g., intentionally defamatory statements, expressing threatening behavior, stating intentional lies that can harm the company).
- What the consequences of an employee's violation of the organization's social media policy may be.
- What the consequences of a user's or visitor's violation of the organization's social media policy may be.
- A requirement that employees should make it apparent that the views expressed on their personal social media sites are their own and not those of their employer, unless clearly stated otherwise.
- Any special expectations or requirements that the company or organization may have based on its respective industry.[41]

FIGURE 5-10: BEST TIMES TO POST ON SOCIAL MEDIA SITES

Analytics app SumAll researched the best time to post to the nine social media platforms listed below. Here are the findings.

- Facebook   1–4 p.m.
- Twitter   1–3 p.m.
- LinkedIn   5–6 p.m.
- Pinterest   8–11 p.m.
- Google+   9–11 a.m.
- Tumblr   7–10 p.m.
- Instagram   5–6 p.m.
- Blogs   10:30–11:30 a.m.
- YouTube   Submit video at 1 p.m. as it will often take up to one hour to upload and process the video. This way your video will be available during peak time which is 2 p.m.

Sources: Lee, Kevan. "Instagram for Business: 12 Answers to the Biggest Questions About Timing, Hashtags, and More," posted online, http://blog.bufferapp.com/instagram-for-business, June 11, 2014. Bonini, John. "What's The Best Time to Publish a Blog Post," posted online, http://www.impactbnd.com/blog/whens-the-best-time-to-publish-a-blog-post, *January 6, 2014. Robertson, Mark R. "YouTube Traffic Patterns and Uploading Recommendations,"* http://www.reelseo.com/youtube-traffic-analysis-seo/*November 12, 2007.*

WRITING BASICS

There are also a number of writing basics that can improve the quality of your social media posts, bios, profiles, and policies. These writing basics categories include:

- Following the Three-Step Writing Process
- Analyzing the Audience
- Choosing the Right Communication Medium
- Overcoming Writer's Block
- Developing Goodwill
- Choosing the Right Words

- Using a Variety of Sentence Types
- Including Images, Photos, Graphics, and Videos
- Editing
- Proofreading
- Writing Collaboratively

The above topics, with the exception of the last one, are discussed in detail in chapters 7 and 8. Information regarding "writing collaboratively" is presented in chapter 14. In addition, detailed writing mechanics rules and guidelines can be found at the textbook student website at the Writing Mechanics Rules and Guidelines resource. There, you will find rules and guidelines pertaining to grammar, punctuation, capitalization, number usage, abbreviations, and spelling as well as numerous examples.

FIGURE 5–11: SOCIAL MEDIA JOBS

With the advent and popularity of social media, new jobs evolved. Eight examples are presented below.

- **Advertising, Promotions, and Marketing Manager.** Employees in these positions plan programs to generate interest in a product or service and work with art directors, sales agents, and financial staff members. They also direct and coordinate advertising and promotion campaigns, as well as introduce new products to the marketplace. In addition, they also manage digital media campaigns which often target customers through the use of social media, websites, and live chats.
- **Blogger.** Employees in this position are responsible for opinionated, stylish writing and frequently posting new content to the Internet. Their duties may also include developing and/or revising text for other venues, including online communities, press releases, Web articles, and video blogs.
- **Community Manager.** Employees in this position create and execute social media strategies to accomplish real business objectives for brands.
- **Content-Marketing Manager.** Employees in this position write and promote business blogs, e-books, and white papers. This includes watching conversations on Twitter to figure out which topics are driving conversations.
- **Meeting, Convention, and Event Planner.** Employees in these positions coordinate all aspects of professional meetings and events which includes being familiar with social media.
- **Public-Relations Manager and Specialist.** Employees in these positions create and maintain a favorable public image for their employer or client. They write material for media releases, plan and direct public relations programs, and raise money for their organizations which includes being familiar with social media.
- **Social-Networking Analyst.** Employees in this position engage with customers and acquire new followers and fans. They also scour the Web finding content that is most relevant to their follower base that will help them get a good conversation started.
- **Social Media Manager.** Employees in this position are responsible for deciding what content to feature on social media channels. Daily tasks include posting, responding to community discussions, and combating spam.

Source: Ricker, Susan. "8 jobs in social media." CareerBuilder. October 23, 2012.

BARRIERS TO EFFECTIVE WRITING FOR SOCIAL MEDIA SITES

Familiarization with the typical barriers will help you write more effective social media posts, bios, profiles, and policies. Here are some of the common writing barriers that can have negative effects on social media posts and content.

- Not having a realistic attitude regarding the importance of writing effectively.
- Not analyzing one's audience sufficiently before crafting social media posts.
- Not choosing the best social media platform(s) for the purpose.
- Not being familiar with and/or willing to apply basic writing fundamentals (e.g., including sufficient details to achieve clarity, writing concisely, using a reader-centered tone).
- Not being familiar with and/or willing to apply writing mechanics (e.g., rules of grammar, capitalization).
- Not concerning oneself with proper spelling.
- Not applying appropriate writing strategies (e.g., persuasive strategy).
- Not posting during the most effective time range.
- Not requesting feedback and/or contact.
- Not being completely honest as described below.

Making false statements and/or exaggerations in social media posts, bios, and profiles is strongly discouraged. Not only is doing so unethical, it can have damaging effects on organizations and even result in expensive legal judgments. Most of us realize that making false statements and exaggerations on social media is unacceptable and unprofessional. If we are not cautious, however, we may knowingly or inadvertently stretch the truth when developing social media content to make our organizations, products, services, and even ourselves sound better than they/we are. For example, some job hunters make false statements and exaggerations on their *LinkedIn* sites and résumés in an attempt to persuade potential employers to grant them job interviews. This is not to suggest that most job candidates do so! However, to suggest that no job hunters do so would be naïve. For example, in a 2015 *Jobvite* survey 20 percent of adults with post-graduate education, 18 percent of adults with a college degree, and 9 percent of adults with a high school education or less admitted to inflating their job skills on social media when searching for jobs.[42] Whether one is searching for a job on social media or developing his or her résumé, the "lies, exaggerations, and land mines analogy" serves as a good reminder to stick with the truth. The analogy suggests that while lies and exaggerations on social media sites and résumés, much like buried land mines, may go unnoticed at first, they can detonate at any moment proving fatal to job searches, job stability, careers, and long-term credibility.[43]

SUMMARY: SECTION 3— SOCIAL MEDIA WRITING SUGGESTIONS

- The following writing suggestions pertain to all social media sites: craft posts that others will find valuable enough to share with friends and colleagues; craft posts that center on your audiences' questions and concerns; write strong, clear headlines; write posts that are long enough to achieve clarity; include images (e.g., photos, graphics) in longer posts to keep readers' attention; and put share buttons at the bottom of every post and page to make it easy for readers to share.
- When writing a professional bio for social media sites: show instead of just telling; tailor your keywords to the specific audience you are targeting; keep your language current; avoid using overused words and phrases such as clichés; answer one question for the reader: "What's in it for me?"; focus on the knowledge, skills, and experiences you bring as a means of gaining and keeping readers' attention; and update your bio frequently, preferably every quarter or so.
- When writing social media policies, include the following: an explanation for why a policy is created in the first place, an explanation for portions of a policy that may be controversial, the importance of employees adhering to existing laws and to consider bringing legal questions or concerns to their supervisor and/or company's attorney, and what the consequences of an employee's violation of the organization's social media policy may be.

SOCIAL MEDIA NETIQUETTE

Social Media Rules for Netiquette video https://www. youtube.com/ watch?v=UOSPFHCROGs

With the advent of the Internet and social media, several new words were added to our collective vocabularies. *Netiquette* is one such word. **Netiquette** refers to "rules about the proper and polite way to communicate with other people when using the Internet."[44] The list of netiquette rules is lengthy and not limited to just those that pertain to social media. Here, however, our interest is focused on those that pertain specifically to social media etiquette; especially those that are writing-related. Here are several such social media netiquette rules.

- Fill out your online profiles completely with information about you and your business.
- Use a different profile or account for your personal connections.
- Create a section on your main profile detailing who you are seeking to befriend and ask visitors to abide by that information.
- Offer information of value. Don't just talk about yourself and your company.
- Pick a screen name that represents you and your company well.
- Don't put anything on the Internet that you don't want your future boss, current clients, or potential clients to read.
- Never write or post social media content when you are overly tired, jet lagged, intoxicated, angry, or upset.
- Compose your posts, updates, and tweets in a word processing document so you can check grammar and spelling before you send them.[45]

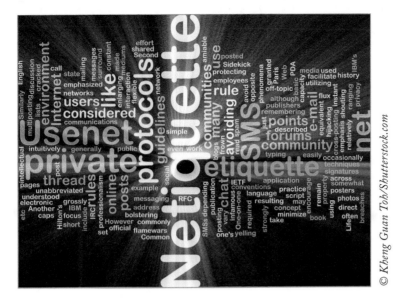

Figure 5-12 contains additional social media etiquette suggestions that are specific to blogs, but most of which are also applicable to other social media platforms.

FIGURE 5–12: BLOGGING ETIQUETTE

- Think before you speak in public.
- Be discreet. Be professional. Be mindful of the future.
- Need therapy? Do not write a blog. Seek counseling instead.
- Do not use your blog to let off steam.
- Watch your language.
- Do not blog anonymously. Stand behind your posted opinions.
- Do not comment unless you have something legitimate to add to the conversation.
- Be 100 percent honest.
- Keep an eye on spelling, grammar, and punctuation.
- Be gracious to readers and commenters.
- Develop a thick skin.

Source: Flynn, Nancy. Blog Rules: A Business Guide to Managing Policy, Public Relations, and Legal Issues. *New York, NY: American Management Association, 2006.*

Nancy Flynn, author of *The Social Media Handbook*, sums up social media etiquette as follows. Adhere to the rules of social media etiquette. Be polite, polished, and professional. Write, post, and publish content that is 100 percent appropriate, civil, and compliant.[46]

SUMMARY: SECTION 4—
SOCIAL MEDIA NETIQUETTE

- *Netiquette* refers to rules about the proper and polite way to communicate with other people when using the Internet.
- *Social media netiquette* refers to rules about the proper and polite way to communicate with other people over social media.
- Examples of social media netiquette rules include offering information of value and never posting social media content when you are overly tired, jet lagged, intoxicated, angry, or upset.
- Examples of blogging etiquette include: do not use your blog to let off steam, do not blog anonymously, do not comment unless you have something legitimate to add to the conversation, and be gracious to readers and commenters.
- Generally speaking, be polite, polished, and professional.

Notes

1. Sara Radicati, Editor, "Email Statistics Report," The Radicati Group, Inc., http://www.radicati.com/wp/wp-content/uploads/2014/01/Email-Statistics-Report-2014-2018-Executive-Summary, April 2014.

2. Hanh Nguyen, "What Is the Definition of Social Media?", http://mysocialmediareview.blogspot.com/2014/08/what-is-definition-of-social-media.html, August 15, 2014.

3. Author unknown, "Social Networking Sites Account for More than 20 Percent of All U.S. Online Display Ad Impressions," September 1, 2009, http://www.reuters.com.

4. Amy M. Young and Mary D. Hinesly, "Social Media Use to Enhance Internal Communication: Course Design for Business Students," *Business and Professional Communication Quarterly*, 24 No. 4, (2014): 426–439.

5. Jim Blasingame, "High Tech or High Touch: It's Really Not Complicated," *The Wall Street Journal*, October 6, 2009.

6. Young and Hinesly, *Business and Professional Communication Quarterly*, 426.

7. Young and Hinsley, *Business and Professional Communication Quarterly*.

8. Mitchell Schnurman, "Schnurman: The great digital hope for ad agencies," *Dallas Morning News*, pp. 1D & 6D, July 21, 2015.

9. M. Miller, *YouTube for Business: Online Video Marketing for Any Business* (Indianapolis, IN: Que Publishing, 2011), 18–25.

10. Chris Anderson, *The Long Tail: Why the Future of Business Is Selling Less of More* (New York: Hyperion, 2006).

11. Bill Eddy, *BIFF: Quick Responses to High Conflict People* (HCI Press, 2012, Kindle edition).

12. Geoff Desreumaux, "10 Tips to Write Engaging Facebook Posts," http://wersm.com/10-tips-to-write-engaging-facebook-posts/, January 13, 2014.

13. Jazeel Ferry, "Tips for Writing Tweets and Facebook Posts Before Your Event or Conference," http://blog.eventifier.com/tips-for-writing-tweets-and-facebook-posts-before-your-event-or-conference/), August 6, 2014.

14. C.G. Lynch, "Twitter Tips: How to Write Better Tweets," http://www.computerworld.com/article/2524316/networking/twitter-tips--how-to-write-better-tweets/, April 30, 2009.

15. Seth Lieberman, "Twitter writing: Five Tips to Win in 140 Characters," http://adage.com/article/btob/twitter-writing-tips-140-characters/287329/), December 19, 2012.

16. Ferry, "Tips for Writing Tweets and Facebook Posts Before Your Event or Conference."

17. Paul Edwards and Sarah Edwards, "Social Media Marketing," *Quick Study,* BarCharts, Inc., 2011.

18. Neal Schaffer, "9 Tips to Writing Posts That Get Read on the LinkedIn Publishing Platform," https://www.linkedin.com/pulse/20140313210407-235001-9-tips-to-writing-posts-that-get-read-on-the-linkedin-publishing-platform/, March 13, 2014.

19. Edwards and Edwards, "Social Media Marketing."

20. Jada A. Graves, "16 Things You're Doing All Wrong on LinkedIn," *U.S. News & World Report,* (June 23, 2014): 1-18.

21. Ariella Coombs, "7 Tips for Writing A Great LinkedIn Invitation," http://www.careerealism.com/linkedin-invitation-tips/, October 25, 2014.

22. Donna Serdula, "What Makes a LinkedIn Profile POWERFUL?", http://www.linkedin-makeover.com/linkedin-profile-samples/).

23. Edwards and Edwards, "Social Media Marketing."

24. William Aruda, "Three Steps To Writing The Perfect LinkedIn Summary," http://www.forbes.com/sites/williamarruda/2014/09/07/three-steps-to-writing-the-perfect-linkedin-summary/, September 17, 2014.

25. Brenda Bernstein, "5 Essential Tips for a KILLER LinkedIn Summary," http://www.careercast.com/career-news/5-essential-tips-killer-linkedin-summary.

26. Graves, *U.S. News & World Report.*

27. Mitt Ray, "6 Tips for Writing Effective Pin Descriptions on Pinterest," http://socialmarketingwriting.com/6-tips-for-writing-effective-pin-descriptions-on-pinterest/, January 6, 2014.

28. Lisa Pluth, "5 Ways Pinterest Success Comes From Great Writing," http://socialfresh.com/writing-on-pinerest/, April 19, 2012.

29. Danielle Cormier, "25 Things That Make You Look Dumb on Pinterest," http://blogs.constantcontact.com/pinterest-for-business/, August 15, 2013.

30. Reba Kennedy, "Google Plus: Tips for Writing Google+ Posts and Why You Should Care About Google+," http://rebakennedy.blogspot.com/2013/09/google-plus-tips-for-writing-google.html, September 11, 2013.

31. Edwards and Edwards, "Social Media Marketing."

32. Jamie Clark, "11 killer tips for a successful Tumblr blog," http://www.creativebloq.com/tumblr/secrets-successful-tumblr-blog-3132101, March 8, 2013.

33. Edwards and Edwards, "Social Media Marketing."

34. "Instagram Tips: Comments," http://blog.instagram.com/post/13978983262/comments.

35. Kevan Lee, "Instagram for Business: 12 Answers to the Biggest Questions About Timing, Hashtags, and More," https://blog.bufferapp.com/instagram-for-business, June 11, 2014.

36. Brittney Helmrich, "Instagram for Business: Everything You Need to Know," http://www.businessnewsdaily.com/7662-instagram-business-guide.html, January 21, 2015.

37. Ed Carrasco, "5 Tips For Effective YouTube Video Descriptions," http:///newmediarockstars.com/2013/06/5-tips-for-effective-youtube-video-descriptions/, June 13, 2013.

38. Nancy Flynn, *Blog Rules: A Business Guide to Managing Policy, Public Relations, & Legal Issues* (New York: American Management Association, 2006).

39. Courtney Seiter, "How to Write a Professional Bio For Twitter, LinkedIn, Facebook, & Google+," https://blog.bufferapp.com/how-to-write-a-professional-bio-for-twitter-linkedin-facebook-google+/, February 5, 2014.

40. Nancy Flynn, *The Social Media Handbook* (San Francisco: Pfeiffer, A Wiley Imprint, 2012), 175–177.

41. Andrea Weckerle, *Civility in the Digital Age: How Companies and People Can Triumph Over Haters, Trolls, Bullies, and Other Jerks* (Indianapolis, Indiana: Que Publishing, 2013), 254–256.

42. Jae Yang and Karl Gelles. "Inflating Job Skills on Social Media," *USA Today*, February 20, 2015.

43. Mark Wrolstad. "Lying on Resumes: Why Some Can't Resist," *The Dallas Morning News*, December 22, 2001.

44. Merriam-Webster Dictionary (online).

45. Lydia Ramsey, "Top 12 Rules of Social Media," http://www.businessknowhow.com/internet/socialmediaetiquette.htm)

46. Sarah E. Needleman, "Firms Get a Hand With Twitter, Facebook," *The Wall Street Journal*, October 1, 2009.

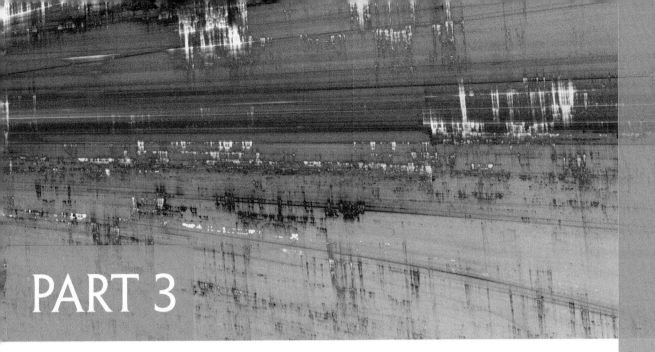

PART 3

BUSINESS WRITING

WRITING ELECTRONICALLY 6

LEARNING OUTCOMES

After reading this chapter, you should be able to:

1. Discuss how to write effective business e-mail messages.
2. Manage an overloaded e-mail inbox.
3. Describe how to write effective business instant messages.
4. Describe how to write effective business text messages.
5. Describe ways to write effective company websites.
6. Discuss netiquette rules that pertain to writing electronically.

© *GaudiLab/Shutterstock.com*

BENEFITS OF LEARNING ABOUT ELECTRONIC WRITING

1. You will understand the impact of electronic writing on the way people communicate in the workplace.
2. You will learn how to communicate effectively using e-mail, instant messaging, text messaging, and websites.
3. You will understand the importance of and how to apply netiquette rules as they pertain to writing electronically.
4. You will learn how to get the Web browser's attention with clear, scannable, and credible content.
5. You will understand the roles of e-mail, instant messaging, text messaging, and websites in the business place.

SELECT KEY TERMS

INTRODUCTION

Writing electronically in the business place has its challenges. First is honing traditional writing skills and acquiring new writing skills as needed. Second is merging the writing process with the speed, convenience, and protocols of electronic communication to achieve effective documents. Third is being realistic about the importance of building relationships. It is important that you are familiar with your employer's e-policies that pertain to electronic communication. In addition, keep in mind that e-mail and texting are considered to be informal communication mediums that are best used for routine matters. Furthermore, do your best to write high-quality material for company websites for obvious clarity and corporate image reasons. Finally, be very familiar with netiquette rules and suggestions that pertain to writing electronically.

The intent of this chapter is to provide you with information on writing electronically. This goal is realized through discussions of the following topics: electronic writing in organizations, writing effective e-mail messages, instant messages, text messages, websites, and choosing the right medium. The information pertaining to the above-mentioned electronic writing topics is reinforced by several student website resources including *PowerPoint slides, preview tests, chapter assessment tests, writing mechanics rules and guidelines, YouTube videos, interactive exercises,* and the *interactive glossary.*

ELECTRONIC WRITING IN ORGANIZATIONS

Electronic writing refers to developing and transmitting messages and documents via electronic communication technologies such as e-mail, instant messaging, text messaging, and websites as well as social media sites which are addressed in chapter 5. Speed, convenience, and cost efficiencies are among the main reasons electronic communication has become so popular in U.S. organizations and elsewhere.

electronic writing Developing and transmitting messages and documents via electronic technologies such as e-mail, instant messaging, text messaging, and websites.

© sebiva/Shutterstock.com

Despite the speed, convenience, and cost efficiencies, electronic writing also has some challenges. Three of these challenges are described below.

1. **Honing Traditional Writing Skills and Acquiring New Skills.** Readers read differently online than offline; thus, you must adapt your online copy to meet readers' needs. Specific writing suggestions are covered in this chapter for *e-mail*, *instant messages*, *text messages*, and *websites*.

2. **Merging the Writing Process with the Speed, Convenience, and Protocols of Electronic Communication to Achieve Effective Documents.** Electronic communication media such as e-mail, instant messaging, and websites encourage the development of short messages and inadvertently invite some to ignore rules of grammar, punctuation, and spelling rules while doing so. In addition, many writers do not edit and revise their electronic messages before sending them. Too often the result is poorly written messages that contain too little detail to achieve clarity, leaving readers with a poor perception of their communication partner's writing abilities. Be careful. Poorly written communications can be career killers.

3. **Being Realistic about the Importance of Building Relationships.** Before expanding on this challenge, please understand that in the U.S. business place strong relationships with stakeholders (e.g., colleagues, clients, suppliers, investors) are crucial to job stability and career growth. Building business relationships is best accomplished through face-to-face interaction. Herein lies the challenge. Avoid doing so much of your communicating (written or otherwise) electronically that you fail to build strong relationships with your stakeholders. Most would agree that communicating electronically is appealing and efficient on several levels. However, communicating too frequently via e-mail, instant messages, text messages, websites, and social media can easily compromise your ability to achieve your career goals. Despite our good intentions, however, we cannot always meet with others face-to-face. When you cannot, but should, at least place a phone call or hold a videoconference instead of e-mailing or texting. Phone calls and videoconferences are more personal and support relationship building better than e-mail and text messages do.

© ARENA Creative/Shutterstock.com

Electronic Methods of Communication in Business
http://smallbusiness.chron.com/electronic-methods-communication-business-2934.html

Formality plays an important role in selecting the best medium for each writing situation. Written documents and messages are frequently viewed as being *formal*, *informal*, or *semiformal*. For example, letters are considered formal documents. Documents and messages developed and transmitted electronically (e.g., e-mails, e-memos, instant messages, and text messages) are generally considered to be informal. Awareness of such differences in perception is important because readers' formality expectations vary and must be taken into consideration. For example, for an important message to an external client, you would be expected to send a formal document, in this case, a hardcopy letter. In contrast, if you need to send a brief message with routine, straightforward information to a subordinate within the company, an informal written medium such as e-mail is a good choice. Or, if you and a fellow worker, who are both on the same job level, need to discuss some points pertaining to a routine, noncontroversial matter, IM would be the informal medium of choice. Before moving on, let's look at one more example that lands you midstream on the formality spectrum. If you need to send a message to subordinates about changes to internal procedures, a semiformal document is necessary. In this case, it would be a memo.

For now, e-mail is the most widely used communication medium in U.S. organizations, which is exactly why it receives the most coverage in this chapter. E-mail will one day be knocked out of the top spot. Humans have a long history of inventing new technologies that, in turn, replace previously popular technologies. PCs replacing typewriters is a good example of this phenomenon. This is not to suggest, however, that e-mail will be replaced in the top spot anytime soon. However, at the rate new electronic communication technologies are being introduced it is always a possibility. As to when this will occur is anyone's guess. In the meantime, if you are preparing for a business career or are already working in the business world, knowing how to use e-mail effectively is very important.

In this chapter you will learn how to write effective, reader-friendly e-mail messages, instant messages, text messages, and website content. Competency in these areas will enable you to capitalize on the potential of each of these electronic communication tools, while avoiding the inherent pitfalls. Since electronic communication will certainly comprise a large percentage of your business communications in the professional workplace, mastering the basics now will give you a competitive edge.

SUMMARY: SECTION 1— WRITING ELECTRONICALLY IN ORGANIZATIONS

- Electronic writing (e.g., e-mail messages, instant messages, text messages, website content) is growing in the business world.
- Electronic writing challenges include honing traditional writing skills and acquiring new skills; merging the writing process with the speed, convenience, and protocols of electronic communication to achieve effective documents; and being realistic about the importance of building relationships.
- Formality plays an important role in selecting the best medium for each writing situation.
- E-mail is the most widely used communication medium in U.S. organizations.

E-MAIL

E-mail is a method of exchanging digital messages from one author to one or more recipients.[1] E-mail is the predominant communication medium in U.S. organizations and elsewhere for that matter, and no wonder why. It is a fast, convenient, and inexpensive way to reach one or multiple recipients with a few clicks of the mouse. Owing to its popularity, e-mail has replaced messages that were once transmitted exclusively through hardcopy letters and memos. E-mail has also replaced the need to send faxes as often. Some even send sensitive correspondence via e-mail, although you must be careful to remember that e-mail is not a private medium.

e-mail
A method of exchanging digital messages from one author to one or more recipients.

© amasterphotographer/Shutterstock.com

Advantages and Disadvantages of Email http://www.workplace-communication.com/advantages-disadvantages-email.html

The prevalence of e-mail means that more workers than ever are writing. Even entry-level employees who used to be exempt from most writing activities now write e-mails to accomplish a host of activities from explaining procedures to coworkers to apologizing to a customer for a billing error.[2]

Where once we picked up the phone to communicate business and personal information, today we routinely send e-mail messages instead. By replacing phone calls with e-mails, however, a process has been created by which informal conversations are recorded and formal business decisions are documented electronically.[3] The result is an unprecedented amount of documented business communication that can be used against an employer or employee should a workplace lawsuit be filed.

The convenience of e-mail comes at a price for employers in the form of increased liability concerns. In response, many companies have reduced their exposure to legal "e-disasters" by establishing and enforcing policies that govern employees' electronic writing. These policies are discussed next.[4] On the employee side, the convenience of e-mail means that much of your relationship with coworkers, customers, and supervisors may rest on your e-mail exchanges.[5] In this writing-centered environment, e-mail is no longer the equivalent of a casual lunch conversation, and your ability to quickly organize and clearly express ideas in e-mail becomes important to your overall success in any organization. In today's electronic workplace, written communication makes a competitive difference.[6]

To write effective e-mail messages, you *must* think before you send. Therefore, the standard rules that apply to all business writing (e.g., appropriate tone, logical organization, grammatical correctness) are important to follow when you write e-mails. When written with consideration for your audience, e-mail is a productive communication tool that allows you to make a direct, positive, and polite connection with your reader. This, in turn, will win you the attention and goodwill of coworkers, customers, and other stakeholders.[7] The trick is to develop an effective e-mail style that supports effective business communication.

SELECTING THE RIGHT MEDIUM: TO E-MAIL OR NOT TO E-MAIL

Not all messages should be sent by e-mail. While corporate e-mail cultures differ, some rules on whether to e-mail the message apply across the board.

Consider the formality or informality of the message context. For instance, when introducing yourself or your product to an organization, the proper route to take is still a formal letter, report, or proposal. In addition, even though e-mailing a thank-you note following a job interview is usually acceptable, sending a promptly mailed, handwritten thank-you note would definitely garner more attention and would be more appropriate.[8]

E-mailing a thank you for a job well done is always appreciated, but a face-to-face thank you is better. Likewise, important job requests, such as requests for a raise or promotion or a resignation announcement, should be done face-to-face.[9] An e-mail that requests a raise would most likely be considered spineless or not be taken seriously. A request for a sick day should be made over the phone in most offices.[10]

On the other hand, e-mail is widely used to communicate routine, daily business messages since it is cost efficient and fast. Direct requests or informative messages to coworkers; companywide announcements, like the time and place of the holiday party or the next staff meeting; or a change in an organization's travel policy can all be sent safely by e-mail as long as everyone in the office has access to it.[11] Equally safe to send by e-mail are major personal announcements, like the happy news of a new mom or dad or the sad news of a death in a coworker's family. Other announcements, like graduations or birthdays, probably do not warrant a companywide e-mail.[12]

Do not use e-mail, however, if your message meets one of the criteria listed below. Instead, make a phone call or immediately hold a meeting. Place a phone call or schedule a meeting if:

- Your message requires an immediate response. You cannot assume that your recipient will answer his or her e-mail right away. It is inappropriate to send a follow-up message demanding to know why a recipient has not responded to your message.[13]
- You want to hear the tone of your communication partner's voice so you can read between the lines.
- Your message has many discussion points and needs an extended response or extended negotiations to resolve.
- You want your comments to be private. No message that is private, confidential, or sensitive should be sent by e-mail.[14] We all know that others can hack e-mail if they really want to. So if we don't want it out there, we shouldn't send it off into cyberspace.
- You are concerned about **phishing**, which is the act of sending an e-mail to a user falsely claiming to be an established legitimate enterprise in an attempt to scam the user into surrendering private information that will be used for identity theft.[15] This is simple. If you question the authenticity of an e-mail that made its way into your inbox, don't respond to it. However, it is best not to open it at all!

phishing
The act of sending an e-mail to a user falsely claiming to be an established legitimate enterprise in an attempt to scam the user into surrendering private information that will be used for identity theft.

When deciding whether to send an e-mail message, ask yourself if your need is for speed, cost efficiency, and/or mass distribution. Speed, cost efficiency, and mass distribution are e-mail's strengths. If you need your reader to receive your communication in a few seconds rather than a few days—especially if you have a tight deadline and want to work up to the last minute—e-mail is the way to go. Remember, though, that a quick message does not necessarily mean a quick reply. The recipient is under no obligation to answer your message quickly even though good e-mail etiquette recommends responding to e-mail promptly.

If you have multiple recipients for that 20-page report, consider e-mailing it as an attachment rather than making 50 copies for distribution. It is a good idea to determine first if your attachment will arrive in its entirety. If not, you might consider sending portions of it as separate attachments.

E-mail is also a good tool for communicating across time zones and continents. Rather than calling your business contact in Germany in the evening, e-mail lets you and your international recipient conduct business during your respective normal business hours.[16]

MANAGING HIGH-VOLUME E-MAIL

Given its many benefits, the following question may sound extremely odd. In regard to e-mail, have we humans created a monster? Well, not in the sense of a Frankenstein monster, but possibly in terms of the number that are sent and received in the business world daily and how much time it has consumed in the daily lives of business employees in the workplace. For example, the number of e-mails sent and received daily in the business world in 2015 was approximately 109 billion—a number which is predicted to increase to approximately 140 billion by 2018.[17] As for the e-mail impact on an individual level, a McKinsey Global Institute poll found that the typical office worker spends an average of 2.5 hours of his or her workday writing, reading, and sorting out e-mail messages.[18] And, e-mail traffic is projected to grow. According to the global computer and telecommuting research company, The Radicati Group, between 2014 and 2018 the number of e-mail messages business employees will send and receive each work day will grow from 121 to 140 which averages out to sending 5 and receiving approximately12 during each working hour.[19] You know the amount of e-mail traffic is high when some employees justify reading and sending work-related e-mails during non-work hours such as evenings and weekends while others hesitate to take all of their allotted vacation time because they dread the thought of facing down overloaded e-mail inboxes when they return to the office.

Help is on the way! Some of the e-mail workload is currently being replaced by text messages, instant messages, and social media. In addition, you might be encouraged by companies such as Yammer, Chatter, Convo, and HipChat that are, according to Leena Rao, "openly waging war on email" by providing and promoting alternative communication approaches for e-mail.[20]

Given the high volume of incoming e-mail activity, you are among the lucky few if you have an assistant who sorts through your incoming e-mail, deletes unnecessary messages, and forwards summaries of the important messages to you. If not, you alone must decide how to deal with all those e-mails that arrive in your inbox daily. Good luck with that! However, help has arrived. The following tips can help you manage that overloaded inbox.

- Follow the Last In, First Out rule. Read the last e-mail in a series of e-mails in case the issues from the previous e-mails have been resolved. If you need to reply to the series, read them all first before you reply.[21]
- If you are away from the office for a few days and return to an overflowing inbox, respond to the last day's e-mail first; these responses will not be late. As for the other e-mails, since you are already late in replying, adopt a last in/first out order after you prioritize by sender or subject.
- On first reading, do something with your e-mail even if it is only to group "Read Later" e-mails into a separate folder rather than leaving them to clutter your inbox.
- Deal with all non-urgent messages at one time rather than taking time out to deal with each message as it comes up during the day.[22]
- Use the archive function to inspect e-mails not previously saved and either delete or archive them. Set up the function to delete nonessential e-mails that are older than a specific number of days.
- Delete chain letters and spam. Unsubscribe to mailing lists that you rarely read.
- Set up other e-mail accounts, outside of your office e-mail, for ordering online and for personal correspondence.
- Use filters to prioritize your mail into separate folders. Some suggestions for ways to organize your mail include:
  - Separate internal office mail from outside mail that does not include your company's domain name.
  - Separate mass mailings from those addressed directly to you. Route messages in which you were cc'd or bcc'd to a mass-mailing folder.

- Create a separate folder for family e-mail after you are sure your company's electronic policy allows you to receive personal e-mail at work.

- If you are going to be away from the office and your e-mail account for an extended period, activate an automatic "Out-of-the-Office" reply. That way, anyone who needs your answer right away will know not to expect it. This feature will help you keep messages from building up in your inbox while you are away.[23]

E-POLICIES AND POTENTIAL E-MAIL LIABILITY ISSUES

To reduce potential liability associated with e-messages, organizations develop e-policies that address matters ranging from corporate-level wheeling and dealing to employee jokes. E-mail with its shoot-from-the-hip qualities of speed and mass distribution exponentially increases this potential for liability. International Data Corp. estimates that millions of U.S. workers send billions of e-mail messages daily.[24] Not all these messages are related to work. According to an Elron Software survey, many employees with Internet access report receiving inappropriate e-mails at work, including e-mails with racist, sexist, pornographic, or inflammatory content. Whether solicited or not, these types of messages in employees' electronic mailboxes can spell e-disaster for the company and the sender.[25]

Evidence of executives and companies stung by their own e-mails abound. One such example is a Chevron Corp. case in which sexist e-mails, like "25 Reasons Beer Is Better Than Women," circulated by male employees cost Chevron $2.2 million to settle a sexual harassment lawsuit brought by female employees.[26]

In another case involving *The New York Times*' shared services center in Virginia, nearly two dozen employees were fired and 20 more were reprimanded for violating the company's e-mail policy. They had sent and received e-mails with sexual images and offensive jokes.[27] In this case, one of the fired offenders had just received a promotion while another had just been named "Employee of the Quarter." These kinds of incidents cost any company negative publicity, embarrassment, loss of credibility, and, inevitably, loss of business.[28]

Another example was a lawsuit against American Home Products Corp. over a rare but often fatal lung condition some consumers developed after taking the company's diet pills. Insensitive employee e-mails contributed to the company's decision to settle the case for more than $3.75 billion dollars, one of the largest settlements ever for a drug company.[29] One e-mail printed in the *Wall Street Journal* expressed an employee's concern over spending her career paying off "fat people who are a little afraid of some silly lung problem."[30] This example shows how important it is to review and revise your e-mails for potentially inflammatory content before sending.

Still another example involves unauthorized use of a company's computer system for a mass e-mailing. At Lockheed Martin, an employee sent 60,000 coworkers an e-mail about a national day of prayer and requested an electronic receipt from all 60,000. The resulting overload crashed Martin's system for six hours while a Microsoft rescue squad was flown in to repair the damage and to build in protection.[31] The company lost hundreds of thousands of dollars, all resulting from one employee's actions. The employee was fired for sabotage. And, the list of corporate e-mail disasters goes on.

Most companies do recognize that careless e-mails can cost them dearly. If one poorly worded, thoughtless e-mail gets in the hands of defense attorneys in a lawsuit, the company may have to pay up to the tune of a six-to-ten-figure settlement. With these kinds of productivity, profit, and public relations disasters resulting from e-mail

e-policies
Guidelines for using electronic communication.

and Internet use, it is not surprising that employers are implementing e-policies. Whether a company consists of two part-time employees or 2,000, the best protection against lawsuits resulting from employees' access to e-mail, IM, and the Internet is a comprehensive, written e-policy, one that clearly defines what is and is not acceptable use of the organization's computers.[32] According to Nancy Flynn, Internet guru and policy consultant, the best policies are straightforward, simple, and accessible.[33] These e-policies inform employees of their electronic rights and responsibilities as well as tell them what they can expect in terms of monitoring. While employees believe they have a right to privacy where their e-mail is concerned, the federal Electronic Communications Privacy Act (ECPA) states that an employer-provided computer system is the property of the employer, and the employer has the right to monitor all e-mail traffic and Internet activity on the system. Currently, over half of U.S. businesses monitor employee e-mail and Internet activity. Monitoring programs can determine if e-mail is being used solely for business purposes.

Some companies monitor every keystroke made on every keyboard by every employee. Electronic monitors screen for words that alert managers to inappropriate content and some monitors can be configured to spot "trigger" words that indicate everything from profanity and sexually explicit or racially offensive language to the exchange of sensitive information, such as trade secrets and proprietary information.[34]

Although sanctioned by the ECPA, monitoring has its downsides. For example, employees may resent being unable to send an occasional personal e-mail to check on their kids or to make dinner reservations online without violating company policies. The feeling of being watched can hurt morale and eventually may cause good workers to quit, which means lost money for the company.[35] Some employees are striking back at e-policies, claiming protection under state statutes that include a right to privacy.

Finally, even monitoring programs cannot ferret out the hostile tone or the badly worded document open to misinterpretation, especially when being dissected by opposing lawyers. The haste and recklessness with which we tend to write e-mail, along with its high volume, exacerbate an old problem: mediocre writing skills. Only careful attention to employees' writing habits can halt the production of bad e-mail documents.[36]

Policies that govern e-mail use often incorporate electronic writing policies, electronic etiquette (netiquette) guidelines, company-use-only guidelines, and retention policies that outline how long e-mails are saved before they are automatically deleted from mail queues and mail host backups.[37] Some companies purge all e-mail messages older than 30 days and do not keep backup tapes of e-mail. Some experts advise companies to retain no e-mail since a lawsuit could require a review of all backed-up e-mail.[38] However, some industries such as financial firms are governed by federal securities laws that require them to retain e-mails relating to the firm's overall business for three years.[39]

What is clear is that more organizations and employers are implementing e-policies. Therefore, as an employee, you need to familiarize yourself with your employer's e-policies and follow them closely. Since every document you write, including e-mail and IMs, is not only a reflection of your professionalism but also a reflection of your organization's credibility, you need to reflect corporate goals by writing clear, clean e-mails that observe company policy. In addition, before firing off that first e-mail at your job, take time to learn your organization's e-mail culture.

GETTING FAMILIAR WITH THE E-MAIL CULTURE OF YOUR ORGANIZATION

Corporate e-mail culture varies greatly.[40] Some companies use e-mail as their main form of communication; others use it only occasionally. Some companies do not mind if you send personal messages via e-mail; in others, it is a dismissible offense. Some top executives welcome e-mails from staff; others follow a strict hierarchy of who can message whom. Therefore, when you move to a new job, take time to observe the e-mail culture for answers to the following questions so you avoid e-mail mistakes or, worse yet, the e-mail career killer (ECK). A good example of an ECK is sending your new boss a jokey "let's get acquainted" e-mail, only to discover his or her dislike for using e-mail except for formal communications.

- Notice the tone of the e-mails among coworkers. Is it formal or informal? Do they use e-mail for socializing, joking, and gossiping, or is it reserved for formal, job-related messages?
- What is the e-mail chain of command? Can staff skip over their supervisors and e-mail suggestions or questions to upper management?
- How are urgent or sensitive messages usually communicated?
- Do all employees have access to e-mail? Do they check it regularly?
- How are staff-wide announcements made, via e-mail? bulletin board? memo? intranet?
- Are personal announcements, such as "My house is on the market" or "I just found the cutest puppy; any takers?" acceptable over companywide e-mail?
- What are the company's written policies on e-mail, IM, and Internet use? Is any noncompany-related browsing allowed? To what extent are e-mail, IM, and Internet use monitored?[41]

Become familiar with your employer's e-culture as soon as possible. If you are uncertain about where the organization stands on such matters, do not guess. Ask your immediate supervisor or an HR representative.

WRITING EFFECTIVE E-MAIL MESSAGES

The fiction that quick, poorly-written business messages are acceptable is fostered, in part, by the medium itself. Unlike writing memos and letters where we tend to be more guarded and take time to write thoughtfully, e-mail often brings out the worst of our bad writing habits. As Gregory Maciag, president and CEO of ACORD, the nonprofit industry standards association, points out, the medium can hamper communication: "In place of thoughtful content, we send and receive short bursts of often grammatically and emotionally challenged communiqués that we sometimes regret."[42] Additionally, writing consultant Dianna Booher laments: "They log on; they draft; they send."[43] To avoid creating confusion, misunderstandings, and hurt feelings with your e-mails and to ensure that you get the busy reader's attention, think and plan before you draft an e-mail message, then revise it before you hit Send.

DRAFTING E-MAIL MESSAGES

Competition for the electronic readers' attention grows daily with tens of millions of e-mail users online. The challenge for those who send e-mails is to get their targeted readers' attention. To help you get your reader's attention, follow the guidelines discussed here, beginning with the all-important subject line.

Subject Line   Some busy executives get hundreds of incoming e-mails a day. To get through them quickly, they look at the subject line. If that grabs their attention, they scan the first screen. Messages that do not get the reader's attention at the subject line run the risk of never being read or of being deleted. To avoid "e-mail triage":[44]

- Always include a clear, informative subject line. It should communicate the topic of the message, and, like the subject line of a memo, it should be specific and brief. A subject line such as "Staff meeting changed to 3 p.m." provides the necessary information. A subject line such as "Meeting," "Information," "Guidelines," or "Hey" convey nothing. If you use "URGENT" or "!" too often, you reduce the urgency of the message in the reader's mind, and he or she eventually ignores it.[45]
- Be brief. Write the important points of your topic in the first half of your subject line. In an inbox, only the first 25–35 characters of the subject line usually appear. In a string (thread) of exchanged e-mails, change the subject line if the subject changes. That way, if you have to refer to an old e-mail, you won't have to reread every message with the same "Re."[46]

e-mailhead
E-mail
letterhead.

Body   The first thing to appear in the body of your e-mail may be your **e-mailhead** (e-mail letterhead; see Figure 6-1 for an example). E-mailheads appear routinely when e-mail is used to transmit formal contracts, proposals, offers, and other business transactions. Companies that provide eletterheads, like Dynamic E-mail Stationery from StationeryCentral.com, offer graphically enriched e-mail that reflects your corporate identity.[47]

When you use an e-mailhead, be sure you have a clear purpose for including it, such as making it clear that the message is from your company. Otherwise, the reader may object to the wasted lines.

Always include a salutation. Including a greeting at the start of your message personalizes it, plus it establishes your role in the message's history.[48] If you normally address a person by his or her title or if you do not know the person well, include his or her title when addressing them: "Ms. Jones," "Dr. Smith," "Prof. James," etc.

FIGURE 6–1: E-MAILHEAD

To: recipient@byco.com
From: Mia Deal (mdeal@herco.com)
Date: 201___
Subject: Offer to Purchase Smartboards
       Her Company Inc.
       3024 Main Street
       Chicago, IL 54890
Dear Mr. Brown:
text
text
Sincerely,
Mia Deal
Marketing Manager
(mdeal@herco.com)

If you are unsure how to address a person, err on the side of formality (this cannot be stressed enough). Being too formal will not offend even the most informal of people and will satisfy the most traditional formalists. However, if you are too informal at the outset, you run the risk of ruining your credibility with that person or organization. You can always change the salutation in subsequent messages if the recipient indicates that informality is fine.

Although business correspondence greetings like "Dear Sirs" are outdated forms in the United States, greetings are more formal in other countries, such as Japan and Germany.

Keep the body of your message short, no more than 25 lines (approximately 250 words) or one screen's worth of words.[49] A sharp contrast to this is the approximately 1,100 word e-mail message an executive vice president at Microsoft sent announcing the layoff of 12,500 employees.

For longer documents, send an attachment. However, some companies do not accept attachments for fear of viruses, so check with your recipient first. If you must attach a document to an e-mail, use clear headings in that document to break up the text and allow for skimming.

Remember there is a live person on the other end of your communication, so get right to the point in the first or second sentence and support your main idea with details in the next paragraph. Begin your e-mail with your main idea or request. Most important, keep the body of the message brief and to the point. Focus on developing one topic only, and make responding easy. For example, phrase a message so that your reader can respond with a quick "yes" or "no."[50]

In summary, make your message reader-oriented to help your recipient grasp your message quickly:

- Begin with your bottom-line, main idea, or a precise overview of the situation. If you want the reader to take action, begin by making your request. Include the requested action in the subject line for emphasis. If the message is for the reader's information only and needs no follow-up, put "FYI" in the subject line.
- Keep messages under 25 lines long, and use short sentences.
- Use white space before and after your main idea to highlight it.
- Use short sentences and short paragraphs that cover one idea. Separate short paragraphs with white space.
- Use bulleted or numbered lists to help readers quickly differentiate multiple points or directions.[51]

Signature Block Always close with something, even if it is only your name. Simple closings, though, like "Regards" or "Best wishes," add a touch of warmth to this otherwise cold medium. Add credibility to your message by adding a signature block after your name. For consistency, create a signature file (.sig) containing, at a minimum, your name, title, and address. You could also include phone and fax numbers; your web address or website; an advertising message, slogan, or quote; your business philosophy; or ASCII art created from text and symbols. However, many organizations have eliminated these slogans and quotes from employees' signature files in an effort to steer clear of potential litigation. The best advice is to know and follow your organization's policy. Avoid duplicating material in the signature that is already in your e-mailhead, if you use one.[52]

The 1,100 Word E-mail Message http://news.microsoft.com/2014/07/17/stephen-elops-email-to-employees/

EDITING AND REVISING E-MAIL MESSAGES

It is in the editing phase that writers have the opportunity to convert an average-to-poor e-mail message into an effective e-mail message. It is not a step to be rushed. Here are some editing tips that should help you produce effective e-mail messages.

- Build some time in between the drafting and editing phases.
- Edit when you are rested.
- Edit when you are not rushed.
- Don't edit when you are upset or noticeably distracted.
- Do several separate editing passes. With each pass, focus on just one or two potential areas of improvement (e.g., *message organization, writing mechanics, spelling*). Identifying 100 percent of the message's weaknesses simultaneously in a single editing pass is difficult to accomplish. By making separate focused editing passes, you are far more likely to identify what should be revised.
- With each editing pass, read the e-mail message word-for-word. Don't just skim over the message.
- If the e-mail message is important, have others edit it also.

While editing, make sure your tone is appropriate to your audience. E-mail is an impersonal medium that is fertile ground for misunderstandings and hurt feelings. Temper your messages with politeness and objectivity. Strive for a professional, yet conversational tone. Use personal pronouns ("I," "you," "me)" to humanize the connection. To humanize your e-mail, avoid the "**e-tone**." Nancy Friedman, a consultant and trainer, invented the term "e-tone" to refer to the miscommunication that occurs when you have one tone of voice in mind as you write e-mail, but your recipient reads it with a totally different tone. Friedman urges e-mail writers to use words that express feelings—"please," "thank you," "I'm happy to report," or "sorry to say"—to tell them how you feel.[53] Friedman contends that even sensitive topics, such as apologies, can be addressed in e-mail if done properly.

Also check to make sure you have not overused punctuation marks that can cause misunderstandings. For example, a subject line in an e-mail to a professor that says "Grades???????" might sound as if you are unhappy with your grade, when your intent was to merely find out what your grade is. Similarly, overuse of the exclamation point can offend people because it can make you sound pushy or overexcited!!!!!!!!

Finally, be sure the e-mail you are about to send does not contain a reckless or emotional outburst. For example, do not send an e-mail in which you stridently complain about your boss to a coworker because the offensive e-mail could get forwarded, accidentally or on purpose, to your maligned boss.

PROOFREADING E-MAIL MESSAGES

Proofread your e-mail carefully. Do not let poor spelling and typos detract from the credibility of your message. Use the grammar and spell checker, but then reread the message yourself before you hit Send. You cannot depend on a grammar or spell checker to catch every error. Some basic proofreading tips that will help you identify those oversights include:

- Proofread when you are not rushed.
- Proofread when you are rested.
- Do separate, focused proofreading passes (e.g., *once for misspelled words, once for spacing problems*, etc.)

e-tone

Refers to the miscommunication that occurs when the writer has one tone of voice when writing the e-mail, but the recipient reads it in a totally different tone.

- With each proofreading pass, read the e-mail message as opposed to merely skimming.
- If the e-mail message is important, have others proofread it also.

Contrary to popular belief, businesspeople do pay attention to typos, no matter what the medium. Typos and grammatical errors undermine your credibility and the credibility of your e-mail message, and they subject the message to misinterpretation. Sloppy writing shows a lack of respect for your reader. Remember that some decision makers go out of their way to catch spelling or grammatical errors in business documents. Catching careless coworkers' errors in office e-mail is a common pastime in many organizations.[54] To avoid being the joke of the day, proofread. Take the following example:

"If emale is writon with speeling mestakes and gramitckal errors, you mite git the meening, however, the messige is not as affective, or smoothly redable."

After proofreading, always ask yourself, Would I want to see this message in a *New York Times* cover story or taped to the office refrigerator? If not, do not send it.

Now let's look at a poorly written, persuasive e-mail message (Figure 6-2). The message situation is based on a request to an individual to be the keynote speaker at the annual conference of the Association for Business Communication. This should be a relatively easy message to write. However, the poorly written sample below reminds us that, when we are careless, we can easily weaken our chances of meeting our objective!

FIGURE 6–2: PERSUASIVE E-MAIL MESSAGE (POORLY-WRITTEN VERSION)

Subject: Keynote Speaker Request

What a beautiful day! Spring is oficially here, and we can finally put away our winter clothes. And, since you are likely in a good frame of mind, it is a good time to ask a favor of you.

The 85th Annual International Conference of the Association for Business Communication will be held in Providence, Rhode Island this coming October 2-5. The theme of the conference focuses on communicating on social media for business purposes. Your name was mentioned as a potential KEYNOTE SPEAKER! We assumed you would like the added publicity. So, how about it? Will you speak at the conference on October 2? We will pick up your travel expenses and put you up in a decent hotel relatively-near the conference site!

Contact us. Have a nice day!

Before reading further, take a few minutes to identify the weaknesses in the poorly written e-mail message above.

Now, let's look at some of some of letter's weaknesses.

- Spelling error: should be "officially" not "oficially" in line one of the message.
- Subject line error: while clear, it signals the request too early
- Strategy error: did not stay on topic in opening paragraph.

- Strategy error: request was strongly hinted at in the first paragraph (". . . ask a favor of you").
- Strategy error: desire was not built adequately before stating request.
- Strategy error: little was done in the way of integrating appeals to build reader desire.
- Netiquette error: the words "keynote speaker" should not be in all caps.
- Netiquette error: overuse of the exclamation point weakens its emphasis.
- Clarity problem: basic details were missing (e.g., location, time of day or evening, length of talk, honorarium, flight details, ground transportation details, meal arrangements, hotel location, etc.).
- The writer's name was not included.

Now, let's look at an improved version of the same e-mail message (Figure 6-3).

FIGURE 6–3: PERSUASIVE E-MAIL MESSAGE (IMPROVED VERSION)

Subject: Your Social Media Expertise Has Come To Our Attention

Your book, *The Social Media Revolution*, is drawing many favorable comments from business managers. Thank you for making such a fine contribution and, in turn, helping so many in the business place keep up to date with social media.

The Association for Business Communication will hold its annual international conference in Providence, Rhode Island on October 2–5. Several of the 600 members currently enrolled for the convention have expressed an interest in meeting you and hearing your thoughts on how to communicate effectively on social media. Those of us on the association's board concur with our members. With this in mind, we are extending to you an invitation to give the keynote speech at the Thursday evening gala dinner from 7–7:30 p.m. on October 2. There, we would like you to share your thoughts regarding how to communicate effectively in businesses on social media. We are prepared to offer you $5,000 honorarium as well as cover your travel, food, and lodging expenses.

We sincerely hope you will accept our invitation. Please contact me with your decision by April 20 at (240) 420-7575 or at rgreer005@gmail.com. We look forward to having you join us in Rhode Island this fall; a time when the weather is pleasant and nature provides added beauty as the leaves change colors.

Ronald Greer, President
Association for Business Communication

Now, take a few minutes to identify the strengths in this improved version of the e-mail message.

- Subject line: on topic and grabs reader's attention without hinting at the request.
- Strategy compliance: the opening paragraph gains attention via complimentary, reader-centered comments.
- Strategy compliance: the opening paragraph is on topic.

- Strategy compliance: the opening paragraph has a friendly tone.
- Strategy compliance: clear, strong desire was built prior to making the request (e.g., *favorable comments, fine contribution, members interested in meeting you*).
- Strategy compliance: request was clearly stated.
- Strategy compliance: made it easy for the reader to respond by giving contact information in the closing paragraph.
- Strategy compliance: the closing paragraph contained forward-looking talk.
- Strategy compliance: the closing paragraph had a positive tone.
- Strategy compliance: building desire continued through the closing paragraph (e.g., *honorarium, Rhode Island is beautiful in early October*).
- Netiquette compliance: no shouting (words in all caps).
- Netiquette compliance: free of abbreviations and emoticons.
- Spelling compliance: no misspelled words.
- Grammar compliance: free of mechanical errors.
- Clarity compliance: message is clear.

OBSERVING E-MAIL NETIQUETTE

We are all encouraged to follow the rules of netiquette (electronic etiquette) when developing and sending e-mail messages. **Netiquette** refers to etiquette rules governing electronic content and use. Netiquette rules apply to all electronic communications—blogs, social media, e-mail, text messages, etc.—business or personal.[55] These rules of polite behavior have sprung up alongside the etiquette that governs our off-line behavior and have quickly become a universally understood behavioral standard that transcends cultures, businesses, and geographical boundaries.[56]

Avoid Flaming Avoid publicly criticizing people in e-mail or discussion groups using inappropriate language. An e-mail **flame** is a hostile, blunt, rude, insensitive, or obscene e-mail. Flames are immediate, heated reactions and have no place in a business environment. If you are upset or angry, cool down and rewrite your hastily written, angry message before it damages you and your organization.[57] Remember that any e-mail you send—whether strictly business, gossip, complaints, or personal issues—could wind up in your boss's inbox.

netiquette
Guidelines for acceptable behavior when using electronic communication via e-mail, instant messaging, text messaging, chat rooms, and discussion forums.

flame
A hostile, blunt, rude, insensitive, or obscene e-mail.

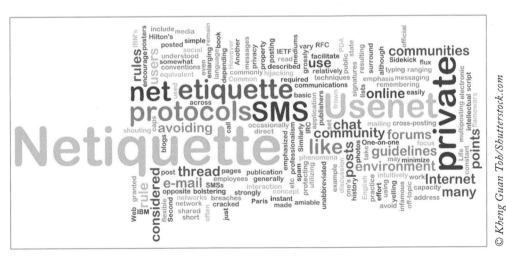

© Kheng Guan Toh/Shutterstock.com

Avoid Shouting   **Shouting** is using all CAPS in your message. An e-mail with the line THE MEETING WILL BEGIN AT 3PM will be interpreted as demanding and obnoxious. Conversely, do not write in all lowercase letters. Stick to standard capitalization in e-mail.

Avoid Spamming   **Spamming** refers to posting junk or unsolicited e-mail posts to a large number of e-mail addresses.

Avoid Acronyms and Abbreviations in E-mail   Do not use acronyms and abbreviations unless you are e-mailing good friends. If you do use them, always explain what they mean. It seems that with increasing volumes of e-mail coming across computer screens daily, the substance of each communication drops, so that the average e-mail message now looks something like this: "OMG did u c K's latest x LOL!!!!!!!!!!" or "I'm on my way. I'll be there soon," has now degenerated to "im on my way!!!!!!!!! Ill be thr son!!!!!"[58] Remember that e-mail not only reflects your level of professionalism, but also lives on in backups that could come back to haunt you.

Watch What You Forward   Forward is perhaps the most dangerous command on your e-mail program, second only to Reply All. While forwarding is a time-saving way to share information, used without thinking, it can turn into an ECK. Think twice before forwarding e-mail. Although forwarding is sometimes necessary for business reasons, most people do it more often than they need to.[59] For example, refrain from passing on chain letters, jokes, rumors, and wacky stories unless you know your recipient shares your love of this Internet flotsam and jetsam.[60] Many e-mail users resent having jokes and stories fill their inboxes. Respect your reader's time and ask before you forward.

Do not forward all or parts of messages without the consent of the sender as well as the intended recipient. Remember that anything a person writes is copyrighted the minute the author writes it, whether it is an article from the *Wall Street Journal* or the musings of your best friend and coworker.[61] Would you send a photocopy of a handwritten letter to someone else? Phillip Zimmermann, creator of Pretty Good Privacy encryption, says the same thought and respect should go into forwarding e-mails.[62]

Ask Before You Send an Attachment   Some organizations prohibit e-mail attachments due to hidden viruses. Before you send an attachment, ask if the reader would prefer receiving the material as an attachment or in the text of the message.[63] In addition, do not simply send an attachment without explaining what it is in the body of the e-mail. "See attached" or a blank e-mail with an attachment raises suspicions that it might be a virus. In such a situation, the recipient will most likely delete the message without opening the attachment.

If You Need an Immediate Response or Action to Your E-mail, Use the "Receipt Notification" Option   *Receipt notification* lets you know when the reader opens the message. However, some readers resent the use of receipts, saying that receipts imply a lack of trust on the sender's part. Your better option might be to phone the recipient, letting them know that a pressing e-mail is on its way and that you would appreciate a quick response.[64]

FIGURE 6-4: INTERNATIONAL E-MAIL NETIQUETTE

- Before you begin writing, determine your reader's needs. You may have to translate your message into your reader's language.
- Be careful with dates and times. Most Europeans would interpret 3/5/17 as May 3, 2017 (with the month appearing in the middle), rather than March 5, 2017. The Japanese, in contrast, sometimes use a year/month/day format. To avoid misunderstanding, write out the name of the month as in March 5, 2017 or 5 March 2017.
- Most countries use a 24-hour system, so be sure to use that time format when setting up videoconferences, conference calls, and IM meetings: "The conference call will begin at 13:00 on 3 March 2017."
- Since most countries use more formal written communications than the United States does, be formal when you e-mail internationally. Address people by their surnames and titles, and use a formal tone throughout your message. To help you sort out titles used in different countries, like *"Monsieur"* or *"Madame"* or *"Herr,"* check a reference work, like Peter Post and Peggy Post's *The Etiquette Advantage in Business.*[70]
- Use specific language and avoid acronyms, abbreviations, business or technical jargon, and humor. They do not translate well.
- Before using monetary denominations, state the currency (e.g., US$10,000).
- Give country codes for phone numbers. The U.S. country code is "1 (e.g., 001-608-123-4567)."
- Use generic names rather than brand names (e.g., photocopy rather than Xerox).
- Be specific when you mention geographical locations: Use New York rather than East Coast.
- When indicating time, be sure to indicate which time zone you mean. For example, "I'll call you at 6 p.m." could mean your time or theirs.

Source: Adapted from Samantha Miller, E-mail Etiquette *(New York: Warner Books, 2001) and Nancy Flynn,* The ePolicy Handbook *(New York: American Management Association, 2001).*

If You Want Your Reply to Go Only to the Sender, Hit "Reply," Not "Reply All." If you hit *"Reply All,"* your message will go to all the recipients on the list. Getting messages not meant for them irritates many listserv members. They might send you a flame for this netiquette breach e-mail. If you want your reply to go only to the sender, type in that person's address. Be considerate of people's privacy.

Only CC People Who Need to Read the E-mail Many managers and executives complain about being copied on messages they do not have to read. Unless your boss has requested it or it is standard practice for your workgroup, keep message CC's to a minimum.

Beware of the blind copy (BCC). BCCing means you can sneak a copy of a message to someone without the main recipient knowing, since the BCC'ed person does not appear in the main recipient's header. You have no assurance that the person BCC'ed will keep the message "secret."[65]

Before E-mailing Over Your Boss's Head to Upper Management, Know What Is Customary in Your Office In most cases, your boss wants to be kept in the loop when you are e-mailing up the chain of command, so let him or her know about ideas, requests, or questions that you plan to send to upper management. Tell your boss before you e-mail up the command chain, rather than by CCing him or her.[66]

Do Not Use Company E-mail to Circulate Personal Requests Instead, use bulletin boards or a Web message board to post personal requests.[67]

International E-mails Pose Language, Culture, Time Challenges Before writing and sending an e-mail message internationally, think about your reader's communication needs.

SUMMARY: SECTION 2— E-MAIL

- The popularity of e-mail in the business community is extensive and growing worldwide.
- When deciding whether to send an e-mail, consider how formal or informal the situation is and your need for speed, mass distribution, and privacy.
- Know the tips on how to manage high volumes of e-mail to avoid getting overwhelmed.
- Employers are developing e-policies to protect themselves from lawsuits. Know your company's e-policies and why they were designed.
- Become familiar with your organization's e-mail culture before you send e-mails.
- Know how to write effective e-mails to communicate your thoughts clearly and to avoid misunderstandings. Rather than drafting and immediately sending a message, take time to plan, draft, and revise before you send it via e-mail.
- Abide by the rules of e-mail netiquette to avoid offending recipients and to support message clarity.
- Before you send messages to international business partners, familiarize yourself with the rules of international e-mail netiquette.

INSTANT MESSAGING

instant messaging (IM)
Exchanging text messages in real time between two or more people logged into a particular instant messaging service.

Instant messaging (IM) involves exchanging text messages in real time between two or more people who are logged into a particular instant messaging service.[68] The two defining characteristics of IM, presence awareness and near real-time operation, make it a compelling alternative to phone calls and e-mail. It has been reported that 60 percent of business phone calls never reach their intended recipients.[71] This obvious deficiency in phone calls helps to explain the growth of instant messaging in businesses.

MAJOR BENEFITS OF IMS IN BUSINESS

Combining the real-time benefits of using the phone with the convenience of e-mail, IM offers a variety of advantages to the corporate communicator.[69] IM's popularity as a business communication tool can be explained by its quickness, flexibility, and versatility.

IM Is Quick A sender can detect whether a user is online, send an IM, and institute a back-and-forth conversation, virtually, in real time.[70] Unlike e-mail that can remain unanswered in someone's overloaded inbox for days, IM can detect someone's presence online, which is good for an for immediate response. IM also eliminates long e-mail threads.[71]

IM Is Flexible Many people can be in on the same conversation. In that way, work groups can use it to get tasks done quickly.

Along with making team communication easier, IM allows users to have more than one message thread going at a time. IMs are so easy to handle that you can be on the phone and still respond to them. In terms of security, with commercial-grade IM software, users have the option of archiving IMs for legal or management reasons or purging them to avoid being susceptible to court-ordered discovery processes.[72]

IM Is Versatile IM facilitates communication among geographically distributed workgroups; it improves communication with business partners and suppliers; it quickens response time between customer service and support departments and customers; and it facilitates cross–business unit communication.[73] Users can even send files via most IM applications when a report, contract, or invoice needs to be quickly reviewed or approved.[74] As a collaborative tool, IM easily enables team members to meet in a dynamic space, share files, set up whiteboards, and discuss changes. The space disappears when users are finished. Collaboration is much easier than in the pre-IM days.[75]

The buddy list, an IM staple first developed by AOL, has become "*presence management*" in business contexts, where detecting who is online to answer a question or to buy a product in real time means increased productivity and profits.[76] **Presence management** refers to being able to determine if others are online and available. Companies like AT&T, IBM, Boeing, the U.S. Army and Navy, the National Cancer Institute, and a host of other high-tech, financial, and retail companies use IM to assemble virtual teams from locations around the world. IMs allow employees to communicate with coworkers, clients, customers, and other business contacts from their virtual offices.[77] Retailers like Landsend.com and 1-800-flowers.com use IM to answer customer questions when they arise. It is faster than e-mail and cheaper because customer reps can reply more quickly.[78] HP, Gateway, and Mail Boxes Etc. also use chat in their sales and service.

presence management Being able to determine if others are online and available.

A good example of a business that thrives virtually by using IM is the CPA firm of Carolyn Sechler. She heads a 14-member virtual office workforce that serves 300 clients, primarily nonprofit organizations and technology entrepreneurs, in several states and countries.[79] From her home office, Sechler works with CPAs from Alabama to British Columbia. She meets with her core team of four every two weeks using her IM service, ICQ. She believes in making people feel comfortable: "At 9 a.m. we all tune in—and we can archive the chats. What's the point of making people go anywhere when they can be comfortable?"

IM is the tool that makes her virtual business possible, a business that has grown 10–15 percent every year. Sechler says that she has used ICQ since its inception. She keeps a "buddy list" of team members up and running on her computer so that they can communicate throughout the day. She can exchange quick messages or files with any of them by IM—a faster service than e-mail—and they can have "impromptu conversations" that bring together four, five, or six members into one chat area. According to Sechler, being accessible online strengthens ties with clients, circumvents crises, and lets the firm find out early about new consulting opportunities.[80]

Despite IM's benefits in the business place, some companies do not allow employees to install IM services because they believe non-work IMs will distract employees from their work. Non-work IM interruptions can be avoided by using the privacy functions on your IM service or by having two IM services—one for work and the other for family and friends.

HOW TO USE IM

Instant messaging works this way: A small piece of client software is loaded onto a PC, smartphone, or other device and maintains a constant connection to a central hosting service. Anyone who is logged onto the service is flagged as online. The software includes a "buddy list" that enables the user to store the nicknames (everyone has a nickname on IM) of clients, coworkers, and other business contacts. When a buddy is online, the name or icon lights up. The user clicks on the icon to send the buddy an IM or a file attachment.[81] After that, messages fly back and forth, all in the same window that scrolls up as the conversation continues. Unlike e-mail, which can take time to reach its destination, IMs reach their destination instantly even if the person is continents away.

You can also control when others can send you a message. Privacy options include saying that you are away at lunch and that you don't want to be bothered. You can even block the fact that you are online.

IM is great for those messages that are too brief to pick up the phone or too urgent to try to play phone tag. In many cases, IM has replaced phone use for short transactions.[82] Since it does not require your full attention, you can even talk on the phone while messaging other people.

Another useful feature allows you to invite several people into the same session. Unless you need the archiving function to save the message, these messages usually disappear when you log off.

© Iculig/Shutterstock.com

FIGURE 6–5: INSTANT MESSAGING BENEFITS THE HEARING IMPAIRED

Instant messaging as well as e-mail, texting, and social media have greatly benefited people with hearing impairments within and outside of the workplace. According to Grant W. Laird Jr., founder, owner, and CEO of the Dallas-based Deaf Network, "Instant messaging has become one of the primary means of communication among members of the deaf community as well as between the deaf and hearing population."[17] Instant messaging is viewed by many in the deaf community as having opened up the lines of communication and leveled the playing field.[18] For additional information, visit these deaf resource websites: www.deafnetwork.com and http://deafcelebration.org/.

WRITING EFFECTIVE INSTANT MESSAGES

Businesspeople typically expect that instant messages be relatively short. With this in mind, be careful not to cause confusion and frustration by taking shortcuts that are ill advised. For example, abbreviations, whether standard or created on the fly, should not be included in business instant messages. Furthermore, a careless writing style (e.g., poor grammar, misspelled words) can leave message recipients questioning your level of professionalism and your credibility. With business instant messages, a careless writing style can easily result in message recipients judging writers' level of professionalism and credibility. In addition, company image is also threatened by poorly written text messages for similar reasons. Here's a list of suggestions to keep in mind when writing business instant messages.

- Write short instant messages. This is what IM recipients expect.
- Start your message with a greeting (e.g., Hello, Hi) and mention your recipient's name.
- Do not include confidential information that you don't want hacked.
- Write clear messages, which means, in part, including enough detail to get the job done.
- Use a polite, friendly tone.
- Adhere to grammar rules.
- Adhere to punctuation rules.
- Adhere to number usage rules.
- Do not type in all caps whether it is a single word or an entire sentence. Doing so looks unprofessional.
- Avoid shorthand measures (e.g., LOL, GR8) because they are typically perceived as being unprofessional and can easily contribute to misunderstandings.
- Avoid acronyms unless you know your reader is familiar with those you use.
- Avoid using technical jargon unless you know your reader is familiar with it.
- Avoid using slang which can easily lead to misunderstandings.
- Don't use abbreviations because they often cause confusion and misunderstandings.
- Don't use emoticons because they are considered to be unprofessional in business writing.

- Avoid misspellings because they speak to a careless, unprofessional writing style.
- Use humor cautiously. If you expect it can be misinterpreted, don't include it.
- Indicate that you are signing off (e.g., Signing off now.).
- Include your name at the end of instant messages.
- Edit, revise, and proofread your instant messages before sending them.

INSTANT MESSAGING NETIQUETTE

You are encouraged to adhere to the following netiquette rules when developing and transmitting business instant messages.

- If someone is marked as unavailable or if you have received an away message from that person, refrain from messaging until they return. Although you may be in a chatty mood, a coworker or family member may be busy and unable to respond promptly. If the recipient uses the same IM service for work and personal messages, the person cannot shut it down since it is a work tool, like the phone. If they are at work and available, be courteous and ask them if they have time to chat, "Got a minute?" If they do not, do not be offended. Ask them to message you when they are free. If you are on the receiving end, don't be afraid to let people know you are busy. Learn to say "no" or ask them to message back later.[83]
- When responding to someone's message, it is a good idea to type your answer, send it, and then wait for the recipient's reply before sending another message. That way, things will not get confusing because you each respond to one idea at a time.
- Know when to stop. Do not let a thread go on and on. A simple "got to go" or "bye" should be sufficient to end the conversation.
- Do not use IMs for long messages. Betsy Waldinger, vice president at Chicago-based OptionsXpress Inc., spends a lot of her day working on an online customer service chat system. She recommends either sending short messages or breaking up long ones over many screens. Typing long messages keeps the person at the other end waiting while you type. IM should not replace e-mail. Use IM for quick-hit messages that require fast responses. Use e-mail for longer discussions.[84]
- If you work in an office where IM is part of the culture, send a message before you drop in on someone. This gives the other person a chance to say whether the visit would be convenient.
- Don't share bad news in an IM.
- Be courteous.
- Log off IM when you are not using it. Otherwise, you may come back to find messages waiting and senders wondering why you are ignoring them.
- Do not hide online. Some managers use the ability to be invisible online as a way to watch employees. This is a quick way to discourage workers from using IM. Being on or off IM is not a good way to determine whether your remote employees are working. Be courteous, and if you are on, be visible. Use the service busy icons, like "Do Not Disturb" or "Busy" to indicate your availability.[85]
- Use two carriage returns to indicate that you are done and the other person may start typing.[86]
- Remember that chat is an interruption to the other person. Use it only when appropriate.

- Be careful if you have more than one chat session going at once. This can be dangerous unless you are paying attention.
- Like e-mail, set up different accounts for family and friends and for work-related IMs.

Instant messaging is a popular communication tool as was previously mentioned. To fully realize its benefits and our purposes for instant messaging, however, you are encouraged to practice the above-mentioned instant message writing suggestions and adhere to the above-mentioned instant message netiquette rules.

Instant Messaging Netiquette
http://www.tafinn.com/andyfinn-us/Writing/Technology/netiquette-im.htm

---

SUMMARY: SECTION 3— INSTANT MESSAGING

- Major benefits of instant messaging include its quickness, flexibility, and versatility.
- IM is a viable alternative to phone calls. It cuts costs and keeps people in touch no matter where they are. IM is great for those messages that are too brief to pick up the phone or too urgent to try to play phone tag.
- When deciding whether to IM, consider how formal or informal the situation is and your need for speed, convenience, and privacy.
- Know how to write effective IM messages so as to communicate your thoughts clearly and to avoid misunderstandings.
- Abide by the rules of instant messaging netiquette to avoid offending recipients and to support message clarity.

TEXTING

A **text message** is a short message that is sent electronically to a cell phone or other device.[87] Text messaging has gained wide popularity in the United States and elsewhere since its inception. The first text message (Merry Christmas) was sent on December 3, 1992. Although usually sent from one mobile phone to another, text messaging is often integrated into IM software so that messages can be sent via an IM, but received on a mobile phone. Text messages are no longer limited to text. Video clips and pictures, which are often captured with a mobile phone, are easily integrated into these messages.

text message
A short message that is sent electronically to a cell phone or other device.

© Fine Art/Shutterstock.com

BUSINESS USES OF TEXTING

Text messaging is popular in the U.S. business community for many reasons. First of all, text messages are relatively inexpensive compared to phone messages. While lengthy and more-involved messages do not lend themselves to text messaging, texting is a practical option for shorter and less-involved messages. Another advantage of texting is its ability to communicate in real time. When sending e-mail messages and instant messages, if the recipient is away from his or her computer or his cell phone lacks Internet capability, they cannot be reached. Generally speaking, text messaging offers mobility as well as e-mail functions such as texting several people simultaneously. Text messaging is used extensively in industries, such as real estate, construction, and transportation. Each of these industries has people working in the field who are not connected to a computer all the time. They are able to receive alerts, updates, and quick messages throughout the day without having to rack up phone bills.

© Mattz90/Shutterstock.com

FIGURE 6-6: TEXTING WHILE DRIVING, WALKING, AND JOGGING

As you know, today's mobile communication technologies and WiFi availability make it possible for drivers to send and receive text messages, as well as participate in phone conversations while operating vehicles ranging from cars, motorcycles, and buses to trains, planes, and helicopters. Unfortunately, there are numerous documented cases of accidents resulting in injuries and fatalities tied directly to such ill-advised use of mobile communication technologies. While some of these drivers lived to tell their side of the story in court, others were not so lucky. Texting and placing phone calls while driving defies both logic and responsible citizenship. It is basically selfish, narcissistic behavior. However, this has not stopped some drivers from taking chances with their fate as well as the fate of others! In response, some countries, as well as several U.S. municipalities and states, are considering or have passed laws making it illegal for drivers to text and/or participate in phone conversations while driving. The U.S. government considers such measures periodically, but has yet to pass such laws.

Drivers in some countries have made great headway on this issue aside from related laws. For example, in the United Kingdom texting while driving is socially unacceptable behavior. In essence, UK citizens are policing themselves on this matter. There appears to be a similar trend in Los Angeles. These are positive signs.

Hopefully you are not risking your safety and the safety of others by practicing such dangerous behaviors. And hopefully the defensive driver in you is constantly on the lookout for other drivers who are not as considerate.

© karen roach/Shutterstock.com

While driving recently, I observed an additional texting-related distraction. It was a humorous, yet serious bumper sticker. It read, "Honk If You Love Jesus. Text While Driving If You Want To Meet Him!" No matter how tasteless you might find this bumper sticker, it is one more reminder to those who read it to be responsible, careful drivers.

Then, there are the potential dangers associated with texting while walking and jogging. The most serious of these is inadvertently stepping out or jogging out onto a street or road into the path of oncoming traffic, stepping through an uncovered manhole, or walking into a light post, tree, or other immobile object. Do you text while walking? If so, you are a *text walker* which is the term used for people who text while walking.

© mimagephotography/Shutterstock.com

Furthermore, the term *text walking* has entered our vocabularies. It refers to the act of texting while walking which apparently is commonplace enough in Belgium that they are adding text walking lanes to their sidewalks. There is also a term that describes specific walking differences between text walkers and other walkers. The term is *text walking gate*, and it reminds us that text walkers typically walk 25 percent more slowly than other walkers, take smaller steps, and raise their feet higher at curbs. The prevailing belief is that text walkers subconsciously take these measures to form a safety bubble around them which frankly won't help a bit if they don't look up before crossing streets and roads!

In the United States the most common business use of text messaging is to communicate with consumers through retail or reality TV shows. Text message marketing has a foreseeable future, whether it be for advertisements or product notifications. Once purchases are made, buyers can then be easily notified of order confirmations, shipping, back orders, etc., through text messages.

WRITING EFFECTIVE TEXT MESSAGES

Writing Great Text Messages to Customers
http://www.onereach.com/blog/6-strategies-for-writing-great-text-messages-to-customers/

In their haste to send short text messages, some writers develop unclear messages that reflect poor writing habits. While using a careless writing style when texting family and friends is typically acceptable, using such a writing style in business text messages is strongly discouraged. With business text messages, a careless writing style can easily result in message recipients judging writers' level of professionalism and credibility. Furthermore, company image is also threatened by poorly written text messages for similar reasons. Here's a list of suggestions to keep in mind when writing business text messages.

- Ask if it is a good time for you and your recipient to have a text chat.
- Write short text messages. This is the standard expectation.
- Do not include confidential information that you don't want hacked.
- Start your message with a greeting (e.g., Good morning) and mention your recipient's name.
- Write clear messages, which means, in part, including enough detail to get the job done.
- Use a polite, friendly tone.
- Adhere to grammar rules.
- Adhere to punctuation rules.
- Adhere to number usage rules.
- Do not type in all caps whether it is a single word or an entire sentence. Doing so looks unprofessional.
- Avoid textese (e.g, LOL, BRB, OMW, W8, CID, GR8) because it is considered unprofessional and can easily contribute to misunderstandings. Recently I noticed a drink coaster in a local restaurant. It had a reminder printed on it that applies to using textese in text messages. It read, "2 much txting mks u 1 bad splr." What an insightful message!
- Avoid acronyms unless you know that your reader is familiar with those you use.
- Avoid using technical jargon unless you know your reader is familiar with it.
- Avoid using slang which can easily lead to misunderstandings.
- Don't use abbreviations because they often cause confusion and misunderstandings.
- Don't use emoticons because they are considered to be unprofessional in business writing.

- Avoid misspellings because they speak to a careless, unprofessional writing style.
- Use humor cautiously. If you expect it can be misinterpreted, don't include it.
- Include your name at the end of text messages.
- Edit, revise, and proofread your text messages before sending them.

TEXTING NETIQUETTE

You are encouraged to adhere to the following netiquette rules when developing and transmitting business text messages.

- Make sure your communication partner is receptive to texting. While millennials are very receptive to texting, that doesn't mean everyone else is. Some people prefer e-mail, others prefer phone conversations. You get the point!
- Don't send text messages regarding important, complex, and controversial business situations and matters. These should be dealt with using more robust, formal communication forms such as face-to-face conversations and videoconferences.
- Text at a time that is reasonable. For example, don't send early-morning (e.g., 6 a.m.) text messages to individuals who are not morning people. And, be sensitive to time differences when texting international business contacts.
- Do not discuss legal matters via text messages.
- Be courteous.
- If you desire an immediate response, consider placing a phone call or sending an instant message rather than texting. While most people respond to text messages, they don't always do so immediately.
- Don't be too quick to get upset with an individual who doesn't respond to your text message. They may have simply overlooked your text message in the midst of juggling all of their responsibilities.
- Don't be a texting nag by resending a text message when you don't feel a person has responded as quickly as you wanted them to respond. Call them instead.
- Do not send bad news via text messages. Sharing bad news warrants a less-casual communication medium such as a face-to-face conversation.
- Don't text in inappropriate settings such as during training sessions, meetings, and presentations. Doing so shows a high degree of disrespect for trainers, fellow meeting participants, and speakers.
- Excessive texting while out to lunch with fellow employees is discouraged.
- Don't text while driving. Doing so is extremely dangerous and inconsiderate of others' safety.
- Before you send a text message, make sure your autocorrect feature has not distorted your message.[88 & 89]

Text messaging certainly has its benefits as mentioned previously and offers businesses a viable communication tool. To fully realize its benefits and our purposes for texting, you are encouraged to practice the above-mentioned text message writing suggestions and adhere to the above-mentioned text message netiquette rules.

WEBSITES

website
A set of interconnected Web pages starting with a homepage.

A **website** is a set of interconnected Web pages that build from a homepage. Websites are commonplace in today's businesses and are used predominately for sharing information, advertising products and services, online retailing, and tracking visitor demographics. *Amazon* and *L.L. Bean* are good examples of online retailing businesses. Whether it is *Amazon, L.L. Bean,* or other company websites, visual features such as photos and videos are powerful tools for attracting customers much like high-quality, color photos are in hardcopy catalogues. Furthermore, many websites also offer audio features which certainly provide additional marketing tools.

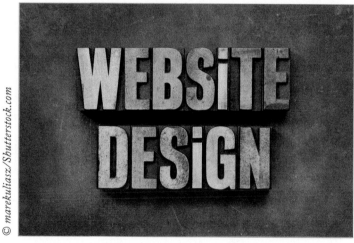

© marekuliasz/Shutterstock.com

WEBSITE WRITING SUGGESTIONS

What follows are some suggestions to keep in mind when developing written materials for business websites.

- **Reduce the Clutter.** Simple, easy-to-navigate websites are typically appreciated, whereas cluttered, hard-to-navigate websites can quickly frustrate potential customers and, in turn, chase them and their consumer dollars to competitors' websites, products, and services.

- **Most People Who Browse the Internet Skim.** This means they do not read content in its entirety. Nor are they big on scrolling. What does this mean to those who write Web content? Write concise, skimmable text. Grab your readers' attention quickly. Make your main points on the first screen. If you don't, your reader will likely be off to one of the millions of other sites, just clicks away.
- **Write Concisely.** Web readers do not want to wade through excess verbiage, so write concisely. However, do not do so at the expense of clarity. Include the level of detail needed to achieve this goal also.
- **Write with Design in Mind.** Include keywords, subheads, bulleted lists, and short paragraphs. Use clear, informational headlines. Then provide objective, supporting details. Experts say that your Web page is too text heavy if you can place your open palm over a block of text on your website without touching a graphic image.
- **Write Comprehensively.** While it seems like a contradiction, Web writing also demands comprehensiveness. Web browsers will stay around if they like what they see.
- **Use Links to Interior Pages Where You Can Tell the Rest of Your Story.** Use links to keep them hooked. However, keep links to a minimum and always provide a link back to your home page.
- **Avoid Puffed, Exaggerated "Marketese" and Stuffy, Bureaucratic Prose.** Write in a conversational voice, do not talk down to Web readers, and do not exaggerate your product or service.
- **Use the Web's Interactivity.** Build your website so your readers can react to your site through e-mail feedback or discussion boards, and use drawings, graphics, animation, audio, or video where they enhance your words.

Writing Great Business Website Content
http://www.openvine.com/small-business-internet-blog/9-tips-for-writing-great-business-website-content

Your website must serve the business community's needs. Knowing how to write effective website content will serve you well in this environment.

SUMMARY: SECTION 5— WEBSITES

- Websites are commonplace in today's businesses.
- Company websites are used predominately for sharing information, advertising products and services, and online retailing.
- The quality and ease of use of company websites contributes greatly to their effectiveness.
- Know how to develop effective websites and write effective website content.

CHOOSING THE RIGHT COMMUNICATION MEDIUM WHEN SO MANY ELECTRONIC WRITING CHOICES ARE AVAILABLE

Imagine you are a businessperson who wants to communicate with existing and/or potential customers or clients. Given the many electronic and non-electronic options available to you, how do you select the right medium? Do you choose e-mail, IM, text messaging, or a website? Or, do you post your message on a social media site such as LinkedIn or Facebook? Do you place a phone call instead or have a face-to-face meeting? Or, do you saturate the market, so to speak, by transmitting your message over digital media, in the hopes that

FIGURE 6–7: POTENTIAL E-WRITING HEALTH THREATS

Excessive electronic writing can potentially cause physical damage. This is not to say that electronic writing technologies are bad or that they should not be used. However, we are reminded that misuse of them can be most serious. Here are three examples of potential health threats for your consideration.

- **Carpal tunnel syndrome.** This is repetitive motion nerve damage that often occurs in individuals' thumbs and wrists as a result of too-frequent keyboarding (e.g., texting) on small smartphone, tablet, and notebook keypads.
- **Chronic Neck and Shoulder Pain.** A form of this has been found to result from excessive keyboarding on electronic tablets during which time our fingers and wrists are hovering above the keypad. It appears that our inability to rest our wrists while keyboarding is the culprit.
- **Vision Problems.** Viewing small screens (e.g., smartphones, tablets, netbooks, etc.) too frequently invite vision problems. Common sense reminds us that straining our eyes frequently while viewing small screens will ultimately take its toll. In addition, there has been an increase in the number of people experiencing detached retinas due to viewing small screens frequently in ill-lighted settings. There is an irony in the detached retinas/digital small screens threat in that the retina acts like an electronic image sensor in a digital camera, converting optical images into electrical signals.

Hopefully you are not going for the potential physical threats trifecta described above. Nerve damage, chronic neck and shoulder pain, and vision problems are not easily and inexpensively repaired. It's worth thinking about!

current and potential customers and clients will spot you? With so many choices, making the right media choice can certainly be overwhelming!

Jim Blasingame, one of the world's foremost experts on small business and entrepreneurship, offers some practical advice to help you make good media choices. He encourages businesspeople to use the following two approaches when making communication media choices: (1) ask yourself which communication medium best suits the circumstance and (2) ask your customers and clients which communication medium they prefer.[90] Regarding Blasingame's second approach, remind yourself that not all of your clients or customers will share your interest in and your ability to use each electronic communication tool you are comfortable using. Nor do they all have access to the technology you prefer to use. For example, many people around the globe lack access to the Internet by circumstance or choice, including some in the United States. Blasingame's advice mirrors some of the basic communication suggestions presented earlier in the book. In chapter 1 you were urged to reflect on the circumstances before selecting a medium. For example, messages about routine matters can typically be communicated effectively via e-mail, while messages involving important and/or controversial matters are best communicated face-to-face. Furthermore, you learned earlier that the better you know your communication partner, the more likely you are to achieve effective communication.

SUMMARY: SECTION 6— CHOOSING THE RIGHT COMMUNICATION MEDIUM

- Making the right communication medium decision is most challenging due to all the options available today.
- In part, making the right communication medium decision should be based on the desired level of informality or formality. For example, e-mail and text messages are considered to be informal media.
- In part, making the right communication decision should be based on the importance of the message or document. For example, important matters lend themselves best to face-to-face conversations and videoconferences, as opposed to e-mail messages, instant messages, and text messages.
- Businesspeople are encouraged to use the following two approaches when making communication media choices: (1) ask yourself which communication medium best suits the circumstance and (2) ask your customers and clients which communication medium they prefer.

Notes

1. Wikipedia.
2. Nancy Flynn, *The ePolicy Handbook* (New York: American Management Association, 2001), 1.
3. Flynn, 49.
4. Ibid, 50.
5. Dianna Booher, *E-Writing: 21st Century Tools for Effective Communication* (New York: Pocket Books, 2001), 1.
6. Ibid., 2.
7. Ibid, 12.
8. Samantha Miller, *E-Mail Etiquette* (New York: Warner Books, 2001), 103.
9. Ibid., 105.
10. Ibid., 103.
11. Ibid., 102.
12. Ibid.
13. Flynn, 101.
14. Booher, 13.
15. Webopedia, http://www.webopedia.com/TERM/P/phishing.html
16. Flynn, 89.
17. Leena Rao, "Email: Unloved. Unbreakable," *Fortune,* 5.1.15 (May 1, 2015): 55-56.
18. Daniel Bates, "You've got (more) mail: The average office worker now spends over a quarter of their day dealing with email," July 20, 2012, http://www.dailymail.co.uk/sciencetech/article-2181680/Youve-got-mail-The-average-office-worker-spends-over-a-quarter-of-their-day-dealing-with-email.

19. Author unknown, "Emails expected to rise to 140 a day in 2018," May 4, 2014, http://www.news.com.au/finance/work/emails-expected-to-rise-to-140-a-day-in-2018/story-e6frfm9r122.

20. Rao, 55.

21. Miller, 22; Booher, 33.

22. Miller, 31; Booher, 36.

23. Booher, 41.

24. Flynn, 3.

25. Ibid., 4.

26. Ibid., 7.

27. Ibid.

28. Ibid.

29. Ibid., 50.

30. Ibid.

31. Ibid., 9.

32. Ibid., 81.

33. Ibid., 34.

34. Michael R. Overly, *E-policy: How to Develop Computer, E-policy, and Internet Guidelines to Protect Your Company and its Assets* (New York: American Management Association, 1999), 27.

35. Alan Cohen, "Worker Watchers Want to Know What Your Employees Are Doing Online," *Fortune* (June 1, 2001): 70–81, http://infoweb7.newsbank.com.

36. Valli Baldassano, "Bad Documents Can Kill You," *Across the Board* 38 (September/October 2001): 46–51.

37. Flynn, 54.

38. Ibid., 52.

39. "Some Wall Street Firms Did Not Retain Required E-mails–NYT," (May 7, 2002), http://www.reuters.com.

40. Miller, 94–95.

41. Ibid., 95.

42. Gregory A. Maciag, "E-mail Might Be the Killer Application, but Poorly Managed, It Could Bury You," *National Underwriter* 106 (March 18, 2002): 33–35.

43. Booher, 9.

44. David Angell and Brent Heslop, *The Elements of E-mail Style* (New York: Addison-Wesley, 2000), 18–19.

45. Ibid., 19–20.

46. Ibid., 19.

47. "Promote Corporate Identity Through E-mail," *Business Forms, Labels & Systems 40* (March 20, 2002): 18.

48. Angell and Heslop, 21–22.

49. Ibid., 20.

50. Ibid., 24.

51. Ibid., 15–32.

52. Ibid., 117.

53. Dawn Rosenberg McKay, "E-mail Etiquette," *Online Netiquette Uncensored: Courtesy #3,* http://www.onlinenetiquette.com.

54. Flynn, 146.

55. Nancy Flynn, *The Social Media Handbook: Policies and Best Practices to Effectively Manage Your Organization's Social Media Presence, Posts, and Potential Risks* (San Francisco: Pfeiffer, 2012), 327.

56. Flynn, 97.

57. Ibid.

58. David Spohn, "E-mail Rules of Engagement" (May 18, 2002), http://webworst.about.com.

59. Miller, 43.

60. Ibid.

61. Ibid., 51.

62. Brian Sullivan, "Netiquette," *Computerworld* 36 (March 4, 2002): 48.

63. Flynn, 99.

64. Ibid., 100.

65. Ibid., 99.

66. Ibid.

67. Ibid., 107.

68. PC Magazine Encyclopedia (online).

69. Mandy Andress, "Instant Messaging," *InfoWorld* 24 (January 7, 2002): 36.

70. Suzanne Gaspar, "RUOK w IM?" *Network World* 19 (February 25, 2002): 40.

71. Matt Cain, "META Report: The Future of Instant Messaging," *Instant Messaging Planet* (April 29, 2002).

72. Ibid.

73. Andress, 36.

74. Brad Grimes, "Peer-to-Peer Gets Down to Business," *PC World* 19 (May 2001): 150–154.

75. David LaGesse, "Instant Message Phenom Is, Like, Way Beyond E-mail," *U.S. News & World Report* 130 (March 5, 2001): 54–56.

76. Laura Schneider, "Is There Room in Your Cubicle for Instant Messaging?" *What You Need to Know About*, http://chatting.about.com.

77. Jim Sterne, "People Who Need People," *Inc.* 22 (2000): 131–132.

78. Michael Hayes, "What We Sell Is Between Our Ears," *Journal of Accountancy* 191 (June 2001): 57–63.

79. Ibid.

80. Bradbury, 41.

81. Lagesse, 56.

82. Laura Schneider, "Instant Messaging: Annoyance or Necessity?" *What You Need to Know About*, http://netconf...about.com.

83. Brian Sullivan, "Netiquette," *Computerworld* 36 (March 4, 2002): 48.

84. Jeff Zbar, "The Basics of Instant Messaging Etiquette," *Net.Worker News* at www.nwfusion. com accessed on May 13, 2002.

85. Ibid.

86. "Netiquette Guidelines," http://www.dtcc.edu.

87. Mirriam-Webster Dictionary (online).

88. Jacquelyn Smith & Vivian Giang, "7 Rules Of Texting Etiquette Every Professional Needs To Know," September 18, 2014, http://www.businessinsider.com/texting-etiquette-rules-every-professional-needs-to-know-2013-9.

89. Dana Manciagli, "Texting etiquette: 6 rules to follow while texting at work," January 23, 2015, http://www.9news.com/story/money/business/2015/01/24/texting-etiquette-6-rules-to-follow-when-texting-at-work/22276643/.

90. Jim Blasingame, "High Tech or High Touch: It's Really Not Complicated," *The Wall Street Journal*, October 6, 2009.

PLANNING & DRAFTING BUSINESS DOCUMENTS

7

LEARNING OUTCOMES

After reading this chapter, you should be able to:

1. Explain how academic writing differs from business writing.

2. Discuss the purposes of various types of written media.

3. Describe the three-stage writing process.

4. Discuss techniques that will help you break through writer's block.

5. Discuss ways to achieve good message organization.

6. Specify drafting techniques that will help you adapt your message to your audience.

© *assistant/Shutterstock.com*

BENEFITS OF LEARNING ABOUT PLANNING AND DRAFTING BUSINESS DOCUMENTS

1. Planning or prewriting is an important part of the writing process. The more front-end loading you can do, the easier it is to draft your document.

2. Knowing the written media options and the strengths and weaknesses of each option helps you decide which form is best for your document.

3. Knowing when to and when not to send a document is as important as knowing how to write it.

4. Drafting is an important part of the writing process. Mastering it allows you to write effective business documents.

5. Learning how to write reader-friendly documents is essential to understanding how to gain your audience's attention and acceptance of your message.

6. Learning how to effectively communicate with international audiences enables you to build strong international business alliances.

SELECT KEY TERMS

INTRODUCTION

Business writing stresses audience awareness, political sensitivity, speed, and fluency. Furthermore, the two usual purposes of business writing are to inform and to persuade.

Good business writers typically follow the three-stage writing process—planning, drafting, and revising. Good planning involves audience analysis, determining the appropriate writing medium, and identifying organizational devices. Drafting involves writing the "rough draft" of the message or document.

The intent of this chapter is to provide you with information on how to effectively plan and draft business documents, including how to move past writer's block and how to manage the drafting process in organizations. These goals will be realized through discussions regarding the following topics: how academic writing differs from business writing, stage one of the writing process (planning, defining your purpose, analyzing your audience, organizing your ideas, and choosing the best medium), and stage two of the writing process (drafting, getting started, moving past writer's block, drafting to support your purpose, types of supporting detail, drafting with your audience in mind, creating goodwill, drafting with organization in mind, building paragraphs, and managing the drafting process in organizations). The information pertaining to the above-mentioned writing steps is reinforced by several student website resources including *PowerPoint slides, preview tests, chapter assessment tests, writing mechanics rules and guidelines, YouTube videos, interactive exercises*, and the *interactive glossary.*

HOW ACADEMIC WRITING DIFFERS FROM BUSINESS WRITING

Although both business writing and academic writing depend on complex thinking and writing strategies, business writing differs in many respects from academic writing. While academic writing encourages you to express yourself, business writing stresses purposefulness, audience awareness, speed, concision, and fluency.

Just as the culture of the writing classroom influences the writing produced in that class, the organization's culture influences how you write each document—its appearance, content, purpose, and tone. A company's internal and external e-mail messages, social media posts, text messages, memos, letters, reports, and proposals not only support the organization's business but also communicate the company's philosophy and public image. For these reasons, good business writing demands that its practitioners develop a social awareness of their organizational environment.

Business Writing
http://writing2.
richmond.edu/writing/
wweb/business/started.
html

THE THREE-STAGE WRITING PROCESS

Another difference between academic and business writing pertains to the writing process. The writing process comprises three stages—*planning, drafting*, and *revising*. In the academic classroom, the writing process is just as important, if not more so, than the final document. In the business world, however, the final product is what matters. The process itself is secondary; but is still important in that it drives the final product.

Business Writing Tips for Professionals
https://www.amanet.
org/training/articles/
Business-Writing-Tips-
for-Professionals.aspx

In business settings "writing" often means only the actual phrasing of ideas into words. In many organizations, prewriting or planning activities, such as creating an outline or gathering information, are not considered part of the writing. This narrow view of writing can cause scheduling problems because, as you know, the actual writing time on a particular document involves more than writing; it also involves planning and revision activities before the document is complete. Therefore, writers in organizations need to define their purpose and audience and organize their ideas quickly in order to move onto the **drafting** process.[1]

As a business writer, you must adapt your writing to the demands of your organizational community, developing several composing styles to fit each writing situation. Your ability to produce well-written documents in an organizational setting will depend to a great extent on how effectively you understand and manage the writing process.

STAGE 1 OF THE WRITING PROCESS: PLANNING

Planning involves defining your purpose, analyzing your audience, organizing your ideas, gathering information, outlining, and choosing the best medium. Document clarity and effectiveness depend, in large part, on the thought and effort put forth in this stage.

Prewriting decisions about purpose, audience, and organization vary from being a matter of a few minutes of reflection before writing a routine letter to performing extensive audience analysis, researching, communal brainstorming, note taking, reviewing previously completed documents, and creating extensive outlines before writing a complex proposal. It is important to generate ideas before you start writing. There are several ways to do this, including freewriting, listing, and clustering.[2]

drafting
The first pass at writing a document.

planning
The prewriting activity; typically includes defining your purpose, analyzing your audience, organizing your ideas, and choosing the right medium.

© Gunnar Pippel/Shutterstock.com

Freewriting occurs when the writer notes all the message ideas that flow through his or her mind without lifting the pen from the paper or pausing at the computer. *Listing* is just that—listing! Simply take a few minutes to list everything you want to include. Clustering involves more focus and attention than freewriting and listing. When you generate ideas through clustering, you establish the relationships among the parts of your message.

DEFINING YOUR PURPOSE

Business writing is done for a purpose. Starting to write without knowing your purpose is like starting on a trip without knowing your destination. Writing without a clear purpose is frustrating for you, but it is even more frustrating for your readers who become impatient and less receptive as they try to figure out what you wrote and what you want. Thus, identifying your purpose is the first step in the *planning stage*.

The cornerstone of good organization is a clearly stated purpose, which is your reason for writing. To determine your purpose, ask yourself, What do I want my audience to do or to learn after reading this message? Put yourself in your reader's place. What would you as a reader ask on receiving this document? Do I read it, route it, or skip it? What's in this for me?[3] To help you determine your purpose, fill in a worksheet like the one presented in Figure 7-1.

<table>
<tr><td colspan="2">

FIGURE 7–1: COMMUNICATION PURPOSE WORKSHEET

The purpose of this (document type) _____

Is to (writer's purpose) _____ [4]

So that (reader's purpose) _____
</td></tr>
</table>

If the document has been requested, a short reminder can lead into your purpose: "Here is the opinion you requested on the recent changes in job descriptions." In contrast, unsolicited writing requires more explanation: "I am writing because I am concerned about the report …" or "I am concerned about the recent report …"

As you identify your purpose, ask yourself, So what? and Who cares? This helps you ensure that what you say has significance for you and for your readers.

The two general purposes of business writing are (1) to inform and (2) to persuade. For example, most memos inform readers, whereas proposals persuade readers. These purposes often exist in a single document. While the central purpose of business proposals is to persuade readers, informing them is a secondary purpose in most. When writing an informational letter to his clients, an insurance agent's central purpose may be to inform them of the products and services his organization offers. However, his secondary purpose is likely to persuade them to take advantage of these products and services.

For experienced business writers, arriving at the document's purpose is a routine part of the writing process because business writing is almost always done in response to a specific request or situation. And certain kinds of documents are written again and again, so your purpose for writing becomes almost second nature.

freewriting
Putting your ideas on paper or computer screen without immediate concern for grammar, spelling, and other matters.

Clustering
Establishing the relationships among the parts of your message.

FIGURE 7–2: PLAN THEN WRITE

In his book, *Write Up the Corporate Ladder*, Kevin Ryan introduces the Plan Then Write method as a process that professional writers use to "achieve the highest standard of excellent business writing." Here are the steps.

Step 1. Plan.
- Choose a format.
- Define your subject by making a bulleted list of your main point and supporting points.
- Determine your audience (Who are your readers? What do they know and not know about your subject?).
- State your purpose (What is your reason for writing?) and state your call to action (What do you want your audience to do?).

Step 2. Write (and keep writing and rewriting until you have a final draft).
Keep these guidelines in mind:
- Start with the easy parts.
- Focus on "thinking clearly on paper," not writing rules. Writing is the act of problem solving using your writer's intuition as a guide.
- Change your plan as you discover new ideas.
- Make liberal use of bulleted lists and subheads.

Step 3. Edit 1. Revise and proofread your final draft.

Step 4. Edit 2. Give your final draft to an experienced or professional proofreader. (If you are unable to give your final draft to an experienced or professional proofreader, a second pass at revising and proofreading it will typically net improvements.)

Source: Kevin Ryan, Write Up the Corporate Ladder: Successful Writers Reveal the Technique That Helps You Write with Ease and Get Ahead. (New York: American Management Association, 2003) 15–16

SUMMARY: SECTION 1— PLANNING YOUR PURPOSE

- Business writing differs from academic writing in that business writing stresses audience awareness, political sensitivity, speed, and fluency as being very important.
- Good writers follow the three-stage writing process: planning, drafting, and revising.
- In the planning stage of writing, you first define your purpose—why you are writing.
- The two usual purposes for business writing are to inform and to persuade.

ANALYZING YOUR AUDIENCE

Your audience is closely tied to your purpose, and analyzing it is the second step in the planning stage. Good business writers write documents from their readers' points of view, asking *who* will read this document and *how* will they use it? Your answers to these questions will help you structure the document so your readers can quickly process the information.

Audience analysis in organizations is more important today than ever before. The lightning speed of the Internet and other communication advances makes information instantaneous and overwhelming. This means business readers must juggle the demands of more information in less time. For business writers this trade-off presents special challenges that did not exist before. Writers must compete for their readers' attention by creating documents that grab their attention and keep it. Every element, from the interest and clarity of the text to the document design, becomes important in the competitive business environment of the 21st century.

Business writers are encouraged to imagine their intended audiences. For example, in the preface to the SEC's *A Plain English Handbook*, Warren Buffet suggests, "Write with a specific person in mind." According to Buffet, when he sits down to write an annual report, he imagines talking to his sisters who "though highly intelligent … are not experts in accounting or finance. They will understand plain English, but jargon may puzzle them."[5] In imagining this kind of "every woman" audience, Buffet succeeds in writing reports that are jargon free and that address what the readers want to know.

CLASSIFYING YOUR AUDIENCE

The first step in audience analysis is to classify your audience in terms of what they will do with your message. Note who will read, route, or make decisions based on your message. These audiences may not be of equal importance, but a successful business message should try to accommodate the needs of all of its readers. The four basic audience classifications are *primary, secondary, gatekeeper,* and *watchdog*.

Primary Audience   Your **primary audience** has the power to make decisions necessary for you to accomplish your purpose and to ensure the appropriate actions are taken. A primary audience may be a single person or many persons and may be from any level in the organization (your peers, your superiors, or your subordinates) or an external reader (a client). The primary audience is the decision maker who acts or does not act on your conclusion and recommendation. The primary audience has the authority to do what you want done.[6]

Secondary Audience   Who else will see your document? Because departments in an organization are interrelated, you involve a number of persons when you send a report to a primary audience. The **secondary audience** is made up of those individuals who will be affected by your message or who will implement your decision or will implement the directive of the primary audience. The secondary audience may have commented on your message in its various drafts and may have to act on the basis of your message even though they were not included in the approval process.[7]

Gatekeeper Audience   The **gatekeeper's** function is to route your message. This person has the power to stop your message before it goes out. Sometimes the gatekeeper is someone higher up in the organization. In some instances, gatekeepers may be first- or

primary audience
The readers for whom you develop your document.

secondary audience
The readers who will be affected by your message or who will implement your decision or the decision of the primary audience.

gatekeeper
People who route and re-route your documents.

second-level managers who must review the document and sign off on it before it is distributed. Often gatekeepers do not read the report; however, they do file it away for future reference.[8]

Watchdog Audience This group is an external audience that is not directly affected by the message, but has substantial political, social, or economic power over the primary audience that will ultimately approve your message. An example of a **watchdog audience** would be industry reviewers whose positive reviews are important to you and to your organization's credibility.[9]

While it is important to classify your readers according to the roles they play in the development of your document, you should also be able to adapt quickly to an audience that you may not immediately recognize as important. For example, the Pacific Gas and Electric's watchdog audience, discussed in Figure 7-3, was ultimately its most important audience.

FIGURE 7–3: THE WATCHDOG AUDIENCE CAN BITE

If your watchdog audience includes Erin Brockovich, watch out. As a clerk for the law firm of Masry and Vititoe, Brockovich was puzzled over why medical records would be included in a real estate file. This led her to the residents of the town of Hinckley, California. The story of her investigation and legal triumph was dramatized in the Oscar-winning movie *Erin Brockovich*.

Brockovich was able to track down internal memos and other documents that connected the corporate offices of Pacific Gas and Electric (PG&E) with PG&E's Hinckley Compressor Station. The Hinckley Station had been contaminating the groundwater with the toxic chemical Chromium 6 for more than 30 years before Brockovich got involved in putting the missing pieces of the case together.

Many of Hinckley's residents and domestic animals that drank the polluted water and breathed the contaminated air were getting or had gotten sick and some had even died by the time Brockovich first visited the town to investigate. In the end, PG&E compensated the named plaintiffs $333 million in damages—the largest legal settlement in U.S. history to that time—in addition to agreeing to clean up the environment and to stop using chromium.

Erin Brockovich is an American legal clerk and environmental activist. She is currently working as a consultant to law firms in the United States and Australia. To learn more about Brockovich, visit her website at www.brockovich.com.

IDENTIFYING THE NEEDS OF YOUR AUDIENCE

The second step in audience analysis is to identify your reader's needs. Analyze your audience to determine what, if anything, in their background or experience might prevent your message from getting through. To do so, determine their background knowledge, experience, and training; what information they need to know; what your audience's attitude is toward you and your message; how interested they are in your message; and which demographic and psychographic characteristics are relevant. After you complete the profile, use the results to adjust your message to meet the specific needs and expectations of your audience.

watchdog audience External critics not directly affected by a message (e.g., an advertisement), but who have substantial political, social, or economic power over an industry.

Consider Your Audience
http://writingcommons.
org/index.php/open-
text/writing-processes/
think-rhetorically/712-
consider-your-audience/

First, what are their background knowledge, their experience, and their training? Recent studies have shown that background knowledge is the key to reader understanding. If you are writing to an audience of your peers, you will probably spend little or no time filling in background information. On the other hand, if your audience has high background needs, you may have to define key terms, eliminate jargon, and use concrete examples that relate your points to things with which your audience is familiar.[10]

For example, if you are developing a new computer program and you are writing a progress report to your immediate supervisor who is familiar with the project, you probably do not need to spend time on background information or definitions. If, however, you are the same programmer faced with the task of writing documentation for a user manual for consumers, you need to use plenty of concrete examples containing little or no jargon to instruct them on how to use your program.

FIGURE 7–4: AUDIENCE ANALYSIS WEB STYLE

As a website visitor you are being watched. Online advertisers have a tool that makes Big Brother seem infantile. Through "cookies" technology, the data collectors—Engage, BroadVision, DoubleClick, and Net Perceptions—collect a mind-blowing amount of information about you, everything from names and addresses to where you are going, what you are doing when you get there, and what you are spending while you do it.

As a website owner and developer, this is great news—if you can afford it. You can make every audience feel like an audience of one as you personalize every customer's experience and serve them ads and special offers they are sure to love. "Hello there, H.T. Customer. Look what we've got for you today!" Try www.broadvision.com or www.doubleclickbygoogle.com or www.perception.net/ for more information on the marketing tools of the future. The U.S. Census Bureau Statistical Abstracts is a helpful source for audience analysis information. Visit www.census.gov/compendia/statab/.

Second, what information do they need to know? Many business writers make the mistake of telling everything they know about the subject rather than considering what their audience really needs or wants to know. Unfortunately, how much you know often has little connection with what your audience wants and needs to know. Some audiences need little supporting information; they want only the bottom line. Others have high information needs. For them provide enough evidence, statistics, and sources to make your message credible and convincing.[11]

For example, if your primary audience comprises busy executives, begin with your purpose, use short paragraphs with clear topic sentences for easy scanning, keep tabular data to a minimum and place it on the same page as the reference whenever possible, and put the detailed information in appendices at the end of the report. Conversely, if your primary audience is your immediate supervisor who must be convinced that your methodology, data quality, and conclusions are correct, provide those details in the body of the report.

Third, what is your audience's attitude toward you and your message? Their attitudes and emotions toward you and your message are important considerations. If they are positive or neutral toward you and your message, you can usually expect a positive reception. In this situation, use direct organization—begin with your main idea first—then reinforce their positive attitude by stating the benefits they will gain from the message.

On the other hand, if tempers have been flaring over recent changes within the organization or over a power struggle between departments, your audience may have a fearful, anxious, or hostile reaction to your message. In this case, use the indirect method to organize your message and begin with your evidence first. This helps your readers understand and accept the recommendations at the end of your message.[12]

For example, when presenting good news about an across-the-board salary increase, use the direct method since you can be fairly sure that your audience will react positively to the news. Conversely, audiences may have a hostile reaction to news about salary cuts unless you can convince them first that salary cuts are needed to prevent across-the-board layoffs.

Fourth, how interested are they in your message? If your audience is neutral or uninterested in what you have to say, you may gain their attention and build their interest by beginning with an attention-getter that emphasizes what's in it for them, build the reader benefits into the body of your message, and in the conclusion make it easy for them to act.[13]

Interest levels typically vary. For example, company managers from a different department may be interested in reading your report on a project they know little about. In contrast, members of your own department may be uninterested in the same report because they are already familiar with the project.

Fifth, which demographic and psychographic characteristics are relevant? Especially when you are directing your message to a large audience composed mainly of strangers, determine their **demographic** characteristics—gender, age, occupation, income—and **psychographic** characteristics—personality, attitudes, and lifestyle. Taking this kind of cultural information into account can help you organize and compose your message in a way that helps your readers accept what you have to say.[14]

Analyzing your audiences for their roles and background expectations helps ensure that the message you send is the one that they receive. If you are already familiar with your audience—your supervisor, your peers of several years—you probably do not need an extensive analysis. At other times, you may find that your audience is too large and diverse to meet each member's needs effectively. In that case, write for the needs of the decision makers and the opinion leaders in the audience.

SUMMARY: SECTION 2— ANALYZING YOUR AUDIENCE

- The first step in audience analysis is to classify your audience according to what they will do with your message. The four major audience classifications are: primary, secondary, gatekeeper, and watchdog.
- The second step in audience analysis is to identify the needs of your audience: (1) What is their background experience? (2) What information do they need to know? (3) What is their attitude toward the subject of your message? (4) How interested are they in your message? (5) What demographic and psychographic characteristics are relevant?

ORGANIZING YOUR IDEAS

The third step in the planning stage is organizing your ideas. After you have analyzed your audience, organize your information with their needs in mind. Find out how your audience will use your document, then organize your information logically from their point of view. If they will use the document for reference only, organize the information to make it easy for them to get in, get their answer, and get out.[15] If you are persuading your readers to take action, organize the information so they can see how taking action will benefit them. Your readers will not appreciate a ricochet approach to writing. They expect a smooth, logical flow of information.

© Nataliya Hoya/Shutterstock.com

ACHIEVING GOOD ORGANIZATION

Achieving good organization is a necessity for any business writer. It helps your audience understand and accept your message. Follow these two steps to organize your material with your audience in mind.

1. Limit your purpose.
2. Organize your ideas using the direct or indirect organization pattern.

Limit your purpose. Suppose your manager asks you, the company's head website developer, to prepare a report about your major competitor's website. You spend five days of grueling research and writing to come up with a 20-page report on every aspect of the site from the size of the graphics on the home page to a description of all 100 links. When you hand him the report, he asks, "What's all this? I only needed to know the size of the graphics on their home page." Save yourself a lot of time and trouble by clarifying the purpose of the document you were asked to produce before planning and drafting. To save yourself and your reader time and trouble, limit your purpose to one main idea that you develop with three or four major supporting points.

Choose the direct or indirect method to organize your ideas. Two ways to organize business documents involve using the direct (deductive) and the indirect (inductive) methods.

Direct Method of Organization When you use the **direct method** of organization, state the purpose of the message—your main idea—at the beginning. In the next paragraph, follow up with supporting details. The direct method is the most efficient way to convey your message to your reader.[16] The memo in Figure 7-5 is organized using the direct method and lets you know up front why you are reading it. The information in this memo is easy to grasp because it is presented in the way that most people comprehend information. Therefore, the direct method is easy to read.

FIGURE 7–5: MEMO ORGANIZED USING THE DIRECT METHOD

As of December 4, we will begin the transformation to a team-based structure. If you are interested in becoming a team leader, please see your department manager for an application. Submit your application to the HR department by December 8.

We will evaluate the applications according to each individual's qualifications. The qualifications we are looking for in a team leader are:

- A willingness to give each project 110%
- An ability to lead coworkers in meetings and projects without causing hostility
- A team spirit as shown in past team projects
- No evidence of hidden agendas on past team projects

Team leaders will have extra responsibilities for which they will receive an additional $2,000 per year. These responsibilities include the following:

- Support and lead a team of 5–7 coworkers
- Act as a liaison between team members and management
- Meet monthly with other team leaders and management to discuss ideas for making teams more productive

Everyone interested is encouraged to apply.

Indirect Method of Organization Using the **indirect method**, begin your message with your evidence or explanation before presenting your purpose or main idea. By working backward, you lead your reader to understand the reasons behind your purpose—the main idea—before you present them with the main idea. The memo in Figure 7-6 is organized using the indirect method. Compare figures 7-5 and 7-6 and how they approach the same situation.

Use the direct method when you expect your audience will be receptive or neutral toward your ideas. Routine and good news, orders and acknowledgments, informational reports, and nonsensitive memos benefit from the direct method of organization. The direct method:

1. Saves the reader time. Messages that take too long to get to the point lose readers who cannot spend time trying to understand them.
2. Sets the details of the message in context. The reader is not left frustrated and wondering, What's the point?

E-mail messages typically follow the direct method. E-mail has become many people's default form of contact, and why not? It's fast, simple, cheap, and independent of time zones and geography.[17]

Use the indirect method when your audience will be unreceptive, displeased, or even hostile toward your message. Use the indirect method when (1) presenting bad news, (2) persuading an audience of strangers, (3) persuading an audience that will be unreceptive or even hostile toward your message, and (4) writing to a superior.[18] The indirect method:

1. Spares the reader's feelings. Since the main idea appears at the end, the reader is more prepared for it.
2. Encourages a full reading. Presenting evidence and explanations first preserves the reader's ego and lessens the negative reaction to the negative purpose, stated at the end of the message.
3. Avoids offending a reader in a superior position and allows the reader to slowly comprehend your sensitive or negative information.[19]
4. Builds suspense, but should be used only when you know your reader will stick with you to that last most important idea.

There are exceptions to choosing the method of organization. For example, if your situation logically calls for the indirect method, but you know your reader prefers reading the message "straight up," use the direct method.

FIGURE 7-7: CHOOSING A FORMAT

In Kevin Ryan's book, *Write Up the Corporate Ladder*, he suggests that the first step in the planning stage is to choose a document format. A *format*, he says, is the outline, layout, or presentation of a document or other publication; the way in which something is presented, organized, or arranged. A format, as described here, is often transformed into a *template* as a means of standardizing document formats. Here are sample subheads for a sample business letter template:

Date
Return Address
Salutation or greeting
Body of the letter
Close
Signature block

Ryan states that templates have many advantages, some of which are:

1. They prevent writer's block by allowing the writer to move around within the document and start writing where he or she has the most immediate information.
2. They speed up the writing process by establishing a logical flow of ideas and information. When you have filled in the subheads, Ryan says, you are done writing.
3. You know which types of information to gather and where to place them.
4. Since each section in the template acts as a prompt for the data you need, templates guarantee your documents will always be complete and that you will not omit important information.
5. Your readers know what to expect and where to quickly find information.
6. Templates help eliminate wordiness by providing structure and guidelines. Wordiness is often a result of not knowing when to stop writing and feeling as if your report or letter needs to be longer.

Ryan reminds us that documents that are produced regularly and contain the same basic information in each are excellent candidates for templates, while documents that include information that changes each time they are created are inappropriate for templates.

Source: Kevin Ryan, Write Up the Corporate Ladder: Successful Writers Reveal the Technique That Helps You Write with Ease and Get Ahead. (New York: American Management Association, 2003) 29–32.

WAYS TO ORGANIZE YOUR IDEAS

Because much business writing is solicited by others, you must read or listen to the request or solicitation carefully. Often the request itself implies a way to organize the document. For example, if your manager asks you to look into the advantages and disadvantages of purchasing a new office printer, your best bet would be to organize your response around the advantages and disadvantages of purchasing a new printer.

If an organization is not implied in the request, use lists, outlines, and planning guides to organize your ideas. For writing projects that require more planning than a routine reflection on the who, why, what, when, where, and how of the message, business writers must decide on the organization ahead of time, especially in light of the constant interruptions and disruptions of writing in the workplace.[20] Even the organization of routine messages can get lost when the writer, plan in head, gets interrupted midsentence and then returns, perhaps hours later, to an incomplete sentence and the original mental plan now gone. Stop-and-go writing, common in the workplace, is frustrating unless you jot down a plan, however rough, before you begin.[21]

If you cannot discern what organization will best serve the reader, then group and unify the document's ideas yourself. In such a situation, the following organizational devices can help you create an organizational plan and stick to it.

Lists   One way to organize a business document is a listing.[22] Many business writers claim to organize their ideas by listing them first. Listing is helpful if it actually arranges the material logically. However, most lists simply note information rather than arrange it. The examples below show the difference between a list and an arrangement. Arrangement here refers to the logical sequencing of items listed. The examples below represent the writer's attempt to organize his ideas regarding an inquiry into health insurance coverage.

List	Arrangement
1. all 50 employees dislike HMOs	1. what information is needed
2. a description of company operations	2. why you need it
3. current provider's limitations	3. when you need it

Comparing the two examples, we instinctively feel that the arrangement is more organized than the list because each item in the arrangement is united by a unifying principle—that of inquiry.

Outlines   In contrast to lists, formal outlines provide an organizational pattern and a visual and conceptual picture of your writing. A well-crafted outline helps you organize a complex document by providing a visual image of how your ideas logically flow. An outline cuts down on your writing time because it provides an ordered overview of your document.

The disadvantage of a formal outline is that it can be too constraining. Many writers complain that outlining takes too long and inhibits their ideas. For example, when writing a report, some writers do not know what they are going to say until they say it. Writers who obsess over creating the perfect outline may be avoiding writing the document itself.

An outline can be written using either topics or complete sentences. A **topic outline** uses words or phrases for all entries with no punctuation after entries. A **sentence outline**

topic outline
Uses words or phrases for all outline ideas with no punctuation after the ideas.

sentence outline
Uses complete sentences with correct punctuation to organize the outline.

uses complete sentences with correct punctuation for all entries. A topic outline is easy and fast to write. A sentence outline presents a more detailed overview—including topic sentences—of your work and makes drafting the actual paper faster and easier.

Planning Guides Another way to organize your ideas is to develop and use planning guides that fit your workplace writing situation. Fred Reynolds, writing consultant and professor at City College, CUNY, helped a writer develop the correspondence planning guide below. Since the writer's work focused mainly on correspondence, Reynolds helped him develop a planning guide that he could fill in prior to drafting. The writer could return to the guide for direction and refocusing when his drafting was interrupted, which it frequently was.

FIGURE 7–8: PLANNING GUIDE

Correspondence Planning Guide
File Reference:

_____

Purpose:

_____

Major Points I Want to Make:

_____

_____

Further Action Needed:

_____

_____

Source: J. F. Reynolds, "What Adult Work-World Writers Have Taught Me about Adult Work-World Writing, in Professional Writing in Context, e. J. F. Reynolds C. B. Matalene, J. N. Magnotto, D. C. Samson, Jr., and L. V. Sadler (Hillsdale, NJ: Lawrence Erlbaum, 1995), 1–31.

No matter what organizational method you use, once completed, it should enable you to move through the drafting stage of the writing process more quickly and efficiently.

SUMMARY: SECTION 3— ORGANIZING YOUR IDEAS

- Achieve good organization in the prewriting stage by limiting your purpose, and choosing the direct or indirect organizational pattern.
- Choose a method to organize your ideas: listing, outlining, or planning guides.

CHOOSING THE BEST WRITING MEDIUM FOR THE SITUATION

The fourth step in the *planning stage* is choosing the best medium. First, let's familiarize ourselves with the most common types of written media in organizations which are e-mail messages, letters, memos, reports, social media, text messages, and websites.

© *patpitchaya/Shutterstock.com*

WRITING MEDIA OPTIONS

E-mail An e-mail message typically deals with routine matters that are not as important as business letters. E-mail is a popular communication medium in organizations for obvious reasons. For example, its speed and ability to reach a number of people at the same time are valued, along with the convenience and permanence of writing.

E-mail's strengths, however, reflect its pitfalls. People often use e-mail as they would a conversation; they react immediately, writing without thinking about organization, grammar, and the effect their words will have. Because it lacks the important nonverbal behaviors that make up face-to-face communication—vocal inflection, eye contact, and gestures—it can generate overreactions and misunderstandings.[23] E-mail is not a private medium so writers must be careful what they include in their messages. E-mail is discussed at length in chapter 6.

Letters Business letters are sent most frequently to external communication partners, but some are also sent internally, most typically to superiors. Business letters speak to a variety of non-routine situations, in contrast to memos that typically address routine matters. In that sense, letters are a more formal medium than e-mails, text messages, tweets, and blogs. They are also more private. According to the late Malcolm Forbes, a good business letter can get you money, get you off the hook, or get you a job.[24] Since business letters frequently go to external audiences, they are important reflections of the company image. According to Emily Post, "[T]hey are the single most impressive written ambassador for your company."[25] Letters are discussed at length in chapter 9.

Memos A memo (memorandum) is an informal written communication sent within an organization for quickly communicating news, policies and procedures, directions, information placed on record, and employment-related information. Memos are the backbone of an organization's daily communication. No matter whether they are hardcopy or e-memos, the fact remains that for brief, one-way communication, the memo remains an efficient form of communication at all levels.[26] Memos are not private. They stay around in filing cabinets and on computers for years. If your message is private, send a letter or communicate verbally. For busy office denizens, make your memos reader-friendly by making your subject line specific, discussing only one topic in each memo, and organizing information around clear topic sentences to allow for skimming. Keep the length to one page or less. Memos are discussed in chapter 9.

Reports These are formal documents that convey information to help others make informed, sound decisions. Reports are typically either informational or analytical, which means some pass along information, while others offer readers conclusions and recommendations based on information gathered. Reports come in many formats and range from a few pages to over a hundred. Reports are discussed at length in chapter 10.

Social Media Posts These are the predominate form of writing at social media sites. Facebook is a very popular social media platform used in businesses predominately for customer service, public relations, and marketing. LinkedIn is a specialty social media platform that caters to business job applicants and professionals. For example, users can upload résumés and present a professional online identity, whereas businesses can search for viable job candidates. LinkedIn is also a good site to bring together employees, clients, suppliers, and other stakeholders. Social media is discussed at length in chapter 5.

Text Messages These are also known as short message service (SMS). Texting is popular in the U.S. business community for a variety of reasons. For example, text messages are relatively inexpensive and enable people to communicate in real time. In addition, employees are able to receive alerts, updates, and quick messages throughout the workday. Texting is discussed at length in chapter 6.

Websites A website is a set of interconnected Web pages. Two common business purposes for websites are sharing information and selling goods and services. Here are some suggestions to keep in mind when writing for business websites: Write concisely, write with design in mind, and make use of the Web's interactivity. These and other suggestions are discussed at some length in chapter 6.

MAKING THE WRITING MEDIUM CHOICE

Choosing the Right Medium
http://www.american-bar.org/newsletter/publications/gp_solo_magazine_home/gp_solo_magazine_index/2009_jun_client-communication.html

Base your medium choice on your audience's expectations and necessity. Do not fall into the habit of simply using the communication medium with which you are most comfortable and skilled. In addition, do not assume that the most cost-effective medium will always get the job done for you and your organization. For example, if you had to communicate to a partner on a sensitive and important matter, you should meet with him or her face-to-face in lieu of communicating via e-mail—a medium devoid of nonverbal cues and privacy.

While electronic communication devices are the right media choice for some situations, they are not the right choice for all situations. We need to be careful not to become so enamored of electronic communication devices that we choose them without thinking, at the expense of effective communication . The concept of information richness (media richness) provides us with a useful way of making effective media choices. *Information richness* refers to how robust a communication medium is. Some communication media are considered to be rich, and some are thought to be lean, while others reside along that continuum. For example, face-to-face communication is the richest form of communication because most people find it to be the most natural way to communicate. In contrast, less-robust media (e.g., text messages, tweets, e-mail messages) are lean media. Such media should be used for routine matters. The trick is to not get too comfortable with any one medium to the point where you use it for most situations without a thought. Let your audience's/receiver's preferences and/or the situation guide you in such decisions.

Finally, there is the question of formality when choosing among the various writing media. Essentially it comes down to determining the level of formality the situation warrants. For example, if the situation you need to address in writing is non-routine and a level of formality is expected, you should turn to business letters and reports and go with a formal tone. On the other hand, if the situation you need to address in writing is routine and formality is not a high expectation, you should consider sending an e-mail message or post to a social media site and go with a less formal, conversational tone.

AUDIENCE EXPECTATIONS

Before sending your message, determine which way your audience would prefer to receive it, then send it that way. Meeting your audience's message expectations helps ensure they receive and read the message promptly. In situations where you are sending written communication to international business partners and are not sure about formality expectations write in a formal style and avoid the conversational tone.

Before sending a message or document, consider whether it is necessary. Most businesspeople are already inundated with too many messages and documents as it is, without having to wade through those that are unnecessary. Here are four tips for deciding when to send a message:

© Korn/Shutterstock.com

1. Avoid writing the message or document if you possibly can.
2. If you must send a message, for every minute you spend considering your message content, spend 10 minutes considering your audience. *How* you say something is *more important* than what you say.[27] Memos and e-mail, especially, are more likely to be perceived as negative and nasty than is verbal communication.[28]
3. Do not assume that written communication is confidential. Assume that your writing will be passed on.
4. Do not falsely equate writing with action. Writing about something is not the same as actually doing something.[29] Do not assume that you are off the hook just because you've written something.

SUMMARY: SECTION 4— CHOOSING THE BEST WRITING MEDIUM FOR THE SITUATION

- There are several media from which to choose when delivering written content. Choose the one that best suits your situation: memo, letter, report, e-mail, text message, blog, website, social networking site (e.g., LinkedIn, Facebook), and Twitter.
- When considering one medium over another, think about your audience's expectations and the necessity of sending the message.

STAGE 2 OF THE WRITING PROCESS: DRAFTING

You have now arrived at Stage 2 of the writing process—the *drafting stage*. You have completed the planning stage and are ready to write.

When writing the *rough draft*, resist that inner English teacher voice. If you analyze and nit-pick each sentence as you write, your writing will be a slow, tortuous process. Instead, focus on writing what you want and need to say; while not forgetting that during the revising stage you can improve how you say it. While drafting, do not stop to worry over the placement of a comma or creating the perfect phrase. Instead, do your best to keep moving forward, guided by the direction and purpose you have already determined in the planning stage. Matters such as comma placement and perfect phrases are best resolved in the revising stage. As draft copy writers we should take comfort in knowing that there is an arsenal of writing support software readily available to assist us during the revising stage.

Most experts agree that writing a rough draft should take less time than revising. Do not waste precious time during the drafting stage that could be better used during the revision stage—the stage that holds the potential of converting a poor-to-average document into a good-to-excellent one. During the *drafting stage*, just let the ideas flow onto your paper or screen as quickly as possible.

GETTING STARTED: MOVING PAST WRITER'S BLOCK

After defining your purpose, profiling your audience, and organizing your ideas, you are ready to draft your document. However, sometimes no matter how much planning you do, you will have trouble getting started. When this happens, you are experiencing **writer's block** which refers to times when writers have difficulty getting started writing.

writer's block
Describes the situation when a writer has difficulty getting started writing.

FIGURE 7–9: COMMON REASONS PEOPLE EXPERIENCE WRITER'S BLOCK

- They do not like to write.
- They lack confidence in their writing skills.
- They are perfectionists, which raises their stress level.
- They let procrastination control the moment.
- They plan poorly so they are uncertain about the document's purpose.
- They know the document is important and must be well written, which raises their stress level.
- They are distracted.
- They are tired.
- They do not want to write the document.

Why does writer's block occur? People experience writer's block for a number of logical and illogical reasons. Some examples are presented in Figure 7-9. Understanding why you experience writer's block will help you recognize the condition and select an approach to help you overcome it.

So, how do you overcome writer's block when it appears to have a stranglehold on you? A good idea is to try an approach that worked for you in the past or that has worked for others. Some examples are presented in Figure 7-10.

Writer's block is something all writers struggle with at times. The trick is to accept that it will happen occasionally, determine the cause, and then control it. In the process, cut yourself some slack. Do not beat up on yourself too much while struggling with writer's block. Instead, tackle the condition logically and move forward with the task at hand.

© Rido/Shutterstock.com

FIGURE 7–10: COMMON WAYS TO OVERCOME WRITER'S BLOCK

- If you do not like to write, give yourself a pep talk and just do it. Just because you do not like to write, does not mean you are a terrible writer.
- If you lack confidence in your writing skills, realize that once you get started and knock out the draft copy, helpful writing assistance software is available.
- If you are a perfectionist, that does not change the fact that you need to knock out a draft copy before working your perfectionistic magic in the revision stage. So, get your hands dirty by writing a typical, imperfect draft copy. In the process of doing so, *freewrite* without concern for spelling, grammar, and punctuation, all of which can be corrected later. Besides, nobody is typically looking at or judging your writing at the draft copy stage. Give your ego a much-needed rest and let the words flow.
- If you are procrastinator, be tough on yourself and do not buy into that cliché that goes, "You do your best writing at the last minute." This is the time for a reality check, which is telling you to get started.
- If you planned poorly and that appears to be at the root of your writer's block, go back and redo the planning stage the right way before attempting to move forward. Your renewed efforts should net you a clear purpose for your writing project, which is an arch enemy of writer's block. While planning, develop an outline. Having an outline in front of you is a good way to overcome writer's block.
- If the document is important and you know it must be well written, do not let fear freeze you. No matter what your hang-ups are, it is likely that you need to get on with it. Much like the procrastinator described above, get tough on yourself. A good starting point is to write the easiest part first, such as the report's cover page or your résumé's contact information section. Those no brainers are painless to write and get your mind and fingers moving.
- If the root of your writer's block is a distraction, either remove the distraction or move to a different location.
- Scheduling uninterrupted blocks of time is a good idea.
- If fatigue is the reason for your writer's block, which is certainly legitimate, set the project down and come back to it when you are rested

13 Famous Writers on Overcoming Writer's Block
http://flavorwire.com/343207/13-famous-writers-on-overcoming-writers-block

© ImageFlow/Shutterstock.com

DRAFTING TO SUPPORT YOUR PURPOSE: TYPES OF SUPPORTING DETAIL

You have come up with your purpose for writing—your main idea—and now you must support it with enough detail to explain your points and support your generalizations. You have to do all this without becoming tedious and losing your reader. Although your supporting details may come naturally to you in routine situations, you should be familiar with the types of support you can use to help your reader understand and accept your purpose. For that reason, make your evidence as specific as possible. Seven common types of supporting detail in business documents are (1) factual evidence, (2) examples, (3) expert opinion, (4) definition, (5) description, (6) analogy, and (7) narration.

Factual Evidence Factual evidence and statistics are the most convincing kinds of support in business documents. To be effective, factual support should clarify and support your purpose.

Examples Giving examples is probably the most common way to develop generalizations, abstract ideas, and unfamiliar concepts. Usually examples do not provide a complete catalog of instances, but give enough to suggest the truth of the idea. In general, the less familiar the concept, the more examples the reader needs to understand the concept.

Expert Opinion The opinion of a recognized authority can add compelling support to your purpose. Expert opinion can be based on primary research (research you have gathered yourself, or expert testimony) or on secondary sources (journals and magazines). Just be sure that the person or source on which you are relying is a recognized authority in your field.

Definition If your audience consists partly or entirely of non-specialists, define technical terms the first time you use them to demystify the reading experience. For example, in a marketing plan to be circulated to an external audience, you would define terms such as *Generation Y* (the 60 million people in the United States born between 1979 and 1994). You might also point out that this population segment is smaller than the 72 million baby boomers that make up their grandparents' generation, but triple the size of Generation X, people born in the United States between 1961 and 1982.

Description Description means using concrete, specific details that appeal to one or more of the five senses (sight, sound, smell, taste, and touch). In business writing, the goal of writing is to convey the information as objectively as possible so the reader and writer interpret the terms and concepts the same way.

Analogy Development of your details by analogy means to draw a comparison between items that appear to have little in common. Business writers use analogies to make the unfamiliar seem familiar, to provide a concrete understanding of an abstract topic, and to help the audience see the idea in a new light.

Narration Supporting with narration means using a story or part of a story to support your purpose. A story is usually arranged in chronological order, starting with what happened first, second, third, etc.

FIGURE 7–11: CAPITALIZING ON WHEN, WHERE, AND WHAT

Writing effectively with a high degree of consistency is challenging for most of us and is even more challenging for those who don't like to write and/or don't feel necessarily skilled at doing so. No matter your attitude about writing and perceived skill level, you can certainly benefit from writing during the time range you do your best writing, at the location where you do your best writing, and using the writing tool with which you do your best writing. That makes sense! Right? In the business place you won't always be able to be as selective, but with the mobility today's electronic communication technologies have provided some of your writing can be done away from the office and even during non-traditional work times.

DRAFTING WITH YOUR AUDIENCE IN MIND: CREATING GOODWILL

unbiased language
Words that do not reinforce a prejudice.

Adapting your message to the needs and wants of your audience contributes to goodwill. You can make your writing reader friendly by developing a tone of goodwill. You create a tone that expresses your goodwill toward your reader by (1) using the you-attitude, (2) emphasizing reader benefits, (3) being positive, (4) using unbiased language, and (5) being polite.

DEVELOPING A YOU-ATTITUDE

Developing a **you-attitude** means writing from your reader's point of view. Just as lawyers create empathy for their clients in the minds of the jurors, visualize what your readers want or need to know and then write your message in terms of them, substituting *you* for the *I* and *we* of the self-centered or company-oriented messages. Compare the following examples.

Company Oriented: Our company can offer you an environment that is always challenging. We've got the best record in the business.

You Oriented: If you are a hard worker, you should do well here.

Company Oriented: Grassbusters is offering one month of free lawn services if you agree to sign up with our service for one year. Call us now to get your free inspection and quote. We are the best lawn service in town.

You Oriented: You can have your yard perfectly clipped and groomed for one month, absolutely free if you sign up with Grassbuster's top-of-the-line lawn service for one year. You deserve the pride and peace of mind that a perfectly groomed lawn brings. Call today for a quote.

I Oriented: I am sending information on peripheral options available for the computer I sold you.

You Oriented: In the next few days, you'll receive complete details on the capabilities and prices of the options available for your new computer.

When you concentrate on the reader, you are putting your empathy skills to work for you. No matter your field, you need to empathize with your audience. For example, accounting firm recruiters use client-responsiveness writing exercises as assessment tools in the hiring of new accountants.[30] Accounting firms believe students need to learn how to respond sensitively to client needs. Similar concerns surface in the insurance industry where writing letters that are legally proper yet still convey a sense of humanity and caring is a constant challenge.[31]

Whatever your goal, your readers will appreciate a warm and sincere tone.

ABUSING THE YOU-ATTITUDE

Overuse of the you-attitude can make you sound pushy: Imagine a staccato voice barking out the following message. "Do you have a job? Do you have 99 dollars? Do you want a new car? Then this is your lucky day, baby!" Sound familiar? This is a good example of how overusing *you* can turn off your audience by making them feel manipulated.

In a more apt example, Brockman and Belanger showed that in letters asking recruiters to participate in a résumé research project, phrases designed to emphasize the reader, like "influential firm" rather than "firm" and "your valuable service" as opposed to simply "your advice," were viewed in many cases as "blatant attempts at flattery and manipulation." In Brockman and Belanger's study, the recruiters preferred the letter without these phrases.[32]

When giving criticism, using *you* can sound too blunt. Using *you* in an accusatory way could offend your reader.

Blunt: You can rest assured that with the old damage on your car, no dealer would ever think of offering you anything near book value.

Less Blunt: The old damage on your car will make it difficult to get full value for your car.

Blunt: You really made a mess of that presentation.

Less Blunt: Presentations can be tricky. Let's see what steps can be taken to improve your next one.

Attitude in Business Writing
http://smallbusiness.chron.com/attitude-business-communication-66988.html

When criticizing another person's performance, it is best to leave out the "you." Concentrate on how your reader can improve, rather than pointing out his or her mistakes.

DEVELOPING READER BENEFITS

A second way to create a tone of goodwill in your message is to emphasize reader benefits. Reader benefits can improve and sustain business relationships with those inside and outside your organization.

© Dirima/Shutterstock.com

Motivation theorists have shown that sources of motivation can be either extrinsic or intrinsic. Extrinsic motivators are external to the person and include tangible rewards like a bonus of $2,000 or a free gift with immediate renewal.

Intrinsic motivators must meet the internal, psychological needs of the person and include:

- stimulating intellectual curiosity by explaining the importance of an action or task

- being aware of your audience's ego needs; giving informal verbal praise or soliciting suggestions can build feelings of self-worth and enhance self-esteem, making the work challenging or interesting.[33]

Identifying reader benefits helps you determine what points to emphasize in your message. First determine how your policy, product, or service will meet your reader's needs. Second, using both intrinsic and extrinsic motivators, determine what will motivate your reader to become interested in your project. Third, choose one or two benefits that will most likely motivate your reader to take action and emphasize them in your supporting points.[34]

EMPHASIZING THE POSITIVE

Another way to create a tone of goodwill is to emphasize the positive rather than the negative. Emphasize what you or your organization can do rather than what you cannot do. In the following examples, the negative and abrupt tone in the first sentence is changed to a positive tone in the second. Words such as *no, do not, cannot, should not, failed*, and *ruined* have no power to change the situation for the better. Whenever possible, then, choose positive language that motivates your audience to new ways of thinking and new courses of action. In the following examples notice how the change from negative to positive changes your attitude about the writer and your motivation to take action.

© StockLite/Shutterstock.com

Negative: *You failed to pay your American Express bill due December 31. Failure to pay this bill by January 10, 20xx will result in your credit rating being negatively affected. You must resolve this matter immediately.*

Positive: *Please check to see whether you have mailed your American Express payment, due December 31. Continuing to pay on time will protect your outstanding credit rating.*

Negative Words	Positive Words
Claim	Appreciate
Blame	Benefit
Cannot	Can
Problem	Pleased
Complaint	Thoughtful reply/request
We cannot	We'll be happy to
We do not	We'll do what we can

Avoid double negatives. Using two or more negatives, like *not, no, except, less than, not less than*, in the same sentence obscures the meaning. Consider the following example from an English newspaper:

It is surely less painful to be unemployed if one is not sober, drug-free, and filled with a desire to work.

The double negative puts a strain on the reader who may give up trying to figure out what's really being said. Put in the positive, the sarcasm behind the message is easier to understand.

It is surely painful to be unemployed if one is sober, drug-free, and filled with a desire to work.

or

It is surely less painful to be unemployed if one is drunk, hooked on drugs, and does not want to work.

This sentence from an insurance policy, "Persons other than the primary beneficiary may not receive these dividends," could easily be rewritten in the positive for clarity: Only the primary beneficiary may receive these dividends.

Use euphemisms with care. To be positive, a writer must sometimes use euphemisms, mild words substituted for words with negative connotations. For example, in the United States you rarely hear someone ask you for directions to the nearest *toilet*. The *restroom, Ladies' or Men's Room*, and *bathroom* are all euphemisms in American culture for *toilet*.

Mild Word	Negative Equivalent
Senior citizen	Elderly
Exfoliate	Wipe off dead skin cells
Bathroom tissue	Toilet paper
Perspiration	Sweat

doublespeak
Language that appears to say something but really does not.

While euphemisms foster positive and polite communication, they also distort the actual meaning of something, making it seem better or worse than it really is. In corporate America the use of euphemisms has been taken to extremes of corporate doublespeak. Doublespeak is a language that appears to say something but really does not. It is evasive and misleading. A company that fires half of its workforce may try to hide that fact behind terms like *cost rationalization* and *volume-related production adjustment schedule*, or more recently, to *rightsize*. In doublespeak, *kickbacks* become *rebates* and *financial losses* become *deficit enhancements*. No one gets fired anymore; instead they are *involuntarily terminated*.[35] When you write ethically, you avoid language that misleads your readers. Avoid using words as a way to circumvent the truth. Be precise when you write.

Popular buzzwords also fit into the doublespeak category, like *empowerment, synergy, competitive dynamics*, and *re-engineering*. Although these examples make euphemisms sound like something writers must avoid, usage experts agree that, on the other hand, euphemisms can be used to avoid causing pain or embarrassment. On the whole, though, cut out the meaningless word or phrase and substitute effective, meaningful content.

USING UNBIASED LANGUAGE

As we settle into the 21st century, discrimination lawsuits are everywhere. With universal efforts to end discrimination, businesses have a responsibility to avoid discriminatory slurs. Misuse of terms is perceived as biased and insensitive behavior. Create goodwill by avoiding language that may offend your readers and that may be construed as bias, sexism, or stereotyping.[36]

Use Sex-Neutral Terms to Avoid Sexist Language   Would you use the following sentence in your annual Christmas message informing your entire workforce—men and women, alike—of their upcoming Christmas bonuses?

> *All saleswomen can expect to receive their bonuses on December 23. As usual you have all done a terrific job.*

You probably would not say this since it likely excludes half your workforce. Similarly, using language like *salesman, businessman*, and *workman* builds a barrier between you and half your readers, a barrier that diminishes the impact of your message. Replace terms that contain the word *man* with words that represent people of either gender. Use the same label for everyone in a particular group. Avoid referring to a woman as a *chairperson* yet calling a man a *chairman*.

Sex-Specific Words	Sex-Neutral Words
Actress	Actor
Authoress	Author
Chairman, chairwoman	Chair or chairperson
Craftsmen	Craft workers, artisans
Foreman, forelady	Supervisor
Hostess	Host
Man, mankind	Human beings, people, humans
Man-hours	working hours, work hours
Salesman	Sales agent, sales representative
Workman	Worker

Avoid *He* to Refer to Both Men and Women

To avoid this, use *he or she* or reword the sentence using the plural form. You can also reword the sentence to leave out the pronoun entirely.

Rather than these:
Each person did **his** job quickly.
The typical accountant … **he**

Write these:
Each person did **his** or **her** job quickly.
The **engineers** did **their** jobs quickly.
The typical accountant … **he or she**
Typical accountants … **they**

Avoid Racial and Ethnic Bias

Avoid identifying someone by his or her race or ethnic origin unless it is relevant to the matter being discussed.

Rather than:
Dr. Mendoza is an intelligent and industrious Hispanic.

Write this:
Dr. Mendoza is intelligent and industrious.

Rather than these:
James Miller, an African-American accountant, will supervise the audit.
Roderick, the Russian stockbroker, saw red when the market crashed yesterday. (The color "red" implies Russia's Communist past.)

Write these:
James Miller will supervise the audit.
Roderick, the Russian stockbroker, was upset when the market crashed yesterday.

Avoid Age Bias

Mention a person's age only when it is relevant, and avoid using adjectives that stereotype the person.

Rather than these:
Jenny Brown, 53 and spry, joined our human resources department yesterday.
Goldie Hawn sure looks great for her age.

Write these:
Jenny Brown joined our human resources department yesterday.
Goldie Hawn sure looks great.

Avoid Disabilities Bias

If you must refer to a person's physical, mental, emotional, or sensory impairments, always refer to the whole person first and the disability second. Avoid outdated usages such as *crippled*, *retarded*, and *handicapped*.

Rather than:
William Robinson, the crippled worker, will start work on Monday.
Please reserve this parking space for disabled customers.

Write this:
William Robinson will start work on Monday.
Please reserve this parking space for customers who are disabled.

Examples of Bias
http://www.writeexpress.com/bias.html

The goal of bias-free writing is to concentrate on an individual's unique characteristics, not on stereotypical assumptions about what or who an individual is or what he or she can or cannot do.

Being Polite A third way to create a positive tone in your message is to be civil and polite. Being polite is a way to enhance your *ethos* (your attitude toward your reader). Ethos is the most important factor in persuading an audience. When you are polite, you project a sincere and credible image to your audience.

Business writing demands diplomacy. A recent study revealed that 90 percent of the American public surveyed felt that incivility is a serious problem. While the business world was thought to be one of the last "bastions of civility," it, too, has started to reflect the informality of society at large, as organizations have flattened and gone casual.[37]

As incivility escalates, so do instances of workplace aggression and violence. Since most people want to do business with those who treat them with respect and courtesy, civility is fundamental to the successful operation of any business.

Some supervisors enjoy intimidating employees by treating them rudely because the supervisors fear losing clout; however, according to management experts, being polite increases employees' and clients' respect. Most people respond favorably to being treated with respect and are more willing to go the extra mile for someone who is courteous and acts professionally. In addition, appropriate business behavior directly and indirectly enhances your company's bottom line, since clients and customers are more likely to do repeat business with a company that makes them feel they are being treated fairly and courteously.[38] Therefore, soften your words when pointing out someone else's mistakes or requesting action.

Blunt: Where's my order? I demand a response within the hour!
Better: I placed order #1254 with you last Friday, May 3. Please let us know as soon as possible when we can expect delivery.
Blunt: You can't go near that stupid copier without jamming it. Maybe you better just stop using it.
Better: The copier jams easily when it is overheated. Please run your copies later when it has cooled down.
Blunt: This is second time you've sent out duplicate billings to Mr. Smith. I can't believe you are this unorganized. Can't you learn the system? Mr. Smith is hopping mad!
Better: Why not let me show you again how we handle billings so that we don't send duplicates. Sending duplicates really annoys some clients.

In terms of writing, politeness means using the common conventions of courteous expression:

- I would appreciate it if you could get back to me before 5 today.
- Thank you for your continued business. We appreciate it.
- Please have the report to me by 5 today.

Writing requires more tact than does speaking. When you are speaking face-to-face, your message can be softened by a smile, a twinkle in your eye, your tone of voice, or your inflection. Plus you have the immediate feedback of the other person's nonverbal behavior.

Usually you can tell if you have inadvertently hurt someone's feelings, in which case you can immediately remedy the situation with a quick apology. In contrast, writing does not provide this kind of immediate feedback. You may never know that you hurt a person's feelings with your hasty and tactless message, as in the following example of an e-mail requesting information for a meeting.

Date: Monday, 7 May 201__ 13:30
From: Jack Crumb
To: Linda Jacobs
Subject: Today's Meeting

Linda,

This afternoon you'd better remember to bring those reports on the Deer Lake project with you. I don't want to waste time like we did at the last meeting while you go back to your office and look for them. We just don't have that kind of time around here.

Jack

In the revised example, the writer communicates his message just as effectively without offending the reader.

Date: Monday, 7 May 201__ 13:30
From: Jack Crumb
To: Linda Jacobs
Subject: Today's Meeting

Linda,

This is just to remind you to please bring the reports on the Deer Lake project with you to the meeting this afternoon. We'll need to go over them right after we get started.

Thanks, and see you there.

Jack

Another way to use courtesy effectively when writing messages is to open your message politely. This is especially good advice when writing to those with higher status and power. As a writer, be aware of the differences in status and power between you and your audience. In general, as differences in status or power increase between the writer and the audience, so does the level of courtesy used by the writer toward the more powerful audience.[40] Words and phrases such as *please, thank you*, and *I would appreciate it if* … go a long way toward softening an overly direct tone.

Avoid using too many indirect strategies in one sentence since doing so sounds like you are groveling: "I apologize ahead of time for asking this, but please, if at all possible, could you submit your report by Friday?"[41]

DRAFTING WITH ORGANIZATION IN MIND: BUILDING PARAGRAPHS

Paragraphs are chunks of information that support the purpose of your message. In business writing, your main concern is writing so that your reader can easily understand your message. Paragraphs signal a pause between ideas. One way to think about paragraphs is as chunks of information in your document. Each sentence in the chunk relates to the other. In general, business paragraphs are short—no more than three or four sentences—unified, and coherent.

PARAGRAPH UNITY

The *topic* or *lead sentence* is the umbrella that covers all the other sentences in the paragraph. It tells your reader what is in the paragraph. A good topic sentence tells readers what is to follow and enables skimming.

Business contexts call for a variety of expository documents, documents that provide information. You might write a proposal to persuade your boss to update your department's computers, or you might explain a newly acquired computer program to your coworkers. In these cases you could start your paragraphs with *It's easy. … It will save us time. … It's fun. … It's secure. …* or *It will improve profits.* The topic sentences tip off your reader to the information in each paragraph before getting into the nitty-gritty details.[42]

Not all paragraphs in business documents are expository, and not all paragraphs need topic sentences. Instead, they might be narrative or process (how-to) oriented. Narratives tell a story about what happened; process messages tell people what to do. In both cases, organize your details chronologically along a timeline: Process—First, do this, second do this. Narrative—First this happened, next this happened, and so on.

Another time that you do not need a topic sentence is when your topic is too long to cover in three or four sentences. Rather than writing a 10–20 sentence paragraph, break the material into information chunks. Just be sure that each chunk conveys only one idea.[43]

Finally, as writing expert Donald M. Murray points out in *The Craft of Revision*, while you should fulfill reader expectations by making clear the main point of the paragraph, don't sacrifice clarity and content to achieve this goal with a "single, superheroic topic sentence."[44] In other words do not lose sight of your message in an effort to fit the content of your paragraph to the topic sentence.

PARAGRAPH DEVELOPMENT

© Igor S. Srdanovic/Shutterstock.com

Develop the idea in your topic sentence with sentences that illustrate or support it. Once you have written your topic sentence, ask yourself, "Why or how do I know this is true?" Your answer will suggest how to develop the paragraph. Just remember that all the sentences in the paragraph should develop or relate to the paragraph's main idea.

You can develop your idea in a variety of ways. Further, a single paragraph may include more than one development method. Use examples and illustrations, comparison and contrast, cause and effect, process, narration, and problem and solution to develop your paragraphs.

These common methods of development reflect our thinking processes. They are not magic.[45] The main point is to stay focused on developing one idea per paragraph, so that you do not overload your readers' comprehension circuits or confuse them by presenting more than one point without developing every one.

Avoid relying on one- to two-sentence paragraphs. The way you develop a paragraph reflects your thought processes, so you probably would not want to write a document, especially a complex one, with a long series of short, one- to two-sentence paragraphs. This suggests inadequate development, which in turn, reflects a need for more thought.

PARAGRAPH COHERENCE

In any business message, sentences and paragraphs should be coherent, that is, they should flow from one to the next without discernible shifts or gaps in thought. Readers new to the material immediately recognize coherence violations, but writers often do not. Why? Because as you write, you make mental connections between your sentences and paragraphs that you may not put down on paper. When you revise, those mental connections are still there, so once again, you may miss shifts and gaps in thought.

You can improve your coherence by thinking in terms of your readers' expectations. As you write from your readers' point of view, strengthen the ties between what the readers have already read and what they are about to read, what you have written and are about to write, and the old and new material.[46] Three techniques for improving your coherence are (1) repeating key words and phrases, (2) maintaining consistency, and (3) providing transitions.

1. Repeating key words and phrases is one of the most common ways to connect thoughts within paragraphs and documents because repetition helps your reader keep the old information in mind while acquiring new information in the next sentence or paragraph. However, too much repetition can be dull. Therefore, use pronouns that refer to the key word (dogs … they) or synonyms (canines).

2. Maintaining consistency in point of view and verb tense is an important part of writing a coherent document. When the writer shifts back and forth from one point of view to another (*one* to *I* to *you*, or third person to first person to second person) and from one verb tense to another (present to past), the reader becomes confused about who is doing what and when. It is less confusing to pick one point of view—first, second, or third person—and stick with it. Similarly, unless there is a reason to use more than one tense, stay with one tense.

3. Transitions are signposts that point your reader in the right direction. Words and phrases such as *first, second, third, and, although, first, however,* and *in addition* show relationships between your ideas and tell your readers how to connect them. Words and phrases such as *consequently* and *as a result* show cause-and-effect relationships, whereas words such as *similarly* and *likewise* show comparisons. In addition, phrases such as *for example* and *in other words* signal that illustrations of points just made are forthcoming.

Be sure to select the transition that fits the overall tone of your document; for example, *in short* has a perfunctory, formal tone, while *so* could be used in more informal writing such as e-mail.

Finally, to link paragraphs within a document, use the same transitional devices that connect sentences within a paragraph. Repeating a key term, using signposts, and maintaining a consistent point of view and tense help you transition smoothly from one paragraph to the next.

SUMMARY: SECTION 7— DRAFTING WITH ORGANIZATION IN MIND: BUILDING PARAGRAPHS

- Paragraphs are chunks of information that support the purpose of your message.
- A good paragraph should be relatively short—no more than 100 words.
- The lead sentence or topic sentence in an expository paragraph lets the reader know what the paragraph is about.
- A paragraph should develop one main idea.
- Paragraphs need transitional devices to connect ideas.

MANAGING THE DRAFTING PROCESS IN ORGANIZATIONS

The process of drafting documents in an organization can be overwhelming if you are inexperienced at doing so. One way writers handle drafting is by document modeling.

DOCUMENT MODELING

document modeling The process whereby workplace writers use documents or parts of documents already written for a similar situation as a template for their own writing.

model document An existing document written for a similar situation

boilerplate language Text used again and again in similar situations.

One of the key ways workplace writers draft documents is through the process of **document modeling**. Document modeling is a process whereby workplace writers use documents or parts of documents that have already been written for a similar situation as a template for their own writing. Because of the pressure to write quickly, writers use **model documents** and **boilerplate language** (language that has been used in other documents of the same type).[47]

Watch for two common problems when using language from other documents. Inexperienced writers often cut and paste whole sections of other documents into their own without attention to the clash of differing writing styles and tones. In this case, the final document will not sound like a coherent, unified document. Instead, it will read like a hodge-podge of documents by different writers. Create smooth transitions between the boilerplate sections and your own ideas so the gaps do not show.[48]

The writing in the "file-cabinet" models may be outdated, bloated, and unorganized, so choose your models carefully with your readers in mind.[53] Do not allow boilerplating to be an excuse for not thinking through the new situation. A hodge-podge results in a document that does not meet the needs of the new audience or the unique needs of the situation. Selling points that you could emphasize in the new proposal are ignored when you use boilerplating as a crutch that offers a seemingly quick and easy solution to a complex rhetorical problem.[50]

SUMMARY: SECTION 8— MANAGING THE DRAFTING PROCESS IN ORGANIZATIONS

- Document modeling is a technique new writers in organizations use to help them adapt to the organizational writing style and document format.
- Using large sections of boilerplate language from other documents is no excuse for not thinking about the new writing situation and meeting its unique requirements. When you don't think things through, your document suffers.

Notes

1. Donald Samson, "Writing in High-Tech Firms," in *Professional Writing in Context*, eds. J. F. Reynolds, C. B. Matalene, J. N. Magnotto, D. C. Samson, Jr., and L. V. Sadler (Hillsdale, NJ: Lawrence Erlbaum, 1995), 97–127.

2. Pamela A. Angell, *Business Communication Design: Creativity, Strategies, and Solutions*, 2nd ed. (Boston, MA: McGraw Hill Irwin, 2007), 193.

3. J. C. Mathes and Dwight W. Stevenson, *Designing Technical Reports* (Needham Heights, NY: Macmillan, 1991), 107.

4. Ibid, 68.

5. Securities and Exchange Commission, *A Plain English Handbook*, http://www.sec.gov/pdf/handbook.pdf

6. Mathes and Stevenson, 42–43.

7. Ibid.

8. Mary Munter, *A Guide to Managerial Communication* (Upper Saddle River, NJ: Prentice Hall, 2000), 11.

9. Kitty O. Locker, *Business and Administrative Communication* (New York: McGraw Hill, 1999), 60.

10. Munter, 12.

11. Ibid.

12. Ibid., 14.

13. Ibid., 13.

14. Ibid., 11.

15. Janice C. Redish, Robbin M. Battison, and Edward S. Gold, "Making Information Accessible to Readers," in *Writing in Nonacademic Settings*, eds. Lee Odell and Dixie Goswami (New York: The Guilford Press, 1985), 129–53.

16. John S. Fielden and Ron E. Dulek, "How to Use Bottom-Line Writing in Corporate Communication," in *Strategies for Business and Technical Writing*, ed. Kevin J. Harty (Boston: Allyn & Bacon, 1991), 179–88.

17. Alec Appelbaum, "The Evils of E-mail," *CIO Magazine* (December 1, 2000), www.cio.com/archives.

18. John S. Fielden, "What Do You Mean You Don't Like My Style?" *Harvard Business Review* (March–June, 1982): 7.

19. Ibid.

20. Fred Reynolds, "What Adult Work-World Writers Have Taught Me about Work-World Writing," in *Professional Writing in Context* (Hillsdale, NJ: Lawrence Erlbaum, 1995), 19.

21. Ibid.

22. Barry Eckhouse, *Competitive Communication* (New York: Oxford University Press, 1999), 28.

23. Marian M. Extejt, "Teaching Students to Correspond Effectively Electronically," *Business Communication Quarterly* 61, no. 2 (1998): 57–67.

24. Malcolm Forbes, "How to Write a Business Letter," in *Strategies for Business and Technical Writing*," ed. Kevin J. Harty (Boston: Allyn & Bacon, 1999), 108–11.

25. Peggy Post and Peter Post, *The Etiquette Advantage in Business* (New York: HarperCollins, 1999), 314.

26. Ruth Davidhizar and Sally Erdel, "Send Me a Memo on It; or Better Yet, Don't," *The Health Care Supervisor* 15, no. 4 (June 1997): 42–47.

27. Richard A. Wueste, "Memos on the Loose," *Manager's Notebook* (September/October 1988): 39–40.

28. Davidhizar and Erdel, 3.

29. Wueste, 39.

30. Faye Bradwick, "Writing Skills of New Accounting Hires: The Message Is Mixed," *The Tax Advisor* 28 (August 1997): 518–21.

31. Gary Blake, "Making Insurance Documents Readable and Friendly," *LIMRA's Market Facts* 18, no.1 (January/February 1999): 15–16.

32. Elizabeth B. Brockman and Kelly Belanger, "You-Attitude and Positive Emphasis," *Bulletin of the Association for Business Communication* 56, no. 2 (June 1993): 1–9.

33. W. Huitt, "Motivation," http://chiron.valdosta.edu/whuitt/col/motivation/motivate.html.

34. Locker, 72–73.

35. "William Lutz Talks about How Doublespeak Has Taken Over the Businessworld," *Business News: New Jersey* 11, no. 4 (January 1988): 13.

36. Judy E. Pickens, "Terms of Equality: A Guide to Bias-Free Language," *Personnel Journal* (August 1985), 24.

37. Lynne Andersson and Christine Pearson, "Tit for Tat: The Spiraling Effect of Incivility in the Workplace," *Academy of Management Review* 24, no. 3 (1999): 453.

38. Ibid, 470–75.

39. Kathryn Riley, Kim S. Campbell, Alan Manning, and Frank Parker, *Revising Professional Writing* (Superior, WI: Parley Press, 1999), 97–99.

40. Ibid., 98.

41. John Clayton, "When to Use a Topic Sentence—and When Not To," *Harvard Management Communication Letter* (March 2001): 3.

42. Ibid., 4.

43. Ibid.

44. Diana Hacker, *The Bedford Handbook for Writers* (New York: St. Martin's Press, 1991), 83.

45. Hacker, 99.

46. Mark Mabrito, "From Workplace to Classroom: Teaching Professional Writing," *Business Communication Quarterly* 62, no. 3 (September 1999): 103.

47. Glenn J. Broadhead and Richard C. Freed, *The Variables of Composition: Process and Product in a Business Setting* (Carbondale: Southern Illinois University Press, 1986), 57–58.

48. Lee Clark Johns, "The File Cabinet Has a Sex-Life: Insights of a Professional Writing Consultant," in *Strategies for Business and Technical Writing*, ed. Kevin J. Harty (Boston: Allyn & Bacon, 1999), 145–76.

49. Broadhead and Freed, 57.

REVISING BUSINESS DOCUMENTS

8

LEARNING OUTCOMES

After reading this chapter, you should be able to:

1. Identify the three stylistic choices for business documents and when to use each.

2. Discuss techniques for revising a document/message's purpose, introduction, and conclusions.

3. Describe ways to revise formatting.

4. Discuss how to revise for tone.

5. Describe several proofreading strategies.

6. Describe how to give and take writing criticism effectively.

© arka38/Shutterstock.com

BENEFITS OF LEARNING ABOUT REVISING BUSINESS DOCUMENTS

1. Taking the time to revise your document saves your manager and your client frustration.

2. Writing reader-centered prose allows the busy reader to find structural cues to help him or her follow your ideas easily.

3. It is essential that you know how to format your document for easy reading.

4. Being 99.9 percent correct is not good enough. Learning the revision and proofreading techniques in this chapter can save you time and money.

SELECT KEY TERMS

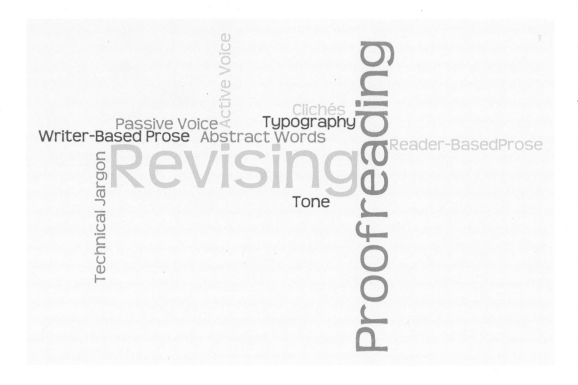

INTRODUCTION

The focus now turns to identifying weaknesses in draft copies of business documents and then making the related revisions. For example, business writers often identify issues pertaining to organization, reader-centered prose, tone, word choice, sentence structure, and/or spelling. By making needed revisions, a business writer typically improves document quality as well as reinforces his or her professional image.

The intent of this chapter is to provide you with information on how to effectively revise draft copies of business documents, including how to manage the revision process in organizations. These goals are realized through discussions of the following topics: stage three of the writing process, revising, revising for organization, revising for your audience: style and tone, proofreading, and managing the revision process in organizations. The information pertaining to the above-mentioned revision steps is reinforced by several student website resources including *PowerPoint slides, preview tests, chapter assessment tests, writing mechanics rules and guidelines, YouTube videos, interactive exercises,* and the *interactive glossary.*

Effective Business Writing
http://www.english-grammar.org/effective-business-writing/

STAGE 3 OF THE WRITING PROCESS: REVISING

You have a rough draft of your document, and now it is time to improve its clarity and quality. Doing so involves three steps: editing, revising, and proofreading. Editing involves reviewing the rough draft with the purpose of determining where it can be improved. Revising involves making written changes/improvements based on what was determined when editing. Proofreading involves conducting a final review of the revised document to catch oversights that need correcting such as misspellings. Most writers revise in tandem with editing. In other words, they identify something in need of change and revise it right then before moving on. It is during the revising stage that the greatest potential for quality writing occurs, which is why writing experts agree that writers should spend more time editing, revising, and proofreading documents than they spend on drafting them.

Lastly, give the document a good proofreading with the purpose of identifying and correcting all those oversights you overlooked while editing. It seems that no matter how thorough we are while editing and revising documents, we often overlook one or more silly errors (e.g., spelling errors, grammar errors, transposed words, etc.). This is where a "last-pass round" of proofreading typically saves the day. Proofreading suggestions are shared later in this chapter.

Some businesspeople finish the draft writing stage with one idea in mind—sending the document out then and there.[1] They believe rewriting is a needless, time-consuming activity. Or, they think that editing and revising means simply moving some words around, correcting a few typos, inserting a comma or two, and then sending the document the second they've made the last change.

Unfortunately, many documents are not ready to go anywhere—least of all to your manager or client—at this stage. While the punctuation may be perfect, the ideas may be confused, the tone may be wrong, and the style may be too ornate to be read easily. The reader of this unrevised document is frustrated and puzzled, rather than informed or persuaded.

To avoid bearing the brunt of your manager's frustration or your client's confusion, revise your document carefully before you send it up the chain of command or to an outside audience. Ideally, you should let your rough draft sit for a while after you finish. This helps you gain perspective on it.

editing Reviewing the rough draft with the purpose of determining where it can be improved.

revising Making written changes and/or improvements to a draft copy of a document.

proofreading A final review of a document to catch oversights in need of correction such as misspellings.

Editing Your Writing: Tips and Tricks
http://syntaxis.com/book/business-writing/editing-your-writing-tips-and-tricks

© Jack Frog/Shutterstock.com

Many times at work, however, you do not have time to let it sit for a day, a few hours, or even a few minutes. In that case, reread your message, but from your readers' perspective. Good editing and revising is the act of anticipating how your readers will respond and adjusting the text to get the response you hope for.[2]

A logical approach to the revision process helps you move through it more quickly. One way to approach revision is to work from the general to the specific, concentrating on the global issues first—content and organization—and then moving to local issues, like style and tone, sentence structure and word choice, and grammar and punctuation. Otherwise, you waste time refining sentences and words that you may eventually cut when you make structural changes.

REVISING FOR CONTENT

The first thing to look at is the clarity of your purpose. Is it clear what you want your audience to do or think after reading your document? Have you immediately answered the reader's question: "What's this all about?" or "So what?"

Sometimes your purpose is hiding in the middle or at the end of your document, rather than at the beginning. In that case, cut and paste your purpose into the first paragraph (unless you are using the indirect organizational plan). Here are some revision tips to help the reader figure out why you are writing.[3]

Problem: As you reread, you find a sentence in the final paragraph that says: "This memo was written to document …" or "… "which is why I have written this letter."

Solution: State the purpose of your memo or letter in the first or second line of the document.

Problem: The first paragraph introduces your topic but does not include your intention. For instance, "I am responding to your letter of January 8, 20xx."

Solution: State your reason for writing along with your topic: "In response to your letter of January 8, 20xx, I am writing to clarify the firm's policy on past due accounts."

Problem: You notice that the subject line of your memo conveys only the topic: "Re: Recommendation."

Solution: Rewrite the subject line to specifically reflect your purpose for writing: "Re: Recommendation--Susan Jones."

Problem: Your letter or memo tells a story but makes no clear point or recommendation about why you are telling the story.

Solution: At the beginning of your memo or letter, state your purpose for telling the story: "In light of Ms. Jones' performance record and in light of a recent customer complaint, I recommend that we terminate Ms. Jones."

REVISING THE INTRODUCTION

After making sure your purpose is clear, reread the introduction. Have you gained your audience's attention in addition to clearly stating your purpose? If you are providing your audience with important information, be sure you included that information in the first or second line of your opening. In an instructional document, proposal, or action-oriented message, you may need to entice your readers to keep on reading. In this case, you want to mention the advantages first—what's in it for them to keep reading—before you discuss the action you want them to take. This gives your readers a reason for taking the action recommended.[4]

The following SkillPath Seminars' letter, addressed to managers and supervisors, correctly opens with examples of what their seminars can do for you:'

© Leah-Anne Thompson/Shutterstock.com

> *When a worker's behavior or performance is not acceptable, it is important that you step in and get things back on track right away.*
>
> *The cost of unsatisfactory job performance is staggering—and often comes in ways that are hard to measure. Performance and behavior problems take their toll in terms of lost productivity, inferior products and services, wasted management time and low worker morale.*[5]

The letter continues with actions you can take to alleviate these problems, all to be revealed by attending their seminar on dealing with problem employees.

REVISING THE BODY

The body can be anywhere from one to hundreds of pages long. Trying to figure out where to fit in a seemingly ill-fitting but essential point or figuring out when to cut a point that pops up in every other section can be a daunting task.[6] However, if you constructed an outline before you began, go through your document, comparing it point for point against the outline. Check to see if your evidence is strong enough to support the point you have made and if it is accurate.

If you have included irrelevant information or omitted essential information, you should be able to catch it as you move through the document. This is also the time to test your original outline. Perhaps you find additional but essential information since constructing the outline. If so, change the outline as you revise the document itself.[7] The main thing here is to ensure your evidence is logical and convincing, and that it clearly supports your purpose.

REVISING THE CONCLUSION

The document's conclusion is your last chance to inform or to persuade your reader. If your reader has had time to read only your opening and closing, then your closing had better be strong. Do not risk a weak, ineffective ending.

The information in your conclusion depends on the kind of document you are writing. A routine letter or memo may simply end positively with a look to the future: "If you need further explanation or more materials, please contact Betty at ext. 321, between 8 and 5, Monday through Wednesday."

On the other hand, if you are writing a substantial report or proposal, include both a summary section, in which you summarize your main points, and a conclusion, in which you draw conclusions from the points you have made. Here are some techniques to help you make your conclusion get results.[8]

1. Be sure your conclusion eases the reader out of the subject gracefully without an abrupt end that leaves the reader wondering, "Where's the rest of the information?"
2. Especially in longer documents, reinforce the main points in your conclusion (since this is the only chance for the skimmer to get them), and use your conclusion to point to the implications of your main points. For example, a memo that offers solutions to the problem of low employee morale could close with suggestions on how these solutions will improve employee morale, which in turn, would eventually improve the company's bottom line.
3. Create document unity and refer to a theme introduced at the beginning of the document, effectively bringing the reader back to where he or she began.
4. Avoid bringing up new issues in your conclusion.
5. Balance your conclusion with the rest of the document. If you have a 300-word document with a 200-word conclusion, you are belaboring your conclusion. On the other hand, do not end a 5,000-word document with a quick sentence. The goal is to achieve a graceful exit, easing the reader out of the message.
6. Revise for ethical lapses.

FIGURE 8-1: WRITER'S CHECKLIST: ETHICAL WRITING

To avoid ethical problems, ask the following questions as you revise your writing:

- Is the document truthful? Scrutinize findings and conclusions carefully. Make sure the data supports them.
- Am I acting in my employer's best interest? My client's or the public's best interest? My own best long-term interest? Your writing reflects on you and your employer. Review it from the perspective of its intended effect. When possible, ask someone outside your company to review and comment on what you wrote.
- What if everybody acted or communicated in this way? Apply the Golden Rule (Treat others as you would like them to treat you). If you were the intended audience, would the message be acceptable and respectful?
- Am I willing to take responsibility, publicly and privately, for what the document says? Will you stand behind what you have written? To your employer? To your family and friends?
- Does the document violate anyone's rights? Have people from different backgrounds review your writing. Have you considered their perspective?
- Am I ethically consistent in my writing? Only by the consistent application of ethical principles can you meet this standard.

Source: Gerald J. Alred, Charles T. Brusaw, and Walter E. Oliu, The Business Writer's Handbook *(New York: St. Martin's Press, 2000), 227.*

REVISING FOR ORGANIZATION

Revising for organization helps your reader better understand your document.

REVISE WRITER-CENTERED WRITING INTO READER-CENTERED WRITING

First drafts often contain writer-based prose. Writer-based prose is writing that focuses on the writer's thinking processes rather than on the readers' questions or needs. One reason first drafts often contain writer-based prose is because that is when writers talk themselves through a problem on paper, exploring their knowledge of the problem, or when writers put their ideas down on paper.[9] The readers' needs are forgotten for the time being. This often happens when writers are uncertain about the topic and are unsure what their readers expect.

One way to spot writer-based prose is to look for loosely connected ideas in narrative form. Sometimes writers record everything they know about the topic or report what they have done rather than what it means, leaving readers to wade through the text looking for the information they need.[10] Or look for places where the writer is trying to answer his or her own question (What will I do?) rather than focusing on the reader's question (What will you do for me?)[11] For example, a new auditor may try to retell the history of an audit rather than offer an analysis of his or her findings. This leaves the busy reader thinking "so what?" or "where's the bottom line?"

Reader-based prose emphasizes the information that the reader needs or expects to find. One way to test your document for a reader-based structure is to check for cues that reveal your plan to your reader. Readers expect to find cues in:

- The introduction, e.g., main idea and preview of points
- The first sentence of each paragraph
- The transition words that you use: *further, finally, nevertheless, to illustrate, first, second, third, etc.*

writer-based prose
Writing that focuses on the writer's thinking processes and needs rather than on the reader's questions or needs.

reader-based prose
Writing that answers the reader's questions and/or emphasizes information the reader needs or expects to find.

- The headings. Readers prefer headings that address the concerns they bring to the document. So rather than "Eligibility Determination" or "Policy Termination," try "Who Is an Eligible Student Borrower?" or "Can This Policy Be Cancelled?"[12]

Another way to test your structure for reader-based prose is to see if you followed through on the promises you made. As you read your text, see that key points are supported with the necessary details.[13]

For example, imagine you are writing an internal report that justifies the expense of an instant messaging service. In paragraph three, you promise to discuss two factors that show how an instant messaging service will save your company money. Check to see if the paragraph does indeed discuss the two factors with the detail necessary to convince even a skeptical audience. If you have not fulfilled your promise to your reader, revise the paragraph, making it reader based.

REVISE THE FORMAT FOR A READER-FRIENDLY DOCUMENT

The format of your document refers to (1) the arrangement of the text on the page—the layout—and (2) the visual features of the print—the typography. While you do not need to be a graphic artist to put together a visually appealing document, giving attention to several features of your document's design as you revise make it easier for the reader to follow the text's organization.[14]

Page Layout   Your document's design not only makes it easier for the reader to follow but also reflects on you as a writer. To design a layout that is internally consistent, reflective of the standard practice in your field, and attractive, observe the following guidelines. These guidelines reflect the standard formatting practices in many organizations. However, if your organization has a style guide of its own, follow those guidelines.

© Alberto Zornetta/Shutterstock.com

- **Margins.** Generally allow a 1–1½-inch margin around your text. Page numbers are placed within the margin, usually in the bottom center or upper outside corner. Header and footer areas are for material that appears on every page in the top or bottom margin, such as chapter titles.

- **Line Spacing.** Most business documents are single-spaced with double-spacing between paragraphs. Extra space is used before and after headings to help the reader follow your organization.

  Sometimes single lines of paragraphs can be "widowed" or "orphaned" at the bottom or top of a page. To eliminate these one-liners, check your word processing program's formatting help for "Widow and Orphan Protection." This protective device groups the outcast line with the rest of the paragraph.

- **White Space.** As with margins and line spacing, careful use of white space improves your text's readability. White space refers to areas in documents that do not contain text, numbers, figures, tables, graphs, and/or images. Margins are good examples of white space. White space is especially effective in setting off vertical lists of items from the surrounding text. This way the information is highlighted for the reader. Use white space to highlight and group details as a unit.
- **Indentation.** Like white space, use indentation to highlight important information, such as long quotations or lists of important details.
- **Justification.** Justified text means that the text is aligned along a vertical margin. Usually text is either full-justified—aligned along both the left and right margins— or left-justified—aligned along the left margin with a ragged right margin.

  The advantage of full justification is that it presents a formal-looking document, but full justification has three drawbacks. (1) If used with a font that has nonproportional spacing, such as Courier or Letter Gothic, it creates distracting gaps between words. (2) Full justification makes corrections difficult since adding or deleting even a few words creates the need to reformat the entire document. (3) Full justification is difficult to read for long periods. The ragged edges of left-justified text are easier on the eyes.

Typographical Effects Once you have revised the layout of your document, create a unified, professional-looking document by using effective typography.

- **Typeface.** The two kinds of typefaces are serif and sans serif. A serif typeface has tiny extenders on the ends of the letters. A typical serif typeface known as Times New Roman is available on most computers.

  In contrast, a sans serif typeface has no extenders. A sans serif typeface known as Arial is available on most computers.

  In general, a serif typeface is easier to read on hard copy, so it is good for extensive prose documents, such as business reports. Sans serif is good for headings or other short elements in documents. Online documents, however, are easier to read if you use a sans serif typeface for both headings and prose.

- **Type Size.** Most business documents use a 10- or 12-point type. Larger type sizes are often used to unify major headings and titles. This unity helps the reader mentally organize the material.
- **Capital Letters.** A text written in all capital letters is hard to read. Reserve all capitals (uppercase type) for headings or short phrases that need particular emphasis.
- **Boldface.** Boldface provides extra emphasis to particular elements in a text. It is often used to unify headings and can even be used to highlight a particular word, phrase, or sentence. The trick with boldface is to be consistent with its use. Putting too much text in bold eliminates the reason for its use—emphasis—and confuses the reader.

white space
Areas in documents that do not contain text, numbers, figures, tables, graphs, and/or images.

justified text
Text that is aligned along a vertical margin. Usually this means text is aligned along both the left and right margins.

serif typeface
Font with tiny extenders on the ends of the letters.

sans serif typeface
Font having no extenders on the ends of the letters.

- **Underlining.** Like boldface, underlining emphasizes and unifies parts of the text, such as second-level headings, which are often underlined rather than capitalized to distinguish them. However, if you are using underlining for emphasis, rather than **boldface**, do not underline technical or foreign terms; instead use *italics* to identify these words: *habeas corpus*. Use underlining sparingly in hard copy documents. Avoid underlining in online text and in professionally produced documents of any type.
- **Headings.** Descriptive headings help readers move through documents quickly. Descriptive headings help the reader follow your ideas more easily. However, to keep your material unified, always use the same typographical features in each heading at each level. For example, use all capital letters (caps) and boldface for first-level headings, use standard capitalization and boldface for second-level headings, and use standard capitalization and italics for third-level headings. You may also want to use a larger typeface for first- and second-level headings. Be consistent throughout the text. Headings are discussed in detail in chapter 9 on business reports.

FIRST-LEVEL HEADING

Text text text text text text text text text text text text text text text text text text text text text text text text text text text text text text text text text text

Second-Level Heading

Text text text text text text text text text text text text text text text text text text text text text text text text text text text text text text text text text text

Third-Level Heading.
Text text text text text text text text text text text text text text text text text text text text text text text text text text text text text text text text text text

- **Lists.** Lists emphasize items within the text or in a stacked (vertical) list. A list can be numbered within a sentence like this: The advantages of e-mail include (1) speed, (2) reliability, and (3) anonymity. You can use symbols like a dash (-) or bullet (·) to create a vertical list. These symbols, however, are not effective for showing chronology or order of importance.

Know when not to use lists. When a report or letter has bullets everywhere, it quickly loses its effectiveness and looks as though you were unable to develop a paragraph of complete sentences. Remember that the two best reasons for using lists are to organize many numerical facts and to emphasize important recommendations.[15]

A Final Word on Formatting. As with most special effects today, word processing programs make creating effects easier than ever before. That's why you should be wary of overdoing it. Overdoing it results in a cluttered and unprofessional appearance, rather than a unified and polished one, and you lose credibility with your readers.

Choose one way to emphasize words, either boldface or italicize (underline only when you do not have a better alternative). Do not use all three. After you make your choice, use it consistently throughout your document. A document that changes typefaces frequently looks unpolished and chaotic.

REVISING FOR YOUR AUDIENCE: STYLE AND TONE

Writing style refers to the strategies we develop for using words or sentences in a particular way. John Fielden defines *style* in business writing as "that choice of words, sentences, and paragraph format which by virtue of being appropriate to the situation and to the power positions of both writer and reader produces the desired reaction and result."[16]

We make many stylistic choices every time we sit down to write. We may decide to use a technical term rather than an ordinary word; we may use active rather than passive verbs; or we may choose to use a series of short sentences rather than one long, cumbersome, complex sentence.

Tone refers to the writer's attitude toward the reader and to the subject matter. Your tone could be sarcastic or straightforward, pompous or accessible, condescending or respectful, impersonal or personal. In general, good business writing should have a confident, conversational, courteous, and sincere tone.

While we are sensitive to the harsh, cold, pompous tone of other people's business writing, we are usually not as alert to our own. Just as their tone offends us and perhaps even costs them our business, our tone can offend them and cost us their business.

Our specific stylistic choices influence a wide range of reader responses, from the reader's willingness to read the document to his or her acceptance of our ideas.[17] CEOs and managers know that clear, simple, and accurate letters and reports save the reader time, translating into increased productivity and higher profits.

Clear language has become a business necessity in the information economy where human attention is a scarce resource.[18] Drowning in information, we attend to the piles of letters, memos, e-mails, text messages, and reports for a few seconds at most.

In such an economy, revising your prose to catch the busy reader's short attention span takes on a new urgency. It becomes essential, since the cost exacted by an unreadable, unorganized, impenetrable document can be estimated in lost business, personal reputation, etc.

Revising for style and tone, then, makes good business sense and can be thought of as strategy building. The next section guides you in making judicious stylistic choices among the available options. Stylistic and tone questions are not about right or wrong; they are about good, better, best.[19]

Revising for Style The three broad styles available to business writers are described below. To be an effective communicator, evaluate your style strategy carefully. Adjust your style to suit the writing circumstances. If you lack a clear sense of the best style, ask yourself what effect you want to produce in your readers, then go with the style that best supports that goal. The answer will help you determine which style is appropriate for your writing situation.

The Impersonal Style. The impersonal style is characterized by a(n):

- Passive voice
- Official, bureaucratic tone
- Excessive nominalization (turning an action verb into a noun)
- Long, convoluted sentence structure
- Superfluous, outdated, and redundant language
- Business and legal jargon
- Abstract words

Although generalizations about when to use a particular style are tricky, a passive style can be appropriate in negative situations and in situations where the writer is in a lower position than the reader.[20] However, because this style is difficult to read and slows down the reader's comprehension, save it for sensitive situations.

The Modern Business Style. The modern business style is characterized by a(n):

- Active voice
- Confident, conversational, courteous, and sincere tone
- Strong verbs
- Parallel structure
- Short sentences
- Everyday words
- Concrete words
- Precise words

This style is appropriate for most business documents, from internal memos to external reports, because it is easy to read and understand. Writers who use this style follow the rules of Plain English. See Figure 8-3 for an explanation of Plain English.

© PePl/Shutterstock.com

The Informal/Colorful Style. The informal/colorful style is characterized by a(n):

- Active voice
- Personal, conversational tone
- Strong verbs
- Colorful use of adjectives and adverbs
- Parallel structure
- Short sentences
- Everyday words
- Concrete words
- Precise words

This style is good for situations where you are familiar with the reader. This style is also effective for delivering good news and in some persuasive action-request situations. Sales letters and advertisements often use a colorful style to capture the reader's attention.

FIGURE 8–2: EXAMPLES OF LETTERS IN THREE WRITING STYLES

1. **Passive and Impersonal Style.** Filled with jargon and difficult to read. Ineffective for routine correspondence as in the following example.

Dear Mr. Smith:

Per your letter of April 7, 20xx, enclosed please find the information in reference to our company that will help in optimizing your choices to build a website. Prices charged are in line with other designers of similar background and experience.

The company objective is to develop end-to-end robust solutions through continued focus on core competencies: Website development, hosting, and maintenance; full access to PHP and CGI; and, of course, SSL encryption. It is believed that the customer deserves the highest quality products and services possible. Through continued expansion of the company's staff and through application of corporate quality programs, such as benchmarking, our establishment of superior processes in each of the core competencies excels over our competitors.

Continued expansion into new, profitable markets will enable the company to provide clients with value-added services and turnkey solutions that will translate into client satisfaction.

Please find herein the company's packages that will endeavor to help the client learn more about the company's superior capabilities and its motivated professional team.

If you have any questions or concerns regarding the above, please feel free to contact Joanne Jones, at 800-543-6677, ext. 213. It is toll free for your convenience.

Very truly and obediently yours,

> **jargon (buzzwords)** Words peculiar to a particular profession that do not necessarily make sense to others outside of that profession.

FIGURE 8-2: EXAMPLES OF LETTERS IN THREE WRITING STYLES

2. Modern Business Style. Uses active voice, strong verbs, short sentences.

Dear Mr. Smith:

Thank you for inquiring about our Web services. Our company specializes in creating websites. Your satisfaction is our priority. We work on projects of any size from large to small. Our prices range from $60 an hour for basic logo design to $100 an hour for designing and implementing a full-featured website.

Our staff includes seven Web designers who will turn your image of a perfect website into reality. We can fulfill any of your Web design needs from developing high-end graphics and animation to incorporating video and sound. We realize that your organization may not yet be clear on what your Web needs are. Our talented staff will work with you to guide you in the right direction.

I have enclosed a brochure that explains the four website design packages we offer. Choose the one that is right for your needs, then give us a toll-free call any time at 800-543-6677. We will be glad to set up a free consultation.

Sincerely,

3. Informal/Colorful Style. Good for communicating with people you know well or for communicating good news to those you are familiar with.

Dear Jack,

Thanks for asking about our Web design services. We have a full range of services and can provide you with just about anything you want in the way of website design. Our prices are competitive. We charge $60 an hour for basic logo design and up to $100 an hour to design and get your site up and running.

As you know, we have seven talented designers who work on all projects. I have included a brochure that explains the various website design packages we offer. If you have a clear idea of what you want on your site, shoot your ideas over via e-mail to bwo@clear.com or give me a call at 800-657-8000. If you're not sure exactly what you want from a website, just give me a call, and we can set up a consult.

It's great to hear from you, and I look forward to working with you again.

Sincerely,

As you can see from the letters in Figure 8-2, the three styles are not mutually exclusive. For example, the modern business style is more personal than impersonal and can be colorful as well. Nevertheless, these general distinctions allow us to learn how to appropriately apply a style and its elements to each writing situation.

Since most business writing situations call for using the modern business style, when you revise your documents, follow the guidelines outlined next to revise for tone, sentence structure, and word choice. Then use your knowledge of each stylistic characteristic to achieve the style that best suits your purpose.

Revising for Tone The right tone for your business document depends on your audience and your purpose. In general, strive for a tone that is confident, but not arrogant; conversational, but not too personal; courteous and sincere, but not condescending. Revising the tone of your writing can be as simple as changing a sentence or choosing a different word. Improving your tone also improves other sentence structure problems, like wordiness or awkward syntax.

1. **Identify the Problem.** I'm confident that our Web design capabilities are far beyond what you could ever imagine and will more than exceed any needs that you could possibly have.
   Problem: Over-confident and arrogant
   Correction: After you read our proposal, I believe you will agree that our Web design capabilities will meet your needs.

2. **Identify the Problem.** Just between you and me, I know you will love our Web design capabilities. Plus I'm a single mom, and I could really use your business.
   Problem: Too personal and unprofessional
   Correction: After you read through the Web design packages we offer, I believe you will find one that meets your company's needs.

3. **Identify the Problem.** Our clothes are made of the finest material. You ruined the material by washing the garment rather than having it dry cleaned. Next time, try ordering clothes that are machine washable.
   Problem: Condescending, rude, and preachy
   Correction: Our clothes are made of the finest material. To maintain their good looks, they need to be dry cleaned.

4. **Identify the problem.** If you have questions or concerns, please feel free to contact us. We look forward to hearing from you.
   Problem: Tired conclusions sound anything but sincere.
   Correction: You may have questions about the restructuring process. We would be glad to clarify your concerns.

REVISING YOUR SENTENCE STRUCTURE

Use Active Voice When writing in the modern business style, use the active voice most of the time rather than the passive voice. **Active voice** means that the subject or agent of the sentence performs the action. This kind of sentence is easy to understand because it mirrors our thinking processes: Subject/Verb/Object is the standard sentence order in English. "Still, we incurred no debt in making these purchases, and our shares outstanding have increased only 1/3 of 1%" (Buffett, 2000).[21]

The **passive voice** is the normal action backward. The subject or agent is acted upon. The person or thing doing the action can be found in the "by" clause at the end of the sentence. Using the passive voice forces the reader to take extra time to mentally convert passive voice into the active voice.

active voice
A sentence in which the subject performs the action; opposite of passive voice.

passive voice
A sentence in which the subject or agent is acted upon; opposite of active voice.

Here are three sentences written in the passive voice.

1. Still, no debt was incurred **by us** in making these purchases, and an increase of only 1/3 of 1% was experienced **by our shares outstanding**. (Here the agent is deleted altogether.)
2. The decision to lay off 50% of the workforce was made yesterday. (Who made the decision?)
3. The proxies solicited hereby for the Heartland Meeting may be revoked, subject to the procedures described herein, at any time up to and including the date of the Heartland meeting. (Who may revoke the proxies?)[22]

Here are these same sentences revised using the active voice.

1. Still, **we incurred** no debt in making these purchases, and **our shares outstanding increased** only 1/3 of 1%.
2. Yesterday, **top management** made the decision to lay off 50% of the workforce.
3. By following the directions on page 10, **you** may revoke your proxy and reclaim your right to vote up to and including the day of the meeting.

In example B, the active version tells you who decided to lay off the employees, which shows management's willingness to take the responsibility.

Example C makes clear who may revoke a proxy. The revised version also replaces the wordy *described herein* with the clear *page 10*. The second examples show how the active voice transforms sentences, making them less wordy and easier to understand.

Sometimes using the passive voice makes sense; for example, when you do not want to blame someone or when the agent is less important than the action. Look at the following three examples. These are appropriate uses of the passive voice.

1. **When you do not want to take responsibility for the action:** Your order was lost but will be immediately replaced and shipped by overnight mail. You will receive it tomorrow, December 1, by 10:30 a.m.
2. **When you do not want to directly blame or accuse the person who acted:** The credit card number for payment was not included.
3. **When the subject or agent who performed the action is not important:** Your order will be shipped overnight mail.

FIGURE 8-3: PLAIN ENGLISH VS. THE BUREAUCRATIC STYLE

Plain English means writing in a style that readers can easily understand. Its original aim was to make formal documents, such as insurance policies, leases, warranties, stock prospectuses, and tax forms published by corporations and government agencies understandable to consumers. In 1998, the Securities and Exchange Commission (SEC) made Plain English official when it released the "Plain English Rule," requiring the issuers of stock prospectuses to write them in a clear and understandable (accessible) manner. The SEC also published *A Plain English Handbook* to assist puzzled corporate writers. You can download a copy of the handbook at www.sec.gov/pdf/handbook.pdf.

Today, many organizations such as Texaco, MBNA American Bank, Procter & Gamble, Ford, General Electric, and governmental agencies have adopted the Plain English style.

FIGURE 8–3: PLAIN ENGLISH VS. THE BUREAUCRATIC STYLE

© auremar/Shutterstock.com

In contrast to the Plain English style, the bureaucratic style is impersonal, wordy, cumbersome, and often passive. It has an "official" sound, however, that some writers prefer because they believe the style lends their writing an authoritative voice.

One of the earliest cases reported under the New York State Plain English law on contracts involved the Lincoln Savings Bank's customer agreement on safe-deposit boxes. State attorney general Robert Abrams sued the bank, demanding that it simplify the following agreement, saying, "I defy anyone, lawyer or lay person, to understand or explain what that means." Here is the 121-word sentence that puzzled Abrams.

The liability of the bank is expressly limited to the exercise of ordinary diligence and care to prevent the opening of the within-mentioned safe deposit box during the within-mentioned term, or any extension or renewal thereof, by any person other than the lessee or his duly authorized representative and failure to exercise such diligence or care shall not be inferable from any alleged loss, absence or disappearance of any of its contents, not shall the bank be liable for permitting a colessee or an attorney in fact of the lessee to have access to and remove contents of said safe deposit box after the lessee's death or disability and before the bank has written knowledge of such death or disability.[23]

The lawsuit ended when the bank settled and changed the passage to the following: "Our liability with respect to property deposited in the box is limited to ordinary care by our employees in the performance of their duties in preventing the opening of the box during the term of the lease by anyone other than you, persons authorized by you or persons authorized by the law."

The revised version is more direct and readable. It uses active voice and the personal pronoun "you" to replace the cumbersome passive voice and the impersonal legalese, such as colessee and lessee. In addition, the second passage eliminates meaningless legal phrases like *renewal thereof, duly authorized representative*, and *within mentioned term*, to name a few. Once pared to its essential meaning, the sentence is much easier to read and understand.

Avoid Nominalizations (Nouns That Hide Verbs) Nouns that end in -ion, -ment, -ship, and -ize hide strong verbs. When released, these strong verbs make your sentence less abstract and more vigorous. So get busy and spring those hidden verbs. Make your sentences vivid and powerful.

> **Before:** The attainment of our goals will be possible this year.
> **After:** We will attain our goals this year.
> **Before:** Company B will have no stock ownership of the company.
> **After:** Company B will not own the company's stock.
> **Before:** We made a determination that Ms. Woods should be hired.
> **After:** We determined that we should hire Ms. Woods.

parallel structure
Two or more sentences are worded such that they have similar grammatical structures.

Use Parallel Structure **Parallel structure** means two or more sentences are worded such that they have similar grammatical structures. Make constructions in a sentence parallel—balanced—by matching phrase with phrase, clause with clause, verb with verb, and so on. Parallel structure provides a rhythm and clarity to your writing that makes it sound polished and easy to read. Items in a series should be parallel, as should the connecting words or phrases (and, but, or, for, nor; either or, neither nor, not only but also, both and).

Here is an example of parallel structure.

The writing team wrote the draft copy, revised the draft copy, and proofread the draft copy.

Keep Sentences Short Short sentences are easier to read than long ones. The average sentence length in business documents should be no more than 20–22 words. A sentence should convey one main idea or two closely related ideas. Here are three sentence types and when to use them.

1. The **simple sentence** is short, direct, and clear. Its form is subject/verb/object.
   Example: Profits collapsed this quarter.
   Use short sentences to add punch to your prose. They are especially useful to emphasize an idea in conclusions or after several complex sentences. However, watch overuse of the short, punchy sentences since they can make your prose sound choppy and monotonous when used again and again.

2. The **compound sentence** comprises two sentences connected by a coordinating conjunction: *and, but, or, for, yet, nor,* and *so.* The subjects or ideas of these sentences should be closely related.
   Example: During the Internet bubble, stocks such as Yahoo, Spyglass, Cyber-Cash, E-Pay, and E-Fax commanded huge sums of money, but the soaring prices of these same stocks collapsed two years later when the speculative bubble burst.

dependent clause
An incomplete sentence.

3. The **complex sentence** is composed of one independent clause and one or several dependent clauses. A **dependent clause** is an incomplete sentence. Complex sentences are good for showing the relationships between ideas. In the following sentence, the less important idea appears in the dependent clause, while the sentence's independent clause emphasizes the main idea.
   Example: Although stocks such as Yahoo, Spyglass, and E-pay commanded huge sums of money during the Internet bubble, their soaring prices crashed when the speculative bubble burst two years later.

REVISING FOR WORD CHOICE

Use Everyday Words   Using familiar, everyday words helps your readers understand your document. Short, familiar words help you get your points across without slowing down your readers. Some beginning business writers mistakenly think that pompous, bureaucratic jargon impresses their supervisors. This could not be farther from the truth. Supervisors fume as they revise employees' wordy prose, eliminating deadwood and bureaucratic jargon.

© Mascha Tace/Shutterstock.com

In short, do not confuse short words with simple ideas. The trick is to express complex ideas in words your readers can easily understand. Revise your sentences to eliminate the deadwood of business and bureaucratic jargon, legalese, trite expressions, and clichés. **Clichés** are overused, worn-out words or expressions. In addition, know when using technical jargon supports your communication goals and when doing so threatens them.

clichés
Overused, worn-out words or expressions.

Eliminate Business and Bureaucratic Deadwood   Substitute shorter, more direct words in place of long-winded words.

Instead of	Use
Terminate	End
Elucidate	Explain
Utilize	Use
Ascertain	Learn
Endeavor	Try
Impact	Affect, influence
Necessitate	Require
Input	Views, comments
Throughput	Material
Prioritize	Rank
Peruse	Review
Remunerate	Pay
Strategize	Plan

Another perpetrator of wordiness is trite expressions, which, like clichés, are words and phrases that have been used for so long they have lost their meaning and punch. Many of the trite phrases remaining in business writing are holdovers from a time when business correspondence followed strict and formal conventions. When you use trite expressions in your letters, memos, and reports, you sound hollow and stuffy. Eliminate the following trite phrases completely or replace each with more up-to-date phrases.

Avoid	Use Instead
Per your request	As you requested
Under separate cover	By overnight mail
Pursuant to your request	As you requested
Enclosed please find	Enclosed
The undersigned	I or me
Permit me to say	Just say it!
At your earliest convenience	Specify a date
Set forth herein	In this agreement

Avoid the following clichés whenever possible. Substitute with meaningful words or fresh metaphors:

grandstand play
hit the nail on the head
worth its weight in gold
solid as a rock
in the ballpark

Every year since 1976, Lake Superior State University has added several words and expressions to its archive of what they refer to as banished words. Since the tradition's inception, words and expressions such as *selfie, perfectly candid, my bad, hunker down, sexting, teachable moment, bromance, a-ha moment, man up, chillaxin, thanking you in advance,* and *ginormous* have made their list along with many others. Unlike most clichés, most of the words and expressions that make Lake Superior State University's banished words list have not been around for a long period of time. Whether we call such words and expressions banished words or clichés, they have apparently overstayed their welcome.

technical jargon
Terms that allow experts within a discipline to speak and write to one another in a technical shorthand that is not necessarily understood by non-experts.

Use Technical Jargon Cautiously Technical jargon allows experts within a discipline—accountants, doctors, lawyers, stockbrokers, information technology specialists—to speak and write to one another in a technical shorthand. Technical jargon refers to terms that allow experts within a discipline to speak and write to one another in a technical shorthand that is not necessarily understood by non-experts. However, the SEC's *Plain English Handbook* recommends we eliminate jargon and legalese in business documents.[24] Why? Because technical jargon, when used in a document to be read by people who do not share knowledge of the jargon, inevitably causes frustration and misunderstandings (see Figure 8-4). Therefore, when writing business documents, avoid technical jargon unless you know your reader understands it.

Here is an example of technical jargon in a letter to a customer: "The account was never reported as a repossession, but was reported as a charge off." Translated into layperson's terms, this means: "Your account was cleared."

Technical jargon may be a natural part of your vocabulary. That's understandable. However, not everyone you communicate with understands such terms. The trick is to determine who would be confused and frustrated by technical jargon, then replace the words you know he or she will not understand.

Use Concrete Rather Than Abstract Words Choose words that are as specific and concrete as your context requires. Concrete terms, such as *cheeseburgers* and *French fries*, help your readers visualize what you say. The more abstract word *meal* would not prompt the *cheeseburger and French fries* image in most readers' minds. When you write, you want the pictures in their minds to match your image. Complex concepts are more comprehensible when readers can form a mental picture.

Avoid Using Abstract Words **Abstract words** refer to language that is often unclear and subject to different interpretations. When you use abstract words—*asset, freedom, love, integrity, liberty, capital appreciation value, zero coupon bond*—you risk reader misunderstanding. To make abstract concepts more comprehensible to your reader (1) use as many concrete terms as you can, and (2) create a hypothetical scenario in which people perform actions.

Here is an example from the SEC *Plain English Handbook*.[25]

Before: Sandyhill Basic Value Fund, Inc. (the "Fund") seeks capital appreciation and, secondarily, income by investing in securities, primarily equities, that management of the Fund believes are undervalued and therefore represent basic investment value.

How to Use (not abuse) Jargon, Slang, and Idioms http://writeitsideways. com/how-to-use-not-abuse-jargon-slang-and-idioms/

abstract words Language that is often unclear and is subject to differing interpretations.

After: At the Sandyhill Basic Value Fund, we will strive to increase the value of your shares (capital appreciation) and, to a lesser extent, to provide income (dividends). We will invest primarily in undervalued stocks, meaning those selling for low prices given the financial strength of the companies.

Make your references clear. Words like *this, that, thing*, and *they* can confuse your readers because the words are vague and imprecise. Substitute vague references with precise equivalents.

Finally, quantify what you mean whenever possible. Words like *few, several, good, interesting, more, small,* and so on have different meanings to you and to your reader. Replace the vague words with specific words, like *two dollars, 200 people, had an intricate plot,* and *two inches tall.*

Increasing the Readability of Business Documents
http://ontariotraining.
net/12-ways-to-increase-the-readability-of-your-business-documents/

FIGURE 8–4: EVALUATE YOUR DOCUMENT'S READABILITY

A document's **readability** refers to the readers' ability to read and understand your document easily. They may even find it interesting. Two key elements of readability are (1) the complexity of the sentence structure and (2) the complexity of the vocabulary. Readability formulas, such as the Fog index and the Flesch-Kincaid Scale, measure the number of words in a sentence and syllables in each word to measure textual difficulty. Each scale makes its determination in terms of grade level.

For the Flesch-Kincaid Scale, you want your text to be somewhere below grade 12, preferably in the single digits. Most routine business documents should score between grades 7–9. Business publications such as the *Wall Street Journal* and *Fortune* rate between 9–11, and technical documents score between 12–14.

Do not get the idea that you want to write at a grade 15 level to reflect your education. Rudolf Flesch, a pioneer in the Plain English movement, developed formulas to predict readability for businesspeople but kept the term *grade level* from his earlier work with grade school students. Do not let the term mislead you; the lower your number, the better your writing, the easier it is to read. Your word processing program should include the results of several readability indexes as part of its grammar checker. Test a section of your writing to see how it rates.

Do not rely solely on readability scales to determine your writing's readability. While word difficulty and sentence length are factors in making your document readable, the indexes overlook other important considerations that contribute to the ease of reading, such as sentence structure, paragraph coherence and unity, logical connection and convincing support of your major ideas, and document design. To fully evaluate your document's readability, check its purpose, content, organization, style, and tone.

Use Precise Words   When you revise, be sure you use each word precisely. Misuse of one word for another can destroy your document's credibility. For example, the misused words in the following sentences express wrong meanings.

- The real estate mongrel made a fortune before he was 30. (*mogul* is intended)
- The CEO's decision was purely obituary. (*arbitrary* is intended)
- Our manager is a man of great statue. (*stature* is intended)
- Irregardless of his decision, I'm staying with the team. (*irregardless* is not a word; regardless is intended)
- The proofreader commentated on my letter. (*commented* is intended; do not make up words because they sound more official)

Besides revising for exact meanings, ensure your words work in context. Make them work for you, not against you. For example, if you are writing a fundraising letter for a cancer research organization, do not use *sick* in your opener: "Are you sick and tired of all the requests asking for your hard-earned money?"

If you are unsure of a word's meaning, look it up in a hardcopy dictionary or a comprehensive online dictionary such as *Merriam-Webster Online, Collins Online Dictionary*, or *Oxford Dictionaries Online*. Or visit www.facstaff.bucknell.edu/rbeard/diction.html where you will find links to online dictionaries in languages ranging from English, German, and French to Spanish, Japanese, and Korean.

Revise for Wordiness Wordiness refers to the fat in your sentences that you could delete to give you sleek, easy-to-read, powerful sentences. Use the following Just-In-Time (JIT) writing tips to check your sentences for extra verbiage.

JIT Tips for Cutting the Fat As you revise for wordiness, check your prose for the following common problems and tighten accordingly.[26]

JIT #1: Watch for the overused impersonal opening. "It is/was," "there is/are." Check your sentences for these wordy beginnings. Cut them out, and replace them with the real subject of the sentence as in the following examples.

It was clear to **the employee** why … (7 words)
The employee knew why … (4 words)
There are **five employees** in this division who were late for flying lessons. (13 words)
Five employees were late for flying lessons. (6 words)

JIT #2: Break up stringy sentences. Avoid too many connectors, such as *and* and *but*, that tie loosely related ideas together in one sentence.

Problem. Regardless of their seniority, all employees who hope to become vampires should start their education by enrolling in the special course to be offered at Vampire U., **and** this course will be offered on the next eight Saturdays, beginning on January 24, **but** you could also begin your apprenticeship by taking approved online-after-dark courses selected from a list available in the Un-Human Resources Office, ext. 123.

Revision. Regardless of seniority, all employees who hope to become vampires should take one of the following steps. (1) Enroll in the special Vampire U. course beginning January 24 and continuing for eight Saturdays. (2) Take approved online-after-dark courses from a list available in the Un-Human Resources Office, ext. 123.

JIT #3: Keep the subject and verb of a sentence as close together as possible.
Difficult to read. Webspeak, pervading everything from the *New York Times Manual of Style* to office e-mail and reminding us that putting the English language in the hands of engineers is like putting Vikings in charge of neurosurgery, **makes** business communication even more vague and stilted.

Unites the subject and verb. Webspeak makes business communication even more vague and stilted, pervading everything from the *New York Times Manual of Style* to office e-mail. The pervasiveness of webspeak reminds us that the English language is now in the hands of computer engineers, something akin to putting Viking marauders in charge of neurosurgery.

JIT #4: Eliminate unneeded prepositions.
I am writing **in order to** list the potential issues **in regard to** the Russell account **in advance of** the client visit. (22 words)
I am writing **about** the Russell account **to** list the potential issues before the client visit. (16 words)

JIT #5: Eliminate Superfluous Words. **Superfluous words** are unnecessary words that can be eliminated or reduced. Correcting them supports clarity and concision. For example, replace the phrase in column one with the word(s) in column two:

Drop this	In favor of this
In order to	To
In the event that	If
Subsequent to	After
Prior to	Before
Despite the fact that	Although
Because of the fact that	because, since
In light of	because, since
Owing to the fact that	because, since
Take into consideration	Consider
Very good	Good
In reference to	About

JIT #6: Eliminate Redundancies. **Redundancies** are words that repeat the same idea in a different word(s). Correcting for them not only eliminates necessary text, but also supports clarity and conciseness. For example, replace the phrase in column one with the word in column two:

Drop this	In favor of this
Absolutely free	Free
Reduce down	Reduce
Cancel out	Cancel
True facts	Facts
Past experience	Experience

How to Spend Less Time Revising
http://www.business-writingblog.com/business_writing/2015/07/how-to-spend-less-time-revising-.html

SUMMARY: SECTION 3—
REVISING FOR YOUR AUDIENCE

- Our stylistic choices influence the way our reader responds to our document, from a willingness to read it to accepting our ideas. As business writers, we have three broad styles to choose from: (1) the passive/impersonal style, (2) the modern business style, and (3) the informal/colorful style. While you should evaluate your purpose and audience before you choose a style, in most cases, the modern business style is the most effective for business documents.
- When we revise for tone, we evaluate how close we have come to having a confident, conversational, courteous, and sincere tone. Improving your tone can be a simple matter of revising a sentence or two and correcting word choices.
- Revising for sentence structure involves looking at the sentence structures that produce the modern business style: active voice, strong verbs, parallel words and phrases, short sentences, and everyday words.

PROOFREADING

After carefully revising your document for tone, organization, sentence structure, and word choice, take the time before sending it out to proofread. **Proofreading** refers to conducting a final review of a document to catch oversights in need of correction such as misspellings. Your focus here will be on looking for grammar, punctuation, spelling, and typographical errors you didn't notice while revising. In addition, double check all figures (e.g., dates, dollar amounts, etc.) and names for correctness, using the original source if possible.

If you think you can get by without this final pass, think again. Being 99 percent correct is not good enough. For example, the need to proofread thoroughly comes to the forefront

proofreading
A final review of a document to catch oversights in need of correction such as misspellings.

© B Calkins/Shutterstock.com

when asked how many spelling errors are too many in a résumé. The typical answer is one! Well, that is also true of other business documents.

At the proofreading stage, you could pull in a proofreading buddy to help you out. A buddy system lets you receive and give help. One way to use a proofreading buddy is to ask the person to read aloud the final draft while you follow along on the recipient's copy. Reading aloud is a powerful proofreading tool because you catch problems in tone as well as sentence structure and word choice problems.

If you do not have a partner, read the material backward, starting from the last word and reading from right to left. This keeps you from getting caught up in the sense of the document so that you do not overlook errors. Look especially for those spelling errors that your spell checker does not catch: to/too/two; their/there; etc.

As you look over your document for formatting, be sure that you have properly located and identified graphics and that your headings at each level match. See Figure 8-5 for more proofreading tips.

FIGURE 8–5: PROOFREADING TIPS

- Always double check the spelling of every proper name—especially those you think you know by heart. One mistake can mean doing the entire job over again, which can easily be a six-figure blooper.

© Thinglass/Shutterstock.com

- Always call every phone number that appears in your document.
- Double check little words: *or* and *of*; *it* and *is* are not interchangeable.
- Do not proof for every type of mistake at once—do one proof for spelling, another for spaces, consistency of word usage, font sizes, etc.
- Have other people read the document.
- Keep a list of your (or the writer's you are proofing) most common errors and proof for those in separate passes.
- Double check boilerplate text like the company letterhead. Just because it is frequently used, does not mean it has been carefully checked.
- Double check whenever you are sure something is right—certainty is dangerous.
- Lay document pages side by side to check for formatting consistency. If your paragraphs look like a Rorschach Inkblot Test, you need some formatting revision.

Source: Adapted from Carl T. Hagberg and Associates, The 1998 Annual Meeting Planner (1998).

GIVING AND TAKING CRITICISM EFFECTIVELY

Criticizing someone else's writing is a tricky business. Many writers take criticism of their writing personally. To avoid hurting someone's feelings, while still making helpful comments, follow these guidelines.

- Preface your comments with *The reader* as in "The reader is confused here." Avoid using *you* or *I*, which personalizes your comments.
- Try to meet face-to-face with the writer to review your comments. This softens the impact of your marks on the page.
- When you edit for content concerns, make your comments specific. For example, if the writer has not answered the reader's questions, point out which ones were unanswered.
- When editing for style and tone, be specific. Writing *wrong tone* is not helpful.
- When you edit for grammar and punctuation, remember that these are usually the last things on the writer's mind. Do not belittle the writer. Point out these mistakes with empathy. Otherwise, you only arouse anger and defensiveness in the writer.

Just as criticizing writing is tricky, taking and digesting criticism is also a tricky business. To avoid getting defensive and feeling that you are now a worthless worm of a human, follow these guidelines as you read through the critical comments and make your changes.

- Do not view criticism as a personal attack on you and your judgment.
- Do not base your self-worth as a writer on negative criticism.
- Ask for examples that illustrate the criticism.
- If you truly believe a critical comment is wrong, talk it over with the editor or proofreader before you make or ignore the suggested change.
- Remember that editors and proofreaders put effort into their reviews to help you improve your documents. Thank them for it.

Giving and Receiving Criticism
https://www.
universalclass.com/
articles/writing/busi-
ness-communication/
conflict-resolution/com-
municating-effectively-
giving-and-receiving-
criticism.htm

MANAGING THE REVISION PROCESS IN ORGANIZATIONS

In a typical organization, documents cycle through many layers of management; each manager adding, deleting, or re-organizing until the top executive signs off, usually as "lead" writer. The final document may not resemble in the least the original written by the junior staff member. However, as each writer leaves his or her stamp on it, the document finally reflects the company's persona, the "accepted" look and feel of the organization's documents.[27]

Although supervisors revise to ensure uniformity in documents that their departments or groups produce, they also bring an understanding of the corporate politics that entry-level employees may be unaware of.

Document cycling is another form of collaborative writing within organizations. Indeed, it is an integral part of organizational writing. **Document cycling** basically involves sending a document to a fellow employee who makes suggestions and then passes the document on to another fellow employee who follows the same process. According to Susan Kleimann at the U.S. General Accounting Office, the review process is what transforms individual products into institutional products.[28] Many staff-level employees see the review process as having a single function—approval of their work—and are frustrated by the document cycling process. Understanding the organization's review process helps you be prepared for its complexities.

document cycling
Involves sending a document to a fellow employee who makes suggestions and then passes the document on to another fellow employee who follows the same process.

In the basic review unit, a staff member sends a completed document to a supervisor, who sends it to a manager, who then sends it back to the employee with notes for revisions to incorporate into the final document. This one-cycle review may turn into several as the employee makes the requested changes and resubmits, only to find the document returned once again for revision. Usually this cycle is not repeated more than three times.[29]

© OtnaYdur/Shutterstock.com

This constant appearance of disapproval can be frustrating to the staff member; the process itself is time consuming. However, supervisors and managers have other reasons besides approval for recycling documents. After years of writing documents that are purposeful, audience sensitive, and politically savvy, the experienced manager revises a subordinate's writing according to the organization's changing needs and the political climate. In these instances, revision requests become a primary means of transmitting corporate values and culture, and the requests play a key role in making the individual's work advance the organization's objectives.[30]

Two factors complicate the review practice in the workplace:

1. The importance of the document to the organization.
2. The presence of multiple internal and external reviewers.[31]

A document with high impact on an organization, such as an executive letter for an annual report or a mission statement, will go through multiple layers of extensive review to assure that the document reflects the company viewpoint and to guard against liability concerns.

In flatter, less hierarchical organizations, where responsibilities and expertise are often fragmented, many readers review a document to ensure that all areas of expertise are represented. A document is reviewed for legality, methodology, content, regulatory compliance, and many other concerns.[32] In addition, many of these reviewers will see a document twice, once as an initial draft on which they make their comments, and again as a final draft that incorporates the comments. The document may also be circulated to external readers with interests in the final draft, such as clients and attorneys.

Although the review process can be overwhelming to the novice writer, as Kleimann's study points out, document cycling serves two important purposes in organizations:

1. To ensure better-written products through the process of vertical review.
2. To provide a form of feedback that works; therefore, the writers improve over time.[33]

Since these documents are not only recycled during the review process but may also become part of other documents over time, the review cycle is one that enhances the final product and sharpens the writer's expertise.

SUMMARY: SECTION 4— PROOFREADING, GIVING AND TAKING WRITING CRITICISM, AND MANAGING THE REVISION PROCESS IN ORGANIZATIONS

- After revising, proofreading is the last pass at your document. Proofreading is intended to catch spelling, grammar, and punctuation oversights as well as typographical errors.
- Knowing how to give and receive writing criticism is important for two reasons: to help others improve their writing and to help you improve your own.
- The revision process varies across organizations. Once you are on the job, become familiar with how your organization manages the revision process.

Notes

1. Susan Benjamin, *Words at Work* (Reading, MA: Addison-Wesley, 1997), 71.

2. Linda Flower and John Ackerman, "Evaluating and Testing as You Revise," in *Strategies for Business and Technical Writing*, ed. Kevin J. Harty (Boston: Allyn & Bacon, 1999), 24.

3. Elizabeth A. Powell, "A Note on Purpose, Voice, and Style in Business Writing" (University of Virginia: Darden School Foundation, Charlottesville, UVA-BC-0113, 1995), 2.

4. Benjamin, 91.

5. *Dealing Effectively with Unacceptable Employee Behavior*, SkillPath Seminars, 1997. Brochure.

6. Benjamin, 94.

7. Ibid., 95.

8. Guidelines for writing conclusions adapted from Richard Bierck, "How to Begin to Write, When to End," *Harvard Management Communication Letter*. Collected in *The Manager's Guide to Effective Business Writing* (Cambridge, MA: Harvard Business School Publishing, 2000).

9. Flower and Ackerman, 24.

10. Ibid., 24–25.

11. Glenn J. Broadhead and Richard C. Freed, *The Variables of Composition: Process and Product in a Business Setting* (Carbondale: Southern Illinois University Press, 1986), 59.

12. John Clayton, "Writing in Scenarios," *Harvard Management Communication Letter* (January 2001): 3.

13. Flower and Ackerman, 33–34.

14. Guidelines for revising document format and typography adapted from Kathryn Riley, Kim S. Campbell, Alan Manning, and Frank Parker, *Revising Professional Writing* (Superior, WI: Parley Press, 1999), 59–64.

15. Bruce Ross-Larson, *Effective Writing* (New York: W.W. Norton, 1999), 137.

16. John Fielden, "What Do You Mean You Don't Like My Style?" *Harvard Business Review* (May/June 1982): 3.

17. Edward P. J. Corbett and Sheryl L. Finkle, *The Little English Handbook* (New York: Longman, 1998), 55–56.

18. Richard Lanham, *Revising Business Prose* (Boston: Allyn & Bacon, 2000), 89.

19. Corbett and Finkle, 56.

20. Fielden, 7.

21. Warren Buffet, *Annual Report* (Omaha: Berkshire-Hathaway, 2000), 3.

22. Securities and Exchange Commission (SEC), *A Plain English Handbook* (Washington, DC: (2001), 20, www.sec.gov/pdf/handbook.pdf.

23. Robert Abrams, "What They Said," *ABA Journal*, 66 (August 1980): 950.

24. SEC, 30.

25. SEC, 30.

26. Just-In-Time (JIT) Tip Sheets idea adapted from Lynn Veach Sadler, "Preparing for the White Rabbit and Taking It on the Neck: Tales of the Workplace and Writingplace," in *Professional Writing in Context*, ed. J. F. Reynolds C. B. Matalene, J. N. Magnotto, D. C. Samson, Jr., and L. V. Sadlert, (Hillsdale, NJ: Lawrence Erlbaum, 1995), 129–178.

27. Susan D. Kleimann, "The Complexity of Workplace Review," *Technical Communication*, Fourth Quarter (1991): 520–526.

28. Ibid., 521.

29. Ibid.

30. Ibid.

31. Ibid., 522.

32. Ibid., 524–525.

33. Ibid., 526.

BUSINESS LETTERS & MEMOS

LEARNING OUTCOMES

After reading this chapter, you should be able to:

1. Identify the various forms of written business communication.

2. Discuss the roles of formality and informality in selecting the best form for each writing situation.

3. Describe key writing principles that affect business letters and memos.

4. Discuss the role of business letters.

5. Describe the three business letter styles.

6. Discuss the role of business memos.

© *korrr/Shutterstock.com*

BENEFITS OF LEARNING ABOUT BUSINESS LETTERS AND MEMOS

1. Being able to write effective business letters supports your message objectives and decreases misunderstandings and other problems associated with poorly written business letters.
2. Being able to write effective business letters supports your job stability and career growth objectives.
3. Being able to write effective business memos supports the objectives of your messages and decreases misunderstandings and other problems associated with poorly written business memos.
4. Being able to write effective business memos supports your job stability and career growth objectives.

SELECT KEY TERMS

INTRODUCTION

Business letters are formal documents that convey information predominately to external stakeholders. The most common business letter styles are the block style and modified block style. The three business letter strategies are the direct strategy, indirect strategy, and persuasive strategy. The direct strategy is recommended for neutral-news and good-news letters. The indirect strategy is recommended for negative-news letters, and the persuasive strategy is recommended for persuasive letters.

Business memos are relatively short, informal and semi-formal documents used to exchange information among people within organizations. Business memos are often sent as e-mail messages, and some refer to these as e-memos.

The intent of this chapter is to provide you with information about how to write effective business letters and memos. The goals of this chapter are realized through discussions on the following topics: written communication in organizations, the roles of letters and memos in organizations, impact of writing basics on letter and memo quality, business letters, business letter styles, business letter components, writing strategies, writing styles, and business memos. The information pertaining to the above-mentioned writing skills is reinforced by several student website resources including *PowerPoint slides, preview tests, chapter assessment tests, writing mechanics rules and guidelines, YouTube videos, interactive exercises,* and the *interactive glossary.*

WRITTEN COMMUNICATION IN ORGANIZATIONS

Written communication is developed and transmitted in many ways in organizations. Common forms of written communication in today's workplace include e-mail messages, text messages, instant messages, letters, memos, and reports. In addition, organizations routinely post written information on company websites and social media sites.

The focus in this chapter is on *letters* and *memos.* The other forms of written communication mentioned above are addressed elsewhere in the book.

Formality plays an important role in selecting the best form of written communication for each writing situation. Written documents and messages are frequently viewed as being formal, informal, or semiformal. For example, letters are considered to be formal documents. Most documents and messages that are developed and/or transmitted electronically (e.g., e-mail messages, text messages, tweets) are considered to be informal. Awareness of such differences in perceptions is important because readers' formality expectations vary and should be taken into consideration. For example, if you need to send an important message to a client, a formal document is typically expected. In this case, you would send a hardcopy letter. In contrast, if you need to send a brief message containing routine, straightforward information to a subordinate within the company, an informal written medium such as e-mail would be a good choice. Or, if you and a fellow worker, who are on the same job level, need to discuss some points pertaining to a routine, noncontroversial matter, instant messaging would be a good choice. Before moving on, let's look at one more example that would land you midstream on the formality spectrum. If you need to send a message regarding changes in procedures internally to subordinates, a semiformal document such as a memo would be a good choice.

Differences Between Business Letters and Memos
http://smallbusiness.
chron.com/difference-
between-business-
memo-business-
letter-57723.html

THE ROLES OF LETTERS AND MEMOS IN ORGANIZATIONS

THE ROLE OF BUSINESS LETTERS

A substantial portion of communication that occurs in the business place is accomplished via letters. Letters are formal documents that convey information mostly to communication partners outside the organization. Examples include customers, clients, investors, suppliers, and government officials. In addition, some **business letters** are sent internally, most often to superiors. Business letters contain messages ranging from routine, informational matters to complex, controversial matters. The goal is typically to share neutral, good, or negative news or persuade readers to take a specific course of action. There are several types of business letters ranging from sales and inquiry letters to adjustment and follow-up letters.

business letter
A formal document typically sent to external communication partners.

10 Types of Business Letters
http://work.chron.com/10-types-business-letters-9438.html

© Zoltan Zempleni/Shutterstock.com

THE ROLE OF BUSINESS MEMOS

A substantial portion of internal communication in the business place is accomplished via memos. Memos most frequently contain routine information. Like letters, the goals of memos range from sharing neutral, good, and negative news to persuading readers to take a specific course of action.

Today's memos come in one of two forms—hardcopy memos and e-memos. On the surface one might think that all memos should take the form of e-memos due to e-mail's efficiencies. Despite the convenience and ease of developing and sending e-memos, they have their shortcomings ranging from general writing quality to privacy concerns. Such shortcomings are discussed in detail in this chapter.

Memo Examples
http://business.lovetoknow.com/wiki/Memo_Examples

© Tatchapbol/Shutterstock.com

IMPACT OF WRITING BASICS ON BUSINESS LETTER AND MEMO QUALITY

No doubt about it, appropriate writing strategies and well-ordered, message-appropriate content are central to effective business letters and memos. However, these features alone do not typically get the job done. Well-written letters and memos are grounded in writing basics. They depend on the writer's mastery of the three-stage writing process (planning, drafting, revising) and the ability to apply appropriate business writing principles and writing mechanics, such as grammar and punctuation.

Think of business writing basics like the bricks-and-mortar analogy. As it relates to writing, our words and thoughts are the bricks, and writing principles and mechanics are the mortar. Much as mortar forms a strong bond with bricks when properly mixed and applied, writing principles and mechanics form a strong bond that unites our words and thoughts in business letters. Will your letters and memos be strong like a well-constructed brick structure, or will they be weak and crumble, resulting in miscommunication and other problems?

Select writing principles that are especially important to developing effective business letters are discussed below. These writing principles are addressed in detail in the "writing process" overview in this chapter and the next.

KEY WRITING PRINCIPLES THAT AFFECT BUSINESS LETTERS AND MEMOS

While all writing principles are important to the development of effective letters and memos, some are especially effective in helping writers achieve their objectives. These particular writing principles are the writer's tone of goodwill, using the you-attitude, emphasizing reader benefits, emphasizing the positive, using unbiased language, and being polite, These writing principles are discussed in detail, along with others, in chapters 6 and 7. Additional writing principles important to the development of letters and memos are: word choice, emphasis and de-emphasis, and writing concisely while including enough detail to support message clarity and purpose. These are discussed below.

Word Choice Appropriate word choice contributes to clear, effective letters and memos. Careless word choice can lead to confusing messages that result in frustration, miscommunication, and other problems. Obviously, you are challenged to take care in your word choice.

Familiar, everyday words help your reader grasp your message. Short, familiar words help you get your points across without slowing down your reader. Some business writers mistakenly think that pompous, bureaucratic jargon impresses their supervisors. This could not be farther from the truth. Supervisors fume as they revise employees' wordy prose, eliminating deadwood and bureaucratic jargon. In short, do not confuse short words with simple ideas. The trick is to express complex ideas with words that your readers understand. Therefore, revise your sentences to eliminate the deadwood of business and bureaucratic jargon, legalese, trite expressions, clichés, and technical jargon.

Emphasis and De-emphasis Techniques The ability and willingness to use emphasis and de-emphasis techniques can make the difference between average and exceptional letters and memos. For example, in a sales letter you would use emphasis techniques to highlight your central selling point. If your central selling point is some feature other than price, then you would use de-emphasis techniques to downplay your price. There are many opportunities in letters and memos to emphasize and de-emphasize information.

Common emphasis techniques include italicizing and boldfacing words, phrases, and sentences. Other examples include placing material you want to emphasize in emphasis positions in short sentences within short paragraphs. (*Emphasis positions* are near the beginning and end of sentences and paragraphs.) Still other examples include writing extensively about something and placing material you want emphasized in *active voice* sentences.

Common de-emphasis techniques include not italicizing and boldfacing words, phrases, or sentences. Other examples include placing material you want to de-emphasize near the center of long sentences in long paragraphs. Still other examples include writing briefly about the material you want to de-emphasize and placing it in a *passive voice* sentence.

Writing Concisely In today's business place, employees who write concisely and clearly are valued. So be careful not to include unnecessary details. Know the depth of detail your reader needs. In addition, use short words instead of long words when short words can get the message across. If necessary, challenge yourself to write a greater number of short sentences. Finally, avoid using surplus words and phrases. *Surplus words* and *phrases* are those that do not affect message clarity when deleted or substituted with a shorter replacement.

Well-written, concise messages promote clarity and save people time. However, in your quest to write concise messages, be careful not to leave out details necessary for message clarity. Message clarity is always more important than conciseness!

SUMMARY: SECTION 1— THE FOUNDATIONS OF EFFECTIVE BUSINESS LETTERS AND MEMOS

- Decisions regarding formality expectations are crucial to selecting the best form of communication for writing situations.
- Business letters and memos are formal documents typically sent to external communication partners, but may also be sent internally to people within your organization.
- Business memos are semiformal documents that convey information to readers within the organization.
- Writing basics—grammar, punctuation, and spelling—impact the effectiveness of business letters.
- Key writing principles, such as appropriate word choice, emphasis and de-emphasis techniques, and concise writing, are critical to writing effective business letters and memos.

BUSINESS LETTERS

As mentioned before, letters are formal documents that are typically used to convey information to communication partners outside the organization. The goal most often is to either share neutral, good, or negative news or to persuade readers to a specific course of action.

Most letters are hardcopy documents sent to readers on company letterhead. Most are one page in length, although two- to three-page letters are not uncommon.

Some letters are developed and sent as e-mail letters, and some are sent as attachments to e-mail messages. Still others are transmitted through fax machines. Keep in mind, however, that sending hardcopy letters on company letterhead is the preferred approach, whether you are communicating with external or internal audiences. Some of this has to do with tradition, some with the formal statement that letters make, and some with the realization that e-mail can be easily hacked, raising privacy and security concerns.

© timquo/Shutterstock.com

FIGURE 9–1: FORM LETTERS

Some letters are sent to many people. This is especially true of sales letters or, for example, debt collection letters. In such situations writing separate, customized letters for each recipient would not be possible or necessary. Such letters are typically referred to as *form letters*. Form letters provide a cost-effective alternative in these letter-writing situations, whether the letter is sent in its entirety to numerous recipients or boilerplate text is inserted.

When the importance of the message escalates and the situation is non-routine, a form letter is the incorrect choice, in large part because it is often seen as too general, unpersuasive, and impersonal. A customized letter is required. A job application cover letter is such a situation. Since no two employers are exactly the same, it would be foolish to send a form cover letter to several recruiters. Cover letters should be customized for each employer and available position. If it is well written, such a letter is specific to the potential employer, persuasive, and personal. To send out form cover letters is like rolling dice—the odds are against you.

BUSINESS LETTER STYLES

The two most common letter styles are the block style and the modified block style. The **block style** is the more efficient of the two styles because all lines begin on the left margin, eliminating the need to set tabs and indent lines. With the block letter style you do not have to worry about forgetting to indent a line, whether it is the first line of a paragraph or another letter component. The **modified block letter style** is the more traditional style. Each style is presented below followed by a brief description of each component.

block letter style
Format for a business letter in which all lines, with the exception of the letterhead, begin at the left margin.

modified block letter style
Format for a business letter in which the date, complimentary closing, written signature, and keyboarded name start at the horizontal center point and the first line of each paragraph is indented one-half inch.

Block Letter Style   The block letter style has gained popularity over the years due to its efficiencies. This style rightfully earns its name because every line of every letter component, with the exception of the company letterhead, starts at the left margin. The company letterhead is typically centered horizontally about one inch from the top of the page, whether keyboarded or preprinted. Standard top, bottom, and side margins are one inch.

The block style does not necessarily mean full justification. For many reasons, there is usually no attempt to have each line end evenly on the right margin. Figure 9-2 contains the block style letter contents.

FIGURE 9-2: BLOCK LETTER STYLE COMPONENTS

Company Letterhead

Return Address – If company letterhead is not used
Current Date
Inside Address – Person to whom you are writing
Attention Line – ATTENTION: Person's Name
Salutation:
Body Paragraphs – Do not indent the first line of each paragraph. Single space the paragraphs. Double space before the first paragraph, between paragraphs, and after the last paragraph.
Complimentary Close, – Followed by three blank lines for the written signature
Written Signature
Keyboarded Name
Sender's Title
Writer/Typist Initials – RW/gt
Enclosure Notation – Enclosed: Photos of new building
Copy Notation – Name(s) of people who also received the letter

---

Modified Block Letter Style   The modified block letter style is a traditional style still used in some businesses. It differs from the block style in that the current date, complimentary closing, written signature, and keyboarded name/title start at the horizontal center point. The first line of each paragraph may start at the left margin as in the block style or may be indented one-half inch. With this style, the company letterhead is typically centered horizontally about one inch from the top of the page, whether keyboarded or preprinted. Standard top, bottom, and side margins are one inch.

As with the block style, there is usually no attempt at full justification. Figure 9-3 shows the modified block style letter contents.

FIGURE 9-3: MODIFIED BLOCK LETTER STYLE COMPONENTS

Company Letterhead

Current Date
Return Address – If company letterhead is not used
Inside Address – Person to whom you are writing
Attention Line – ATTENTION: Person's Name
Salutation:
Body Paragraphs – Do not indent the first line of each paragraph. Single space the paragraphs. Double space before the first paragraph, between paragraphs, and after the last paragraph.

Complimentary Close, – Followed by three blank lines for the written signature
Written Signature
Keyboarded Name
Title

Writer/Typist Initials – RW/gt
Enclosure Notation – Enclosed: Photos of new building
Copy Notation – Name(s) of people who also received the letter

© Lichtmeister/Shutterstock.com

SECOND-PAGE LETTER HEADINGS

When you write business letters that exceed one page, include a standard heading on succeeding pages. This way if the pages get separated or mixed up, they can be easily reordered.

The three components you should include in a standard second-page heading are the name of the person or company you are writing to, the page number, and the letter date. The most common second-page headings are the *vertical heading* and the *horizontal heading*.

Vertical Second-Page Heading This heading should start one inch from the top of the page on blank paper (or second-page stationery if your company uses it). Each heading component should begin at the left margin in a block format and should be single spaced. Triple space after the third line (current date), then continue with the body of the letter. Figure 9-4 contains an example of a vertical second-page heading.

Horizontal Second-Page Heading This heading should also start one inch from the top of the page on blank paper (or second-page stationery if your company uses it). With this heading style, all three heading components are on the same line. The name starts at the left margin, the page number is centered horizontally, and the current date is positioned so that it ends at the right margin. Triple space after that line, then continue with the body of the letter. Figure 9-5 contains an example of a horizontal second-page heading.

BUSINESS LETTER COMPONENTS

The typical business letter contains the following standard components: *company letterhead, current date, inside address,* **salutation**, *body,* **complimentary close**, *written signature,* and *keyboarded name/title.* Each is described below. In addition, some business letters contain one or more other components. Common among these are **attention line**, **subject line**, *enclosure notation, copy notation,* and *postscript.* Each of these is also described below.

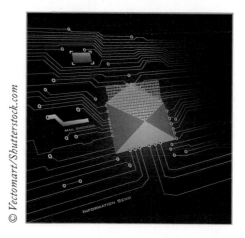

© *Vectomart/Shutterstock.com*

Company Letterhead This is typically preprinted on company stationery and contains information such as company logo, company name, post office box address, physical address, e-mail address, telephone number, and fax number.

Current Date This sounds simple enough, but certain standards should be adhered to. When writing letters to U.S. communication partners, spell out the month followed by the date and year (June 5, 2014). Do not use the digital version (06-05-14 or 6-5-14 or

6-5-2014). When writing letters to international communication partners, it is more typical to start with day followed by the month and year (5 June 2014).

Inside Address The inside address (or letter address) contains the name and mailing address of the person or company the letter is being sent to.

Salutation This is the greeting to the reader. If you are writing to a specific individual, the typical salutation is the word *Dear* followed by the receiver's title (Ms., Mr., Dr., etc.) and surname followed by a colon, for example, Dear Ms. Garcia:. If you are writing to a company and do not have a specific individual's name, use a salutation such as Human Resources Department or To Whom It May Concern.

Body This is the message. Most business letters contain three parts: an *opening paragraph*, one or more *body paragraphs*, and a *closing paragraph*. Each of these parts is discussed at some length in the Writing Strategies section.

Complimentary Close As the term suggests, this closes the letter. It is typically a word or phrase followed by a comma. Examples of popular complimentary closes include *Sincerely* and *Respectfully*. Although they are less widely used, complimentary closings such as *Sincerely yours* and *Very truly yours* are still used by some.

Written Signature This is the writer's written signature. It is typical to leave three blank lines between the complimentary close and keyboarded name components for the writer's written signature.

Keyboarded Name/Title At minimum, this component contains the keyboarded name of the writer. In addition, the writer's job title should follow his or her name either to the right of it (e.g., William G. Rogers, Project Director) or below it. If your title appears on the line below, omit the comma after your name on the line above.

salutation
The letter's greeting (e.g., Dear _____).

complimentary closing
The letter's closing (e.g., Sincerely).

OTHER BUSINESS LETTER COMPONENTS

Attention Line Use this when you will send your letter to a company, but want to direct it to a specific person (Attention: Mr. Kuo), position (Attention: Marketing Director), or a department within the company (Attention: Information Systems Department). It is the second line of the inside address.

Subject Line As the term implies, the subject line tells the reader, in brief, the nature of the letter. It starts with the word *Subject*: followed by colon, then a five- or six-word message description. The subject line is located between the salutation and the first paragraph of the body.

Enclosure Notation This notation indicates to the reader that you have sent along one or more items with the letter. If you enclose one item, either type Enclosure (the word only) or type Enclosure followed by a colon and the item enclosed (Enclosure: Sale Flyer). If you enclose two or more items, type Enclosures followed by a colon and the number of enclosures (Enclosure: 2). The enclosure notation is located one blank line below the keyboarded name/title component.

Copy Notation This tells the reader the name(s) of others the letter was sent to. Here are some examples: cc: Tamara Jones, cc: Tamara Jones & Jennifer Maxwell. The copy notation is located one blank line below the enclosure notation. If there is no enclosure, the copy notation is located one blank line below the keyboarded name/title component.

Postscript The postscript typically contains an afterthought or a brief reminder of information that the writer wants to emphasize. Type PS followed by the entry. The

attention line
In the address block, drawing attention to a specific person or position.

subject line
Brief statement that specifies the letter's subject.

postscript is located one blank line below the copy notation. If there is no copy notation, the postscript is located one blank line below the enclosure notation. If there is no enclosure notation or copy notation, the postscript comes one blank line below the keyboarded name/ title component.

WRITING STRATEGIES

Business letters and memos typically have one of three purposes. The purpose may be to (1) share neutral or good news, (2) share negative news, or (3) persuade the reader to take some action. Each letter-writing strategy is discussed and presented in detail.

But first, a practical reminder is in order. Even if a specific letter-writing strategy is the clear and logical choice for a message, do not use that strategy if you know your communication partner wants the message structured differently. For example, when conveying negative news, writers typically avoid sharing the bad news until later in the letter for reasons that are explained shortly. However, if you know your communication partner (reader) wants you to get to the main point early in the letter, then overlook the dictates of the preferred writing strategy. While letter-writing strategies are both logical and effective, reader expectations and desires must also be taken into consideration.

© YanLev/Shutterstock.com

Now, let's look at the recommended letter-writing strategies for the three business letter categories—neutral or good news, negative news, and persuasive messages. When properly integrated, these strategies typically improve your ability to accomplish your message objective. The three strategies are most frequently referred to as the *direct strategy*, the *indirect strategy*, and the *persuasive strategy*. Before doing so, however, it is especially helpful to remind you of the roles de-emphasis and emphasis techniques play in the development of effective business letters. This is especially true of indirect strategy (negative news) and persuasive strategy (persuasive) business letters. Figure 9-6 contains several de-emphasis and emphasis techniques.

FIGURE 9-6: DE-EMPHASIS AND EMPHASIS TECHNIQUES

De-emphasis Techniques

In regard to indirect strategy (negative news) business letters, writers are challenged to not only share the negative news with the reader, but to do so in such a way that the reader won't take their business elsewhere permanently. Appropriate letter-writing strategy and tone are critical to achieving this goal. Appropriate use of de-emphasis techniques plays an important role also. Business writers obviously need to state the negative news in such letters, but they do not have to put the spotlight on it, which many readers would find annoying. Instead, they should use de-emphasis techniques that lower the spotlight. Here are some de-emphasis techniques that will help you do so when you are writing indirect strategy business letters.

- State the negative news in a paragraph located near the middle of the letter
- State the negative news in the middle of a paragraph
- State the negative news in the middle of a reasonably long sentence
- State the negative news using the passive voice
- Avoid repeating/restating the negative news
- Avoid using emphasis techniques such as boldfacing and italicizing

Emphasis Techniques

In regard to persuasive-strategy (persuasive) business letters, writers are challenged to persuade readers to buy, do, or support something. Creating reader desire is the central goal when writing these letters and using appropriate emphasis techniques will help you achieve it. Essentially, you would use emphasis techniques in persuasive-strategy business letters to emphasis (put the spotlight on) qualities that will build reader desire (e.g., *central selling point in a sales letter*) Here are some emphasis techniques that will help you do so when you are writing persuasive-strategy business letters.

- State desire-building qualities near the beginning and/or end of paragraphs
- State the desire-building qualities in short sentences
- State the desire-building qualities using the active voice
- Restate the desire-building qualities where appropriate
- Use emphasis techniques where appropriate (e.g., *boldfacing, underscoring, italicizing*)

DIRECT STRATEGY

The **direct strategy** works well with business letters meant to share neutral or good news. Neutral- and good-news letters include a wide range of letter types, including letters providing or requesting routine information and responding favorably to requests for action. Examples range from claim letters, thank-you letters, and job-offer letters to letters providing credit information, letters of appreciation, and letters of condolence.

direct strategy
Letter-writing style used for positive or neutral news in which the main idea is presented at the beginning of the letter.

This is the easiest strategy and message type to write because you are satisfying your reader's needs and, in the case of good-news messages, putting him or her in a good mood. Believe it or not, it is possible to write ineffective neutral- and good-news letters by careless handling of writing strategy, tone, clarity, grammar, and/or punctuation. This is unfortunate when it happens because writing these letters effectively is not difficult.

Central to the direct strategy is sharing the neutral or good news in the first paragraph, thus placing the reader in a positive frame of mind. This vastly increases the likelihood that the reader's interest and attention will be maintained to the end of the letter. The direct strategy is outlined below.

Direct Strategy Outline

- **Opening Paragraph.** Present the main idea—the neutral or good news—and develop a friendly tone.

Specifically, state the news in the first sentence of the opening paragraph so you can capture the reader's interest from the outset.

- **Body Paragraph(s).** Present the supporting information and maintain a friendly tone.

The central purpose of the body is to logically and clearly present information that supports the main idea (the neutral or good news).

- **Closing Paragraph.** Maintain a friendly tone and include some forward-looking talk when applicable. End the letter positively.

The tone in neutral-news and good-news letters should be positive, sincere, and conversational. It should be devoid of negative words.

Now, let's look at a poorly written, direct strategy, good-news letter (Figure 9-7). The letter makes a job offer to a candidate following his interview. Sounds like an easy letter to write—right? They are easy letters to write if we know how to write them and care about doing a good job.

FIGURE 9-7: DIRECT STRATEGY, GOOD-NEWS LETTER (POORLY WRITTEN VERSION)

Advanced Energies
22 Harris Drive
Houston, TX 77003
(713) 436-9102

April 2, 201X

1078 First St.
Austin, TX 78702

Dear Chao:

It was a pleasure visiting with you on March 15. Advanced Energies is a leader in the energy industry, and I am certain you were impressed with all you learned about us during your visit. While Advanced Energies has focused predominately on oil and natural gas exploration in the past, we are currently entering the solar energy market with plans for expansion. With all this growth and diversity, we are adding to our ranks of employees and that's where you come in. We would like you to come to work for us.

We will start you out with a two-day orientation next month. Then, we will place you in one of the areas where we have the most need of help. I hope you are flexible in regard to the type of work you do. During your orientation we will discuss your starting pay rate and benefits package.

See you in May.

Very truly yours,

Juan Lopez
Legal Department

Enclosures: 3

Before reading further, take a few minutes to identify the weaknesses in the poorly written letter above. You should be able to identify a number of weaknesses in all three letter parts.

Now, let's look at some of some of letter's weaknesses.

Opening Paragraph. While the tone is friendly, there are three noticeable weaknesses. (1) The good news should have been shared in the first sentence, not the last. The reader may have tossed the letter before getting to the last sentence, assuming a rejection was forthcoming. (2) All the hype about the company in sentences 2 and 3 is unnecessary, making the letter longer than necessary. (3) The you-attitude is weak. The opening is writer centered instead of reader centered and is reinforced by the inclusion of several *I's*, *we's*, and *our's*.

Body Paragraph. There are three noticeable weaknesses. (1) The tone is semifriendly at best. (2) The you-attitude is weak. (3) Many details are missing, thus leaving questions. When will the orientation take place? Where will the orientation take place? What type of work will the reader do? What is the starting pay? What are the starting benefits?

Closing Paragraph. There are three noticeable weaknesses. (1) The tone is not friendly. (2) The closing is writer centered. A you-attitude is nowhere to be found. (3) There is no

"We look forward to …" statement at the end. In addition, the complimentary closing *Very truly yours* is outdated. *Sincerely* is a friendly close that is appropriate for this letter.

Now let's look at an improved version of the letter (Figure 9–8).

FIGURE 9–8: DIRECT STRATEGY, GOOD-NEWS LETTER (IMPROVED VERSION)

Advanced Energies
22 Harris Drive
Houston, TX 77003
(713) 436-9102

April 2, 201X

Mr. Chao Yung
1078 First St.
Austin, TX 78702

Dear Chao:

We are pleased to offer you the position of Research Director in the Legal Department at Advanced Energies. You have the exact qualifications and personality we hoping to find in a candidate for this position and believe we are a good fit for you also.

As mentioned during our March 24 interview, orientation will take place on April 17–18. Plan to arrive at my office (2024B, second floor, Progressive Tower) at 9 a.m. on April 17. We have much information to share with you, and know you will have questions. Please develop a list of questions you have and e-mail it to me by April 16 so I have time to review it prior to meeting with you. In addition, please review the attached benefits information and be prepared to make selections from the benefits options. Finally, please review the Legal Department's policy handbook, which can be found at AEpolicies@lgldept.com prior to April 17.

We are excited about having you as a member of the Advanced Energies team. During the upcoming days, please contact me at (713) 436-9102, ext. 32 or at juan.lopez27@ AE.org. See you on the 17th.

Sincerely,

Juan Lopez
Legal Department

Enclosures: 3

Before reading further, take a few minutes to identify the strengths of this improved version.

Now, let me share some of the strengths in the improved letter.

Four strengths are particularly noticeable in this improved version of the opening paragraph. (1) The good news is shared in the first sentence, placing the reader in a good frame of mind. He will read more! (2) There is a strong you-attitude. The opening is reader centered, as it should be. (3) The writer compliments the reader. (4) The tone is friendly.

Body Paragraph. Three strengths are evident in this improved body paragraph. (1) The you-attitude is strong. (2) Supporting information is included, which removes guessing and frustration from the equation. (3) The tone is friendly.

Closing Paragraph. Four strengths should jump out in the closing paragraph of this improved version. (1) The you-attitude is strong. (2) The tone is friendly. (3) Practical, forward-looking talk is included. (4) Contacting the company is made clear and easy.

In addition, using *Sincerely* for the complimentary closing was the right choice. It is friendly and right on the mark.

Now let's look at another poorly written, direct strategy, good-news letter (Figure 9-9). The situation the letter is based on grows out of a farmer's request to a farm equipment distributor for a line of credit so he can purchase global positioning systems for his combine and tractors. The equipment distributor decided to grant the farmer's request and is writing to inform him of the good news. Sounds like a simple letter to write—right? The poorly written sample below reminds us that, when we are careless, we can weaken even an easy letter!

FIGURE 9–9: DIRECT STRATEGY, GOOD-NEWS LETTER (POORLY WRITTEN VERSION)

Hanley Farm Equipment
213 Lima Avenue
Findlay, OH 45840
(419) 724-6153

June 12, 201X

Mr. Robert G. Conway
CR347
Arcadia, OH 44804

Dear Mr. Conway:

We are pleased with your interest in the Global Star global positioning system. Our Global Star global positioning system is revolutionizing the farming industry! Our global positioning system can save users enough money to pay it off quickly with increased profits. This is why we are happy to grant you credit to purchase the equipment you expressed interest in.

Our field representative, Tom Holman, will call you soon to get you on his installation schedule. Following this initial meeting, contact Tom any time you have questions.

Thanks for giving us your business.

Cordially,

Sharon Tyler
Accounts Manager

Before reading further, take a few minutes to identify the weaknesses in the poorly written letter. You should be able to identify a number of weaknesses in all three letter parts.

Now, let me share some of the letter's weaknesses.

Opening Paragraph. While the tone is friendly, there are four noticeable weaknesses. (1) The good news should have been shared in the first sentence, not the last. The reader may have tossed the letter before getting to the last sentence, assuming a rejection was forthcoming. (2) All the unnecessary sales talk leading up to the good news makes the letter longer than necessary. (3) The you-attitude is weak. The writer-centered opening (instead of being reader centered) is reinforced by the inclusion of several *we's* and *our's*. (4) More detail is needed in the last sentence. Credit is being granted, but the amount is not specified. This farmer could be left guessing and wondering if he received the full amount he applied for or less or more.

Body Paragraph. While the tone is friendly and a you-attitude is evident, there are two noticeable problems. (1) The word *soon* is vague and can be improved by being specific. Farmers often live by tight schedules, especially around planting and harvest times. They need specifics. (2) Lots of details are missing, thus leaving questions. How long will the installation take? Will time be set aside for training and, if so, how long will it take? What is the preferred way to contact Tom?

Closing Paragraph. While the tone sounds friendly on the surface, there are two major problems. (1) The closing is writer centered. A you-attitude is nowhere in sight! (2) There is no attempt to offer some forward-looking talk. This situation is ripe for forward-looking talk. For example, the writer could mention future increases in the farmer's credit line or include a brochure describing other equipment the farmer might find of interest. In addition, the writer could offer the farmer discounts on future purchases based on referred customers (fellow farmers). Oh, the missed opportunities!

The complimentary closing *Cordially* is cold. *Sincerely* is a friendlier close, and a friendly close is appropriate for this letter.

Now, let's look at an improved version of the letter (Figure 9-10).

FIGURE 9–10: DIRECT STRATEGY, GOOD-NEWS LETTER (IMPROVED VERSION)

Hanley Farm Equipment
213 Lima Avenue
Findlay, OH 45840
(419) 724-6153

June 12, 201X

Mr. Robert G. Conway
CR347
Arcadia, OH 44804

Dear Mr. Conway:

Your request for a $20,000 line of credit toward farm equipment purchases has been approved. This clears the way for you to move ahead and purchase the global positioning systems for your combine and tractors and get them installed before it's time to harvest your wheat crop next month.

Our field representative, Tom Holman, will call you on June 16 to schedule a day and time convenient for you to install your new systems. If you have questions regarding the credit conditions, equipment, installation, or training that you want to ask Tom about before he calls you on the 16th, please contact him at (419) 724-6153, ext. 5 or at tholman@globalstar.org. It will take approximately four hours to install the systems and approximately one hour to train you on them.

We really appreciate that you came to us with your equipment needs, and we trust that the global positioning systems will exceed your expectations! The $20,000 credit line will easily cover the cost of the equipment you expressed interest in; leaving you an extra $5,000 for future purchases. With this in mind, consider visiting our website to learn about other farm equipment products you may find useful. If you have questions or want to explore your next equipment purchase, stop by our store in Findlay or call me at (419) 724-6153, ext. 2.

Sincerely,

Sharon Tyler
Accounts Manager

Before reading further, take a few minutes to identify the strengths in this improved version.

Now, let me share some of the strengths in the improved letter.

Opening Paragraph. Four strengths are noticeable in this improved version of the opening paragraph. (1) The good news was shared in the first sentence, placing the farmer in a good frame of mind. He will read on! (2) There is a strong you-attitude. The opening is reader centered, as it should be. (3) The specific amount of credit approved is stated, leaving no room for confusion or frustration. (4) The tone is friendly.

© svinka/Shutterstock.com

Body Paragraph. Four strengths should be evident in this improved version of the body paragraphs. (1) The you-attitude is strong. (2) Vague words such as *soon* have been omitted. (3) Supporting information is included, which removes guessing and frustration from the equation. (4) The tone is friendly.

Closing Paragraph. Three strengths should jump out in the closing paragraph of this improved version. (1) The you-attitude is strong. (2) The tone is friendly. (3) Practical, forward-looking talk is included that ranges from mention of the excess available credit to the invitation to explore other product lines online.

Using *Sincerely* for the complimentary closing was the right choice. It is a friendly complimentary close and right on the mark.

INDIRECT STRATEGY

The **indirect strategy** works well with negative-news business letters. Examples of negative-news letters include request refusals, claim refusals, credit refusals, job rejection letters, and a host of other situations requiring a negative response.

For many, this is the most difficult strategy and message type to write because you are sharing information that your reader does not want to see, all the while doing your best to maintain goodwill. This is no small challenge! These letters require special attention to writing strategy and tone.

Central to the indirect strategy is delaying the mention of the negative news until after you have laid out the reasons supporting the negative outcome. The attempt here is to set a logical base for the decision that the reader can understand. The reader may not be pleased with your negative decision, but should understand on a logical level why the decision had to be made as it was.

Indirect Strategy Outline

Delivering a Negative News Message
http://catalog.flat-worldknowledge.com/bookhub/15?e=mclean-ch17_s01

- **Opening Paragraph.** Present neutral, on-topic talk and develop a friendly tone.

Key to this strategy is not stating or hinting at the negative news in the opening paragraph. Not hinting that the outcome is good news is also equally important. To state or hint at the negative news in the opening paragraph turns off your reader to the rest of the letter. To hint at good news would only result in a harder fall for the reader when he or she reads the negative news later. Remain neutral and friendly and do not hint!

- **Body Paragraph(s).** Present reasons supporting the negative news, state the negative news, offer alternative(s) to the original request where applicable, and maintain a friendly tone.

This is the section where most of the work is accomplished in this type of letter. Start this section with the reasons leading up to the negative-news decision, all the while not giving away the negative news. That is a tough job! Then state the negative news clearly and tactfully. However, do not end the body at that point if possible. When applicable, follow up the negative news with one or more alternatives. Alternatives tell readers you care and give them choices in an otherwise uncontrollable situation.

- **Closing Paragraph.** Maintain a friendly tone and include some forward-looking talk when applicable.

Your goal here is to ease your reader in a forward-looking direction. This means you do not apologize and do not repeat the negative news. After all, you stated and explained the negative news clearly and tactfully in the body paragraph(s) and started easing the disappointment with offers of alternatives. Why would you now in the closing paragraph want to circumvent all that good effort by reminding the reader of the negative news? Finally, end the paragraph with a friendly tone and some forward-looking talk.

As previously mentioned, your tone in negative-news letters is crucial. Keep the tone positive, sincere, and tactful. Avoid using negative words or coming across as preachy, cold, defensive, condescending, patronizing, or arrogant.

Now let's look at a poorly written, indirect strategy, negative-news letter (Figure 9-11). The situation involves a ski resort and a job applicant. The ski resort has received below-average snowfall going into December, which has reduced customer traffic. As a result, it is unable to hire this job applicant at this time. Thus, we are looking at an employment rejection letter.

FIGURE 9–11: INDIRECT STRATEGY, NEGATIVE-NEWS LETTER (POORLY WRITTEN VERSION)

Sunny Valley Resort
14 Timberlane Rd.
Sante Fe, NM 87594
(505) 331-2424

December 2, 201X

Mr. Nicholas P. Brunsell
2400 Brumly St., Apt. 27
Santa Fe, NM 87504

Dear Nick,

The weather sure hasn't been very cooperative this fall. Here we are in early December, and we've had only one decent snowfall. It dropped enough snow for us to open a few runs, but we are nowhere close to full operation. We are really hurting because of this situation. This is not what you want to hear because the situation has caused us to initiate a hiring freeze.

Conditions will change if we get some more snow soon, but I am not holding out much hope with all this talk about global warming. If by some miracle we do get two or more significant snowfalls soon, everything will be good for us, and we will consider hiring additional help. I guess we will see what happens.

Sorry to have to share bad news. Thanks for your interest in working for the Sunny Valley Resort.

Sincerely,

Ron Baker
Operating Manager

Before reading further, take a few minutes to identify the weaknesses in the poorly written letter. You should be able to identify a number of weaknesses in all three letter parts.

Now, let me share some of the weaknesses in the letter.

Opening Paragraph. Very little positive can be said about this opening paragraph except that the grammar, punctuation, and spelling are in pretty good shape. Otherwise, it is loaded with weaknesses. Three main weaknesses come to mind. (1) The writer uses the direct strategy instead of the indirect strategy, giving away the bad news in the opening paragraph. (2) There is too much detail in the first two sentences, contributing to unnecessary wordiness. (3) The you-attitude is weak.

Body Paragraph. As was the case with the opening paragraph, little positive can be said about it. The paragraph contains numerous weaknesses. (1) It opens with pessimistic news. (2) The you-attitude is nonexistent. (3) The writer does not offer any tangible alternatives.

Closing Paragraph. The closing paragraph also contains several weaknesses. Four are evident. (1) The writer reminds the reader of the negative news from the first paragraph. (2) The writer apologizes to the reader. (3) The closing is not especially friendly. (4) There is no forward-looking talk.

Now, let's look at an improved version of the same letter (Figure 9-12).

FIGURE 9–12: INDIRECT STRATEGY, NEGATIVE-NEWS LETTER (IMPROVED VERSION)

Sunny Valley Resort
14 Timberlane Rd.
Sante Fe, NM 87594
(505) 331-2424

December 2, 201X

Mr. Nicholas X. Jackson
2400 Brumly St., Apt. 27
Santa Fe, New Mexico 87504

Dear Nick,

We have finally been blessed with a long-overdue snowfall. For snowboarding enthusiasts, such as yourself, this is certainly good news.

We plan to open approximately half of our beginner and intermediate runs and one-quarter of our advanced runs this coming Saturday, with the hope that there will be enough new snowfall during the next three weeks to open the remaining runs by Christmas. In the meantime, we plan to supplement as much as possible with man-made powder. Even then, at least one significant snowfall will be needed to ready the remaining runs. At the time that we are able to open at least 80 percent of the runs, we will be able to hire on additional help. Until then, the volume of business will not support hiring additional seasonal staff. Despite this temporary setback, if you are still interested in working at the Sunny Valley Resort this winter, please e-mail me at Ron-Baker12@sunnyvalley.org. As soon as snow conditions are right to support opening most of the remaining runs, we will bring you onboard. If for some reason this doesn't occur, we would like you to consider joining our summer whitewater rafting staff. Doing so would then secure you a guaranteed position with us for next winter.

I believe you will be a valuable member of Sunny Valley team and look forward to working with you. Please stay in touch.

Sincerely,

Ron Baker
Operating Manager

Before reading further, take a few minutes to identify the strengths in the improved version.

Now, let's look at some strengths in the improved letter.

Opening Paragraph. Five strengths are particularly noticeable in this improved version of the opening paragraph of the letter. (1) The negative news is not stated in the opening paragraph. (2) There is no hint of negative or positive news in the opening paragraph. The writer remains neutral. (3) There is a strong you-attitude. (4) The subject matter is on topic. (5) The tone is friendly.

Body Paragraph. Five strengths are particularly evident in this improved version of the body paragraph of the letter. (1) The you-attitude is strong. (2) Reasons supporting the negative news are presented in appropriate order and stated clearly. (3) The negative news is stated clearly, yet tactfully. (4) Alternatives are presented following the negative news, thus de-emphasizing the negative news. (5) The tone is friendly.

Closing Paragraph. Five strengths should jump out in the closing paragraph of this improved version of the letter. (1) The reader is not reminded of the negative news nor did the writer apologize in the closing paragraph. (2) The you-attitude is strong. (3) The tone is friendly. (4) The writer compliments the reader and expresses interest in working with him. (5) Forward-looking talk is included in such a way that the writer can be easily contacted.

Using *Sincerely* for the complimentary closing is the right choice. It is friendly and right on the mark.

Now let's look at another poorly written, indirect strategy, negative-news letter (Figure 9-13). The letter situation grows out of a researcher's request to access some of a company's data for a research project. The company has decided not to grant the researcher's request. Thus, the letter is a negative-news letter informing the researcher that she cannot access the desired company data. The poorly written sample below reminds us of the damage to goodwill that can result from a carelessly written, negative-news letter.

FIGURE 9–13: INDIRECT STRATEGY, NEGATIVE-NEWS LETTER (POORLY WRITTEN VERSION)

DD&D Corporation
10 Franklin Avenue
Boston, MA 02103
(617) 558-9867

February 16, 201X

Ms. Nancee L. Reid
457 Hartford Lane
Boston, MA 02105

Dear Ms. Reid:

This letter is being written to inform you that DD&D Corporation has no interest in taking part in your corporate sales projections research project. We will not grant you permission to access our sales projections figures.

In fact, our company has a policy that prohibits its participation in external research projects such as yours. If we were to provide sales projection figures to you for your proposed project, it would cause us numerous problems because other researchers would then expect the same treatment!

We are sorry we couldn't meet your request. However, if we can help you in any other way, please let us know.

Cordially,

Jeff Oliver
Public Relations Manager

Before reading further, take a few minutes to identify the weaknesses in the poorly written letter. You should be able to identify a number of weaknesses in all three letter parts.

Now, let me share some of the weaknesses in the above letter.

Opening Paragraph. Very little positive can be said about this opening paragraph except that the grammar, punctuation, and spelling are in pretty good shape. Otherwise, it is loaded with weaknesses. Five weaknesses come to mind. (1) The writer uses the direct strategy instead of the indirect strategy, giving away the bad news in the opening paragraph. (2) The second sentence is unnecessary, contributing to unnecessary wordiness. (3) The tone is unnecessarily negative, abrupt, and unfriendly. (4) The writer implies that the researcher's project is unimportant. (5) The you-attitude is nonexistent.

Body Paragraph. As is the case with the opening paragraph, little positive can be said about the body paragraph. It also contains numerous weaknesses. Four weaknesses come to mind. (1) The opening phrase, *In fact*, rubs salt into the wounds already opened in the first paragraph and is a continuation of an unwarranted negative tone. (2) The you-attitude is nonexistent. (3) The writer does not provide the reader much to base the denial on. (4) The writer hides behind a company policy he doesn't explain.

Closing Paragraph. The closing paragraph also contains several weaknesses. (1) The writer reminds the reader of the negative news in the closing paragraph. (2) The writer apologizes to the reader in the closing paragraph. (3) Attempts at being friendly and the brief forward-looking talk come off as insincere in light of the unnecessarily negative tone throughout the opening and body paragraphs.

Cordially is a cold closing. *Sincerely* is a friendlier close, and a friendly close is more appropriate for this letter.

Now, let's look at an improved version of the same letter (Figure 9-14).

FIGURE 9–14: INDIRECT STRATEGY, NEGATIVE-NEWS LETTER (IMPROVED VERSION)

DD&D Corporation
10 Franklin Avenue
Boston, MA 02103
(617) 558-9867

February 16, 201X

Ms. Nancee L. Reid
457 Hartford Lane
Boston, Massachusetts 02105

Dear Ms. Reid:

We appreciate your interest in using DD&D Corporation data in your corporate sales projections research project. The project sounds very interesting.

Each year we receive several requests asking for our assistance with research projects similar to yours. As a result, we established guidelines to determine which requests we can honor and which we cannot. One such guideline is that we only permit sales projections figures to leave corporate headquarters after they are announced publicly through press releases. The timing of your request is such that the sales projections figures you are requesting will not be released until April 15. Thus, we are unable to grant your request at this time. However, if you can wait for another two months, we should be able to grant your request then.

Your project has piqued my interest, and I look forward to seeing your findings once you finish. Please contact me at oliver@dd&dcorp.org if you have questions or other research needs.

Sincerely,

Jeff Oliver
Public Relations Manager

Before reading further, take a few minutes to identify the strengths in the improved version.

Now, let's look at some strengths in the improved letter.

Opening Paragraph. Five strengths are particularly noticeable in this improved version of the letter's opening paragraph. (1) The negative news is not stated in the opening paragraph. (2) There is no hint of negative or positive news in the opening paragraph. The writer remains neutral. (3) There is a strong you-attitude. (4) The subject matter is on topic. (5) The tone is friendly.

Body Paragraph. Five strengths are evident in this improved version of the body paragraph. (1) The you-attitude is strong. (2) Reasons supporting the negative news are presented in appropriate order and stated clearly. (3) The negative news is stated clearly, yet tactfully. (4) An alternative is offered following the negative news, thus de-emphasizing the negative news. (5) The tone is friendly.

Closing Paragraph. Five strengths should jump out in the closing paragraph of this improved version. (1) The reader is not reminded of the negative news nor does the writer apologize in the closing paragraph. (2) The you-attitude is strong. (3) The tone is friendly. (4) The writer makes a complimentary statement about the research project and expresses interest in seeing the findings. (5) Forward-looking talk is included in such a way that the writer can be easily contacted.

Using *Sincerely* for the complimentary closing is the right choice. It is friendly and right on the mark.

PERSUASIVE STRATEGY

persuasive strategy
Letter-writing style used for persuasive letters in which the request is made after the reason(s) have been presented.

The **persuasive strategy** works well with business letters that are meant to persuade the reader to take a specific course of action. Examples of persuasive business letters include sales letters, collection letters, recommendation letters, job offer letters, and letters ranging from requesting a favor to requesting some form of support. The persuasive letter-writing strategy is similar to the indirect strategy in that the request is made later in the letter, just as the negative news is stated later in the negative-news letter.

Many find writing persuasively a challenging strategy and a difficult message approach to write because persuading others to a course of action is not easy. Writing persuasively is no small challenge! These letters require special attention to writing strategy and tone.

Central to the persuasive strategy is delaying the request until after you have laid out reader benefits. This involves not only capturing the reader's attention, but also building his or her interest and, ultimately, desire before making the request. Using the persuasive strategy properly increases the odds that your reader will act on your request in the desired fashion. The persuasive strategy is outlined below.

- **Opening Paragraph**. Gain the reader's attention and develop a friendly tone.

AIDA: Attention-Interest-Desire-Action
http://www.mindtools.com/pages/article/AIDA.htm

Key to the persuasive strategy is not making the request in the opening paragraph. To state the request here would likely turn your reader off to your objective. It is also important that you capture your reader's attention in the opening paragraph so he or she will want to read on. A question is a good sentence structure for capturing readers' attention. Here is an example that I bet will catch your attention: How would you like to reduce your costs?

- **Body Paragraph(s)**. Build the reader's interest, then their desire. Next, state your request.

The body paragraph is an important section in persuasive letters. Here you start by building reader interest and ultimately desire before stating your request. Building interest and desire are at the heart of your ability to persuade your reader to respond positively to your request. Essentially, you are challenged to determine one or more ways to appeal to your reader, realizing that different situations and people are persuaded by different appeals. Common appeal categories include *direct gain*, *prestige*, and *altruism*. Specific examples of appeals include profit, recognition, pride, usefulness, and savings. As you might guess, the list of appeals is long. Once you have built desire, state your request clearly and make sure you make it easy for the reader to respond.

- **Closing Paragraph**. Restate your request or make the request if you didn't do so in the body. Make it easy for your reader to respond and include some forward-looking talk when applicable. Maintain a friendly tone.

The closing paragraph of a persuasive letter is more involved than the closing paragraph of direct and indirect strategy letters. For example, you would start the closing paragraph in a persuasive letter by stating the request if you did not do so in the body. Or, you might choose to open the closing paragraph with a restatement of the request if you made it in the body section. Make it easy for the reader to respond. End with a friendly tone and forward-looking talk.

As previously mentioned, your tone in persuasive request letters is important. Keep it positive, sincere, and tactful. Avoid negative words and do not come across as patronizing, condescending, arrogant, or pushy.

Let's look at a poorly written persuasive letter (Figure 9-15). This is a basic sales letter written with the goal of persuading the reader to choose Shooting Star Airlines the next time he or she takes a commercial flight. The poorly written sample will likely do little to convince the reader to fly Shooting Star Airlines.

FIGURE 9-15: PERSUASIVE STRATEGY LETTER (POORLY WRITTEN VERSION)

Shooting Star Airlines
217 North State Street
Chicago, IL 60604
(312) 852-6311

August 18, 201X

Ms. Leslie Koval Tanner
319 Bradford Lane
St. Louis, MO 63105

Dear Ms. Koval Tanner:

Tired of all the hassle and expense involved in flying commercial? We are here to offer you a much more pleasant and affordable travel experience. We want you to fly Shooting Star Airlines.

Shooting Star doesn't nickel and dime you to death with all those fees like most of the other commercial airlines, with the exception of luggage. Luggage is something that we can't even avoid charging you extra for. While we are disappointed that we have to charge for luggage, we trust you understand our position.

We know you are going to want to fly Shooting Star Airlines when you hear about our food and beverage offering. Unlike our competitors, on Shooting Star flights you will receive a free refill on soft drinks, tea, and coffee and an extra bag of peanuts or pretzels. We even let you use a small blanket for free when you get cold, which is typical on those northern routes. One of the ways we are able to offer so many extras, free of charge, is that all our flights have stopovers at two or more small, regional airports where we pick up additional passengers. Each of these stops will provide you with an opportunity to stretch your legs and, in some cases, buy a snack in the airport lobby. And if all that is not enough to impress you, every passenger on our flights can use the restroom at the front of the plane. There is no discrimination against passengers who fly coach!

Are you ready to fly Shooting Star Airlines? I bet you are, and we are ready to book your next flight. Just go online and look us up. Our service agents are standing by. Have your credit card ready, and thanks for the business!

Sincerely,

Miranda Krause
CEO & President

Before reading further, take a few minutes to identify the weaknesses in the poorly written persuasive letter above. You should be able to identify a number of weaknesses in all three parts.

Now, let's look at some weaknesses in the poorly written letter.

Opening Paragraph. There are three major weaknesses in the opening paragraph. (1) The writer follows a direct strategy by making the request in the opening paragraph instead of the less direct persuasive strategy. (2) The tone is neutral. (3) The you-attitude is weak at best.

Body Paragraphs. There are two problems with the body paragraphs. (1) While the writer builds interest, she did not build desire. For example, stating that there is a luggage fee and two or more stops at regional airports is a turnoff to most. (2) The request is not stated in the body as the persuasive strategy dictates.

Closing Paragraph. The closing paragraph contains three major weaknesses. (1) The you-attitude is weak. (2) The tone is cheesy and sounds like a cheap radio or TV commercial. (3) Contact information is not provided.

Now look at an improved version of the same letter (Figure 9-16).

FIGURE 9-16: PERSUASIVE STRATEGY LETTER (IMPROVED VERSION)

Shooting Star Airlines
217 North State Street
Chicago, IL 60604
(312) 852-6311

August 18, 201X

Ms. Leslie Koval Tanner
319 Bradford Lane
St. Louis, MO 63105
August 18, 201__

Dear Ms. Koval Tanner:

Do you remember the last time you enjoyed a commercial airline flight? It has probably been several years since you used words such as *enjoyable* and *pleasant* to describe your flying experience. Fortunately, enjoyable, pleasant commercial flights have not been lost to the past!

You may have heard about Shooting Star Airlines. We are "the new kids on the block" in the commercial airline industry, having provided service for slightly more than six months. Shooting Star Airlines currently flies routes to all major metropolitan airports and select regional airports in the United States and leads the industry in on-time flight arrivals and customer satisfaction.

From the outset, Shooting Star Airlines set a goal to be noticeably different than its competitors. Specifically, we set out to put the fun back into flying by making it a more enjoyable and pleasant experience so people would look forward to flying. The first step was to hire positive people who have a strong desire to serve customers. Next, we built more comfort into our airplanes, resulting in more legroom and bigger seats than our competitors. Shooting Star didn't stop there. We also provide flat screen monitors at each seat, along with headphones. We provide electrical outlets at each seat for your convenience, and the restroom at the front of each airplane is not off limits to coach passengers. Shooting Star Airlines also offers free blankets and pillows to passengers and serves free sandwiches, cookies, and non-alcoholic beverages on all flights.

The combination of above-average services and amenities, combined with friendly, helpful flight attendants, removes much of the drudgery from 21st-century flying and puts fun back into the experience. Learn more about Shooting Star Airlines by visiting our website at ShootingStarAirlines@fun.org. And the next time you are going to fly a U.S. route, consider giving us a try. We think you will be pleasantly surprised, and we guarantee that you will arrive at your destination relaxed.

Sincerely,

Miranda Krause
CEO & President

Before reading further, take a few minutes to identify the strengths of the improved letter.

Now, let's look at some strengths in the improved letter.

Opening Paragraph. Four strengths are noticeable in this improved version of the opening paragraph. (1) Appropriately, the request is not made in the opening paragraph. (2) The tone is friendly. (3) The you-attitude is strong. (4) The writer does a good job of gaining the reader's attention (e.g., opens with a question, piques the reader's interest with talk about enjoyable, pleasant commercial flights).

Body Paragraphs. Four strengths should be evident in this improved version of the body paragraphs. (1) The you-attitude is strong. (2) The tone is friendly. (3) The body paragraphs contain several statements that build interest and desire (e.g., free sandwiches and cookies, flat screen monitors at each seat). (4) Sufficient details are included.

Closing Paragraph. Three strengths should jump out in the closing paragraph of this improved version. (1) The request is clearly stated. (2) The tone is friendly. (3) Sufficient contact information is included so the reader can make contact easily.

Using *Sincerely* for the complimentary closing is the right choice. It is friendly and right on the mark.

Now, let's look at another poorly written persuasive strategy letter (Figure 9-17). In this letter the conference chairperson asks an expert in the real estate appraisal field to be the keynote speaker at an annual conference. The poorly written sample below will likely do little to convince the reader to say yes to the request.

FIGURE 9–17: PERSUASIVE STRATEGY LETTER (POORLY WRITTEN VERSION)

The Society of Real Estate Appraisers
1405 Wilson Dr.
Portland, OR 97205
(503) 784-3288

February 20, 201X

Dr. Kobe B. Evans
576 Vista Lane
Reno, Nevada 89503

Dear Dr. Evans:

We would like you to speak at the annual conference of The Society of Real Estate Appraisers. The conference will be held on August 13–15, and we would like you to join us and be this year's keynote speaker.

We hate to bother you because we know an important, busy person like you has many commitments. This is why we are contacting you well in advance of the conference—approximately six months. We're not picky about the topic of your talk. Pick one of interest to you. In addition, audience members take well to handouts, so make sure to bring plenty.

Please send your confirmation and the topic of your talk promptly so we can get the information printed on the conference flyers.

Cordially,

Yolanda Jordan
Conference Chairperson

Before reading further, take a few minutes to identify the weaknesses in the poorly written letter. You should be able to identify a number of them in all three paragraphs.

Now, let's look at some weaknesses in the above letter.

Opening Paragraph. There are four weaknesses in the opening paragraph. (1) The writer follows a direct strategy by making the request in the opening paragraph instead of the less direct persuasive strategy. (2) The tone is rather vanilla. It is not negative, but it's not overly friendly, either. (3) The you-attitude is nonexistent. (4) The opening does little to gain the reader's attention.

Body Paragraph. There are several problems with the letter's body paragraph. (1) At the heart of the problem, the writer does not build reader interest at the outset, then does nothing to build desire. (2) The request is not stated in the body as the persuasive strategy dictates. (3) Opening statements give the reader an out. (4) Details are scarce, for example, the talk topic and length.

Closing Paragraph. The closing paragraph contains several weaknesses. (1) The you-attitude is weak. (2) The tone is neutral. (3) Contact information to send along acceptance or denial is not provided.

Now, let's look at an improved version of the same letter (Figure 9-18).

FIGURE 9–18: PERSUASIVE STRATEGY LETTER (IMPROVED VERSION)

The Society of Real Estate Appraisers
1405 Wilson Dr.
Portland, OR 97205
(503) 784-3288

February 20, 201X

Dr. Kobe B. Evans
576 Vista Lane
Reno, Nevada 89503

Dear Dr. Evans:

Your recent article "Are Appraisers Talking to Themselves?" in the *Appraisal Journal* has drawn many favorable comments from local real estate appraisers. Congratulations on your publication.

The Society of Real Estate Appraisers wants to share with its members more information about appraisal report writing from the point of view of a specialist in real estate education and hopes to do so at the President's Dinner Session during the upcoming Annual Conference in Phoenix on August 13–15. Approximately 400 members will attend the dinner meeting, and we know they would be especially interested in hearing your thoughts and experiences regarding appraisal report writing. With this in mind, we extend to you an invitation to be our keynote speaker at the President's Dinner Session. This would be a wonderful opportunity for you to meet several members of the society and expand your professional network. In addition to covering your travel expenses, we will pay you an honorarium of $10,000.

The post-dinner meeting will be held from 7–9 p.m. at the McGallister Hotel in Phoenix on Thursday, August 14, with your talk running from 7:45 to 8:15 followed by 15 minutes of audience questions. We can promise you a pleasant evening and a receptive audience.

Along with your acceptance, we would like to have a photograph of you for display purposes. Please send your acceptance and photo to me by March 15 at yjordan@ scsrea.org. I look forward to hearing from you.

Sincerely,

Yolanda Jordan
Conference Chairperson

Before reading further, take a few minutes to identify the strengths in the improved letter.

Now, let's look at some strengths in the improved letter.

Opening Paragraph. Four strengths are particularly noticeable in this improved version of the opening paragraph. (1) Appropriately, the request does not come in the opening paragraph. (2) The tone is friendly. (3) The you-attitude is strong. (4) The writer did a nice job of gaining the reader's attention (e.g., publication, favorable comments).

Body Paragraphs. Four strengths should be evident in this improved version of the letter's body paragraph. (1) The you-attitude is strong. (2) The tone is friendly. (3) The body paragraphs contain several statements that build interest and desire (e.g., audience size, networking opportunities, honorarium). (4) Sufficient details are included.

Closing Paragraph. Three strengths should jump out in the closing paragraph of this improved version. (1) The acceptance is restated. (2) The tone is friendly. (3) Sufficient contact information is included to make it easy for the reader to respond.

Using *Sincerely* for the complimentary closing was the right choice. It is friendly and right on the mark.

A FINAL LETTER-WRITING STRATEGIES REMINDER

Now that we have reviewed the three letter-writing strategies, you are reminded that exceptions to these strategies are made at times and for logical reasons. The most common exception occurs when a writer knows with certainty that his or her reader wants the information presented directly (get to the point), even if the message contains negative news or if its goal is persuasion.

FIGURE 9–19: EMOTICONS AND EMOJIS IN BUSINESS LETTERS

Emoticons and *emojis* are visual images of facial expressions and objects. Emoticons and emojis are common in some e-mails, which is not to suggest that they are always welcome there. For example, including emoticons and emojis in personal e-mails is generally accepted; however, including emoticons and emojis in business e-mails is discouraged.

The general rule is that when you are writing business letters, do not include them. Otherwise, you may leave your reader with one or more negative perceptions about you and the organization you represent. You and your organization will be perceived by some as being unprofessional. Some readers will be distracted by them, while others will question your maturity.

WRITING STYLES

Writing style is often dictated by company policy or personal preference. Some styles are effective; others are not. Some styles target specific audiences (readers). Do you have a writing style? If so, can you describe and/or identify it? Is it an effective style? Are you open minded enough and skilled enough to switch writing styles when necessary to enhance your written communication?

Examples of letters written in three writing styles are presented here.

Passive/Impersonal Style   This style is filled with jargon and clichés and is difficult to read. This style is ineffective for routine correspondence as you can see in the example in Figure 9-20. This is an outdated style that not only invites miscommunication, but results in unnecessarily long messages. See if you can identify the jargon and clichés in the sample letter.

---

passive/impersonal style
Language characterized by official, bureaucratic tone; passive voice; excessive nominalization; convoluted sentence structure; superfluous, outdated, and redundant language; business and legal jargon; and abstract words.

FIGURE 9–20: SAMPLE PASSIVE/IMPERSONAL
STYLE BUSINESS LETTER

Davis Consulting
12 Second Ave.
Birmingham, AL 35203
(205) 222-4993

May 4, 201X

To Whom It May Concern:

As per your request, enclosed please find the information in reference to our company that will help in optimizing your choices to build a website. Prices charged are in line with other designers of similar background and experience.

The company's objective is to develop end-to-end robust solutions through continued focus on core competencies: website development, hosting and maintenance, full access to PHP and CGI, and of course, SSL encryption. It is believed that the customer deserves the highest quality products and services possible. Through continued expansion of the company's staff and through application of corporate quality programs, such as benchmarking, our establishment of superior processes in each of the core competencies excels over our competitors.

Continued expansion into new, profitable markets will enable the company to provide clients with value-added services and turnkey solutions that will translate into client satisfaction.

Please find herein the company's packages that will endeavor to help the client learn more about the company's superior capabilities and its motivated professional team.

If you have any questions or concerns regarding the above, please feel free to contact Joanne Jones, at ext. 213, 1-800-543-6677. The number is toll free for your convenience.

Very truly and obediently yours,

Scott Davis, President

© slava17/Shutterstock.com

Modern Business Style This style uses the active voice, strong verbs, and short sentences. This style typically results in concise messages that are clear and professional. It is a good style and works well with external audiences (readers) and others you are unacquainted with. The letter in Figure 9-21 is an example of a modern business-style letter.

FIGURE 9-21: SAMPLE MODERN BUSINESS STYLE LETTER

Carter Web Design
24 Sea Side Drive
Fort Lauderdale, FL 33302
(954) 3276

January 20, 201X

Mr. Marshall M. Smith
Mass Spectrum Plastics
142 South Seabay Drive
Sea Island, FL 33617

Dear Mr. Smith:

Thank you for inquiring about our Web services. Carter Web Design specializes in creating websites. Your satisfaction is our priority. We work on projects of any size from large to small. Our prices range from $75 an hour to design a basic logo to $150 an hour to design and implement a fully featured website.

Our staff includes seven Web designers who will help you turn your image of a perfect website into reality. We can fulfill any of your Web design needs, from developing high-end graphics and animation to incorporating video and sound.

We realize that your organization may not be clear on what your Web needs are. Our talented, insightful staff will work with you to develop a vision and implement your strategy.

I have enclosed a brochure that explains the four website design packages we offer. Choose the one that is right for your needs and give us a call anytime at 1-800-543-6677. We will be glad to set up a free consultation.

Sincerely,

Sarah Carter, President

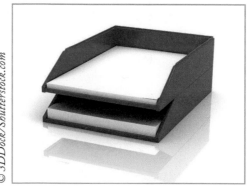

© 3DDock/Shutterstock.com

Informal/Colorful Style This style is good for communicating with people you know well or for communicating good news to those you are familiar with. The letter in Figure 9-22 is an example of an informal/colorful style letter.

informal/colorful style Language characterized by personal, conversational tone; active voice; strong verbs; colorful adjectives and adverbs; parallel structure; short sentences; everyday, concrete, and precise words.

FIGURE 9-22: SAMPLE INFORMAL/COLORFUL STYLE LETTER

Basic Website Options
101 Fremont St.
Tombstone, AZ 85638
(520) 832-0038

August 17, 201_

Jack Jackson
Jack's Cactus Grill
2600 University Plaza Dr.
Dead Gulch, AZ 85733

Dear Jack,

Thanks for asking about our web design services. We have a full range of services, and we can provide you with just about anything you might want in the way of website design. Our prices are competitive. We charge $75 an hour to design a basic logo and up to $150 an hour to design and get your website up and running.

As you know, we have seven talented designers who work on our projects. I have included a brochure that explains our website design packages. If you have a clear idea of what you want on your site, shoot your ideas over via e-mail to bwo@clear.com or give me a call at 1-800-657-8000. If you're not sure exactly what you want from a website, just give me a call, and we can set up a consult.

It's great to hear from you, and I look forward to working with you again.

Sincerely,

Morgan Neely, President

As you can see, these three styles are not mutually exclusive. For example, the modern business style is likely to be more personal than impersonal and can be colorful. Nevertheless, the three general categories let us learn how to appropriately apply a style and its elements to each writing situation.

FIGURE 9-23: CARELESS WRITING STYLES AND BUSINESS LETTERS

Let's first establish what careless writing means. On its simplest level, *careless writing* speaks to a disregard for the rules of grammar and spelling. Careless writing can also result in inclusion of too little information or too few details, leading to confusion or misunderstandings. Careless writing can also take the form of a poorly structured letter in which the message does not flow logically.

In regard to business letters, careless writing is not appreciated. Business letters are formal documents, and there is an expectation that they be written with care. In contrast, carelessly written business letters often result in miscommunication and all the related problems they cause, as well as the negative perceptions about their writers and the organizations they represent.

Why do some people have careless writing styles? For some, it is because they never learned to write properly. For others, it is because they do not value or feel the need for such a level of care. Some people are probably too lazy to put forth the effort. Still others have been influenced by other writing methods that did not call directly for careful writing. For example, some people have so much experience at writing e-mails, IMs, and tweets that these experiences have negatively influenced how they write other messages such as letters. In other words, they have become so accustomed to writing messages that comprise incomplete sentences, single-paragraph messages, nonstandard abbreviations, and punctuation and capitalization errors that they appear to know no better or don't care when it is time to write a business letter. They write on autopilot, based on their past writing experiences. The result includes letters that are difficult to read, hard to understand, and frustrating. And, their readers are left not appreciating their communication partner's careless writing style and not feeling positive toward the writer's employer.

© Jennifer Nicole Buchanan/Shutterstock.com

BUSINESS MEMOS

As mentioned earlier, hardcopy memos and e-memos are commonplace written documents in the U.S. business place. Memos are semiformal documents used to exchange information among people within an organization. Memos most frequently contain routine information. Much like letters, the goal of memos also ranges from sharing neutral, good, or negative news to persuading readers to take a specific course of action.

© marekuliasz/Shutterstock.com

Memos
http://writingcommons.org/index.php/open-text/genres/professional-business-and-technical-writing/memos

Joe LoCicero offers good examples of when to use memos. He states, "Internally, memos may inform their recipients of:

- Announcements for such diverse happenings as hirings or holidays.
- Changes in such aspects as policies, procedures, and prices.
- Confirmations of verbal discussions, decisions, and meeting times.
- Documents to follow, such as reports, gathered research, and survey results.
- Recommendations for action.
- Requests for further information, further research, or reports.
- Solicitation[s] for opinions."[3]

Electronic memos, sent via e-mail, are commonplace in many organizations and are most commonly referred to as *e-memos*. Despite the convenience and ease of developing and sending e-memos, be cautious! They have several shortcomings typically not associated with hardcopy memos. Some of these shortcomings are listed here.

- Receivers are more likely to read hardcopy memos than e-memos because e-memos can be so easily filtered out or deleted before receivers get past the subject line.
- E-memos are often poorly written, with problems ranging from including too little detail, careless tone, and misspelled words to grammatical mistakes and lack of clarity.
- E-memos can be easily hacked, thus raising privacy and security concerns. After all, even deleted e-memos (e-mail) can be resurrected! For example, if you need to relay information regarding a sensitive or private matter (e.g., health conditions, salary), do not do so in an e-memo. Instead, send a hardcopy memo.

FEATURES OF MEMOS

When you look at the features listed below, notice that in some ways the features of both memos and letters are identical. However, you will also notice that other memo features differ from those of letters.

Memos are typically:

- Written in a less formal style than letters. (E-memos are more conversational and there is greater use of first-person pronouns.)
- Written more often using a direct strategy. (Memos can be and still are developed using the indirect and persuasive writing strategies.)
- Tone should be courteous no matter what the receiver's level in the organization.
- Conciseness is desired more so than in letters.
- Clarity is as important in memos as in letters.
- Message completeness is as important in memos as in letters. Degree of completeness directly impacts clarity.
- Message correctness is as important in memos as in letters. In other words, are facts, dates, names, etc., correct? If not, we cause confusion, misunderstandings, and mistakes.
- Subheadings are more prevalent in memos than in letters.
- Lists are more common in memos than in letters.
- Writing mechanics (e.g., grammar, punctuation, spelling) are just as important in memos as in letters.

MEMO FORMAT

From a formatting standpoint, memos look noticeably different than letters. Here are some memo format observations.

- Some are produced on standard, full-size pieces of paper (8½ x 11 inches).
- Some are produced on half-size paper (8½ inches wide x 5½ inches long).
- They may have a preprinted, standardized, company, department, or division header, but this is not as typical as the preprinted company letterhead found on company letter stationery.
- Top and side margins are typically one inch.
- There is a pre-printed, standardized routing header to expedite internal routing. Here is an example of a typical routing header:

MEMORANDUM or MEMO
(centered horizontally)
Date: (starts at left margin)
To: (starts at left margin)
From: (starts at left margin)
Subject: or **Re:** (starts at left margin)

Of course, paper size, margins, and routing headers vary based on companies' preferences.

- As with letters, you can include a copy notation following the message.
- In place of the enclosure notation used with letters, an attachment notation (Attachment:) often follows the message.

How to Write a Perfect Memo video http://curious.com/davidtaylor/how-to-write-a-perfect-memo

SAMPLE MEMOS

The following memo (Figure 9-24) was written by the president of Right Ideas, Inc. to the company's employees to announce a policy banning tobacco use on company grounds. The purpose of the message is to share the policy's main points. Since most employees do not use tobacco products, this message will be perceived by most to be good news; thus, it follows the direct writing strategy.

FIGURE 9-24: SAMPLE DIRECT WRITING STRATEGY, GOOD-NEWS MEMO

MEMORANDUM

Date: October 2, 201X
To: Right Ideas, Inc. Personnel
From: Mac Steiner, President
Subject: Tobacco Use Policy

Starting January 1, 201X a companywide ban on the use of tobacco products will go into effect. The intent of the policy is to promote a healthy workforce and work environment.

Employees and visitors will not be allowed to use cigarettes, cigars, pipes, or smokeless tobacco products anywhere on company grounds, including the parking lots and parking garage. In addition, tobacco use will not be allowed in company vehicles or in personal vehicles parked on company grounds. Electronic cigarettes are prohibited inside company buildings, but may be used outside of the buildings on company grounds, as long as they are used 30 feet or more from building entrances.

The detailed tobacco use policy (policy #107b) can be found in the policies folder at the company website. Please contact Lillian Cole in Human Resources if you have questions regarding this policy. Lillian's telephone extension is 327. You can also contact her at lilliancole@rightideas.org.

The following memo (Figure 9-25) was written by the director of the Human Resources department at Graham and Rudley, a Midwest food distributor, to associate recruiters in the employment division about an upcoming series of training sessions on interviewing skills. This is a direct strategy, neutral-news message.

MEMORANDUM

Date: September 16, 201X
To: Graham and Rudley Associate Recruiters
From: Jan Bishop, HR Director
Subject: Interviewing Skills Training

On October 1 the first of three interviewing skills training sessions will be held from 1–4 p.m. in the training room. The remaining two training sessions will be held in the same location from 1–4 p.m. on October 3 and October 10.

The training sessions are designed to enhance your interviewing skills and to gain a greater awareness of job candidates' expectations. In addition, existing and new employment laws relating to job interviews will be discussed. In addition to the session trainer, our veteran recruiters will join in on some of the discussions and share some sage advice.

The training sessions are mandatory, so mark your calendars accordingly. We scheduled the sessions between the traditional summer vacation period and the busy winter holiday season to avoid schedule conflicts. If you have questions, contact me at extension 554 or at janbishop@gr.org.

Much like e-mails, memos are typically short, but not to the extent that text messages and tweets are. In your quest to write short memos, include enough detail to clearly transmit the message you set out to communicate.

SUMMARY: SECTION 3— WRITING STRATEGIES AND STYLES

- The direct writing strategy works well with neutral-news and good-news business letters and memos.
- The indirect writing strategy works well with negative-news business letters and memos.
- The persuasive writing strategy works well with persuasive business letters and memos.
- Business letter and memo styles include the passive/impersonal style, the modern business style, and the informal/colorful style.

Notes

1. H. J. Leavitt, *Managerial Psychology* (Chicago: University of Chicago Press, 1978), 122.

2. Robert Kreitner and Angelo Kinicki, *Organizational Behavior*, 5th ed. (Boston: Irwin McGraw-Hill, 2000), 486.

3. Joe LoCicero, *Business Communication: Deliver Your Message with Clarity and Efficiency* (Avon, MA: Adams Media, 2007), 93–94.

BUSINESS REPORTS

LEARNING OUTCOMES

After reading this chapter, you should be able to:

1. Describe what a business report is.

2. Discuss the role of business reports in organizations.

3. Discuss the importance of using reliable, valid data and information when writing business reports.

4. Discuss the purpose of business proposals.

5. Describe the key components of long, formal business reports.

6. Describe a number of electronic tools that support business report development.

© Dragance137/Shutterstock.com

BENEFITS OF LEARNING ABOUT BUSINESS REPORTS

1. An understanding of the role of business reports in organizations is critical to your ability to develop them effectively.

2. An understanding of the characteristics that differentiate business reports from other business documents is necessary for you to decide which written document is the appropriate choice.

3. The ability to gather data and information from reliable, valid sources is critical to your ability to develop effective business reports.

4. An understanding of the key components of formal business reports enables you to not only write the components, but also determine which of these components are needed for various report-writing situations.

5. Being able to use coherence techniques in business reports facilitates your readers' comprehension tasks and keeps you organized.

6. Being familiar with and able to use electronic tools that support report development will make you a more efficient report writer.

SELECT KEY TERMS

INTRODUCTION

A **business report** is a document containing information designed to assist others in making an informed decision. Within organizations, business reports travel upwardly, laterally, and downwardly. In addition, some travel to external sources. Some business reports are only a few pages in length whereas others are significantly longer. Electronic tools such as mindmaps, *Qualtrics, and RefWorks* hold the potential of helping business report writers develop reports more effectively and efficiently.

Business report categories include informational reports, analytical reports, and persuasive reports. The two major types of business reports are periodic reports and non-periodic reports. Periodic reports are reports that are submitted at regular intervals such as annual reports, sales reports, and financial reports. Non-periodic reports are not submitted on regular intervals, but instead are developed and submitted when needed. Business proposals are non-periodic reports.

The intent of this chapter is to provide you with instruction on how to write effective business reports. The goal of this chapter is realized through discussions of the following topics: description of business reports, the role of business reports in organizations, characteristics of business reports, conducting research for business writing purposes, business report categories and types, the key components of formal business reports, business report coherence, and electronic tools that support business report development. The information pertaining to the above-mentioned report-writing steps is reinforced by several student website resources including *PowerPoint slides, preview tests, chapter assessment tests, writing mechanics rules and guidelines, YouTube videos, interactive exercises,* and the *interactive glossary*.

business report
A business document containing information designed to assist others in making an informed decision.

WHAT IS A BUSINESS REPORT?

Business reports represent a class of business documents that are developed for the purpose of assisting others in making informed decisions. Business reports contain relevant, factual information that is organized so that it is relatively easy for readers to move about within them and comprehend the data and information presented.

THE ROLE OF BUSINESS REPORTS IN ORGANIZATIONS

In short, reports are vital to organizations. They help businesspeople make informed decisions when planning, organizing, and controlling their operations.

© Pressmaster/Shutterstock.com

How to Write a Business Report
https://www.wikihow.com/Write-a-Business-Report

REPORT REQUESTERS' EXPECTATIONS

There are five things those who request reports want report writers to do. Report writers are expected to: (1) gather reliable, on-topic data and/or information; (2) reduce the data/information collected to a practical quantity so it can be presented concisely without compromising clarity; (3) use structural techniques (e.g., table of contents, headings) that enable the readers to move within the report easily and quickly; (4) analyze and interpret the data and information logically if asked to do so; and (5) complete and submit reports on time. Since report writers are often subordinate to those requesting the report, writers are wise from both job stability and career growth standpoints to meet the above-mentioned expectations.

INTERNAL FLOW OF REPORTS

While some reports are developed for external audiences, many reports circulate within organizations. Internal reports typically travel in three directions—upward, laterally, or downward. Predictably, the specific purposes they serve vary. These purposes often vary based on their directional flow. For example:

- **Reports Moving Upwardly.** These reports typically contain information that assists higher-level decision makers.
- **Reports Moving Laterally.** These typically contain information that assists in the coordination of work activities.
- **Reports Moving Downwardly.** These reports typically contain policies and instructions concerning how to implement them.

EXTERNAL FLOW OF REPORTS

Some reports are developed for external audiences. A company's annual report to stockholders is an example, as are business proposals. Characteristics of Business Reports

---

SUMMARY: SECTION 1—
THE ROLE OF BUSINESS REPORTS IN ORGANIZATIONS

- Business reports are written to serve a business purpose.
- Business reports should be relevant, factual, and organized.
- There are five specific things end users expect writers to do when writing reports.
- Business reports flow both externally and internally. Internally they move in an upward, lateral, or downward direction.

CHARACTERISTICS OF BUSINESS REPORTS

There are several characteristics that distinguish business reports from other business documents. Five of these characteristics are discussed below—report length, level of formality, listings, headings, and visual aids.

REPORT LENGTH

Business reports are often classified by length. They are typically considered to be either short reports or long reports.

Short reports are 1–9 pages long and are typically based on routine matters. They are frequently memo and letter reports that are often informal, usually without prefatory or appended components.

Long reports are 10 pages or more. Some long reports can be hundreds of pages in length or longer. Long reports are typically based on non-routine, special matters. They are often formal, **analytical reports** having several prefatory and appended components.

The general rule is, the longer the report, the greater the number of prefatory components (e.g., executive summary) and appended components (e.g., index) that should be included to aid the reader. The prefatory and appended components serve useful and important purposes. They help writers present a more organized and thorough reporting of data and information than they might otherwise do. They also provide efficient and effective guidance to readers as they navigate the report. This latter point is important given how most people use/read long reports. Essentially, the longer the report, the more likely the reader will not read it in its entirety from start to finish as one would read a novel. For example, a reader may only read the Executive Summary or specific sections that are of interest to him or her. In addition, readers will often move in and out of prefatory or appended components, such as the Table of Contents and Indexes that help him or her to locate specific portions of interest.

> **short reports** Reports of 1–9 pages; typically presenting routine matters.
>
> **long reports** Reports of 10 or more pages.
>
> **analytical report** A document identifying an issue or problem, presenting the relevant information, and interpreting that information.

LEVEL OF FORMALITY

Another characteristic of business reports is their level of formality. Business reports are often categorized into one of two general levels of formality—informal reports and formal reports.

Informal reports are usually short, informational reports. If your end user prefers informality in documents, write them accordingly with regard to report structure, word choice, etc. Sales reports and quarterly financial reports are examples of informal reports.

Formal reports contain less conversational language and more structural elements designed to reinforce clarity and guide the reader (e.g., headings, summaries). Formal reports can be either informational or analytical. The main features that define a business report as formal include length, number of topics and subtopics addressed, information complexity and/or data shared, and data interpretation content. For example, if you send a report to a high-ranking decision maker in the organization or an external business partner or stakeholder, you would probably write a formal report.

A good general rule regarding informality and formality is "when in doubt, write a formal report." Unnecessary formality features are rarely viewed negatively, whereas unwanted informality can result in poor perceptions about the writer, his or her company, and the report.

> **informal reports** Short, informational reports employing conversational language.
>
> **formal reports** Informational or analytical reports employing formal language.

LISTINGS

Another characteristic of business reports is the use of lists. However, do not develop reports that are predominately lists. Doing so is unprofessional. Furthermore, most topics and data cannot be reduced to bulleted lists. Lists would contain too little detail and compromise clarity.

HEADINGS

Another characteristic of business reports is the use of headings, which serve as efficient guides for report readers and writers, alike. The two major types of headings are topic caption headings and talking caption headings.

Topic caption headings identify the topic of discussion. Topic caption headings are typically 1–4 words long. For example:

Store Locations

Talking caption headings identify the specific topic of discussion. They are typically longer than topic caption headings. For example:

Sales Figures Are Typically Correlated with Store Location

As mentioned before, headings help report readers and report writers locate a page or specific information they are interested in. Report writers also benefit from report headings during the organization phase, which is especially important with longer reports addressing numerous topics. Headings here provide the basic outline for the report. By developing an outline composed predominately of headings, the report writer is more assured of the logic of the report's structure. Having headings in place, in turn, offers one more assurance that the writer will not omit necessary sections and information.

topic caption headings
Headings that identify the topic of discussion in a report; typically 1–4 words long.

talking caption headings
Headings that identify the specific topic of discussion in a report; headings are typically longer than topic caption headings.

General Rules for APA Format
http://psychology.about.com/od/apastyle/a/apageneral.htm

MLA Style Guide—Quick & Easy
http://library.csun.edu/egarcia/documents/mlacitation_quickguide.pdf

FIGURE 10–1: WRITING STYLES

Writing styles such as the APA style and the MLA style provide guidelines that writeers often find helpful when developing business reports. Each of these styles is described below.

APA (American Psychological Association) style guidelines were developed to assist reading comprehension in the social and behavioral sciences, for clarity of communication, and for word choice that best reduces bias in language. The sample APA style article at the website in the side margin contains a number of APA guidelines as well as links to additional APA style articles.

MLA (Modern Language Association) style guidelines focus on writing and documentation in the humanities. Sample websites containing a number of MLA style guidelines are located in the side margin. The sample MLA style article at the website in the side margin contains a number of MLA guidelines.

The American Psychological Association and the Modern Language Association both publish style manuals. The American Psychological Association's manual is titled *Publication Manual of the American Psychological Association,* and you can learn more about it by visiting the following website: https://en.wikipedia.org/wiki/APA style. The Modern Language Association's manual is titled *The MLA Style Manual,* and you can learn more about it by visiting the following website: https://en.wikipedia.org/wiki/MLA_Style_Manual. You should be able to access both of these manuals at your your university, community college, or junior college library and writing assistance center.

Source: APA style. https://en.wikipedia.org/wiki/APA_style
Source: MLA Style Manual. https://en.wikipedia.org/wiki/MLA_Style_Manual

VISUAL AIDS

© hanss/Shutterstock.com

Yet another characteristic of business reports is the regular and extensive (when appropriate) use of visual aids. The good news is that there has never been a time when it has been as easy and fast for writers to develop visual aids for business reports, thanks to the availability of computers, scanners, and graphics software. On the downside, there has never been a time when report readers have had such high expectations of the professional quality of visual aids in terms of appearance and communication accuracy. This means report writers are expected to know how to develop professional-quality visual aids and be willing to do so.

Why do writers include visual aids in business reports? Visual aids serve a number of purposes, such as:

- Sharing messages that are communicated more clearly visually than they are verbally.
- Capturing report readers' attention.
- Helping readers form quick mental images of the data through visual images, charts, tables, diagrams, etc. (See Figure 10-2.)
- Presenting complex information visually to enable quick comprehension.
- Providing an interesting and appealing break for readers from the ongoing drudgery of sentence after sentence and page after page of text.
- Efficient presentation of quantitative data via tables versus paragraphs of text explanation.

FIGURE 10–2: TABLE

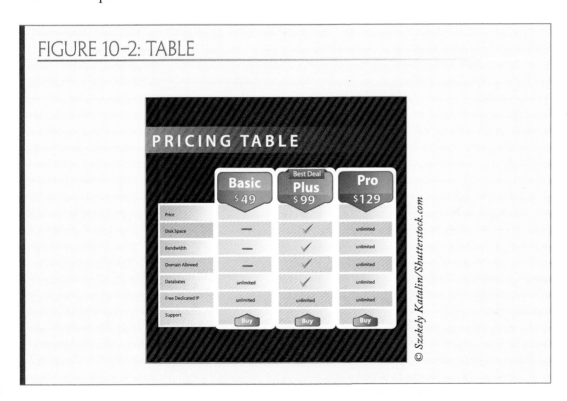
© Szekely Katalin/Shutterstock.com

- Showing comparisons with bar charts. (See Figures 10-3 & 10-4.)

FIGURE 10-3: BAR CHART

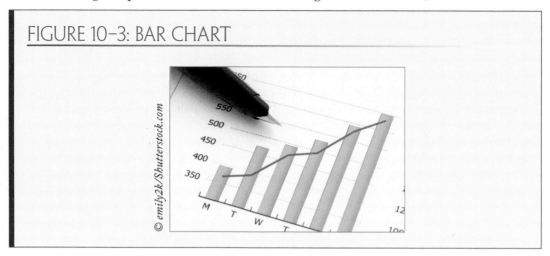

© emily2k/Shutterstock.com

FIGURE 10-4: BAR CHART

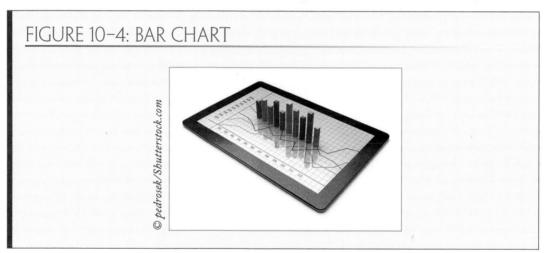

© pedrosek/Shutterstock.com

- Showing relationships of the parts to the whole with pie charts. (See Figure 10-5.)

FIGURE 10-5: PIE CHART

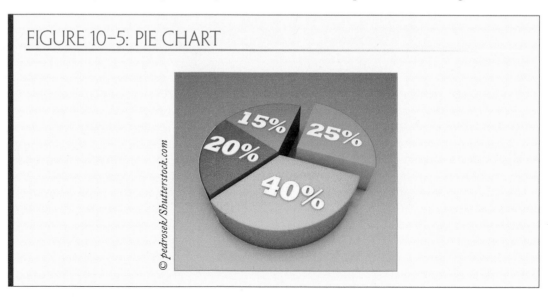

© pedrosek/Shutterstock.com

- Showing trends with line charts. (See Figure 10-6.)

FIGURE 10-6: LINE CHART

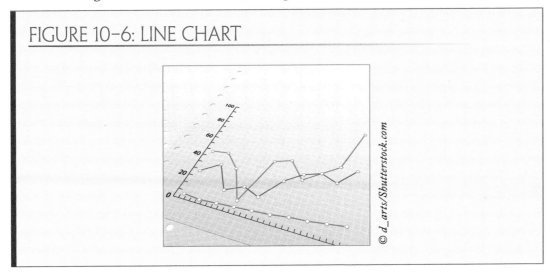

© d_arts/Shutterstock.com

Visual aids included in business reports should never be mere add-ons or afterthoughts, inserted randomly to appease readers' expectations. Each visual aid should serve one or more specific purposes and be an integral, logical component of the report.

Effective business reports are not composed predominately of visual aids strung together with a minimal amount of text. Some novice business report writers who know how to develop visual aids fall into this trap. Be careful!

So, what techniques help writers develop effective visual aids for business reports? Here are several good tips to consider:

- Include a visual aid only if it serves a purpose.
- Strive for clarity in your visual aids so as not to cause confusion, frustration, and misunderstandings.
- Give each visual aid a title, not only a chart or figure number (e.g., Chart 1. Retail Sales by Quarters, 2016–2017).
- Introduce each visual aid in the report text.
- When appropriate and natural, follow up on visual aids with a brief summary in the text.
- Avoid developing visual aids that are too busy. In other words, don't include too much information or show too many comparisons on a single visual aid. Today's technology makes it easy to include far too much information on a single visual aid, or throw in a number of audio and video features simultaneously, all of which can contribute to miscommunication.

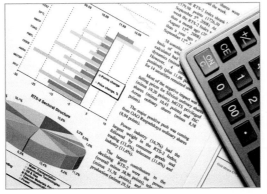

© Borodaev/Shutterstock.com

A good analogy for visual aids that are too busy can be drawn from the film *Unstoppable*. The story is about an unmanned, runaway freight train that gains speed as it barrels down on a tight turn on elevated tracks above refinery tanks in a populated area of Stanton, Pennsylvania. The film's stars, Denzel Washington and Chris Pine, stopped the train before an environmental catastrophe occurred. Unfortunately, the film contained a number of unnecessary, annoying distractions. For example, news station helicopters flying too low crisscrossed each other over crowds of townspeople while an incessant stream of law enforcement vehicles with lights flashing and sirens blaring drove up and down the roads parallel to the train tracks. At one point, several law enforcement vehicles crashed into each other for no apparent reason.

Report writers are encouraged to design visual aids in ways that do not distract readers. The KISS Principle provides a practical reminder of this point. The *KISS* Principle stands for *Keep it short and simple.* For what it's worth, the less polite interpretation is *Keep it simple, stupid.*

Here are some more tips:

- Stick with one font style in a visual aid. In fact, use the same font style in all the visual aids you include in a business report. Otherwise, readers may be distracted from your message or purpose.
- Change type size in visual aids as needed. For example, the type size for table headings should be 1–2 points larger than the type size used for table body contents.
- Be careful when presenting visual aids that are produced in a 3-dimensional image. While the 3-D feature produces attractive, attention-grabbing visuals, they can be difficult to interpret accurately and quickly. Make sure the image does not interfere with your reader's ability to accurately interpret the information or data.
- When possible, include color in your visual aids. Business report readers like to see color. Color captures most readers' attention and assists in building reader interest and comprehension. However, don't overdo it! For example, you are less likely to distract readers from your message or purpose if you use five or fewer colors in any one visual. Remember that while color is desirable, you should avoid visual aids that are colorfully chaotic!

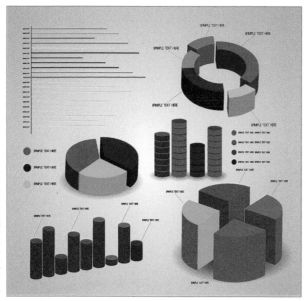

There is so much more to know about visual aids (such as tables, graphs, diagrams, charts, illustrations, maps, etc.) that is beyond the scope of this book. If you have the interest and time, there are two excellent visual aids books you should consider. The first of these is *Information Graphics: A Comprehensive Illustrated Reference—Visual Tools for Analyzing, Managing, and Communicating* by Robert L. Harris. This book contains numerous examples and descriptions of charts, graphics, maps, diagrams, and tables. The other book is *The Visual Display of Quantitative Information* by Edward R. Tufte. The focus of Tufte's book is on displaying quantitative information in ways that do not compromise and/or distort the data. These two books contain a wealth of sound information about visual aids. If you are planning a business career, you are strongly encouraged to read these books.

One closing thought and it's a big one. Long gone are the days when report writers' visual aids were limited to tables, graphs, diagrams, charts, and basic illustrations. Today's technologies, combined with the Internet, have unleashed an ever-growing number of electronics-based visual aids options. Many of these options are discussed later in this chapter in the section on Electronic Tools That Support Report Development. They range from Prezi and Mindmaps (e.g., Mindomo) to Wordle and GoAnimate, to mention a few. Examples of several of these are included in that section of the chapter. Such programs challenge us to rethink how we integrate and display visual information in reports.

SUMMARY: SECTION 2—
CHARACTERISTICS OF BUSINESS REPORTS

- Business reports vary in length from short (1–9 pages) to long (10+ pages).
- Business reports are typically informational, analytical, or persuasive.
- Business reports are informal or formal.
- Bulleted lists are used frequently in business reports.
- Headings and subheadings are used frequently in business reports.
- Visual aids are expected, integral components of business reports.

Prezi
Cloud-based presentation software program for exploring and sharing ideas on a virtual canvas.

mindmaps (e.g., Mindomo)
Diagramming software for organizing projects visually.

Wordle
Visually appealing word clouds.

GoAnimate
Software that enables creators to develop short, animated videos and visual aids.

CONDUCTING RESEARCH FOR REPORT-WRITING PURPOSES

Most report writers must conduct research prior to writing reports. Data and information are typically collected either through primary sources or secondary sources or some combination thereof. *Primary sources,* such as interviews, focus groups, and surveys, are used to obtain firsthand accounts regarding research topics. *Secondary sources,* such as journals and books, are used to obtain secondhand data or information that was originally presented elsewhere.

University and college business librarians are great resources for research guidance and suggestions. In addition, your university may have a media center or media library that has useful business information. There are numerous business research sources and much to know. Do not be shy! Contact your business librarian or media center staff and get on with your research.

As mentioned earlier, decision makers rely on reports when making some of their decisions. They must be able to trust the reliability (trustworthiness) of the data and information they are presented with. They also must be able to trust the validity (soundness) of report writers' conclusions and recommendations. Here are several ways to ensure the reliability of data and information you collect during your research phase.

- Consider the date of publication, scope of information, the author, and publisher. Double-check citations, footnotes, appendices, and other sources to be confident the information is from a recognized authority.
- Use Internet sources cautiously. Remember, anyone can put anything on a website. There may be no editor, publisher, or other means of quality control.
- Determine how search engines such as Google and Yahoo prioritize displayed information. Some Internet search engines "sell" top billing to advertisers.
- Do not assume that an Internet search engine retrieves and evaluates information the same way librarians do.

- Examine how often the search engine updates its information.
- Look for information describing the methodologies used to gather data and information presented on the Internet.
- Seek out the sources or links within the bibliography to the actual documents to ensure accuracy.
- Paid subscriptions to databases are often used by researchers and libraries because of their up-to-date and valid information. One such source is Lexis-Nexis (www. lexisnexis.com).[1]

Fortunately, a wealth of data and information is available. The challenge, however, is knowing how to access the specific information you need. That is where the information presented in this section comes into play.

Before presenting a list of potential business research sources by category (e.g., journals, databases, etc.), here are some specific sources. If you want to locate:

- Industry codes, access SIC code (Standard Industrial Classification) and NAICS code (North American Industry Classification System).
- Benchmark industry ratios, access the Almanac of Business & Financial Ratios, Dun & Bradstreet (D&B), Industry Norms & Key Business Ratios, and RMA (Risk Management Association) Annual Statement Studies.
- Company numbers, access Business & Company Resource Center, Hoover's Online (click on SEC filings), LexisNexis Academic (click on Companies, then click on SEC Filings), Morningstar Document Research, and SEC Edgar Database.
- Industry information, access Business & Company Resource Center, Hoover's Online, and NetAdvantage – Standard and Poor's.
- Articles about companies and industries, access ABI Inform, Business & Company Resource Center, Business Source Complete, and Predicast's PROMT – Predicast's Overview of Markets and Technology.

The following section lists potential business research sources by category—journals, periodicals, books, databases, websites, and other sources.

JOURNALS

Hundreds of journals contain articles on a wide variety of business topics. Here is a sampling.

- *Journal of Management*
- *American Business Review*
- *Business Horizons*
- *Harvard Business Review*

Then, there are journals that frequently contain an international forum section or publish articles pertaining to international business issues. Examples include:

- *The International Executive*
- *International Journal of Intercultural Relations*
- *International Journal of Public Relations*
- *International Journal of Research and Marketing*
- *Foreign Language Annals*
- *Journal of International Studies.*

Thanks to the widespread availability of the Internet, WiFi, and affordable computers and tablets, conducting searches for journal articles is fairly painless!

PERIODICALS AND NEWSPAPERS

Newsstand periodicals, such as *Forbes, BusinessWeek, Fortune, and Newsweek,* and newspapers such as *The Wall Street Journal,* contain articles on a wide variety of business topics. Most of these periodicals and their articles can also be accessed over the Internet.

One of the major advantages periodicals and newspapers have over books is the currency of the information reported. Given how rapidly economic and political conditions change in some countries and regions of the world, this is an important consideration.

BOOKS

Books offer yet another business research source. Fortunately there is no shortage of these book titles pertaining to business. Some are specialized, while others are more general. Examples of these include:

- *The Standard Industrial Classification Manual*
- *NAICS Manual*
- *Business Plans Handbook*
- *RMA* (Risk Management Association) *Annual Statement Studies*
- *Industry Norms and Key Business Ratios* (D&B)
- *Almanac of Business and Industrial Financial Ratios*
- *Craighead's International Business, Travel, and Relocation Guide to* ... various countries
- *Mergent International Manual*
- *Kiss, Bow, or Shake Hands: Sales and Marketing* by Terri Morrison and Wayne A. Conaway (McGraw-Hill).
- *Kiss, Bow, or Shake Hands* by Terri Morrison, Wayne A. Conaway, and George A. Borden (Adams Media Corporation).

Just keep in mind that such books become dated as circumstances and customs change. Of course, this is not always the case, but it is a consideration to keep in mind.

DATABASES

Many databases contain information on business topics. A sampling of such databases is listed below.

- ABI/Inform
- Business & Company Resource Center
- Business Source Complete
- EBSCOhost
- EconLit
- Emerald FullText
- Hoover's Online
- IMF Publications
- LexisNexis Academic
- PAIS International
- Plunket Research
- Predicast's PROMT

- Reference USA
- STAT-USA
- World-Newspapers.com

Databases provide an efficient information-gathering option. We are fortunate to have databases so readily available as well as the computing power to access them. Gathering information has not always been so fast and efficient.

WEBSITES

As can be expected, a number of websites contain information pertaining to business topics. Here are some examples.

- **DoingBusiness.org (World Bank) www.doingbusiness.org**. This site is sponsored by the World Bank. This site provides objective measures of business regulations of individual countries and their enforcement. Indicators cover topics such as starting a business, employing workers, paying taxes, getting credit, etc.
- **Import/Export Guide (Business.gov) business.usa.gov.** Contents include getting started in exporting, how to obtain export financing, importing goods, trade agreements, business travel, and importing/exporting specific products.
- **Business & Company Resource Center.** It has a very long URL. The best way to get to it is by Googling it. This site provides full abstracts and full-text articles from journals, periodicals, and newspapers covering a wide range of business and industry topics. It also provides company and industry information for more than 300,000 companies.
- **Yahoo! Finance finance.yahoo.com.** The site contains quotes, financial news, stock market statistics, and more.
- **Reuters.com reuters.com/finance/stocks.** This site provides financial ratios of industries in addition to market news and company and industry figures.

As the Internet continues to grow, we can anticipate that even more such websites will become available. Locating information pertaining to business topics should not be a problem as long as you know where to look. In addition, many companies have their own websites with information that may meet your needs.

OTHER SOURCES

There are several other ways to locate information on intercultural communication and international business topics. Here are some examples:

- *Quick Study Reference Guide* titled *Business Research,* BarCharts Publishing, Inc., www.quickstudy.com.
- Standard & Poor's Industry Surveys
- *Encyclopedia of American Industries*
- Company websites and annual reports
- SEC filings
- *Standard & Poor's 500 Guide*
- Moody's Manual
- *Who's Who in Finance and Industry*
- *Who's Who in Finance and Business*
- *Financial Yellow Book*

- Standard Industrial Classifications manuals
- *Encyclopedia of Associations*
- Statistical Census information
- *Thomas Register of American Manufacturers*
- Business.com
- Wall Street Executive Library
- D&B Small Business Solutions
- CEO Express

You now have quite a number of sources to start with when you need data and information on business topics.

FIGURE 10-7: WHY SOME REPORT WRITERS PLAGIARIZE

Plagiarism is theft of another person's ideas or writings. It occurs when a person passes off another person's ideas or writings as his or her own. Here's a list of the common reasons why plagiarism occurs.

© marekuliasz/Shutterstock.com

- Some writers procrastinate to the point that they have too little time to handle citations properly.
- Some writers are too lazy to cite when required.
- Some writers are too careless to cite or cite properly when required.
- Some writers are unscrupulous and plagiarize knowingly.
- Some writers think they do not have to cite information they find on the Internet.
- Some writers simply do not understand when they are plagiarizing. For example, they do not understand what a paraphrase is, so they are unable to identify one. If you are confused about what quotations and paraphrases are, read these descriptions.

Quotation To quote an author means you used his or her exact words. A writer typically quotes an author when the writer feels that the author has stated the idea most effectively or clearly. A writer also quotes another person when the writer feels the quote will strongly or clearly emphasize a point or because that person is a respected expert in his or her field.

Paraphrase To paraphrase an author is to restate the meaning or substance of that person's ideas and words. A writer typically paraphrases an author when the writer believes that by restating what the author has said, the writer's document can achieve greater clarity. The writer knows that even when not using the author's exact words, the writer is using enough of the author's ideas and thoughts to warrant giving the author credit by citing his or her work. Identifying a paraphrase is not as easy as identifying a quotation. A safe bet is to cite when you are unsure whether something is or is not a paraphrase. In such situations, it is better to err on the side of caution than to gamble.

One of the best ways to avoid plagiarizing is to be familiar with the common reasons some people plagiarize and then don't repeat their actions.

SUMMARY: SECTION 3— CONDUCTING RESEARCH FOR REPORT-WRITING PURPOSES

- Business reports should be based on reliable and valid data and information.
- Business research should come from reliable and valid sources.
- Business research comes from primary and secondary sources.
- Conducting business research increasingly involves databases and online sources.

BUSINESS REPORT CATEGORIES AND TYPES

BUSINESS REPORT CATEGORIES

Generally speaking business reports fall into the following three categories: informational, analytical, and persuasive.

informational report A document presenting facts, observations, and/or experiences only.

Informational Reports These reports present facts, observations, and/or experiences only. The report writer makes no attempt to interpret the data by drawing conclusions or offering recommendations. Sales reports and quarterly financial reports are good examples of informational reports. Some are form reports that only require the report writer to fill in blanks.

analytical report A document identifying an issue or problem, presenting the relevant information, and interpreting that information.

Analytical Reports These reports identify an issue or problem, present relevant information, analyze that information, and interpret it. The interpretation results in conclusions and recommendations for action. Conclusions are drawn from report findings, and recommendations are based on report conclusions. A performance review report is an example of an analytical report.

© hanss/Shutterstock.com

Persuasive Reports These reports aim to move their readers to some desired action. A logical presentation of information is central to these reports. People who write **persuasive reports** must capture their readers' attention and then convert it to interest and ultimately desire. A business **proposal** is an example of a persuasive report.

BUSINESS REPORT TYPES

There are two major types of reports—**periodic reports** and non-periodic reports. Each is described below.

Periodic Reports These are reports that are submitted at regular intervals (e.g., monthly, annually). Examples of periodic reports include annual reports, sales reports, and financial reports.

- **Annual reports** are distributed to a number of stakeholders ranging from stockholders to regulatory agencies. Essentially these reports inform corporate constituencies as to how the business is doing, anticipated changes, and potential problems and opportunities in the offing. Annual reports typically include items such as a balance sheet, profit and loss sheet, cash flow statement, board of directors' statement, and auditors' report.

© maxuser/Shutterstock.com

- **Sales reports** are typically developed for managers. Basically they contain sales figures for a past, specified time period, which could be the past week, month, or quarter. In addition, they often contain comparison sales figures for a previous, equivalent time period(s). Client/customer contact histories are typically included, as well as data on marketing costs. Sales reports help managers determine if adjustments ranging from changes to sales personnel to changes to service or product lines and prices need to be made to meet company objectives and goals.

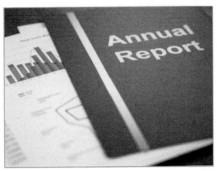

© nasikhan/Shutterstock.com

5 Brands That Nailed Their Annual Reports
http://www.forbes. com/sites/ross-crooks/2014/09/15/ 5-brands-that-nailed-their-annual-reports/

How to Write a Weekly Sales Report
http://smallbusiness. chron.com/write-week-ly-sales-report-42969. html

- **Financial reports** are distributed to a number of stakeholders ranging from stockholders and potential investors to government agencies, including the SEC and IRS. Essentially, they inform these constituencies about the financial condition of the company during a specific period (e.g., quarter, year).

Non-periodic Reports These are reports that, unlike periodic reports, are not submitted on regular intervals. Instead, non-periodic reports are developed and submitted when needed. They contain data or information that decision makers need to address special situations. Proposals and special-situation reports are examples of non-periodic reports.

- **Proposals** are reports that propose (recommend) ways specific needs can be met or problems can be solved. Proposals are commonplace in both the private and public sectors. For example, in the business sector, one might submit a proposal that addresses ways employee use of electronic communication devices for personal reasons at work can be reduced. In the public sector, proposals are often written when government agencies issue RFPs (requests for proposals) for grants targeted at solving problems. When developing a grant proposal, be especially diligent about following instructions. To do otherwise typically results in a denial of your grant request.

Successful proposals meet a need or solve a problem. They contain a clearly stated purpose and are honest, factual, realistic, and objective. Successful proposals are written at a formality level appropriate to their audience and are professional. They are clear and incorporate headings to assist in the proposal's clarity and ease of use. Successful proposals are convincing, in part, because they demonstrate how benefits can outweigh costs. Well-written proposals contain a timetable and appropriate illustrations and visual aids.

Here are some additional important points to keep in mind when writing proposals.

- Use persuasive communication techniques. After all, your goal is to persuade your readers. For example, emphasize reader benefits while de-emphasizing cost.
- Write concisely. This means developing a proposal that is no longer than necessary.
- Eliminate errors ranging from grammar and punctuation to typos and misspellings. Ask someone to proofread your proposal.

FIGURE 10-8: SAMPLE BUSINESS PROPOSAL

Customer Service Assessment: Great Toppings Pizza

Proposal by Todd Shaner, Shaner Consulting Group
www.ShanerConsultingGroup.com
719-378-5682
July 8, 201X

Congratulations on the growth Great Toppings Pizza has experienced this past year. This is certainly a testimonial to the fine pizza you serve and to your employees also. Despite strong competition, your sales continue to grow. However, now is not the time to become complacent. Great Toppings needs to continue to do all it can to remain competitive and grow. That is where Shaner Consulting Group can help.

Opportunity

Great Toppings Pizza currently operates 112 stores across the western half of the United States. Like most businesses that operate many outlets over a wide geographic area, some of Great Toppings Pizza's outlets are more profitable than others. Increasing sales in your less-profitable outlets is certainly important.

Shaner Consulting Group is prepared to help you make Great Toppings Pizza's less-profitable stores more profitable. Our company specializes in all matters to do with customer service. We propose to determine whether customer service shortcomings in your company's less-profitable outlets are directly correlated with sales. We realize that other factors such as store location, local economic conditions, and tax rates also influence sales. While factors such as local economic conditions and tax rates are not easily controlled, Great Toppings Pizza can exercise control over customer service.

Procedures

Given the opportunity, Shaner Consulting Group (SCG) will assess Great Toppings Pizza's customer service situation as follows.

1. SCG will conduct assessments in 25 percent of Great Toppings Pizza's outlets that have been identified as being sufficiently profitable with the purpose of identifying outstanding customer service behaviors that are relatively consistent across these outlets. These assessments will be accomplished through (1) anonymous in-store observations; (2) focus group sessions with current customers, outlet employees, and outlet managers; and (3) questionnaires sent to current and potential customers, outlet employees, and outlet managers.

FIGURE 10–8: SAMPLE BUSINESS PROPOSAL

2. SCG will conduct assessments in all Great Toppings Pizza outlets that have consistently reported substandard sales figures with the purpose of identifying poor customer service behaviors. SCG will also identify best practices that were identified in the profitable outlets that are not apparent in the unprofitable outlets. These assessments will be accomplished through (1) anonymous in-store observations; (2) focus group sessions with current customers, outlet employees, and outlet managers; and (3) questionnaires sent to current and potential customers, outlet employees, and outlet managers.

Proposed Timeline

SCG will complete all the above-mentioned assessments by November 30, 201X and report our findings to you via a written report and presentation by December 15, 201X.

Benefits of Proposed Actions

Great Toppings should realize the following benefits if it implements the proposed actions.

1. SCG findings should ultimately contribute to increased sales and profits for Great Toppings Pizza, assuming steps are taken to improve the quality of customer service in stores currently reporting substandard sales.
2. Great Toppings Pizza will be able to direct its attention to other matters important to the company such as expansion into new markets.

Costs

These are open for discussion and negotiation based on the extent of the investigation Great Toppings Pizza is interested in pursuing.

Shaner Consulting Group opened its doors for business in Pueblo, Colorado in 1987. Since then, we have served numerous businesses of all types and sizes by helping them improve customer service. We look forward to also meeting Great Toppings Pizza's existing customer service needs. If you are interested in seeing a sampling of companies we have served, as well as comments submitted by prior clients, please visit us at www.ShanerConsultingGroup.com.

I look forward to visiting with you.

Sincerely,

Todd Shaner, President
Shaner Consulting Group

- **Special-situation** reports are reports that address decision makers' data or information needs that are not met via proposals and periodic reports. Here, the report writer is not asked to attempt to persuade the reader, but instead to provide relevant data and/or information.

Some special-situation reports are true informational reports in that their purpose is to present facts, observations, and/or experiences only and not to interpret the data or information, draw conclusions, or make recommendations. Other special-situation reports are analytical reports that identify an issue or problem, present relevant data or information, analyze the data or information, and interpret it. The interpretation stage requires the writer to draw conclusions and make recommendations for a specific course of action.

SUMMARY: SECTION 4— BUSINESS REPORT CATEGORIES AND TYPES

- Business report categories include informational, analytical, and persuasive reports.
- Business report types include periodic reports and nonperiodic reports.
- Proposals and special-situation reports are examples of nonperiodic reports.

This chapter's next section describes the components of a long, formal business report, along with an example of each component based on a common business situation. As you piece together the example, you will see a special-situation, analytical report unfolding. This sample report could easily be converted into an informational report by removing the analysis and interpretation components. To do so, remove any mention of key findings, conclusions, and recommendations from the Executive Summary; remove the Summary Paragraphs at the end of each Topic Chapter; and remove the Report Summary chapter.

FORMAL BUSINESS REPORTS

Formal business reports typically contain numerous components. Some of these components are necessary in order to report the needed data or information (e.g., Executive Summary, Report Body). Other components are included to help readers navigate their way through the report (e.g., Table of Contents, Report Preview, Index). On the surface, some components often found in formal business reports might appear to be unnecessary. However, each has its purpose and the interesting thing about many of these components is that they are beneficial to report writers and report-writing teams, as well as to the readers. For example, the Report Preview benefits readers as they head toward reading the Report Body by telling them what major topics will follow and in what order. The Report Preview is also beneficial to writers because, once it is written, it sets out the Report Body topics and topic order for them. Even if extended periods of time pass between writing sessions, the Report Preview helps the author(s) avoid leaving a topic out or presenting topics out of the intended order. And if multiple writers are working on the Report Body, you can see the need and benefit of having the Report Preview to turn to.

Long, formal report components typically fall into one of three categories—prefatory parts, report proper, and appended parts. Each of these categories and report components are presented Figure 10-9, followed by a description of each component.

How to Write a Formal Business Report video
http://www.youtube.com/watch?v=F-c9PRInPZw

FIGURE 10-9: KEY COMPONENTS OF FORMAL BUSINESS REPORTS

Prefatory Parts
- Title Page
- Letter of Transmittal
- Table of Contents
- Executive Summary

Report Proper
   Introduction
- Statement of Purpose
- Statement of Problem
- Sources of Information
- Report Preview

Report Body
- Report Topic Chapters
- Report Summary

Notes

Appended Parts
- Glossary
- Index
- Additional Data

KEY COMPONENTS OF A FORMAL BUSINESS REPORT

What follows is a description of each of the formal business report components listed in Figure 10-9. Examples are included for most of the report components. Each example is based on the business scenario presented in Figure 10-10. This scenario portrays an ongoing challenge many businesses face routinely worldwide.

FIGURE 10-10: STORE PROFITABILITY SCENARIO

All Sports, Inc. owns a chain of retail sporting goods stores located throughout the United States. As can be expected, some of the company's stores are less profitable than others. Management wants to determine how to make its less-profitable stores more profitable. They suspect poor customer service is at the heart of the problem, but understand that other factors likely contribute also. Imagine you are a member of a team charged with investigating the situation and developing a formal, analytical report in which you make recommendations to management regarding how to turn their less-profitable stores toward greater profitability.

PREFATORY PARTS

This is the first of the five report categories. This category contains standard prefatory parts, which are the components that precede the report proper section.

Title Page The Title Page typically contains the report title, name of the person requesting the report, name of the writer(s), and date the report is submitted. This is also the typical order of the Title Page contents. Figure 10-11 contains a sample Title Page based on the store profitability scenario.

FIGURE 10–11: SAMPLE TITLE PAGE

Store Profitability: Making Substandard Stores More Profitable

Prepared for
Maria Sanchez, Vice President
All Sports, Inc.

Prepared by
Jonathan Reynolds, Director of Operations
All Sports, Inc.

Date
July 27, 201_

Letter of Transmittal This is a brief letter that serves to transmit the report to the reader by communicating who requested the report, when it was requested, the key findings, and words of appreciation for being asked to develop the report. The Letter of Transmittal is a direct strategy letter. Figure 10-12 contains a sample Letter of Transmittal based on the store profitability scenario.

FIGURE 10–12: SAMPLE LETTER OF TRANSMITTAL

July 27, 201_

Dear Ms. Sanchez:

On January 7, 201X you asked our project team to investigate and report on All Sports, Inc.'s less-profitable stores for the purpose of determining ways to bring these stores to greater profitability.

The key findings growing from our investigation of the matter clearly pointed to several customer service behaviors that need to be addressed. Central to these behaviors is how customers are greeted when they enter the store, store employees' willingness to help customers locate merchandise and answer customers' questions, and store employees' overall level of friendliness.

We would like to thank you for this opportunity to investigate the situation, which is of great importance to our company. Please contact us if clarification or additional information is needed.

Sincerely,

Jonathan Reynolds
Director of Operations

---

letter of transmittal Brief letter that transmits a report to its reader(s) by stating who requested the report, when it was requested, the key findings, and words of appreciation for being asked to develop the report.

Table of Contents The Table of Contents typically presents the primary and secondary report headings, along with the page numbers to indicate where each section starts. Figure 10-13 contains a sample Table of Contents based on the store profitability scenario.

FIGURE 10–13: SAMPLE TABLE OF CONTENTS

Table of Contents

While the following tables are not included in long, formal business reports as frequently as is the Table of Contents, consider including each when there are three or more such items in the report.

- Table of Tables
- Table of Figures
- Table of Charts
- Table of Illustrations
- Table of Photos

Include these sections in the Table of Contents only when you have placed several tables, figures, charts, illustrations, or photos in your report, and you believe your readers will find the their listings helpful. These additions to the Table of Contents present the numbers, titles, and their page numbers.

Executive Summary The **Executive Summary,** referred to by some as the synopsis, provides a summary of all of the essential report ingredients, including the Statement of Purpose, Statement of Problem, Data Collection Process, Key Findings, Conclusions, and Recommendations. Figure 10-14 contains a sample Executive Summary based on the store profitability scenario.

executive summary
A section of a document providing a summary of a report's essential facts and recommendations. Also known as *synopsis*.

FIGURE 10-14: SAMPLE EXECUTIVE SUMMARY

Executive Summary

The purpose of this study is to determine how to make the company's less-profitable stores more profitable. To do so, we set out to determine which specific customer service behaviors are correlated with greater store profitability. How are customers greeted when they enter the store? How are customers assisted while in the store? What are customers' perceptions of how they are treated while in the store?

Data for this study were gathered from a number of sources. Observations were made at 70 percent of the most-profitable as well as 70 percent of the most-unprofitable stores. We carried out these activities:

- Employee surveys were distributed.
- Employee focus group sessions were conducted.
- Customer satisfaction surveys were distributed.
- Customer focus group sessions were conducted.
- Books and journals that address customer service themes were delved into.

The study resulted in two key findings, which were the basis for two conclusions and two recommendations.

Key Finding #1: Based on store observations, we determined that employees in our most profitable stores greet customers with a smile as they enter the store 96 percent of the time.

Conclusion #1: The willingness of employees in profitable stores to greet customers with a smile appears to contribute, in part, to higher profit levels in these stores.

Recommendation #1: Management should strongly consider encouraging employees in all stores to greet customers with a smile when they enter their stores.

Key Finding #2: Based on store observations, we determined that employees in our least-profitable stores greet customers with a friendly word only 22 percent of the time.

Conclusion #2: The infrequency with which customers are greeted with a friendly word in the least-profitable stores appears to contribute, in part, to low profit levels in these stores.

Recommendation #2: Management should strongly consider encouraging employees in all stores to greet customers with a friendly word when they enter the store.

The purpose of the executive summary is to give report readers an overview of the high points of the report. Some report readers read only the Executive Summary when they do not have the time or feel the need to read the entire report. For obvious reasons, the Executive Summary should be well written!

Even though the Executive Summary is located near the beginning of the report, most of it cannot be written until the Report Body has been completed. A good way to determine whether your Executive Summary is too short or too long is to compare its length to that of the Report Body. The Executive Summary should be approximately 10–15 percent of the length of the report.

REPORT PROPER

This is the second of the five report categories. This category is broken into two subsections—Introduction and Report Body. The Introduction contains the Statement of Problem, Sources of Information, and Report Preview.

statement of purpose The report's main goal.

Introduction **Statement of Purpose** The statement of purpose identifies the main goal of the report. Figure 10-15 contains a sample statement of purpose based on the store profitability scenario.

FIGURE 10-15: SAMPLE STATEMENT OF PURPOSE

To determine how to make the company's less-profitable stores more profitable.

It is obviously important that the writer(s) have a clear understanding of their assignment before moving ahead with their research and writing efforts. Otherwise, the result is likely to be wasted time and effort, followed by a weak report that does not serve the readers/decision makers well.

statement of problem The report's specific topic(s) or concern(s).

Statement of Problem The statement of problem identifies the specific topic(s) or concern(s) linked directly to the statement of purpose. Figure 10-16 contains a sample statement of problem based on the store profitability scenario.

FIGURE 10-16: SAMPLE STATEMENT OF PROBLEM

To determine which specific customer service behaviors are correlated with higher store profitability. Specifically: How are customers greeted when they enter the store? How are customers assisted while in the store? What are customers' perceptions of how they are treated while in the store?

It is equally important that report writers have a clear understanding of the specific concern(s) they are attempting to address before moving forward with their research and writing efforts. Otherwise the result will be wasted time and effort, followed by a weak report that does not serve the readers/decision makers well.

Sources of Information The sources of information section lists the sources you accessed while gathering data and information for the report. The entries in this section do not need to be in full citation form as you would when you cite paraphrases and quotations in the notes section. Readers like to browse the sources of information to determine if the sources you used are reliable, current, and best suited to the report's needs. After all, if your reader is going to make decisions based in large part on your report, then he or she needs to have faith in the sources you used. Figure 10-17 contains two sample sources of information based on the store profitability scenario.

FIGURE 10-17: SAMPLE SOURCES OF INFORMATION

Customer Service Done Right by William Meador (2015)
Satisfied Customers Contribute to the Bottom Line by Geoff Goffield, in the *Journal of Customer Service* (2015)

Do not confuse the sources of information section with the notes section as they have different purposes. The purpose of the notes component is to give credit to those authors you quoted and/or paraphrased in your report. Cite sources in full citation form (e.g., APA style, MLA style) for those sources from which you quoted or paraphrased authors.

Report Preview The report preview briefly lays out the topics presented in the report body in the same order as they appear in the report, followed by some discussion of why they are included. The report preview provides the reader with a brief overview that serves as a topic base, leading to the extensive specifics and details in the report body. The report preview also provides the reader with insights into why a topic was included and why it was addressed in a specific location. This section also helps the report writer. As the writer develops the report body, he or she can use the report preview as a guide, so he or she does not forget to include a topic and includes the topics in the correct order. Figure 10-18 contains a sample report preview based on the store profitability scenario.

report preview
Brief text laying out the topics presented in the report body in the same order that they appear in the report, followed by a discussion of why each topic is included.

FIGURE 10–18: SAMPLE REPORT PREVIEW

Chapter 1, Substandard Stores, identifies company stores that reported substandard profit figures during the past six quarters. Identification of these stores was necessary before we could explore what could be done to make them more profitable. Chapter 2, In-Store Customer Service in Profitable Stores, reports how employees in the company's profitable stores greet customers as they enter the store (e.g., a smile, a friendly word). Chapter 3, In-Store Customer Service in Substandard Stores, reports how employees in the company's substandard stores greet customers as they enter the store (e.g., don't look up at them, don't say anything to them). Etc.

REPORT BODY

This is the third of the five report categories. This category is broken into two subsections—Topic Chapters and Report Summary. The Topic Chapters contain the findings. The Report Summary contains the key findings, conclusions, and recommendations.

Topic Chapters Topic chapters have three parts—Introductory Paragraph, Body, and Summary Paragraph.

Introductory Paragraph You are encouraged to start each topic chapter with an introductory paragraph that tells the reader which specific topics will be discussed in the chapter and the order they will be discussed. This section prepares the reader for what he or she is about to read and also helps the report writer stay organized. As the writer develops each topic chapter, he or she can use the introductory paragraphs as a guide so as not to forget to include a topic and to report on the topics in the order designated in the report preview. For an abbreviated sample introductory paragraph based on the store profitability scenario, see paragraph 1 in Figure 10-19.

Body Here is where you present the data or information you gathered that you believe is pertinent to the report's objective. In doing so, you perform some data (information) analysis. After all, every piece of data or information you collect is not included. You will go through the process of choosing what you think is most pertinent and should be included. The data or information you include is called *findings*. For an abbreviated sample body paragraph based on the store profitability scenario, see paragraph 2 in Figure 10-19.

Summary Paragraph You are encouraged to end each topic chapter with a summary paragraph in which you present the key findings for that chapter. To do so, you must first analyze the findings presented in the body of each topic chapter to identify the key (most important) findings from among all those you presented in each body section. Key findings are what the findings (raw data) reveal when analyzed. For an abbreviated sample summary paragraph based on the store profitability scenario, see paragraph 3 in Figure 10-19.

FIGURE 10-19: ABBREVIATED SAMPLE TOPIC CHAPTER

In this chapter we explore in-store customer service behaviors pertaining to how employees greet customers when they enter the store. Specifically, we explore whether employees greet customers with a smile and a friendly word.

Based on observations, we found that **96 percent** of the time, employees in All Sports, Inc.'s most-profitable stores greet customers with a smile as they enter the store. Based on observations, we found that employees in All Sports, Inc.'s least-profitable stores greet customers with a friendly word only **22 percent** of the time.

Ninety-six percent of the time, employees in All Sports, Inc.'s most profitable stores greet customers as they enter the store with a smile. Only **22 percent** of the time, employees in All Sports, Inc.'s least profitable stores greet customers with a friendly word.

Topic chapter summary paragraphs ultimately provide the starting point for the report summary.

Report Summary The report summary chapter contains three components—key findings, conclusions, and recommendations. Key findings, as you know, come from the summary paragraphs of the topic chapters. Conclusions are an outgrowth of the key findings, and recommendations evolve from conclusions.

Key Findings Key findings are what the findings (raw data) reveal when analyzed. When writing the report summary chapter, you do not need to rethink the key findings. After all, you already decided on these when you wrote the summary paragraphs for each topic chapter. For an abbreviated sample of key findings based on the store profitability scenario, see paragraph 1 in Figure 10-19.

Conclusions Conclusions are logical inferences based on the key findings. For an abbreviated sample of conclusions based on the store profitability scenario, see paragraph 2 in Figure 10-19.

As you draw conclusions, you move farther from the objectivity associated with key findings and find yourself relying increasingly on your perceptions regarding what the findings mean. Subjectivity enters the process in varying degrees.

Here are some ways you can reduce subjectivity in your conclusions:

- Conclusions should be relevant to the report's statement of purpose and statement of problem.
- Conclusions should be as objective as possible and flow logically from the analysis of the key findings.
- Conclusions should not introduce new material. They must be based on the analysis of the key findings.

report summary
Section of a report containing the key findings, conclusions, and recommendations.

key findings
What the report's data reveal.

conclusions
Logical inferences based on key report findings.

Here are some additional guidelines for writing conclusions:

- Do not assume each key finding will generate one conclusion! One key finding may generate one conclusion or it may generate two or more conclusions. Conversely, several key findings may be needed to generate a single conclusion. Then, too, some key findings do not warrant a single conclusion.
- Number the conclusions so readers can identify and refer to them easily while reading and discussing the report.
- Present conclusions in a meaningful order. For example, most-to-least important, easiest-to-most difficult, or immediate-to-long-term.

Recommendations These are confident statements of proposed actions based on report conclusions. Recommendations propose actions about which the writers are confident. They believe strongly enough in their data collection, analysis, and interpretation to encourage others to act on their recommendations. For an abbreviated sample of recommendations based on the store profitability scenario, see paragraph 3 in Figure 10-120.

As is the case with drawing conclusions, subjectivity is part of the process when making recommendations. When determining recommendations, it is helpful to bring to the process logical thinking, experience, knowledge, and a good dose of common sense. Keep in mind that recommendations must respond to the report's purpose and be appropriate for the audience.

Here are some ways you can reduce subjectivity in your recommendations:

- Recommendations must be relevant to the statement of purpose and the statement of problem.
- Recommendations should be as objective as possible and flow logically from the analysis of the conclusions.
- Do not introduce new material in the recommendations. They must be based on analysis of the conclusions.

Here are some additional guidelines for writing recommendations:

- Do not assume each conclusion will generate one recommendation! One conclusion may generate one recommendation or two or more recommendations. Conversely, several key conclusions may be needed to generate a single recommendation. Then too, some conclusions do not warrant a single recommendation.
- Begin each recommendation with an action verb. For example: Establish an ad hoc committee to determine ways to resolve the problem.
- Number the recommendations so readers can identify and refer to them easily while reading the report and making decisions about their implementation.
- Present recommendations in a meaningful order. For example, most-to-least important, easiest-to-most difficult, or immediate-to-long-term.
- Suggest additional research to investigate unanswered questions that become evident during the report-writing process.

recommendations Confident statements of proposed actions based on a report's conclusions.

> ## FIGURE 10-20: ABBREVIATED SAMPLE REPORT SUMMARY
>
> **Key Findings Ninety-six percent** of the time, employees in All Sports, Inc.'s most-profitable stores greet customers when they enter the store with a smile. Only **22 percent** of the time, employees in All Sports, Inc.'s least-profitable stores greet customers with a friendly word.
>
> **Conclusions** The willingness of employees in All Sports, Inc.'s profitable stores to greet customers with a smile appears to contribute, in part, to the higher profit levels in these stores. The infrequency with which employees in All Sports, Inc.'s least-profitable stores greet customers with a friendly word appears to contribute, in part, to the low profit levels in these stores.
>
> **Recommendations** Employees in all All Sports, Inc.'s stores should be encouraged to greet customers with a smile as they enter the store. Employees in every All Sports, Inc.'s store should be encouraged to greet customers with a friendly word as they enter the store.

NOTES

This is the fourth of the five report categories. The purpose of the notes section is to give credit to the authors you quoted and or paraphrased in your report. Be sure to give credit where credit is due. Figure 10-6 contains a list of the common reasons some writers plagiarize, including definitions of the terms quotation and paraphrase. None of us should plagiarize intentionally or unintentionally. For an abbreviated sample of the notes section based on the store profitability scenario, see Figure 10-21.

> ## FIGURE 10-21: ABBREVIATED SAMPLE NOTES SECTION
>
> ### Notes
>
> 1. W. C. Collins, *Customer Service* (New York: Cannon Press, 2012).
> 2. Sarah Wilfred, "Greeting Customers," *Fortune* 243, no. 8: 43–49.

APPENDED PARTS

This is the fifth of the five report categories. The appended parts section of your report may include an Index, a Glossary, or Additional Data/Information that include items such as spreadsheets, financial reports, policies, architectural drawings, maps, or schematics that you chose not to include in the report body, but want to make available to your reader. For an abbreviated sample of the index based on the store profitability scenario, see Figure 10-22.

FIGURE 10-22: ABBREVIATED SAMPLE INDEX

Index

SUMMARY: SECTION 5— FORMAL BUSINESS REPORTS

- Formal business reports are broken into five categories—prefatory parts, report proper, report body, notes, and appended parts.
- Prefatory parts include the title page, letter of transmittal, table of contents, table of tables, table of figures, table of charts, table of illustrations, table of photos, and executive summary.
- The report proper contains an introduction. The introduction section contains the statement of purpose, statement of problem, sources of information, and report preview.
- The report body contains the report presentation and report summary.
- The notes section contains the citations for paraphrases and quotations.
- The appended parts section contains the glossary, index, and additional data/information.

REPORT COHERENCE: TYING IT ALL TOGETHER

Given the length and complexity of many long, formal reports, writers are encouraged to integrate several coherence techniques into the writing process that assist their readers and themselves. Coherence techniques are critical to a document's flow, logic, clarity, and ultimately its overall effectiveness.

Coherence, as discussed here, refers to consistency and logical connections built into a report. Consistency and logical connections help readers see the relationships among the report's sections.

GUIDELINES FOR INCLUDING COHERENCE TECHNIQUES

Writers include coherence techniques in their business reports for a number of reasons. Major factors that guide their decisions to include coherence techniques include:

- **Length of the Report.** The longer the report, the greater the need to include coherence techniques to guide report readers and writers.
- **Number of Topics Addressed in the Report.** The greater the number of topics addressed in a report, the greater the need to include coherence techniques to guide report readers and writers.
- **Difficulty Level of the Information in the Report.** The more difficult the topics addressed in a report, the greater the need to include coherence techniques to guide report readers and writers.

COHERENCE TECHNIQUES

There are several coherence techniques that assist report readers and writers. Here are some of the major coherence techniques used by business report writers.

- **Start With a Strong Outline.** This establishes the report structure for the writer. Ultimately readers benefit from this effort.
- **Include a Report Preview.** This briefly presents the topics discussed in the report, the order in which they are presented, and the reasons they are included.
- **Include Topic Chapters Introductory Paragraphs.** These opening paragraphs present the topics discussed within each topic chapter and indicate the order in which they are presented.
- **Include Topic Chapters Summary Paragraphs.** These closing (summary) paragraphs present the key findings based on the findings presented in the topic chapters' body sections.
- **Use Basic Transitional Tools.** These bridging tools include the use of transition words, repetition of key words, topic sentences, and tie-in sentences, to name a few.

SUMMARY: SECTION 6— REPORT COHERENCE

- Coherence refers to consistency and logical connection throughout a report.
- Major factors that guide report writers' decisions to include coherence techniques are based on report length, the number of topics addressed, and the difficulty level of the information in the report.
- Business report coherence techniques include starting with a strong outline and including a report preview, sectional introductory paragraphs, sectional summary paragraphs, and basic transitional tools.

ELECTRONIC TOOLS THAT SUPPORT REPORT DEVELOPMENT

Every year, creative individuals and companies add to the list of electronic tools that support report development. Electronic tools that you likely use routinely include word processing software and research databases. (Several computer- and Internet-based databases and sources were mentioned earlier in this chapter.) If you have developed quantitative, analytical reports, you have probably used one or more statistical software programs. Here are some other electronic tools you may consider using if you have not already done so.

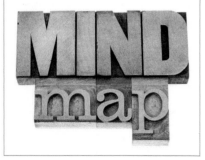

FOR PLANNING, OUTLINING, AND ORGANIZING YOUR REPORT

Mindmaps such as *Mindomo* provide a great way to organize your project visually.

Such programs are good for brainstorming the report components, including topics and subtopics, and then determining relationships and connections. If you are on a report-writing team, developing a mindmap on a smartboard is the way to go! (See Figure 10-23.)

FIGURE 10-23: MINDOMO MINDMAP

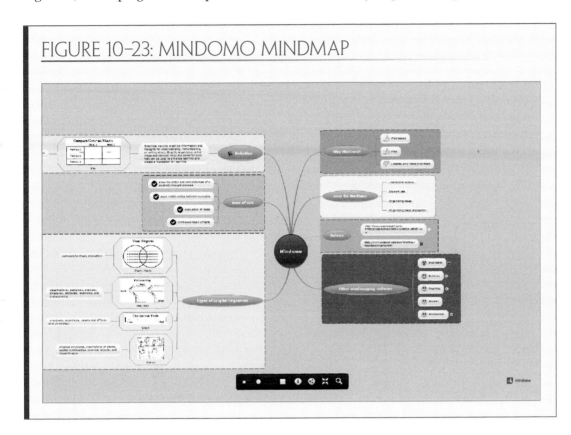

FOR DEVELOPING AND ADMINISTERING SURVEYS AND QUESTIONNAIRES

Qualtrics is a powerful, user-friendly tool for designing, developing, and administering surveys and questionnaires. This program also has so much more.

FOR CAPTURING, STORING, AND ACCESSING REFERENCE CITATIONS

Programs such as **EndNote** and **RefWorks** are reference management tools. With these programs you either scan the ISBN number of a book or key it into your laptop or tablet. The result is you capture the full citation information digitally without having to write it down. Then you can instruct the program to convert it into your preferred citation style (e.g., APA, MLA) and drop it into your Notes section. How cool is that! These programs help you store and organize your citations and references. They also make it easy for you to share your citations and references.

Qualtrics Powerful software for designing, developing, and administering surveys and questionnaires.

EndNote Bibliographic management system software.

RefWorks Web-based references management software package.

FOR STORING DATA AND INFORMATION

OneNote
Electronic
three-ring binder
software with
tabs for data
organization
and storage.

To organize and store your information, try **OneNote**. Essentially it is an electronic three-ring binder with tabs. You can easily share the data and information with others if you are on a report-writing team.

FOR DEVELOPING AND DISPLAYING VISUAL AIDS

There are many electronic tools that develop and display static and active visual aids. A good starting point is to discover the tools available on your word processing program. For example, you should have features that let you create and display tables, charts, graphs, and spreadsheets. You can easily import basic *PowerPoint* slides into your reports or liven up the look by developing *Prezi* slides. When appropriate, you could include one or more *YouTube* videos as live links in reports sent digitally. You might even find practical application for *Wordle* visuals, which let you produce word clouds for emphasis. (See Figure 10-24.)

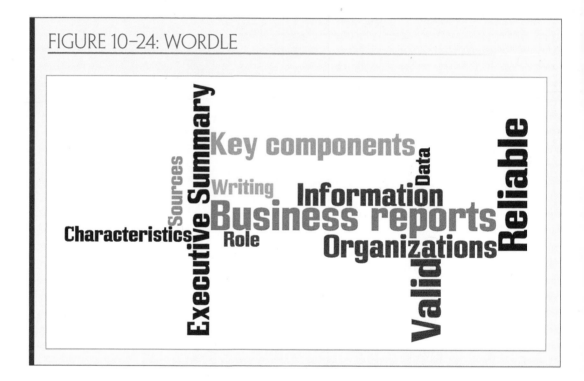

FIGURE 10–24: WORDLE

Certainly, it is easy to import photos into your reports also. You could also insert mind-maps for illustrative purposes. You might even find practical applications for short animated video clips (e.g., *GoAnimate*), and screen capture software that helps you record and overlay audio (e.g., *Camtasia Studio*). (See Figure 10-25.)

FIGURE 10-25: GOANIMATE

Visual Aids to Overcome Barriers to Communication http://smallbusiness. chron.com/visual-aids- overcome-barriers- communication-10134. html

FOR DEVELOPING REPORTS ON WRITING TEAMS

Writing reports with others is not uncommon in the business place. The good news is that there are many electronic tools to aid writing teams in areas ranging from meetings to report writing. Electronic support tools for teams and meetings are discussed in chapters 14 and 15. Electronic tools that support collaborative writing are addressed at length in chapter 14. For example, programs such as *PBworks SharePoint*, and *Google Drive* are three among many such programs that make it possible for writing team members to share, write, and edit individually and collectively without having to work together in a single location at the same time.

We are fortunate that so many creative, practical electronic tools are available to us, and the cool thing is that most of them are free or reasonably priced. You are encouraged to use the full range of electronic tools available when writing reports and to keep an eye open for new tools that will appear on the scene in the future.

Notes

1. *Quick Study Business: Business Research Guide*, BarCharts, Inc., Boca Raton, February 2002, 1.

PART 4

BUSINESS PRESENTATIONS

DEVELOPING BUSINESS PRESENTATIONS

11

LEARNING OUTCOMES

After reading this chapter, you should be able to:

1. Describe common purposes of business presentations.

2. Discuss the types of business presentations you will make in the business place.

3. Describe how organizations, businesspeople, and audiences benefit from effective business presentations.

4. Identify the basic components of effective business presentations.

5. Discuss how to manage and use speaking anxiety while planning and preparing business presentations.

6. Describe the activities involved in planning business presentations.

7. Describe the activities involved in preparing business presentations.

© Dean Drobot/Shutterstock.com

BENEFITS OF LEARNING ABOUT DEVELOPING BUSINESS PRESENTATIONS

1. Organizations prefer to hire and retain individuals who have good presentation skills because of the persuasive potential of good presentations and the positive role effective speakers play as representatives of their companies.

2. The ability to plan and prepare professional, persuasive, effective presentations contributes to your career and earning goals. An inability to do so hinders your advancement potential and job stability.

3. Good presentation skills position you to give effective presentations throughout your life in a host of non-work settings as well as in the workplace.

SELECT KEY TERMS

INTRODUCTION

Business presentations are given for purposes ranging from sharing information and persuading others to instructing and making position statements. In turn, your ability to give effective presentations should have a positive influence on your job stability and career growth. Aside from learning effective presentation techniques, it is important that you are able to manage your speaking anxiety effectively. Most of us experience some degree of speaking anxiety predominately due to self-pride, lack of familiarity with our presentation topic, and/or poor preparation. Several practical techniques for managing speaking anxiety while planning and preparing business presentations are shared in this chapter.

Practicing business presentations is very important to the process and is increasingly important when the presentation is a team presentation. In either case, you are strongly advised to make a video/audio recording of your practice sessions in order to better learn from any presentation strengths and weaknesses you notice. In addition, you are encouraged to prepare and practice question-and-answer (Q&A) sessions which typically occur immediately following business presentations.

The intent of this chapter is to provide you with information about planning and preparing effective business presentations. The goal of this chapter is realized through discussions on the following topics: why business presentations are given, why you should develop good presentation skills, benefits of effective presentations, components of effective presentations, your feelings about giving presentations, planning business presentations, and preparing business presentations. The information pertaining to the above-mentioned topics is reinforced by several student website resources including *PowerPoint slides, preview tests, chapter assessment tests, YouTube videos, interactive exercises,* and the *interactive glossary.*

WHY BUSINESS PRESENTATIONS ARE GIVEN

Millions upon millions of business presentations are given each year in organizations worldwide. The purpose for each presentation typically falls into one of four categories: *sharing information, persuading, instructing, and making position statements.*

Some business presentations are given for the purpose of sharing information. For example, a human resources director may give a presentation before the company's employees to convey information and entertain questions about a new benefits policy. Other presentations are given for the purpose of persuading audience members to a course of action. For example, a company representative may give a presentation to employees encouraging them to contribute generously during the upcoming United Way fund drive. Still other presentations are given for the purpose of instructing audience members. For example, an information technology representative may give a presentation to select employees teaching them to navigate a new, online purchasing system. Other presentations are given for the purpose of making official position statements. For example, a company's CEO may give a presentation to employees to announce and explain a merger with another company.

The Main Purpose of Presentations
http://westsidetoast-masters.com/resources/powerspeak/lib0026.html

MAIN TYPES OF BUSINESS PRESENTATIONS

The three main types of business presentations are face-to-face presentations, webcasts, and poster presentations. *Face-to-face* presentations have speakers and their audiences in the same room/space, whereas webcasts are media presentations transmitted over the Internet. *Poster presentations* bring interested audience members together in the same room or space where they discuss the topic addressed on presentation posters. You can develop professional quality poster presentations using programs such as *Adobe Illustrator* and *CorelDraw Graphics Suite*. If you must travel to another location to give a poster presentation, should consider producing a cloth poster instead of a paper stock poster. You can fold it up and transport it easily in your briefcase, computer bag, or suitcase. This is a much more practical option for poster presentations on the go!

WHY YOU SHOULD DEVELOP GOOD PRESENTATION SKILLS

Giving business presentations is not that far off for you. Do not fool yourself into believing that once you are on the job you will not be required to give presentations right away. Some students have the inaccurate perception that new hires in the business place are not required to give presentations. They believe that presentations are given only by middle- and upper-level executives, so their involvement in presentations is several years off. Hence, they are in no rush to develop their presentation skills. What an inaccurate perception! On average, a typical white-collar worker in the United States gives one or two work-related presentations per year for the first several years of his or her business career. These presentations are typically made before relatively small audiences of 30 or fewer people, and the composition of the audience members at any one presentation is often similar (e.g., similar job status, occupations, etc.).

Those individuals whose careers take them past middle-management level typically find themselves giving several presentations per year, and company leaders, such as presidents, CEOs, CIOs, and CFOs, typically make numerous presentations annually. Their audiences often vary in size from very few to several thousand, and the composition is often diverse. Company leaders are also likely to have some of their presentations broadcast to audiences at remote sites. The higher your rank in the company, the greater your audience's expectations are that you are an excellent presenter. So work now at preparing for such a future.

Wise students and businesspeople work continuously on improving their presentations skills. So, how can you grow both your presentation skills and speaking confidence to levels of excellence? Get started now if you are not already doing so. In other words, do not wait until you reach middle management to begin working seriously on your presentation skills. That's too late! Instead, work on them from this point forward. Doing so will serve you well as you move through the early stages and years of your career and will, in turn, prepare you for that point in your career when you will make high-stakes presentations.

ACQUIRING PRESENTATION TRAINING

Unfortunately, just giving one or two presentations each year during the early stages of your career will do little to develop your presentation skills. Most of us need several years of training, practice, and experience to gain sufficient confidence and develop excellent presentation skills. Do not be discouraged. You can develop excellent presentation skills by acquiring training and additional presentation experiences on a regular basis. Consider these suggestions:

- Attend workshops and take speech classes at universities, junior colleges, and private business schools.
- Take Internet-based, distance learning, presentation skills courses.
- Take Internet-based, continuing professional education, presentation skills courses.

- Read presentation skills books. They range from full-coverage books to those that focus on specific elements of the process, such as those that focus on overcoming speaking anxiety.
- Learn from presentation skills audio tapes, videotapes, and online programs.
- Attend Toastmasters and **Toastmasters International** meetings and training sessions. The purpose of these organizations is to help people become good speakers.

ACQUIRING PRESENTATION EXPERIENCE

- Volunteer to give presentations at work. Since most people do not like to give presentations, your gesture will be welcomed. This approach might even help you earn promotions.
- Speak at professional conferences. Professional conferences provide you with the opportunity to practice in front of both small and mid-sized audiences. Furthermore, you gain valuable experience managing question-and-answer sessions, including an occasional aggressive audience member. For starters, consider presenting at a regional or national conference of the Association for Business Communication (http://businesscommunication.org/).
- Make a presentation before friends or family members. However, instruct them to inform you honestly of your specific shortcomings and strengths. If all they say is "good job," that's not helpful.
- Speak before college, high school, middle school, and elementary school classes. Simply contact the schools and express your interest in speaking. Colleges typically have you talk about your company or career. Schools ranging from elementary schools to high schools may have you speak on the above topics or about your personal interests (e.g., hobbies). Be aware that children at the elementary school level will often interrupt you mid-sentence. This gives you good practice. Of course, adults in your audiences will also interrupt you occasionally. You need to be able to think on your feet, stay on schedule, and pick up on your presentation where you left off at the time of the interruption.
- Speak at senior citizen centers, assisted care facilities, and nursing homes. Your efforts will be greatly appreciated.
- Speak at meetings of public service organizations such as Girl Scouts, Boy Scouts, Kiwanis, Rotary, etc. The audiences are friendly and appreciative of your efforts.
- Speak at personal interest meetings and conferences. For example, each year several people who hold a special interest in studying and analyzing the Battle of the Little Bighorn share their perspectives regarding the battle at meetings and conferences.

There is no great secret to becoming a good presenter. Persistence, hard work, and following the right course of action are the keys to developing the necessary skills and confidence. The good news is that you can become an excellent speaker and actually enjoy giving business presentations!

Toastmasters
Well-respected organization that helps members improve their speaking abilities.

Toastmasters International
http://www.toastmasters.org/

© Elena11/Shutterstock.com

BENEFITS OF EFFECTIVE PRESENTATIONS

Several parties typically benefit from effective presentations. Among the beneficiaries are organizations, presenters, and presentation audiences. The ways each benefit are presented here.

Organizations Benefit from Effective Presentations Organizations typically benefit from good presentations in three ways. First, organizations benefit when outside speakers give good presentations to their employees. Second, organizations realize benefits when their employees give effective presentations to audiences of fellow employees. Last, organizations benefit when their employees make effective presentations to external audiences on behalf of the organization.

When outside speakers give effective presentations to your employees, your organization typically benefits from the added information, knowledge, and understanding the speakers impart to employees. This occurs, in part, because good speakers capture and keep their audience's attention. As a result, audience members typically focus on the information being presented. The outcome is that the audience members understand, learn, and retain more than they would if they were listening to an inept speaker.

When speakers make good presentations before fellow employees, benefits such as those described above are also typical. With good presentations, organizations benefit from a reduction in miscommunication and the related losses that often result from poor-quality presentations.

When employees give good presentations to external audiences on behalf of their organizations, their organizations stand to benefit. The connection here pertains to the speaker's role as a representative of his or her organization. When organizations allow poor or average speakers to represent them before outside audiences, they risk negative outcomes in terms of poor public relations and lost business. If a speaker has poor or average presentation skills, what impressions do the audience members form about not only the speaker, but also about the speaker's organization? If the speaker is a good presenter, however, the audience members are more likely to be persuaded by the presentation, think well of the speaker's organization, and do business with the speaker's organization in the future.

Speakers Benefit from Giving Effective Presentations Speakers with good presentation skills realize benefits also. Most managers appreciate the impact such employees can have on their organizations. This is why managers place such a high value on presentation skills. In turn, you are encouraged to (1) appreciate the importance the business community places on good presentation skills, (2) develop good presentation skills as early as possible, and (3) continue to develop and refine your presentation skills throughout your career.

One of the times good presentation skills will serve you well is during the job hunting process. It is not uncommon for employers to look for evidence of job applicants' presentation skills on their college transcripts or in their résumés and cover letters. In addition, some recruiters require job applicants to give one or more presentations during the application process to determine the level of their actual presentation skills.

Good speakers also benefit in other ways. For example, organizations often take employees' presentation skills into account when making employment termination, demotion, transfer, pay raise, bonus, and promotion decisions. As can be expected, good speakers often experience higher levels of job security and larger, more-frequent pay raises, performance bonuses, and promotions. There is nothing like a well-delivered, "knock-their-socks-off" presentation to get the attention of those who make the big decisions.

FIGURE 11–1: PRESENTERS' ETHICAL RESPONSIBILITIES

Good speakers understand that adhering to ethical standards is also important. Here are several suggestions on how to be an ethical speaker. Good speakers:

- Avoid sharing inaccurate, misleading, or manipulative information.
- Develop visual aids that avoid distortion of facts and statistics.
- Avoid color and other design techniques that distract audience members' attention from points the speaker wants to gloss over.
- Use visual aids that are visible. Speakers leave the visuals up long enough so the audience has enough time to understand the information, without feeling they are being rushed for less-than-professional reasons.
- Refrain from highly persuasive nonverbal cues, such as gesturing, voice inflection, pauses, and inviting facial expressions, to mask inaccurate, misleading, or manipulative information.
- Avoid using their friendly, inviting personality to mask inaccurate, misleading, or manipulative information.
- Do not use their language in ways that manipulate foreign audiences whose command of the speaker's language is weak.

Individuals with good presentation skills benefit from the increased self-confidence that comes with knowing they have mastered an activity that many people never master. Their self-confidence makes it possible for them to be open to presentation opportunities, address audience questions without hesitation, and enjoy giving presentations. Furthermore, their self-confidence radiates in presentations, making them dynamic speakers.

Audiences Benefit from Effective Presentations How often have you sat through a presentation during which you spent more time looking at your watch or texting than focusing on the speaker? Or you daydreamed, doodled, or did some work. That speaker likely did not have good presentation skills. While we cannot always avoid being subjected to poor speakers, each of us can and should work at not subjecting others to such torment. We owe it to the organizations that provide us with a livelihood, we owe it to our audiences, and we owe it to ourselves.

So how do audiences benefit from effective speakers? They typically learn and retain more information from a good speaker than from one who is less skilled. Audience members may learn how to be better speakers simply by observing the techniques of those who are proficient at their craft. In addition, dynamic, effective speakers are capable of inspiring individual audience members to truly desire to improve their own presentation skills.

Yet another audience benefit is simply the enjoyment factor. Most of us enjoy listening to dynamic, effective speakers. After all, it sure beats the boredom we experience when subjected to a poorly skilled, unenthusiastic speaker. Face it, the topics addressed in business presentations are not always interesting, let alone exciting. With such topics, effective speakers have the ability to help their audiences bridge the gap between disinterest and interest.

Presentation Benefits
http://smallbusiness.
chron.com/benefits-
presentations-business-
professional-set-
tings-72176.html

BASIC COMPONENTS OF EFFECTIVE PRESENTATIONS

What makes one presentation successful and another mediocre? Is one presentation successful because the speaker effectively covered all of his or her information in the allotted amount of time or was it because he or she was dynamic and interesting? Is another presentation considered mediocre because the speaker appeared disorganized and did not imbue his or her voice and expressions with enthusiasm? Numerous factors contribute to the effectiveness or ineffectiveness of presentations. Each of the basic elements that affect the quality of presentations is presented below.

UNDERSTANDING THE PURPOSE OF THE PRESENTATION

Good speakers have a clear understanding of their purpose before planning and preparing a presentation. Their purpose may be to share routine information or provide some form of instruction to their audience members. Or, the intent of the presentation may be to persuade the audience to make an official position statement.

A good speaker understands that familiarization with the purpose impacts the effectiveness of the planning and preparation as well as the presentation itself. Knowing one's purpose is at the heart of good communication.

Determining Audiences' Information Expectations and Needs Good speakers understand the importance of presenting information that their audiences perceive as useful. When planning and preparing presentations, good speakers take time to determine their audience's information expectations and needs.

Sharing the right information does not preclude the need to be a skilled, dynamic speaker. However, good presentation skills alone are typically not enough to produce an effective presentation. Choosing the right information to share is also important.

Selecting the Right Amount of Information Good speakers understand the importance of selecting the right amount of information. This means they share the information their audiences expect and need. Furthermore, they share this information within the recommended time frame. This implies that they understand their audience's information expectations and needs well enough to make such decisions.[1]

When we do not pay adequate attention to selecting the right amount of information, problems arise. When we select too little information, we do not meet our audience's information expectations and needs. When we select too much information, we compromise our audience's ability to understand and retain information. The key to selecting the right amount of information involves diligent planning, preparation, and practice.

Organizing Information Logically Good speakers understand the need to organize their presentations in ways that help their audiences understand and retain the information shared. It is important that speakers do so because their audiences do not have an opportunity to hear the presentation a second time (unlike a written document that they might read two or more times to achieve understanding and retention). Thus, good speakers organize their presentations so the points they are making are clear and flow logically.

To help their audiences comprehend and retain the information presented, good speakers often share it three times. First, they introduce the presentation topic by giving an overview of the main points to be shared. Second, they present the information in detail. Third, they summarize the main points made.

Choosing the Right Type and Number of Visual Aids Good speakers know that visual aids are expected in business presentations and understand the importance of choosing the right type and number for each presentation. While visual aid types vary significantly (e.g., handouts, PowerPoint slides, mindmaps, graphs, YouTube clips, flip charts), be aware of the growing popularity of professional-quality, colorful visual aids. In a world where we are bombarded by so many visual images (e.g., TV, video games, movies, the Internet), business audiences have come to expect professional-quality, colorful visual aids.

The most common computer-generated presentation tool by far is Microsoft's **PowerPoint**, but it is not the only tool of its kind. **Corel Presentations** and Sun Microsystem's **Apache Open Office Impress** are similar tools. Then there are web-based tools such as Trellix, a program that supports presentations made for the Web, teleconferences, and live electronic presentations. Many freeware programs have been designed to support business presentations. For example, Google has developed a documents and spreadsheets program that lets you share projects online with the general public or specific people.[2]

Be careful not to overdo it with the visual aids. Since computers and presentation software make it easy to produce visual aids, you have time to end up with more visual aids than you can present effectively. Produce only the number needed to communicate and support the points you are making—no more, no less.

Staying on Schedule Make it a point to respect your audience's need to stay on schedule. Plan, prepare, and practice for a designated length; start the presentation on time; keep an eye on your watch; and end on time.

Work to eliminate those obstacles that can cause you to start or end late, such as (1) not planning, preparing, and practicing properly; (2) selecting too much information; (3) developing too many visual aids; (4) arriving at the presentation site late; (5) not understanding how to use the equipment and software; (6) lacking a backup plan to cope with equipment or software that is not working properly; (7) getting away from your notes and rambling; and (8) not controlling question-and-answer sessions.

Presenting Professionally Good speakers understand the importance of good presentation skills. They know that good presentation technique alone does not produce a truly effective presentation. They do know, however, that when good presentation skills are combined with the right content, a good presentation is the result. So, give each of these components sufficient attention, and you will be on the right track.

PowerPoint
A popular presentation software package.

Corel Presentations
Presentation software similar to Microsoft PowerPoint.

Apache Open Office Impress
A presentation program analogous to Microsoft PowerPoint and Apple Keynote. Can export presentations to Adobe Flash (SWF) files, allowing them to be played on any computer with a Flash player installed. Impress lacks ready-made presentation designs but this can be overcome by downloading free templates online.

Key Components in Business Presentations http://www.melrosemac.com/blog/bid/323077/4-Key-Components-Included-in-Every-Memorable-Business-Presentation

In all presentation phases—planning, preparing, practicing, presenting, and Q&A sessions—acknowledge and control your presentation anxiety. Most people experience some level of presentation anxiety. If you do, take comfort in knowing that you are not alone! The trick is to learn to control anxiety and use it to your and your audience's advantage. The next section contains information about why most of us experience *presentation anxiety* and some techniques to control it during the planning, preparation, and practicing phases. The benefits of managing and using presentation anxiety are addressed in chapter 12, along with some techniques to control speaking anxiety shortly before and during presentations, as well as during Q&A sessions.

HOW DO YOU FEEL ABOUT GIVING PRESENTATIONS?

Do you enjoy giving presentations? Do you know many people who do? Do you know anyone who does? Is it humanly possible to enjoy giving presentations? Believe it or not, some people actually do. Many others who may not necessarily use the word *enjoy* to describe their feelings about giving presentations still embrace the task wholeheartedly when necessary.

SUMMARY: SECTION 2— THE COMPONENTS OF EFFECTIVE PRESENTATIONS

- Understanding the purpose
- Determining the audience's information expectations and needs
- Selecting the right information
- Organizing the information effectively
- Choosing the right type(s) and number of visual aids
- Staying on schedule
- Determining appropriate appearance
- Making a professional presentation

If you do not enjoy giving presentations, challenge yourself. When you become skilled, experienced, and confident enough, then you will enjoy making dynamic, effective presentations and gain the satisfaction of knowing that you have mastered a challenging skill set.

PRESENTATION ANXIETY: WILL YOU CONTROL IT OR WILL IT CONTROL YOU?

Let's cut to the chase and put the bad news out there. Most people do not like to give presentations. Are you surprised? Are you like most people? Given the choice, most people would rather have someone else speak. When asked why they do not like to give presentations, most people are quick to cite presentation anxiety as the reason. Some call it *presentation anxiety*, while others call it *speaking anxiety* or *stage fright*. No matter what they call it, they are all talking about the same uncomfortable feelings. In general terms, **presentation anxiety** (*glossophobia*) is a tense emotional state resulting from one's apprehension of speaking before groups. The degree of anxiety varies from person to person, with typical symptoms ranging from heightened nervousness, poor sleep patterns, and sweaty palms to overwhelming feelings of fear and self-doubt.

presentation anxiety
A tense, emotional state resulting from one's attitude and feelings about speaking in front of a group. Also known as *glossophobia*.

© benchart/Shutterstock.com

Even though we understand on a logical level that others also experience presentation anxiety, most of us convince ourselves that other speakers are either not nervous or far less nervous than we are. Take solace in knowing that you are not alone when it comes to presentation anxiety. While this awareness alone will not resolve your nervousness, it will help you keep your feelings in perspective. You are faced with the same challenges as everyone else—the challenges to face up to your presentation anxiety and to learn to manage and use it productively.

WHY DO MOST OF US EXPERIENCE PRESENTATION ANXIETY?

What makes us anxious about public speaking? There are a number of reasons, and not surprisingly, the reason or reasons that plague one person do not necessarily plague others. So, each of us is faced with the challenge of determining specifically what makes us anxious. Knowing the reasons behind our speaking anxieties is a good starting point. We may even discover that some of the reasons are unwarranted. For those that are not, however, we are then in a better position to identify relaxation techniques and presentation anxiety control techniques that will help us control our fears.

Now, let's look at the typical reasons behind presentation anxiety. Self-pride is the main reason most of us experience presentation anxiety. We simply do not want to embarrass ourselves before a group of people. Most of us want our audience to think we are knowledgeable, competent people who have our act together. We certainly do not want people to laugh at us or pity us when we say or do something embarrassing. Even comedians and clowns want people to laugh with them, not at them. Most speakers want to do a good job.

Self-pride is not the only reason most people experience speaking anxiety. Here are some other reasons.

- Insufficient planning
- Insufficient preparation
- Insufficient practice
- Lack of familiarity with the presentation topic
- Lack of confidence in the presentation topic
- Tension associated with knowing that big stakes are riding on the outcome of the presentation
- Tension associated with knowing the boss or other influential people will be in the audience
- Fear of certain sizes of audiences
- Realization that you have been ill or tired leading up to the presentation
- Realization that you have been stressed about other matters leading up to the presentation
- Fear that you will not finish in the allotted time or that you will finish too early
- Fear that the microphone or visual aid equipment or software will not work properly or that you are not familiar enough with it to fix it on the fly
- Fear of audience apathy
- Fear of not having a response for an audience member's question
- Fear of having to deal with aggressive audience members

Hopefully, your presentation anxiety level was not heightened as you read the above list. Good speakers come to grips with their fears and learn to control them. They appreciate the importance of understanding the reasons behind the fears. Understand that most of the reasons for presentation anxiety can be controlled through careful planning and preparation.

BENEFITS OF MANAGING AND USING SPEAKING ANXIETY WHILE PLANNING AND PREPARING PRESENTATIONS

The trick is to learn to manage and use your presentation anxieties, instead of struggling to eliminate them. Most of us naturally seek to eliminate our anxieties and fears as quickly as possible, which is understandable because they make us uncomfortable and appear to threaten our perceived sense of control. However, good speakers know they can derive benefits from presentation anxiety experienced during the planning and preparation stages. For example, presentation anxiety can motivate you to:

- Start planning and preparing early
- Gain a clear understanding of your objective
- Learn about your audience
- Learn your presentation topic thoroughly
- Gain confidence in your presentation topic
- Derive your information from reliable sources
- Determine the right amount of information to include in your presentation
- Check out the presentation site and equipment well in advance of the presentation date
- Develop backup plans for equipment and software malfunctions
- Practice extensively
- Prepare for question-and-answer sessions

MANAGING AND USING SPEAKING ANXIETY WHILE PLANNING AND PREPARING PRESENTATIONS

© iQoncept/Shutterstock.com

Although presentation anxiety is typically most noticeable shortly before and during presentations, most speakers experience some anxiety while planning and preparing their presentations. Fortunately, you can do several things to manage and use presentation anxiety during the planning and preparation stages. Some relaxation strategies and strategies for managing and using presentation anxiety while planning and preparing presentations follow.

RELAXATION STRATEGIES WHILE PLANNING AND PREPARING PRESENTATIONS

Relaxation helps us keep a reasonable perspective on our presentation anxiety. It also allows us to be more objective and thorough as we plan and prepare presentations. Finally, relaxation helps us look to the presentation day with optimism, not dread.[3] Consider the following suggestions.

- **Exercise**. Choose a type of exercise you enjoy, then have fun while working off some of that speaking anxiety.
- **Listen to relaxing music**. Listen to relaxing music while you plan and prepare your presentation or take a break, sit back, close your eyes, and take it in.

- **Meditate**. Use meditation to calm down, give your mind a rest, and place yourself in a positive frame of mind.
- **Visualize your presentation**. Visualize yourself giving a dynamic, effective presentation. Build self-confidence by visualizing yourself moving successfully through the presentation, from your introduction to your closing.
- **Watch movies, read, and play computer games**. Give your mind a break from your fears by getting lost in a good movie, book, or computer game.
- **Volunteer**. Step away from your presentation anxiety for a few hours and do some volunteer work for a charitable organization. This will take your mind off your fears for a while and put your presentation anxiety in perspective.
- **Treat yourself**. Be especially kind to yourself. This may mean treating yourself to that dessert you might not normally eat or buying a special item of clothing that makes you feel good.

Lists of strategies for relaxation and for managing and using presentation anxiety shortly before and during presentations, as well as during Q&A sessions, are presented in chapter 12 .

PRESENTATION ANXIETY CONTROL STRATEGIES TO CONTROL SPEAKING ANXIETY WHILE PLANNING AND PREPARING PRESENTATIONS

Use one or more of the following suggestions to reduce anxiety while planning and preparing your presentation.

- **Identify and embrace the reasons you are anxious**. Write them down on paper, rank them, then decide how you will manage and use them as you plan and prepare your presentation.
- **Begin planning and preparation early**. Waiting until the last minute to do these things simply adds to your anxiety.
- **Gain a clear understanding of your presentation objective**. Remove any doubt regarding your objective.
- **Familiarize yourself with your audience**. Remove unknown elements that might otherwise feed your fears.
- **Learn your presentation topic well**. Gain confidence in knowing that you are secure in your understanding of your presentation topic. The audience looks to you as the expert!
- **Determine the appropriate information to include**. Take comfort in knowing you are choosing information that your audience needs to know.
- **Select information you will share from authoritative sources**. Remove concerns that you will either not be sharing good-quality information or that your audience will question your sources.
- **Determine the right amount of information to include**. Remove fears that you will share too much or too little information, which will result in your presentation running over or falling short of the allotted time.

- **Check out the presentation site and equipment well in advance of the presentation**. Familiarize yourself with the presentation setting, hardware, and software to remove unknown elements about which you might otherwise worry.
- **Develop backup plans for potential equipment or software malfunction**. Reduce your fears by knowing how you can proceed if your equipment or software does not work properly.
- **Get extremely comfortable with the first couple minutes of the presentation**. Knowing that your presentation will get off to a good start reduces your fears and builds your self-confidence.
- **Practice extensively**. Practice often using good practice techniques. If you can, practice in a room similar in size and shape to the room in which you will give your presentation. In addition, practice your speech in front of people with whom you are comfortable, such as family or friends. They can provide you with priceless feedback regarding your presentation. If necessary, public speaking coaches are available to help you with your presentation and anxiety.[4]
- **Prepare thoroughly for question-and-answer sessions**. Anticipate questions and prepare your responses and reactions in advance to reduce your fear of intimidation by audience questions.
- **Prepare yourself physically**. Eat right, get enough sleep, and exercise some. This makes you alert and objective while planning and preparing, as well as during your presentation.

SUMMARY: SECTION 3— PRESENTATION ANXIETY

- Presentation anxiety refers to a tense emotional state resulting from one's attitude toward and feelings about speaking in front of groups.
- The main reason for presentation anxiety is self-pride. Other causes of anxiety range from insufficient planning and preparation to fear of equipment failure to audience apathy.
- The trick to benefiting from presentation anxiety is to manage it instead of struggling to eliminate it.
- Relaxation techniques include exercising, listening to relaxing music, meditating, visualizing your presentation, watching movies, reading, playing computer games, doing volunteer work, and treating yourself.
- Anxiety control techniques range from thoroughly planning and preparing your talk to preparing yourself physically.

PLANNING BUSINESS PRESENTATIONS

Planning is the foundation on which effective presentations are built. Good planning contributes to presentations in which speakers meet their objectives and their audience's needs. The following website contains information about all presentation skills components: www.abacon.com/pubspeak/histsit.html.

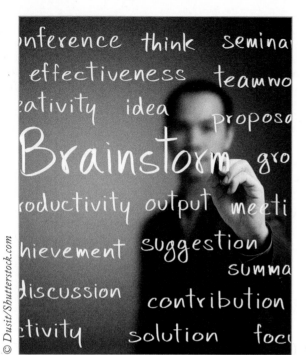

© Dusit/Shutterstock.com

*Planning an Effective
Presentation*
http://www2.le.ac.uk/
offices/ld/resources/
presentations/planning-
presentation

Planning a presentation involves determining what it is you need to accomplish and how you will do it. Think of the planning process as being one of answering a series of questions. The questions and answers discussed here provide a sense of the activities involved in planning presentations.

WHAT IS MY PRESENTATION OBJECTIVE?

At the heart of this question is determining if your task is to share routine information, provide instruction, persuade audience members toward a specific objective, or make an official position statement. Write out the specific purpose so that it remains clear in your mind as you plan and prepare.

WHAT DO I NEED TO KNOW ABOUT MY AUDIENCE?

Familiarizing yourself with your audience and its needs is critical to planning and preparing effective presentations. The idea here is to analyze your audience so you will be able to achieve a good fit between your objectives and your audience's needs and expectations.

For example, determine your audience's information needs and expectations. This involves determining what information they already know, what information they expect, and what information they need. While making such determinations, do your best to identify their level of understanding and anticipate their probable reaction to your presentation—both content and presentation style.

It is useful to determine audience size for a variety of reasons. Such information makes it possible for you to select appropriate types of visual aids and font sizes. While flip charts and whiteboards may work for small audiences, to get the job done properly with large audiences, computer-generated visual aids are the more appropriate choice. Determining audience size in advance also makes it possible to decide whether you will need to use a microphone. When your audience size exceeds 100 people, expect to use a microphone.

Determining audience type is a crucial step in organizing your presentation. For example, if you have a friendly audience you want to be warm in your presentation and include a little humor. If your audience is neutral, you might want to present both sides of an issue using a pro-con pattern and employ more facts, statistics, and expert opinions. And if your audience is hostile, you might use a noncontroversial, chronological pattern, objective data, and expert opinions that are more appropriate than anecdotes and humor.[5]

FIGURE 11–3: PLANNING AND PREPARING PRESENTATIONS FOR DIFFERENT LEARNING STYLES

When planning for a business presentation, it is important to remember that individual audience members have one of three learning styles: visual, auditory, or kinesthetic/tactile. Simply put, visual learners learn through seeing; auditory learners learn through listening; and, kinesthetic/tactile learners learn through hands-on activities. To effectively meet the needs of your entire audience, you must address all three learning styles. Here are some techniques for doing so.

To reach out to **visual learners** in your audience, lace your presentation with:

- Photos
- Graphics
- Colorful charts

© snapgalleria/Shutterstock.com

To reach out to the **auditory learners** in your audience, make sure to include:

- Personal stories
- Analogies and metaphors
- Tangible examples, facts, and figures
- Variation in pitch and volume of your voice and the speed of your presentation to keep the auditory learners engaged.

FIGURE 11-3: PLANNING AND PREPARING PRESENTATIONS FOR DIFFERENT LEARNING STYLES

© Graphicworld/Shutterstock.com

To reach out to the **kinesthetic/tactile learners** in your audience, provide opportunities for audience members to:

- Take notes
- Raise their hands and ask questions

© Batshevs/Shutterstock.com

To achieve the most effective presentation possible, you should include everyone in the audience. If you do not reach out to all three types of learners, you risk leaving people behind during your presentation.

Source: Carmine Gallo. "Presentations with Something for Everyone." Business Week Online. (2006).16-16. http://www.businessweek.com/stories/2006-12-05/presentations-with-something-for-everyonebusinessweek business-news-stock-market-and-financial-advice

FIGURE 11-4: PLANNING AND PREPARING PRESENTATIONS FOR INTERNATIONAL AUDIENCES

Here are some general suggestions for planning and preparing presentations to be given to international audiences.

- Learn about your audience's culture, especially its business customs.
- Gain a clear understanding of your audience's expectations.
- Determine the level of formality that your audience expects. (Most expect a high level of formality and professionalism.)
- Determine if your status and age are important to the audience.
- Practice speaking more slowly than you would if you were giving a presentation in the United States.
- Identify your accent characteristics (e.g., drawl, speed) and practice controlling them so they do not interfere with clarity.
- Avoid slang and profanity. You do not want to confuse or offend your audience.
- Use technical jargon sparingly. If you have to use jargon, explain it.
- Use humor sparingly. Humor translates poorly into other languages and cultures.
- If you will not be speaking in your audience's native language, plan to sprinkle a few words and phrases in their language into your presentation, but first test these words with a native speaker before the presentation.
- As you practice, be aware of your nonverbal communication habits and how they will be interpreted by your international audience (e.g., eye contact, gestures, etc.).
- Determine the type of visual aids your audience prefers (e.g., computer-generated, handouts) and whether they should be prepared in advance (e.g., PowerPoint slides) or they can be developed during the presentation (e.g., whiteboards, flip charts).
- Be extremely clear and specific with your host regarding your equipment needs. Test your equipment ahead of time to ensure it works properly and meshes with any hardware or software you plan to use. Plan for a worst-case scenario.
- Determine your audience's appearance expectations. (Most foreign audiences expect the speaker's appearance to be professional and conservative.)

Finally, determine the composition of your audience. Are the members similar or diverse in terms of job title, education, age, gender, cultural backgrounds, etc.? Given their composition and expectations, what level of formality will your audience expect? Should you give your entire talk and then entertain questions? Or, should you encourage discussion throughout your presentation? Should you dress formally and remain behind the podium during the presentation? Or, should you dress casually and move around before your audience?[6] Additional information pertaining to understanding your audience is available at this website www.abacon.com/pubspeak/histsit.html.

WHAT INFORMATION DO I NEED TO SHARE?

This question really pertains to two separate issues. You should be concerned about sharing the right information, and you should be concerned about doing it within the suggested time frame.

First, identify the information needs of your audience. This suggests that you will determine who your audience is and what information your audience expects and needs. Your audience may know what information they expect, but they may not realize they need additional information. This is where you plan the information needs accordingly and fill in the gaps.

Having identified your audience and its information expectations and needs, you are now faced with the challenge of determining how to organize and present the information in a way that is consistent with the amount of time allotted for the presentation.

Selecting too little information often results in ineffective presentations. The problem is further compounded when a presenter speaks more rapidly during the presentation than he or she does during the practice sessions. The result is an ineffective presentation that falls noticeably short of its recommended time frame.

Selecting too much information also contributes to ineffective presentations. When you include too much information in your presentation, one of the following four problems typically occurs. (1) You speak at a recommended rate, but disrupt audience members' schedules when your presentation runs long. (2) You speak at a recommended rate, but must skip important points in your quest to finish on time. (3) You speak at a recommended rate, but skip or rush through the summary. (4) You speak too fast and rush through visuals in your quest to include all your information and still finish on time.

WHAT INFORMATION SHOULD I PRESENT VISUALLY?

To answer this question, ask yourself how your audience will benefit from your visual aids. For example, is the purpose of your visual aids to help your audience understand and retain information presented? Is the purpose to simplify complex or detailed information? Is the purpose to emphasize specific information or show a trend? Is the purpose to introduce your presentation or is it to highlight key points in the summary? Assign a purpose to each visual aid you consider including. If you see no clear, driving purpose to a proposed visual aid, drop it. Visual aids should be developed in conjunction with development of the talk. They should not be developed as an afterthought or included for show.

WHAT TYPES OF VISUAL AIDS SHOULD BE INCLUDED?

The answer is: those that best support your presentation. The good news here is that you have several visual aid types to choose from. The bad news is that you have more types of visual aids to become familiar with and consider when planning presentations. Here are several examples.

- **Handouts.** Are a good choice when you have more information to share with your audience than you are able to include. Handouts are most frequently used with small, informal audiences.
- **A flip chart or whiteboard.** Is a practical choice if your intention is to develop lists during presentations. Flip charts and whiteboards are most frequently used with informal audiences. They do not provide a practical alternative for large audiences,

Creating Effective Visual Aids
http://www.mindtools.com/pages/article/creating-presentation-visuals.htm

due to the obvious lack of visibility and because formal audiences expect professionally prepared visual aids.

- **Items**. Refers to tangible things a speaker would hold up before an audience, for example, a prosecuting attorney might show a murder weapon to a jury in a criminal trial. Items are an appropriate type of visual aid for both informal and formal audiences. In either case, the audience must be small or some will not be able to see the item.

- **Demonstrations**. Provide a practical way to communicate visually when you want to walk your audience through a particular action. For example, a speaker could invite a colleague or friend to the front of the room and the two could demonstrate the proper way to shake hands at a job interview. Demonstrations are also limited to small audiences due to the restricted visibility factor.

- **Bar charts**. Are used to show numerical comparisons. Bar charts are typically computer-generated and displayed digitally. Keep them simple. For example, 3D bar charts are often confusing. There is too much going on, and the 3D angles often distort clear comparisons. Use distinctly different colors for each comparative bar in multiple-bar charts. They are equally effective for informal and formal audiences, as well as small and large audiences. (See Figure 11-5.)

bar charts
Graphs that show numerical comparisons.

FIGURE 11–5: BAR CHART

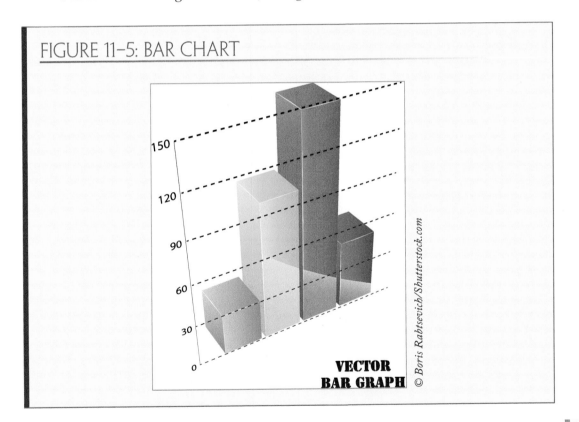

- **Line charts** are is used to show trends. Line charts are typically computer-generated and displayed digitally. Use different color lines in multiple-line charts. They are equally effective for both informal and formal audiences, as well as small and large audiences. (See Figure 11-6.)

line charts
Graphs that show trends.

FIGURE 11-6: LINE CHART

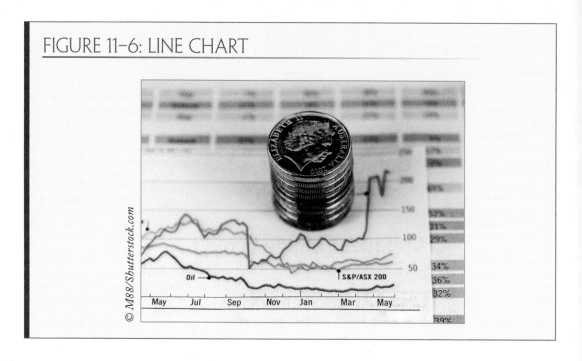

© M88/Shutterstock.com

- **Pie charts** are used to show comparisons of a whole (100 percent), such as budgets. Pie charts are typically computer-generated and displayed digitally. Use distinctly different colors for each slice of the pie. They are equally effective for both informal and formal audiences, as well as for small and large audiences. (See Figure 11-7.)

FIGURE 11-7: PIE CHART

© ra2studio/Shutterstock.com

- **PowerPoint.** The main idea with regard to PowerPoint slides is to keep them simple. Avoid including too much information on a PowerPoint slide. Select a font style and a type size that are legible and easy to read from a distance. Document cameras, also known as digital overheads, provide a good alternative to overhead transparencies.

FIGURE 11–8: DEVELOPING POWERPOINT SLIDES

How familiar are you with developing effective PowerPoint slides? The following questions will help you answer the question if you are unsure.

A. Is it better to select a relatively simple background design and then use it across all of your presentation PowerPoint slides <u>or</u> is it better to select a background design that has a lot of components (very busy) as a means of holding your audience's attention?

B. Is it better to use a legible font (e.g., *Arial, Times New Roman, Calibri*) <u>or</u> is it better to use a scripted font (e.g., *Freestyle Script, Segoe Script*) as a means of adding additional interest to your PowerPoint slides?

C. Is it better to use a 13-point type size for PowerPoint slide titles and 9-point type size for PowerPoint body information <u>or</u> is it better to use 40- and 26-point type sizes instead?

D. Is it better to use six or more colors on a PowerPoint slide <u>or</u> is it better to use five or fewer?

E. Is it better to include one emphasis technique (e.g., *italicizing*) in each PowerPoint slide <u>or</u> is it better to use emphasis techniques on PowerPoint slides sparingly so their emphasis is not compromised?

<u>Key:</u> A - question #1, B - question #1, C - question #2, D - question #2, E - question #2

- **Document cameras.** Magnify images of two-and three-dimensional objects, documents, photographs, etc.
- **Guidance Reminders.** Reminders that speakers include in their presentation notes.
- **Transparencies.** Provide an alternative to PowerPoint slides and not long ago were a common way to present information visually prior to the advent of computer-displayed visuals. Transparencies work best with small, informal audiences.
- **Drawings and illustrations.** Sometimes that adage, "A picture is worth a thousand words," is spot on when making visual aid decisions. For example, if you want to display all or a portion of an architectural drawing or schematic, a drawing or illustration would be a practical choice. They are equally effective with informal and formal audiences, but need to be used with small audiences due to limited visibility.
- **Spreadsheets.** Portions of spreadsheets are often used when the speaker wants to display specific numbers or groups of numbers. Spreadsheets are equally effective with informal and formal audiences, but work best with small audiences due to limited visibility.
- **Photos.** Like drawings and illustrations, photos are at times the most effective way to say what you want to say. They are equally effective for informal and formal audiences, as well as for small and large audiences.

document cameras magnify images of two-and three-dimensional objects, documents, photographs, etc.

guidance reminders Reminders that speakers include in their presentation notes.

- **YouTube videos.** At times a short video clip is the right visual aid choice. For example, you could show a short YouTube video that displays the proper way two businesspeople would greet each other in a given country or culture. If possible, use YouTube video clips in the 1–3-minute range. Short video clips are equally effective for informal and formal audiences, as well as for small and large audiences.
- **Wordles.** Wordles are word clouds. If you want to display several terms at once, including them in a wordle is an interesting and colorful way to do so, since the terms are displayed at different angles and in different type sizes and colors. Wordles are equally effective for informal and formal audiences, as well as for small and large audiences. (See Figure 11-9.)

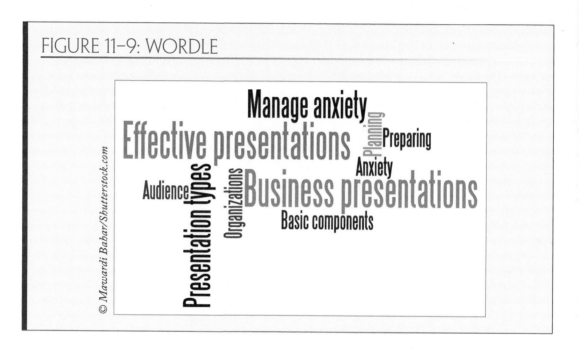

FIGURE 11-9: WORDLE

- **Mindmaps.** Mindmaps are created using diagramming software used for planning and organizing. *Mindomo* is a popular online mindmap program. From a presentation perspective, mindmaps provide a visual aid alternative if you want to display an entire process. You can focus your audience's attention on portions of mindmaps by enlarging and bringing forward those portions. Mindmaps are equally effective for informal and formal audiences, as well as for small and large audiences. (See Figure 11-10.)

FIGURE 11-10: MINDMAP

http://www.mindomo.com/mindmap/ mindomosample-d6ec73f153f44571b83e1d0 01b8cc988

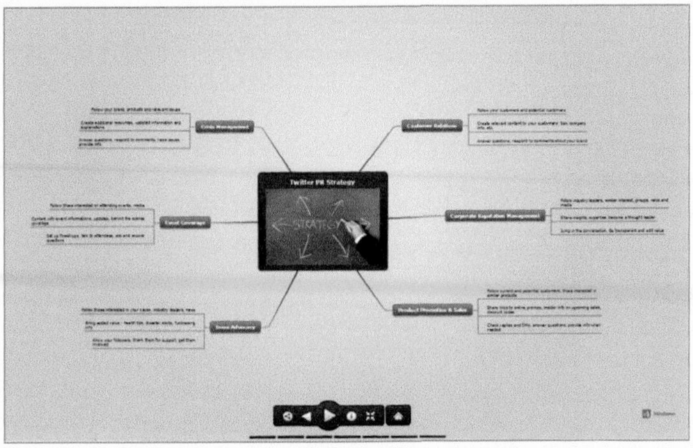

- **Prezi.** Prezi is an open canvas that allows users to navigate between a number of different media forms (e.g., text, video, images, etc.). Essentially users can zoom in and out of various media. To really liven up some of your visual aids, include some Prezi slides. However, do not include too many because they can be busy and distracting. Prezi slides are equally effective for informal and formal audiences, as well as for small and large audiences.
- **GoAnimate.** GoAnimate helps you make animated video clips using pre-made or user-designed animated characters (e.g., people, animals). You can even develop animated characters that look like you in animated form. You can have them standing still or moving around and they can be silent, talking, or making sounds. You can even give animated characters your voice via audio-/video capture programs like Camtasia Studio. You can even take photos of scenes and use animated forms of them as your backdrops. GoAnimate provides interesting and colorful ways to capture and keep your audience's attention. GoAnimate clips are equally effective for informal and formal audiences, as well as for small and large audiences. (See Figure 11-11.)

HOW MANY VISUAL AIDS SHOULD BE INCLUDED?

Audiences expect to see visual aids in business presentations. They are not optional. Fortunately, today's affordable technology and presentation software make it possible for us to create professional-quality visual aids in a matter of minutes at little cost. The challenge, however, is to produce simple, clear visual aids in a quantity you can present effectively and professionally in your allotted time.

Do not develop too many visual aids. Sharing, displaying, and discussing visual aids during presentations is time consuming if done correctly. In addition, audiences need sufficient time to take in, comprehend, and retain the information on each visual aid. The general rule is that it is better to do a good job of presenting too few visual aids, than a poor job of rushing through too many.

FIGURE 11–11: GOANIMATE

goanimate.com

Determining which visual aids to use typically depends on one or more of the following three characteristics.

1. **Audience and Room Size**. If the audience is small (25 or fewer), visuals aids presented on flip charts, whiteboards, and overhead transparencies are typically visible to all audience members. As the audience size increases, computer-generated visual aids, films, and slides are more readily visible to the entire audience.

2. **Expected Formality Level**. If your audience expects a formal presentation, prepare professional-quality visual aids (e.g., PowerPoint slides, video clips) in advance. If it is an informal presentation, then handouts and pre-prepared and unprepared flips charts are sufficient.

3. **Purpose of Your Presentation**. If your purpose is to make an official declaration before your employees, investors, etc., prepare high-quality, computer-generated visual aids and other multimedia. If your presentation is instructional, whiteboards and unprepared flip charts provide you with the flexibility to accomplish your goals.

WHAT ARE MY EQUIPMENT AND SOFTWARE NEEDS?

A number of factors govern your equipment and software needs. They include audience and room size, expected level of formality, and presentation purpose.

By planning equipment and software needs early, you position yourself to assure your needs will be met. Your host may supply some or all of your equipment requirements. In this case, you must clearly communicate your specific needs to him or her in advance. Do so in writing so he or she will have a checklist to work from and so there can be no doubt about what you need. Or, you can take responsibility for arranging all or some of your equipment and software needs. This is often the preferred approach, simply because it eliminates (often unjustified) concerns that the host will not have the requested equipment or forget to make the requested arrangements. Even if you arrange for your equipment and software needs, it is still a good idea to create a checklist.

WHAT APPEARANCE DOES MY AUDIENCE EXPECT?

Appearance as it relates to business presentations is interesting. If your appearance is consistent with your audience's expectations, it typically goes unnoticed. However, if your appearance is inconsistent with their expectations, it will typically be judged unfavorably. Some will even form a less-than-favorable impression of you and your presentation before you get started. They will assume that since you did not adhere to appropriate appearance guidelines, your professional stature and presentation information are suspect. At minimum, inappropriate appearance will distract some of your audience members from the information you are sharing.

What is appropriate appearance for a business presentation? Well, it varies based on the presentation situation. Some business presentations warrant conventional, conservative (formal) appearance (e.g., dark suit, white blouse or shirt, conservative necktie or scarf, well-polished shoes, well-kept hair and fingernails, moderate make-up and jewelry). In some presentation settings, however,

© Monkey Business Images/Shutterstock.com

less-conventional (casual) appearance (e.g., casual business attire, well-kept hair and fingernails, moderate make-up and jewelry) is preferred by audiences. Then, there are those occasional presentation settings where either a formal or a casual appearance is acceptable. Unless you know differently, when speaking to upper-level executives in your organization or to external and international audiences, the general rule is to go with formal appearance as described above.

Figure 11-13 contains four presentation scenarios that remind us that preferred presentation appearance does, indeed, vary from setting to setting.

FIGURE 11–13: PRESENTATION APPEARANCE SCENARIOS

1. **Presentation to Management**
   Imagine a scenario in which you are a distribution center employee for a package delivery company. You have figured out a way to do your job more efficiently, thus saving the company money. You have been asked to give a presentation to some of the company's upper-level managers describing your new approach to doing your job. Would you dress in formal business attire (e.g., suit, dress shoes, etc.) or business casual attire?

2. **Professional Conference Presentation**
   Imagine you have been asked to give a presentation at a professional conference. Would you dress in formal business attire (e.g., *suit, dress shoes*, etc.) or business casual attire or would either formal business or business casual attire be equally acceptable?

3. **Presentation Outside of the United States**
   Imagine you have been invited to give a presentation on behalf of your company in a business setting outside of the United States. Would you dress in formal business attire (e.g., *suit, dress shoes*, etc.) or business casual attire?

4. **Presentation to United Auto Workers (UAW)**
   Imagine you have been invited to give a presentation to a group of UAW members at a large automobile assembly plant in the greater Detroit, Michigan area. Would you dress in formal business attire (e.g., *suit, dress shoes*, etc.) or business casual attire or would either formal business or business casual attire be equally acceptable?

Key: Scenario #1 - formal business attire, Scenario #2 - either formal business attire or casual business attire, Scenario #3 - formal business attire, Scenario #4 - business casual

It is always best to identify in advance your audience's appearance expectations. In some instances, this is fairly easy to do. However, with today's trend toward casual dress in the business place, it can be unclear just how "dressed up" you should be. If you cannot identify your audience's expectations, lean toward dressing more conservatively. If you are still confused as to what is meant by conventional, conservative appearance, read some of John Malloy's thoughts on the matter. He has published a number of "dress for success" books for women and men. Or, you could visit your campus career center for additional advice.

FIGURE 11–14: FORMAL BUSINESS APPEARANCE SUGGESTIONS

Appearance Suggestions for Women
- Moderate jewelry: earrings (one per ear), bracelets, necklaces, rings, and watches are acceptable
- Moderate makeup, moderate perfume if you choose to wear any (none is better)
- No visible tattoos
- No visible piercings in eyebrows, nose, and/or tongue
- Manicured nails
- Non-distracting hair style
- Natural hair color
- Dark-colored suit or pants suit
- Dress shoes with lower heels, polished
- Briefcase, portfolio, or purse of good-quality leather

Appearance Suggestions for Men
- Moderate jewelry: rings and watches are acceptable; no earrings, bracelets, or necklaces
- No makeup
- Moderate cologne or aftershave if you choose to wear any (none is better)
- No visible tattoos
- No visible piercings in eyebrows, nose, and/or tongue
- Clean, well-trimmed fingernails
- Conservative hair style
- Natural hair color
- Conservative-style, dark-colored suit (not a sports coat and slacks)
- Solid color shirt, preferably white
- Necktie, conservative pattern
- Socks same color as suit
- Dress shoes, polished
- Briefcase or portfolio of good-quality leather

In summary, the time and effort invested in planning presentations are not wasted. Careful planning provides a strong foundation on which to prepare and ultimately give effective presentations.

SUMMARY: SECTION 4—
PLANNING BUSINESS PRESENTATIONS

Planning business presentations involves:
- Determining the presentation objective
- Learning about the audience
- Determining what information needs to be shared
- Determining what information should be presented on visual aids
- Identifying the types and number of visual aids
- Determining equipment and software needs
- Preparing for equipment and software problems
- Determining appropriate appearance

PREPARING BUSINESS PRESENTATIONS

Once you have devoted adequate time to planning your presentation, the next steps involve preparing and practicing. Before moving on, however, consider visiting speeches.com/index.shtml. This website contains information on how to prepare presentations.

Preparing presentations involves several steps. If done right, each step takes time—some more than others. Build quite a bit of time into your schedule for these activities. You do not want to be rushed as you approach the day of the presentation. This only fuels your presentation anxieties, resulting in a less-effective presentation. Follow these preparation steps.

VISIT YOUR PRESENTATION SITE

If possible, visit your presentation site well in advance of the day of your presentation. If you cannot visit your presentation site physically, try to visit it virtually. This involves asking your host to send you a video of the room or, at minimum, photos. If this is not possible, ask your host to send you information such as room dimensions, whether you will need a microphone, audience size, and number and location of electrical outlets. Visiting your presentation site prior to the presentation, in person or otherwise, is the smart thing to do. Here are some sample benefits of doing so.

- You remove one unknown element from the process, which should reduce some of your presentation anxiety.
- You become familiar with the seating arrangement. Make sure to ask if the seating arrangement will be different on the day you are scheduled to speak and if so, how so.
- You gain an appreciation for how loudly you need to speak and whether you need to use a microphone. Then you can practice accordingly.
- You can determine the extent to which you can move around based on the room size and design and the location of the podium and equipment.

- You can determine appropriate font size for your visual aids.
- You become familiar with the location of the podium, equipment, and electrical outlets. For example, you might decide that you need to take along a laptop, a portable projector, a power strip, some three-prong adapters, or an extension cord.
- You become familiar with the light and dimmer switches and how they operate.
- You become familiar with how the screen is raised and lowered.
- You can determine the distance between you and your audience and how to best deliver eye contact based on the room dimensions and design.

© razihusin/Shutterstock.com

By removing so many unknown elements, you greatly enhance the effectiveness and efficiency of the preparation process, conduct more realistic practice sessions, and reduce some of your speaking anxiety.

If you are able to visit your presentation site in person, then practice your presentation there. It's a great wonderful opportunity to become familiar with the surroundings, while getting somewhat comfortable at the same time.

GATHER THE PRESENTATION INFORMATION

During the planning stage, you determined your audience's information expectations and needs. Now, it is time to gather the necessary information.

The information may come from a variety of sources ranging from company records and interviews to the Internet. Remember to gather valid information from reliable sources. Be especially careful about information you locate on the Internet. It is difficult to confirm the reliability of some Internet sources. It is equally difficult to confirm the validity of the information from those sources. For obvious reasons, you do not want to create a situation where audience members question the validity of your information and the reliability of your sources during your presentation or during the question-and-answer session.

ORGANIZE THE INFORMATION

Once you have gathered the information, structure it so it is clear and flows logically.[7] Do not make your audiences struggle to keep up or figure out your logic. Remember, they are hearing the information for the first time and do not have the opportunity to hear it a second and third time to aid in understanding and retention. Your efforts to logically organize the information may go unnoticed, but audiences will notice a presentation that is illogical or unorganized.

Organize your information into the following three presentation components.

1. **Introduction**. Introduce yourself (name, job title, affiliation, etc.), mention the purpose of your presentation, tell your audience when you will entertain questions, and share a brief overview of your talk so your audience has a framework to follow.
2. **Body**. Present the information in detail, with special emphasis on key points.
3. **Closing**. Announce the close, briefly recap the key points, extend a call for action if the purpose is to persuade, and close with a memorable statement. Finally, extend an invitation for questions.

As you organize the information, give some thought to where visual aids will logically support your goal. Determine specific visual aid types and contents after you have organized the information.

FIGURE 11–15: PLANNING AND PREPARING TEAM PRESENTATIONS

Here are some general suggestions for planning and preparing team presentations.

- Plan together by defining clear objectives, audience characteristics, appropriate information.
- Divide the work fairly, based on each team member's strengths and interests. Determine who will speak, who will handle equipment and visual aids, etc.
- Assign a leader to coordinate each member's segment and make sure everyone stays on schedule.
- Agree on the approximate number of visual aids to include in each segment and the type that all team members will use. Consider using a single visual aid template for all members.
- Determine appropriate dress and appearance. Then, agree that all team members will adhere to the same standard.
- Visit the presentation site and, among other things, decide where members will stand during the introduction and where they will sit or stand while other members are speaking.
- Determine how each speaker will introduce the next speaker and segment.
- Prepare for the question-and-answer session together. Encourage each member to be prepared to respond to all audience questions so no one is caught flat footed without an answer.
- Practice together. Be especially alert to inconsistencies among speakers (e.g., speaking style, level of formality, vocabulary level, degree of eye contact, visual aids, transition between speakers).
- Teach and coach each other. Help teammates improve their presentation skills and learn to manage and use presentation anxiety.
- Determine who will step in and give another team member's portion of the presentation if that team member is ill on the presentation day.

DEVELOP AN OUTLINE

Business audiences typically prefer that speakers present their information naturally in what some describe as a conversational tone. Therefore, you are discouraged from reading from a written or memorized script. Presenters who read their script typically sound stilted and even rigid. Furthermore, with a script you run the risk of losing your place and not finding it again if you are interrupted or otherwise distracted (which happens). This is especially true if you work from a memorized script.

Write your outline on 5x7-inch notecards.[8] As you write your outline, keep the following suggestions in mind:

- Write words and phrases, not sentences and paragraphs.
- Use a large enough print or font size so you can read them clearly and not lose your place.
- Write on one side of each notecard only to eliminate concerns about whether you covered the material on the reverse side.
- Write a page number on each card in case you drop your cards and need to quickly reorder them.
- Write personal guidance reminders on your note cards. **Guidance reminders** refer to presentation techniques you suspect you will perform inadequately. For example, if you are concerned that you will not give your audience enough eye contact, draw an eye here and there on your notecards as a reminder. If you worry that you will speak too fast, write *slow down* occasionally in a different ink color.

Some speakers find it helpful to start by writing a script, then converting it to an outline. Doing so helps them avoid overlooking information they want to include and also helps them get comfortable with the information to be presented.

DEVELOP YOUR VISUAL AIDS

Your goal is to develop visual aids that can be quickly and easily understood by your audience. The **KISS Principle** (Keep It Short and Simple) applies to developing visual aids for business presentations. Avoid developing "busy" visual aids that have too much going on. Be careful not to overuse visual aids such as clip art, animations, and YouTube clips. Ask yourself, Does the visual aid serve a purpose? Is it appropriate? Will it distract my audience? Does it compromise the amount and quality of information presented on a visual aid? Avoid distracting your audience by using more than one font style on a visual aid. In addition, be sensitive to how you use colors. For example:

KISS Principle
Keep It Short and Simple, which reminds speakers to design and develop visual aids that are short and simple.

- Limit the number of colors used on a visual aid to no more than five.
- Use bright colors such as yellow to emphasize key information.
- Understand color and mood associations. For example, red is associated with operating at a loss, yellow is associated with positive themes, blue and green are neutral, red and yellow combinations raise people's blood pressure, and color blind people are affected by the red-green combination. Note that not all cultures make the same color associations.
- Avoid placing similar colors next to each other.
- Ensure effective contrasts. Use light-colored text on dark backgrounds in darkened rooms, dark-colored text on light backgrounds in rooms where the amount of light filtering in cannot be controlled. Avoid dark colors on dark backgrounds and light colors on light backgrounds.

Business audiences react positively to colors in visual aids. Just be careful to reap the benefits by following the basic color selection rules. In addition to the suggestions presented above, consider the following when developing visual aids:

- Make the print or font size large enough to be seen by everyone in your audience. The size and dimensions of the presentation room will determine the appropriate size. A 24-point type size works well in most settings.
- Use legible font styles (e.g., Times New Roman, Arial). Avoid flamboyant fonts (e.g., English Gothic).
- Do not use fill patterns (diagonal lines, dots, etc.) with colors to distinguish between slices in pie charts and bars in bar charts. Colors are preferred over fill patterns.
- Use three-dimensional, multiple bar charts cautiously. They are susceptible to mis-reading. The three-dimensional feature works best with pie charts.

Develop back-up visual aids for those unwanted times when the equipment or software malfunctions. For example, make one or more soft copies of your PowerPoint slides to use just in case your main copy does not work properly. Make a hardcopy set of your PowerPoint slides to display on a document camera. Make handouts containing your slides. None of us want the equipment or software to fail us; however, it does at times. Backup visual aids help us move past these unwelcomed, uncomfortable moments without getting overly frustrated.

PREPARE FOR EQUIPMENT AND SOFTWARE PROBLEMS

Anticipate and take measures to effectively contend with equipment and software problems. Equipment and software do not always work as planned; however, such unwanted situations do not have to doom your presentation. Do some pre-planning to work through such situations. Here are some troubleshooting suggestions:

- If you are using electrical equipment, collect one or more extension cords, power strips, and three-prong adapters.
- If you are using battery-operated electrical equipment, purchase spare batteries.
- If you are going to use a portable projector, get some spare light bulbs.
- If you are using a computer, arrange for a backup computer (e.g., notebook, tablet, etc.).
- If you are using a projection system, arrange for a backup portable projector.
- If you are using an overhead project, get a portable projector and some spare light bulbs.
- If you are using software, make backup copies to take to the presentation.
- If you are using a whiteboard, assemble some extra dry-erase pens and an eraser.
- If you are using a flip chart, take along extra marker pens, an extra flip chart, and a portable tripod stand.

Like it or not, equipment and software will fail at the least opportune times. Your preparations will pay big dividends when these times occur.

PREPARE FOR THE QUESTION-AND-ANSWER SESSION

The two best approaches to prepare you for the "Q&A" session are learning your presentation topic thoroughly and anticipating questions.

1. Become very knowledgeable of the facts in your presentation and comfortable with your topic so you will be relaxed as you respond to audience questions. Of course, this means you must learn more about the topic than you plan to share in the presentation.
2. To the extent that your intuition and experience allow, anticipate the questions most likely to be asked. Next, determine your responses. Finally, write out the questions and answers and take them with you to the presentation.

As you prepare, remind yourself not to take audience questions personally and, in turn, get defensive. There is no need to be overly anxious about Q&A sessions. Remind yourself that you are the expert on the topic; otherwise, you would not have been asked to speak. Furthermore, as you prepare, remind yourself that if you are asked a question for which you do not have an immediate answer, it is acceptable to pause and reflect on it before responding. If you are unable to give an adequate answer, offer to contact the audience members later with an answer. Finally, you may be concerned about the possibility of aggressive audience members. Like it or not, they come with the territory. You will not necessarily enjoy the experience, but you will survive and live to speak another day. If you have aggressive audience members, plan to keep your responses brief, but complete. Also plan to use a courteous tone and maintain pleasant facial expressions. However, avoid prolonged eye contact with such individuals; it is viewed as aggressive. In addition, have a plan so you do not let aggressive individuals dominate your Q&A.[9, 10] For example, it is acceptable to remind the individual that, since time is limited, you would be happy to discuss his or her concerns following the session. Alternatively, do not call on the individual if he or she continues to try to dominate the session.

Finally, conduct some Q&A practice sessions. Practice in front of some of your colleagues, friends, or family members. Ask them to play an active role, asking you some questions you cannot immediately answer. Also, instruct someone to get aggressive in their questioning, so you get some practice dealing with that type of situation. It is far too common for speakers to overlook preparing and practicing for Q&A sessions and quietly worry about their outcome instead.

PRACTICE YOUR PRESENTATION

Once you have prepared your presentation, it is time to practice. Practice will help you achieve the required presentation length, get comfortable with the topic, sharpen your skills, control your presentation anxiety, and build your confidence.

When possible, practice in a room similar in size and dimensions to the actual presentation site. In addition to reducing some of your presentation anxiety, you will be better able to determine appropriate eye contact, voice volume, and font size on

Presentation Practice Tips
http://www.forbes.com/
sites/forbesleadership-
forum/2013/06/19/the-
only-way-to-prepare-to-
give-a-presentation

visual aids as well as the extent to which you can move around in front of your audience. Practice your presentation in its entirety each time so your delivery is ultimately consistent and predictable (to you) and you develop a realistic sense of its length.

One of the best approaches for practicing presentations is to give them in front of others. However, this approach is only effective if your practice audience members are willing to provide you with honest, candid feedback. While you want them to point out your specific presentation strengths, more importantly you want them to point out your specific shortcomings so you know what you need to improve on. You can help them help you by providing each with an easy-to-use presentation feedback form that reduces their chances of overlooking important presentation feedback weaknesses and strengths. Figure 11-16 contains a sample feedback evaluation form.

FIGURE 11–16: PRESENTATION FEEDBACK FORM

Speaker: _____ Date: _____ Evaluator:_____

Visual Aids

Yes	No	Constructed properly
Yes	No	Spoke to audience as opposed to talking to screen, whiteboard, etc.
Yes	No	Used a pointing device when presenting visual aids (e.g., laser pointer)

Nonverbals

Yes	No	Displayed appropriate facial expressions (e.g., pleasant, occasional smile)
Yes	No	Gestured some
Yes	No	Gave appropriate eye contact
Yes	No	Avoided distracting nonverbal behaviors (e.g., fiddling with pointer, jewelry)

Voice Qualities

Yes	No	Volume appropriate
Yes	No	Pitch/voice inflection appropriate
Yes	No	Rate appropriate
Yes	No	Speaking enthusiasm evident in speaker's voice
Yes	No	Speaker included pauses in appropriate locations
Yes	No	Enunciation was appropriate
Yes	No	Speaker avoided verbal fillers (e.g., ah, um, er)
Yes	No	Speaker avoided junk words (e.g., ok, you know, like)

Overall Perception (circle one)

Excellent Presentation   Average Presentation   Poor Presentation

Comments:

_____
_____
_____

Taping your practice sessions is another excellent practice tactic. Set up a video camera in the back of the room, turn it on, and then forget that it is there. Or, record your practice session using an NCast System if one is available at your college or university. In either case, do not look directly at the camera throughout your practice session(s). Instead, imagine you are looking out on a roomful of people and make imaginary eye contact with your imaginary audience. The beauty of taping practice sessions is that you and others can review the tape later for feedback purposes. You might even sit together with them and evaluate your performance. Actually you are encouraged to view the recording at least once with the monitor turned off so you can focus your full attention on the audio qualities of your presentation only, such as your volume, voice inflection, rate of speech, use of pauses, enthusiasm, etc. Then replay the recording at least once with the monitor turned on and the audio turned off. By doing so, you can focus your full attention on only the visual components, such as eye contact, gestures, and facial expressions. Finally, replay the recording with both the audio and video on, which will provide you with a good sense of how you are doing overall.

NCast system
Technology for recording a presentation that can then be downloaded.

FIGURE 11–17: PRACTICING AND ASSESSING A PRESENTATION WITH A VIDEO CAMERA

Carmine Gallo has helped many executives prepare presentations for the International Consumer Electronics Show. Speakers at this show have included Bill Gates from Microsoft, Michael Dell from Dell, and John Chambers from Cisco. When aiding in presentation preparation, Gallo encourages his clients to devote a lot of time to rehearsing. He also recommends taping practice sessions. When reviewing the tape, Gallo helps his clients look for the following eight specific issues to be corrected and/ or improved on for an out-of-the-park presentation:

1. **The Hook.** Speakers have 30–90 seconds to catch the audience's attention. **The hook** pertains to the words you speak and visuals you display at the very beginning of your presentation that are intended to capture your audience's attention. Begin your presentation by telling the audience why they should spend their time listening to you. Gallo says, "I prefer to hear speakers start with the end in mind."
2. **Brevity.** After 18 minutes, your audience's attention span is going to radically drop, and that, Gallo says, is why you should not wait until 15 minutes into your presentation to present your hook. If your presentation is going to take more than 20 minutes, then you should break it up with a video or demonstration after 15–20 minutes to keep your audience from tuning you out.
3. **Visual Impact.** When speaking about a product or service, use PowerPoint slides to display an image of the product or service. Do not use slides to present text or else you risk diverting your audience's attention from you to the slides.
4. **Eye Contact.** Maintain eye contact with audience members to connect with them and make them feel as though you are directly addressing each one of them.

5. **Gestures.** Don't put your hands in your pockets during a presentation or else you might, and probably will, lose your audience's attention. Gallo once interviewed a professor who studied body language who suggested that "complex thinkers use complex gestures," meaning two hands gesturing above the waist.

6. **Movement.** Standing in one place on the stage or behind a podium does little to keep your audience's attention. Pace back and forth or move into the audience during your presentation. Doing this, along with eye contact and gestures, will help keep your audience interested.

7. **Wardrobe.** Gallo once received a valuable piece of advice from a military leader about dressing for a presentation: "Always dress a little better than everyone in the room." It is important to present yourself as a professional if you want to be taken seriously!

8. **Closing.** It would be such a waste to end an engaging presentation with a dud of a closing statement. Gallo suggests memorizing a closing statement with a reminder of the theme of your presentation.

Source: Carmine Gallo. "The Camera Doesn't Lie." Business Week Online. (2007). 24–24. http://www.businessweek.com/stories/2007-01-03/the-camera-doesnt-liebusinessweek-business-news-stock market-and-financial-advice

Practicing in front of a full-length mirror is another approach that some people find helpful. However, be careful not to stop and start your presentation over from the beginning each time you notice something in the mirror that does not please you (e.g., too little eye contact or gesturing). Otherwise, the quality of your overall delivery will become inconsistent.

In summary, good speakers are not simply gifted with the ability to give dynamic, effective presentations. They understand the importance of effective planning and preparation, including the need to control speaking anxiety. The good news is that giving effective presentations gets easier and more enjoyable with time and experience. Even then, giving effective presentations requires each of us to plan and prepare thoroughly.

Notes

1. M. Munter and L. Russell. *Guide to Presentations*. (Upper Saddle River, NJ: Prentice Hall, 2002), 8–9.

2. S. H. Gale and M. Garrison. *Strategies for Managerial Writing*. (Mason, OH: Thomson/South-Western, 2006), 279.

3. Tim Hindle. *Making Presentations*. (New York, NY: DK Publishing, 1998), 47–48.

4. S. Xavier. "Effective Presentations Take More Than Skill." *U.S. Business Review* 7, no. 8 (2006): 6–7.

5. M. E. Guffey. *Essentials of Business Communication*, 6th ed. (Mason, OH: South-Western, 2004), 336.

6. Andrew D. Wolvin, Roy M. Berko, and Darlyn R. Wolvin, *The Public Speaker/The Public Listener* (Boston: Houghton Mifflin, 1993), 71–78.

7. Hindle, 26–27.

8. Ibid., 29.

9. Wolvin et al. 218–219.

10. Hindle, 60–61.

DELIVERING BUSINESS PRESENTATIONS

12

LEARNING OUTCOMES

After reading this chapter, you should be able to:

1. Discuss how to manage presentation anxiety immediately before and during business presentations as well as during question-and-answer (Q&A) sessions.

2. Explain the importance of starting and ending business presentations on time.

3. Describe recommended business presentation techniques.

4. Describe webcasting and how it is used in the business place.

5. Describe podcasting and how it is used in the business place.

6. Explain how to conduct effective Q&A sessions.

7. Describe ways to evaluate your presentations and Q&A sessions.

© *Rawpixel.com*

BENEFITS OF LEARNING ABOUT DELIVERING BUSINESS PRESENTATIONS

1. Organizations prefer to hire and retain individuals who are effective speakers because of their persuasive potential and their positive impact as company representatives.

2. The ability to give effective presentations typically contributes to a businessperson's career growth potential because he or she is able to persuade audiences and represent the organization well. An inability to speak publicly hinders career advancement potential as well as job stability.

3. The ability to give effective presentations typically leaves individuals with a strong sense of accomplishment, pride, and confidence because they realize that few people master this skill.

4. Good speakers often reach the point of becoming confident public speakers; they also come to enjoy giving presentations.

5. The ability to give effective presentations can have a positive effect on individuals' personal lives by providing them with the desire and ability to be involved in public speaking outside the workplace.

SELECT KEY TERMS

INTRODUCTION

The closer you get to the presentation, the more likely your speaking anxiety will increase. Several practical techniques for managing speaking anxiety shortly before and during presentations as well as during Q&A sessions are presented in this chapter. It is important to respect your audience members' schedules by starting and finishing your business presentations on time.

Wear a pleasant facial expression and smile occasionally. In addition, make sure your posture is good, gesture frequently, and make occasional eye contact with audience members. Use your voice qualities to the fullest. For example, use a conversational tone, change your volume intermittently, and vary your speaking rate. Furthermore, your visual aids should be of professional quality and left before your audience long enough for them to grasp. Finally, expect a Q&A session will occur immediately following your business presentation. Here are some sample suggestions for conducting effective Q&A sessions: relax and maintain a positive attitude, know how you will handle questions you are unable to answer, repeat or paraphrase each audience member's question before responding, do not embarrass anyone, and do not get defensive.

The intent of this chapter is to provide you with information on how to deliver effective business presentations and conduct effective question-and-answers sessions following those presentations. The goal of this chapter is realized through discussions of the following topics: the final hours leading up to the presentation, presentation anxiety, delivering business presentations, conducting effective question-and-answer sessions, and evaluating your presentations. The information pertaining to the above-mentioned topics is reinforced by several student website resources including *PowerPoint slides, preview tests, chapter assessment tests, YouTube videos, interactive exercises*, and the *interactive glossary*.

THE FINAL HOURS LEADING UP TO THE PRESENTATION

As your presentation date grows closer, it becomes increasingly important for you to do those things that keep you healthy and alert. Eat right, get an appropriate amount of rest and sleep, relax some, and exercise. You know the drill! This is especially true the day and night preceding the presentation.

Most speakers find it helpful not to be rushed the morning of the presentation. They understand that being rushed that day contributes to speaking anxiety as well as increases the chance that they might forget something essential. Seasoned speakers build enough time into their schedules to dress appropriately, eat a good breakfast, gather and organize their presentation materials, and find a quiet place to collect their thoughts and relax.[1]

If you must travel a distance to reach your presentation site, learn the route ahead of time and leave early so you have a cushion of time to offset delays. It is even a good idea to travel the route at least once before the presentation date, so you are familiar with it. You will likely be a bit anxious as it is, so you do not want to add to these feelings by misjudging travel time and conditions.

While the following suggestion applies to some speakers more than others, it is not a good idea to arrive at your presentation site immediately before you are scheduled to begin. As a general rule, arriving 15 minutes early should get the job done. Arriving much later hardly gives you enough time to get set up, visit the restroom if needed, and relax before the presentation begins. Furthermore, it is unprofessional and discourteous to start the presentation late. On the flip side, arriving more than 15 minutes early may work against you. If you have too much extra time, you may become nervous.

Once in the room, busy yourself with those activities necessary to giving your presentation. For example, go ahead and open computer files if using presentation software and check your microphone if you intend to use one. In addition, get out the pointing device you plan to use. If you are using a laser pointer, make sure the batteries are strong. If not, replace them before you start your presentation. This is also a good time to get out your notecards and make sure they are in order. If you still have a few minutes to spare before the presentation is scheduled to begin, visit with some of the audience members who arrived early. You should find that calming.

SUMMARY: SECTION 1—
THE FINAL HOURS LEADING UP TO THE PRESENTATION

- Eat right, get enough rest and sleep, and relax.
- Build enough time into your schedule the morning/day of the presentation so you can achieve the expected appearance, eat a proper meal, gather your materials, and relax.
- If you are traveling to your presentation site, leave early enough to offset traffic delays, to locate parking, etc.
- Arrive at the presentation site approximately 15 minutes early.
- Set up your equipment and software—both preferred and backup.
- Walk around the room and visit with some of the audience members.

PRESENTATION ANXIETY: BEFORE AND DURING PRESENTATIONS

The discussion concerning presentation anxiety continues here with the focus directed toward four distinct time periods near and including the presentation: the night before the presentation, the day of the presentation, the few minutes on site before the presentation begins, and the presentation.

PRESENTATION ANXIETY—THE NIGHT BEFORE THE PRESENTATION

People who are nervous about giving presentations often notice an increase in their apprehension level beginning the night before they are to speak. If this describes you, do what you can to avoid adding to your speaking apprehension. For example, do not spend the entire evening practicing the presentation and fretting about the event. Instead, plan a relaxing evening! Have a nice dinner, then spend the evening with friends or family or lost in a good book or movie. The idea is to replace your feelings of apprehension with enjoyable, relaxing thoughts. This approach reduces, not adds to, your speaking anxieties. It can also leave you more rested for the presentation. Of course, get a good night's sleep.[2]

30 Ways to Manage Speaking Anxiety
https://counseling.
studentlife.uiowa.edu/
self-help/30-ways-
to-manage-speaking-
anxiety/

PRESENTATION ANXIETY—THE DAY OF THE PRESENTATION

No matter what time your presentation is scheduled, it is good technique to start the day positively. Following a good night's rest, go out for a morning walk or run and make it a point to enjoy your surroundings. Follow up your walk or run with a long, refreshing shower, then treat yourself to a good, healthy breakfast. The result will be that you feel better about yourself and more positive about your presentation. There is nothing to be gained from starting your day worrying about the presentation. Activities like those recommended above truly help you manage your presentation anxiety and redirect anxious feelings and thoughts in positive ways. Keep the same positive theme going if your presentation is later in the afternoon or evening.

Making sure that you have gathered all the materials on your checklist that you need to take to the presentation helps you control nervous feelings. Knowing that you have what you need (e.g., notecards, visual aids, backup software, handouts) has a calming effect.

Be careful not to overuse medication as a way to control your nervousness. Some speakers suggest that taking a couple of aspirin 15 minutes before they speak has a calming effect. This may be worth a try. However, drinking alcohol and taking other drugs shortly before giving a presentation could spell disaster for the presentation and may also turn into a destructive habit that you repeat before every presentation.[3]

Get an early start, so you do not worry about arriving on time. This is especially true if you have to travel to your presentation site. As you know, roads, streets, and highways are often crowded, and commercial airline flight delays and cancellations are common. There is a lot of stress and nervousness associated with any form of travel. So, control it instead of letting it work against you. It is a good technique, when feasible, to travel the route in advance of the presentation date to eliminate some of the unknowns. It is not uncommon for many of us to be challenged by locating the correct parking garage and then navigating our way through it and onto the elevator that will deliver us to our destination.

FIGURE 12-1: RELAXATION EXERCISES FOR MANAGING ANXIETY

Patricia Fripp, a San Francisco-based executive speech coach and former president of the National Speakers Association (http://www.nsaspeaker.org/), suggests that when dealing with speaking anxiety, seek out a secluded area and go through the following relaxation exercises:

- Stand on one leg and shake the other. Upon putting your foot back down, it should feel lighter. Switch, and do the other leg.
- Shake your hands quickly. Hold your arms above your head, bend them at the wrist and elbow, and then lower them. This will help your hand gestures feel more natural.
- Relax your face muscles by chewing in a highly exaggerated way.
- Do neck and shoulder rolls.

Source: Patricia Fripp. "Presenting Your Talk." Women in Business, 58, no. 5 (2006): 43–45.

PRESENTATION ANXIETY—THE FEW MINUTES BEFORE THE PRESENTATION

Imagine you are scheduled to give a presentation, and you are about to arrive at the presentation site. You are anxious and hope to control these nervous feelings during the final few minutes before the presentation begins. The following paragraphs contain some good suggestions for controlling anxiety.

Arrive Early Doing so will provide you with a few minutes to calm down and settle in before the presentation begins. This way you will not feel rushed as you set up for the presentation. Do not just stand still or sit down. Move around as you set up and, if time allows, walk around the room and visit with some of your audience members. These activities should reduce your anxiety level as you near the start of the presentation.

first impression
An audience's initial reaction to a speaker; may occur prior to the start of the presentation.

Make the Right First Impression As you enter the presentation room, audience members will form **first impressions** of you. You want these first impressions to have a positive effect on your presentation anxiety. First impressions really center on your audience's perceptions of how confident you are, how you are dressed, and how willing you are to connect with them. So, walk confidently into the room with normal strides, as opposed to shuffling in. Maintain good posture; do not slouch. Wear a warm, pleasant expression on your face; do not show doubt or apprehension. You might even smile occasionally as you make eye contact with audience members who are already there. Extend the same courtesies to those who enter later. Such actions help your self-confidence and warm up your audience to you. When you share pleasant facial expressions and smiles, audience members typically do the same. This relaxes you.

Make Sure Your Appearance Meets Audience Expectations If you have studied your audience, you will arrive at the presentation site confident that your appearance is appropriate. In essence, you will have eliminated one more thing that might contribute to presentation anxiety. Appearance refers to several characteristics, ranging from dress and hair style to the amount, type, and location of make-up, jewelry, tattoos, and body piercings.

Check Out Your Equipment and Adjust the Curtains/Blinds and Lighting Make sure the equipment works properly, load up software, close the curtains or blinds, and adjust the lights. If necessary, switch to backup equipment or backup approaches without making a fuss about it in front of the audience. You control the situation. Do not let them see you sweat! The combination of the physical movements involved in performing the above-mentioned activities and the knowledge that the equipment and lighting are ready will reduce your presentation anxiety.

Q&A session
Discussion following a business presentation in which the audience asks questions of speakers, and speakers respond to audience questions.

Visit with Audience Members Before the Presentation Allow enough lead time that you can move away from the front of the room and visit with some of the audience. This may sound like an unnerving suggestion; however, making relaxed contact with audience members prior to a presentation typically makes us less anxious about them. You may choose to visit with a small group of two or three or sit down and visit with one individual followed by another. Simply have a casual visit, small talk about topics such as the weather, an upcoming holiday, current news or sporting events, and the like. You might consider learning some of their names so you can call on them by name during the **Q&A session.**

Use Silence Immediately Before You Start Both you and your audience need time to settle down immediately before you start your presentation. Tell them that you are about to start your presentation, then allow 5–10 seconds of silence before you begin. During these few seconds do not shuffle papers like newscasters often do immediately before going off camera. Instead, make eye contact with several members of your audience while maintaining a pleasant facial expression.

Acknowledge Your Presentation Anxiety Accept the fact that you are nervous. Most speakers admit to experiencing some degree of presentation anxiety. The trick is to manage and use it properly, which can result in your giving a more dynamic, persuasive presentation than you would otherwise. Recognize that your feelings of nervousness are normal; then take a drink of water followed by a deep breath, relax, and move ahead.

PRESENTATION ANXIETY—DURING THE PRESENTATION

© Sam72/Shutterstock.com

Now it's time to start. The following suggestions will help you manage anxiety during your presentation.

Start on Time Assume your audience members are on a tight schedule and must be elsewhere immediately following your presentation. Avoid giving them a reason to think poorly of you and feel anxious about their own schedules simply because you did not start on time. They know that if you start late, you are likely to end late.

Introduce Yourself, Your Topic, and the Purpose and Structure First This is painless information to share, especially during those first few awkward seconds.

Be Familiar with the Information You Will Share During the First Few Seconds after Introductions This helps move you through the beginning of the presentation—the time when many of us are the most nervous.

Use Humor Throughout the Presentation Only If Appropriate Appropriate humor has the potential of warming up your audiences. When you see them smile or laugh, you relax and become less apprehensive. Keep in mind that the best humor in business presentations is humor related to your topic.

Remember, too, that humor backfires easily. If one or more audience members find the humor offensive or in bad taste, you might find yourself facing a cold audience during the remainder of the presentation. Of course, in settings where the topic is serious or controversial, avoid humor altogether.

Make Eye Contact with Supportive People As you begin speaking, use eye contact to establish rapport with audience members. Locate some friendly faces. They could be people you visited before the presentation or others with whom you feel you are connecting. When you feel nervous, return to those faces for a moment's moral support.

Present from Notecards or a Tablet Outline but not from a Memorized Script Presenting from memorized scripts often contributes to presentation anxiety, because speakers worry—subconsciously or consciously—about forgetting what they want to say or losing their place. You are actually relaxed presenting from notecards or a tablet since you have something to refer to that helps keep you on track.

Know What Information to Omit or Summarize If You are Running Out of Time The realization that we must complete our presentation by a given time contributes to presentation anxiety. If you go into a presentation knowing what information is expendable, you will be more relaxed. As you move through presentations, be sensitive to the time and whether you are falling behind schedule. If you do fall behind, either omit or summarize predetermined information so you can end on time. Do not be unnerved by this technique. After all, the audience does not know you have cut off part of your presentation.

Insert Pauses Throughout Your Presentation As you move through your presentation, pause when you feel you need a moment to collect yourself. This also provides a good opportunity to take a drink of water. Do not view pauses (silence) as scary interludes. Instead, think about how they are beneficial to you and your audience.

Move Around During Your Presentation Some speakers appear to anchor themselves to the floor and hold their bodies rigid. This adds to their presentation anxiety. Most speakers find that moving around while speaking reduces nervousness. Some of this movement occurs naturally in the course of handling visual aids and pointing at information displayed on screens, whiteboards, and flip charts. Consider moving away from the podium and taking a couple steps periodically.

Use Visual Aids Using visual aids reduces presentation anxiety. On one hand, they give you an opportunity to move away from your notecards, which often relaxes you. In addition, the physical movement associated with presenting visual aids tends to relax you.

Be Enthusiastic Enthusiastic speakers are dynamic, effective speakers. They have learned to harness their nervous energy and reroute it in a productive direction (e.g., voice qualities, gesturing, facial expressions, movement).

Avoid Digressions You made an outline and notecards for a reason, so use them. When stories and anecdotes occur to you during the presentation, avoid telling them. Digressions throw off your timing and rhythm, so you may lose the point you were trying to make.[4]

Slow Down! When speakers have little experience or are nervous, they tend to talk too rapidly, which causes difficulties for audience members in following and understanding the presentation. Make a conscious effort to slow down and listen to what you are saying.[5]

Maintain a Positive Mental Image See yourself giving a successful presentation.

SUMMARY: SECTION 2— MANAGING YOUR PRESENTATION ANXIETY

- **The Night Before.** Relax (have a nice dinner, get together with friends, watch a movie) and get a good night's sleep.
- **The Day of the Presentation.** Start the day positively with a relaxing walk or run, a refreshing shower, and a good, healthy breakfast. Organize your materials and allow extra time to travel to the presentation site so you do not feel rushed.
- **The Few Minutes before the Presentation.** Arrive early. Make the right first impressions; check out the equipment and software; adjust curtains, blinds, and lighting; and visit with some audience members. Use silence immediately before you start and acknowledge your presentation anxiety to yourself.
- **During the Presentation.** Start on time, introduce yourself, your topic, and the purpose and structure of your presentation. Use humor if appropriate, make eye contact with supportive audience members, present from notecards or a tablet, and know what information to omit or summarize if pinched for time. Pause occasionally, move around, use visual aids, and be enthusiastic.

DELIVERING BUSINESS PRESENTATIONS

Well, it is finally time to start the presentation! All of the effort, energy, and time you invested in planning, preparing, and practicing are about to pay off. All you have to do is either turn on the microphone or raise your voice and say, "Let's begin." Suggestions pertaining to delivering your presentation follow.

START AND FINISH YOUR PRESENTATION ON TIME

It is safe to assume that your audience will appreciate it if you start and finish your presentation on time. After all, they probably have other activities scheduled following the presentation and do not want to have to leave late because you did not start or finish on time.

As a general rule, you should be able to stick to your presentation time frames if you plan, prepare, and practice. Your actions during the final few hours leading up to the presentation, including arriving at the presentation site early, increase the probability that you will meet your objective.

Even so, you can take steps to avoid being knocked off schedule. Even the best-laid plans can go awry, so consider the following suggestions:

- Start on time even if all of your audience members have not arrived. You want to avoid the hassle and nervousness associated with "playing catch-up" that comes with starting late.
- Start on time using your backup visual aids if necessary. All equipment and software issues should be dealt with beforehand. Do not delay the start of a presentation because your visual aid equipment or software is not functioning properly. Also keep in mind that if your preferred visual aid equipment or software does not function properly, it is not professional to mutter a profanity. This point is stressed in Figure 12-2.

Tips for Starting Presentations
http://www.customshow.com/start-presentation-tips-tricks/

© *Karramba Production/Shutterstock.com*

- Ask audience members to hold all their questions and comments for a Q&A session that will be held after the presentation. Entertaining questions and comments during the presentation can throw your schedule way off, resulting in finishing late, rushing through, and/or leaving out large amounts of information you had hoped to share.

Keep in mind that both you and your audiences will have a more positive and relaxing experience if you make it your business to start and finish your presentations on time.

MAKE SPEAKER INTRODUCTIONS

Once you have announced to your audience that it is time to begin, pause for a few seconds so they can finish their side conversations, sit down, and settle in. Then, make some brief introductory remarks.

This is the point in the presentation when you mention your name and job title, the organization you represent, and your topic. This sounds simple enough! However, do not do like some nervous speakers and omit the speaker introductions or rush through them. Consider presenting this information on a PowerPoint slide. You could even display it for a few minutes before the presentation begins.

In the case of team presentations, the person scheduled to speak first should begin by introducing him- or herself, his or her job title, organizational affiliation, and presentation topic. Next, this speaker should introduce each of the other team members, having each stand or step forward one step when introduced. Then, repeat the presentation topic and mention specific portions he or she will address. After each team member speaks, he or she should reintroduce the next speaker and mention their specific contribution.

As was recommended with individual presentations, with team presentations, present speakers' names and job titles, organizational affiliation, and the presentation topic on a Power Point slide. It is also a good idea to display it a few minutes before the presentation begins, listing the team members' names in the order they will speak.

GIVE A PRESENTATION OVERVIEW

Before sharing detailed information, outline your presentation for your audience. Doing so sets the stage for the audience to know what to expect. If done properly, it also increases audience attention, understanding, and information retention.

It is at this point that you should clarify the presentation's purpose or objective, as well as describe the presentation's structure. Tell your audience that you will begin with an introduction in which you will share an outline of your talk. Then, tell them that in the body of your presentation, you will give a detailed talk based on the outline, followed by a summary of the key points you made.

Finally, clarify how questions will be handled. You may choose to entertain questions and comments during your presentation or handle all of them during a Q&A session following the presentation. You might even do both. No matter which approach you choose, communicate it to your audience before going farther.

USE NOTECARDS AND TABLETS EFFECTIVELY

As a rule, business audiences prefer speakers present from notecards or small tablets as opposed to presenting from memorized or written scripts. Working from outlines on notecards or tablets results in a conversational tone. Audiences greatly prefer this because they find such presentations to be more interesting than those read from scripts. Giving presentations from outlines on notecards and small tablets forces speakers to become very familiar with their topics and practice more than they might have otherwise.

Most speakers find it most practical to write their presentation outlines on notecards or tablets rather than 8½x11-inch paper which is clumsy to handle and distracting for audience members.

Here are some suggestions pertaining to presenting from outlines on notecards.

© Adam Tinney/Shutterstock.com

- Most speakers prefer 5x7-inch notecards, instead of 3x5-inch cards. The latter are too small to hold much information, and speakers tend to write so small or reduce the font size to the point that they are difficult to read.
- If your notecards are keyboarded, use a minimum font size of 14 points to improve ease of reading.
- Use a dark ink and boldface so it is easier to read at a glance.
- Double space the lines on the notecards so you are less likely to lose your place.
- If your notecards are handwritten, print so the material is clearer.
- If your notecards are keyboarded, select a legible font. Fonts such as *Times New Roman* and *Calibri* are easy to read, whereas scripted fonts are not necessarily readable at a glance.
- Write or keyboard on only one side of each card. This way you do not have to worry about whether you have already covered the material on the flip side.

- Write a page number on each notecard to help you keep them in order.
- Include presentation guidance reminders in your notecards. You do not share these reminders with the audience; they are there to help you. First, acknowledge to yourself your presentation shortcomings. Then, remind yourself of them in your notecards. For example, if you know that you do not give your audiences the degree of eye contact they expect, draw an eyeball on every notecard. Seeing these during the presentation will remind you to look up and make eye contact. Whether you use symbols or words as reminders, produce them in a color other than the color of your presentation outline. This way you will not accidentally mix them up with the outline material. Furthermore, by writing them in another color, you increase the chance that you will notice them.

Here are some suggestions pertaining to presenting from outlines on tablets.

© Stuart Jenner/Shutterstock.com

- For obvious reasons, make sure your tablet is fully charged before your presentation.
- If possible, use a smaller tablet such as the 6x3-inch Galaxy Note tablet or smartphone with a good-size screen instead of one of the many larger tablets on the market. Doing so will be less distracting for your audience.
- If your tablet has a cover, make sure the color or pattern will not be a potential distraction.
- Type your outline using a minimum font size of 14 points to improve ease of reading.
- Boldface your entire outline so it is easier to read at a glance.
- Double space the lines on your outline so you are less likely to lose your place.
- Keyboard your outline using a legible font. Fonts such as *Times New Roman* and *Calibri* are easy to read, whereas scripted fonts are not necessarily readable at a glance.
- Include presentation guidance reminders in your outline. You do not share these reminders with the audience; they are there to help you. First, acknowledge to yourself your presentation shortcomings. Then, remind yourself of them in your outline. For example, if you know that you do not give your audiences the degree of eye contact they expect, draw an eyeball on every notecard. Seeing these during the presentation will remind you to look up and make eye contact. Whether you use symbols or words as reminders, produce them in a color other than the color of your presentation outline. This way you will not accidentally mix them up with the outline material. Furthermore, by writing them in another color, you increase the chance that you will notice them.

- Familiarize yourself with public speaking apps that you can use to create and use tablet-based presentation outlines.

Finally, presenting from notecards and small tablets typically reduces presentation anxiety. As they move through their presentation, speakers do not have to worry about losing their place, which can so easily occur when we present from memorized or written scripts!

DISPLAY APPROPRIATE BODY LANGUAGE

Body language (nonverbal language) is an important component of audiences' first impressions of business speakers—the way they walk, their posture, their facial expressions, and the amount of eye contact they share. Body language is also very important during presentations! Specifically, presentation body language includes facial expressions, eye contact, posture, gestures, and moving around, which are discussed next.

Facial Expressions Speakers should wear a pleasant facial expression. In addition, they should smile and laugh when appropriate. Such expressions help capture and hold audiences' attention and, in general, warm them up to speakers. Audiences perceive the speaker as being friendly, approachable, knowledgeable, and sincere.

Audiences are more likely to be persuaded by friendly looking speakers than by speakers who wear a blank expression or an expression of anger or annoyance. However, be careful not to wear a fixed smile throughout presentations. Most people find this distracting and even annoying. In addition, do not wear a forced smile. You've seen that smile on the faces of adolescents who are asked to smile for photographs. That smile looks unnatural and phony.

Apps for Public Speakers http://appadvice.com/ applists/show/apps-for-public-speakers

© Karramba Production/Shutterstock.com

Eye Contact Eye contact is important to American business audiences. They expect business speakers to share the same degree of eye contact with them that we share with each other in daily lives—not too much, but not too little. Good speakers do not stare at individuals during their presentations, nor do they avoid making eye contact by focusing on their notecards or the ceiling, floor, or back wall. Speakers who make too little or no eye contact are often perceived as manipulative, unnecessarily nervous, unprepared, or unsure of what they are saying. None of these interpretations may be accurate, but it is what the audience perceives that counts. If your audience is small (30 people or fewer), you are encouraged to make eye contact with each person several times during your presentation. The larger the audience, the more unlikely it becomes that you can make eye contact with every audience member.

How should you make eye contact with large audiences? Two practical suggestions come to mind. One approach is to mentally divide your audience into sections and make eye contact with one or two friendly faces in each section. This way your entire audience will feel as though you are making eye contact with them. Another approach involves locating a friendly face or two in the left-most section, the center section, and the right-most section of your audience about one-third of the way back from the front. Sweep your eye contact back and forth across the room from friendly face to friendly face, which gives your entire audience the impression that you are making eye contact with them. Just be careful not to favor a certain section of the room with your eye contact. For example, some speakers will make all of their eye contact with those in the center section of their audience, whereas others focus solely on audience members seated near the front of the room. The name of the game when it comes to eye contact is to make sure it is balanced.

As can be expected, audience expectations regarding eye contact vary among cultures. Be sure you learn about these differing cultural expectations before presenting in other countries. For example, in most Middle Eastern countries male speakers should make little or no direct eye contact with female audience members.

Posture Audience members form perceptions based on speakers' posture. Speakers who exhibit good posture are thought to be confident, knowledgeable, and interested in their topic. They are also viewed as individuals who know how to carry themselves professionally. On the other hand, speakers who do not square off their shoulders, do not stand up straight and slouch, stand on one foot, or lean on the podium are perceived as uninterested, lacking confidence, and generally not knowing how to carry themselves professionally.

Mary Munter and Lynn Russell, business communication experts, offer the following advice regarding your formal "opening stance": (1) Place your feet shoulder-width apart, rather than close together or far apart. (2) Distribute your weight evenly, using both legs equally for support. (3) Divide your weight between your heels and the balls of your feet, rather than leaning back on your heels or up on your toes. (4) Position your feet straight out, avoiding a "duck" stance by making sure your toes are not farther apart than your heels. (5) Do not lock your knees.[5]

While good posture is necessary, keep in mind that we refer to a "relaxed" good posture. This means you should avoid being physically rigid. Rigid posture is awkward for the speaker as he or she attempts to move and gesture and is often noticeable to the audience.

Gestures Much like appropriate facial expressions, gesturing holds the potential of capturing and holding your audiences' attention. Gestures, like appropriate facial expressions, contribute to dynamic presentations that persuade audiences to action. Imagine how much more interested you are in observing a speaker who captures your attention with gestures and uses them to stress information he or she is sharing than one who does not gesture at all.

Gesturing occurs when speakers raise their forearms, moving them slightly from the left or right, much like a conductor directs an orchestra or concert band. In addition, gesturing involves speakers opening up their hands and fingers. Gesturing is done for the purpose of emphasizing points. It has also been suggested that "complex thinkers use complex gestures" during presentations, meaning two handed gesturing above the waist.[7] But do not overdo the gestures in an attempt to look like a complex thinker because you might just end up looking funny. Remember to keep it as natural as possible. Several helpful suggestions regarding gesturing during presentations are listed here:

Gesture with a purpose in mind. American audiences find constant gesturing distracting and annoying. As was mentioned above, gestures are used for emphasis; thus they should be used sparingly. To do otherwise greatly reduces their attention-getting, persuasive qualities.

Gesture with both hands. When you do so, you give more balanced attention to your audience. Speakers who gesture with only one hand tend to favor the portion of the audience closest to that hand. Speakers actually turn their body and head slightly in that direction. Their eye contact and attention fixes on that portion of the audience, leaving the remainder of the audience wondering where they fit in. In addition, there is a tendency for speakers who gesture with only one hand to place their other hand in their coat, skirt, or pants pocket, which is distracting.

Keep all fingers open to the audience. What this means is avoid pointing one of your index fingers at the audience. This is more likely to happen if you are gesturing with one hand only. Many of us conjure negative feelings or memories when another person points an index finger at us. Such an action is associated with being lectured to, scolded, etc.

Avoid quick, jerky gestures. Speakers who make abrupt movements are perceived as being nervous. In turn, they make audience members apprehensive, all of which distracts from the presentation.

Gesturing is critical to effective presentations. Keeping in mind that many speakers do not gesture, gesture too little, gesture too much, or gesture inappropriately, you are reminded to practice gesturing. Make it as much a part of your practice sessions as practicing your talk, displaying your visual aids, eye contact, etc. Appropriate gesturing is not as simple as it sounds but can be achieved if you are willing to make it part of your practice sessions.

Moving Around Speakers are encouraged to move around during their presentations. This is helpful in capturing and recapturing audiences' attention.[8] It is similar to what happens when a speaker raises or lowers his or her voice or pauses before making a point. Audiences pay attention. Moving around also helps speakers manage presentation anxiety. The physical movement is relaxing.

Be careful not to wander aimlessly, dance back and forth, bounce up and down, or pace back and forth predictably like a dog in a backyard dog run. Such movements distract your audience from your message. In addition, be sensitive about moving too close to audience members and running the risk of invading their spatial comfort zones. For example, most Americans feel uneasy when another person moves closer than an arm's length from them. Others prefer an even greater distance. For example, most Japanese prefer a greater distance than Americans.

Of course, there are situations where you may not be able to move around. If you are speaking to a large audience and must use a microphone attached to the podium, you have no choice. Even then, you may be able to take a step in either direction, assuming the microphone is powerful enough to still pick up your voice. At minimum, move your head periodically and gesture as a way to capture and recapture your audience's attention.

AVOID DISTRACTING NONVERBAL BEHAVIORS

While nonverbal elements such as facial expressions, eye contact, posture, gestures, and moving around enhance the quality of presentations, several nonverbal behaviors are counterproductive (e.g., leaning on the podium, fiddling with a rubber band, tugging on jewelry) because they distract the audience's attention from the speaker's message.

Speakers are typically unaware that they are exhibiting these distracting behaviors. When speakers put their hands in their pockets, they probably do not realize they are distracting their audience. In turn, when speakers continuously tap pencils or pens on the podium, they are equally unaware of their actions.

So what can speakers do to eliminate such distracting behaviors? First, they must identify them. Suggestions for identifying distracting nonverbal presentation behaviors are presented in Figure 12-3.

FIGURE 12–3: IDENTIFYING DISTRACTING NONVERBAL PRESENTATION BEHAVIORS

- **Videotape your presentation.** Watch the videotape to identify your distracting, nonverbal behaviors.
- **Have a colleague or a friend sit in on one or more of your presentations.** Ask this person to note your distracting, nonverbal behaviors. You may even give him or her a list of the more common distracting behaviors before the presentation, so he or she is better prepared.
- **Following presentations, ask one or two audience members if they observed any distracting, nonverbal behaviors.** If you were exhibiting the behaviors, they should be fresh in the minds of these individuals.

Notice that none of these suggestions pertain to practice sessions. Speakers rarely exhibit these behaviors when practicing. Instead, they typically exhibit them during presentations. Such behaviors are the byproduct of speaking anxiety not being channeled in more-productive directions.

Once you have identified your specific counterproductive behaviors, commit them to writing so you do not forget them the next time you prepare for a presentation. This is a good time to prioritize them if two or more have been identified. This way you can get a start first on those behaviors that are most damaging.

Some distracting nonverbal behaviors, such as fiddling with a rubber band or paper clip, can be easily eliminated. Other behaviors, such as rocking from foot to foot, require ongoing effort to conquer.

Those that are not as easily eliminated include tugging on one of your ears, crossing your arms, resting your chin in your hand, leaning on the podium, rocking back and forth from one foot to the other, clasping your hands as if praying, placing your hands on your hips, fiddling with your pointer, holding your hands behind your back, and crossing your hands in front of your body in what is typically referred to as the "fig leaf" position. These are the types of nonverbal behaviors we must eliminate. An effective technique is to periodically remind yourself of such behaviors via "guidance" (reminder) notes or symbols included in your notecards. This "guidance" approach helps you recognize and immediately deal with these behaviors as you move through your presentations.

Then there are those nonverbal behaviors that can easily be prevented. For example, putting your hands in your pockets, playing with keys or change in your pockets, fiddling with rubber bands and paper clips, tapping pencils and pens, fiddling with jewelry and neckties, and twisting your hair. What makes these behaviors easier to avoid is that they can be dealt with (prevented) before the presentation. You can sew your pockets shut; put your keys and change in your purse or briefcase; place rubber bands, paper clips, pencils, and pens out of sight; leave dangling jewelry at home; wear a tie pin and button your coat to restrict access to your necktie; and tie your hair back if it is long enough to twist.

USE YOUR VOICE EFFECTIVELY

How a speaker uses his or her voice holds incredible potential. Used effectively, it can capture audience attention, gain their interest, excite them, thrill them, and persuade them to accept and act on the speaker's message. How you use your voice plays a major role in whether your presentations are viewed as dynamic and effective or monotonous and ineffective. Here are several suggestions on using your voice effectively.

Use a Conversational Tone U.S. audiences prefer speakers who use a conversational tone because they find it more interesting than the rigid tone and monotone voice of a speaker who reads from a written script.

Speak Clearly Use good diction. Pronounce words clearly. Speakers are unclear because they do not know how to pronounce some words properly, have too little practice, speak too fast, mumble, slur words, fade away near the end of sentences, or have strong regional or foreign accents.

Speak Loud Enough so Everyone in the Audience Can Hear Ask your audience shortly after you begin if everyone can hear you. Also ask them if you are speaking too loudly. Invite them to tell you during the presentation if the volume of your voice needs adjusting. Ask these questions even if you are using a microphone.

Change Your Volume Intermittently Changing your volume periodically during presentations serves several productive purposes. If you want to really capture your audience's attention or emphasize a point, raise or lower your volume. Varying your volume helps you avoid sounding monotonous.

Use Pitch Effectively Switch your voice back and forth periodically from high to low. This helps you avoid sounding monotonous.

Vary Your Speaking Rate Switch your voice back and forth periodically between faster and slower. This also helps you avoid sounding monotonous.

Avoid Speaking Too Fast When speakers speak too fast, audience members have trouble processing and retaining the information. For one, information is presented too quickly. For another, the fast speaker is more likely to slur and mispronounce words. Speaking too fast rarely occurs during practice sessions. Instead, it rears its ugly head at presentations, where we are more likely to be nervous.

Make Sure Your Voice is Sincere Doing so can go a long way in winning your audience's trust and support. Be aware that nonverbal cues (e.g., facial expressions) that communicate insincerity are damaging. Even if your words and tone of voice promote sincerity, your nonverbal cues are judged as the most honest form of communication.

Project Friendliness and Enthusiasm in Your Voice Audiences prefer friendly, enthusiastic speakers. Your enthusiasm makes you a more dynamic, persuasive speaker.

Insert Pauses Throughout Your Presentations Pauses provide you with an occasional breather and a chance to take a drink of water. Furthermore, they give you an opportunity to collect your thoughts before moving to a new topic or point.[9] They also provide your audience with a chance to catch up or take a quick mental break. Pauses help presenters who have a tendency to speak too fast because pauses force the speaker to stop. Finally, pauses are effective emphasis tools. Some speakers pause immediately before making an important point as a way to capture their audience's attention. Other speakers pause immediately after an important point so the audience can reflect on what was just said.

Eliminate Verbal Fillers and Junk Words Verbal fillers, also referred to as *verbal tics*, are verbal sounds that serve no purpose. The most common among these "filler sounds" are *um* and *ah*. Junk words refer to words or phrases that, like verbal fillers, serve no purpose. The most common among these filler words are *ok*, *like*, and *you know*.

Speakers use verbal fillers and junk words when they are struggling to come up with their next words or are in the midst of switching to their next topic or point. Verbal fillers and junk words are rooted in presentation anxiety, but can be controlled. The simplest suggestion is to replace them with pauses. Slowing down your speaking rate can also help. Remind yourself of this problem via reminder notes or symbols on notecards. Of course, the trick is to first become aware of your verbal fillers and junk words. Like distracting nonverbal behaviors, we are rarely conscious of these habits. Have others tune into yours and then work on eliminating them from your presentations.

Getting Tongue Tied If you stumble over your words, pause to collect your thoughts, and move forward. There is no need to apologize.

> **verbal fillers**
> Sounds that serve no purpose; speakers often include them while searching for their next words or switching to their next topic or point. Same as *junk words*.
>
> **junk words**
> Words and phrases such as *ok*, *like*, and *you know* that serve no purpose; speakers often include them while searching for their next words or switching to their next topic or point. Same as *verbal fillers*.

FIGURE 12–4: GIVING TEAM PRESENTATIONS

Here are some general suggestions for giving team presentations.

© Janos Levente/Shutterstock.com

- The first speaker should greet the audience, introduce him- or herself, and state the presentation topic.
- Next, the first speaker should introduce his or her teammates (names and job titles). Do not rush this.
- Before sharing information on his or her specific portion of the presentation topic, the first speaker should give an overview (outline) of the entire presentation.
- When handing off the talk to a teammate, the speaker should mention the next speaker's name and tell the audience briefly what the next speaker will present.

- Before mentioning the Q&A session and ending the presentation, the last speaker should briefly summarize the high points of entire presentation.
- Immediately before ending the presentation, the last speaker should tell the audience that a Q&A session will follow.
- Next, a predetermined team member should start the Q&A session by telling the audience how long the session will last, followed by session rules, such as each audience member will be given the opportunity to ask a question before an audience member can ask a second question. The speaker will invite the first question from the audience.
- Finally, a predetermined team member will announce the end of the Q&A session followed by thanking the audience for their attention and input.

USE VISUAL AIDS EFFECTIVELY

Audiences have come to expect visual aids in presentations. In a world of visual images (e.g., TV, Internet, movies, presentation software, video games), people have grown to expect visual aids in presentations.

Each visual aid should serve a purpose beyond meeting audience desires.[10] Presenting a point visually may be the clearest way to communicate it. Visuals also simplify large amounts of information or numbers. Other times, visual aids display comparisons (bar charts and pie charts) and show trends (line charts). Visual aids reinforce, emphasize, or clarify information. They are also used to preview and summarize presentations. Visual aids are integral presentation components, not afterthoughts tossed in for visual effect. Purposes such as these are introduced in chapter 11, along with suggestions regarding colors, fonts, three-dimensional features, fill patterns, length, simplicity, and backups. Here are several recommendations for using visual aids.

Number Your Charts, Figures, Tables, Graphs, Diagrams, and Illustrations This comes in especially handy during the Q&A portion of your presentation. Numbering makes it easier for audience members to refer to specific visuals and for you to return to a specific visual, rather than wasting time trying to figure out which visual about financial aid, for example, the audience member is referencing.[11]

Make Sure Your Visual Aids are Visible If you follow the guidelines suggested in chapter 11, this should not be an issue. However, ask your audience to tell you if there is a visibility problem. Some speakers try to cram too much information onto a single visual aid, which results in readability and clarity problems. Similar problems occur when speakers misjudge the color combinations they use in graphics and visual aid backgrounds. For example, using yellow text on a white background does not work. Neither the slide with too much text nor the slide with a poor color combination appears as if it would cause a readability problem for the audience when we look at it on our computer screens. However, such problems are noticeable on large screens.

Do not block your audience's view with your body, the podium, or the equipment. Project information higher on screens and stand to the side of screens, whiteboards, and flip charts.

Introduce Each Visual Aid Do this so your audience members know how that information fits into the presentation.

Explain Each Visual Aid Explain and discuss each visual aid. Do not merely display the visual aids and expect your audience members to figure them out on their own.

Display Visual Aids Long Enough Leave each visual aid up long enough so audience members can comprehend the content. Do not be in a rush to move onto the next visual aid. Be especially careful if you project several visuals through a computer and have them set on a timer whereby one disappears and the next appears automatically every few seconds. Having the technology available to do this is impressive; however, it takes a very skilled speaker to use it effectively.

Talk to Your Audience; Do Not Talk to Your Visual Aids Some speakers talk with their backs to their audiences while explaining visual aids. They literally talk to their screens, whiteboards, or flip charts. Stand to the side so your body is turned slightly sideways in the direction of the screen, whiteboard, or flip chart. Use a pointer to focus your audience's attention.

Paraphrase the Contents of Each Visual Aid Do not read the contents of each screen word for word. To do so is redundant and monotonous.

Focus Audiences' Attention on the Point You are Making You can use laser and extension **pointers**, fade-in and fade-out features on presentation software, and cover up information not being discussed on overhead transparencies. Figure 12-5 suggests several ways to use pointers properly.

pointers
Devices that allow speakers to point to portions of visual aids to focus audience attention.

© Andresr/Shutterstock.com

FIGURE 12–5: USING POINTERS EFFECTIVELY

- Extension pointers (radio antenna pointers) work well in settings where the screen is low, and the room and audience are small.
- Laser pointers and pointers built into presentation software work well in settings where the screen is high, and the room and audience are large.
- Presentation software features such as fading in and fading out serve the function of more traditional pointing devices.
- Laser pointers, while inexpensive and popular, require some practice and a steady hand. If used improperly, audience members are easily distracted by the somewhat erratic dot jumping around the screen.
- Be careful not to aim laser pointers at people's eyes and be careful to keep them away from children who would view them as toys. Lasers can injure eyes if pointed directly at them.
- If you give presentations in a variety of settings, purchase a combination extension/laser pointer. This lets you can adapt to any setting.

Effective Presentations with Laser Pointers www.color-blindness.com/2006/05/22/effective-presentations-with-laser-pointers/

Remove Visual Aids after Discussing Them You do not want to distract your audience with old information after you have moved on to new information. Erase the previous information from the whiteboard, turn the flip chart page to a blank page, advance the PowerPoint to a blank slide, or turn off the overhead projector. You get the idea. It is easy to plan ahead for this.

Figure 12-6 contains a number of tips for presenting visual aids effectively.

FIGURE 12–6: TIPS FOR PRESENTING VISUAL AIDS EFFECTIVELY

- **Handouts.** Distribute handouts following your presentation. If you distribute them sooner, your audience may read them while you are speaking. In addition, take along extra copies for audience members who would like to take an extra copy to someone back at the office. Instead of taking along hardcopy handouts, consider posting your handout on a website and then share the website with your audience. Yet another option is to make your handout accessible via a QR code audience members can scan with their smartphones. The website and QR code approaches are especially practical if you travel a distance to deliver your presentation and/or your audience is large.
- **Flip Charts.** Use good quality, felt-tip markers in a dark ink. Print in a size large enough that all can see. Make sure everyone has had a chance to absorb the contents of one page before you flip to the next.

© CandyBox Images/Shutterstock.com

- **Transparencies.** Make sure you know how to switch to the spare light bulb and how to focus the image. Place the transparency on the projector print side up and facing you. Glance at the screen to make sure the transparency is straight, right side up, and in focus. If people cannot see, move the projector farther from the screen to increase size and then refocus.
- **Document Cameras.** Make sure you know how to focus the image as well as zoom in and out on portions you want to emphasize. Glance at the screen to make sure the item you are projecting is straight, right side up, and in focus.
- **Whiteboards.** Make sure they are well cleaned before you use them. Use good quality, dry-erase pens in a dark ink exclusively. Print in a size larger than you would use on a chalkboard. Even then, periodically ask your audience if they can see.

FIGURE 12–6: TIPS FOR PRESENTING VISUAL AIDS EFFECTIVELY

- **Items.** The most important thing here to keep in mind is to make sure everyone in your audience can see the item you are displaying. Sweep your audience with it much like you give sweeping eye contact. Make it available for viewing following the presentation.
- **Demonstrations.** Three suggestions here. (1) Introduce the demonstration so your audience knows what they are about to witness, (2) make sure everyone in your audience can see the demonstration, and (3) do not rush the demonstration. You want to be sure your audience has had enough time to observe and understand what you are trying to communicate.
- **Bar Charts, Line Charts, and Pie Charts.** Leave them up long enough for your audience to learn from them. Point to portions you want your audience to focus on using a laser pointer or software-based pointing feature.
- **Presentation Software.** Visual aids generated with presentation software such as PowerPoint are professional looking and capture your audience's attention. However, always be prepared to switch to backup visual aids if either your computer or software gives you fits. Keep your electronic visuals clear and simple. Remember, including too many multimedia features (e.g., text, graphics, animation, voice overs, background music, photos) on a single visual aid will distract and/or confuse your audience. Do not expect slick, computer-displayed visual aids alone to carry your presentations. Visual aids are meant to be support tools for presentations, not substitutes for them.
- **Drawings and Illustrations.** Point to portions you want your audience to focus on using a laser pointer or software-based pointing feature.
- **Spreadsheets.** Point to portions you want your audience to focus on using a laser pointer or software-based pointing feature. Do not simply throw a spreadsheet up on the screen, stand back, and talk numbers. Since most spreadsheets contain quite a bit of data, make sure to leave them up long enough for your audience to absorb.
- **Photos.** Introduce photos before presenting them so audiences understand why you are showing the photos. If need be, point to portions you want your audience to focus on using a laser pointer.
- **YouTube Videos.** Introduce YouTube videos before showing them so audiences understand why you are showing them, what they should look for, and what the main message/purpose is. Summarize the key points immediately following each video.
- **Wordles.** These can be overwhelming to an audience, so be sure to use a laser pointer to focus their attention on those specific terms you want to highlight.
- **Mindmaps.** Mindmaps, like wordles, can be overwhelming, so introduce each before showing it to your audience. Focus your audience's attention on portions you want to emphasize using a laser pointer or the software's zoom-in feature.

Using PowerPoint Effectively
http://www.thinkoutsidetheslide.com/ten-secrets-for-using-powerpoint-effectively/

FIGURE 12-6: TIPS FOR PRESENTING VISUAL AIDS EFFECTIVELY

© concept use/Shutterstock.com

- **Prezi.** These slides can be busy and distracting, so make sure information is not zooming in and out so quickly that your audience cannot keep up. Like mind-maps, introduce Prezi slides before showing them.
- **GoAnimate.** The uniqueness of GoAnimate characters and creatures can quickly capture an audience's attention, but can also distract their thoughts from your message. With this in mind, introduce each before showing it. In the process of doing so, tell your audience what you want them to look for in the way of the message.

BE PREPARED, SKILLED, SINCERE, AND ENTHUSIASTIC

Dynamic speakers share the information their audiences need, do so skillfully, and are sincere and enthusiastic. They capture their audiences' attention, persuade them, and move them to action. Such speakers bring vitality and genuine believability to their presentations. They understand that the goal of most business presentations is to convince and persuade their audiences. Effective business speakers know they can do so not only by sharing the right information, but also by being prepared, skilled, sincere, and enthusiastic. For example, they know the value of moving around, maintaining normal eye contact, gesturing, emitting friendly facial expressions, and projecting genuine sincerity and enthusiasm through their voices. An effective business speaker also knows how to choose the right medium for her or his needs and audience. Recent choices in those mediums include both webcasting and podcasting.

Webcasting is the term used to describe audio or video presentations broadcast over the Internet that are either downloaded or streamed live.

There are several versions of webcasts, including presentations. For example, executives located around the world can all log on to view the same presentation. Or, professors can upload video lectures so that online students can view them. The other side of webcasts

webcast
Audio or video broadcast over the Internet, either down-loaded or streamed live.

includes full-fledged TV shows that are viewable online and newscasts that are available online rather than on TV. No matter what the purpose, Figure 12-7 lists some tips for presenting webcasts.

© fotoscool/Shutterstock.com

FIGURE 12-7: WEBCASTING TIPS

- **Don't bury the lead (the first few paragraphs of a story).** It's difficult to get viewers to watch an entire webcast. Fail to grab their attention in the first 90 seconds, and you'll lose them for good to a myriad of distractions. Establish the benefit to the audience right out of the gate. If you're going to help viewers make money, save money, or make them more productive, let them know it immediately.
- **Speak in sound bites.** A *sound bite* is a short quote or statement edited from a longer interview. Sound bites used in newscasts keep getting shorter. When I studied journalism at Northwestern, it was acceptable to edit an interview into 20-second sound bites. Today, I notice newscasts carry sound bites of as little as 3–6 seconds. Of course, that's acceptable for a news story that lasts 60–90 seconds, but not in the case of most webcasts, which can last up to an hour. However, it's still important to speak in short, crisp quotes. If you're asked a question and you ramble for several minutes, the listener will fail to retain much of your answer. If, however, you edit your answers to keep them concise, you will keep the conversation moving along and make it easier for your listeners to digest key points.
- **Use lists.** One easy way to speak in sound bites is to use lists to outline your responses to questions. During a typical webcast, you will know most questions in advance, so answers should be prepared ahead of time. For example, you might say, "This product comes with three important features our customers will love." Outlining the key features could take 30 seconds. That's a sound bite. Leave additional explanation of the details for later.

FIGURE 12-7: WEBCASTING TIPS

- **Pump up the energy.** When viewers must view you in a pop-up box on their computer screens, they lose the benefit of being in your physical presence. The energy that might be evident in person is lost. It's important to pump up your energy level a few notches, even to the point where you might feel uncomfortable having such high energy in a normal conversation. To the webcast viewer, it will look and sound fine.
- **Make your wardrobe pop.** In an interview with CNBC's Donnie Deutsch, real estate mogul Donald Trump talked about how much attention he pays to his wardrobe. His suit is his "uniform," and he likes to wear colorful ties to play up his personality. He also notices what other people wear and what that says about them. Don't take wardrobe for granted. Wear complementary color combinations. I once interviewed a man who has tailored the suits of every U.S. president since Lyndon Johnson. He says the best colors for television are dark navy suits, a blue shirt, and a burgundy tie.
- **Lean forward 20 degrees.** This is a technique broadcast journalists know well. When they are seated in an anchor chair or doing a "stand up" in the field, the good ones lean slightly toward the camera. The key word is *slightly*. It might feel a little awkward but you will appear more engaged to the viewer. Lean back and you will appear disengaged, disinterested, and unenthusiastic.
- **Smile—It's not that painful.** Webcast viewers are tuning in because you have information that they want. Use a warm, friendly smile from time to time. It won't hurt you and will endear you to your viewers!

Used with permission of Bloomberg Businessweek Permissions Copyright © 2016. All rights reserved.

A major challenge when making webcast presentations is holding onto your audiences' attention. Webcasts are similar to conference calls in that others know they cannot be seen. Thus, they are tempted to do other things (multi-task) during your presentation like they often do during conference calls. However, you would prefer that they give your presentation their full, undivided attention. Figure 12-8 contains a number of tips for overcoming the webcast distraction factor.

© Andrey_Popov/Shutterstock.com

FIGURE 12-8: TIPS FOR OVERCOMING WEBCAST DISTRACTIONS

- Grab your audience's attention from the start by asking them a question.
- Make sure there is genuine enthusiasm in your voice.
- Gesture some. Doing so grabs audience members' attention.
- Wear a pleasant, inviting facial expression. In addition, smile occasionally.
- Vary your speaking rate and volume.
- Pause occasionally so audience members can keep up.
- Include visual aids such as charts, photos, video clips, etc., in contrast with your audience simply watching you talk at them the entire presentation.
- Share interesting, useful information.

podcast
An audio file, usually in MP3 format, that can be delivered to a computer through an RSS feed, like the text entry of a blog.

Podcast refers to a series of audio and video files that are downloaded or streamed to computer or mobile devices such as smartphones and tablets. The users' convenience is really the advantage of the podcast. One of the biggest advantages to podcasts is their mobility. For example, you could listen to a presentation in your car, on an airplane, or while riding the subway home from work.

© marekuliasz/Shutterstock.com

Podcasts vary in length, as could be expected, and do not have to be listened to at the time they are recorded. If you cannot listen to a presentation in its entirety, you can easily come back to the remainder of it later.

FIGURE 12-9: PRESENTING TO INTERNATIONAL AUDIENCES

© Kheng Guan Toh/Shutterstock.com

Here are some general suggestions to keep in mind when delivering presentations to foreign audiences.

- Match your appearance to your audience's expectations (e.g., dress, jewelry, etc.).
- Provide audience members with a written, detailed outline before you begin.
- Be aware of your nonverbal communication and how it will be interpreted.
- Smile periodically! Smiles are well received by people around the globe.
- Avoid slang and profanity. Doing so may confuse or offend your audience.
- Minimize technical jargon. If you must use jargon, explain it.
- Slow your speaking rate.
- Enunciate clearly.
- Control your accent so it does not interfere with clarity.
- If you are presenting in English and it is not your audience's native language, sprinkle a few words and phrases in their native language into your presentation, but first test these words with a native speaker before the presentation.
- Use professional-quality visual aids developed in advance of the presentation.
- To focus your audience's attention on what you are explaining, use a pointer with your visual aids.
- If you use an interpreter, be sure he or she is communicating your intended message.
- Use humor cautiously! Humor is usually lost in translation.
- Maintain a high level of formality and professionalism throughout presentations to foreign audiences.

If you want to expand your knowledge of presentation skills as well as work on improving your delivery skills, contact Toastmasters or Toastmasters International at www.toastmasters.org and arrange to attend some meetings and training sessions. The purpose of these organizations is to help people become effective speakers.

CONDUCTING EFFECTIVE QUESTION-AND-ANSWER SESSIONS

Q&A sessions are an inevitable component of most business presentations. Do not allow the unpredictable nature of them to unnerve or frustrate you. We all know that, unlike the presentation itself, you do not have complete control over what the audience will say. However, there are many things you can do to ensure the success of your Q&A sessions as well as build your confidence. Focus your energies and attention on what you can control.

If you find the thought of conducting Q&A sessions to be unnerving, you are in good company. Most speakers feel the same way. Unlike the presentation itself, you do not have much control over what happens. However, there are some things you can do to reduce your apprehension about Q&A sessions. Several suggestions are presented in Figure 12-10.

FIGURE 12–10: TIPS FOR CONTROLLING ANXIETY DURING Q&A SESSIONS

- **Maintain a Positive Attitude.** Remind yourself that they invited you to speak because you have information they want. The likelihood that you are about to face a hostile audience is slim. Even if one or two audience members are a bit aggressive, most of your audience will be supportive.
- **Remind Yourself That You are the Expert.** Give yourself a confidence boost by reminding yourself that you are the expert. In other words, you should be able to answer most questions. Of course, it is to your advantage to anticipate and prepare for audience questions.
- **Do Not be Alarmed by Questions You are Unable to Answer.** Be realistic. You will probably be asked a couple of questions for which you do not have an adequate response. Avoid the urge to guess or base an answer on insufficient information. Instead, say that you need to look into the topic further and that you will get back to him or her with a response shortly. Ask the questioner to stop by after the Q&A session to share contact information with you, such as a business card. It is a good idea at that time to write the question on the back of the business card.
- **Be Prepared to Control Difficult Audience Members.** The two types of people most speakers least like to have in their audiences during Q&A sessions are those who want to dominate the conversation and those who are aggressive in their questioning and reactions to your responses. As for the dominator, remind yourself that you are in control. Respond to others' questions, but do not feel obligated to respond to all of the dominator's questions or comments. As for the aggressive person, keep your responses brief and do not become defensive. If he or she asks you a question you are unable to answer adequately, follow the suggestions mentioned above. If the individual continues to be rude, ignore him or her. Refuse to be intimidated by such a person and do not acknowledge his or her presence.

As with presentations, Q&A sessions should be planned, prepared, and practiced. Chapter 11 covered suggestions on how to do these things. There are techniques you can use to manage nervousness while conducting these sessions, several of which were discussed earlier in this chapter. What follows are suggestions on how to conduct Q&A sessions to ensure success.

Inform the Audience of the Time Frame At the start of the Q&A session, tell your audience exactly how many minutes it will last and what time it will end. Since you do not want anyone to leave the session feeling short changed, make it easy for audience members to contact you later. Tell your audience at the start of the session that you may not get to answer all their questions and that they should contact you if they have unanswered questions. Of course, you need to share your contact information (e-mail address, phone number, fax number, etc.) on a handout or by distributing business cards. In addition, you might invite them to write down unanswered questions and their contact information. You can collect this information immediately following the Q&A session and get back with your responses on a later date.

Control Smartphone and Cell Phone Distractions It is safe to assume that most audience members have a smartphone or cell phone. These devices may ring during your Q&A session, distracting you and your audience. To forestall those interruptions, ask the audience at the start of your presentation to switch these devices to vibrate. If they feel the need to respond to an incoming call, encourage them to leave the room quietly.

Relax and Maintain a Positive Attitude Remind yourself that they invited you to speak because you have information they want. It is safe to assume that most of your audience, if not the entire audience, will be friendly and supportive.

Also remember that your audience views you as the expert on your topic. If you have planned, prepared, and practiced for your presentation and the Q&A session as recommended, you should be able to answer most questions adequately.

Have a List of Anticipated Questions and Answers You can Turn To It is a good idea to go into Q&A session already familiar with questions you anticipate will be asked and the responses you will share if asked. Take a written list of these anticipated questions and answers to the presentation. If you get nervous or feel especially rushed for time, you have the written list to fall back on. You can simply say, "I know I have the information you want here in my notes."

Be Ready for Questions You are Unable to Answer or to Answer Thoroughly Do not be alarmed if you are asked a question you are unable to answer at all or at least thoroughly. It happens to the best of speakers, so why should you be spared the thrill?

When you find yourself in this situation, avoid the urge to say something for the sake of taking a jab at a response. Instead, tell the person who asked the question that you need to look into it further or reflect on it a little longer, and you will get back to him or her with a response as soon as possible. Of course, you want to ask that individual to see you immediately following the Q&A session so the two of you can share contact information. It is a good idea at that time to write down the question so you do not forget it.

Be a Good Listener Good listeners communicate to others that they respect them and what they have to say. You can win audience members over to your side and enjoy a more successful, relaxed Q&A session by showing such respect. Give each speaker your full, undivided attention, being careful not to interrupt or finish his or her sentences in your haste to respond.

Ask Audience Members to Repeat or Restate Questions When Necessary Sometimes you simply did not hear the full question. Other times an audience member asks a several-part question that needs to be broken down and clarified. Still other times, you may want to "buy a little more time" to reflect on your response before giving it. Asking the questioner to repeat or restate the question buys you those extra seconds.

Repeat or Paraphrase Each Audience Member's Question Before Responding This serves two major purposes. (1) The person who asked the question knows you heard exactly what he or she asked, and (2) you know your audience members have also heard the question.[12]

Keep Discussions on Track In addition to responding to questions and even asking the audience an occasional question, speakers are responsible for facilitating Q&A sessions. That means starting and finishing the sessions on time, as well as keeping discussions on track. Speakers need to intercede when they see the conversation is drifting too far off topic. How do you intercede tactfully and move the conversation back on track? Probably the single best approach is to wait until the person speaking comes up for a breath of air or ends one thought. At this juncture, jump in and politely compliment the speaker on his or her response. This leaves the speaker feeling good and not necessarily cut off. Then, immediately redirect the conversation back on track or ask if there are other questions.

Do Not Embarrass Anyone Most people do not like being embarrassed, especially in public. If they are, they will typically not say anything more or will get up and leave the Q&A session. Others in the audience may react similarly. They see they are at risk of having the speaker publicly humiliate them also.

Most speakers do not intentionally set out to humiliate audience members. However, it can occur unintentionally. For example, an audience member asks a question about something you spoke about at length during your presentation. You are surprised by the question and respond in an abrupt, condescending tone: "I believe I covered that topic thoroughly during my presentation!" Now, visualize the audience member sliding down in his or her seat, feeling humiliated and possibly even angry.

Do Not Get Defensive Snapping back and even arguing with audience members serves no useful purpose. You will get upset and likely discourage other audience members from asking questions. After all, they just saw you snap back at one of them, and they do not want to be on the receiving end of that behavior.

Control Difficult Audience Members The two types of difficult audience members most speakers least prefer to interact with during Q&A sessions are: (1) those who want to *dominate the conversation* and (2) those who *get aggressive* when asking questions and hearing the responses.

Those who dominate. It is likely you will have at least one person in your audience who, if allowed to do so, will dominate the conversation. This individual will ask far more questions and share far more responses than anyone else, if not controlled. Your job is to control him or her, thus allowing and encouraging others to get involved. The best thing to do is control these individuals before they control you. For example, at the start of the session tell the audience that due to time limitations each person can ask one question and then, if time allows, each can ask more. Or, at the start of the session ask audience members to raise their hand when they wish to ask a question or get in on a conversation. This way you can control who you call on and, in turn, how much each person is involved.

Those who get aggressive. As much as you may want to, you cannot ignore aggressive audience members. However, you can choose not to call on them frequently. If they are not controlled, they typically try to dominate the session. They are not only aggressive, they are typically aggressive dominators!

Your best bet is to try to calm them down. How? Practice good listening techniques. Maintain a pleasant facial expression. Maintain normal eye contact, instead of glaring at them. Use a courteous tone when speaking to them even though you would rather use a defensive or aggressive tone. Avoid raising your voice even though your aggressive audience member is probably doing so. Keep your responses to them brief, while complete. Finally, if the person continues to be a jerk, ignore him or her. Do not be intimidated by such a person. Simply do not acknowledge his or her presence in the room! Remind yourself that, as a speaker, it is your responsibility to maintain control.[13]

Conduct Effective Team Q&A Sessions If you just completed a team presentation, all members of your team should participate in the Q&A session. As a rule, all members should be prepared and willing to jump in to respond to all questions asked, not only those directed to him or her or those pertaining to his or her portion of the presentation. For example, each member should also be able and willing to speak up when an audience member directs a question at the entire team as opposed to an individual. The same holds true when he or she sees a teammate struggling with providing a clear and thorough response.

SUMMARY: SECTION 4— QUESTION-AND-ANSWER SESSIONS

- Control your apprehensions about Q&A sessions.
- Inform your audience of the time frame.
- Control smartphone and cell phone distractions.
- Relax and maintain a positive attitude.
- Take along a list of anticipated questions and responses.
- Anticipate being asked questions you will be unable to answer or to answer thoroughly.
- Be a good listener.
- Ask audience members to repeat or restate questions when necessary.
- Keep discussions on track.
- Be careful not to embarrass anyone.
- Do not get defensive.
- Control difficult audience members.
- Conduct effective team Q&A sessions.

EVALUATING YOUR PRESENTATIONS

If your goal is to either become or remain a good speaker, you must work at it continuously. Otherwise, your presentation skills and confidence will grow rusty. Working at speaking skills continuously is only part of what it takes. The other part involves identifying your strengths and weaknesses so you know what to work on. As the old saying goes, "You can't fix it unless you know it's broken." Good speakers understand the value of evaluating each presentation they give as a way of identifying and better understanding their strengths and weaknesses. While recognizing our presentation strengths brings each of us a sense of satisfaction and boosts our confidence, it is important that we also recognize and accept our shortcomings.

© Rawpixel.com/Shutterstock.com

Speakers use several approaches to evaluate their presentations. Keep in mind that the suggestions here also pertain to evaluating question-and-answer sessions, which should be viewed as a component of the presentation.

Evaluate Your Presentation Skills While Speaking You do not have to wait until a presentation ends to evaluate your efforts. Do so as you work your way through each talk. Awareness of speaking strengths boosts your confidence. Acknowledging weaknesses helps you avoid repeating them later in the presentation.

Ask a Friend or Colleague to Sit in on Your Presentations and Evaluate Them Provide this person with an evaluation form that will make his or her job easier and more thorough. Prior to your talk, brief your volunteer about your most consistent weaknesses so he or she can look for them. Shortly after the presentation, sit down with your friend or colleague and discuss his or her observations.

Ask a Friend or Colleague to Videotape Your Presentations Ask a friend or colleague to set up a video camera on a tripod in the back of the room and record your presentation and Q&A session. Shortly after the presentation, view the video alone and reflect on your observations. Or, view it with others and discuss your observations as you work your way through the video or after you watch it in its entirety. Whether you watch it alone or with others, use an evaluation form. If you view it with others, compare evaluations as a way to identify both consistent and inconsistent perceptions regarding your presentation strengths and weaknesses.

Ask Your Audiences to Evaluate Your Presentation Another way to identify your presentation strengths and weaknesses is to ask willing audience members to complete an anonymous evaluation form immediately following your presentation. The challenge is to develop an evaluation form that is short and easy to complete. Check-off items (questions) and those requiring numerical ratings or rankings work well. The first and fifth sample presentation evaluation forms presented at the URL in the side margin provide good options. Avoid asking general questions such as, "How was my presentation?" and "Were my visual aids helpful?" The evaluators are likely to leave such questions blank, respond in such general terms that you learn little of any value, or simply answer yes or no, which does little for you.

Sit Down Shortly After Each Presentation and Evaluate It You could conduct a self-evaluation shortly after each presentation. Find a quiet spot where you can sit down and relax. Once you are settled in, develop a written list of strengths and weaknesses while the presentation is still fresh in your mind. Like presentation videotapes and evaluation forms gathered through other evaluation approaches, your written list will be helpful when you plan and prepare for future talks.

Evaluate Your Presentation Skills While Watching Others Present You have an opportunity to evaluate your own skills each time you watch another person give a presentation. During and immediately after these presentations, contrast your own approach and skills with their performances. Every speaker exhibits some strengths and some weaknesses against which you can contrast your own. There is usually much to learn about our own skills by observing others.

Sample Presentation Evaluation Templates http://www. sampletemplates.com/ business-templates/ presentation-evaluation. html

FIGURE 12–11: PRESENTING ETHICALLY TO INTERNATIONAL AUDIENCES

As part of your self-evaluations, ask yourself if you presented ethically. Suggestions such as those listed here will help keep you on the right track.

- Learn and respect international audiences' expectations (e.g., level of formality, cultural understanding, nonverbal behavior, appearance).
- Avoid speaking rapidly, using slang, or using technical jargon as a way to mislead, manipulate, or mask inaccurate information.
- Do not mask inaccurate, misleading, or manipulative information with an inviting, friendly personality.
- Do not use your language in ways that manipulate foreign audiences whose command of your language is not strong.
- Make sure your information translates clearly and accurately to avoid misunderstandings, no matter how unintentional.
- Do not share inaccurate information when responding to audience questions.
- Make sure all audience members' questions are answered, and provide future contact information if necessary to get the job done.

In summary, what is important is that you conduct some form of evaluation of your presentations to help you grow your speaking skills and confidence so you can become an effective speaker. You will not use all of the above-mentioned approaches. None of us do. It is important; however, for you to choose one or more from the list and take charge of your presentation destiny!

Top 10 Presentation Videos
http://www.
presentation-process.
com/top-10-youtube-
videos-for-presentation-
skills-training.html

SUMMARY: SECTION 5— EVALUATING YOUR PRESENTATIONS

- Evaluate your presentation skills while speaking.
- Ask a friend or colleague to sit in and evaluate your presentation.
- Ask a friend or colleague to videotape your presentation.
- Ask your audiences to evaluate your presentations.
- Sit down shortly after each presentation and evaluate your performance.
- Evaluate (reflect on) your presentation skills while watching others present.
- Ask yourself if you presented ethically.

Notes

1. Tim Hindle. *Making Presentations*. (New York, NY: DK Publishing, 1998), 47.

2. Ibid.

3. L. Todd Thomas. *Public Speaking Anxiety: How to Face the Fear*. (Fort Worth, TX: Harcourt Brace College Publishers, 1997), 29–30.

4. Mary Ellen Guffey. *Essentials of Business Communication*, 6th ed. (Mason, OH: Thomson/South-Western, 2004), 353.

5. Ibid.

6. James V. Connor. *Cuss Control: The Complete Book on How to Curb Your Cussing*. (New York, NY: iUniverse, 2006).

7. Carmine Gallo. "The Camera Doesn't Lie." *Business Week Online http://www. businessweek. com/stories/2007-01-03/the-camera-doesnt-liebusinessweek-business-news-stock-market-and-financial-advice*.

8. Andrew D. Wolvin, Roy M. Berko, and Darlyn R. Wolvin. *The Public Speaker/The Public Listener*. (Boston: Houghton Mifflin Company, 1993), 195.

9. Rich Sorenson, Grace DeBord, and Ida Ramirez, *Business and Management Communication*, 4th ed. (Upper Saddle River, NJ: Prentice Hall, 2001), 222.

10. Michael Osborn and Suzanne Osborn. *Public Speaking*, 3rd ed. (Boston: Houghton Mifflin), 360.

11. T. Leech. *How to Prepare, Stage, and Deliver Winning Presentations*, 3rd ed. (New York: American Management Association, 2004).

12. Osborn and Osborn, 354.

13. Hindle, 61.

PART 5

COMMUNICATING COLLABORATIVELY

LISTENING

13

LEARNING OUTCOMES

After reading this chapter, you should be able to:

1. Discuss how organizations benefit from good listening.

2. Discuss how organizations are harmed by poor listening

3. Explain how good listening skills can potentially affect individuals' careers.

4. Identify the fundamental qualities of good listeners.

5. Describe common listening barriers.

6. Describe recommended listening techniques.

© *Pressmaster/Shutterstock.com*

BENEFITS OF LEARNING ABOUT LISTENING

1. Good listening skills increase your chances of being hired, retained, and promoted. Organizations prefer recruits and employees with good listening skills because good listeners typically cause fewer misunderstandings and problems. In turn, good listeners contribute to better employee morale and more positive business relations with customers, clients, suppliers, and investors.

2. Good listening skills typically contribute to your job stability and career growth while poor listening skills can hinder both.

3. Good listening skills can have positive effects on your personal life by strengthening your communications and relationships.

SELECT KEY TERMS

INTRODUCTION

Organizations benefit from good listening; good listening results in better business relationships and fewer misunderstandings and problems. In contrast, organizations suffer from poor listening; poor listening results in poor employee morale, more problems, and poor hiring decisions. Good listening skills benefit individuals during the job search process as well as on the job.

There are several listening styles—some effective and some relatively ineffective. The active listener style is considered to be the most effective style. Common barriers to effective listening range from failure to work at listening and closed mindedness to failure to listen for nonverbal cues and interrupting those speaking. In contrast, recommended listening techniques range from having the right attitude toward listening and giving your full attention to the person speaking to being open minded and fighting the urge to interrupt.

The intent of this chapter is to provide you with an appreciation for the importance of effective listening as well as a number of effective listening techniques. These goals are realized through discussions of the following topics: the role of listening in organizations, the effects of good listening on individuals' careers, listening effectively when communicating electronically, the nature of listening, common barriers to effective listening, and recommended listening techniques. The information pertaining to the above-mentioned topics is reinforced by several student website resources including *PowerPoint slides, preview tests, chapter assessment tests, YouTube videos, interactive exercises*, and the *interactive glossary*.

Effective listening will be encouraged throughout this chapter. With this in mind, let's clarify what this means before moving forward. Here are the main qualities of effective listeners.

- They give their full attention to the person speaking.
- They listen for emotions and nonverbal cues as well as for facts and details.
- They are open-minded; thus, they are not quick to judge what is said.
- They position their body such that they give full attention to the person speaking.
- They avoid the urge to interrupt the person speaking.

These qualities, along with others, are described in detail later in this chapter.

THE ROLE OF LISTENING IN ORGANIZATIONS

Listening typically ranks among the most frequently used forms of communication in U.S. organizations. In fact, listening has long been considered the most frequently used form of communication by managers.[1] The large amount of time managers spend listening makes sense when you consider how often they participate in business meetings, face-to-face conversations, and telephone conversations.

While some recent technology developments have contributed to a reduction in the amount of listening activity (e.g., texting, e-mail), the importance of effective listening in organizations has not diminished. Many of today's electronic communication devices require users to be exceptionally focused listeners. For example, listening to another on a smartphone requires a disciplined approach to focused listening. Or, imagine the need to be a focused listener when participating in conference calls.

The Importance of Listening in Businesses http://smallbusiness. chron.com/listening-important-business-organisation-24040. html

HOW ORGANIZATIONS ARE AFFECTED BY LISTENING

Organizations and their stakeholders benefit from good listening, and they suffer from poor listening. Here are six ways organizations and their stakeholders can benefit from good listening or be harmed by poor listening.

1. **Employee Morale**. Most people in today's workforce appreciate the attention and respect they receive when others truly listen to their thoughts and feelings. This is especially true when it is apparent that a supervisor or manager is listening willingly. Employees who are listened to typically feel more appreciated and respected. In turn, they are more likely to complete tasks successfully, making fewer mistakes. Overall, the effect on employee morale tends to be positive, which reduces absenteeism, tardiness, and employee turnover, while making the organization look even more attractive to potential job candidates and the public at large.

   No matter what their job title, employees typically develop feelings of frustration and resentment when they believe that others are not truly listening to them. Such feelings have a negative effect on employee morale, which typically leads to a host of problems. Among these problems are reduced productivity, increased tardiness and absenteeism, and increased turnover. When employees are disgruntled, the word gets out, which can mean the organization can have problems recruiting good job candidates.

2. **Misunderstandings**. Good listeners typically make fewer mistakes because they experience fewer misunderstandings. While speakers have a responsibility to share clear messages, listeners have a responsibility to be good listeners, so they do not contribute to misunderstandings. The best bet is to "listen right" from the start and be willing to request clarification if you are unsure of what you heard.

   Misunderstandings typically result in mistakes—mistakes that cost organizations time, money, and productivity. In addition, misunderstandings and the ensuing mistakes frustrate people and often lead to hard feelings.

3. **Team Success**. Active listening contributes to team success. When team members listen actively to each other, the "talk of the team can be richer and both more efficient and more effective." In addition, active listening reduces or eliminates unnecessary interruptions and long-winded contributions from team members.[2]

4. **Relationships with External Stakeholders**. Listening effectively to customers, suppliers, and investors is crucial to every organization. External stakeholders who believe that insiders listen to them feel respected and appreciated. This increases the likelihood that those stakeholders will continue to maintain a business relationship with those organizations. Stakeholders are also more likely to encourage others to work with those organizations.

   Poor listening affects organizations' external stakeholders negatively. For example, poor listening can result in incomplete orders or improperly routed orders. Investors and suppliers may stop doing business as a result of unnecessary costs and hassles resulting from poor listening. Poor listening when interacting with upset customers results in lost future business from the disgruntled customer.

© Odua Images/Shutterstock.com

5. **Hiring Decisions**. A major element of the hiring process is the employment interview. An organization's major purpose for interviewing job candidates is to gather enough additional information about the candidates' knowledge, skills, experiences, attitudes, values, and personality to make good hiring decisions. Good listening is obviously critical to achieving this goal.

   When recruiters listen poorly during the hiring process, they are more likely to make poor hiring decisions. Whether the recruiters are poor listeners due to ignorance, carelessness, apathy, a rushed schedule, or selective listening (hearing only what they want to hear), poor and costly hiring decisions are often the outcome.

6. **Communicating with People from Other Cultures**. Organizations benefit when their employees listen effectively to people from other cultures, which is especially important when language differences exist. Effective listeners tune into nonverbal cues as well as spoken words, which is challenging as people around the globe assign different meanings to nonverbal cues.

   Of course, all kinds of problems are likely to occur when workers do not make a good effort to listen to people from other cultures. Such actions are fraught with potential problems, ranging from mistakes to broken relations.

selective listening
Occurs when a person hears what he or she wants to hear.

FIGURE 13–1: LISTENING TO PEOPLE FROM OTHER CULTURES

Here are some general suggestions for listening to people from other cultures.

- Give the speaker your full, undivided attention. This is a sign of respect that is valued in most cultures.
- Be open-minded. Attitudes, values, and practices differ greatly among cultures, requiring listeners to be empathetic and attentive.
- Request clarification if the speaker's English is unclear or broken.
- Learn in advance whether you are or are not expected to interrupt the speaker for clarification or to interject your thoughts.
- Realize that people from some cultures, even when speaking English, may speak faster than you are accustomed to and have challenging accents.
- Accept some environmental distractions as the norm in the speaker's culture. For example, it is not uncommon for speakers in business meetings in Saudi Arabia to be interrupted and for participants to leave the meeting.
- Learn about the emotional and nonverbal customs of the speaker. They are probably different than what is customary in the United States. When the speaker is talking, observe his or her emotions and nonverbal cues, but be careful not to misinterpret them.
- Familiarize yourself with speaker qualities that, if you are not careful, could interfere with your listening effectiveness. For example, if the speaker's appearance, voice qualities, or mannerisms are different than U.S. norms, they can easily distract you.

Active Listening: Cross-Cultural Business Communication Skills
www.kwintessential.co.uk/read-our-blog/active-listening-cross-cultural-business-communication-skills.html

In summary, effective listening plays an important role in organizations. When done the right way, good listening contributes to fewer misunderstandings and problems, better employee morale, and better business relations with customers, clients, suppliers, and investors. Unfortunately, when good listening is not encouraged in organizations, there are misunderstandings, problems, instances of poor employee morale, and compromised business relations.

SUMMARY: SECTION 1— THE ROLE OF LISTENING IN ORGANIZATIONS

- Listening plays an important role in organizations. In fact, it is the most frequently used communication skill among managers.
- The ways organizations benefit from good listening include better employee morale, fewer misunderstandings, fewer problems, better business relationships with external stakeholders, and better hiring decisions.
- Organizations suffer as a result of poor listening through poor employee morale, more misunderstandings, more problems, poor business relationships with external stakeholders, and poor hiring decisions.

THE EFFECTS OF GOOD LISTENING ON INDIVIDUALS' CAREERS

The quality of an employee's listening affects his or her performance in an organization, which in turn affects his or her career growth. Employees at any organizational level enjoy some level of career growth due in part to good listening skills. In today's business place, where senior managers are responsible for the company's success and their job security depends on the return to stakeholders, many use listening as an integral tool which benefits both their companies and their careers.

Poor listeners, due to ignorance, carelessness, or apathy, do not enjoy the same level of career growth realized by their colleagues who take listening seriously. This can also be said about those who shirk their ethical responsibilities when listening. Figure 13-2 contains several reminders regarding listeners' ethical responsibilities.

© Aaron Amat/Shutterstock.com

While the basic act of hearing, and possibly listening, is believed to begin for most of us in the womb, it is your current attitude regarding listening and your listening skills that will affect your career growth. Even before most young children enter elementary school, their parents and other caretakers typically encourage them to be good listeners. When promoted and reinforced, these early efforts build a strong listening foundation capable of serving us well throughout our school years and beyond. Some of the more noticeable ways your career will be affected by good listening skills are listed in Figure 13-2.

FIGURE 13-2: LISTENERS' ETHICAL RESPONSIBILITIES

While listeners typically cannot control the ethical behavior of speakers, listeners can at least control their own listening. Some general suggestions regarding how to listen ethically are listed below.

- Do not be a selective listener who hears only what he or she wants to hear, ignoring or distorting the rest of the message.
- Do not rush to judgment. Be open-minded and hear the person out before responding.
- Avoid entering the communication with preconceived notions that will interfere with giving the person speaking your full attention.
- Do not let prejudice play a role in the listening process. People who allow prejudice and stereotypes to interfere are not ethical listeners.
- Respect speakers by removing environmental distractions under your control (e.g., let voicemail pick up any calls).
- Respect speakers from other cultures by learning about and accepting their customs, values, and mannerisms.

WAYS GOOD LISTENING AFFECTS EMPLOYEES' CAREERS

Individuals Learn More Throughout their years of formal education (K–12 or K–college), good lis\teners typically learn more than their peers as a direct result of their ability and willingness to listen effectively. This helps them be successful students. The added knowledge they take to employers, along with their good listening attitude and skills, typically helps them succeed on the job.

Individuals Improve Their Odds In The Job Search Process The step in the job search process in which listening plays the largest role is the employment interview. This is true whether it is a face-to-face, videoconference, or telephone interview. Job candidates need to recognize how much they are under the microscope during interviews and practice excellent listening techniques. Many white-collar job applicants do not receive job offers following employment interviews because of poor communication skills, which include poor listening.

Individuals Are More Successful On The Job When individuals come to organizations with the right attitude toward listening and good listening skills, career success often follows. Part of this success is the result of making fewer mistakes and causing fewer problems for their employers, colleagues, and other stakeholders. Part of their success can also be attributed to human relations. Good listeners typically develop stronger relationships with others.

Individuals Are Better Prepared To Succeed In Upper-Level Management Positions Individuals in the upper-level management ranks are typically expected to be good leaders and exceptional communicators. Listening is at the top of that long list of expected communication skills. Those who have the right attitude toward listening and who continuously refine their listening skills are better prepared for promotion when their time comes and to succeed in those positions.

In summary, effective listening is important to individuals' careers. Employees who are good listeners learn more in school and in other training forums, listen more effectively during employment interviews, realize greater success on the job, and meet the listening expectations of their many constituencies if and when they assume upper-level executive positions.

Ways Effective Listening Can Make You a Better Leader
http://www.
forbes.com/sites/
glennllopis/2013/05/
20/6-effective-ways-
listening-can-make-
you-a-better-leader

SUMMARY: SECTION 2—
THE EFFECT OF GOOD LISTENING ON EMPLOYEES' CAREERS

- Listening is important to employees and to organizations.
- An employee's job stability and career growth potential are affected directly by his or her ability and willingness to be a good listener.
- The ways employees' careers are affected by good listening include learning more, improving their chances in the job search process, being more successful on the job, and being prepared to succeed in upper-level management positions.

LISTENING EFFECTIVELY WHEN COMMUNICATING ELECTRONICALLY

Prior to the invention of the telephone in 1876, listening was limited to face-to-face exchanges and shouting from a distance. The popularity telephones have enjoyed for more than a century certainly changed all that.

The potential of telephones as listening devices continues to grow as more electronic features are added. The popularity telephones have enjoyed for over one and one-half centuries certainly changed all that. Standard features, such as automatic redial, caller ID, call waiting, call forwarding, and voicemail, would surely astonish the telephone's inventor, Alexander Graham Bell, if he were alive today. Today's developers continue to design additional features.

There are other popular electronic devices that support listening activity also. These include smartphones, cell phones, conference call technology, and various forms of videoconferencing.

ELECTRONIC COMMUNICATION TECHNOLOGIES: HAVE THEY IMPROVED OUR ABILITY TO LISTEN EFFECTIVELY?

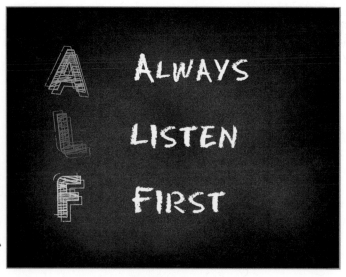

© Vaju Ariel/Shutterstock.com

Despite the many communication technology developments, the communication method that still best supports good listening is face-to-face communication because most people are comfortable in this setting. In addition, with face-to-face communication listeners are not limited to just the spoken message. They also have access to the full range of emotions and nonverbal cues their communication partners transmit. If an oral message is important, complex, or controversial, good listening is critical. Thus, communicating face-to-face is advised whenever possible in such situations.

Despite their numerous benefits, several electronic communication devices pose challenges to listeners. For example, with some electronic devices, the listener's ability to detect and interpret a speaker's emotions and nonverbal cues is extremely limited (e.g., phone calls, conference calls, voicemail). Even videoconferences pose a challenge to listeners. While videoconferences and similar technologies (e.g., Skype, Facetime, video chat) add the visual elements to the communication process, most people are still not very experienced or as comfortable with these media. This lack of experience and the accompanying discomfort level pose threats to effective listening. Furthermore, participants in videoconferences are not able to pick up on as many of the speaker's emotions and nonverbal cues as they are in face-to-face meetings. Videoconferencing on mobile electronic devices presents even greater limitations to listening effectiveness because most laptop, netbook, and tablet screens are relatively small.

FIGURE 13-3: LISTENING ELECTRONICALLY CAN COMPROMISE COMMUNICATION

When communicating electronically, listening effectiveness is too often compromised by polyphasic activity. *Polyphasic activity* refers to doing more than one thing at a time.[3] As you should know by now, effective listening is hard work that requires sustained focus. However, many of today's electronic communication devices support polyphasic activity, which directly weakens listening effectiveness.

© pupunkkop/Shutterstock.com

What follows are some examples of situations where too much polyphasic activity interferes with good listening.

- People with call waiting on their phones often jump back and forth between two or more conversations. Their attention is split, which does not support good listening.
- Speakerphones threaten effective listening by placing listeners in hands-free environments where they are tempted to do other work while listening.
- Some businesspeople do business on their smartphones and cell phones while driving. Needless to say, these speakers are not getting the listener/driver's full and undivided attention.
- Conference calls and traditional phone calls also threaten effective listening. In these settings, it is tempting and easy to check your e-mail or catch up on other work while talking on the phone.

Naturally, multitasking as just described undermines effective listening.

USING ELECTRONIC TOOLS IN WAYS THAT SUPPORT EFFECTIVE LISTENING

Here are a number of ways electronic communication tools support effective listening.

Telephones and Conference Calls Since telephones by their very nature reduce listeners' ability to fully identify all the speaker's emotions and nonverbal cues, it is even more important that the listener remain focused. In addition to listening closely for facts and details, focus on identifying emotional and nonverbal qualities in your communication partner's voice. For example, is his or her voice breaking or tense? Listen for the long pause that may signal that the speaker said something important, is about to say something important, or is seeking a response from you. Finally, do not work on other tasks while on telephone and conference calls. You cannot fully concentrate on the speaker's message if you are simultaneously doing other things such as sorting through your e-mail.

Mobile Phones (Smartphones and Cell Phones) The foregoing suggestions also apply to smartphones and cell phones. While many people conduct business regularly on smartphones and cell phones, they pose some additional listening challenges. Listeners need to stay focused during smartphone and cell phone conversations. Being a good listener during such conversations presents challenges due to all the potential distractions. The most obvious example is that of the businessperson who is trying to listen effectively on such devices while driving. Not only is this person compromising his or her listening effectiveness, he or she is creating a potential safety hazard! This particular safety issue is discussed at length in chapter 4.

Videoconferences Videoconferences, in the traditional sense, are conducted in rooms designed for and dedicated to this activity. Such facilities include a wall-mounted or drop-down screen, a good speaker system, and a conference table. Now videoconferences are also conducted on desktop PCs, laptops, netbooks, tablets, and smartphones. While these approaches provide the listener with more opportunities to observe speakers' emotions and nonverbal cues than is possible with traditional phone calls, there are shortcomings. For example, the visual and audio features are compromised when cameras and speaker systems are of poor quality or are not operating properly. Small screens pose an obvious difficulty due to size. Furthermore, when videoconferencing in today's multiple-windows environment, the ability to distinguish visual emotional and nonverbal cues is often compromised when screens are split into small viewing spaces. Finally, listening effectiveness is compromised when listeners are inexperienced with videoconferencing. The newness and the novelty of the medium are distracting, resulting in less-effective listening.

© Artistico/Shutterstock.com

THE NATURE OF LISTENING

Listening is a complex process that extends beyond simple hearing. Next we discuss the differences between hearing and listening.

HEARING AND LISTENING—WHAT'S THE DIFFERENCE?

Do not confuse the term *hearing* with the term *listening*. So how do hearing and listening differ? The two terms are not synonymous. **Hearing** refers to the reception of sound through sensory channels. Hearing is one of the five human senses and is a biological process. Hearing is obviously a critical component of the listening process. However, how each of us values and processes speakers' words, emotions, and nonverbal cues—rather than how we hear—are what ultimately determine if we are effective listeners.

Listening refers to the accurate perception of the message being communicated through a combination of words, emotions, and nonverbal cues.[4] This definition implies that we should listen for emotions and nonverbal cues as well as for words. For example, when a speaker's voice breaks frequently or he or she is mumbling, good listeners sense emotional tension. When a speaker frowns or pauses often, good listeners sense that the speaker lacks familiarity with or confidence in his or her message. Good listeners do not only listen for words, they also listen for emotions and nonverbal cues that are often more telling than the spoken words.

hearing
The reception of sound through sensory channels.

listening
The accurate perception of a message being communicated through a combination of words, emotions, and nonverbal cues.

© StockPhotosLV/Shutterstock.com

The Listening Process The listening process breaks the listening activity into five distinct steps. The process begins with **receiving,** which refers to hearing (the biological reception of sound). The second step involves **focusing,** which suggests the listener is limiting his or her attention to that stimulus. Step three is **interpreting,** which involves decoding and assigning meaning to what is heard. The fourth step is **accepting,** which suggests the listener interprets the meaning of the message as the speaker intended it to be interpreted. This implies that the message is accepted free of bias, but does not suggest that the listener agrees with what is being said. The fifth and final step is **storing,** which refers to depositing in our minds all or part of the message.[5]

How Good of a Listener Are You? Most people believe they are good listeners whether or not they really are. It is a reasonable perception, since most of us have been listening at least since birth. Some even suggest that babies listen while still in the womb. By the time we reach adulthood, we must be good listeners, right?

The Fundamental Qualities of Good Listeners

- Good listeners have a realistic attitude about the importance of being good listeners.
- They are familiar with effective listening techniques.
- They are familiar with common listening barriers.
- They listen for emotions and nonverbal cues as well as spoken words.
- When assuming the role of listener, they view themselves as active participants, which helps them focus on their responsibilities in the communication process.
- They are willing to work continuously at refining and improving their listening skills.

In summary, individuals are not born good listeners. To be a good listener requires continuous, conscious, and purposeful effort. However, the personal and professional rewards resulting from this invested effort are numerous.

LISTENER STYLES

Not all people listen the same way. We differ. Some individuals are poor listeners, while others are excellent listeners. Then, there are all those people who fit somewhere in between. Even then, we do not always listen consistently from day to day no matter our most prevalent listening style. Each of us has good days and bad days. For example, an employee who is usually a good listener may, on a given day, due to too little sleep or too much stress, exhibit poor listening skills, leading to mistakes. It is a good idea not to generalize about others when it comes to listening.

© Gustavo Frazao/Shutterstock.com

At least eight styles of listeners have been identified. As you work your way through the list, identify which style or combination of styles describes how you listen most of the time. Then ask yourself if there is room for improvement.

Casual listeners "listen for pleasure, recreation, amusement, and relaxation."[6]

Non-listeners make no attempt at listening and can often be recognized by their blank stare and nervous mannerisms. These individuals are not taken seriously. This is the least effective listening style.

Marginal listeners are superficial listeners who hear sounds and words, but rarely their meaning and intent. There is a fine line between marginal listeners and non-listeners, and for obvious reasons, both are highly susceptible to misunderstanding the messages.

Message content listeners tend to focus their energies on listening mainly for message content. While people do need to listen for message content, they also need to listen for emotions and nonverbal cues that reinforce and add meaning and importance to the speaker's words. Many people believe men have a greater tendency than women to listen almost exclusively for message content at the expense of the emotional and nonverbal cues, while women listen more closely for emotions and nonverbal cues at the expense of message content.

Critical listeners focus on both understanding and evaluating (analyzing) the message.[7] In their quest to evaluate the soundness of the speaker's message, however, they typically overlook the need to process emotional and nonverbal cues.

© Michal Kowalski/Shutterstock.com

Results-style listeners are "interested in hearing the bottom line or result of a message."[8] The shortcoming of this listening style is the tendency to tune out much of the message and to rush speakers to get to the point.

Process-style listeners "like to discuss issues in detail."[9] Possibly the greatest shortcoming of this listening style is the tendency to interrupt speakers in their quest to discuss.

casual listener
Someone who listens for pleasure, recreation, amusement, or relaxation.

non-listener
Someone who makes no attempt to listen; can often be recognized by his or her blank stare and/or nervous mannerisms.

marginal listener
A superficial listener who hears sounds and words, but rarely absorbs their meaning and intent.

message content listener
Someone who focuses his or her energies on listening mainly for message content.

critical listener
Someone who focuses on both understanding and evaluating (analyzing) a message.

results-style listener Someone who is interested in hearing the bottom line or result of a message.

process-style listener A detail-oriented listener who likes to discuss issues in detail and often interrupts speakers to do so.

Active listeners possess the most comprehensive and effective listening style. Active listeners give speakers their undivided attention. They listen for emotions and nonverbal cues as well as message content. They also hear the speaker out before evaluating the soundness of the message. Finally, they attempt to understand the speaker as well as the message to the point of respecting the speaker's feelings and point of view even when it is inconsistent with their own.[10]

© Gustavo Frazao/Shutterstock.com

In sum, the three least-effective listening styles are the *non-listener,* the *marginal listener,* and the *casual listener,* with the *non-listener* style being the worst of the three. The *message content, critical, results-style,* and *process-style* listening styles each have merits, but be cautious of their shortcomings. The *active* listening style is the best listening style to practice.

SUMMARY: SECTION 4— THE NATURE OF LISTENING

- Hearing and listening are different activities. Hearing is the reception of sound; listening is the accurate perception of the message being communicated through a combination of words, emotions, and nonverbal cues.
- The listening process involves five steps: receiving, focusing, interpreting, accepting, and storing.
- Fundamental qualities of good listeners include a realistic attitude, a familiarity with effective listening techniques and common listening barriers, and the willingness to work continuously to refine and improve one's listening skills.
- The eight basic listening styles are casual listener, non-listener, marginal listener, message content listener, critical listener, results-style listener, process-style listener, and active listener. The strongest of these is the active listener style.

COMMON BARRIERS TO EFFECTIVE LISTENING

There are plenty of barriers to effective listening. The listening comprehension of the typical U.S. worker is low. On average, 75 percent of what people hear is forgotten within 48 hours or is distorted.[11] Listening comprehension can be increased by controlling or eliminating the listening barriers presented below and by practicing the recommended listening techniques presented later in this chapter.

Unquestionably, maintaining a realistic attitude about the importance of good listening, learning and practicing good listening techniques, and continuously working at refining one's listening skills are among the admirable qualities shared by effective listeners. However, even well-intentioned listeners are human enough to be susceptible to listening barriers. Familiarize yourself with the common listening barriers and identify those to which you are most susceptible so you can control or eliminate them. The most common listening barriers are discussed here.[12]

INAPPROPRIATE ATTITUDE TOWARD LISTENING

This problem can be viewed in several ways. First, there are people who do not understand the importance of effective listening in organizations. As a result, they make no effort to learn the common listening barriers and effective listening techniques. Even when such information is brought to their attention, they shrug it off, failing to improve their listening abilities. Finally, they make no attempt to refine or improve their listening skills because they assume good listening is nothing more than a byproduct of the biological function called hearing.

FAILURE TO WORK AT LISTENING

Good listening is work and requires genuine effort to learn, develop, practice, and refine. Poor listeners have not learned—or at least have not reminded themselves of—the most common barriers and effective listening techniques. They do not work at improving their listening abilities. Finally, poor listeners often assume they are good listeners merely because they have two ears and have been able to hear since birth.

FAILURE TO GIVE FULL ATTENTION TO THE PERSON SPEAKING

For a variety of reasons, we all fail at times to give speakers our full attention. The range of reasons extends from exhaustion and clock watching to doodling and daydreaming. At times, we fail to give our full attention to speakers by not controlling the difference between the speaking rate and processing rate. Indeed, the average speaking rate for most people is 125–150 words per minute, while most people can process 500–800 words per minute.[13] This rate difference leaves listeners with a large gap to fill either effectively or ineffectively. Poor listeners fill the gap by daydreaming or doodling instead of redoubling their listening efforts.

Poor listeners fail to give speakers their full attention in other ways. For example, they compromise their listening effectiveness when they multitask simultaneously or allow interruptions (e.g., answering phone calls or responding to knocks on their door).

FAILURE TO LISTEN FOR EMOTIONS AND NONVERBAL CUES

Some people fail to achieve balanced listening by devoting too much of their attention and energies to listening for facts and details—the message content—and not enough to emotions and nonverbal cues. Emotions and nonverbal cues are important components of the message and should not be overlooked. Balanced listening is the answer.

FAILURE TO LISTEN FOR FACTS AND DETAILS

Some people fail to achieve balanced listening because they devote too much of their listening attention and energies to the speakers' emotions and nonverbal cues and not enough to facts and details—the message content. Facts and details are also important components of the message and should not be overlooked. Balanced listening again is the answer.

CONFLICTING NONVERBAL CUES

A speaker creates a barrier to effective listening when his or her nonverbal cues differ from his or her spoken words. If a coworker verbally congratulates you on a recent promotion while frowning and glaring at you, you experience a conflict between spoken words and facial expressions. As a listener, look for conflicting cues and incorporate them into your interpretation of the speaker's message.

CLOSED MINDEDNESS

Closed-minded listeners refuse to relate to and learn from speakers' ideas. These listeners go into the communication setting with opposing, preconceived ideas and opinions about what the speaker will say. While the speaker talks, the listener is interrupting, silently developing a rebuttal, sighing, daydreaming, or looking at the clock. The listener's mind is like a closed parachute and just about as effective.

URGE TO INTERRUPT OR DEBATE

Poor listeners often fail to control their urge to voice their thoughts. Instead of waiting until the speaker finishes, these listeners continuously interrupt, not for clarification, but to share their own thoughts, to "one up" the speaker with a better story, or to finish the speaker's sentences or thoughts before he or she can finish them. Some listeners want to turn listening sessions into debates. They think nothing of constantly interrupting the speaker with challenges to what he or she is saying.

FAILURE TO CONTROL EMOTIONS

When a listener dislikes the speaker or strongly disagrees with what he or she is saying, poor listening is typically the result. In such situations, the listener often interrupts the speaker. Even if the listener does not interrupt, he or she is typically developing a rebuttal instead of listening carefully. These listeners often sigh, fidget, and make facial expressions while the speaker talks.

© Pressmaster/Shutterstock.com

FAILURE TO CONTROL SELECTIVE LISTENING

Selective listening occurs when listeners listen for only what they want to hear and/or attach their preferred interpretation to the message even if it is inconsistent with the speaker's desired intention.

ALLOWING STATUS TO INTERFERE

Some people do not listen as effectively to people whose job titles or status is lower than theirs. These people are typically good listeners when communicating with people of equal or greater job status because they believe that has a positive effect on their career growth. Conversely, they seem to believe that people of lower job status are unworthy of their full attention, in part because those people have little ability to affect their career success.

ALLOWING ENVIRONMENTAL DISTRACTIONS TO INTERFERE

Listeners who fail to control avoidable environmental distractions interfere with effective listening. Examples include allowing noises, talking, and visual distractions to interfere when doors and windows can be closed and chairs can be repositioned; allowing others to interrupt the speaker so they can talk to you; and answering phone calls, including accepting incoming call-waiting calls, while the speaker is talking. It is rude to allow avoidable environmental distractions to interfere.

FAILURE TO PUT THE SPEAKER AT EASE

Some listeners exhibit behaviors that interfere with effective listening and make the speaker tense. Examples of such behavior include failure to give your full attention to the speaker, closed mindedness, interrupting and debating, failure to control emotions, status interference, and allowing environmental distractions.

MESSAGE ORGANIZATION BARRIERS

Speakers can even interfere with listening effectiveness. This is likely to occur when they fail to organize their thoughts before speaking. In such instances, even a good listener may have trouble understanding the message.

ALLOWING CONTENT-RELATED BARRIERS TO INTERFERE

Several listening barriers are associated with the speaker's message content. Here the listener's attitude toward the speaker's message may compromise his or her listening abilities. The following examples of message content barriers produce the same result: The listener tunes out the speaker. Examples of content-related listening barriers include believing there is little or nothing to be learned, believing the speaker's message is boring, believing you have too little knowledge or experience to understand the speaker's message, and believing that what is about to be said or is being said is not interesting or entertaining.

ALLOWING SPEAKER-RELATED BARRIERS TO INTERFERE

Several speaker-related barriers interfere with effective listening. Here, the listener allows some aspect of the speaker to distract him or her from listening to the speaker's message. Typical examples include being distracted by the speaker's appearance, mannerisms, voice qualities, gestures, or facial expressions. Most humans observe each other and form

opinions about what is appropriate appearance, normal voice qualities, etc. We all need to be careful not to allow speaker-related barriers to compromise listening effectiveness.

We are all susceptible to any number of the above-mentioned listening barriers, and it is good to know about them so we can watch for and control them. A good starting point is to reflect on your own listening behavior with the purpose of determining which barriers are typical components of your listening style. If there are some, which is common, get to work and fix them. You could ask those around you to point out instances when you have allowed listening barriers to interfere. In addition, it's good technique to periodically review a list of listening barriers, such as the one above. Doing so refreshes your memory, giving you yet another opportunity to improve your listening skills.

Listening skills typically become listening habits no matter whether they are poor, average, or good. Poor listening skills left uncorrected result in poor listening habits that are difficult to break. While some people may get away at times with being poor listeners when communicating with subordinates, they will likely get in trouble quickly when they exhibit poor listening skills before superiors and external stakeholders.

SUMMARY: SECTION 5— COMMON BARRIERS TO EFFECTIVE LISTENING

- People are susceptible to many of the common barriers to effective listening.
- Individuals should first identify which barriers affect their listening effectiveness, then work on changing them.
- Some of the common listening barriers are inappropriate attitude toward listening, failure to work at listening, failure to listen for speakers' emotions and nonverbal cues, closed mindedness, urge to interrupt or debate, and failure to control emotions.
- The most damaging barrier to effective listening is an inappropriate attitude toward listening. Individuals with a careless attitude typically do not familiarize themselves with listening barriers and recommended listening techniques and do little to improve and refine their listening skills.

RECOMMENDED LISTENING TECHNIQUES

Let's end this chapter on a positive note by discussing several effective listening techniques. You should recognize many of them; hopefully several of them are already a part of your regular listening regimen. You should learn some new techniques by reading the following material.

© Gustavo Frazao/Shutterstock.com

DEVELOP AND MAINTAIN THE "RIGHT ATTITUDE" TOWARD LISTENING

You are encouraged to develop the "right attitude" toward listening. Appreciate how much good listening is valued by organizations and how good listening skills can affect your career, job stability, and personal life. A sound, realistic attitude toward listening is similar to the foundation of a house. The foundation provides the base on which the house is built. With listening, a realistic attitude is the base on which good listeners build their skills. The right attitude is at the heart of their willingness and desire to be good listeners.

GIVE YOUR FULL ATTENTION TO THE PERSON SPEAKING

First, remember that the speaker deserves your full attention. Avoid those actions that divert your attention, such as daydreaming, faking attention, answering your telephone, responding to a text message, making judgments about the speaker's appearance, etc. Be especially careful to avoid framing your response to what a speaker is saying while he or she talks. Hear the speaker out before developing and sharing your response. This way you can focus on all the facts, details, emotions, and nonverbal cues he or she shares.

© Pressmaster/Shutterstock.com

LISTEN FOR EMOTIONS AND NONVERBAL CUES AS WELL AS FOR FACTS AND DETAILS

Facts and details are important components of any oral conversation; however, they alone do not comprise the total message. Good listeners understand that a speaker's emotions and nonverbal cues also contribute to the total message. The general perception is that men listen more for facts and details than do women, and women listen more closely for emotions and nonverbal cues. While these perceptions sound interesting, there is nothing physically unique or restrictive about either gender that prohibits people from being thorough listeners.

CAPITALIZE ON THE SPEAKING/LISTENING RATE DIFFERENTIAL

Most people are able to listen at a much faster rate than others can speak. Thus, when a person speaks to you, you are left with spare time that you can use productively or unproductively. Instead of allowing this spare time to be consumed with counterproductive activities like daydreaming, clock watching, and doodling, use it productively. Fill the voids with activities that not only help you focus your attention on the speaker but also help you better understand the message. For example, mentally outline what is being said, relate what is being said to the purpose of the conversation, and focus some of your attention on the speaker's emotions and nonverbal cues.

BE OPEN-MINDED

View listening situations as learning experiences. Avoid a quick dismissal of some or all of what a speaker says because it is inconsistent with your way of thinking. For example, a customer may voice a negative opinion about a product that you think is wonderful. Instead of tuning out the customer's opinion, take the opportunity to understand it and learn about the product's defects or drawbacks and ways to improve it. Closed mindedness and preconceived ideas about what the speaker is saying typically interfere with good listening. Keep in mind that old saying, "Minds are like parachutes, they only function when open."

© Peter Bernik/Shutterstock.com

CONTROL YOUR EMOTIONAL BLIND SPOTS

Everyone has emotional buttons that can and will be triggered when least expected. When emotions flare and are left unchecked, communication suffers. Here are some ways to control your emotional blind spots when you are the listener. In advance of meeting with the speaker, anticipate what he or she might say that could set you off emotionally. Mentally review the downsides of allowing your emotions to control your words and actions. If the speaker's message is emotionally charged, avoid fueling an already raging fire. When a speaker upsets you, take a couple of deep breaths before responding. Finally, know when to walk away from a heated or potentially heated conversation before saying things you and your organization will regret.

EMPATHIZE WITH THE SPEAKER

The better you understand the speaker and the message, the greater the chance you will listen effectively. For example, learn about the speaker and his or her concerns, needs, or objectives in advance of your meeting. In addition, imagine yourself in the speaker's position and think about how you would feel and react. Avoid saying to the speaker that you know exactly how he or she feels. Such statements are perceived as patronizing and insincere. Be sure your voice as well as your words expresses empathy.

REMOVE ENVIRONMENTAL DISTRACTIONS

There are several benefits associated with removing environmental distractions. First and foremost is the respect shown to the speaker. For example, you communicate respect for a speaker when you allow your incoming phone calls to be picked up by your voicemail. You and the speaker are better able to maintain a consistent train of thought during conversation if avoidable distractions are removed or controlled.

FIGURE 13–4: NONVERBAL SUGGESTIONS TO IMPROVE YOUR LISTENING SKILLS

The following nonverbal suggestions for listeners fall into two categories: putting your speaker at ease and positioning your body for effective listening.

Put your speaker at ease. Speakers typically feel more relaxed and confident when you put them at ease. For example, an attentive, pleasant facial expression communicates to the speaker that you are interested in what he or she is saying. In turn, you benefit from your added efforts through an increase in the quality and quantity of information the speaker shares. Other techniques that you can use to put speakers at ease include:

- Maintaining normal eye contact
- Smiling periodically
- Providing a variety of reassuring nods
- Providing supportive verbal utterances, such as *uh-huh*

Position your body for effective listening. The ways you position your body while listening determine to a great degree how effectively you listen and how the speaker perceives you. Several positions that will enhance your listening effectiveness are listed here.

© dotshock/Shutterstock.com

- When standing or sitting, square off with the speaker. Position your body to directly face him or her.
- Turn your head so your face is toward his or hers. This helps you focus on the speaker and avoid being distracted by peripheral activities.
- Sit where you will have direct eye contact with the speaker. When in such a position, you have to stay tuned into the speaker because you know that eye contact with him or her is unavoidable.
- When you and the speaker are sitting down, lean forward slightly from the waist. This is a sign of attentiveness.
- When you and the speaker are sitting down, avoid crossing your legs at the knee or ankle. When you cross your legs, you tend to slide down in the chair, which makes you appear inattentive.

AVOID THE URGE TO SPEAK TOO SOON

It is natural for most people to want to have their thoughts heard, and oftentimes, they want them heard right now. This urge and ensuing behavior can often be traced to infancy. As babies, most of us were conditioned to speak out (cry) when we had a need, and for most of us, our needs were met immediately.

In your zeal to share your thoughts, be careful not to interrupt speakers. Interrupting speakers tends to derail their train of thought and leaves them feeling that they and their messages are unimportant. In the United States, who interrupts the most: men or women? Men interrupt speakers of both genders with greater frequency than do women.

Of course, it is appropriate to interrupt a speaker if clarification is necessary. However, be courteous in regard to when you interrupt a speaker for clarification. At minimum, wait until he or she has finished a sentence or thought before jumping in. Ideally, you should wait until the speaker has finished his or her presentation before asking.

DO NOT ALLOW STATUS TO INTERFERE

Good listeners give their full attention and listen equally well to all internal and external stakeholders, no matter what their job title or status happens to be. Good listeners understand that this is appropriate and respectful. They do so despite the temptation to rush a speaker who has little potential to affect their career growth and success.

DO NOT EAVESDROP

Good listeners are also ethical listeners and, in turn, do not eavesdrop.

© Artisticco/Shutterstock.com

AVOID MESSAGE CONTENT-RELATED BARRIERS

Good listeners control content-related listening barriers such as those listed here.

- **Believing there is little you can learn.** A poor listener often tunes out speakers when he or she believes the speaker is saying something that is too elementary or already known. Instead, listen for added information by doing your best to stay focused on the speaker's message. In addition, work at remaining open-minded.
- **Believing that you have too little knowledge or experience to understand.** A poor listener often tunes out speakers when the listener believes what the speaker is saying is beyond his or her comprehension. In such situations, rather than tune out the speaker, challenge yourself to apply your best focusing techniques. Ask the speaker for clarification as needed. Finally, do not hesitate to restate some of the speaker's main points so you can determine if your perceptions and interpretations are accurate.
- **Believing that what is being said is uninteresting or unentertaining.** Most people understand and accept the fact that not all the information shared in business is going to be interesting or entertaining. When the message is not interesting or entertaining, redouble your focusing efforts and fight the urge to daydream or doze off.

AVOID SPEAKER-RELATED BARRIERS

Good listeners control speaker-related listening barriers, such as being distracted by the speaker's appearance, mannerisms, voice, gestures, facial expressions, and so forth. For example, overcome the urge to focus even a small portion of your attention on a male customer's unusually high voice or a female customer's excessive makeup. To do otherwise threatens your ability to fully receive and understand the speaker's message. Instead, keep your attention focused on the speaker's words, emotions, and nonverbal cues.

As with many other skills, listening skills diminish if we do not use them regularly. We may even forget practical listening techniques if we do not use them for extended periods. Keep a list of good listening techniques, such as the list above, close at hand. Then make a point to review the list periodically so you do not forget or under-use the techniques. By combining this approach with the right attitude toward listening, you increase the number of effective listening techniques you use.

As you reflect on the list of recommended listening techniques, you can understand the importance of the technique that topped the list—developing and maintaining the right attitude toward listening. This is the key to effective listening, while the wrong attitude is the single greatest obstacle. The right attitude about the importance of good listening and the amount of effort it takes to be a good listener are what opens people's minds to learning, practicing, refining, and using effective listening techniques.

Effective Listening Tips
http://www.forbes.com/
sites/womensmedia/
2012/11/09/10-steps-
to-effective-listening/

> ## SUMMARY: SECTION 6—
> ## SUGGESTED LISTENING TECHNIQUES
>
> - People can learn effective listening techniques.
> - Individuals are advised to first identify which listening techniques they are currently using and add those techniques they are not using.
> - Some of the suggested listening techniques include having the right attitude toward listening, observing speakers' emotions and nonverbal cues, capitalizing on your listening rate, staying open-minded, controlling emotional blind spots, positioning your body for effective listening, and removing environmental distractions.
> - The right attitude toward listening is the common denominator in good listeners. It is the base from which they willingly familiarize themselves with and watch for listening barriers, learn effective listening techniques, and continuously improve and refine their listening skills.

Notes

1. Valerie Priscilla Goby and Justus Helen Lewis. "The Key Role of Listening in Business: A Study of the Singapore Insurance Industry." *Business Communication Quarterly*, 63, no. 2 (June 2000): 42–43.

2. L. Rehling. "Improving Teamwork through Awareness of Conversational Styles." *Business Communication Quarterly*, 67, no. 4 (2004): 475–82.

3. Kristen Bell DeTienne. *Guide to Electronic Communication*. (Upper Saddle River, NJ: Prentice-Hall, 2002), 5.

4. Kevin J. Murphy. *Effective Listening: Your Key to Career Success*. (New York: Bantam Books, 1987), 11.

5. James Benjamin and Raymie E. McKerrow. *Business and Professional Communication*. (New York: Harper-Collins College Publishers, 1994), 93–94.

6. Carol M. Lehman and Debbie D. Dufrene. *Business Communication*, 13th ed. (Cincinnati: South-Western Publishing), 55.

7. R. T. Bennett and R. V. Wood. "Effective Communication via Listening Styles." *Business* (April–June 1989), 47.

8. Ibid., 46.

9. Ibid.

10. Don Hellriegel, John W. Slocum Jr., and Richard W. Woodman. *Organizational Behavior*, 9th ed. (Cincinnati: South-Western Publishing), 399.

11. Ibid.

12. S. Golen. "A Factor Analysis of Barriers to Effective Listening." *Journal of Business Communication*, 27, no. 11 (1990): 25–36.

13. M. P. Nichols. *The Lost Art of Listening*. (New York: Guilford, 1995).

COMMUNICATING IN BUSINESS TEAMS

14

LEARNING OUTCOMES

After reading this chapter, you should be able to:

1. Discuss the effect your attitude toward working in teams will have on your career.

2. Describe positive and negative business team member roles.

3. Discuss the key factors that affect business team developments.

4. Discuss communication techniques that contribute to successful business teams.

5. Describe effective business team collaborative writing techniques.

6. Describe online collaborative writing tools and effective techniques for virtual writing teams.

© Rawpixel/Shutterstock.com

BENEFITS OF LEARNING ABOUT COMMUNICATING IN BUSINESS TEAMS

1. You will increase your chances of receiving job offers and achieving your desired career goals if you can communicate effectively in teams.

2. You will increase your ability to make useful contributions by being able to communicate effectively in teams.

3. You will increase your chances of achieving your desired career and earning goals if you can communicate effectively in teams.

4. You will appreciate the value the business community places on your ability to communicate effectively in teams.

5. You will know how to be an effective member of a collaborative writing team.

SELECT KEY TERMS

INTRODUCTION

There are three types of business teams—informal teams, formal teams, and virtual teams. Informal teams develop out of day-to-day activities, interactions, and members' sentiments for the purpose of meeting their social needs. Formal teams are created by management to accomplish certain organizational goals. Virtual teams comprise individuals in different locations who collaborate through information technologies.

Key factors that affect team development include conflict, norms, cohesiveness, group-think, and team size. Positive team member roles include task roles which are behaviors that are directly related to accomplishing team tasks, and maintenance roles which are behaviors that express the social and emotional needs of team members. Negative team member roles refer to behaviors that threaten task completion and/or relationships among team members. Communication techniques that typically contribute to team success include clear goals, open communication, good listening, and adherence to team meeting agendas.

The intent of this chapter is to provide you with a clear understanding of the role of teams in organizations and of how you can perform effectively in teams. These goals are realized through discussions regarding the following topics: the role of teams in organizations, team development, team member styles, team member roles, effective communication in teams, writing teams, online collaborative writing tools, and virtual writing. The information pertaining to the above-mentioned topics is reinforced by several student website resources including *PowerPoint slides, preview tests, chapter assessment tests, YouTube videos, interactive exercises,* and the *interactive glossary.*

THE ROLE OF TEAMS IN ORGANIZATIONS

A **team** is a small number of people with complementary competencies (abilities, skills, and knowledge) who are committed to common performance goals and working relationships for which they hold themselves mutually accountable.[1] For example, a product development team may be formed with the purpose of exploring new product opportunities.

© Dragon Images/Shutterstock.com

team
A small number of people with complementary competencies (abilities, skills, knowledge) who are committed to common performance goals and working relationships for which they hold themselves mutually accountable.

There is a good chance you have already participated on several teams at school, in the workplace, in the military, and/or in other settings. Hopefully many of these experiences were positive.

Teams are used extensively in organizations. They are formed for a variety of reasons, including addressing and solving problems, overcoming obstacles, embracing challenges, analyzing opportunities, gathering information for decision makers, and accomplishing routine tasks. Sometimes employee involvement on a team is voluntary, but more often teams are assigned.

Individuals and organizations benefit from team efforts. For example, team participants typically outperform individual efforts in terms of quantity and quality of ideas generated and work performed. In addition, team participants typically make better decisions and perceive their contributions to be more highly valued. Finally, some participants even report social benefits such as psychological intimacy and integrated involvement. *Psychological intimacy* refers to the emotional and psychological closeness to other team members, whereas *integrated involvement* refers to the closeness achieved through sharing enjoyable tasks and activities.[2]

Possessing a good attitude about teams is important, as is the ability to communicate effectively in such settings. If you already have a good attitude about working as part of a team and can communicate effectively in such a setting, you are off to a good start. The information in this chapter should further strengthen your ability to communicate effectively in teams. However, if your attitude about working on a team is negative or your requisite communication skills are lacking, it is time for you to make some serious changes, since your attitude toward and ability to communicate effectively on teams will have a profound effect on your career. Team involvement will play a major role throughout your professional career, so you stand to gain much from putting forth the necessary effort to make teams positive, productive experiences for you and your coworkers. This chapter provides you with numerous opportunities to reflect on your attitude toward teams and teamwork and to learn ways to communicate effectively in these settings.

This chapter also includes some talk about barriers to effective team communication. Once you know what the common barriers are, you know what to look for and avoid. Becoming familiar with barriers to effective team communication also provides us with an opportunity to reflect on our own team communication skills. While doing so, it is likely that most of us will identify one or more counterproductive techniques that we are guilty of practicing. Possibly, we didn't even know we were doing it or didn't realize doing it caused problems. The good news is, is that by identifying counterproductive team communication behaviors you have been practicing, you are less likely to repeat them.

TYPES OF TEAMS

There are many types of teams at work in organizations. While their purposes and goals may differ vastly, they do have two things in common: (1) each comprises two or more people, and (2) each is formed for some specific purpose(s) and goal(s). Essentially, there are informal and formal teams and beyond that, there are virtual teams. Each of these is described below.

Informal Teams Informal teams exist to meet a portion of employees' social needs. For example, two or more friends may form a bowling team as a way to interact socially. At the same time, some informal teams form with the purpose of discussing work-related issues. The size may vary, and members often come and go at will. Informal teams are created by their members and are neither company sanctioned nor under management direction.

informal teams Teams that develop out of day-to-day activities, interactions, and members' sentiments for the purpose of meeting their social needs.

© Boguslaw Mazur/Shutterstock

© Artisticco/Shutterstock.com

Formal Teams When most of us hear about teams in organizations, formal teams come to mind. **Formal teams** are created by management to accomplish certain organizational goals.[3] For example, management may create an *ad hoc team* to deal with an immediate problem. An ad hoc group might be formed to gather information and ideas (and report to management) on how to contend with a recent spike in energy prices that affect utility and transportation costs. Several of the more common formal teams are described below.

© Monkey Business Images/Shutterstock.com

- **Work Units** or **Functional Teams.** They comprise members who work together daily on a cluster of ongoing and interdependent tasks.[4] For example, a five-member team that moves from house to house laying brick is a functional team, as is a four-member auditing team that travels from business to business.
- **Problem-Solving Teams.** These teams focus on specific issues in their areas of responsibility, develop potential solutions, and often are empowered to take action within defined limits.[5] For example, if the majority of grinders in a foundry were not reaching minimal quota standards, it is likely that a problem-solving team, comprising grinders and foremen, would be formed to address the problem. Or, high employee turnover rates would likely trigger the formation of a problem-solving team that, at minimum, would conduct employee satisfaction surveys and interviews.

Chapter 14: Communicating in Business Teams **479**

- **Quality Circles** or **Quality Control Circles.** These are small teams of employees who strive to solve quality-related and productivity-related problems.[6] They typically meet a few hours each week. Quality control circles propose solutions to management and often manage the implementation of these solutions in their work area.[7]

© Macrovector/Shutterstock.com

- **Task Forces** or **Cross-Functional Teams.** These are teams composed of individuals from different departments and work areas who are brought together to identify and solve mutual problems.[8] For example, if a company is considering transforming 40 percent of its workforce into telecommuters, a task force or a cross-functional team would be formed to determine the appropriateness and feasibility of the goal.
- **Transnational Teams.** These are multinational work teams composed of members whose activities span multiple countries.[9] In addition to the typical challenges inherent to the team process, transnational teams are challenged to overcome cultural differences, language fluency, and leadership style issues among team members.[10] Thompson suggests that the likelihood of success in the transnational team is increased when there are a clearly shared goal, well-articulated team member roles, shared values, and agreement on performance criteria.[11]

© Rawpixel.com/Shutterstock.com

- **Skunkworks.** These are teams that form to develop products and solve complex problems. While skunkworks might sound like ad hoc teams, there are two differences. Ad hoc teams are typically temporary, while skunkworks may not be. In addition, ad hoc teams form to solve an immediate problem; skunkworks form to develop products and solve complex problems.
- **Affinity Groups.** These groups (teams) are composed of individuals who "meet on a regular basis to exchange information, ideas, opinions, and experiences on a variety of issues in a safe and supportive atmosphere, resulting in personal and professional growth."[12] While some complaints may be aired in affinity groups, holding gripe sessions is not the purpose of their existence. The potential for the personal and professional growth of members is their central focus.
- **Boards of Directors** or **Boards of Trustees.** These are top-level organizational teams. Their main responsibilities are to represent corporate stockholders and oversee the well-being of the organizations that appointed them.

Virtual Teams According to Duarte and Snyder, a **virtual team** includes team members in different locations who collaborate through various information technologies (IT) on one or more projects.[13] IT advances, such as the Internet, e-mail, instant messaging, videoconferencing, teleconferencing, groupware, and fax machines, have made virtual teams a reality.[14] Virtual teams provide a practical option in global companies where team members may work in two or more countries. Likewise, virtual teams offer cost- and time-saving advantages to companies with team members spread across a city, state, or country.

© Gigra/Shutterstock.com

The amount and sophistication of IT that supports collaborative, virtual team efforts vary. For example, some virtual teams accomplish their tasks via some combination of phone conversations, tweets, text messages, social media posts, e-mail messages, and faxes. Others use electronic systems that re-create some aspects of face-to-face interaction or typical group processes. Three categories of information technologies that do so to varying degrees are discussed next.[15]

Videoconferencing Systems Videoconferencing apps and programs such as *Skype, Go-To-Meeting,* and *video chat* that work in conjunction with PCs, laptops, notebooks, tablets, and smartphones, provide a degree of face-to-face interaction and, in the case of most, a great degree of mobility. Small video cameras, speakers, and microphones built into or attached to these devices get the job done.

skunkworks
Teams formed to develop products or solve complex problems.

affinity groups
Groups composed of individuals who meet regularly to exchange information, ideas, opinions, and experiences on a variety of issues in a safe and supportive atmosphere, resulting in personal and professional growth.

boards of directors or boards of trustees Top-level organizational groups in corporations

virtual teams Team members in different locations who collaborate through information technologies.

How to Lead Remote Teams
http://www.management.co.nz/articles/top-tips-how-lead-remote-teams

Group Software Systems These systems typically allow virtual team members to communicate with each other, share data and documents, set schedules, e-mail each other, and work on common documents independently or together.[16] *Lotus Notes* is an example of a popular group software product.

Internet/Intranet/Extranet Systems Internet, intranet, and extranet technologies provide virtual teams with the ability to interact with each other and share documents and data. Intranets, in particular, make it possible for virtual teams to share organizational information with minimal security concerns. According to Hellriegel, Slocum, and Woodman, Internet, intranet, and extranet technologies allow virtual teams to archive text, visual, audio, and numerical data in a user-friendly format.[17] Finally, Internet, intranet, and extranet technologies provide virtual teams with a practical way to keep fellow employees and important stakeholders up-to-date on their progress.[18]

Among other useful features, Internet, intranet, and extranet technologies have enabled teams, organizations, and others to participate in electronic discussion groups or forums that range from e-mail and bulletin board discussion groups to real-time discussion (chat) groups. A virtual team can now set up a private electronic discussion group or groups to meet its communication needs and, at the same time, maintain security, whether on the Internet or intranet or extranet. For example, a virtual team might set up one electronic discussion group site that can be accessed only by team members, while another virtual team might provide communication with select internal and external sources.

From a virtual team perspective, the purpose of using electronic bulletin board discussion groups and e-mail discussion groups is similar: to send and receive messages and support materials. With electronic bulletin board discussion groups, team members post and access written messages, pictures, and audio files.[19] Virtual and traditional teams are encouraged to set up electronic bulletin board discussion groups.[20]

A virtual team can also set up one or more real-time discussion (chat) groups as a means of communicating with each other and select others. These real-time chat groups provide a practical alternative to conducting conference calls and videoconferences. Virtual and traditional teams are encouraged to set up their own real-time discussion (chat) groups.[21]

While virtual teaming sounds attractive, no single electronic approach or combination of electronic approaches used to support virtual teams has duplicated the effectiveness of face-to-face group and team communication. Thus, if you define your reasons for forming a team as being extremely important or critical, a virtual team format is not recommended, no matter how efficient and cost effective it may appear. However, when used for the right purposes and conducted properly, virtual teams provide a practical alternative for accomplishing group-related tasks. With this in mind, several strategies for enhancing virtual teams are presented here.

Tips for Virtual Collaboration
http://www.forbes.com/
sites/carolkinseygoman/
2012/06/05/5-tips-for-
virtual-collaboration/

- Provide top management support.[22]
- Set specific objectives, schedules, and deadlines.[23]
- Provide adequate hands-on training.[24]
- Provide essential face-to-face contact, especially during the early phases of the group development process.[25] Doing so allows members to attach faces to names.
- Work together face-to-face for a short time. This approach gives members a chance to become acquainted with each other's personalities and to develop the beginnings of a working relationship.[26]

- Introduce and determine initial work via videoconference if the virtual team is unable to get together initially face-to-face.[27]
- Engage in one or more get-acquainted e-mail or IM exchanges as a way to establish relationships with fellow virtual team members.[28] Doing so increases the quantity and quality of team communication and builds rapport.
- Providing the positive impact that inspirational leadership can have on creativity in electronic brainstorming teams.[29]

In recent years lift-outs have gained attention. A *lift-out* is when one company hires an entire team, rather than a single employee. The team hired is one that has worked well together in another company and is able to quickly catch up in a new environment. An effective lift-out occurs over four consecutive, interdependent stages—courtship, leadership integration, operational integration, and full cultural integration.[30] Descriptions of each follow. *Courtship* occurs prior to lift-out. During this stage, the team leader and the hiring company discuss the advisability of the move. Business goals and strategies for accomplishing those goals are also discussed. It is during the courtship stage that the team leader addresses his or her team about the potential move to assess whether they are interested. *Leadership integration* occurs after lift-out. During this stage, the team leader is integrated into the hiring company's top employees. It is vital that access to senior executives is ensured during this time. *Operational integration* occurs during the lift-out. At this point in the lift-out process, the team leader ensures that the team has the resources it needs to complete its day-to-day work and thrive in its new work environment. *Full cultural integration* occurs during the lift-out. During this stage, relationships are built between members of the lift-out team and new colleagues. The team is integrated into the social network.

Companies benefit from lift-outs because they know they are hiring a highly effective team. No time is wasted on team members getting to know each other and learning how to work well together. The longstanding relationship and trust present within a lift-out team help it quickly make an impact in the new environment.

SUMMARY: SECTION 1— THE ROLE OF TEAMS IN ORGANIZATIONS

- A team is a small number of people with complementary competencies who are committed to common performance goals and working relationships for which they hold themselves mutually accountable.
- Informal teams develop out of the day-to-day activities, interactions, and sentiments of the members for the purpose of meeting their social needs.
- Formal teams are created by management to accomplish certain organizational goals. Formal teams include work units or functional teams, problem-solving teams, quality circles or quality control circles, task forces or cross-functional teams, transnational teams, skunkworks, affinity teams, and boards of directors or boards of trustees.
- Virtual teams are groups of individuals who collaborate through various information technologies on one or more projects while being at two or more locations.
- A lift-out occurs when one company hires an entire team, rather than a single employee.

TEAM DEVELOPMENT

Team development often occurs in stages. The best-known development process goes through these steps: *forming, storming, norming, performing,* and *adjourning.*[31] Each stage is described below. A quick review of these stages gives you a sense of teaming norms and expectations.

1. **Forming.** During this stage members familiarize themselves with each other and the team's task. They also determine which leadership style is best for the team. Members are typically cordial during this stage.[32]

2. **Storming.** During this stage some team members, but not all, express strong feelings and attitudes. Some even get confrontational regarding how tasks should be accomplished, teams should be led, and who should be assigned which responsibilities. If this stage is managed improperly, ongoing resentment, bitterness, and/or withdrawal can result, which could doom the team to failure.[33]

3. **Norming.** During this stage, the team members who endured the storming stage attempt to function as an effective team. They replace counterproductive feelings and behaviors with cooperation, compromise, and collaboration.

4. **Performing.** During this stage team members move ahead with accomplishing the team's task. Communication is open and informal, and members embrace their shared responsibility for completing the task at hand.

5. **Adjourning.** This signals the completion of the team's task and termination. During this stage, team leaders have an opportunity to prepare members for future team efforts by emphasizing team dynamics lessons experienced and learned.

Teams do not always experience the storming and norming stages, which suggests they move directly from the forming stage into the performing stage without conflict.

© Kirill Wright/Shutterstock.com

KEY FACTORS THAT AFFECT TEAM DEVELOPMENT

Conflict, norms, cohesiveness, groupthink, and team size are the five factors of particular importance in team development. *Conflict* is clearly most evident in the storming stage but may also appear in the performing stage. *Norms* are most evident in the norming and performing stages. *Cohesiveness* is most evident in the norming, performing, and adjourning stages. *Groupthink* is the tendency of highly cohesive teams to value consensus at the price of decision-making quality. *Team size* is detrimental when too large or too small.

Conflict Conflict is defined as "a condition of opposition and discord."[34] This particular definition sums up what is meant by team conflict. While conflict is viewed in negative terms and often poses a threat to effective communication, it also plays an important role in teams. In fact, some level of conflict is natural in the forming stage. It is healthy for members to air their differences and concerns so they can ultimately move on to the norming stage. Conflict is also important in the performing stage as it is productive to debate ideas and question others as a means of fully exploring issues. Of course, good communicators are tactful in their choice of words, tone, and body language during these discussions.

© Rafal Olechowski/Shutterstock.com

Take a moment now to think about conflict in teams. Figure 14-1 presents several personal conflict styles that appear in teams.

conflict
A condition of opposition and discord.

FIGURE 14–1: PERSONAL CONFLICT STYLES IN TEAMS

As you study each of the following personal conflict styles, identify those you use most frequently when serving on teams. Then, determine if you need to make some adjustments in order to become a more effective team member.

- **Competitive or Aggressive Style.** Team members who exhibit this style pursue their own interests aggressively, often at the expense of individual participants and the team as a whole.
- **Collaborative or Problem-Solving Style.** Team members who exhibit this style seek to find mutually acceptable solutions.
- **Compromising or Viable Solution Style.** Team members who exhibit this style work to find effective solutions, because they believe that everyone stands to lose if the conflict goes unresolved.
- **Accommodation Style.** Team members who exhibit this style feel that harmony is of utmost importance; thus, they are quick to neglect their own concerns to address others' concerns.
- **Avoidance or Impersonal Style.** Team members who exhibit this style dislike conflict, so they shy away from uncomfortable situations by refusing to be concerned.[35]

Norms Norms are behaviors to which team members are expected to adhere. They might even be thought of as standards and rules. The point is that teams eventually arrive at a set of spoken or unspoken, expected behaviors that guide members' actions and communication. Examples include the expectation that members will arrive at team meetings on time and prepared, not leave early, be tactful even when disagreeing with others, and not allow disagreements to become personal. Norms contribute to effective team communication, intergroup relations, and overall productivity. Norms are clarified and solidified in the norming stage and put into practice most visibly in the performing stage.

Cohesiveness Cohesiveness refers to the degree to which members are committed to a team and its goals.[36] Team cohesiveness is desirable because it suggests that members cooperate, communicate openly, and participate in their common task. If a team achieves cohesiveness, it is typically most noticeable in the performing and adjourning stages. The likelihood that team cohesiveness will be high is influenced by several factors. Cohesiveness is typically high when members share similar attitudes, have similar needs, respect each

norms
Behaviors to which team members are expected to adhere.

cohesiveness
The degree to which members are committed to a team and its goals.

© kirill_makarov/Shutterstock.com

other, hold one another's competencies in high esteem, relate to each other, interact frequently, agree on the team's goals and purpose, and are few in number.[37]

Achieving cohesiveness in large teams is challenging but possible. Doing so just takes more time and effort. Consider virtual teams such as electronic discussion forums and newsgroups that meet in cyberspace. Even in these settings, where great distances often separate members and teams are often extremely large, some people still feel a sense of community.[38]

Groupthink Groupthink is the tendency of some highly cohesive teams to be too agreeable, which can result in poor decisions. Groupthink can also occur when groups and teams are rushing to closure. Essentially, members do not challenge and debate each other's ideas and contributions to an extent that is prudent. In fact, they may not gather enough information to make the right decisions.

From a communication perspective, groupthink in a cohesive team is not always obvious. Members get along fine, disagreements are minimal, and communication is open and frequent. On the surface all appears well. These teams need to be reminded that effective communication is not compromised by professional disagreements. Challenges and debates are essential and useful, especially when done tactfully and in the spirit of achieving a team's objectives.

Janis, the originator of the *groupthink* concept, described several symptoms of groupthink. Teams are encouraged to look out for these symptoms, especially when cohesiveness exists. Figure 14-2 lists Janis's eight symptoms of groupthink.

groupthink
The tendency of highly cohesive teams to value consensus at the price of decision-making quality.

FIGURE 14-2: SYMPTOMS OF GROUPTHINK

While reading about each of the groupthink symptoms below, reflect on times you saw each one occur. Then, think about what was done to counter each.

1. **Illusions of invulnerability.** Members feel they are incapable of making mistakes.
2. **Collective rationalization.** Members ignore contradictory data and warnings. Alternatives are not considered thoroughly, and members do not reconsider the team's assumptions.
3. **Shared illusion of unanimity.** Members accept decisions prematurely, often assuming that silence implies consent.
4. **Sense of team morality.** Members feel their actions are inherently right, thus they ignore the ethical implications of their decisions.
5. **Self-censorship.** Members do not express their questions and concerns about the course of action, which prevents critical analysis.
6. **Stereotyping competitors.** Members view competitors as evil, inept, or stupid.
7. **Peer pressure.** The loyalty of members who express doubts or concerns is questioned by the other team members.
8. **Mindguards.** Members shelter each other from exposure to information that might lead them to question their assumptions.[39]

Groupthink does not need to be the end result of team cohesiveness. Teams can take some preventative measures to either eliminate the possibility of groupthink or at least minimize its impact on the decision-making process. For example, schedule realistic amounts of time to discuss, evaluate, and vote on ideas; conduct a second-round vote; and have a colleague sit in on meetings for the purpose of informing the team when groupthink symptoms are evident. Janis offers the following guidelines for preventing groupthink.[40]

- Ask each team member to assume the role of the critical evaluator who actively voices objections or doubts.
- Have the leader avoid stating his or her position on the issue prior to the team decision.
- Create several teams that work on the decision simultaneously.
- Bring in outside experts to evaluate the team process.
- Appoint a devil's advocate to consistently question the team's course of action.
- Evaluate the competition carefully, posing as many different motivations and intentions as possible.
- Once consensus is reached, encourage the team to rethink its position by reexamining the alternatives.

Wyman suggests that to avoid groupthink, a process that uses more than one technique for decision making should be used. He offers the following steps as another way to curb groupthink.[41]

1. **Take time at the beginning of meetings to have a dialogue about the problem.** Drawing out the problem helps the team develop shared meaning.
2. **Clarify the goal.** The leader needs to describe the authentic purpose of the meeting and then align the subsequent process to support that goal.
3. **List the criteria for the decision.** If the team's criteria are identified in the meeting, unrecognized criteria may surface that provide a new perspective on the problem. From the two or three essential criteria that everyone can agree on, unity is created.
4. **Use straw votes as initial polls, not as final decision makers.** After an initial straw vote, the reasoning behind the decision should be explored. "They should be focused on sharing their perspectives in alignment with the agreed-upon criteria, not to defend their vote."
5. **Ask probing questions.** Good leaders should ask open-ended questions. For example: What are the short and long-term risks of this solution?

Team Size   The size of a team has the potential to positively or negatively affect the quality and quantity of communication, as well as team cohesiveness. Stetch and Ratliffe captured the essence of effective team size when they stated, "A team should have the smallest number of members possible who have all the resources and points of view needed to meet the goal or mission of the team."[42] Business teams can be found in a variety of sizes, ranging from two members to several. However, all team sizes are not equally effective. When possible, form 5–7-member teams, which is considered to be an effective size. Figure 14-3 contains the typical advantages of 5–7-member teams and the potential problems associated with smaller and larger teams.

FIGURE 14–3: IMPACT OF VARYING TEAM SIZE

Effective Team Size (5–7 members)

Teams composed of 5–7 members are typically most effective. Here are some of the reasons.

- Members typically feel the workload is evenly distributed.
- Cohesiveness is more likely to occur.
- Members share more ideas and opinions.
- Members are more involved in discussions.
- Members ask for and give more feedback.
- Members feel more involved.
- Members show more agreement.
- Less time is needed to make decisions.
- Members tend to be more friendly.
- Members tend to be less formal.

Large Teams (8+ members)

Teams composed of eight or more members are typically less effective than preferred. Here are some of the reasons.

- Cohesiveness is less likely to be achieved.
- Members share fewer ideas and opinions.
- Not all members participate in the discussions.
- Fewer members ask for and give feedback.
- Members feel less involved.
- Members show less agreement.
- More time is needed to make decisions.
- Members tend to be less friendly.
- Some members engage in side social conversations.
- Some members text, check their e-mail, etc.
- Members tend to be more formal.
- Members are less satisfied.

Small Teams (4 or fewer members)

Teams composed of four or fewer members are typically less effective than preferred. Here are some of the reasons.

- Members often feel the workload is excessive.
- Members bring fewer skills (e.g., research, drafting, editing).
- Fewer ideas and opinions are shared.
- Less discussion occurs.
- Members feel too involved.
- Members are less satisfied.

Unfortunately, team size cannot typically be dictated. Sometimes, for example, you end up with a large team. If fate deals you this hand, divide the team into subteams if possible. Each subteam should then appoint a subleader. Subleaders meet periodically with each other and ultimately with the entire team. This approach is used routinely and successfully in the public sector when public school systems determine redistricting guidelines or formulate bond packages. These situations require representation from a vast cross-section of the community, often resulting in large teams. Forming subteams is the key to making it possible for large teams to work effectively and efficiently.

The value of limiting teams to a reasonable size or breaking large teams into subteams cannot be overstated. When teams are too large or too small, communication, productivity, and goal achievement suffer.

Multicultural teams are relatively common in businesses and can pose unique challenges. Several of the more common potential challenges are discussed in Figure 14-4.

Multicultural Teams Tips
http://hbr.org/2012/04/
leveling-the-playing-
field-on/

© Vadym Dobot/Shutterstock.com

FIGURE 14–4: MULTICULTURAL TEAM CONFLICTS

A study done by Brett, Behfar, and Kern found differing styles of communication to be only one of four barriers that can stand in the way of success when dealing with a multicultural team. These four challenges are:

1. **Direct versus Indirect Communication Styles.** When communicating, it is common for members of Western cultures to take a direct approach. On the other hand, in non-Western cultures, the meaning of a message often depends on the way the information is presented. Due to the Westerner's direct presentation, it is often unnecessary for the message receiver to know much about the information or the speaker. In a cross-cultural exchange of information, the non-Westerner has little or no difficulty understanding the Westerner's direct communications, whereas the Westerner is likely to have difficulty understanding a non-Westerner's indirect method of communicating.

2. **Trouble with Accents and Fluency.** In a multicultural team, a non-native member's trouble with fluency, accent, or translating may lead to misunderstandings and frustration. This is true, despite the fact that the language of international business is English. Such problems might influence the perception of one's status and competence. Non-native speakers experiencing this problem may become less involved in the team and worry about performance evaluations and future career prospects.

3. **Differing Attitudes toward Hierarchy and Authority.** "A challenge inherent in multicultural teamwork is that by design, teams have a rather flat structure. But team members from some cultures, in which people are treated differently according to their status in an organization, are uncomfortable on flat teams.

FIGURE 14-4: MULTICULTURAL TEAM CONFLICTS

If they defer to higher-status team members, their behavior will be seen as appropriate when most of the team comes from a hierarchical culture; but they may damage their stature and credibility—and even face humiliation—if most of the team comes from an egalitarian culture."

4. **Conflicting Norms for Decision Making.** Cultures vary when it comes to making decisions; specifically, how fast decisions should be made and how much analysis there should be before a decision is made. It is not surprising to note that American managers tend to make decisions faster and with less analysis than do managers from several other countries.

When presented with any of these problems, it has been discovered that leaders of multicultural teams typically deal with the problem in one of the following four ways:

1. **Adaptation.** Acknowledging cultural gaps openly and working with them.
2. **Structural Intervention.** Changing the shape of the team.
3. **Managerial Intervention.** Setting norms early or bringing in a higher-level manager.
4. **Exit.** Removing a team member when other options have failed.

Source: K. Behfar, J. Brett, and M. C. Kern. "Managing Multicultural Teams." Harvard Business Review, 84, no. 11 (2006): 84–91.

SUMMARY: SECTION 2—
TEAM DEVELOPMENT

- Teams pass through developmental stages; the more common being forming, storming, norming, performing, and adjourning. Many do not travel through the storming and norming stages.
- The key factors affecting team development are conflict, norms, cohesiveness, groupthink, and team size.
- Conflict refers to conditions of opposition. Norms are behaviors to which team members are expected to adhere. Cohesiveness refers to the degree to which members are committed to the team and its goals. Groupthink is the tendency of highly cohesive groups to value consensus over decision quality. Team size affects cohesion and productivity.
- Cross-cultural team conflicts result from direct versus indirect communication, trouble with accents and fluency, differing attitudes toward hierarchy and authority, and conflicting norms for decision making.

TEAM MEMBER STYLES

Just as personalities vary, a variety of personal communication styles typically emerge in teams. Some of these styles contribute to team success, while others impede efforts and threaten goals. Stech and Ratcliffe suggested four basic personal communication styles that emerge in teams. They are the team player, the fighter, the nice gal/nice guy, and the individualist[43] (see Figure 14-5).

FIGURE 14–5: CHARACTERISTICS OF PERSONAL COMMUNICATION STYLES IN TEAMS

Style	Talking vs. Listening Behavior	Typical Group Behavior
Team Player	Balances talking and listening.	Much interaction; much statement making, information seeking, agreeing, and disagreeing.
Fighter	Prefers talking and asserting.	Much statement making and disagreeing; much interrupting.
Nice Gal/ Nice Guy	Prefers listening and accepting.	Much information seeking and agreeing; not much interrupting. Few interactions.
Individualist	Prefers minimal communication.	Few interactions.

Source: Ernest Stech and Sharon A. Ratliffe. Effective Group Communication: How to Get Action by Working in Groups. *(Lincolnwood, IL: National Textbook, 1985), 133.*

So which of the four styles best supports team efforts and which impede them? Of the four styles, the team player is thought to make the strongest contributions to team efforts because the style combines the best qualities of the fighter and the nice gal/nice guy styles. Fighters make contributions to team efforts by questioning and debating ideas and opinions. By doing so, they contribute to better decisions and counter potential groupthink behaviors. Nice gals/nice guys contribute by helping their teams achieve answers that are acceptable to everyone. They are harmonizers. Individualists typically make the smallest contributions because they are often silent and uninvolved when the team is not doing what they want.[44]

In summary, you are challenged to monitor your personal communication style in team settings. Strive to be a team player, and adjust your communication style as needed to support team efforts.

TEAM MEMBER ROLES

Another way to understand team interaction is to recognize the various roles members assume. The roles members assume, either purposely or out of habit, profoundly affect overall team communication, team efficiency, and team effectiveness. Some roles can be viewed as having positive qualities that contribute to the achievement of team goals, while others possess negative qualities that pose a threat.

Roles of Individuals on Teams
http://artsfwd.org/9-team-roles/

Positive Team Member Roles The two general categories of positive team member roles are task roles and maintenance roles. Organizational behavior experts Bowditch and Buono state that **task roles** "are those actions and behaviors that are related to productivity and are concerned with accomplishing the team's task," and **maintenance roles** "are those actions and behaviors that express the social and emotional needs of team members."[45]

While it is natural to focus your attention on completing team tasks, you need to keep your focus balanced. In your quest to complete tasks, be careful not to spend an inordinate amount of time on task actions and behaviors at the expense of team maintenance actions and behaviors.

© Monkey Business Images/Shutterstock.com

Being supportive, encouraging, and keeping the peace are examples of maintenance roles that support team cohesiveness, thus setting the stage for the team to complete its tasks successfully. Willingness to clarify and share information and give constructive criticism are examples of task roles.

Identify which task and maintenance roles you typically exhibit in team settings. You might be surprised by how many are already a part of your style. In turn, you will likely learn of other roles that you should add to your portfolio of team roles.

Negative Team Member Roles Just when you thought you had this team interaction thing figured out, along come some obstacles in the form of negative team member roles to make your life even more challenging. Some individuals, either intentionally or subconsciously, assume negative, disruptive roles in teams (e.g., sarcasm, chronic interrupting, etc.). Since these individuals pose a serious threat to team efficiency and effectiveness, their actions cannot be disregarded. Ross suggests that such individuals be reminded of the seriousness of their actions (criticized or threatened), then ignored, isolated, rejected, and finally ejected.[46]

task roles
Those actions and behaviors related to productivity and concerned with accomplishing the team's task.

maintenance roles
Those actions and behaviors that express the social and emotional needs of team members.

FIGURE 14–6: NEGATIVE TEAM MEMBER ROLES

Do you exhibit any of the following negative team member behaviors? If you do, it is in your best interest professionally to eliminate them.

- **Aggressor.** Deflates the status of others, puts down team values, and jokes aggressively.
- **Airhead.** Attends team meetings unprepared.
- **Blocker.** Stubbornly resists, disagrees, and opposes beyond reason.
- **Detractor.** Constantly criticizes, gripes, and complains.
- **Digressor.** Deviates from the team's purpose.
- **Dominator.** Attempts to dominate discussions and viewpoints. Is manipulative.
- **Free Rider.** Does not do his or her fair share of the work.
- **Isolate.** Psychologically leaves the team by showing a lack of interest and by not participating.
- **Nit Picker.** Focuses on insignificant details.
- **Recognition Seeker.** Calls attention to him- or herself.
- **Self-Confessor.** Uses the team forum to express feelings and insights not relevant to the team's goals.
- **Socializer.** Pursues only the social aspects of the team.

Sources: Raymond S. Ross. Small Groups in Organizational Settings. *(Englewood Cliffs, NJ: Prentice-Hall, 1989), 155–56; Debbie D. Dufrene and Carol M. Lehman.* Building High-Performance Teams. *(Cincinnati: South-Western, 2002),6.*

You are encouraged to do some serious soul searching as a way to identify any negative roles you exhibit in team settings. If you are unaware of any, consider getting the opinions of those who have served on teams with you. If you do not exhibit any of the negative behaviors discussed above, congratulations! If you do, it is time to work on eliminating them.

FIGURE 14–7: TEAM MEMBERS' BILL OF RIGHTS AND RESPONSIBILITIES

What can you do to become a better team member? The following list provides some good advice that will be helpful. It is likely that you are already doing some of the techniques below, but it is also likely the list contains some additional techniques you can work on.

- To be heard and not be ignored
- Not to be exposed to crude stories and jokes
- To have cultural differences respected
- To select meeting times, locations, and methods that are convenient for all members
- To contribute to the development of the team's goals
- To contribute to the division of work among team members
- To contribute to the determination of deadlines
- To expect that all team members will do their fair share of the work
- To confront team members who are not doing their fair share of the work

FIGURE 14-7: TEAM MEMBERS' BILL OF RIGHTS AND RESPONSIBILITIES

- To expect fellow team members to be active participants
- To expect constructive feedback on your work from fellow team members
- To expect that team meetings begin and end promptly
- To expect that the team will follow the agenda during meetings
- To expect team members will listen to you respectfully
- To ask team members to keep conversations on topic/task
- To complete the work assigned to you on schedule
- To be an active participant
- To provide constructive feedback on fellow team members' work
- To contribute to getting meetings started and ended on time
- To participate in teams that work together cooperatively
- To participate in teams that handle disagreements constructively
- To listen to team members respectfully
- To help the team stay on task
- To keep your conversations on topic/task

Source: Maryellen Weimer, The Teaching Professor Blog, Faculty Focus, February 8, 2012. Pages 1-2, http://www.facultyfocus.com/articles/teaching-professor-blog/group-work-a-bill-of-rights-and-responsibilities-for-all-members/

TEAM LEADERS

Team leaders play a number of important roles in teams. Good team leaders not only help teams succeed in terms of achieving their goals in a time manner, but also contribute to good teaming experiences.

A good team leader assumes several responsibilities related to his or her role. This fact should be kept in mind when work assignments are made. In some team settings the team leader is needed to also take on some of the other tasks in order to get the job done. They may very well be the case in team settings in which there are few team members and a lot to be accomplished in a relatively short period of time. In contrast, some team settings are such that the only task that should be assigned to the team leader is that of performing his or her leadership role. This may be the case in team settings where there a sufficient number of team members and the project is complex. In such settings, the team leader's attention and efforts need to be fully focused on leading in order to manage the team and the work that needs completed. A team would be foolish to attempt its charge without having a team leader (or co-leaders) on board! After all, somebody needs to coordinate the efforts and keep an eye on the progress being made. That's the team leader.

So, what responsibilities do team leaders assume? Here are some examples:

- Team leaders should make sure everyone clearly understands the goals and work at hand.
- Team leaders should communicate deadlines and keep team members on schedule.
- Team leaders should facilitate making work assignments.
- Team leaders should coordinate team technologies decisions.
- Team leaders should oversee the development of back-up plans to prevent loss of materials.
- Team leaders should keep team meetings on schedule and on topic.
- Team leaders should keep an eye out for groupthink symptoms.
- Team leaders should assure common quality standards and writing style across reports written collaboratively.
- Team leaders should deal with problem member (e.g., those who attempt to dominate meeting conversations).
- Team leaders should inspire team members when they are in a slump.

If you have not accumulated any leadership experience thus far, you really need to do so. You may be able to acquire some at your place of work, while doing internships, while participating in team projects at school, in a student chapter of a professional organization, and in a team setting in your community. By doing so, you will begin to build an important professional skill set that is highly valued by business recruiters who are routinely look for looking for job candidates who have leadership experience.

SUMMARY: SECTION 3—
TEAM STYLES, TEAM ROLES, AND TEAM LEADERS

- Basic personal communication styles that emerge in teams include the team player, the fighter, the nice gal/nice guy, and the individualist.
- Members with the team player communication style typically make the strongest contributions to teams.
- Members with the individualist communication style typically make the least contributions to teams.
- Team member roles include both positive and negative roles.
- Positive team member roles include task roles and maintenance roles.
- Negative team member roles include roles that threaten the team's efforts.
- Team leaders play a number of import roles in teams.

EFFECTIVE COMMUNICATION IN TEAMS

Members of successful teams understand the importance of effective communication in accomplishing their goals. In turn, they practice communication techniques that support team efforts. You are encouraged to learn and practice these communication techniques. Here is a list of communication techniques that contribute to team success.

- The team's goal is clearly communicated to all members.
- Members are polite to and respectful of their fellow team members. In turn, they build trusting, informal relationships.
- Communication is open among members. They are free to express their feelings regarding the tasks and how well the team is functioning, without concern of being ridiculed.
- Members are encouraged to participate in discussions and are given ample opportunities to do so.[47] In turn, members are discouraged from dominating discussions.

- Members ask questions openly and do not hesitate to ask others to repeat or restate them for clarification purposes.
- Members exercise good communication skills (e.g., *supportive listening, proper eye contact, positive tone of voice*).
- Members know how to communicate in conflictive situations and keep disagreements focused on the tasks at hand and not on personalities and people.[48]
- Members share information with each other openly instead of hoarding it for their own personal or professional gain.
- Members exhibit verbal and nonverbal behaviors that support team efforts, while controlling those who do not.
- Members communicate with each other frequently.
- Members use a variety of communication methods ranging from face-to-face meetings/conversations to technology-based methods (e.g., conference calls, video chat, e-mail, social media).
- Members resolve conflicts as they arise.
- Members teach each other and learn from each other.
- Member accept criticism as well as praise.
- Members control counterproductive behaviors in themselves and in fellow members (e.g., *chronic interrupters, chronic whiners/complainers*).

- Members cooperate rather than compete.
- Members limit their comments to the team's agenda items and recommended timelines so they stay on topic and schedule, thus, accomplish their goals in a timely fashion.

© merzzie/Shutterstock.com

What Makes Teams Succeed?
http://www.trilliumteams.
com/articles/41/what-
makes-teams-succeed

FIGURE 14–8: HELPFUL ELECTRONIC TOOLS FOR PROJECT TEAMS

Teaming
- **Sharing Ideas and Information with Teammates**
  phone, e-mail, texting, Facebook, LinkedIn, Dropbox, OneDrive, OneNote, TeamViewer
- **Scheduling Team Meetings**
  Doodle, TimeBridge, Meet-O-Matic, NeedToMeet, World Clock Meeting Calendar, World Meeting
- **Conducting Virtual Team Meetings**
  conference calls, Skype, TeamViewer, video chat, Go-To-Meeting, Zoom, Google Talk

Planning Team Projects: Brainstorming, Outlining, & Organizing Them
- mindmaps (e.g. *Mindomo*), smartboards, conference calls, e-mail, texting, Facebook, LinkedIn, TeamViewer

Conducting Research
- **Developing Surveys and Questionnaires**
  Qualtrics, SurveyMonkey, SurveyGizmo, SoGoSurvey, AskNicely, QuestionPro
- **Conducting Electronic Searches**
  electronic subject guide searches, e-books, Scoop.it, Google

Reference Management Tools
- RefWorks, EndNote, Referencer, Reference Manager

Writing Team Documents
- SharePoint, Dropbox, Google Drive, RefWorks, EndNote, smartboards

Planning, Developing, Practicing, & Giving Team Presentations
- NCast Presentation Recorder Systems

Are you communicating as effectively as you can in teams? If you have not already done so, reflect on the prominent role communication plays in teams. Finally, identify the communication techniques presented above that you currently practice, as well as those you do not.

Nonverbal cues inherently affect how effectively team members communicate with each other. Nonverbal communication is most prevalent in settings where participants can see and hear each other (e.g., face-to-face meetings and videoconferences). To a lesser degree, nonverbal cues are present in conference calls in vocal qualities (e.g., vocal inflections, tone, pauses). However, when teams communicate predominately through e-mail and text messages, nonverbal cues are nonexistent. A number of nonverbal suggestions that should help you navigate more successfully in teams are presented in Figure 14-9.

FIGURE 14–9: NONVERBAL CONSIDERATIONS

Your attitude about nonverbal communication, a willingness to acknowledge nonverbal cues emitted by teammates, and a willingness to use nonverbal cues will strengthen communication within your teams.

- Show up on time for team meetings and avoid leaving early. Arriving late and leaving early are typically perceived negatively.
- Respect fellow members' space desires. For example, most U.S. businesspeople prefer an arms-length distance between themselves and their counterparts.
- Give appropriate nonverbal cues. For example, sighing and looking disgusted when you disagree with what a fellow member just said is inappropriate.
- Give supportive nonverbal cues. For example, a smile or nod offers support.
- Maintain normal eye contact with the person speaking. Don't avoid the speaker or stare at him or her.
- Realign your body so your face, head, and shoulders face the speaker. This communicates to him or her, nonverbally, that you are attentive and interested.
- Display pleasant facial expressions.
- Provide supportive gestures (e.g., a nod of approval).
- Look for signs of confusion and/or misunderstanding in fellow members' facial expressions and listen for these signs in their voices also.

You are challenged to understand the important role nonverbal communication plays in teams. Furthermore, you are challenged to be aware of your nonverbal behaviors and understand how they affect your contribution to teams. Finally, you are challenged to read the nonverbal cues of fellow team members with the goal of understanding them more clearly.

SUMMARY: SECTION 4— COMMUNICATING EFFECTIVELY IN TEAMS

- Communicating effectively is important to team success.
- Communication techniques that contribute to team success include a clear goal, open communication, good listening, information sharing, and adherence to the agenda.

WRITING TEAMS

Collaborative writing occurs when two or more people work together to produce a written document. Business **writing teams** typically collaborate on reports, but rarely on letters, memos, e-mail messages, text messages, and tweets. Business writers collaborate in many ways, ranging from informal oral discussions with colleagues about the document to working as a coauthor to produce a single document. Collaboration can also involve critiquing the rough draft of a peer or subordinate, a process known as *document cycling*. Colen and Petelin posit that 90 percent of business professionals produce some of their documents as part of a writing team."[49]

COORDINATING SUCCESSFUL WRITING TEAMS

In some organizations, planning, drafting, and revising a document may be done by a technical writer who works with a programmer, a product designer, a user or the audience, a graphic artist, members of other departments—legal, marketing, accounting, public relations—and editors at various stages of a document.

© *Tribalium/Shutterstock.com*

As a writer moves through the writing process for a particular document, different groups and teams are concerned with different aspects. Technical staff is concerned with technical accuracy. Managers look at documents from a cost and quality perspective as well as from a corporate view; they want to assure that the document reflects the company's goals and strategies. Editors look for consistency and adherence to the company's standards and norms as well as clarity.[50]

In contrast, collaborative writing involves a group of people who are responsible for planning, drafting, and revising a document. To be successful, the group must have a sense of what is involved in the writing process itself, be aware of how people write successfully in teams, and be adept at negotiating through team conflicts to reach consensus.[51]

COLLABORATIVE WRITING STAGES SUGGESTIONS

Collaborative writing projects have three stages: (1) planning documents, (2) drafting documents, and (3) revising documents. Writing process stages are discussed at length in chapters 7 and 8.

The team writing suggestions based on the three writing stages are not simply a repeat of writing stages information shared in chapters 7 and 8. Instead, the writing stages suggestions here are for collaborative writing teams. They do not nullify the writing stages information and suggestions shared in the earlier chapters, but add to the information needed by business writing teams.

1. **Planning Documents**
   - Determine who will be the writing team leader or co-leaders.
   - Schedule as many sessions as needed to plan the document and determine how the work will be apportioned.
   - Don't be in such a rush to get started on the work that the planning is poor.
   - Define a timeline specifying intermediate and final due dates.
   - Build some leeway into your deadlines.
   - Set up a timeline specifying meeting dates, times, and locations.
   - Determine each individual's project-related strengths and weaknesses as well as project-related likes and dislikes to support wiser work assignment decisions.

- Make work assignments.
- If more than one team member will write, determine the preferred writing style and encourage each writer to adhere to it.

2. **Drafting Documents**
   - Keep in mind that even though drafting alone is typically faster, team drafting typically reduces revision time.
   - Have each team member who is drafting use the same word processing product and version number to make it easier to revise and merge files.
   - Use writing support software such as outliners and idea generators to assist team writers when structuring reports.
   - Use groupware software to coordinate each team drafter's efforts with fellow team members.
   - Have the team's best writer write the first draft if the writing quality is crucial.

3. **Revising Documents**
   - Use writing support software such as spell checkers, electronic thesaurus, and grammar checkers (document analysis programs) to assist you in identifying areas that need revision.
   - Have each member read the entire document independently and suggest revisions.
   - Have all members meet and discuss areas where revision should be done.
   - If more than one team member drafted a portion of the document, recognize that there are likely variations in writing styles that needed to be identified.
   - Have one team member (preferably your best writer) make the recommended changes.
   - Have the writing team member who has the best English skills take a final look at the document for overlooked writing mechanics problems, such as grammar and punctuation, and consistency in the way that format elements (e.g., headings), names, and numbers are written.
   - Have one writing team member read the document to identify overlooked spelling errors and typos such as transposed letters.
   - Have one team member (preferably your best writer) make the revision and/or proofreading changes recognized.

COMMON REASONS FOR WRITING TEAM FAILURE

Common reasons for failure of writing teams include poor definition of the writing task (different interpretations of the document's purpose, different conceptions of the intended audience), too little planning time, little knowledge of each other's capabilities, unclear leadership, poorly planned meetings, and poor division of labor resulting in duplicated efforts.[52] Additional examples of reasons collaborative writing teams fail include:

- Writing team tries to complete its work too quickly (e.g., rushing the planning stage)
- Sporadic meetings
- Poor attendance, preparation, and participation at meetings—leading to resentment among members
- Too much leadership involvement and overly authoritarian leadership
- Too little leadership, which is especially problematic in noncohesive teams
- Writing team is too cohesive, which often results in groupthink
- Members function as individuals, instead of as a team

- An open communication environment is not established and maintained (too little communication and lack of trust, respect, and empathy)
- Inadequate time to merge individual drafts and to revise and proofread allowed in the project timeline
- Lack of confidence among some team members about other members' expertise
- Team members afraid to offer constructive criticism because of others who do not take constructive criticism well
- No procedures or poor procedures for assessing progress
- Lack of appreciation for each other's contributions
- Failure to record suggestions or incorporate changes suggested by members
- Difficulties with compromising
- Failure to control counterproductive displays of emotion such as irritation and anger

Good luck! Knowing the common reasons writing teams fail is a good start in the right direction.

FIGURE 14-10: TEAM WRITING TIPS

In her book *Business Communication Design*, Pamela Angell offers these practical tips for team writing. Several of these are listed below.

- Make sure collaborative writing is clearly oriented toward shared and defined goals.
- If a team leader is not designated beforehand, ask the team to choose a leader or coordinator. The leader needs to be a decent writer, but also needs to have a comprehensive vision of the project.
- The leader should be responsible for compiling the written input from each team member and sharing successive drafts with the team.
- Encourage the team to focus on substantive matters (facts, policies, processes).
- Make sure the writing produced has a uniform and consistent voice. Help the team understand that concerns for specific phrasing are often matters of individual taste.
- Whenever possible, avoid that most tedious exercise—team editing. Meetings set aside for final editing (revising) must be strictly time limited.

Source: Pamela A. Angell. Business Communication Design: Creativity, Strategies, and Solutions, 2nd ed. (Boston, MA: McGraw-Hill Irwin, 2007), 219–20.

DETERMINING WRITING TEAM WORK ASSIGNMENTS

© Bimbim/Shutterstock.com

Here are five strategies writing teams often use to coordinate work assignments.

1. **Parallel collaborators** divide the writing task into subtasks, so each writer writes a part of the document at the same time and sends his or her draft to each team member for comments. Each part is merged at the integration stage to produce a single document that sounds as though it was written by a single author. The limitations of this process are that each writer has a different perception of (1) his or her writing task and (2) what the other writers are producing. These different perceptions can produce different-looking and -sounding parts, which are difficult to meld into a whole, coherent document in the final stages. In addition, the review process is time-consuming. When each writer individually reviews a draft, there is no chance to negotiate and resolve issues. This increases the number of review passes before an issue is resolved, if it ever can be.

2. **Sequential collaborators** divide the writing task among the writers so that the output from one writer is passed on to the next individual who writes a new draft that incorporates his or her changes, and then passes that draft to the next writer who writes a new draft incorporating feedback from all team members. Successive drafts advance the team's thinking, with each complete revision more closely reflecting the team's goals. The last writer in the team does a near-to-final draft on which all writers give feedback. Someone does a final editing as the last step in document production.

3. **Reciprocal collaborators** work together to create a common document, by using online collaboration tools or software that allows several collaborators to simultaneously modify a central document from their computers. Lacking group software, a team could meet and compose a document together out loud, as one person writes down each person's contributions. Collaborators plan, draft, and revise a document in real time. They adjust their writing to take into account each other's changes.

4. **Independent collaborators** each writer drafts the entire document independently and simultaneously. In other words, each writing team member writes his or her version of the document independently. Once each writer has a complete document, team members meet to discuss each version and select the best one or a combination of the best portions as their working draft. The entire writing team then edits, revises, and proofreads the entire document.

5. The **single writer strategy** is an approach whereby the best writer on the team writes the entire document. The other team members serve in support roles: gathering information, developing graphic aids, and editing. The idea is to tap into each member's strengths and interests.

No matter which approach your writing team uses, it is important that each member perceives the work assignments to be reasonable and fair. Good advice is to determine work assignments based on individual strengths and interests.

GUIDELINES FOR BUILDING A SUCCESSFUL WRITING TEAM

The following guidelines present the problem-solving and decision-making skills needed in collaborative writing efforts. These skills will produce a writing team with a shared understanding of the document and the capability to produce it in a unified voice.[53]

- Maintain a writing team that coordinates its writing efforts before beginning to write the document, thus creating a sense of ownership among team members.
- Select writing team members with strong interpersonal and negotiating skills and a tolerance of others' perspectives.
- Ensure that each writer has the same purpose and audience in mind for the document.
- Determine what tasks each team member should undertake, manage communication concerning individually generated work, and integrate that work into the whole.
- Maintain open, ongoing communication to address division of labor, resource allocation, and integration of work. These decisions should be made in light of each person's abilities, areas of expertise, time constraints, and place in the organizational hierarchy.
- Maintain a high level of planning among team members regarding the organization of their work, plans, and schedules.
- Encourage face-to-face collaborative writing to successfully negotiate intentions, set constraints, generate ideas and text, and air conflicts during the collaborative writing process.

Writing team success depends on a number of things. With this in mind, here are some additional guidelines for collaborative writing team success.

- Be realistic about the amount of time needed to produce an effective document, especially the time needed for planning, revising, and proofreading.
- Get to know your fellow team members to build a sense of mutual accountability and team loyalty. By doing so, members typically work harder and the final document is better.
- Allow plenty of time to discuss problems and solutions during the planning stage.
- Plan well-structured meetings.
- All members attend meetings regularly and arrive punctually, are prepared and ready to participate. Even then, build in some realistic flexibility to deal with the inevitable time conflicts and illnesses.
- The leader is neither passive nor overbearing.
- Use co-leaders when the need is obvious.
- Encourage cohesiveness but avoid groupthink.
- Members respect and support each other's capabilities and contributions.
- The work is divided and assigned evenly, tapping into the best of each member's capabilities, strengths, and interests.
- Assess progress using agreed-on procedures.
- Maintain a good record of suggestions.
- Base changes on appropriate suggestions.
- Use feedback liberally to reduce misunderstandings and hard feelings.
- Control counterproductive emotions, such as anger.
- Hold how-are-we-getting-along meetings to routinely discuss personal concerns to support cohesive, positive efforts.
- Understand the need to compromise for the good of the team.

independent collaboration Independent writers who each draft an entire document independently and simultaneously; then they compare the versions

single writer strategy The best writer on the team writes the entire document.

FIGURE 14–11: INTERPERSONAL SKILLS THAT SUPPORT BUSINESS TEAM WRITING SUCCESS

Interpersonal skills play an important role in teams. Several skills that support effective business writing team efforts are listed below.

- Self-reflection skills
- Active listening skills
- Trust-building skills (reliability, responsiveness, empathy)
- Management of defensiveness
- Ability to process multiple perspectives
- Ability to distinguish others' interests, issues, and positions
- Ability to respond to others' communication, learning, and conflict styles
- Ability to manage one's assumption-making processes and to resolve conflicts that arise when wrong assumptions are made
- Decision-making skills
- Team-reflection skills (to encourage the awareness of composition processes, individual strengths and weaknesses, preferences, and personal perceptions of what constitutes "good writing")
- Ability to assume multiple roles throughout the writing project (sometimes simultaneously) including writer, editor, reader, consultant, stakeholder, manager, document designer, and publisher
- Ability to identify and prioritize audiences
- Ability to "satisfice": to select the "most satisfactory solution" within a specific corporate context

Source: K. Colen and R. Petelin. "Challenges in Collaborative Writing in the Contemporary Corporation." Corporate Communications: An International Journal, *9, no. 2 (2004): 136–45.*

Good luck! Even when we are familiar with how writing teams succeed, we are all human enough to overlook some of the techniques that would help us. Obviously it is best to incorporate as many of the above techniques as possible.

PLANNING FOR THE UNEXPECTED WHEN WRITING COLLABORATIVELY

Writing teams often experience unexpected problems. Some distractions can be anticipated and planned for, thus making them manageable and less disruptive. It is no secret that with more collaborative writing team experience, you become better equipped to anticipate and plan for surprises. Here are some examples:

- **Due to a number of circumstances, both individual team members and collaborative writing teams fail to meet deadlines.** Missed deadlines can usually be avoided in the planning stage by incorporating a cushion of extra days.
- **Documents or drafts are lost or misplaced.** This doesn't have to be your worst nightmare! Make extra copies and distribute them to team members routinely. Back up your work on your internal hard drive, on an external hard drive, and/or on a USB drive. You could also send it to yourself as an e-mail attachment.

- **A member of the writing team leaves.** A member is pulled from the team and put on another project team. Another leaves the company. Yet another member has an extended illness. The team should consider planning in advance on how they will deal with such a situation if it transpires.
- **The person requesting the document changes the project goal, requiring you to take a different approach to your task or to reformat the report.** Convene a meeting of the writing team to develop a revised plan and timetable.

No one wants to be surprised by the unexpected. That is all the more reason to do your best to anticipate and plan for unexpected collaborative writing issues.

FIGURE 14–12: COLLABORATIVE WRITING PROS AND CONS

Collaborative writing has its pros and cons, and it is helpful to know the more common among them. The pros appear to outnumber the cons, or we would not use writing teams as frequently as we do in U.S. organizations.

Collaborative Writing Pros
- Higher-quality documents due to a range of perspectives, knowledge, and skills
- Higher levels of motivation, because participants encourage each other to give their best
- Cowriters who operate as readers provide valuable feedback while the document is in the draft stage
- Opportunities for less-experienced writers to improve their skills and to become acculturated to organizational norms, values, and standards by working with more-experienced senior colleagues
- Enhanced work relationships among colleagues
- Higher levels of acceptance of their final document, because a range of staff or sections of an organization have worked together

Collaborative Writing Cons
- Coordinating a collaborative process is more complex than producing an individual document
- Collaboratively written documents typically take longer to write
- Collaboratively written documents are not necessarily higher quality
- Participants' personal communication, learning, and conflict styles can interfere with their receptivity to the ideas of others
- Personal conflict may arise because of agenda, status, and power differences, and lack of diplomacy and sensitivity
- The revising-editing process can continue ad nauseam, because so many people "own" the document
- Different participants with different writing styles can lead to stylistic inconsistencies that may—or may not—be eliminated in a final edit.

Source: K. Colen and R. Petelin. "Challenges in Collaborative Writing in the Contemporary Corporation." Corporate Communications: An International Journal, 9, no. 2 (2004): 136–45.

SUMMARY: SECTION 5— COLLABORATIVE WRITING

- Collaborative writing is an important way to generate documents in organizations.
- Face-to-face collaborative writing is difficult. Lots of work in the planning stage is essential to making a team writing project go well.
- Collaborative writing stages include planning the document and work assignments, proposing draft copies of the document, editing the document, and revising and proofreading the document.
- Coordinating the work of a collaborative writing team can be reduced to five strategies—parallel collaborators, sequential collaborators, reciprocal collaborators, independent collaborators, and single writer collaborators.
- Collaborative writing teams should plan for the unexpected.

ONLINE COLLABORATIVE WRITING TOOLS AND VIRTUAL WRITING TEAMS

As often happens with complicated projects, meetings are not satisfactory or not possible. In either case, available online collaborative writing tools are a staple in today's business place. These online writing tools range from **SharePoint** and wikis to blogs and collaborative software such as Google Drive.

Wikis are popular online collaborative work sites. A **wiki** is a type of website that allows participating users to add, remove, and edit content quickly and easily. Wikis are usually open source, meaning anyone can add information. A wiki is ideal for collaborative work because it uses a simple markup technique to denote changes. One of the key aspects to wikis is the rollback function that allows users to decide if older material is better than new material. If someone tries to add incorrect information, it is up to the wiki user community to notice and roll back the wiki page to the correct information. It is easy to see how this is well suited for projects that require input from multiple sources. Wikis have become a mainstream collaboration tool in many companies, and they continue to grow in popularity.

There are wikis for all sorts of topics and uses. One of the largest and most popular wikis, wikipedia.com, is an online encyclopedia created and maintained by users. There are topic-specific wikis created for various external uses, but not all wikis are public. Even when a wiki is public, there are some that are open for anyone to change without a review process or accountability. Then there are those that allow only registered users to add or change content. Because of wikis' openness, there are many critics who believe the information is of no value. While information from wikis is not considered scholarly material acceptable for formal papers or presentations, because of their wealth of information and ease of use, wikis are a good resource for informal learning.

SharePoint
An online site that aids writing teams with content and document management.

wikis
A website that allows participating users to add, remove, and edit the content of a document quickly and easily.

Wiki Advantages	**Wiki Disadvantages**

Wiki Advantages

- Greater transparency
- Increased participation
- Inexpensive
- Frees up e-mail
- Easy to use
- Keeps a record

Wiki Disadvantages

- Unstructured
- "Anyone" can edit
- Needs a dedicated manager
- Pages can become tangled and overgrown

Wikis provide a platform where the best ideas can prevail, and everyone can contribute to and benefit from them. Although quickly becoming one of the most popular collaboration tools, a wiki is not the only tool. A website formerly known as Writely.com was bought by search engine giant Google.com and transformed into Google Documents, or Google Docs for short. Wikis can be used for large-scale projects, whereas Google Docs is limited, so there are pros and cons to both applications, and they are intended for different uses.

Google Drive, which is the home of Google Docs, is a file storage and synchronization service that provides cloud storage to users. Google Docs is essentially an online word processing and spreadsheet application available for Google users that also allows users to manage presentations. It lets users upload or create text documents and spreadsheets into a personal set of online folders and then edit, save, and download them as needed. Google Docs also has a collaborative function. Users who create or upload their documents can enable certain users access to view the selected documents and/or edit them.

Blogs are an equally important form of online collaboration. Blogs are a more restricted form of collaboration. Where wikis have many creators and many viewers, blogs have one creator and many viewers. As the most-structured collaborative tool, a blogger can make a post and then many people can comment on it, adding suggestions and elaborating on certain points. It is then up to the blogger to incorporate those comments as he or she feels is appropriate. In this form everyone can participate, but ultimately one person has the final say. While blogging may not facilitate the same discourse of ideas, as SharePoint and wikis do, blogs do have their place.

Here are some additional online collaboration tool websites for your consideration—PBworks.com, BlueTie.com, ContactOffice.com, Projectspace.com, TeamWorkLive.com, and WebOffice.com. Other online collaboration tools you should consider using are Slack, Dropbox, Skype, Trello, and Google Hangouts.

Google Drive
Software that allows writing teams to create and edit documents online while collaborating in real time.

virtual writing teams
Writing groups that complete all or portions of their work virtually using support tools ranging from wikis and Share-Point to Google Drive and blogs.

WRITING IN VIRTUAL WRITING TEAMS

Collaborative writing support software systems, such as Quilt, SharedBook, and MULE, have provided significant productivity gains. When implemented in a tightly structured process, computer-supported collaborative writing can raise the productivity of a team of writers by allowing them to write at the same time, bringing multiple writers together for synchronous writing to shorten the time it takes to complete a document (since resolving issues that come up in various drafts is instantaneous), and increase the degree of ownership felt in the final product. [54]

© Manczurov/Shutterstock.com

USING WRITING TEAM SOFTWARE EFFECTIVELY

Writing team software can result in a more productive, effective outcome when it is used correctly. Here are some techniques that will help you maximize the benefits of using writing team software:

- Hold a face-to-face or chat discussion to develop the objectives and the general scope of the document before outlining the document
- Generate a document outline using a team outlining tool to develop main sections and subsections
- Interactively generate and discuss the document content in each section of the outline using parallel discussion with a team outlining tool
- Compose different parts of the document by subteams using a collaborative writing tool to organize and complete the first draft
- Take advantage of online feedback and discussion using either a collaborative annotation tool or a parallel discussion tool
- Perform a team review of each section, making suggestions in the form of annotations or comments. Section editors accept, reject, or merge suggestions to improve the document.
- The team completes a verbal walkthrough of the document. This stage requires heavy verbal and nonverbal interaction.

Even when using team writing software, talk is important to the collaborative writing process. Computer groupware experts recommend using a system that enables informal discussion as an integral part of the process. By discussing the written outline and text, the team gains insights that are fed into new writing in a progressive cycle of talk and text that leads to an effective final document.[55]

Since time spent working online simultaneously may be limited, writing teams should spend the greatest part of informal discussion time adding to and refining the document content.

The tightly structured process of using collaborative writing software can alleviate disputes that arise during collaborative writing sessions. The process itself helps to identify, focus, and structure the document and, thereby, resolve most disputes. However, when team members have different philosophical approaches to an issue, disputing team members can be assigned to a subteam to negotiate their differences and work out the issue without pulling the entire team off-task. After resolving an issue, subteam members can return to the full team with a compromise text that the full team willingly accepts.[56]

If you are either headed for the professional workplace or already there, participating on teams is in your future. Being an effective team member will serve you well and be appreciated by others. The article located at the URL in the margin serves to remind us of admirable qualities of effective team members.

SUMMARY: SECTION 6—
ONLINE COLLABORATIVE WRITING
TOOLS AND VIRTUAL WRITING TEAMS

- A wiki is a type of website that allows participants to add, remove, and edit the content quickly and easily. Multiple people come together to reach the best solution to a problem through edits and revisions.
- Other tools such as Google Docs and blogs are more restrictive forms of online collaboration, but they are more controlled as far as who can contribute and what they can do.
- Used effectively, collaborative writing support systems increase writing team productivity.
- Virtual writing teams are becoming more common and have some advantages over face-to-face writing. These include increasing team productivity because everyone can write at the same time and reducing the time it takes to complete a document because resolving conflicts among various drafts can be done in real time. Careful planning at the beginning is the key to a successfully completed document.

Ten Qualities of an Effective Team Player
http://www.dummies.com/how-to/content/ten-qualities-of-an-effective-team-player.html

Notes

1. Don Hellriegel, John W. Slocum Jr., and Richard W. Woodman. *Organizational Behavior,* 9th ed. (Cincinnati: South-Western College Publishing), 226; J. E. Henry. *Lessons from Team Leaders: A Team Fitness Companion.* (Milwaukee: ASQ Quality Press, 1998).

2. Debra L. Nelson and James C. Quick. *Organizational Behavior,* 4th ed. (Cincinnati: South-Western College Publishing), 302.

3. Hellriegel, 224.

4. Hellriegel, 228.

5. E. Rose and S. Buckley. *50 Ways to Teach Your Learner: Activities and Interventions for Building High-Performance Teams.* (San Francisco: Jossey-Bass, 1999).

6. Robert Kreitner and Angelo Kinicki. *Organizational Behavior,* 5th ed. (Boston, MA: Irwin McGraw-Hill, 2000), 426.

7. Steven L. McShane and Mary Ann Young Von Glinow. *Organizational Behavior.* (Boston, MA: Irwin McGraw-Hill, 2000), 228.

8. Ernest Stech and Sharon A. Ratliffe. *Effective Group Communication.* (Lincolnwood, IL: National Textbook, 1985), 8; Hellriegel et al., 229.

9. C. C. Snow, S. A. Snell, S. C. Davison, and D. C. Hambrick. "Use Transnational Teams to Globalize Your Company." *Organizational Dynamics,* 24, no. 4 (1996): 50–67; Leigh Thompson. *Making the Team: A Guide for Managers.* (Upper Saddle River, NJ: Prentice-Hall), 250.

10. Ibid., 253

11. Thompson, 253.

12. H. Dan O'Hair, James S. O'Rourke IV, and Mary John O'Hair. *Business Communication: A Framework for Success.* (Cincinnati: South-Western College Publishing), 294.

13. D. L. Duarte and Tennant Snyder. *Mastering Virtual Teams: Strategies, Tools, and Techniques That Succeed.* (San Francisco: Jossey Bass, 1999); Hellriegel et al., 229.

14. K. Kiser. "Tools for Teaming." *Training* (March 1999): 32–33.

15. Hellriegel et al., 231–32.

16. Ibid., 231.

17. Ibid., 232.

18. J. Lipnack and J. Stamps. *Virtual Teams: Reaching Across Space, Time, and Organizations.* (Somerset, NJ: John Wiley & Sons, 1997).

19. Kristen Bell DeTienne. *Guide to Electronic Communication.* (Upper Saddle River, NJ: Prentice Hall, 2002), 45.

20. Ibid.

21. Ibid., 45–46.

22. K. Kiser. "Building a Virtual Team." *Training* (March 1999), 34.

23. Ibid.

24. Ibid.

25. Kreitner and Kinicki, 428.

26. Thompson, 249.

27. Ibid.

28. Ibid., 250.

29. Based on J. J. Sosik, B. J. Ovolio, and S. S. Kahai. "Inspiring Group Creativity: Comparing Anonymous and Identified Electronic Brainstorming." *Small Group Research* (February 1998): 3–31.

30. R. Abrahams and B. Groysberg. "Lift Outs: How to Acquire a High-Functioning Team." *Harvard Business Review,* 84, no. 12 (2006): 133–40.

31. Bowditch and Buono, 144.

32. Ibid.

33. Hellriegel et al., 234.

34. *The Reader's Digest Great Encyclopedic Dictionary.* (Pleasantville, NY: Reader's Digest Association, 1975), 284.

35. Raymond S. Ross. *Small Groups in Organizational Settings.* (Englewood Cliffs, NJ: Prentice Hall, 1989), 168–69.

36. Hellriegel et al., 138.

37. Bowditch and Buono, 139.

38. S. C. Herring. *Computer-Mediated Communication: Linguistic, Social, and Cross-Cultural Perspectives.* (Amsterdam: John Benjamins, 1998).

39. I. L. Janis. *Crucial Decisions.* (New York, NY: Free Press, 1989), 56–63; I. L. Janis. *Groupthink: Psychological Studies of Policy Decisions and Fiascoes,* 2nd ed. (Boston: Houghton Mifflin, 1982); Nelson and Quick, 340; Ibid., Nelson and Quick, 244–45.

40. I. L. Janis, *Groupthink*, 56–63.

41. W. Whyman and R. Ginnett. "A Question of Leadership: What Can Leaders Do to Avoid Groupthink?" *Leadership in Action,* 25, no. 2 (2005): 13–14.

42. Stech and Ratliffe, 118.

43. Ibid., 119.

44. Ibid., 132.

45. Bowditch and Buono, 150.

46. G. M. Parker. *Team Players and Teamwork: The New Competitive Business Strategy.* (San Francisco: Jossey Bass, 1990), 33.

47. Hellriegel et al., 289.

48. Mary Beth Debs. "Recent Research on Collaborative Writing in Industry." *Technical Communication*, no. 4 (1991): 479.

49. K. Colen and R. Petelin. "Challenges in Collaborative Writing in the Contemporary Corporation." *Corporate Communications: An International Journal,* 9, no. 2 (2004): 136–45.

50. Debs, 480.

51. Ibid., 481.

52. Guidelines adapted from Marjorie Horton and Kevin Biolsi. "Coordination Challenges in a Computer-Supported Meeting Environment." *Journal of Management Information Systems,* 10, no. 3 (Winter 1993–94): 7–25. Retrieved from http://www.proquest.umi.com.

53. Guidelines adapted from J. F. Nunamaker, Robert O. Briggs, Daniel Mittleman, Douglas Vogel, and Pierre Balthazard. "Lessons from a Dozen Years of Group Support Systems, Research: A Discussion of Lab and Field Findings." *Journal of Management Information Systems,* 13, no. 3 (Winter 1996–97): 163–207.

54. Mike Sharples. "Using CommonSpace as a General Purpose Writing Environment." Retrieved from http://www.sixthfloor.com/sharples.html.

55. Susan Benjamin. *Words at Work.* (Reading, MA: Addison-Wesley, 1997), 18.

56. Scenario adapted from Karl Smart. "'The Wreck': Meeting the Needs of the Audience." *Business Communication Quarterly,* [63] (September 2000): 73–79.

COMMUNICATING IN BUSINESS MEETINGS

15

LEARNING OUTCOMES

After reading this chapter, you should be able to:

1. Discuss the reasons business meetings are held.

2. Describe a variety of business meeting approaches.

3. Discuss obstacles to effective business meetings.

4. Discuss the use and contents of effective business meeting agendas.

5. Describe techniques for communicating effectively in business meetings.

6. Describe how business meeting preferences differ around the globe.

© Robert Adrian Hillman/Shutterstock.com

BENEFITS OF LEARNING ABOUT COMMUNICATING IN BUSINESS MEETINGS

1. You increase your chances of receiving job offers as a result of communicating effectively in business meetings (interviews).

2. You increase your chances of persuading others of your ideas and goals by communicating effectively in business meetings.

3. You increase your chances of achieving your desired career and earning goals as a result of communicating effectively in business meetings.

4. You gain an appreciation of the value the business community places on your ability to communicate effectively in business meetings.

5. You gain an appreciation of how much meeting preferences vary globally and the importance of learning and adhering to international business partners' meeting preferences.

SELECT KEY TERMS

Conferences
Electronic Meeting Systems   Virtual   Agenda
Business Meetings
Holoconferences   GoToMeeting   Videoconferences
Conference Calls   NetMeeting
Web   Skype
Meetings

INTRODUCTION

Business meeting are held for a variety of reasons such as solving problems, developing policies, analyzing strategies, and discussing potential opportunities. Business meeting types range from face-to-face meetings and conference calls to virtual meetings. Of these, face-to-face meetings are considered to be the most effective when dealing with serious matters.

When developed properly and distributed in advance of business meetings, agendas are powerful tools for guiding business meetings. In addition, it is typically helpful when meeting participants arrive for meetings on time and prepared to contribute. Furthermore, it is typically helpful when meeting leaders keep discussions on topic, clear up misunderstandings, summarize participants' input, and keep meetings on schedule.

The intent of this chapter is to provide you with a clear understanding of the role of meetings in organizations and how to communicate effectively during meetings. These goals are realized through discussions regarding the following topics: the role of meetings in organizations, reasons for holding business meetings, business meeting approaches, obstacles to effective business meetings, business meeting agendas, and communicating effectively in business meetings. The information pertaining to the above-mentioned topics is reinforced by several student website resources including *PowerPoint slides, preview tests, chapter assessment tests, YouTube videos, interactive exercises,* and the *interactive glossary.*

THE ROLE OF MEETINGS IN ORGANIZATIONS

According to management communication authority James O'Rourke, "A **business meeting** is a gathering in which a purposeful exchange or transaction occurs among two or more people with a common interest, purpose, or problem."[1] As can be expected, some business meetings are necessary, while others are not. Similarly some business meetings are effective, while others are a waste of time due to ineffective leadership, poor planning, poor preparation, and/or lack of involvement.

business meeting
A gathering during which a purposeful exchange or transaction occurs among two or more people with a common interest, purpose, or problem.

© Stuart Miles/Shutterstock.com

During your business career, you will attend numerous meetings in the workplace and elsewhere. Millions of business meetings are conducted daily. Middle- and upper-level managers report spending somewhere between 40 and 70 percent of their work time in meetings.[2] Meetings' popularity, as a communication medium, is further evidenced by figures that suggest that most U.S. organizations spend between 7 and 15 percent of their personnel budgets on meetings.[3]

Don't you just love meetings? Unfortunately, most people do not. Those who do not enjoy meetings have typically attended one too many poorly planned and/or poorly conducted meetings, which formed their negative perceptions. Our reasons for liking or disliking meetings obviously vary. One reason that supports negative perceptions about meetings is tied soundly to poor productivity. According to survey results from The Microsoft Office Personal Productivity Challenge survey of 38,000 office workers across 200 countries, 71 percent of U.S. office workers feel meetings are unproductive, compared to 69 percent outside the United States. Obviously there is plenty of room for improvement when it comes to planning and conducting productive business meetings! The sad thing about such high percentages is that with the right knowledge and a professional attitude, we can all plan and conduct productive meetings. The information contained in this chapter can help us achieve those outcomes.

Like them or not, you will participate in meetings in the professional workplace. In fact, you will participate in lots of meetings, and the higher you advance, the greater the number of meetings. Sometimes you will chair the meeting and other times you will be a non-leader participant. It might seem odd to you that so many meetings are conducted despite a general disliking for them. You will see that meetings provide a setting in which the right mix of people can quickly accomplish objectives that typically cannot be accomplished quickly by people working individually. For example, a meeting to resolve a problem or consider an opportunity is best left in the hands of several people in a meeting. Together they hold the potential to generate more ideas, creativity, and analysis regarding the situation than a single individual could.

© Rawpixel/Shutterstock.com

Individuals and organizations typically benefit from well-planned, well-conducted meetings. Individuals also benefit from the pride associated with doing a good job—making valid, useful contributions. They also benefit from being viewed more favorably when choice projects are assigned, pay raises are distributed, and promotions are made.

Possessing a good attitude toward business meetings is important, as is the ability to communicate effectively in them. If you already have a good attitude about meetings, you are off to a good start. The information in this chapter should strengthen your knowledge of how to plan and conduct effective meetings. However, if your attitude toward meetings is negative or your requisite communication skills are lacking, it is time to make some serious changes. Without a doubt, your attitude about and your ability to communicate effectively in meetings will affect your career. Undoubtedly, your ability and willingness to communicate effectively in meetings will play a major role throughout your professional career. Thus, you stand to gain from putting forth the necessary effort to make meetings productive experiences for you and your coworkers. This chapter provides you with some opportunities to reflect on your attitude toward meetings and to learn ways to communicate effectively in them.

This chapter includes some discussion of obstacles to effective business meetings. As with teams, there is much to learn from knowing the obstacles to effective meetings. For example, knowing the obstacles gives us a clear sense of what to look for. In other words, they remind us of what not to do. A familiarity with the obstacles also gives us an opportunity to do some self-reflection. While reviewing the list of obstacles, most of us identify with one or more that we are guilty of. Or, we might not even know we were guilty of causing a problem. The good news is that by identifying which obstacles you are guilty of, you will probably not repeat them.

No matter your personal attitude toward meetings, you are challenged to give them your best effort. After all, during your business career you will be involved in a significant number of meetings, so why not make the best of them? By doing so, you will help your organization and earn the respect of your colleagues. In addition, you will enhance your job stability and career growth.

REASONS FOR HOLDING BUSINESS MEETINGS

Businesspeople hold meetings for a variety of reasons. Here are some of them. Business meetings are held to:

- Solve problems
- Discuss and analyze potential opportunities
- Develop policies
- Analyze strategies
- Hammer out budgets

Why Have a Meeting?
http://www.meetings.org/meeting1.htm

As you can see, there are valid reasons to hold meetings. No matter why they are held, business meetings all have one thing in common: communication. The central activity in all meetings is communication—lots of communication.

SUMMARY: SECTION 1— MEETINGS AND REASONS FOR HOLDING THEM

- A business meeting is a gathering in which a purposeful exchange or transaction occurs among two or more people with a common interest, purpose, or problem.
- Middle- and upper-level managers typically spend 40–70 percent of their work time attending meetings.
- Business meetings are typically held to talk about goals, hear reports, train people, inform people of what they are supposed to do and how they are to do it, build morale, reach a consensus, and analyze and solve problems.

BUSINESS MEETING APPROACHES

Business meetings are conducted using a variety of approaches. While face-to-face meetings are still commonplace, many of today's meeting methods involve technology. The most common electronic approaches include videoconferences, conference calls, and web conferences. **Electronic meeting systems** merge technology and participants in face-to-face meetings in productive ways.

FACE-TO-FACE MEETINGS

conference calls Phone conversations involving three or more people.

electronic meeting systems Software that provides meeting participants with a way to communicate simultaneously and sometimes anonymously via computers during face-to-face meetings, videoconferences, and web conferences.

© Monkey Business Images/Shutterstock.com

videoconferencing A videoconference involving two or more participants in two or more geographical locations viewing each other on screens or monitors.

videoconferences Virtual meetings between two or more participants in two or more geographical locations during which they hear each other and view each other on screens or monitors.

Face-to-face meetings are the most effective way to meet. Most participants in face-to-face meetings find this approach to be the most natural approach and the one that best promotes effective communication. Participants typically appreciate the full range of communication signals (spoken words and nonverbal cues) available to them. Participants tend to be more relaxed; thus, they participate more freely and creatively. As a rule, if your reason for holding a meeting is that the topic is important, controversial, sensitive, critical, or complex, take a pass on the electronic approaches and hold a face-to-face meeting. Do not compromise your goal by choosing a less-effective method.

VIDEOCONFERENCES

Videoconferencing was introduced at the New York World's Fair in the early 1960s. Since then, videoconferencing has increased in popularity due to technological improvements and reduced costs. **Videoconferencing**, as referred to here, is a conventional videoconference that involves two or more participants in two or more geographical locations viewing each other on wall-mounted screens or large-screen monitors. Videoconferencing enables meeting participants to meet simultaneously with real-time audio and video feed.

Holcombe and Stein offer a number of suggestions that contribute to effective **videoconferences**. Some of these include establishing a relationship with other participants before the videoconference; keeping a friendly, open expression; introducing yourself before you speak; listening carefully; and avoiding side conversations and doodling.[4]

In addition, create short, simple visual aids using a legible font and dark colors on off-white backgrounds (white backgrounds cause a glare).[5] Avoid wearing bright-colored clothing and bright jewelry. While videoconferences offer the advantage of relieving participants' need to travel to meetings, videoconferences are not as robust a meeting method as face-to-face. Participants do not enjoy the full range of communication signals (spoken words and nonverbal cues) available to them in face-to-face meetings. In addition, participants are not as relaxed; thus, do not share as freely and creatively as they do in face-to-face meetings.

WEB CONFERENCES (VIRTUAL MEETINGS)

Web conferencing allows meeting participants in different locations to meet over the Web. **Web conferences** are frequently referred to as *virtual meetings*. There are a large number of virtual meeting providers such as GoToMeeting, Skype, Zoom, MegaMeeting, TalkPoint, Microsoft Office Live Meeting, and ACT Conferencing, to name a few. Virtual meetings are conducted over a number of electronic devices such as PCs, laptops, netbooks, tablets, and smartphones. Even though these meetings are conducted over the Web and use different technologies, the videoconferencing suggestions presented in the previous section apply here as well.

web conferences Meetings conducted over the Web.

Skype Software that allows users to communicate with others by voice, video, and instant messaging over the Internet.

© nmedia/Shutterstock.com

The least-expensive approach to virtual meetings involves purchasing a webcam and Web conferencing software such as Adobe Connect, GoMeetNow, or LiveOn. Most of today's PC monitors, laptops, netbooks, tablets, and smartphones have built-in webcams. Web conferencing works well if one or two people gathered around a PC, laptop, or a tablet at one site conduct a virtual meeting with one or two people gathered around a PC, laptop, or tablet at another site.

A second popular approach to virtual meetings is to use a conferencing service. According to Jan Ozer, to do so "provides a collaborative environment, complete with application sharing and whiteboard, as well as audio and video."[7] This approach provides a full range of services that supports working meetings and collaborative group and team projects. **GoToMeeting and Zoom** are a popular videoconferencing services, You can learn more about these services by visiting www.GoToMeeting.com and www.zoom.us/. Companies such as Centra and WebEx also provide Web conferencing services.

GoToMeeting Remote meeting software that enables the user to meet with other computer users, customers, clients, or colleagues via the Internet in real time.

FIGURE 15–1: RUNNING SUCCESSFUL VIRTUAL MEETINGS

Julia Young of Facilitate.com offers six critical success factors for running a successful virtual meeting.

1. **Plan a viable agenda or series of agendas**. Virtual meetings should be short. Holding several short meetings is more productive than holding one long one. Keep the number of participants to a minimum. Large virtual meetings are unwieldy and do not support meaningful interaction and collaboration.

2. **Use technology effectively**. Be aware of the full range of electronic meeting tools and become proficient in their use. Make sure the technology you want to use is accessible to all participants and easy to use. Match electronic meeting tools with your meeting objectives.

3. **Prepare participants and pre-work**. Provide information to be reviewed and commented on ahead of real-time virtual meetings. Distribute meeting notices and remind participants of pre-meeting activities.

4. **Engage and focus participants**. This is a major challenge in virtual meetings! Here are some suggestions. Start meetings by asking participants to remove distractions (e.g., smartphones). Make multitasking difficult by keeping participants interested and occupied. Call on people often. Do frequent polling. Stick to the agenda. Keep the meeting on schedule.

5. **Build trust and social capital**. Here are some suggestions. Minimize power differentials—up front and throughout the life of the team. Create norms for areas that do the most to build trust and avoid distrust—handling conflict, fulfilling commitments, etc. Meet face-to-face at the start-up of an ongoing virtual team. Build in reasons to communicate with each other frequently.

6. **Maintain momentum between meetings**. Keep shared goals in sight. Track progress visibly via a dashboard which is a computer interface that displays key performance indicators. Celebrate achievements with rewards and awards. Recognize great, unforeseen performance. Check in with individuals frequently to express appreciation, identify issues, take a pulse, etc.

Source: From "Six Critical Success Factors for Running a Successful Virtual Meeting" by Julia Young. Copyright © 2009 by Facilitate.com. Reprinted by permission.

Although on the surface virtual meetings and videoconferences may appear similar, they have a couple of major differences. One difference between them is that the ability of virtual meeting participants to see fellow participants' nonverbal cues and the visual aids they display is restricted by the size of their viewing screens. Such restrictions are even more pronounced when participants split their screens to view other functions while meeting. Whenever possible, dedicate your full screen to the meeting. While large PC monitors are more prevalent now than in the past, they are small compared to the wall screens used for videoconferences. The viewing screens on most laptops, netbooks, and tablets are even smaller. And, the screens on smartphones are extremely small, as you are well aware.

Another difference between virtual meetings and videoconferences has to do with distractions. Videoconferences are typically held in dedicated rooms where outside distractions are limited. However, this is not always the case when virtual meetings are conducted in open-concept office cubicles on PCs and mobile devices. For example, participating in a virtual meeting at an airport would be complicated by competing sound and visual distractions. This is not to say you should not conduct virtual meetings in public places. However, know going into such meetings that they are going to be compromised by external distractions and that they are not private. Others nearby will know your business. The more important the meeting topic is and/or the more private conversation should be, the more you should consider a videoconference or a face-to-face meeting.

While virtual meeting participants benefit from not needing to travel to meetings, virtual meetings are not as robust as meeting face-to-face. Participants do not enjoy the full range of communication signals (e.g., visual nonverbal cues) that are available to them in face-to-face meetings. In addition, participants are not as relaxed; thus, they do not share as freely and creatively as in face-to-face meetings.

How to Run a Great Virtual Meeting
http://hbr.org/2015/03/how-to-run-a-great-virtual-meeting

© nmedia/Shutterstock.com

CONFERENCE CALLS

Conference calls link together three or more people for a joint phone conversation. This meeting method is popular due to the convenience, ease of use, and relatively low cost. Events such as the 9/11 terrorist attacks in the United States, combined with rising energy and travel costs, have fueled growth in the popularity of conference calls among businesspeople seeking safer, less-expensive meeting alternatives.

The visual elements of the videoconferences and Web conferences are absent in conference calls. Thus, participants cannot observe and learn from the visual nonverbal cues of others. In addition, sharing visual aids during a conference call is more challenging than doing so during face-to-face meetings and videoconferences. However, it is possible to share visual aids during conference calls using electronic whiteboards and other technologies. Possibly a more practical way to share visual aids involves simply distributing copies in advance of the meeting.

© bikeriderlondon/Shutterstock.com

Kristen Bell DeTienne, author of *Guide to Electronic Communication*, suggests that conference call leaders should:

- Inform participants about the day, time, duration, and purpose of the conference call
- Provide agendas and information relevant to the call
- Provide copies of visual aids
- Call from a quiet location
- Introduce all participants at the beginning of the conference call
- Make sure all participants are near a speaker and can hear.[8]

In turn, conference call participants should speak clearly, identify themselves, not interrupt others unnecessarily, pause regularly so others can comment, and listen carefully.[9]

At their best, conference calls are not as effective a meeting approach as face-to-face meetings, videoconferences, or Web conferences. However, they are inexpensive and convenient to set up—even on short notice.

ELECTRONIC MEETING SYSTEMS

Electronic meeting systems (EMS) provide meeting participants with a way to communicate simultaneously and anonymously via computers during face-to-face meetings, videoconferences, and Web conferences. Also referred to as *electronic meeting software* and *meetingware*, EMS first appeared as prototypes in 1979. The real catalyst behind EMS didn't occur until IBM and AT&T each awarded $1 million grants to the University of Arizona and the University of Maryland in 1985 and 1990, respectively, to fully develop the technology.

Using EMS technology, participants can simultaneously share their thoughts, ideas, reactions, and opinions anonymously using a combination of networked computers and electronic meeting software. Some groups even vote this way. EMS is an especially practical approach when the group wants a record of all ideas, when time is of the essence, when members are hesitant to speak up because people of higher organizational status are participating or they worry that others will find their ideas irrational, when discussions need to be kept on track, and when several ideas and alternatives are needed. On this last point, EMS lends itself nicely to *brainwriting*, defined here as the electronic equivalent of brainstorming. Brainwriting is an approach that results in meeting participants writing (keyboarding) their ideas and alternatives simultaneously. *Stormboard* is a really cool online brainstorming and collaboration platform that you should check out (http://stormboard.com/).

On the other hand, do not use an EMS when group efforts are just beginning and the goal is to establish rapport and emotional ties.[10] Establishing rapport and emotional ties typically requires some level of verbal and visual interaction not provided with electronic meeting systems.

TELEPRESENCE SYSTEMS

Telepresence systems offer marked improvements over traditional videoconferencing, thus providing meeting experiences that are more closely aligned with face-to-face meetings. Most telepresence systems use a series of screens much like those in the image below. The screens are positioned at sitting height or otherwise to create a more natural environment. Essentially it is as if your virtual meeting partners are right across the conference table from you.

Improvements in the ability to create and transmit real-time holograms of people from and to different locations mark even further improvement over traditional videoconferencing and traditional screen-based telepresence systems. Having holograms (3D images) of virtual meeting partners in the chairs across the table from you is truly the next best thing to having everyone in the conference room. Conference rooms equipped to support holoconferences are often referred to as immersion rooms or immersive rooms. This is pretty cool stuff no matter what it's called! This is a relatively new approach to conducting business meetings that, while yet to be commonplace, will become more common as costs come down and greater numbers of businesses learn about this approach and become aware of its benefits. The major benefit of holoconferences is that they capture the full range of qualities of face-to-face meetings while eliminating the need for travel. Holoconferences have the potential of one day eliminating the need for conference calls and videoconferences.

SUMMARY: SECTION 2— MEETING APPROACHES

- The most effective meeting approach is face-to-face, while the least effective method is PC conferencing.
- The most commonly used meeting approaches include face-to-face meetings, videoconferences, virtual meetings, and conference calls.
- Electronic meeting systems greatly enhance the effectiveness and efficiency of face-to-face meetings and videoconferences.
- Telepresence systems have recently been added to the list of meeting approaches, leading to improvement over conventional videoconferencing.

OBSTACLES TO EFFECTIVE BUSINESS MEETINGS

Many people walk away from a meeting feeling it was not as effective as they thought it should have or could have been. In some instances, we go into meetings with unrealistic expectations regarding how much can be accomplished and how much time is needed. Naturally, we walk away disappointed and frustrated. Other times, we enter meetings with realistic task and time expectations, only to be disappointed and frustrated because they were poorly planned, prepared, or managed by the meeting leader. Yet other times, our disappointment and frustration result from the level of meeting participants' involvement and behavior. Effective meetings don't just happen. They require well thought-out planning and preparation, as well as careful management. They also require that participants enter them with realistic expectations, be involved, and exhibit behaviors that support group efforts.

FIGURE 15–2: COMMON CAUSES OF FAILED BUSINESS MEETINGS

- Too many people are invited.
- Some people are invited even though they are not necessary.
- The meeting is poorly structured/organized.
- A poor meeting location is chosen (e.g., too small, poor lighting, insufficient ventilation).
- An ineffective meeting time is selected (e.g., right after lunch, 8 a.m. or earlier, 4 p.m. on a Friday).
- The meeting is too long. Face-to-face meetings should not exceed 90 minutes and virtual meetings should not exceed 30 minutes.
- The wrong meeting method is chosen. When meeting regarding important matters, hold face-to-face meetings. When meeting regarding routine matters, consider a conference call or Skype meeting.
- The meeting agenda contains too little information to guide the meeting adequately.
- The meeting agenda is not distributed in advance of the meeting, leaving the participants unprepared.
- The meeting chairperson and participants do not follow the agenda or do not stick to the recommended time limits for each topic.
- The meeting chairperson and/or participants with the highest job status monopolize the conversation.
- There is a hidden agenda.
- The meeting chairperson and participants do not trust each other.
- Suggestions and ideas are not welcomed.
- Participants create distractions (e.g., arriving late, leaving early, texting, conducting extensive side conversations).
- Participants are rude (e.g., overly argumentative, disrespectful, chronic interrupters).
- Participants are too nice (e.g., do not question others, avoid the rough issues).

Did any of these sound familiar? Have you ever been the guilty party, so to speak? Even if you have, being reminded of the common causes of failed meetings increases the odds that in the future we won't cause such problems as frequently.

Meeting Pet Peeves
http://www.amanet.
org/training/articles/
The-Top-Meeting-Pet-
Peeves-That-Plague-
Organizations.aspx

What bothers people about meetings? What are the obstacles to effective meetings? As you look at the reasons discussed here, remember that everyone involved in meetings may in some way compromise the outcome. Some obstacles to effective business meetings result from the actions, inactions, or behaviors of the leaders, while others result from the actions, inactions, or behaviors of the participants.

FIGURE 15-3: COUNTERPRODUCTIVE MEETING BEHAVIORS

Counterproductive Leader Behaviors

- **Allowing Interruptions.** Constantly interrupting others and allowing others to do the same.
- **Showing Favoritism.** Allowing select individuals to dominate the meeting.
- **Monopolizing the Meeting.** Doing most of the talking and forcing decisions.
- **Chastising Participants.** Ridiculing and embarrassing participants during meetings.
- **Losing Control.** Not sticking to the agenda or controlling negative behaviors.
- **Following the "Same Old, Same Old."** Meetings tend to follow a basic format of presentations or large group discussions that can get old. Leaders need to devise creative ways to get people involved to increase participation.[13]
- **Anticipating the Mindset People Have about Your Meeting.** Feeling that the leader has decided in advance what they will think, feel, and imagine could hinder their participation.[14]
- **Failing to Choose Carefully Whom You Want at Your Meeting.** Make sure there are good reasons for inviting each person.[15]

Counterproductive Participant Behaviors (Meeting leaders may also exhibit these behaviors.)

- **Displaying Apathy.** Communicating a lack of interest through one's words and actions.
- **Participating in Side Conversations.** Ignoring those speaking, distracting others, passing notes, etc.
- **Rambling.** Talking about either unrelated matters or matters so remotely related to the topic at hand that they are an ineffective use of meeting time.
- **Opposing or Blocking.** Constantly opposing others' ideas and opinions and picking them apart.
- **Seeking Attention.** Dominating the discussion for attention and recognition purposes.
- **Monopolizing Discussions.** Dominating the discussions.
- **Competing Too Aggressively.** Some competition leads to more creativity, ideas, and discussion; whereas too much threatens group efforts.
- **Acting Out Personality Clashes.** Allowing personality conflicts to override clear thinking, group responsibilities and protocol, and the ability to perform effectively.
- **Remaining Quiet.** Not offering suggestions or opinions and not involving oneself in discussions.
- **Clowning Around.** Finding humor in what is being said and in others at the expense of making valid contributions to the group efforts.

One study concluded that the most bothersome meeting characteristics include drifting off subject, poor preparation, questionable effectiveness, poor listening, participants' verbosity, meeting length, and lack of participation, in that order of importance.[11] Other obstacles to effective business meetings include holding unnecessary meetings, meeting when the same objectives could have been accomplished a better way, and failure to guide discussions.[12] Failure to develop thorough agendas, distribute them far enough in advance, and stick to them also interferes with successful outcomes, as does failure to start and end on time. Effectiveness is also compromised when leaders and participants do not eliminate, minimize, or control nonproductive, disruptive behaviors. A number of the more common counterproductive meeting behaviors are presented in Figure 15-3. Of course, you should avoid such behaviors yourself when participating in meetings.

Meeting leaders and participants who have difficult personalities also pose obstacles to effective business meetings. Prevalent among these are angry people, aggressive people, chronic interrupters, submissive people, and whiners. Angry people become an obstacle when they do not control their emotions. They typically upset fellow participants, invite defensive responses, and waste meeting time. Aggressive people come off as pushy, rude, and overbearing, posting obvious threats to meetings. Chronic interrupters are disrespectful and rude. They irritate fellow participants who want their thoughts heard without constant interruption. Submissive people are difficult in that they rarely have an opinion and are quick to give into others' ideas. Thus, they contribute little to meeting objectives. For whiners, nothing is ever right, and it seems their life's mission is to tell everyone else. After a short time, most people tire of whiners' complaints and no longer want to be around them.

© Volt Collection/Shutterstock.com

Unfortunately, we cannot snap our fingers and rid the world of angry, aggressive, or submissive people, chronic interrupters, and whiners. Some people just seem to be wired those ways, and the rest of us are challenged to figure out how to best communicate with them. And, that is how it is in the workplace. As much as we might wish difficult people would leave voluntarily, be transferred, or possibly even be dismissed, we are challenged to move forward with them as best we can. The suggestions presented in Figure 15-4 are helpful. Here a number of communication suggestions for interacting with angry, aggressive, and submissive people and chronic interrupters and whiners are presented. Some of these suggestions can improve communication with fellow meeting participants exhibiting difficult personalities, while others can improve communication if you are the person exhibiting one of these difficult personalities.

FIGURE 15-4: COMMUNICATING EFFECTIVELY WITH DIFFICULT PEOPLE

When the Other Person Is Angry
- Treat them with respect. Do not yell at them, cross your arms, get in their face, etc.
- Listen well. Show them you care about their concerns.
- Detach yourself emotionally so you do not respond with anger.
- Remain calm and task-oriented.
- Stay on topic. Do not get personal.
- Do not insist on getting in the last word and/or one-upping them.
- Know when to walk away if they are not calming down.

When You Are the Angry Person
- Walk away and cool down.
- Put what you want to say in writing, then walk away from it. Come back later and revise it. Then, have someone else read it before saying or sending it.
- Focus on your tone, word choice, and nonverbal cues so they do not communicate anger.
- Stick to the topic. Do not get personal.
- When it is over, let it be over.

When the Other Person Is Aggressive
- Detach yourself emotionally so you do not respond with aggression.
- Remain calm and task-oriented.
- Do not be pressured into a decision.
- Treat them with respect.
- Listen well.
- Do not let them dominate the conversation.
- Compliment the person's competence.
- Do not insist on getting in the last word and/or one-upping them.

When You Are the Aggressive Person
- Show respect to other people by not being aggressive.
- Force yourself to be an active listener. This reduces your aggression.
- Control your nonverbal cues (tone, volume, physical distance, etc.) so you are not communicating aggression.
- Do not abuse your job status when you outrank the others.
- Learn why you are a bully.
- If all else fails, see a therapist.

When the Other Person Is a Chronic Interrupter
- Set some rules up front. For example, remind everyone not to interrupt others when they are sharing and to save their thoughts until after the speaker is finished.
- If the individual insists on interrupting, consider responding with a comment such as "I would like to respond to that, but first I need to finish the point I was making." After a few such comments, most chronic interrupters get the point.

FIGURE 15-4: COMMUNICATING EFFECTIVELY WITH DIFFICULT PEOPLE

When You Are the Chronic Interrupter
- Ask others if you are a chronic interrupter. You may not realize you are.
- Practice exceptional listening. Good listeners hear other people out before forming opinions and responses, let alone interrupting them.
- Observe the speaker's facial expressions, tone of voice, and even the number of times he or she sighs. Such nonverbal cues will signal their disgust with your constant interruption.
- Set a goal to not dominate conversations by constantly interrupting others.

When the Other Person Is Submissive
- Fight the urge to dominate them, even though they are an easy target.
- Be supportive (e.g., be a good listener; project pleasant, supportive nonverbal cues). This helps them open up.
- Encourage/solicit their input. Compliment them on their contribution (e.g., That's a good idea.).
- Help them improve their confidence, like a good teacher or coach would.

When You Are the Submissive Person
- Do your homework so you are prepared to contribute.
- Give yourself a pep talk before meetings to build up your confidence.
- Be confident of the contributions you plan to share.
- Before meetings, practice a confident voice and confident facial expressions.
- Sit upright in in your chair. Doing so makes you feel more professional and confident. Do not slump or slouch.
- If the situation involves negotiations, be prepared to do some give and take. However, be careful that for you it is not mostly or all give and no take.

When the Other Person Is a Whiner
- Listen well and use supportive nonverbal cues.
- Show some empathy (e.g., I see your point.), but do not feed the individual's pessimistic mindset.
- Try to get the individual to see the other side of the story or situation.
- Jump in as often as possible with some "positive talk."
- Keep the conversation short.

When You Are the Whiner
- Get a grip! Being a whiner is unhealthy for you and, whether they tell you or not, others are not that thrilled to be around you. Whiners damage their careers, personal relationships, health, overall happiness, and quality of life.
- Do volunteer work at soup kitchens, homeless shelters, the Red Cross, etc. Doing so should reduce your whining by making you more thankful for what you have.
- Ask yourself why you are so pessimistic. Identify it, embrace it, then fix it.
- If all else fails, see a therapist.

Good luck with communicating effectively with meeting participants who have difficult personalities. Challenge yourself to move past your personal feelings about them, control your emotions, and do your best to communicate with them effectively. The suggestions presented in Figure 15-4 provide a good starting point, no matter whether the difficult person is someone else or is you.

BUSINESS MEETING AGENDAS

© Krasimira Nevenova/Shutterstock.com

Running Effective Meetings
http://www.forbes.com/sites/forbesleadershipforum/2014/02/05/seven-steps-to-running-the-most-effective-meeting-possible

Some people perceive an agenda as nothing more than a list of topics to be discussed and things to be accomplished during a meeting. However, the contents of an effective agenda surpass that. An effective meeting agenda includes the following information.

meeting agenda
A document that serves to guide a meeting.

- Date of the meeting
- Start and end times
- Meeting location, including maps to building, parking garage, and meeting room if necessary
- Name of the meeting leader, including title, department, division, branch, and organization
- Names of participants, including titles, departments, divisions, branches, and organizations
- Meeting objective and purpose
- List of topics to be discussed or things to be accomplished plus the purpose of each (e.g., share information, make a decision, arrive at a consensus). Sequencing the list from least difficult or controversial topics to most difficult and controversial topics typically nets more ideas and discussion because more people participate from the start of the meeting
- Allotted time for each topic to be discussed or thing to be accomplished
- Names of presenters for each agenda item if applicable

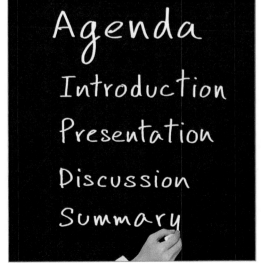

© Dusit/Shutterstock.com

FIGURE 15-5: SAMPLE AGENDA

Meeting Agenda

Date: November 18, 201__   **Time:** 10-11 a.m.

Location: Windcrest Tower, Room 943, 242 Tower Dr., Atlanta, Georgia
(maps attached)

Chairperson
Rachel Wilkens, IT director, Fly, LLC, 412 Windcrest Tower, 404-833-7241,
R.Wilkens@clarity.org

Participants
Erik Satler, HR director, Fly, LLC, 404-833-9838, E.Satler@clarity.org
Jill Stanton, Marketing director, Fly, LLC, 404-833-4862, J.Stanton@clarity.org
Stan Lee, Communications director, Fly, LLC, 404-833-1154, S.Lee@clarity.org

Purpose
To discuss potential virtual meetings technology updates

Topics:
- Conference Call Technologies (10-10:15)   discussion leader: Rachel Wilkens
- Videoconference Technologies (10:15-10:35) discussion leader: Rachel Wilkens
- Telepresence Technologies   (10:35-11)   discussion leader: Rachel Wilkens

Agendas play a critical role in ensuring that meetings are carefully planned, participants are informed and prepared, and meetings run effectively and efficiently. Agendas should be distributed to participants, along with related documents such as financials, far enough in advance to ensure they have time to review them, formulate ideas and opinions, gather needed information, and ask questions. In addition, well-thought-out agendas are instrumental in keeping participants on topic and meetings on schedule.

SUMMARY: SECTION 3— MEETING OBSTACLES AND AGENDAS

- Some obstacles to effective business meetings result from the actions, inactions, and behaviors of meeting leaders, while others result from the actions, inactions, and behaviors of meeting participants.
- Effective agendas are distributed in advance of meetings, not at the beginning of meetings.
- Effective agendas are more than a list of the topics to be discussed. For example, include the purpose of each topic and the amount of time to be allotted to each topic.
- Meeting leaders and participants should do their best to stick to the agenda during the meeting.

COMMUNICATING EFFECTIVELY IN BUSINESS MEETINGS

© Monkey Business Images/Shutterstock.com

Leaders of and participants in successful meetings understand the importance of effective communication in accomplishing goals. They practice communication techniques that support effective group interaction and the achievement of the goals. You are encouraged to learn and practice the communication techniques (presented below) that contribute to successful meetings.

COMMUNICATION TECHNIQUES FOR MEETING PARTICIPANTS

- **Practice the communication techniques that support team efforts.** The recommendations are as applicable to business meetings as they are to teams.
- **Come to meetings with well-thought-through suggestions and supporting information.**[16] By doing so, you will be better able to communicate clearly and convincingly.
- **Communicate with fellow participants in such a way that everyone believes his or her contributions are important to the meeting's objectives.** Otherwise, individuals will clam up and refuse to share their ideas and opinions.
- **Use visual aids when appropriate.** In addition to being preferred by meeting participants, visual aids increase participant understanding and retention, while reducing meeting length.
- **Eliminate and control counterproductive meeting behaviors that threaten effective communication** (e.g., interrupting others, showing favoritism, monopolizing, chastising, holding side conversations, rambling, opposing, dominating, silencing, clowning around, etc.).

FIGURE 15-6: EXCHANGING BUSINESS CARDS

Businesspeople frequently exchange business cards at meetings. Here are some examples of business card preferences around the globe.

- **Argentina.** Spanish on one side and your native language on the other side.
- **Australia.** English on one side and your native language on the other side.
- **Brazil.** Portuguese on one side and your native language or English on the other side.
- **Germany.** They should be in German.
- **India.** English on one side and Hindi on the other side. Present and receive cards with your right hand.
- **Japan.** Japanese on one side and your native language on the other side. Always start with the most senior member of the Japanese team. Present your business card with both hands, with the Japanese language side up and facing forward.
- **Saudi Arabia.** Arabic on one side and your native language on the other side. Do not keep your business cards in a pigskin card case or wallet since pork products are prohibited under Islamic law.
- **South Korea.** Korean on one side and your native language on the other side. Present with the Korean side up and forward. Present with the right hand. To convey respect, support your right hand with your left hand.
- **Turkey.** Turkish on one side and your native language on the other side. If your cards are in your wallet, do not keep your wallet in your back trouser pocket. (This is true in a number of other countries also!)
- **United States.** Information in English. Present it with either left or right hand. Can be kept in wallet in back trouser pocket.

Source: Terri Morrison and Wayne A. Conaway. Kiss, Bow, or Shake Hands: Sales and Marketing. (New York: McGraw-Hill, 2012), 6, 17, 27, 82, 94, 136, 178, 205, 221, 257.

COMMUNICATION TECHNIQUES FOR MEETING LEADERS

In addition to the techniques for meeting leaders presented in Figure 15-6, meeting leaders are encouraged to do the following.

- **Schedule meetings** at times when participants are most likely to communicate at the level needed to accomplish the meeting's goals. For example, it is unproductive to schedule an important meeting during early morning hours with people who are not morning people and thus are not fully alert. In addition, scheduling important meetings immediately following big lunches is a bad idea. Some people get drowsy, compromising the quantity and quality of communication. Finally, avoid scheduling Friday late afternoon meetings. Participants are anxious to get their weekends started, and thus may keep their comments too brief.
- **Understand the connection** between meeting length and the quantity and quality of communication. Essentially, participants reach a point where their contributions decline rapidly. For example, the communication exchange is best when face-to-face meetings do not exceed 90 minutes—about the length of a typical

movie. Most people tire more quickly and easily in videoconferences and other electronic meeting approaches; thus, they are most productive when they do not exceed 30 minutes.[17]

- **Distribute agendas** far enough in advance of meetings that participants understand the meeting objectives. This helps keep discussions on track.
- **Invite participants to share** their ideas, viewpoints, and concerns with you and fellow participants before the meetings.
- **Keep discussions on topic** so the objectives can be met and all participants have an opportunity to share their thoughts.

Leading Meetings Effectively
http://www.inc.com/eric-morgan/7-tips-for-leading-meetings-more-effectively.html

© Rawpixel.com/Shutterstock.com

FIGURE 15–7: MEETING LEADERS' ETHICAL RESPONSIBILITIES

Meeting leaders often have a real or perceived degree of power over participants. This is especially true when meeting leaders outrank their fellow participants. In such instances, meeting leaders must be careful not to use their leadership position or organizational rank unethically. Several recommendations to help leaders avoid such behaviors are listed here.

- Do not arrange the meeting so that all or the voting majority of the participants will automatically support your ideas and decisions, while opposing those of others.
- Do not monopolize meetings to force through your ideas and decisions.
- Do not be unnecessarily aggressive as a way to intimidate participants and force through your ideas or decisions.
- Do not show favoritism as a way to support your ideas and decisions.
- Do not display apathy when ideas and decisions with which you do not agree are presented.
- Do not ridicule and embarrass participants with whom you disagree.
- Do not rush the vote to force through your ideas and decisions.

FIGURE 15–7: MEETING LEADERS' ETHICAL RESPONSIBILITIES

Leading meetings ethically is typically appreciated and has the effect of motivating meeting participants to be involved.

- **Clear up misunderstandings** as they arise through further explanation, detail, and examples.
- **Communicate the link** between participants' input so everyone is clear on how the ideas and information are connected.
- **Summarize participants' input** where appropriate throughout and at the end of meetings.
- **Allow time at the end of the meeting** to clear up misunderstandings that may still exist.
- **Invite participants to share** with you and fellow participants their ideas, viewpoints, and concerns that arise following meetings.

Are you communicating as effectively in business meetings as you would like? If you have not already done so, reflect on the prominent role communication plays in business meetings. Identify the communication techniques presented above that you currently practice, as well as those you do not.

FIGURE 15–8: LEADING A SUCCESSFUL BUSINESS MEETING

Gilbert and Field suggest that pre-meeting planning and involving every person present at the meeting can lead to a successful business meeting. When leading a meeting, you may find the following tips from Gilbert and Field helpful:

- Prepare a timed agenda to assist in guiding the meeting—but be flexible. Decide how much time you are prepared to spend on each item and allocate time slots on the agenda.
- Include any related documents, such as financials, with your agenda.
- Allow time in your meeting for multiple responses. People naturally agree with the first good suggestion proposed. If you allow time for multiple responses, you may find that the first good suggestion was not the best one.
- Ensure that all agenda items are relevant to the purpose of the meeting.

© wongwk/Shutterstock.com

FIGURE 15-8: LEADING A SUCCESSFUL BUSINESS MEETING

- Prepare the process for each agenda item in advance. Once you have defined the desired outcome of the agenda item, consider how you can most effectively achieve it with the available resources.
- Too many meetings follow the same format of presentations or large-group discussion. Find ways to involve everybody. For example, a simple two-minute pairs exercise will give quieter members a chance to contribute and will produce a larger number of responses.
- Anticipate people's likely mindset about your meeting. Ask yourself what they are likely to be thinking, feeling, and imagining, and how this will help or hinder the meeting.
- Think carefully about who you want at the meeting. What are your reasons for inviting them? Reasons might include their knowledge or skills, their positive attitude, or their ability to motivate a group.
- Consider what other people need to bring or what you want from them. Is it something tangible like information or statistics, or something less tangible like a sense of humor or creativity?
- Ensure that everyone understands his or her role at the meeting.

Source: From "How to Generate and Think Creatively" by G. Field and A. Gilbert. Copyright © 2005 by British Journal of Administrative Management. *Reprinted by permission.*

Now that you know all there is to know about what to do and what not to do in business meetings, do not forget that businesspeople in other countries have their own ideas about what constitutes appropriate meeting protocol. Figure 15-9 provides several examples of differing preferences and offers a strong reminder to learn and respect international business partners' meeting preferences.

© Rawpixel.com/Shutterstock.com

FIGURE 15-9: CULTURAL DIFFERENCES—MEETINGS VARY AROUND THE GLOBE

- In **Italy,** most business meetings are conducted over lunch, which helps Italians get to know their foreign counterparts. The **French** also prefer luncheon business meetings.
- **Mexican** businesspeople prefer to meet in relaxed, neutral settings, such as a restaurant or at conferences where they can create an atmosphere of trust and friendship prior to discussing business.
- In **China,** do not interrupt others during meetings. In contrast, this is not a hard and fast rule in the **United States.**
- In the **United States,** business meetings are expected to start and stop on time, which is also true in **Denmark, Germany, Nigeria,** and **Venezuela. U.S.** businesspeople like to get right down to business, quite the opposite of Indian businesspeople.
- **Irish** businesspeople like to meet at restaurants and pubs or on the golf course.
- **Brazilian** businesspeople prefer not to meet over meals.
- In **Middle Eastern** and **Latin American** countries meetings start out with small talk as a means of getting to know communication partners. The same is true in **Australia.**

© diplomedia/Shutterstock.com

- **Finns,** like U.S. businesspeople, like to skip the small talk and get down to business.
- In **South Africa,** meetings are typically held in formal settings. The structure is similar to U.S. meetings, and 10–20 staff members are typically present.
- **Chinese** businesspeople expect that during meetings most of the speaking is done by the highest-ranking person representing the company. Subordinate participants should not interrupt one of higher rank, and the participants should show little emotion.18
- In **Saudi Arabia,** meetings do not always start on time and frequently run over schedule. Participants come and go as needed.

FIGURE 15–9: CULTURAL DIFFERENCES—MEETINGS VARY AROUND THE GLOBE

- **Japanese** and **Kenyan** businesspeople expect meeting participants will dress in business attire.
- In **Middle Eastern countries**, do not cross your legs such that the soles of your shoes are visible and remember that the left hand is considered unsanitary.

You are strongly encouraged to learn about and adhere to international business partners' meeting preferences. Doing so is a sign of respect and goes a long way in building strong relationships.

International Business Meetings
http://www.culturosity.com/articles/effective-meetings.htm

SUMMARY: SECTION 4— TECHNIQUES FOR COMMUNICATING EFFECTIVELY IN MEETINGS

- Communication techniques for meeting leaders and participants include practicing supportive communication, using visual aids, and eliminating counterproductive communication behaviors.
- Additional communication techniques for meeting leaders include scheduling meetings at productive times, limiting them to an effective length, keeping discussions on topic, clearing up misunderstandings, summarizing participants' input, and inviting participants to share their ideas, viewpoints, and concerns that come to mind following meetings.
- Meeting preferences vary around the globe.

Notes

1. James S. O'Rourke IV. *Management Communication*. (Upper Saddle River, NJ: Prentice Hall, 2001), 205.

2. Georganna Hall and Gemmy Allen. *The Internet Guide for Business Communication*. (Cincinnati: South-Western College Publishing), 101.

3. Taggart E. Smith. *Meeting Management*. (Upper Saddle River, NJ: Prentice Hall, 2001), 2.

4. Marya W. Holcombe and Judith K. Stein. *Presentations for Decision Makers*, 2nd ed. (New York: Van Nostrand Reinhold), 185–91.

5. Anne Fisher. "Lights! Camera! Action! How Can We Do a Great Videoconference?" *Fortune.com* (January 25, 1999): 1–2.

6. Ibid.

7. Jan Ozer. "The Next-Best Thing to Being There." PC Magazine (November 13, 2001): 32.

8. Mary Munter and Michael Netzley. *Guide to Meetings*. (Upper Saddle River, NJ: Prentice Hall, 2002), 41; Kristen Bell DeTienne. *Guide to Electronic Communication*. (Upper Saddle River, NJ: Prentice Hall, 2002), 82.

9. DeTienne, 86.

10. Ibid., 87.

11. Bradford D. Smart. "Achieving Effective Meetings—Not Easy But Possible." *Training and Development Journal*, 28, 1 (1974): 12–17.

12. Smith, 124, 141.

13. K. Roberts. "How to Generate Ideas and Think Creatively." *British Journal of Administrative Management*, (2005) 47: 28.

14. Ibid.

15. Ibid.

16. Marcia Zidle. "Meetings: Don't Just Show Up, Stand Out and Shine." *Professional & Technical Careers* (October 19, 1997): 2.

17. Holcombe and Stein, 187.

18. T. Morrison, W. A. Conway, and G. A. Borden. *Kiss, Bow, or Shake Hands: How to Do Business in Sixty Countries*. (Holbrook, MA: Adams Media, 1994).

PART 6

EMPLOYMENT COMMUNICATION: THE JOB SEARCH PROCESS

JOB SEARCH: PRE-INTERVIEW STEPS

16

LEARNING OUTCOMES

After reading this chapter, you should be able to:

1. Describe the seven steps in the job search process.

2. Discuss the role of internships in the job search process.

3. Describe how to research organizations and jobs effectively.

4. Describe how knowing the qualities employers look for in job candidates can affect the outcome of your job searches.

5. Describe how to write an effective cover letter.

6. Describe how to write an effective résumé.

7. Discuss the role of electronic approaches in the first five steps of the job search process.

© donskarpo/Shutterstock.com

BENEFITS OF LEARNING ABOUT THE PRE-INTERVIEW JOB SEARCH STEPS

1. You improve your ability to make a career choice that results in you doing the type of work that best suits you.

2. You improve your chances of working for the type and size of organization that best suits you in the geographic location you desire.

3. You increase your chances of achieving your desired career and earning goals.

4. You know how to write effective cover letters and résumés.

5. You understand the role of electronic approaches in the first five steps of the job search process.

SELECT KEY TERMS

INTRODUCTION

There are seven steps to the job search process ranging from making the right career choice to developing effective follow-up correspondence. The seven-step process can be likened to the "chains and links analogy" which suggests that a chain is only as strong as its weakest link. This suggests, in turn, that you should not reduce your employment offers by performing one (or more) of the job search steps poorly. If done correctly, the job search process is very time consuming and should be started early.

You can increase your odds by being familiar with skills (e.g., communication, interpersonal, and problem-solving skills) and personal attributes (e.g., honesty, politeness, open-mindedness) employers look for and then communicating those you possess to them in cover letters, résumés, and job interviews. In addition, communicate your merchandising qualities, which are those qualities that make you an "exceptional fit" for a job or organization.

The key elements of cover letters include communicating your general familiarity with the organization, your awareness of the organization's needs, and that you possess the qualifications and desire to meet the organization's needs. Key elements of résumés range from the key words section and career objective to work history and education.

The intent of this chapter is to provide you with information about Steps 1–5 of the job search process—making the right career choice, locating job prospects, researching organizations and jobs, writing cover letters, and developing résumés. The role of electronic approaches in the job search process is also discussed. These goals are realized through discussions about the first five steps of the job search process: Step 1—Making the Right Career Choice, Step 2—Locating Job Prospects, Step 3—Researching Organizations and Jobs, Step 4—Writing Persuasive Cover Letters, and Step 5—Developing Effective Résumés. The information pertaining to the above-mentioned job search steps is reinforced by several student website resources including *PowerPoint slides, preview tests, chapter assessment tests, writing mechanics rules and guidelines, YouTube videos, interactive exercises,* and the *interactive glossary.*

JOB SEARCHES: YOU WILL LIKELY PARTICIPATE IN SEVERAL

Before reading about the seven steps of the job search process, take time to consider the role the information presented in chapters 16 and 17 will play throughout your working years. The point is that the information you are about to read will be important to you for a long time to come! This is because you will likely conduct several job searches throughout your working years. Few people build their entire careers around one employer. Most people work for several employers, switching careers one or more times during their working years. Current predictions suggest that once you graduate from college you will likely work for eight different employers in three to four different careers before retiring.

In addition, you will most likely retire at age 75 or even later based on your circumstances and financial needs. Even

today, not all U.S. workers retire at age 65, the age long thought to be the norm although the current average retirement age is 66. In 2009 approximately 3 million Americans bypassed retiring in their mid-60s and were working into their 70s, 80s, and some beyond and this number is growing. In a 2012 survey, 25 percent of respondents said they did not plan to retire until age 70 or older.[1] In another 2012 survey, 9 percent of respondents indicated they planned to work full-time and 44 percent part-time after retiring.[2] Currently, 54 percent of Americans age 60+ say they plan to work past age 65. Centenarians (people age 100+), numbering approximately 100,000 in the United States, also make up a portion of the workforce. Some even work more than one job. For information about centenarians, visit www.adlercentenarians.org. Of course, the above retirement projection of 75 may change significantly if medical researchers are successful in slowing the aging process as some predict will happen. The outcome, then, may well surpass age 75!

Why do so many workers choose to work beyond the conventional retirement age? Some people continue to work into their senior years due to financial necessity. Others do so for the personal satisfaction they get from being around others. Still others say they enjoy what they are doing. Some say they like where they work, while others need the health insurance. There are even some who continue to work because they are afraid retirement will be boring. Finally, there are some who continue to work because they have known people who died shortly after retiring, and they do not want to chance the same outcome! Retirement may one day be right for you, but for many it is not an option or is something they simply choose not to do.

Hopefully you will make good career choices and find yourself enjoying what you do for a livelihood. Matters such as retirement age then will not necessarily be of concern to you, whether you retire at age 75 or 105 or never. Life is short enough as it is and to waste a single day of it working at a job you do not find satisfying would be most unfortunate. Think about it. It makes sense.

THE JOB SEARCH PROCESS—AN OVERVIEW

The **job search process** refers to the seven steps you are encouraged to take when seeking professional employment. The steps are listed here.

The Seven Steps in the Job Search Process:
1. Making the right career choice
2. Locating job prospects
3. Researching organizations and jobs
4. Writing persuasive **cover letters**
5. Developing effective résumés
6. Interviewing convincingly
7. Developing effective follow-up correspondence

If you are preparing for a new career, you will want to begin with Step 1 (making the right career choice). If you have already made your career choice or are currently established in your chosen career, begin the job search process with Step 2 (locating job prospects).

Have you ever heard the expression "A chain is only as strong as its weakest link"? If you have worked with chains on construction sites, farms, or elsewhere, you know the seriousness of this expression. In comparison, the job search process is only as successful as its weakest step. Successful job searches are more likely to occur when you devote an adequate amount of attention and effort to each step.

We often weaken our job search efforts by not expending the necessary time and effort to perform the process effectively. Furthermore, sometimes we base career choices on potential earning power rather than on what we suspect we would be successful at and happy doing. Other times, we don't bother to research companies or customize cover letters and résumés. Still other times, we weaken our job search efforts by sending/transmitting poorly developed cover letters with well-written résumés. Sometimes, we even forget to brush up on our communication skills and manners before going into interviews. And if we do get interviews, many of us simply don't bother to send thank-you notes or check back with recruiters following interviews. Then we wonder why potential employers don't call us in for interviews or make job offers. Get the idea? The process is not only about getting a job; it is about putting adequate time, attention, and effort into the seven steps of the job search process. Doing so increases your chances of landing a job with a company you really want to

Job Hunting Mistakes
http://money.usnews.
com/money/blogs/
outside-voices-
careers/2014/05/15/
its-not-them-its-you-
10-major-mistakes-
youre-making-in-your-
job-hunt/

SUMMARY: SECTION 1— THE JOB SEARCH PROCESS

- The job search process refers to the seven steps job seekers are encouraged to take when seeking professional employment.
- The job search process includes the following seven steps: (1) making the right career choice, (2) locating job prospects, (3) researching organizations and jobs, (4) writing persuasive cover letters, (5) developing effective résumés, (6) interviewing convincingly, and (7) developing effective follow-up correspondence.
- The effectiveness of the job search is contingent on the degree of attention and effort given to each step in the job search process.

---

work for doing the type of work you want to do in the geographical area you prefer. Many people around the world don't have the luxury of making such choices. You do! Don't allow the opportunity to slip through your hands.

STEP 1: MAKING THE RIGHT CAREER CHOICE

Step 1 is the most important step in the job search process. Making the right career choice is likely to have the most pronounced effect on the success of your job search, your career, and your overall happiness. Making a career choice that is right for you will motivate you to put forth the time and effort necessary to complete the remaining six steps of the search process effectively. Furthermore, by choosing a career path that is right for you, you significantly increase the likelihood that you will enjoy your chosen line of work and be successful at it. In addition, you should be a fairly happy, optimistic individual in your personal life as well as at work. Making the right career choice will affect both your quality of life and standard of living.

© Kheng Guan Toh/Shutterstock.com

YOUR CURRENT CAREER CHOICE STATUS

You may have already made your career choice. If you have and you are happy with your choice, congratulations! You can still use the career choice material presented in this section to confirm your choice. On the other hand, you may have made your career choice but still have some doubts. If so, you are not alone! Use this material, then, to confirm your tentative choice and/or explore other career paths. Then too, you may have no idea what career path to follow. If this is your situation, then the career choice material presented in this section will help you move in the direction of making a sound decision.

THE BASIS FOR A GOOD CAREER CHOICE

The basis for a good career choice is a good fit. A **good fit** implies not only that you know what you want to do for a livelihood, but you are right for it and it is right for you. Making a career choice that is a good fit is somewhat analogous to choosing a lifelong mate. Most of us hope that over the years we will continue to love our career as we do our mate and will remain enthused with and committed to both for the duration.

Be careful not to rush your decision. Avoid gravitating to a career simply because job openings abound in that line of work, the earning potential is high, and/or on the surface it looks attractive. While all these things may be true, choosing the career path that is right for you requires more exploration.

HOW TO DETERMINE WHAT IS RIGHT FOR YOU

Start out by focusing on you—your needs, your interests, your abilities, your values, and your work ethic. Below is a list of some considerations to reflect on when deciding what is right for you.

- The degree of stress and challenge you can realistically tolerate
- The degree of autonomy you enjoy
- The amount of variety you need
- The opportunity for creativity a job offers
- Your need to make a difference with your work
- Your preferred social environment[3]

Other examples of personal preferences include:

- The amount of money you really need to earn to make to be happy and meet your financial obligations.
- The degree to which you are comfortable taking risks
- Your openness to traveling for work
- Your willingness and ability to make effective decisions
- Your attitude about teams and your ability to work effectively on them
- How much you enjoy working with people
- Your attitude about involuntary and voluntary job transfers
- Your desire to work around others
- Your attitude regarding telecommuting
- Your willingness and ability to supervise and manage
- Your leadership skills, experience, and potential
- How much career growth you require and how often you require it

Take time to reflect on your preferences as thoroughly as possible before choosing a career. It would be a good idea to visit your campus counseling and testing office and undergo some career profile tests. You don't want to wake up one day only to discover that you invested a considerable amount of time, effort, and money preparing for a career that you cannot succeed at and that you find unrewarding. For example, preparing for a career in business would not be realistic if you do not enjoy taking risks, making decisions, attending meetings, making presentations, and supervising people. You want to know what you are getting into and whether it is right for you.

Unfortunately, it is possible to determine your response to each of the items listed above and still make a poor career choice. To reduce the probability of this happening, choose a career you think is important, you will enjoy, you are capable of succeeding at, and to which you can commit for the long run.

Another way to determine which career paths are right for you is taking personality tests that link personality traits with specific careers. The article mentioned in the side margin contains a personality test you might find of interest.

A practical way to test whether you are on the right course with your career choice is to participate in one or more internships or co-ops. These give you first-hand work experience in the career path you are considering, which may either confirm your career interests or remind you that it is in your best interest and beneficial to your overall happiness to choose a different path.

Does Your Personality Fit Your Job?
http://time.com/3915807/personality-fits-job/

LEARNING ABOUT CAREER OPTIONS

There are many ways to learn about careers. Some of the more popular ways include visiting your campus career center, talking with college advisors, and talking to professors. In addition, attending career exploration classes and workshops as well as student and professional association career workshops can help steer you in the right direction. Talking to people who currently work in the career area you are considering is also helpful.

Numerous websites contain a wealth of information about careers. A sampling includes www.careers.org, www.iccweb.com, www.quintessentialcareers.com, www.assessment.com, and www.careerbuilder.com.

Another career discovery option involves exploring current and projected trends impacting career opportunities. For example, the health care industry is growing in the United States as the large post–World War II baby boom population ages. In addition, people are living longer and enjoying more active retirements, which support related career paths.

© dizain/Shutterstock.com

Finally, consider a real hands-on approach to learning about careers by doing one or more internships or co-ops. There is no substitute for actually performing the work. While it is useful to hear people talk about "a day in the life" of their career, it is even better to work around these folks and observe firsthand "several days in their career."

© Krasimira Nevenova/Shutterstock.com

FIGURE 16–1: INTERNSHIPS AND CO-OPS

Internships and co-ops provide practical ways to learn firsthand about careers that interest you. In addition, they provide you with practical work experience in your major field of study and often open doors to job opportunities. For example, interns are typically offered fulltime jobs with the companies they have interned with if they have proven themselves to be capable and reliable. In addition, some companies hire almost exclusively from their intern/co-op pools because they know these candidates' capabilities and personal qualities, having worked with them.

Other reasons to consider doing an internship or co-op include:
- They provide a practical way for you to determine if the major you chose is the right choice for you.
- They provide you the opportunity to expand your professional network.
- They provide you a practical way to grow your professional skills and knowledge.
- You can often earn academic credit for participating in them.
- They provide you with networking opportunities you wouldn't have otherwise.
- They are often paid (salary or hourly rate) positions, although they rarely offer benefits.
- The practical work experience you gain adds persuasive strength to your résumé in the eyes of most recruiters.

For additional information about internships and co-ops, visit your campus internship office or career/employment center. Also consider visiting www.internships.com. Internship resources for students, employers, and faculty are provided at this site.

IS MAKING A CAREER CHOICE A ONCE-IN-A-LIFETIME DECISION?

You may not want to hear this, but you will likely make several career choices during your life. Not only will you likely change employers more often than your parents and grandparents did, you will also make more career changes. The typical reasons for changing employers within the same career path include better pay, better benefits, career growth opportunities, downsizings, firings, layoffs, desire to learn more, personality conflicts, work schedule, and the need to move geographically for various reasons. In turn, the most common reasons we change careers include career burnout, lack of career growth opportunities, career becomes obsolete, desire to be "one's own boss," pay, benefits, desire to try something new, transfers, firings, layoffs, and downsizings.

© iQoncept/Shutterstock.com

While frequent job and career changes are disruptive for most U.S. workers, they have become a fact of life for many. After all, we are living and working longer, and seem to be a bit more restless than our predecessors. So, it should come as no surprise that most of us are not starting and ending our professions with the same employer or even in the same career for that matter. Of course, what is often said about changing employers is also true about changing careers: Looking for another job (and another career) is typically best done while you are still employed if for no other reason than financial stability.

SUMMARY: SECTION 2— MAKING A CAREER CHOICE

- Making the right career choice is likely to have the most pronounced effect on the success of your job search, your career, and your overall happiness.
- The basis for a good career choice is a good fit, which suggests that you know what you want to do for a livelihood, you are right for it, and it is right for you.
- Determining what career is right for you involves identifying a career that you think is important and that you will enjoy, at which you are capable of succeeding, and to which you will remain committed.
- Sources for learning about career options include career advice books, magazines, and websites; professors and college advisors; campus career opportunities centers; workshops; jobs; internships and co-ops; those with established careers; and observing trends impacting career choices and opportunities.
- Most Americans revisit the career choice step more than once during their working years, sometimes by choice, other times out of necessity.

STEP 2: LOCATING JOB PROSPECTS

The second step in the job search process is identifying job openings that are a good fit for you. Some of your peers will attempt to simplify this step by identifying any and all openings their schedule allows them time to locate. You are encouraged to approach Step 2 with more focus. By now, you have invested too much time, energy, and money into choosing

and preparing for your career to merely throw your future randomly to the four winds. Instead, seek job prospects that are a good fit for you as well as for your target employer.

KNOW WHAT YOU WANT

Before spending a single minute of your limited time trying to locate job prospects, know what it is you really want to do. You made a start on this by choosing your career. However, there are many questions you should ask yourself that will ultimately help you secure a job doing exactly what you want with the type of organization that suits you. For example, are there career growth opportunities? Will the position I am applying for have me doing the type of work I want to do? What type of organization do I want to work for (e.g., nonprofit, for-profit, public company, government agency, etc.)? What size organization do I want to work for (e.g., small, mid-size, large)? TheLadders.com surveyed job seekers regarding the size of company (based on number of workers) they prefer to work for. Twenty-seven percent reported that they preferred to work for a company with fewer than 200 employees, 21 percent preferred a company with 201–500 employees, 28 percent preferred 501–1,000 employees, and 24 percent said 1,001 or more employees.[4] What's your preference? Which geographical areas are you open to living in either temporarily or long term? Are you receptive to some business travel and, if so, how much? Are you receptive to telecommuting and, if so, how much? If you are uncertain regarding such questions, you are strongly encouraged to do one or more internships to help clarify where you stand on such matters. For obvious reasons, knowing the answers to such questions will help you direct your job search more effectively. In turn, your ability to land a position that mirrors your preferences will greatly influence your happiness and overall quality of life.

FIGURE 16–2: JOB SEARCH SOURCES FOR MILITARY VETERANS

Transitioning from the military to the civilian workforce can be challenging. With this in mind, here is a sampling of job search sources that focus on helping veterans make the transition.

- *Expert Résumés for Military-to-Civilian Transitions,* Wendy Enelow and Louise Kursmark
- *Out of Uniform: Your Guide to a Successful Military-to-Civilian Career Transition,* Tom Wolfe
- *Military-to-Civilian Résumés & Letters: How to Best Communicate Your Strengths to Employers,* Ronald L. Krannich and Carl S. Savino
- Job Search: Marketing Your Military Experience, David G. Henderson
- The article "10 Resources That Help Veterans Get Jobs" offers several good options for veterans transitioning from the military to the civilian workforces. You can access this article at http://www.skilledup.com/articles/resources-help-veterans-get-jobs.

WHAT IF YOU DON'T KNOW WHAT YOU WANT TO DO?

What if you find yourself, degree in hand, but not thrilled with the career choice you made, or you recognize that you chose a major that is not marketable? In either case, you sense that marketing yourself is going to be a struggle. While such situations are difficult to accept, there is help out there. Good examples include Donald Asher's books *How to Get Any Job: Life Launch and Re-Launch for Everyone under 30 (or How to Avoid Living in Your Parents' Basement)* and *How to Get Any Job with Any Major: A New Look at Career Launch and Re-Launch for Everyone Under 30.*

START EARLY

Don't wait until the last minute to look for job prospects. Start at least one year before your anticipated college graduation date, if not sooner. Job search activities such as identifying job prospects, researching potential employers and jobs, writing cover letters and résumés, and preparing for interviews are time-consuming activities when approached seriously.

TECHNIQUES AND SOURCES FOR IDENTIFYING JOB PROSPECTS

Numerous techniques and sources are available for identifying job prospects. These are broken out below into two categories—electronic approaches and traditional (non-electronic) approaches.

Electronic Approaches Electronic job search approaches are popular and appealing to many job hunters due to their ease, time efficiency, and relatively low cost. Even though the benefits of electronic approaches are obvious, you are discouraged from using them exclusively. Why? The reason is that all job prospects cannot be located using electronic approaches. The same is also true of traditional job search approaches. By using both, you will be less likely to overlook job opportunities.

© kpatyhka/Shutterstock.com

Because the Internet is so vast in its offerings, it is important to know exactly what career you are looking for before you start an Internet search. Robert Lock, author of *Job Search*, got 71,800,000 matches when he Googled *"jobs."* Lock suggests knowing the names of occupations you're interested in, the skills you can honestly claim, the geographic areas you prefer, and the names of organizations that interest you before starting an online job search.[5]

Without a doubt, social media sites like *LinkedIn* and *Facebook* are popular in our personal lives, in the public sector, and in businesses. Such social media sites are also helpful in the job search process. However, the content we post on them can also be detrimental to our job search efforts if we are not careful. Figure 16-4 expands on this very important reminder.

FIGURE 16-4: SOCIAL MEDIA SITES CAN WORK AGAINST YOU IF YOU ARE NOT CAREFUL!

Be careful what you post, download, or say on social media sites such as *LinkedIn*, *Facebook*, and *Twitter*. Once that information goes out into cyberspace, it is out there for the taking. Recruiters routinely scan such sites and if what they see or read leaves them questioning your judgment, behavior, maturity, and/or character, you may not be considered a viable job candidate. Examples of questionable judgment, maturity, and character include stories and images ranging from those involving violence, drug use, and excessive drinking to those of a sexual nature and of unethical behavior and attitudes. Other candidates limit their job opportunities when they post information regarding serious personal issues such as recovery programs and divorces or dangerous recreational pastimes like mountain climbing and skydiving. Still other candidates remove themselves from the running when they post negative and critical comments about prior or current employers. Some have even had job offers pulled due to questionable posts made after receiving job offers. For example, shortly after receiving a job offer an individual tweeted a friend that the job was not really his dream job and he would be moving on to a better job in a few months. The recruiter who hired him read his tweet and pulled the job offer.

Some individuals view social media sites as private, personal-use sites where anything goes. Unfortunately some of these individuals forget that once they post to the Internet, the content is likely indexed in one or more search engines and is available for all to access in perpetuity. This is where recruiters come into the mix. In growing numbers, recruiters visit social media sites to identify potential job candidates who they believe would be a good fit for their organizations and to screen job applicants.

Approximately half of recruiters today also screen job applicants' social media sites because they are able to do so both quickly and inexpensively. They look specifically for content that either speaks to a sound job candidate or suggests a job candidate who exhibits questionable behavior, judgment, maturity, or character. Hopefully you are in the first camp! That is not the case for all, however. About one third of recruiter visits to job applicants' social media sites lead to rejections either before job interviews, following job interviews, or even after job offers are made as evidenced by the previous example. Furthermore, about two-thirds of recruiters say they did not hire a job applicant based on information they viewed about him or her online.

Whether you have one or more social media sites, ask yourself if the image that you are presenting to your friends and family will also be viewed favorably by recruiters, assuming your family and friends find it acceptable. If not, make some changes while you still have time! What we are talking about here is your *digital personal identity*. What's yours? It will very likely affect you in the professional workplace—hopefully in good ways.

Most job search books on the market today devote either a portion or all their coverage to information on electronic job searches. If you turn to books for such information, make sure the information is current. Such information is always subject to change, so you need to do your best to stay current.

Many organizations of all types and sizes have phone job lines available to job seekers. Among the more familiar are Opportunity Network and Executive Connection. Check at your college or university career/employment center for other listings and phone numbers.

There are also electronic versions of traditional job fairs. A number of interactive virtual career/job fairs are advertised routinely. Look for that information at your university career/employment center, in trade journals, or in the employment section of your local newspaper.

Electronic job boards that can be accessed on the Internet are common. Here are some examples: www.indeed.com, www.monster.com, www.glassdoor.com, www.careerbuilder.com, www.jobbankusa.com, and www.TheLadders.com which specializes in positions starting at $100K+.

The U.S. government also provides assistance to job hunters. Visit the U.S. Bureau of Labor Statistics website at www.bls.gov, where you will find a list of fastest-growing jobs. Of course, this information changes constantly.

Another electronic job search option to consider is tweeting. Many big companies now list job openings on Twitter. This approach provides a way for companies to identify job candidates who have social networking skills if that is the type of candidates they are targeting. If you are going to use this approach to locate job opportunities, make a good first impression by developing professional messages. Otherwise, you will likely be passed over for being too casual. One of the downsides of this approach, however, is its growing popularity. Just as online job boards have become crowded, so has the Twitter approach.

Among other websites that can assist you in the job search process is Job-Hunt. The Web address for this site is http://www.job-hunt.org/.

In addition, LinkedIn, eHarmony, and TerraTal target services that better match job seekers and employers predominately in the areas of skills requirements and personality traits.

Traditional Approaches While electronic job search approaches are popular, don't overlook the need to also use one or more traditional approaches when searching for jobs. For example, answering job advertisements in professional and trade journals, local business journals and newspapers, and national newspapers such as *The Wall Street Journal* is encouraged. Your college or university career center is another good source, as is making direct contact with employers by phone, mail, or in person.

Another traditional approach involves seeking out the services of employment agencies. One of the most effective traditional approaches grows from networking. This involves

Matchmaker for Job Seekers and Employers
http://working-womanreport.com/dallas-startup-terratal-plays-matchmaker-for-job-seekers-employers/

learning of job leads from friends, family members, fellow members of professional associations, former coworkers, and even current coworkers. Finally, do not overlook job fairs. It is likely your college or university sponsors such events periodically. City- and community-wide job fairs are also commonplace. Dress appropriately, take a stack of résumés, and be prepared to shake a lot of hands.

As can be expected, there are also job search books that you may find helpful. Good examples include *What Color Is Your Parachute? A Practical Guide for Job Hunters and Career Changers* (Richard N. Bolles) and *Knock 'Em Dead: The Modern Job Search—How to Succeed* (Martin Yate).

FIGURE 16–5: COMMON JOB SEARCH MISTAKES AMONG NEW COLLEGE GRADUATES

Landing good jobs with good employers in favorable geographic locations is challenging. If you have identified such attractive opportunities, it is safe to say quite a few fellow job hunters have also. In addition, such employers can be more selective when deciding which job candidates to call in for interviews and which will receive job offers. Essentially, you really need to be on your game and avoid making job search mistakes that will take you out of the running. What follows is a list of common job search mistakes among new college graduates.

- Not fully utilizing their university career center. At some universities such services are available for free or for a minimal charge following graduation.
- Not developing custom cover letters for each potential employer.
- Not developing custom résumés for each potential employer.
- Not using professional-sounding voicemail messages.
- Not using social media sites wisely. For example, some new college graduates fail to capitalize on the networking potential of LinkedIn. Then, there are others who compromise their job search efforts by having questionable content on social media sites such as Facebook.

Each of the above mistakes can be avoided. Knowing what they are is a good start!

HOW WHITE-COLLAR JOB HUNTERS CAN IMPROVE THEIR CHANCES

Landing an interview and eventually a job offer with an organization you find attractive because of the company's reputation, geographic location, or otherwise are always challenging. Typically other job hunters identify the same attractive job opportunities that are on your radar. Professional job hunting is all about navigating your way through the competition by marketing yourself more skillfully and successfully than others.

No one can guarantee that you will always land one of the jobs you target. However, the suggestions presented in Figure 16-6 will improve your chances, no matter whether the job market is dismal, rosy, or somewhere in between.

FIGURE 16–6: HOW TO IMPROVE YOUR JOB SEARCH CHANCES

- Diversify your job search approaches. Here are some recommended approaches:
  - Do not wait until you graduate from college to begin your job search
  - Do internships and co-ops, even if they are unpaid.
  - Familiarize yourself with campus career center services and resources.
  - Attend internship fairs, career fairs, and job fairs.
  - Conduct online searches, but not to the exclusion of other approaches.
  - Post a "hire me" website (e.g., *TwitterShouldHireMe*).
  - Conduct traditional (non-Internet) searches.
  - Make some cold-call searches.
  - Use recruiting agencies.

FIGURE 16-6: HOW TO IMPROVE YOUR JOB SEARCH CHANCES

- Practice basic job search skills. (See Steps 1–7 in chapters 16 and 17.)
- Conduct targeted job searches using tailored cover letters and résumés.
- Target industries and employers that are stable or growing or that appear to have good growth potential.
- Target job opportunities in geographic locations that are economically stable or are experiencing economic and job growth.

© Thinglass/Shutterstock.com

- Be flexible in regard to pay, benefits, work location, type of work, type of company, and size of company, especially during tough economic times.
- Be willing to consider a temp position or contract work as a way to earn some money and get your foot in the door.
- Don't miss important persuasive opportunities. In cover letters, résumés, and interviews:
  - Share your merchandising qualities.
  - Communicate awareness of skills that employers desire in employees.
  - Communicate awareness of attributes that employers desire in employees.
  - Share success stories.
- Communicate that you are technologically current and savvy. For example, social media skills (e.g., *LinkedIn, Facebook*) are valued particularly in areas such as public relations, sales, marketing, and technology.
- Be well spoken whether at job fairs and career events or during phone conversations and interviews.
- Make sure there are no typos or other errors in your written correspondence with recruiters. The adage "One spelling error on a résumé is too many" is true.
- Communicate community involvement in your résumé and during interviews.
- Be an active member in one or more professional associations. It is even better to be an officer.
- Remove content from social networking sites that leaves recruiters questioning your behavior, judgment, maturity, and/or character.

FIGURE 16–6: HOW TO IMPROVE YOUR JOB SEARCH CHANCES

- Especially during recessionary times, expand your job search strategies (e.g., "hire me" websites) as a means of locating potential job opportunities. Jay Conrad Levison and David E. Perry, authors of *Guerrilla Marketing for Job Hunters*, suggest that during economic downturns job hunters need to be part detective, part consultant, and part salesperson.[7]
- Do volunteer work as a way to network and keep your skills current.
- Seek work in public service programs such as AmeriCorps, the Peace Corps, or Teach for America as a way to network and keep your job skills current.[8]
- Further your education and training (e.g., licenses, certificates, Master's degree).
- Network via social media (e.g., *LinkedIn, Facebook*) as well as in traditional ways.

© *dolphfyn/Shutterstock.com*

FIGURE 16–7: TIPS FOR NETWORKING ON SOCIAL MEDIA

- Make sure your content is interesting and/or relevant.
- Stay professional. Do not get too casual or personal.
- Use the tools to your full potential. For example, use the "join groups" feature on LinkedIn.
- Don't spam.
- Don't post too frequently.
- Don't post the same information across different platforms.
- Keep your content fresh.
- Follow up with connections.

Source: From "How to Network via Social Media" by Susan Ricker. Copyright © 2012 by Careerbuilder. Reprinted by permission.

16 Things You're Doing All Wrong on LinkedIn
https://www.yahoo.
com/tech/16-things-
youre-doing-all-
wrong-on-linke-
din-89653015534.html

LinkedIn is a highly recommended media platform for professionals interested in networking and improving their hiring potential. To achieve these goals, however, one needs to do more than simply establish a LinkedIn account. There are things you need to know if you want LinkedIn to be an effective resource for you. In addition, you might recall the "Social Media Writing Suggestions" section in chapter 5 of this textbook. A number of LinkedIn writing suggestions, including several that pertain to developing LinkedIn profiles, are included in this section. It is also good to know what not to do, as well as what to do, to benefit from LinkedIn's potential.

Effective job searches require patience, persistence, flexibility, and effective job search skills. More often than not, there is a correlation between the outcome and how much effort and time we put into our job searches. Be both realistic and smart about how you go about conducting your job searches.

STEP 3: RESEARCHING ORGANIZATIONS AND JOBS

Step 3 of the job search process involves researching organizations and specific job openings. Some job hunters skip this step of the search process, claiming they do not have the time for it. You are strongly encouraged to find the time.

GENERAL ADVICE

Start early. Researching organizations and jobs typically takes more time than most of us would prefer. Thanks to a host of electronic approaches, you can conduct some of this research more efficiently and thoroughly than was possible in the past. A variety of electronic and non-electronic techniques for researching organizations and jobs are discussed next.

Be realistic about how many organizations and jobs you can research adequately. If you target only a few potential employers, the likelihood that you will research them effectively is fairly high. If you target too large a number, you will likely research some too little and skip others altogether. So, what is the right number and how many are too many? Your level of commitment to the job search process and your career, your schedule, and your research skills will determine how many employers you can research effectively.

Begin with an understanding of what items of information you want to gather. Then, gather similar information regarding each organization and job. Develop a checklist. This helps you in two ways. First, you are less likely to overlook information needed to make a sound decision. Second, you are better able to compare employers and jobs, which will help you determine which are right for you.

The information collected can get disorganized quickly. Develop a system to help you keep all that information organized. For example, set up a separate manila or pocket folder for each organization or job. Or, you might scan the information you collect into your computer and organize the files in a way that works efficiently and effectively for you.

Basically, you should learn as much about the position you are applying for and the employer as possible. Such information ranges from job descriptions to company size, growth strategies, and product lines.

WHAT WILL YOU GAIN FROM RESEARCHING ORGANIZATIONS AND JOBS?

There is no denying that researching organizations and jobs involves a major time commitment. However, the benefits are enormous! Two major benefits follow.

First, from a short-term perspective, your efforts set the stage for you to be more competitive in the remaining steps of the job search process. How so? Imagine for a moment that you are a recruiter who needs to fill a position. You hope to recruit and hire someone who will be a good fit for both the job and your company. You will most likely be persuaded by job applicants who are familiar with the job and your company and are also a good fit. As a job applicant, the only way you can write truly persuasive cover letters and résumés and be persuasive in interviews is to first do your homework—research jobs and organizations.

Second, from a long-term perspective, your efforts will help you determine in which organizations you will most likely achieve the level of career happiness, growth, and success you desire. As was mentioned earlier in this chapter, choose a career that you think is important, doing what you enjoy, doing work that you can do well, and doing work to which you will remain committed. Think similarly when choosing organizations and jobs. In other words, researching organizations and jobs will help you decide which employers are the right fit for you.

TECHNIQUES FOR RESEARCHING ORGANIZATIONS AND JOBS

There are many techniques for researching organizations and jobs. These techniques can be easily broken into two categories—traditional approaches and electronic approaches.

Traditional Approaches A good starting point for researching organizations and jobs is your college or university career center. Journals such as trade journals, local business journals, *The Wall Street Journal*, *BusinessWeek*, and *Fortune* are also good sources. There are also directories such as *Dun and Bradstreet's Million Dollar Directory* that you can access at your campus career center or library. Still other sources include visiting with people at trade shows, job fairs, professional association meetings, and chambers of commerce. You might even want to pick up some firsthand knowledge by doing an internship or co-op with a company or simply hiring on part time or during the summer. In addition, networking always holds the potential of netting information.

Many job search books contain a wealth of information regarding specific companies and industries you may be interested in. You can find many of these books in your campus career center and libraries.

Electronic Approaches Electronic approaches also offer opportunities for researching organizations and jobs. A good starting point for learning about your electronic choices is to visit your college or university career center.

Most organizations have a website where you can find at least some of the information you seek. If you cannot track down a Web address in your career center, ask your professors or conduct an Internet search. Information about companies can also be located at www.companiesonline.com, www.corporateinformation.com, www.hoovers.com, and www.sec.gov.

Finally, keep in mind the electronic job search books mentioned in Step 2. They also contain a wealth of information on researching organizations and jobs.

SUMMARY: SECTION 3— LOCATING JOB PROSPECTS AND RESEARCHING ORGANIZATIONS AND JOBS

- Seek out job prospects that are a good fit for you and your target organizations.
- Don't wait until your last term in college to begin these phases of the search process. They are time-intensive activities.
- Use networking, the Internet, your college career center, recruiting firms, newspapers, and trade journals to locate prospects.
- Be aware of the negative perceptions most recruiters attach to questionable materials on social networking sites such as LinkedIn, Facebook, and Twitter.
- Be realistic about how many organizations you can research effectively.
- Determine exactly what information you are seeking. Develop a checklist.
- Constantly remind yourself how important researching organizations and jobs is to your ability to persuade recruiters to grant you a job interview and offer you a job.
- Use networking, the Internet, your college career center, books, part time and fulltime jobs, internships and co-ops, newspapers, trade shows, local business journals, mainstream business journals (e.g., *Fortune*), newspapers, and trade journals as means of researching organizations and jobs.

© Rawpixel.com/Shutterstock.com

OPPORTUNITIES TO PERSUADE RECRUITERS

Steps 4 and 5, which focus on writing cover letters and résumés, are the next two steps in the job search process. Before moving on to these steps, some discussion about two persuasive opportunities that hold the potential of enhancing the effectiveness of cover letters and résumés is needed.

Let's use a hypothetical situation to set the stage. Imagine you learn about a job opening in a company that interests you. Luckily, the opening is a good match with your interests and qualifications. As you can imagine, many other people are also interested in the job. In fact, you are one of 487 people who eventually apply for the job. In this not-so-uncommon scenario, what can you do to improve the persuasive power of your cover letter and résumé to increase the chances you will be asked to interview? Assuming most of the candidates have similar educational and training backgrounds, work histories, licenses, etc., what will separate you from the pack?

In such situations, focus your efforts on developing persuasive, error-free cover letters and résumés. To do so, forgo the urge to make your cover letter and résumé stand out by using gimmicks such as bright-colored paper and nontraditional fonts. Instead, communicate your understanding of the skills and personal attributes employers are looking for in job candidates. Another persuasive technique involves merchandising yourself in your cover letter and résumé. This involves showing recruiters that you are familiar with what they value in the way of skills and personal attributes.

SKILLS EMPLOYERS LOOK FOR IN JOB CANDIDATES

Knowing which skills employers look for in job candidates can work in your favor during the search process and beyond. That is the first step. Then, identify which of these skills you possess. Finally, emphasize the desired skills you possess in your cover letters, résumés, and interviews. By doing so, you tell recruiters two things: that you know what skills they are looking for and that you have them. Such an approach goes a long way in persuading employers to grant you an interview and make you a job offer. The following list contains several skills valued by most business employers.

- Communication skills—especially listening, presentation, and writing skills
- Interpersonal skills (people skills)
- Social skills
- Teamwork skills
- Analytical skills
- Decision-making skills
- Problem-solving skills
- Leadership skills
- Management skills
- Technology skills

So, where do you locate information on the skills employers want in job candidates? In addition to the information presented above, look for such lists in newspapers, business journals, etc. Such information is also shared frequently in job skills workshops, classes, and books. Other sources include college career centers, recruiting firms, and job websites such as www.monster. com. When determining specific skills desired by specific employers and industries, talk to businesspeople familiar with the company and browse company literature. Do not overlook your own work experience and common sense when determining the skills employers want in candidates. Finally, as you move through your career, stay current regarding employers' desired skills. Some will remain the same over the years, while others will come and go.

In summary, do not give up an opportunity to persuade potential employers that you are the right choice. Emphasize their desired skills that you possess in your cover letters, résumés, and interviews.

PERSONAL ATTRIBUTES EMPLOYERS LOOK FOR IN JOB CANDIDATES

Knowing which personal attributes employers look for in job candidates can work to your favor during the search process and beyond. That is the first step. Then, identify which of these you possess. Finally, emphasize the desired personal attributes you possess in your cover letters, résumés, and interviews. By doing so, you tell recruiters two things: that you know which personal attributes they value and that you possess them. Such an approach goes a long way in persuading recruiters to grant you an interview and make you a job offer. The following list contains several personal attributes recruiters routinely look for in job candidates. Employers want job candidates who are:

- Honest
- Ethical
- Polite
- Tactful

- Self-motivated
- Self-starters
- Flexible/adaptable
- Open-minded
- Ambitious
- Willing to take risks
- Creative thinkers
- Receptive to business travel
- Aware of and open to other cultures

FIGURE 16–8: EXECUTIVES' PERCEPTIONS OF THE TOP 10 SOFT SKILLS

While "hard skills" such as analytical skills, computer skills, etc., are valued in job candidates, you do not want to overlook the value placed on "soft skills" such as interpersonal skills and several others presented below.

- **Communication.** Listening, written, oral, presentation
- **Courtesy.** Manners, etiquette, business etiquette, graciousness, says please and thank you, respectful
- **Flexibility.** Adaptable, willing to change, lifelong learner, accepts new things, adjusts, teachable
- **Integrity.** Honest, ethical, high morals, has personal values, does what's right
- **Interpersonal Skills.** Nice, personable, sense of humor, friendly, nurturing, empathetic, has self-control, patient, warm, has social skills
- **Positive Attitude.** Optimistic, enthusiastic, encouraging, happy, confident
- **Professionalism.** Businesslike, well-dressed, good appearance, poised
- **Responsibility.** Accountable, reliable, gets the job done, resourceful, self-disciplined, wants to do well, conscientious, common sense
- **Teamwork.** Cooperative, gets along with others, agreeable, supportive, helpful, collaborative
- **Work Ethic.** Hard-working, willing to work, loyal, has initiative, self-motivated, punctual, good attendance

Source: Marcel M. Robles. Business Communication Quarterly (75, 4). Copyright © 2012 by Sage Publications, Ltd. Reprinted by permission of Sage.

Six Soft Skills Everyone Needs
http://www.monster.com/career-advice/article/six-soft-skills-everyone-needs-hot-jobs

So, where do you locate information about the personal attributes employers look for in job candidates? In addition to the information presented above, look for similar lists in newspapers, business journals, etc. Such information is also shared frequently in job skills workshops, classes, and books. Other sources include information presented in lists provided by college career centers and recruiting firms and at jobs websites such as www.monster.com. Another good online source is www.values.com since personal attributes also encompass values. When determining personal attributes that specific employers and industries want, talk to businesspeople familiar with the company and browse company literature. And, don't overlook your own work experience and common sense when determining the attributes employers value in job candidates. Finally, stay current as to what personal attributes employers want as you move through your career. While some will remain the same, others will change.

In summary, do not overlook the opportunity to persuade potential employers that you are the right choice. Emphasize desired personal attributes you possess in your cover letters, résumés, and interviews.

PROMOTING YOUR MERCHANDISING QUALITIES

Merchandising qualities are those qualities that make you an "exceptional fit" for a job or an organization. Your first task is to identify your merchandising qualities that are an exceptional fit for the career you are preparing for. Once you have identified your merchandising qualities, mention those that are applicable in your cover letters, résumés, and job interviews as frequently as possible. Keep in mind that the merchandising qualities you highlight for each potential employer will differ somewhat because jobs and employers differ in their needs.

merchandising qualities
Promoting those qualities that make you an "exceptional fit" for a target job or organization.

At this point, you might find some examples useful. Individuals who wish to perform public relations work should emphasize their communication and human relations training, along with work experiences involving public contact. Individuals applying for computer programming or information systems positions should emphasize their familiarity with those programming languages, operating systems, networks, etc., used by their potential employers. An individual who wants to work for the federal government would be encouraged to emphasize government internships (e.g., regional offices, Capitol Hill, the White House) as well as community volunteer work. Accounting majors would be wise to emphasize such qualities as a strong GPA, their CPA license, internship experience, ethical behavior, and a willingness to work long hours when necessary. Job hunters who are fluent in two or more languages should emphasize their language skills, foreign travels, willingness to travel, and willingness to relocate abroad when applying with companies that conduct global business.

In summary, do not overlook the opportunity to persuade potential employers that you are the right choice. Emphasize applicable merchandising qualities you possess in your cover letters, résumés, and interviews.

Searching for professional positions is all about persuasion. With this in mind, do not overlook the persuasive opportunities discussed in this section.

SUMMARY: SECTION 4— PERSUASIVE OPPORTUNITIES

- View cover letters and résumés as being persuasive documents, not merely listings of your education and work histories.
- Be familiar with the skills employers look for in job candidates.
- Merchandise yourself by promoting those qualities that make you an exceptional fit for a target job/organization.

STEP 4: WRITING PERSUASIVE COVER LETTERS

Step 4 of the job search process involves developing persuasive cover letters. While some people refer to them as job application letters, they are usually called cover letters because they are placed on top of résumés. Generally speaking, cover letters are paired with résumés for the purpose of convincing recruiters to grant job interviews. Specifically, the purpose of cover letters is to convince recruiters to read job candidates' résumés.

© Keith Bell/Shutterstock.com

WHAT PURPOSES DO COVER LETTERS SERVE?

Understanding the purposes of cover letters from both the job hunter's and recruiter's perspectives will help you appreciate the role they play in the job search process. From a job hunter's perspective, a cover letter has two purposes: (1) introduce his or her résumé and (2) persuade recruiters to grant him or her a job interview. From a recruiter's perspective, a cover letter has four purposes: (1) provide information not presented in the accompanying résumé, (2) determine if the candidate is familiar with his or her organization, (3) better determine if the candidate is a good fit for the organization and a particular job opening, and (4) decide if he or she will look at the résumé.

SHOULD YOU ALWAYS INCLUDE A COVER LETTER?

No, but you should most of the time! If you know for a fact that a recruiter does not want you to send a cover letter with your résumé, don't do so. Some recruiters simply don't want to take the time to glance at one more piece of paper. It is unfortunate that some do not desire a cover letter, thus robbing you of one more opportunity to persuade them to grant you a job interview.

Most résumé databases do not accept cover letters. Similarly, most college career centers do not accept cover letters for your files. When you are not supposed to submit a cover letter, a lot obviously rides on the quality of your résumé.

The good news is that most recruiters do prefer you submit a cover letter with your résumé because of the benefits mentioned above. This is also standard practice when answering a "help wanted" ad. If you know that a recruiter prefers a cover letter or if you do not know where he or she stands on the issue, submit one. These are the most ideal situations for you because you are able to submit two distinctly different documents, which, in their own ways, contribute to the central purpose of persuading the recruiter to grant you a job interview.

THE IMPORTANCE OF A READER-CENTERED TONE IN COVER LETTERS

reader-centered tone
Refers to developing a tone in a letter that gives the reader the impression that he or she is "center stage."

A **reader-centered tone** refers to developing a tone that gives the reader the impression that he or she is "center stage." For example, when using a reader-centered tone in a sales letter, you focus on how your product or service will benefit the reader, as opposed to how your company would profit from the sale.

The same principle applies to cover letters. The tone, as well as the content of a cover letter, should communicate what you can do for a potential employer, not what you want the potential employer to do for you. This is at the heart of how you persuade recruiters to read further, to look at your résumé, and to give you a job interview.

As logical as this sounds, it is easy to end up with cover letters with a writer-centered tone. It is too easy to think solely in terms of what you have accomplished and what you want. The result is letters that have a real "give me, give me, give me" ring to them. Be careful not to produce cover letters that really center on a "here I am" and a "I want this, this, and this" tone and content. In addition, avoid using the word *I* frequently in cover letters. This technique helps you develop reader-centered cover letters. The information presented in the next section should assist you.

Figure 16-9 is a poorly written example of a cover letter for a 24-year-old person about to complete a five-year combination Bachelor's/Master's program in accounting. This letter is based on the sample résumé presented in Figure 16-13. The letter's main weakness is that it has a writer-centered tone, which would very likely contribute to its failure to get the reader's attention and gain his or her interest.

FIGURE 16-9: POORLY WRITTEN COVER LETTER

4722 Riley, Apt. 23
College Park, MD 20740
April 10, 201_

Mr. William Garret
Managing Partner
William Garret & Co., P.C.
Columbia, MD 21045

Dear Mr. Garret:

I just learned from a friend that you will have an opening in the tax division in late May for an accountant. This is exciting news. I am about to graduate from college with a degree in accounting, and I know I am the right person for the job.

Your firm has been experiencing unprecedented growth during recent years, which must be exciting and challenging. With current population and business growth in the greater Washington, D.C./Baltimore metropolitan area, your firm's future looks very bright. I want to be part of that bright future and believe that my education has prepared me to be placed immediately on the fast track for a partner position, which I am certain I can reach within five years.

I have worked my way through school, so I have proven that I know how to work. Thus, I know I would not have any problems working for you.

I am willing to start at an annual salary of $55,000. In addition, I would expect a standard benefits package including dental insurance and three weeks of paid vacation. Given my qualifications, I believe these to be reasonable expectations.

I would like to meet with you to discuss the position. Let's plan on doing so on Friday afternoon in your office. Please e-mail me the time you can meet with me. My e-mail address is swilk18@gmail.com.

Sincerely,

Shondra Wilkins

The sample cover letter presented in Figure 16-9 is so writer-centered that it is doubtful that the recruiter will read the candidate's résumé, let alone call her for an interview. The letter included little mention of what she can do for the firm. Instead, it was all about what she wanted the firm to do for her.

COVER LETTER STRATEGY AND STRUCTURE

Cover letters are a form of persuasive messages. Job hunters' purpose in writing cover letters is to persuade recruiters to read their résumés and grant them an interview.

You are advised to use a persuasive strategy when developing cover letters. This suggests that you will not actually make your request for a job interview until later in the letter. In the early sections of the letter, focus on gaining your reader's attention, building interest, and creating desire. Once you have accomplished these objectives, you request an interview. By using the persuasive strategy, you increase the likelihood that your ultimate objective will be realized.

The structure of a cover letter is linked directly to the persuasive strategy. Any type of letter, including a cover letter, can be viewed as containing three components—opening, body, and closing. Typically, the opening component is one paragraph—the first paragraph. The body is typically one to three paragraphs long, and the closing is one paragraph. Each component serves one or more purposes.

The opening section should project a positive, upbeat tone and be on topic. Most important, it should capture your reader's attention. Cover letters, like résumés, are often glanced at quickly on first pass. This means you must capture the readers' attention immediately so they will want to read further.

The body section is where most of the serious work is done. Your objectives in this section are to maintain your reader's attention, build interest, and create desire. In cover letters, you build interest and create desire by sharing information that persuades the recruiter that you possess the qualifications and desire to meet the company's needs. You may request an interview at the end of the body, then restate the request in the closing paragraph. However, it is more usual to make the request only once, in the closing paragraph.

Your main objective in the closing section is to request a job interview. This is the logical next step after piquing your reader's interest and building desire. Begin by expressing your desire to learn more about the company and eventually work for it. Then, state your request clearly. Furthermore, make it easy for the recruiter to contact you. Provide them with a host of contact numbers and addresses (e.g., cell phone number, fax number, e-mail address, and street address). Do not make recruiters struggle to get in touch with you. You don't have to sit by your phone around the clock, but do have to check your contact sites at least daily. (Don't dictate to recruiters when they can contact you. Some job applicants actually do this! They try to force recruiters to fit into their schedules.) Finally, end your closing by restating your desire to work for the company, followed by a statement to the effect that you hope to hear from them soon.

7 Tips for Writing a Winning Cover Letter
http://www.moneytalk-snews.com/7-tips-for-writing-a-winning-cover-letter/

THE PERSUASIVE ELEMENTS OF COVER LETTERS

Some people believe they will persuade recruiters to grant them interviews by restating most of the content of their résumés in their cover letters. Others believe they will persuade recruiters to grant them job interviews by restating the high points from their résumés in their cover letters. Both approaches leave it up to recruiters to sort and sift through the cover letters to determine what is useful to them. Most recruiters will not do so. They simply stop reading.

There are specific, persuasive elements you can include in your cover letters. To include these elements effectively in a cover letter, you need to have completed Steps 1 and 3 of the job search process. In other words, you need to know your own career goals as well as have researched the organization and job thoroughly. You should integrate three interrelated elements into your cover letters. Incorporate them predominately in the body section where you are trying to build reader interest and create desire. Communicate these three persuasive elements in your cover letters.

1. **Communicate your general familiarity with the organization** you are applying to and its industry. While it is imperative that you research the specific organization (e.g., number of employees, product lines, financial stability, etc.), it is also advantageous to research the industry it is part of (e.g., current and future trends, economic stability, customer preferences, etc.). Since so few job hunters bother to research beyond learning about the specific organization, those who also research industries typically impress recruiters. Here is one of those golden opportunities to build greater interest.

2. **Communicate your awareness of the organization's needs** as they relate to the job. By being able to discuss the finer points of specific jobs, you once again position yourself to impress recruiters. Here, you benefit from your ability to build recruiter interest.

3. **Communicate that you possess the qualifications and desire** to meet the organization's needs. Up to this point you have been building recruiter interest. Now you include information that, combined with the preceding information, has the strong potential of creating desire and persuading the recruiter to grant you a job interview. This is because you have communicated that you are familiar with the industry, organization, and specific job needs and that you have what it takes to meet the organization's specific needs. In other words, you persuade the recruiter to give you an interview by convincing him or her that you are a good fit for the job. This approach is appropriate to the type of message you are writing.

The fruits of your labors will pay off when you are developing résumés and interviewing. For example, you make your résumés more persuasive by including qualifications that are a good fit with an organization's specific needs. You also increase your level of persuasiveness during interviews by integrating all three of the above-mentioned persuasive elements into responses to recruiters' questions when appropriate, as well as into questions you may have an opportunity to ask.

Figure 16-10 is an example of a well-written cover letter for a 24-year-old person who is about to complete a five-year, combination Bachelor's/Master's program in accounting. This letter is based on the sample résumé presented in Figure 16-13. Consider contrasting this well-written version with the poorly written version of this letter in Figure 16-9.

FIGURE 16–10: WELL-WRITTEN COVER LETTER

4722 Riley, Apt. 23
College Park, MD 20740
(202) 555-4326
swilk18@gmail.com

April 10, 201_

Mr. William Garret
Managing Partner
William Garret & Co., P.C.
1347 Main Street
Columbia, MD 21045

Dear Mr. Garret:

My interest in working for your firm was piqued last Monday when Maria Jiminez, the director of your tax division, encouraged me to send you the attached résumé. Maria mentioned that there would be an opening in the tax division in late May for a person with my credentials. This is exciting news as I have worked part-time for the past three months as an intern in your tax division and have enjoyed both the experience and the people.

Your firm has experienced unprecedented growth in recent years, which must be exciting and challenging. With current population and business growth in the greater Washington, D.C./Baltimore metropolitan area, your firm's future looks very bright. I believe I can bring to your firm the benefits of a strong education in tax accounting as well as related experience. On May 11, I will graduate from the University of Maryland with a Master of Science degree in Accounting. While working on my degree, I developed computer skills important to the accounting industry and made the Dean's list several semesters. In addition, I was active in Beta Alpha Psi and the College of Business Administration's Professional Leadership Program. I am scheduled to take Parts 1 and 2 of the CPA exam on April 30 and the remaining two parts on May 15.

I have worked my way through college. My most current job is that of tax intern in your firm. This experience has provided me valuable work experience in tax accounting specific to your firm as well as an appreciation for what an exciting, dynamic organization it is. To date, I have gotten along well with those I work with and have received positive progress reports.

I feel I would be an asset to William Garret & Co., P.C. and am excited about the prospect of working fulltime in the tax division. I look forward to hearing from you soon regarding an interview where we can further discuss the firm's goals and how I might fit into them. In addition to the contact numbers and addresses at the top of this letter and on my attached résumé, I can be contacted at the firm at ext. 4301 from 1–5 p.m. on weekdays or at (202) 555-4326 at all other times.

Sincerely,

Shondra Wilkins

Figure 16-11 is an example of a well-written cover letter from a 22-year-old college senior who is majoring in human resource management. This letter is based on the sample résumé presented in Figure 16-14.

FIGURE 16-11: WELL-WRITTEN COVER LETTER

1204 Mountainview Dr.
Aurora, CO 80016
(303) 225-8664
ShObrien7@hotmail.com

March 17, 201_

Ms. Julia Mathason, Director
Human Resources Department
Randall, Inc.
142 South Segoe Road
Denver, CO 80012

Dear Ms. Mathason:

Yesterday afternoon we visited briefly at the career fair held at the Denver Convention Center. I was intrigued by your company's growth plans and plans for expansion into European markets. Most of all, I was impressed by your helpful demeanor and mention of the friendly, supportive work environment at Randall, Inc.

The anticipated growth and market expansion at Randall, Inc. should also signal growth in your human resources department. This is where I come in. I have a strong interest in human resource management and will be graduating from the University of Colorado with a Bachelor's degree in Human Resource Management on May 14. While working toward my degree, I have been an active member of the campus chapter of the Society for Human Resource Management. Last year I served as vice president of the chapter, and I currently serve as the chapter president.

During recent years I have worked a variety of jobs to pay for my college education. The most beneficial of these jobs was the semester-long internship in the human resources department at Getchle Electronics in Boulder where I assisted predominately in the area of corporate training. My experience at Getchle Electronics was time well spent. I learned a lot, received positive progress reports, and confirmed my interest in pursuing a career in human resource management.

I believe I would be an asset to Randall, Inc. and am most interested in discussing the possibility of a fulltime position in the human resources department. I hope to hear from you soon regarding an interview.

Sincerely,

Shawn O'Brien

FORMAT CONSIDERATIONS FOR COVER LETTERS

Keep the following list of format considerations in mind when developing cover letters.

- Avoid developing cover letters of more than one page. Longer letters are rarely read.
- Print cover letters with black ink on white or cream-colored, high-quality, 8½x11-inch paper.
- Select a legible font such as Times New Roman or Helvetica/Arial. Scripted fonts are difficult to read, especially if using a small font size.
- Select fonts that scan completely. For example, Times New Roman, Helvetica/Arial, Optima, New Century, Futura, Schoolbook, or Palatino fonts scan well.
- Use a 12-point font size and stick to that size throughout the letter. This is a standard size that most people have little difficulty reading. Don't give recruiters a reason to discard your cover letter because they must struggle to read it.
- Be conservative in your use of emphasis features, such as boldfacing and italicizing. Avoid underscoring. Along the same lines, do not type words or entire sentences in all capital letters. Use only one color of ink and font style. To do otherwise is distracting, which reduces the effectiveness of your cover letters. Finally, overuse or misuse of any of the features mentioned here may sow seeds of doubt in recruiters' minds over your understanding of appropriate job search protocol.
- Make sure your cover letter is free of all mechanical errors (e.g., grammar, punctuation, spelling, typos).

The job search process provides each of us with numerous opportunities to impress and persuade recruiters. In contrast, you have many opportunities to undermine your efforts. Using the wrong strategy, structure, or content in a cover letter or overlooking important format considerations will undermine your efforts. Be careful. You have invested too much time and money into earning an education to be your own worst enemy during this step.

COVER LETTER BOOKS

As you could imagine, there are a number of cover letter books on the market. These books typically provide information on how to write cover letters, followed by numerous sample letters. Looking at sample cover letters in such books can help you decide how to best convey your message and even move you past writer's block. However, don't look to these books to provide you with that one sample cover letter that is the perfect fit for you and all your job-hunting situations. That sample letter doesn't exist. If you do force the issue, the result will very likely be ineffective cover letters that sound like generic, non-persuasive form letters.

ARE COVER LETTERS AS IMPORTANT AS RÉSUMÉS?

Yes! Don't weaken the job search process by giving less attention to developing cover letters than you give to developing résumés. Too often, individuals second-guess themselves by assuming that the résumé is the more important of the two job search documents. Those people pay too little attention to developing persuasive cover letters. Sometimes in their quest to be efficient, they develop cover letters that sound generic rather than individualized. In addition, they often send identical copies of their cover letter (form letter) to numerous employers. As you can imagine, such an approach is unfruitful because their cover letters are typically not very persuasive and/or are generic which gives recruiters no reason to glance further at accompanying résumés.

STEP 5: DEVELOPING EFFECTIVE RÉSUMÉS

Step 5 of the job search process involves developing résumés. A **résumé** is a marketing tool that's purpose is to convince a recruiter to grant you a job interview.

Be careful not to harbor an oversimplified view of résumés. Résumés are essential to the job search process and deserve your full attention. Some people view them as simply condensed autobiographies that cover their education/training and work experiences. While these components should be included, other components are also important. For example, sections such as key words, career objective, honors and awards, activities, and personal interests help recruiters determine candidates' career goals, personal interests, and to some extent, their personalities. Résumés are typically short, yet each section and word should be thought through carefully.

résumé

An individual marketing tool, whether paired with a cover letter or not, that's purpose is to convince a recruiter to grant you a job interview.

HOW MANY RÉSUMÉS DO YOU NEED TO DEVELOP?

If you approach this step of the job search process realistically, the correct answer to this question is *several*. If you develop a traditional résumé, then customize your résumé for each potential employer. If you develop an electronic résumé, develop two versions of the same résumé for each potential employer—one for an independent résumé database service and one for your web page. These different electronic résumés are discussed later in this chapter.

When you develop traditional résumés, submitting a customized résumé to each employer greatly increases your chances of being granted a job interview. Developing more than one résumé doesn't mean you have to develop a completely different version for each potential employer. While your contact information often remains the

© nasirkhan/Shutterstock.com

same, some of the remaining components should be revised to varying degrees (e.g., removed, replaced, reordered, reworded). For example, your career objective may vary, as will the work experiences you choose to include. You may even find it advantageous to revise your personal interests section to make a more favorable impression on a potential employer.

The purpose of developing a customized résumé is to communicate as specifically and clearly as possible that you are a good fit for an organization and job. These points are elaborated on later in this chapter.

WHAT PURPOSES DO RÉSUMÉS SERVE?

Understanding the purposes of résumés from both the job hunter's perspective and the recruiter's perspective helps us appreciate the role each plays in the job search process. From a job hunter's perspective, a résumé serves one purpose: to persuade an employer to grant him or her an interview. From a recruiter's perspective, résumés have four purposes: (1) to supply information not presented in the cover letter, (2) to determine if the candidate is clear on his or her short-term and long-term career goals, (3) to determine if the candidate possesses enough of the right qualifications to be a good fit for the organization and a particular position, and (4) to determine if the candidate's interests and personality are compatible with the organization.

THE CHANGING NATURE OF RÉSUMÉS

Résumés evolve over time. Over the years, some previously standard résumé components have justifiably dropped off of résumés, while others have been added. For example, a few decades ago, U.S. job hunters attached small photos of themselves to their résumés. Now, U.S. recruiters discourage applicants from including them out of fear of discrimination charges. In contrast, recruiters in the Philippine Islands expect job candidates to attach a small photo. They also expect job candidates to report their height and weight for the purpose of sizing work uniforms. Another résumé expectation that has changed over the years for U.S. job hunters is the references section. Several years ago, U.S. job hunters listed their references on their résumés. When they quit doing so, due to concerns over a résumé's length, applicants included a statement such as "References provided upon request." Today, such a statement is left off because it is considered to be redundant. If recruiters want job candidates' references, they will ask for them. A Computer Skills section provides us with yet another example of how U.S. résumés have evolved. Before computers became ubiquitous in organizations, job hunters did not include a Computer Skills section in their résumés. Today, Computer Skills sections are prevalent for obvious reasons.

Do your best to keep up with changing résumé expectations. Attend résumé writing workshops or read current résumé writing books and articles. Job hunters who are not current with changing expectations are typically less successful in their job searches than they would have otherwise been. When such people find themselves back on the job market, some merely dust off the résumé they last used, update the Work Experience section, and send it off. No matter the circumstances, if you do not remain current regarding résumé components, then you are simply not as persuasive and competitive as job candidates who have remained current.

FIGURE 16-12: VIDEO RÉSUMÉS

Video Résumés, also referred to as Video Profiles, Visumes, and Video CVs, are not replacements for traditional hardcopy and electronic résumés and curriculum vitas (CVs). They are, instead, a separate tool that provides job hunters with a means of making first impressions on potential employers. Most job hunters who submit video résumés believe that by doing so they will stand out in the eyes of recruiters in positive ways that will separate them from others applying for the same positions. Here are some tips pertaining to video résumés.

- Your video résumé should be relatively short. The typical length is 60 to 90 seconds.
- Don't merely summarize or read your hardcopy or electronic résumé.
- Highlight information not included in your cover letter and hardcopy or electronic résumé.
- At minimum, prepare an outline you can work from. In contrast, don't prepare a script! Most of us are tempted to read scripts which we typically do with an uninspiring, monotonic voice. You want to breathe life into you voice, not put recruiters to sleep.
- Practice several times. Record each practice session so you can identify areas that need strengthened.
- Make sure you appearance is appropriate. Professional appearance is strongly encouraged. For example, dress like you would for a job interview.
- Wear a pleasant, inviting facial expression and smile occasionally.
- Don't let nervousness interfere. For example, instead of speaking too fast, as many do when nervous, remind yourself to speak more slowly.

Now that you know how to create a video résumé, consider whether doing so is a good idea and a wise use of your time. Not really! Most companies don't even accept video résumés due, in part, out of fear of bias claims from applicants. If you still feel inclined to create one, however, consider the following advice from Max Messmer, chairman and CEO of Robert Half International. "Before submitting a video résumé, job candidates should check with the hiring manager to ensure the company does not have a policy against their us in evaluating candidates."

Source: "Video Resumes: Let the Applicant Beware" by Caroline M.L. Potter, Yahoo! Hot Jobs.

WHAT IS THE DESIRED LENGTH?

The answer to this question is, it depends. Be careful not to automatically assume that everyone requires a one-page résumé.

Résumé length is analogous to the old expression, "When in Rome, do as the Romans do." For example, when you open a file with your college career center, you will probably be required to limit your résumé length to one page. The same is true of most college internship offices and many résumé databases. Some organizations help us answer the length question by reporting the maximum length they expect. It may be one page or more, but at least in such situations you aren't left guessing.

But what about those situations when you don't know how long a résumé you should submit? This is not uncommon. When you don't know an organization's preferred preferences, keep yours in the 1–3 page range. The ideal length is one page and if you can reduce your résumé to one page, do so. If you are nearing graduation and have little work experience, you should be able to develop one-page résumés. However, if you have an extensive work and training history, keeping your résumé to one page may be nearly impossible. In such situations, your résumé length can extend out to three pages if necessary.

FIGURE 16–13: DEVELOPING RÉSUMÉS FOR INTERNATIONAL EMPLOYERS

If you are developing a résumé for international employers, don't assume the one-page length guideline automatically applies. Learn about international employers' preferences and adapt accordingly. For example, some foreign recruiters prefer a longer résumé (often called a *curriculum vitae* or *CV*). A foreign recruiter might expect you to devote 3–4 pages to your life history (e.g., age, marital status, number of children) and your personal interests, before presenting traditional information such as education/training, and work history.[9] The recruiter wants to understand what you are like as a person before reading about your qualifications and credentials.[10] Good communicators do their best to learn about and adhere to their communication partners' preferences no matter whether their partners are domestic or foreign.

© ruigsantos/Shutterstock.com

RÉSUMÉ TYPES

Selecting the résumé type that will best serve you is a decision you must make each time you conduct a job search. The two most common résumé types are chronological résumés and functional résumés. Each type is described below, followed by some pointers regarding which one to select.

chronological résumé
A type of résumé in which the focus is on work and experience.

Chronological Résumé The **chronological résumé** is a format that focuses on work experience and education. Both of these sections should be clearly labeled so recruiters can spot them quickly. Furthermore, entries in each section should be presented in reverse chronological order. Thus, your Education section should begin with your most recent degree, certificate, or training, and your Work Experience section should begin with your most recent job. The chronological résumé is considered to be the traditional-looking résumé.

The chronological résumé is the type more frequently used by relatively inexperienced job hunters just launching their careers. This does not mean that you have to switch from a chronological résumé to a functional résumé as you move through your career. Individuals with little work experience who are nearing college graduation typically place their Education section before their Work Experience section. As time passes and they accumulate professional work experience, they are encouraged to switch the order of the sections so the Work Experience section precedes the Education section. Even then, the question regarding how to order these two sections should always come down to which one is more likely to capture a recruiter's attention and persuade him or her to grant you an interview.

Develop a chronological résumé when:

- You want to call attention to a stable work history.
- You want to call attention to consistent upward mobility and promotions in your career.

- You believe the name of your last employer is an important consideration.
- You believe prior job titles are impressive.
- You know the recruiter is most comfortable with a traditional-looking résumé.

Figure 16-14 is an example of a chronological résumé for a 24-year-old person who is about to complete a five-year, combination Bachelor's/Master's degrees program in accounting.

FIGURE 16–14: SAMPLE CHRONOLOGICAL RÉSUMÉ

Shondra Wilkins
4722 Riley, Apt. 23
College Park, MD 20740
(202) 555-4326
swilks18@gmail.com

KEY WORDS

accounting	tax accounting	Master's degree
tax internship	officer in Beta Alpha Psi	taxation scholarship

CAREER OBJECTIVE

Seeking a staff position in an accounting firm in the area of taxation that provides a career path to a partner position

EDUCATION

Master of Science in Accounting with specialization in taxation, May 11, 201_
Five-year combination Bachelor's/Master's degrees program, GPA: 3.83/4.0
University of Maryland, College Park, MD, Earned 100% of college expenses
Key courses: *Corporate Taxation, Tax Research, Managerial Accounting, Business Ethics*

LANGUAGE SKILLS

Fluent in Spanish, French, and Japanese as well as English

WORK HISTORY

Tax Intern, *William Garret & Co., P.C.*, August–December 201_
Responsibilities include: assisting in researching tax issues, compiling financial statements, reviewing and preparing federal tax returns for partnerships and corporations
Sales Associate, *Red Barn Apparel Outlet*, June 201_–August 201_
Assisted customers, worked at the customer checkout counter, assisted with inventory, stocked shelves
Assistant Manager, *The East Coast Kitchen*, June 201_–May 201_
Supervised 12 employees, trained new hires, closed the restaurant at night, handled customer complaints, performed other administrative duties

HONORS & ACTIVITIES

Current president of the student chapter of Beta Alpha Psi (accounting honorary fraternity).
201_–1_ recipient of the Department of Accounting taxation scholarship.
Dean's List the past 6 semesters.
Volunteer work for the Red Cross and a number of homeless shelters in the area.

PERSONAL INTERESTS

Enjoy traveling, reading, golf, and racquetball.

Figure 16-15 is an example of a chronological résumé for a 22-year-old college senior majoring in human resource management.

FIGURE 16–15: SAMPLE CHRONOLOGICAL RÉSUMÉ

Shawn O'Brien
1204 Mountainview Dr.
Aurora, CO 80016
(303) 225-8664
ShObrien7@hotmail.com

KEY WORDS

human resource management	compensation & benefits	multi-lingual
bachelor of science degree	SHRM chapter president	scholarships
management experience	training materials development	trainer
professional leadership program	customer service experience	inventory

JOB OBJECTIVE

Seeking an entry-level position in the Human Resources Department at Randall, Inc. that will lead to career growth opportunities in the compensation and benefits division

EDUCATION

Bachelor of Science Degree in Human Resource Management, May 14, 201_
University of Colorado, Boulder, GPA: 4.0/4.0 in major, 3.67/4.0 cumulative
Earned 75% of college expenses

LANGUAGE SKILLS

Fluent in Spanish and English

WORK HISTORY

Intern *Getchle Electronics* (Boulder, CO) August–December 201_
Responsibilities included assisting in development of employee training materials, assisting with employee training sessions, analyzing the employee benefits package vis-à-vis competitors' benefits packages, assisting in updating compensation policies.
Assistant Manager, *Rapid Fire Gaming Outlet*, June 201_–August 201_
Assisted customers, worked at the checkout counter, analyzed the merits of new games, updated inventory records, reordered stock, stocked shelves
Sales Associate, *The Jolly Roger Costume Shop*, June 201_–June 201_
Supervised 4 employees, trained new hires, addressed customer complaints, performed other administrative duties

HONORS & ACTIVITIES

Current president of the student chapter of the Society for Human Resource Management.
201_–201_ recipient of the Department of Management human resources scholarship.
Member of the College of Business Professional Leadership Program.
Dean's List the past 4 semesters.
Volunteer routinely for the Habitat for Humanity program and local food bank.

PERSONAL INTERESTS

Enjoy photography, hiking, snowboarding, and traveling

Functional Résumé The **functional résumé** is a format that emphasizes functional experience, focusing on transferable skills and accomplishments. Individuals making a major career change should develop a functional résumé in which they highlight transferable skills and accomplishments from previous jobs or careers.

This is not to suggest that you would not include Education and Work Experience sections in functional résumés. You should, however, include and place special attention on a section titled Relevant Skills & Accomplishments. By highlighting skills and accomplishments relevant to your target job and organization, you communicate to the recruiter what you can do for the organization. This is an opportunity to capture the recruiter's attention and persuade her or him to grant you an interview. This section is not included in a chronological résumé.

The Relevant Skills & Accomplishments section in a functional résumé precedes the Work Experience and Education sections. This section should be clearly labeled so recruiters can find it quickly. Include in this section the top three or four skills relevant to your target job and organization, making a point to prioritize them from most-to-least important. Below each skill include three or four accomplishments that demonstrate this skill, again prioritizing them.

Develop a functional résumé when:

- You are making a major career change.
- Your job titles do not do justice to your accomplishments and responsibilities.
- Your most relevant accomplishments are not from your most recent jobs.
- Your work history has stretches when you were unemployed.
- You have been away from the workforce for several years and do not want your age known.
- Your most impressive (relevant) skills and accomplishments are from unpaid or volunteer work.

Figure 16-16 is an example of a functional résumé for a 38-year-old person who worked for 10 years as an auditor in a public accounting firm before deciding to make a major career change. He returned to school, earned a Ph.D. in accounting, and is now searching for a university faculty position.

GENERAL SUGGESTIONS ABOUT RÉSUMÉS

Before discussing specific résumé contents, a few general suggestions are in order.

Include cross-functional information. The natural inclination when writing a résumé is to focus your attention, almost exclusively, on your major area of training and experience. While you should present information pertaining to your major area(s) of training and experience, you should also include information pertaining to your cross-functional training, knowledge, experiences, and expertise.

Cross-functional information refers to areas outside your major area(s) of training and experience that have some relationship to the job for which you are applying. An accounting major who envisions herself or himself as a managing partner in a large public accounting firm should also include information pertaining to her or his management and marketing training, knowledge, experiences, and expertise. When you communicate your cross-functional qualities to recruiters in your résumés, you paint a picture of a flexible employee who understands organizations and what is needed to help them succeed.

functional résumé A type of résumé that emphasizes functional experience, focusing on transferable skills and accomplishments.

cross-functional information Information about areas outside of your major areas of training and experience that have some relationship to the job for which you are applying.

FIGURE 16–16: SAMPLE FUNCTIONAL RÉSUMÉ

James Fullerton, Ph.D., CPA
648 Poolside Way
Austin, TX 78705
(361) 392-5806
jfullerton27@gmail.com

KEY WORDS

accounting auditing	Ph.D. in accounting	university teaching experience public
accounting experience	CPA	managed
coached	supervised	published

CAREER OBJECTIVE

Seeking a tenure-track faculty position in an Accounting Department in a university that has an AACSB-approved College of Business

SUMMARY OF QUALIFICATIONS

- Worked in public accounting for 10 years.
- Worked in accounting in a corporate setting for 3 years.
- Developed 2 national training programs for Ernst & Young.
- Instructed management- and staff-level accountants in 14 workshops.
- Taught three different accounting courses while serving as a teaching fellow.
- Presented research papers at 2 professional conferences.
- Wrote one research article, which was published in a professional accounting journal.

RELEVANT SKILLS & ACCOMPLISHMENTS

Teaching
- Taught *Accounting Principles* and *Auditing* classes at UT.
- Trained management- and staff-level accountants in corporate training programs.
- Developed 2 national training programs for Ernst & Young.

Research Abilities

- Wrote "Internet-Related Auditing Challenges," James Fullerton, *Journal of Accountancy*, 68, no. 3: 17–32.
- Conducted extensive research on auditing issues in both business and university settings.

Management
- Supervised up to 50 people routinely.
- Coached and mentored several accountants.
- Managed large and small client projects for Ernst & Young.

WORK HISTORY

Teaching Fellow, Dept. of Accounting, U. of Texas, Austin, 201_–present
Tax Manager, Ernst & Young, Houston, 20__–201_

EDUCATION

Doctor of Philosophy in Accounting, May 11, 201_
The University of Texas at Austin, Austin, Texas, GPA: 3.8/4.0
Master of Science in Accounting with specialization in Auditing, Dec. 11, 20__
Five-year combination Bachelor's and Master's degrees program, GPA: 4.0/4.0 University of Michigan, Ann Arbor, Michigan
Fluent in Spanish and German as well as English.

FIGURE 16–17 HONESTY IS THE BEST POLICY ON RÉSUMÉS

Do not make false statements and exaggerations on your résumé. Including false statements and exaggerations on résumés is unethical and, in some cases, illegal. Doing so misleads potential employers.

While it is natural to want to sound your best, if you are not careful, self-pride or a strong desire to persuade potential employers to grant you an interview can give way to lies and exaggerations. One way to avoid doing this is to keep the following "lies, exaggerations, and land mines" analogy in mind when preparing résumés. The analogy suggests that lies and exaggerations on résumés can sit undetected indefinitely, much like buried land mines. And just like land mines, lies and exaggerations on résumés can detonate at any moment, proving fatal to job searches, careers, and long-term credibility.[10] Many people, including college students, coaches, CEOs, and high-profile politicians, have been called out in recent years for including lies and exaggerations on their résumés. No one is exempt.

Include leadership training and/or experience. Include leadership training and/or experiences in your résumés. Recruiters look favorably on candidates who have leadership training and experience. These qualifications come from a variety of sources. You may be in a leadership role in your current job, or you may have taken a leadership class or workshop. You may have gained some leadership experience as an officer of a club, association, church group, classroom team project, or sports team. You likely have some leadership experiences in your background and should communicate them in your résumés in the Education/Training, Work Experiences, Honors, Clubs, or Personal Interests sections.

Communicate what you can do for potential employers. Be careful not to produce résumés that read like your obituary. In other words, don't write résumés in which you chronologically present all your education, training, and work experiences without regard to which should be included and how they should be organized. Instead, include and highlight information in your résumés that clearly communicates what you can do for the potential employers. This is the same persuasive technique recommended in the discussion of cover letters. Your résumés are another opportunity to benefit from the time and energy expended researching jobs and organizations.

Use action verbs. Use action verbs in your résumés to capture recruiters' attention and create with words visual images of your skills and accomplishments. Begin each phrase with an action verb. Action verbs lend themselves well to descriptive phrases, which allow you to say "Reduced project costs" instead of "I reduced the costs associated with an information-retrieval project." Figure 16-18 contains several examples of action verbs.

FIGURE 16-18: ACTION VERBS

administered	directed	judged	predicted
advised	established	led	presented
arbitrated	forecasted	managed	recruited
budgeted	guided	mediated	redesigned
communicated	handled	mobilized	supervised
coordinated	hired	negotiated	trained
designed	implemented	organized	tracked
designed	inspired	originated	volunteered

In contrast, avoid including overused phrases that most recruiters find annoying in your résumés. Several such phrases are listed in Figure 16-19.

FIGURE 16-19: DEADLY RÉSUMÉ PHRASES

When job hunting we want to impress and persuade recruiters to call us in for interviews once they have read our résumé. Achieving this goal, however, can be easily sidetracked if we irritate recruiters by using phrases such as those listed below

- Results-oriented professional
- Proven track record of success
- Strong work ethic
- Team player
- Bottom-line orientation
- Excellent communication skills
- Best-in-class anything
- Strong attention to detail
- Meets or exceeds expectations
- Visionary, strategic thinker

Why are these phrases discouraged? Here are some reasons: they are dreadfully unoriginal, they say nothing, they are made of thin air, and they are self-praising terms.

Source: Liz Ryan, "Ten Deadliest Resume Phrases," glassdoor.com, September 23, 2009, http://www.glassdoor.com/blog/ten-deadliest-resume-phrases/)

RECOMMENDED RÉSUMÉ COMPONENTS

The way you choose to order your résumés components varies based on the type of résumés you develop and the extent of your relevant work history. Figure 16-20 presents the components most business recruiters prefer you include.

Name & Contact Information Your name should be centered at the top of your résumé followed by your address, phone numbers, fax number, and e-mail address. If you are living at a temporary address, append the date you will move. If you live in a temporary place, also include a permanent address (e.g., parents' or friend's address or your future address). Place the temporary address closer to the left margin with the title *Temporary Address* above it and the permanent address closer to the right margin with the title *Permanent Address* above it.

FIGURE 16–20: RECOMMENDED RÉSUMÉS COMPONENTS

- Name & Contact Information
- Key Words
- Career Objective
- Summary of Qualifications
- Relevant Skills & Accomplishments
- Education
- Computer Skills
- Work Experience
- Honors & Activities
- Personal Interests

Key Words Key words refers to a list of words/phrases that focus on business skills, accomplishments, and personal qualities especially relevant to a potential employer. The "key words" section is especially critical in résumés that are submitted electronically. Thus, you will find a more extensive discussion of key words in that section of this chapter. However, all résumés are not submitted electronically (online), but the "key words" section is still important in them because often times hardcopy résumés are scanned into résumé databases. In turn, those hardcopy résumés that are scanned into résumé databases are far more likely to be pulled out for job interview consideration if they contain key words.

Career Objective Your career objective, also referred to as the Job Objective, is the first major section following the contact information. A good career objective clearly states an applicant's job and career interests. It distinguishes between short-term and long-term career goals. The following career objective meets these recommendations: "Seeking a staff position in tax accounting with the long-term goal of becoming a partner." Avoid a career objective that provides no specific information and leaves recruiters wondering if you know what you want to do. The following career objective is a typical, yet ineffective example: "Seeking a challenging position that will allow for growth and the opportunity to use my educational background to secure employment with a company where I can use my training and skills to make a contribution to the profitability of my employer."

© NAN728/Shutterstock.com

Summary of Qualifications This section may be included in chronological résumés or in lieu of the Relevant Skills & Accomplishments section in functional résumés. Here you have the opportunity to provide the potential employer with a summary of what specifically makes you a good fit for the job and organization. Talk briefly about skills, relevant work experiences, and credentials (e.g., degrees, workshops, licenses). In addition, present two or three accomplishments directly related to your job objectives and the position for which you are applying. Finally, mention your willingness to travel or transfer (relocate), languages you have mastered, and key personal qualities important to the job and organization. Even though this section is located near the beginning of the résumé, do not write it until you have written all the other sections. You need to see this other information before writing an effective summary.

Relevant Skills & Accomplishments This section is typically included only in functional résumés. Include the top three or four skills relevant to your target job and organization, making a point to prioritize them from most-to-least important. Below each skill include three or four accomplishments that demonstrate this skill. Prioritize them.

Education & Training Present your post-secondary education in reverse chronological order. Do not include information about your high school experience unless you believe it will help persuade a recruiter to grant you an interview.

Include in the following order your degree, major, minor, university or college, city, state, graduation date or anticipated graduation date, and GPA(s). For example: "Bachelor of Science Degree, Major: Human Resource Management, Minor: Economics, University of Colorado, Boulder, Colorado, Anticipated Graduation Date: May 14, 201_, GPA: 3.67/4.0."

If you decide not to include your GPA, then be prepared to discuss it during interviews. By not including your GPA in your résumé, you run the risk of having your résumé discarded! Some employers believe that candidates who do not include their GPA are hiding something or being manipulative. While this may not be the case, the result is the same. The way the GPA is presented in the example above implies that this is the candidate's cumulative GPA. If you are not as pleased with your cumulative GPA as you are with your GPA within your major or the GPA for your last two years of school, clearly label and report one of them. You may be pleased with both your GPA within your major and your cumulative GPA, in which case you should clearly label and include both.

Include in this section any digital badges you have earned and where they are hosted. *Digital badges* certify a form of online training you have acquired.

If you have financed all or a significant portion of your college education, mention this in your résumé. The education section is a logical place to do so.

If room allows, include a subsection in which you mention four or five relevant courses. These courses are not necessarily limited to those in your major and minor. For example, if you are a Human Resource Management major, you may decide to include the psychology course you took your freshman year.

If you have mastered more than one language, mention this in a subsection. Given the ongoing growth in global business activity, languages (aside from English) that you read, write, or speak fluently are a bonus. If you are an international student, mention English, if you are proficient in it.

Include training sessions relevant to the target job and organization in the Education & Training section. State the training topic, training sponsor or school, city, state, and date(s) taken.

One more thing. Include any professional certifications and licenses you've earned (e.g., CPA license).

© mindscanner/Shutterstock.com

Computer Skills Make sure you have a working knowledge of the items you include in this section. You may be expected to exhibit your proficiency during the interview process. Include in this section the hardware, application software, computer programs, operating systems, and research databases with which you are proficient. Increase the effectiveness and decrease the length of this section by including only those computer skills most relevant to the target job and organization. Prioritize this information.

Work History Present your jobs in reverse chronological order: job title, employer, city, state, starting and ending employment dates, and key job responsibilities.

You do not need to include all the jobs you have had. Only include those most relevant to your target job and organization. You may wonder how far back in your work history you should go. If you are only one to four years out of high school, then report high school and post-secondary jobs. If you are one to five years out of college, report relevant college and post-college jobs. If you have been out of college for six or more years, only report those jobs that you have had since graduation. If you worked for a number of years before attending college, you probably have an extensive work history. If this describes you, report relevant pre-college and college jobs. Do not worry about leaving gaps of time in your work history. These can be easily explained during interviews if the question arises.

Do not be too quick to leave off jobs that you don't feel sound classy enough or even remotely related to your future career. Many college students who have worked for fast food restaurants leave them off their résumés. By doing so, they miss out on the chance to communicate a number of transferable skills that are valued by most businesses, including customer service, communication and interpersonal skills, money handling, and supervisory, management, and leadership skills.

Once you have decided which jobs to include, select specific responsibilities and experiences from each to list. Do not get lazy and skip such information or merely list all job responsibilities and experiences for each job in chronological order. Instead, choose those most relevant to your target job and organization. Then, prioritize them from left to right.

Imagine you are a Human Resource Management major who worked for a fast food restaurant while in college. You are nearing graduation and have decided to include this job on your résumé. Your responsibilities and experiences at the fast food restaurant included, in chronological order, mopping floors, emptying trash cans, and cleaning restrooms; placing condiments on hamburgers, frying hamburgers, preparing drinks, and making fries; working the main counter, working the drive-up window, and serving as shift manager. Based on the career path for which you are preparing, which of the above should you include and in which order should you prioritize them? You probably eliminated all but the last three. The last three are relevant to human resource management because they involve people skills, customer service, leadership, and management opportunities. As for the prioritization question, place the shift manager responsibility in the first position.

Honors & Activities Include honors and activities relevant to the target job and organization. In addition, include activities and honors that show you are a well-rounded, involved person. Prioritize the honors and activities you decide to include.

Honors typically come in the form of honors bestowed by employers and professional associations. Honors speak highly of a candidate's performance potential, attitude, and ability to learn. See Figure 16-21 for examples.

Include such activities as memberships in student chapters of professional associations (see Figure 16-21 for examples), campus clubs, musical and theater groups, church-related groups and functions, and athletic teams. Mention any officer position or leadership roles in any of the above. In addition, include community service (volunteer) work you have done. Many organizations promote volunteerism among their employees and are impressed by individuals who share their feelings about voluntarily giving back to their communities.

FIGURE 16-21: PROFESSIONAL ASSOCIATIONS AND HONORARY FRATERNITIES

- American Marketing Association
- Association for Information Technology Professionals
- Association for Operations Management
- American Logistics Association
- Beta Alpha Psi (honors fraternity for accounting, finance, and information systems)
- Beta Gamma Sigma (honor society for business students and scholars)
- Financial Management Association
- Hispanic Business Association
- National Association of Black Accountants
- Phi Chi Theta (business and economics fraternity)
- Society for Human Resource Management

Personal Interests Many recruiters prefer you include a Personal Interests section in your résumé so they can see how you spend your time away from school and work. Include five or six personal interests such as hobbies, physical fitness, and other relaxation pastimes. Keep the following guidelines in mind.

- Include interests that are a good match with the organization. For example, if you are applying for a position with a firm or a company, mention interests such as golf and softball.
- Do not include interests that are perceived as being physically unsafe, unless the potential employer prefers extreme risk takers. For example, do not mention interests such as sky diving, rock and mountain climbing, or auto and motorcycle racing that have the potential of landing you in a hospital or morgue.
- Avoid including interests that may be viewed negatively by some employers. For example, mentioning that you have or plan to have several children is not

advised. The potential employer may believe you will miss work frequently due to family demands.

- Prioritize your personal interests from left to right representing what you believe to be the most persuasive followed by others in descending order.

If you are unsure whether a potential employer wants you to include a Personal Interests section in your résumé, go ahead and include it. Recruiters who are not looking for such information will not hold it against you for including it.

FORMAT CONSIDERATIONS FOR NON-ELECTRONIC RÉSUMÉS

While persuasive content is important in résumés for obvious reasons, don't overlook that format expectations also influence recruiters' decisions to call candidates in for job interviews. Several format considerations are presented below.

- Take into account the résumé length guidelines discussed above.
- Print résumés using black ink on white or cream-colored, high-quality, 8½x11-inch paper.
- Select a legible, nondecorative font such as Times New Roman or Arial/Helvetica. Scripted fonts are difficult to read, especially if you use a small font size.
- If you suspect a potential employer may scan your résumé into its database, use a font that scans completely such as Arial/Helvetica, Optima, New Century, Futura, Times New Roman, Schoolbook, or Palatino.
- Use a 12-point font size, with the exception of your name and section titles which may be slightly larger (13 or 14 points). Twelve points is a standard size that most people have little difficulty reading. Don't give recruiters a reason to discard your résumé because the type size is too small.
- Be conservative in your use of features, such as boldfacing and italicizing. Do not overdo it by typing words or entire sentences in all capital letters. In addition, don't use more than one ink color or font style. Typing main section headings in all capital letters or boldfacing them is all right, as is boldfacing or italicizing subheadings. Just be careful not to overuse such techniques elsewhere. Otherwise, the text becomes a distraction, reducing the effectiveness of your résumé. Furthermore, overuse or misuse of these features may sow seeds of doubt in recruiters' minds about your understanding of appropriate job search protocol.
- Use clear, boldfaced headings so it is easy for recruiters to spot the sections they want to read. For example: **CAREER OBJECTIVE, WORK EXPERIENCE**, etc. Recruiters don't read résumés from top to bottom. Instead, they scan them looking for sections of interest to them. Make it easy for them. Part of this challenge involves positioning sections in expected locations and part of it involves adhering to the suggestions above that standardize your résumé.
- Make sure your résumé is free of all mechanical errors (e.g., grammar, punctuation, spelling, typos).

As you develop résumés, don't overlook the impact of format. It is easy to get so engrossed in making sure the right content is included that format considerations are overlooked. Résumés do get tossed due to inappropriate formatting as well as noticeable spelling and grammatical errors. In such cases, recruiters are left to believe the candidate is unfamiliar with appropriate résumé writing expectations or is careless. While these may not be accurate perceptions, the damage is done.

RÉSUMÉ BOOKS

There are a number of books on the market that discuss résumés. Such books typically provide information on how to write résumés, followed by numerous examples. Looking at sample résumés can help you decide how to best say things, locate components, and move you past writer's block. However, don't look to these books to provide you with that one sample résumé that is the perfect fit for you to plug into and use for all of your job-hunting situations. That perfect template, form résumé doesn't exist! If you do force the issue, the result will very likely be an ineffective résumé that reads like too many others and gets you nowhere.

RÉSUMÉ SOFTWARE

There are several résumé software programs on the market. Among the more popular programs are Résumé Maker Professional, WinWay Résumé Deluxe, Résumé Maker Professional Ultimate, EasyJob Résumé Builder, Easy Résumé Creator Pro, and Power Résumés. These programs range in price from $20 to $40.

As long as you have access to a word processing program and the information in this chapter, you do not really need a software program to develop your résumés. However, you may find that a software program works for you and keeps you from overlooking important components and formatting requirements.

Résumé software programs offer some writing suggestions, present sample résumés, and provide templates for a variety of styles, including chronological and functional résumés. As good as they sound, consider these cautionary reminders:

- Make sure the advice, samples, and templates for traditional résumés are consistent with the suggestions pertaining to traditional résumés presented above. Then, make modifications as necessary.
- Make sure the advice, samples, and templates for electronic résumés are consistent with the suggestions about electronic résumés presented in the following section. Modify as necessary.
- Make sure that using a software program does not result in a generic or formulaic résumé. Effective résumés are customized for each employer and do not have a generic ring to them.

The good thing about today's résumé software programs is that they provide more than résumé writing assistance. Most also provide career advice; help you create cover and thank-you letters; help you build and manage contacts databases (e.g., store, search, and retrieve names, addresses, phone numbers, e-mail addresses); provide information about businesses, executive recruiters, professional search firms, and employment agencies; provide links to employer websites; and provide you with a way to post your résumé electronically.

SUBMITTING RÉSUMÉS ELECTRONICALLY

Many companies now prefer that job applicants submit résumés electronically or at least submit a hard copy that can be scanned into a résumé database. Electronic résumés are popular with companies because of the cost and time efficiencies associated with receiving, storing, managing, and accessing them. Before describing the common ways résumés find their way to recruiters electronically, an important question must be raised: Are electronic résumés the only form employers accept these days?

Don't assume that every employer, domestically and abroad, wants only an electronic résumé. Some employers, either by choice or size, don't have their own résumé databases. They still accept cover letters and résumés predominately by mail. In addition, they may subscribe to one or more independent résumé database services or electronic job boards that help them locate job candidates.

No doubt, submitting cover letters and résumés electronically is more convenient, less time consuming, and less expensive than submitting them the traditional ways. The downside, however, is in embracing the electronic approach so fully, you overlook potential employers who are not searching for you electronically.

So, which companies want job candidates to submit electronic résumés and which don't? Some make it easy by asking in job ads, at job fairs, or in person for an electronic résumé. If no mention is made, however, call the company and ask which approach they prefer, or check their website to see if they specify their preference there. The size of the company can also be helpful when answering this question. Small companies are less likely than midsize and large companies to expect electronic résumés. If all else fails, cover your bases by submitting your cover letter and résumé electronically and in hardcopy form.

There are several ways to transmit your résumé to recruiters electronically. The more common ways include e-mailing your résumé, submitting a hardcopy of a scannable résumé, and posting it on an electronic job board and at your web page.

E-mailing Your Résumé   Some recruiters ask you over the phone, via e-mail, or in person to e-mail them your résumé. Other times you are instructed to do so in help wanted ads, in trade journals, in newspapers, or in job listings posted on the Web. Still other times, you submit an unsolicited résumé via e-mail because you are interested in the company and want to make sure you will be considered for current and future job openings.

Now you have two choices. (1) Do you e-mail a cover letter along with your résumé? (2) Do you attach your résumé to a separate file containing a cover note/letter or do you send it along in the file containing the cover note/letter?

1. **Should you send a cover letter with your résumé?** Unless you are instructed not to send a cover letter, send one. From your perspective as a job hunter, the ideal situation is when you are invited to e-mail a cover letter and résumé. If you are asked to e-mail a résumé only, you still have an opportunity to send a brief cover letter. In such instances, communication etiquette dictates that you e-mail a cover note with your résumé. As long as you are reminding an individual or a company of who you are, why you are contacting them, and what you are sending, benefit from the note by adding some key persuasive material you would normally include in a cover letter.

   Some recruiters are irritated by cover notes that are too brief and informal. Here we are referring to the one-line notes that simply say, "Here is my résumé" or "See the attached file." Applicants who submit such notes communicate ineffectively, overlook standard professional expectations, and miss an opportunity to persuade recruiters to give them an interview. Be careful if you send cover notes. Many of us have become too informal and careless when developing e-mail messages as the example one-liners above describe. Furthermore, too many grammatical and spelling errors crop up in e-mail messages. This raises the question, How many grammatical or spelling errors are too many in cover letters and résumés? The answer is, one.

2. **Should you attach your résumé to a file containing your cover note/letter?** You are strongly encouraged not to attach your résumé as a separate file. Instead, send it with your cover letter as part of the e-mail message. Sending attachments is risky business. It is not uncommon for receivers to have trouble opening attached files, in which case

they will consider you no further. In addition, many recruiters will not open attachments for fear of computer viruses.

Just as scanners do not scan all fonts accurately, there are occasions when there are compatibility problems between e-mail and word processing programs that ruin a résumé's appearance or readability. In addition, including such items as symbols (e.g., bullets, Wingdings), graphics, and pictures also interfere with clean transmission.[11]

In addition, e-stalking is discouraged. Here *e-stalking* refers to job hunters who send an electronic copy of their résumé several times. Another example refers to applicants who do not capitalize any letters or mysteriously capitalize some words while not capitalizing proper names and the first words of sentences.[12]

Given the large number of online résumés submitted to most companies, be realistic about how quickly and how frequently recruiters are able to respond. Just because the technology makes quick responses possible (e.g., instant messaging), recruiters' workloads and schedules may not. This is not to say you should not contact the company to which you e-mailed your résumé. Just be realistic regarding how soon they can respond and be polite. It is all right to inquire about the status of an opening, but it is counterproductive to scold recruiters for not getting back in touch with you quickly.[13]

Submitting a Scannable Résumé A **scannable résumé** is one that can be scanned into a résumé database clearly, accurately, and completely. Here are some tips on how to develop scannable résumés, which are discussed later in this section.

Submit a scannable version of your résumé when (1) you are asked to, (2) you are mailing or dropping off a regular hardcopy résumé, and (3) when you are submitting your résumé to an independent résumé database service.

If you are uncertain whether a company scans résumés into a résumé database, call and ask or check for such information at its website. If you are still uncertain, mail or drop off two résumés—a regular version and a scannable version. Attach a note to each indicating which one is the regular (mail version) and which one is the scannable version.

Independent résumé database services provide job hunters with the opportunity to have their résumés scanned into (posted on) résumé databases that are viewed by literally thousands of potential employers. Job hunters pay a fee for the service. It is typically $50 or less, and some are free. If you use one or more of these services, ask if you can update your résumé at will, whether there is a charge, and if your résumé will be dropped after a specified period of inactivity.

Employers access these services' résumé databases in search of candidates who meet their needs. Employers may query databases in their entirety or only those portions containing the résumés for specialized areas (e.g., accounting, engineering, marketing, medicine, sales).

Immediately below the Name & Contact Information section of your scannable résumé, include a major section titled Key Words. This section on scannable résumés is critical. Key Words refers to a list of 10–20 words/phrases that focus on business skills, accomplishments, and personal qualities especially relevant to a potential employer. Furthermore, you are advised to present the key words in three subsections—business skills, accomplishments, and personal qualities. Your *business skills* subsection might include key words such as: leader, motivator, and team player. Your *accomplishments* subsection might include key words such as: Bachelor's Degree, MBA, and CPA. Your *personal qualities* subsection might include key words such as: open-minded, risk taker, and decisive.

Whether your résumé is pulled for further consideration depends greatly on the key words you include and the order in which they are presented. Choose 10–20 key words/phrases that you believe are a good fit between your qualifications, interests, and work attitudes and the needs and interests of potential employers. In other words, choose key words that focus on relevant skills and accomplishments as well as qualities employers typically value. For example, if you want to work for a creative, competitive company, then early in this section include key words such as *creative* and *competitive*. Once you have selected your key words, prioritize them from most-to-least important, left-to-right or top-to-bottom.

When writing your Key Words section, develop two key words lists. One is a list of words that describe your qualifications and work-related attitudes. The other list contains words you think employers would use to find a match in the résumé database. This helps you better understand employers' needs and, in turn, you are more likely to include key words/phrases that will result in bringing up your résumé for consideration.

Aside from the Key Words section, scannable résumés are not noticeably different in content from regular résumés, although scannable résumés do have some formatting requirements (listed below). Before looking at the list, however, remind yourself that the requirements vary from company to company because they use different scanning equipment and software. Contact each company's human resources department in advance and ask for specific guidelines.

- Print hard copies of scannable résumés and cover letters on a laser printer.
- Print hard-copies of scannable résumés on white paper (with no dark speckles), and use black ink.
- Delete headers and footers.
- Use a font size of 10–14 points.
- Use a simple font such as Optima, Ariel, Palatino, Times New Roman, or Helvetica. Avoid scripted fonts where the characters are too close together.
- Do not use multiple columns like a newspaper. Instead, use a standard paragraph format starting all lines at the left margin.
- Place your name at the top of each page on a separate line starting at the left margin.
- Don't center any information. Don't right-justify your lines.
- Place contact information (home, work, and cell phone, fax number, and e-mail address) on separate lines below your name starting at the left margin. (City, state, and zip code can be on the same line.)
- Put section headings in all capital letters and start each at the left margin.
- Leave one blank space before and after a diagonal (/) so it doesn't touch numbers or letters on either side.
- Don't use percent signs, ampersands, boxes, graphics, or clip art.
- Use simple, round, solid bullets. Hollow bullets may be read as the letter *o*.
- Don't fold or staple scannable résumés. Mail or hand deliver them to recruiters in flat 9x12-inch envelopes. As an extra precaution, send them in cardboard, express mail envelopes.

Posting Your Résumé on Your Web Page This approach is helpful in one of the following not-so-uncommon situations:

- Assume you are at a social function or professional association meeting and someone expresses work-related interest in you. You could easily hand the person a business card containing your URL address and mention that both an ASCII version and traditional version of your résumé are posted on your web page. If you don't have business cards, have some made at a copy shop or design and print your own using one of several business card software programs on the market (e.g., My Professional Business Cards by MySoftware Company and 20,000 Business Cards by Data Becker).

- Assume you are interested in job possibilities with a company. Send them a job-inquiry letter containing your URL address. In the letter, clearly state that both an ASCII version and a traditional version of your résumé are posted on your web page.

Be sure to include a link to an ASCII version of your résumé on your home page. This enables employers to download your résumé into their résumé database.

Include a link to your traditional résumé. This copy will have that professional appearance and will be easy to read, whether on computer screen or printed out. In your traditional résumé, you can set up hyperlinks based on key words that tie into relevant skills, training, accomplishments, attitudes, etc. These hyperlinks enable you to provide additional information that recruiters may or may not choose to read. Here are several points about setting up hyperlinks in your résumé.

- Select them based on key words that are most likely to capture the interest of recruiters.
- Make sure the quality of the material at each hyperlink is well-organized and of good quality (e.g., content, grammar, spelling).
- Don't place too much information in a hyperlink. If recruiters feel overwhelmed by the quantity of information, they may not spend any more time on your résumé.
- Don't include hyperlinks containing personal information that may lend itself to discrimination. For example, don't mention your age, marital status, race, or religion.
- Make sure each hyperlink works and takes the recruiters to the right starting point.
- Don't assume recruiters will open your hyperlinks. They may not have the time. That's understandable. Just make sure your résumé, less the hyperlink information, is sound enough on its own to persuade recruiters to grant you an interview.

Proceed with Caution! The issue of privacy cannot be overlooked whether you are posting your résumé with an independent résumé database service or on your web page. Like it or not, your posted résumé will likely end up at unanticipated sites. This may please you because the potential is there for it to be looked at by a greater number of employers. However, there are a couple downsides. First, the increase in the number of databases your résumé is in increases the likelihood that your résumé may show up on your current employer's job board, which may get you dismissed. (2) Second, it is a major hassle once employed to have your résumé removed from independent résumé database services that post your résumé without your knowledge. If you have privacy concerns, specify who should have access to your résumé or determine if you can lock out your current employer.

ELECTRONIC RÉSUMÉ RESOURCES

There is much to know about electronic résumés and how to submit them. The information presented above will go a long way in helping you, but it is good to know that there are numerous books and websites available to offer in-depth information and guidance.

Books with Information about Electronic Résumés Résumé writing books typically contain extensive sections on electronic résumés. Be sure you access current books.

How to Keep Your Resume From Getting Lost in Cyberspace
http://fortune.com/2014/08/22/how-to-keep-your-resume-from-getting-lost-in-cyberspace/

Websites with Information about Electronic Résumés A number of websites contain information on electronic résumés. Most of these sites also allow users to post résumés to advertised positions or résumé data banks. Three of these websites are www.jobcenter.com, www.4resumes.com, and www.provenresumes.com.

Should You Use a Résumé Writing Service to Create Your Résumé? If you would rather not develop your own résumés, you could use a résumé writing service. This is a fairly expensive alternative. Such services typically have you come in for an interview so they can learn what your career goals are as well as your education, training, work history, and the like. Then they develop a résumé for you based on the information you shared with them during the interview. Sounds easy enough, assuming you don't mind spending the money.

However, there is a potential downside to having a service develop your résumé. If the person who interviews you and writes your résumé is careless, important information may be omitted. Your résumé may also have a generic ring to it, which will do little to attract recruiters' attention.

No matter your personal view of résumé writing services, you are still the best person to develop your résumé. You know your career aspirations, qualifications, experiences, and personal interests better than anyone else. Furthermore, you are the one most familiar with the organizations and jobs you are interested in pursuing. So, follow the résumé writing suggestions shared in previous sections and write your own.

THE NEED TO TAKE CARE WHEN DEVELOPING RÉSUMÉS

There are many reasons why recruiters do not give résumés serious consideration. Several of these reasons are presented in Figure 16-22.

FIGURE 16-22: DO NOT GIVE RECRUITERS A REASON TO TOSS YOUR RÉSUMÉ!

- **Difficult to read.** Type size is too small (9-point font or smaller); ornate font style is not clear; print is fading.
- **Length concerns.** Recruiter expected a shorter or a longer résumé.
- **Mechanical errors.** Typos, grammar, punctuation, and spelling errors.
- **Format problems.** Too little white space, hard to locate desired sections, and unclear organization due to unclear or nonexistent headings or unconventional ordering of information.
- **Appearance problems.** Cheap paper, poor-quality copy, smudges, soft drink or coffee stains, folded, crumpled, torn, tattered, overuse of emphasis features (e.g., boldfacing, italicizing, underscoring), too many font sizes, etc.
- **Gimmicks.** Paper color other than white or off-white, clip art, using several colors of ink, using an ink color other than black for the entire résumé, and wasting precious space by including ornate borders.
- **Incomplete contact information.** It's a struggle to contact you.
- **Personal pronoun use.** Avoid pronouns such as *I* and *me*.

FIGURE 16-22: DO NOT GIVE RECRUITERS A REASON TO TOSS YOUR RÉSUMÉ!

- **Unprofessional contact information (e.g., e-mail address).** E-mail addresses such as *PresciousMissy@* . . . . will leave most recruiters questioning your professionalism and maturity. Since we are called for interviews at times, it is good to remind ourselves that our phone voicemail greetings should also be professional. Avoid greetings that force recruiters to listen to even a few seconds of music before they are able to leave a message. Do not chance turning off a recruiter with a cute or funny greeting message on your voicemail. Keep your greeting short and to the point.
- **Immature additions.** Examples include emoticons (e.g., smiley faces), photos, and cartoons.
- **Ineffective job or career objective.** No specifics, does not communicate what you want to do, does not communicate career goals.
- **Irrelevant information provided.** If the information does not relate to the position you are applying for, leave it out.
- **Accuracy and honesty concerns.** If a recruiter suspects the résumé contains false statements or exaggerations, it will be thrown out.
- **Relevant transferable skills missing.**
- **References included.** That space can be better used to present other information. If a recruiter wants to see your references, he or she will ask you.
- **Familiarity with the job and organization missing.** If it is evident that you did not do enough research, your résumé may be set aside.
- **Inappropriate language.** Slang, profanities, abbreviations, and first- and third-person pronouns are reasons for going on to the next résumé.
- **Personal information of a potentially discriminatory nature.** Leave out information such as your age, gender, disability, ethnicity, marital status, children, height, weight, and religion.
- **Desired salary and benefits included.** Save this topic for the second interview. Even then, let the recruiter initiate talk about these matters.
- **Extra documents attached.** Unless asked to do so, don't include reference letters, transcripts, etc.
- **Key Words section missing on an electronic résumé.**
- **Résumé sent as an e-mail attachment.** Recruiters may have difficulty opening the attachment. E-mail your cover letter and résumé as the e-mail message.
- **Failure to follow scannable résumé requirements.**
- **URL address and ASCII version with posted résumés missing.**

The Biggest Mistakes I See on Resumes, and How to Correct Them https://www.linkedin.com/pulse/20140917045901-24454816-the-5-biggest-mistakes-i-see-on-resumes-and-how-to-correct-them

Mechanical errors (e.g., typos, grammar, punctuation, spelling) are especially costly, no matter if they are on the résumé, cover letter, or thank-you note. In a recent survey, the majority of responding executives said that just one or two inadvertent strokes of the keyboard will eliminate a job applicant from consideration.[14] Recruiter concerns regarding mechanical errors are pretty basic. Most recruiters assume that if a job applicant has mechanical errors on the résumé or other documents, if hired, he or she will probably make work errors as well. Do you want to avoid making these potentially costly mistakes? Of course you do!

FIGURE 16-23: HOW TO AVOID EMBARRASSING AND COSTLY WRITING MISTAKES

- **Ask for help.** Search your friends and family for someone who is detail oriented to review and offer input on your application materials.
- **Give yourself a break.** Leave the project for a while and come back to it refreshed.
- **Print it out.** You might miss something on the computer screen that you'll see on hard copy.
- **Look at things differently.** Try reading your résumé backward to catch errors. Sometimes the work is so familiar, you think a word is there and it's not.
- **Read it out loud.** You may hear mistakes you didn't see.

Source Adapted from: The Associated Press. "Want to get hired? Watch out for typos," The Dallas Morning News, July 29, 2009, 11A.

After spending so much time, money, and effort earning a degree, don't let your opportunities slip away due to silly, manageable typos and the like. This is not the time and place to allow the informal writing style so common in text messages, tweets, and e-mail to sabotage your job search efforts. Be careful and good luck!

UPDATE YOUR RÉSUMÉ PERIODICALLY

If you are like most people, after graduation you are busy professionally and in your personal life. In the midst of all this activity, develop a habit of updating your résumé periodically. Do not wait until you find yourself back on the job market to do it. It is too easy to forget past activities that would enhance your résumé's effectiveness, especially if a few years have passed since you were last on the job market.

Updating your résumé is not difficult to do or overly time-consuming. The challenge lies in forming the habit of doing so periodically. Set up a schedule and then get into the swing of adhering to it. Your approach may be to open your résumé file every three, four, or six months and update it. Or, you may simply choose to keep a running list of activities that you update periodically. Then you can update your résumé using your activities list annually or when the need arises.

DO NOT STRETCH THE TRUTH ON YOUR RÉSUMÉ

When developing your résumé, it might be tempting to stretch the truth a bit to make yourself sound better than you are or fill in employment gaps with fictitious jobs to show a continuous work history. Some even tell lies such as claiming they have earned educational credentials they don't have. Even though it is tempting and seems easy to get away with, it is not worth it! Recruiters are likely to verify previous employment and education before making job offers. If during the verification process something appears suspicious, they will ask the specific and potentially embarrassing (to you) questions to get to the truth. To avoid ending up in this position, do not include inflated education statements, grades, or honors, enhanced job titles, puffed-up accomplishments, or altered employment dates on your résumé.[15]

SUMMARY: SECTION 6—
DEVELOPING EFFECTIVE RÉSUMÉS

- Résumés are one of two major documents used by job hunters to persuade recruiters to grant them job interviews.
- Be willing to develop a slightly different or uniquely different résumé for each potential employer.
- Over the years, keep up with changing expectations for résumés.
- Résumés submitted to U.S. organizations should be one-to-three pages long, while those sent to foreign employers may be longer.
- Whether you develop a chronological or a functional résumé, include cross-functional information and leadership experience and training.
- The recommended résumé sections include name and contact information, career (job) objectives, summary of qualifications, relevant skills and accomplishments, education and training, computer skills, work experience, activities and honors, and personal interests.

The last two steps of the seven-step job search process—interviewing convincingly and developing effective follow-up correspondence—are addressed in chapter 17. Checking back with recruiters, reasons for rejection following interviews, and managing your career are also discussed in chapter 17.

Notes

1. Jae Yang and Paul Trap. "When Do You Expect to Retire?" *USA Today*, February15, 2012.

2. Jae Yang and Karl Gelles, "After I retire, I …" *USA Today*, February 23, 2012.

3. Martin Yate. *Career Smarts: Jobs with a Future*. (New York: Ballantine Books, 1997), 6.

4. Jae Yang and Paul Trap. "The Ladders.com Survey of 250,000 Job Seekers." *USA Today*, March 19, 2012.

5. R. D. Lock. *Job Search: Career Planning Guide, Book 2*, 5th ed. (Belmont, CA: Thomson Brooks/Cole, 2005), 41.

6. Sue Shellenbarger. "The Next Youth-Magnet Cities." *The Wall Street Journal*, September 30, 2009.

7. Jia Lynn Yang. "How to Get a Job." *Fortune* (April 13, 2009): 49–56.

8. Sakina Rangwala. "Graduates Should Rethink Job Options." *Denton Record-Chronicle*, May 24, 2009.

9. Joyce Lain Kennedy. "Overseas Recruiters Look for More Information in Résumés." *The Dallas Morning News*, December 4, 1994.

10. Jennifer Vessels. "Diplomacy Is Required When Seeking a Job Abroad." *National Business Employment Weekly*, (September 28–October 4, 1997): 15–16.

11. Mark Wrolstad. "Lying on Résumés: Why Some Can't Resist." *The Dallas Morning News*, December 22, 2001.

12. Joyce Lain Kennedy. "Online Résumés Present Pitfalls." *The Dallas Morning News*, November 25, 2001.

13. Stephanie Armour. "Employers: Enough Already with the E-Résumés." *USA Today*, July 15, 1999.

14. Associated Press. "Want to Get Hired? Watch Out for Typos." *The Dallas Morning News*, July 29, 2009.

15. M. E. Guffey. *Essentials of Business Communication*, 6th ed. (Mason, OH: Thomson South-Western, 2004), 386–87.

JOB SEARCH: INTERVIEWS & BEYOND

17

LEARNING OUTCOMES

After reading this chapter, you should be able to:

1. Discuss the differing goals of job hunters and recruiters with regard to job interviews.

2. Describe the various types of job interviews.

3. Discuss how to prepare for job interviews.

4. Describe the materials job hunters should take along to job interviews.

5. Describe how job hunters can be effective in job interviews.

6. Discuss the major types of follow-up correspondence.

7. Discuss recommended career strategies.

© *Alexander Raths/Shutterstock.com*

BENEFITS OF LEARNING ABOUT THE POST-RÉSUMÉ JOB SEARCH STEPS

1. You increase your chances of working for the type and size of organization that best suits you and in the geographic location you desire.

2. You increase your chances of achieving your desired career growth opportunities and earning goals.

3. You understand recruiters' goals in the interviewing process; thus you are in a better position to persuade them to make you a job offer.

4. You learn what to do and not do when preparing for and participating in interviews.

5. You understand the importance of follow-up correspondence in the search process.

6. You understand how and how often to check back with recruiters following interviews.

7. You learn about several career management strategies that increase your chances of achieving your desired career goals.

SELECT KEY TERMS

INTRODUCTION

A wise job hunter enters into a job interview planning to learn more about the organization and position, determine if the organization and job are a good fit for them, and persuade the recruiter that he or she is a good fit. In turn, a good recruiter enters into a job interview planning to acquire enough additional information about the job candidate to help him or her make an informed hiring decision, which includes determining if the job candidate is a good fit for the job and the organization. Job interviews range from on-campus and phone interviews to group face-to-face interviews and online interviews.

Common types of job interview questions include behavioral-based and closed-ended questions, and commonly asked questions that you can acquire examples of online and at campus career centers. Then, there are the unusual or odd questions some recruiters ask to see if you can think on your feet while remaining composed. Finally, there are the illegal questions you should anticipate being asked which you should determine in advance how you will respond to.

You are strongly encouraged to send thank-you notes following job interviews. Most recruiters appreciate receiving them, while far too many job candidates do not do so. Furthermore, it is ok to check back with recruiters following job interviews regarding the status of hiring decisions. However, do not contact them too frequently, thus becoming an annoyance!

The intent of this chapter is to provide you with information regarding Steps 6 and 7 of the job search process—interviewing convincingly and developing effective follow-up correspondence. Advice on checking back with recruiters and career management, along with a discussion regarding reasons why candidates are rejected following interviews, are included. These goals are realized through discussions regarding the following topics: Step 6—Interviewing Convincingly: interviewing goals, job candidates and recruiters, types of interviews, preparing for job interviews, job interviews—on deck, job interviews—on stage, and interviewing suggestions; Step 7—Developing Effective Follow-Up Correspondence; checking back with recruiters; reasons for rejection following interviews; and managing your career. The information pertaining to the above-mentioned job-search steps is reinforced by several student website resources including *PowerPoint slides, preview tests, chapter assessment tests, writing mechanics rules and guidelines, YouTube videos, interactive exercises*, and the *interactive glossary*.

STEP 6: INTERVIEWING

Interviewing convincingly is Step 6 of the job search process. While job hunters have a fair amount of control over submitting cover letters and résumés, interviews are not guaranteed. Whether you are granted an interview depends, in large part, on the effectiveness of your cover letter and résumé. Since the majority of job offers are made following interviews, it is critical that you work diligently on the previous five steps (covered in chapter 16) to increase your chances of being granted an interview.

INTERVIEWING GOALS: JOB CANDIDATES AND RECRUITERS

Knowledgeable, prepared job hunters and recruiters approach employment interviews with a number of goals in mind. Both parties understand that their time is limited and there is much to be accomplished.

Possibly the only goal both job hunters and recruiters have in common is that of gathering information. Whether you are a job hunter or a recruiter, understanding and appreciating the goals of both parties helps you achieve your specific goals.

JOB CANDIDATES' INTERVIEWING GOALS

Does your first thought concern receiving a job offer following a job interview? That is the usual goal for many job candidates entering interviews, but that should not be your only goal. You may get to the end of an interview and find you are no longer interested in working for that potential employer even if you are made a job offer. It is not uncommon for job candidates to learn things during interviews that sour them on the idea of working for the organizations they are interviewing with. Just as good employment recruiters set out to identify job candidates that are potentially a good fit for their organizations, wise job candidates should set out to determine which organizations are a good fit for them. With this in mind, here are four basic goals you should have when entering into job interviews.

1. Learn more about organizations you are considering.
2. Learn more about the specific job positions you are considering.
3. Determine if you really want to work for the organizations to which you are applying. For example: Is its value system consistent with yours? Is its organizational climate a good fit with your personality? Are the career growth opportunities consistent with your career goals?
4. Persuade the recruiter that you are a good fit for the organization and job opening so he or she will be persuaded to either call you back for another round of interviews or make you a job offer.

RECRUITERS' INTERVIEWING GOALS

Good recruiters have a number of goals in mind as they prepare for and enter into job interviews. They understand the amount of time and money being invested in the recruiting process and the potential impact on their organization resulting from making either an excellent or a poor hiring decision. Here are recruiters' typical goals going into job interviews:

1. Acquire information they were unable to gather from the candidate's cover letter and résumé.
2. Prompt a candidate to explain or elaborate on information in the cover letter, résumé, or grade transcript.
3. Determine the accuracy and honesty of information received previously.
4. Determine if the candidate is qualified for the specific position for which he or she is applying.
5. Decide if the candidate is a good fit for the organization (e.g., Is the candidate's personality appropriate for the organization, coworkers, clients, and other stakeholders?).
6. Use the interview as a way to decide if they will call the candidate back for a second interview, make him or her a job offer, or keep the information on file for future consideration.

You will be a stronger job candidate if you make it a point to understand and appreciate recruiters' needs and goals in addition to your own. Understanding job candidates' needs and goals will also make you a more effective recruiter if you find yourself assuming that role in the future.

TYPES OF INTERVIEWS

Screening interviews and selection interviews are the two major types of job interviews. Screening interviews are short (approximately 20–30 minutes), during which recruiters weed out unacceptable job applicants. Selection interviews typically follow successful screening interviews. However, recruiters may bypass the screening interviews and move straight into selection interviews. Selection interviews are longer than screening interviews, often lasting an entire day (or longer) during which candidates meet with a series of interviewers.

Within the two major types of job interviews discussed above, there are a variety of types or approaches. Several of these are described here.

- **On-Campus Interviews.** These are relatively short screening interviews that provide a convenient, cost-effective means of interviewing with a large number of potential employers.
- **On-Site Interviews.** These are selection interviews that give you an opportunity to visit potential employers' facilities and meet with several people.
- **One-on-One Interviews.** This is the most common interview format. Here you have one interviewer meeting with one job candidate.
- **Panel (Team, Board) Interviews.** These interviews involve two or three interviewers meeting at the same time with one job candidate.

© wavebreakmedia/Shutterstock.com

- **Group Interviews.** These interviews are uncommon. Here you have a single recruiter or a panel of recruiters interviewing two or more candidates simultaneously.
- **Structured Interviews.** During these interviews, interviewers ask predetermined questions. Their goal, by asking the same questions of all job applicants, is to make sure the interviews are nondiscriminatory, thus avoiding potential lawsuits.
- **Unstructured Interviews.** Here interviewers have no set agenda for questions. These interviews are a casual exchange of questions and answers between interviewers and job candidates.

screening interviews Short interviews during which the recruiter's goal is to weed out unacceptable job applicants.

selection interviews Longer interviews where the goal is to select a job candidate for hiring consideration.

on-campus interviews Relatively short screening interviews held on college campuses.

on-site interviews Selection interviews held at employers' work sites.

one-on-one interviews An interview of a job candidate by an individual recruiter.

panel interviews An individual candidate interviewed by two or more recruiters. Also known as team or *board interviews*.

group interviews One recruiter or a panel of recruiters in one session interviewing two or more job candidates simultaneously.

- **Stress Interviews.** This type of interview determines how well job candidates handle pressure. Candidates are asked tough questions. In addition, interviewers are often intentionally sarcastic and/or aggressive. They tend to interrupt, to stare, to ask questions in rapid succession, to criticize answers, and to allow long periods of silence to pass before asking the next question. If you find yourself on the receiving end of a stress interview, stay calm, do not get angry or defensive, and do your best to answer as many questions as possible.
- **Phone Interviews.** These are interviews conducted over the phone. They are conducted in a one-on-one, panel, or group interview format. In his book, *Job Search*, Robert Lock maintains that "the phone interview is being increasingly used as the first screening interview."[1] Phone interviews should be taken as seriously as face-to-face interviews right down to wearing appropriate business attire!
- **Computer Interviews.** These are screening interviews that involve candidates sitting at a computer keying in responses to a set of questions. The computer program used by the recruiter keeps track of the time needed to answer each question, length of pauses, and changed answers.
- **Videotaped Interviews.** These are taped interviews of the applicant set in professional studios, then sent to prospective employers. When recruiters request this format, they typically send job applicants a written list of questions in advance.
- **Videoconferencing Interviews.** These are screening interviews during which job candidates and interviewers meet simultaneously from different locations. One day videoconferencing interviews, as we now know them, will be improved with telepresence (hologram) technology. In such instances, holograms (3-D images) of both parties would replace 2-D images on screens.
- **Online Interviews.** These interviews include a video component, but differ from computer interviews. Here interviewers and candidates visit online in an instant messaging format.
- **Video Online Interviews.** These interviews can be conducted by recruiters from their desktop, laptop, or tablet computers. Given their Web-based format, video online interviews can be multicast to several locations simultaneously.

7 Tips for Mastering the Phone Interview
http://blog.sfgate.com/gettowork/2014/06/25/7-tips-for-mastering-the-phone-interview/

© phpatbig/Shutterstock.com

INTERVIEWING RESOURCES

There are numerous ways to learn more about interviewing. For example, visit your campus career center or your campus internship office. The people at these offices will share extensive information and advice regarding interviewing. Some professors, especially business communication professors, can share similar information and advice. You could also attend interviewing workshops. These are sponsored by student and professional associations or by your campus career center.

Several good books focus exclusively on the topic of interviewing. A sampling of these includes *Knock 'Em Dead Job Interview Guide: How to Turn Job Interviews Into Job Offers* (Martin Yate), *The 10 Most Common Interview Questions* (Alison Green), and *101 Great Answers to the Toughest Interview Questions* (Ron Fry).

Numerous websites contain a wealth of information regarding interviewing, including www.job-interview.net and www.interviewcoach.com.

SUMMARY: SECTION 1— STEP 6: INTERVIEWING

- Interviewing, Step 6 of the job search process, offers no guarantee.
- Job hunters' interviewing goals include learning more about organizations and jobs, determining if they really want to work for the organization, and convincing recruiters they are a good fit.
- Recruiters' (interviewers') interviewing goals include gathering information, prompting candidates to expand on information, determining the accuracy and honesty of information previously received, deciding if candidates are truly qualified and a good fit, and determining candidates' ongoing viability in the hiring process.
- The two major types of job interviews are screening interviews and selection interviews.
- Within the two major types of interviews, we find the following types: on-campus, on-site, one-on-one, panel, group, structured, unstructured, stress, phone, computer, videotaped, videoconferencing, online, and video online interviews.

PREPARING FOR JOB INTERVIEWS

Preparing properly for job interviews is a time-consuming process involving careful thought and focused effort. Do not sabotage your interviewing opportunities by assuming little preparation is needed, like some who believe it involves nothing more than developing canned responses to a list of the 50–100 most commonly asked questions. You owe it to yourself to do better than that.

THE GOOD NEWS

If you were diligent in Steps 3–5 of the job search process (detailed in chapter 16), you have a huge head start on the interview preparation process.

Step 3 involves researching industries, organizations, and jobs. Your ability to convince an interviewer that you are familiar with his or her organization, the industry in which his or

computer interviews Typically screening interviews that involve candidates sitting at a computer keying in responses to a set of questions.

videotaped interviews Interviews in which recruiters typically send advance guidelines and questions to a candidate who responds in a professional studio setting and then sends the video to prospective employers.

videoconferencing interviews Screening interviews typically conducted using videoconferencing.

online interviews Computer interviews conducted over the Internet.

video online interviews Online interviews with a video component.

her organization is positioned, and the job for which you are applying influences the interviewer's perception of you either favorably or unfavorably when the hiring decision is made.

Step 4 of the job search process involves writing persuasive cover letters. While part of doing so involves communicating familiarity with organizations, industries, and specific jobs, one of the key components of an effective cover letter involves communicating your qualifications and desire, and how they meet a potential employer's needs. During job interviews, you should not only re-emphasize your qualifications and desire, but also clearly indicate that you understand the connection between what you have to offer and their hiring needs.

Step 5 of the process involves developing effective résumés. If you approach developing résumés as was discussed in chapter 16, you cannot help but gain better insight into yourself in terms of your short- and long-term career goals, your strengths and weaknesses, your special talents, your academic capabilities, your learning goals, your thoughts on work, and your personal interests. Awareness of all this helps you immensely when answering and asking questions during interviews. Your ability to do so will not only help you control typical nervousness, but will also leave interviewers with the perception that you are a prepared, confident candidate.

ANTICIPATE A SHORT SMALL-TALK SESSION BEFORE THE INTERVIEW

Before jumping into the conventional question-and-answer phase of job interviews, recruiters often engage you in a few minutes of small talk on a topic or topics unrelated to the job opening and the company. You may end up talking about one of your hobbies or pastimes, the outcome of a current sporting event, or your thoughts regarding a recently released movie. It is probably best to avoid talking about politics or religion during the small-talk session.

Recruiters initiate small-talk sessions for a specific purpose. They are trying to relax job candidates. Most recruiters understand that relaxed job candidates share more and better-quality information during the question-and-answer phase than overly nervous candidates share. Anticipate these small-talk sessions at the start of job interviews and go with the flow. Go to your interviews with one or two topics in mind that you could easily visit about during the small-talk sessions. These might be hobbies or enjoyable pastimes. Avoid mentioning potentially life-threatening pastimes such as skydiving and rock climbing, because most organizations would not want to lose you shortly after hiring you. Be tasteful in your input and do your best to keep your responses brief. Finally, during the small-talk sessions, be careful not to verbally or nonverbally dismiss (put down) one of your interviewer's hobbies or interests. Doing so may get you eliminated as a viable candidate before the question-and-answer session begins.

ANTICIPATE THE MAJOR TYPES OF QUESTIONS THAT MAY BE ASKED

The most common type of interview question asked by U.S. recruiters is the behavioral question. Behavioral questions require job candidates to respond based on past situations or experiences. The belief is that such responses are good predictors of future performance and behavior. Here is an example of a behavioral question: Describe a time when you had to deal with an angry customer and you achieved a mutually agreeable outcome. If asked such a question, you would be expected to share specifics regarding a time when you were in the midst of such a situation during which you calmed the customer and arrived at a successful outcome.

In contrast, imagine being asked a hypothetical question about a similar situation—one not based on experience. Let's use the same example here: If you were confronted by an angry customer, would you be able to deal with him or her successfully? In response to such a question, you would say that you would be able to handle the situation successfully without being certain you would be able to do so. For that matter, your interviewer cannot say, with any degree of certainty either, that you would be able to do so. The behavior-based format at least gives interviewers some past experience on which to base their perceptions of job candidates' responses.

Behavioral questions are open-ended questions. This type of interview question requires more than a yes or no answer. Most interview questions are open ended because they net interviewers more information. Here are some examples. What two things would your former/current supervisor like you to improve on? Tell me about a work-related accomplishment you are proud of. What motivates you to excel?

Interviewers also ask closed-ended questions. Closed-ended questions illicit short, limited responses. Candidates are able to answer closed-ended questions with two-or-three word responses or a simple yes or no. Here are some examples. How long have you worked for your current employer? Do you get along well with fellow employees and customers? Do you smoke?

While the closed-ended format is needed to gather some information during interviews, good interviewers limit the number of these questions because they net little information. For that matter, many closed-ended questions are unnecessary because the information can often be found in cover letters or résumés. For example, why ask a candidate how many years he or she worked at his or her last job when this information is typically included on the résumé?

As a job candidate, expect to be asked some closed-ended questions. However, when the opportunity presents itself, expand on your short responses to provide recruiters with additional information they did not anticipate receiving. Doing so will be appreciated. For example, if you were asked if you are a take-charge person, your initial response would likely be yes. Do not stop there. Give an example of time when you stepped forward and took charge of project or situation when others appeared unwilling to do so.

Remember, recruiters go into interviews with the intention of gathering as much information about job candidates as possible. As a job candidate, help recruiters achieve this goal and impress them in the process by providing them with more useful information.

open-ended questions Recruiter questions that require more than short, limited responses.

closed-ended questions Recruiter questions that result, by design, in short, limited responses.

© wavebreakmedia/Shutterstock.com

ANTICIPATE COMMONLY ASKED QUESTIONS

Every job search book, job search website, and campus career center provides a list of the 50–100 most commonly asked interview questions. With the exception of the varying length of these lists, the questions are fairly similar. Here are some examples along with suggestions on how to answer them.

- **Tell me about yourself.** Limit your response to relevant facts about your education and career. Do not set out to tell your entire life story.
- **Why do you want to work for this company?** Show the connection between your career goals and the position you are applying for as well as the company. This is one of those times when researching the job and company will really pay off.
- **Give me an example of one of your weaknesses.** Give a work-related example that you have been working on overcoming. It is important that you move your response quickly to describing what you are doing to overcome the weakness and the progress you have made.
- **Tell me why we should hire you.** Share those skills, attributes, and qualities you possess that are a good fit for the job and company.
- **Tell me one of your workplace success stories.** Share a success story that grew out of adversity. In other words, you faced down a tough situation, took hold of it, and turned it into a success. Such an answer will speak to your tenacity in a positive way.
- **Are you a team player?** You will likely answer yes, but don't stop there. Share an example of a team you served on by describing how you got along with your teammates and what your specific contributions were.
- **What do you see yourself doing in 20 years?** This is not a difficult question to respond to if you have some sense of where you want to take your career over the long term. If today you could not answer this question quickly and confidently, get busy and reflect on where you think you want to take your career over the next few decades.[2]

You are encouraged to familiarize yourself with lists of commonly asked questions. This is not to suggest that you memorize insincere-sounding, canned responses for these questions. It is good preparation, however, to reflect on each question so you have a general sense of how to answer it.

ANTICIPATE UNUSUAL OR ODD QUESTIONS

Do not be surprised by an occasional question that appears to have no relationship whatsoever to the job or organization you are targeting in your job search. Interviewers have their reasons for asking such questions. Just do your best not to get flustered.

unusual (odd) questions Recruiter questions that appear to have no relationship to the position for which the candidate is interviewing.

One of the classic examples of an **unusual question** is: Why are manhole covers round? Unless you are applying for a specific type of engineering position, being asked this question will probably make little sense to you. The same is true of the following odd question: Why is it common in most high-rise hotels and many high-rise office buildings for the numbering system for the floors to bypass floor #13? These questions and others like them provide recruiters an opportunity to determine (1) if you can remain calm, (2) if you can think on your feet, and (3) if you can think analytically and logically. Responding to such questions is not totally about coming up with the right answer. However, recruiters prefer you at least make a reasonable attempt. No doubt about it, responding to off-the-wall questions can be challenging. As for the manhole cover question, they are round so they cannot fall through the hole. In regard to the 13th-floor question, it has to do with perceived bad luck.

ANTICIPATE ILLEGAL AND UNETHICAL QUESTIONS

Federal law dictates that there are certain questions recruiters cannot ask job applicants without threatening their equal opportunity for employment. For example, asking a woman how many children she plans is potential discrimination. The major federal laws that support equal opportunity employment include the following:

- Title VII of the Civil Rights Act of 1964 and the Equal Employment Opportunity Act of 1972, which state that job applicants cannot be discriminated against on the basis of race, color, religion, sex, or national origin.
- The Age Discrimination Act of 1968 prohibits hiring discrimination against anyone aged 40 or older.
- The Americans with Disabilities Act of 1990 protects individuals from hiring discrimination based on their disabilities.

As opposed to including a lengthy list of sample illegal questions, the main categories or topics that are discriminatory in nature are listed in Figure 17-1.

11 Common Interview Questions That Are Actually Illegal
http://www. businessinsider.com/ 11-illegal-interview-questions-2013-7

FIGURE 17–1: POTENTIALLY DISCRIMINATORY CATEGORIES OR TOPICS

- Age
- Gender
- Height
- Weight
- Health conditions
- Disabilities
- Marital status (e.g., married, single, divorced, separated)
- Family status (e.g., number of current or planned children)
- Sexual orientation
- Race
- Birthplace
- National (ethnic) origin
- Ancestry
- Religion
- Memberships in organizations
- Record of offenses (e.g., arrests, convictions)

An exception to asking **illegal questions** exists. This exception is the bona fide occupational qualification (BFOQ). A *BFOQ* is a characteristic that is integral to the job itself. For example, a job might require heavy lifting. This requirement might legally eliminate some potential job candidates incapable of heavy lifting.

Even though the information presented above is commonplace, some interviewers intentionally or unintentionally still sneak in the occasional impermissible question. Watch

illegal questions
Questions that interviewers are legally prohibited from asking unless the questions fit the guidelines of bona fide occupational qualifications.

for interviewers who not only slip illegal questions into the question-and-answer phase, but also during small-talk sessions when candidates might let their guard down.

Whether recruiters ask you illegal or unethical questions intentionally or unintentionally, you should have considered in advance how you will respond to them. Here are some suggestions on how to handle them.

- You may choose to answer such questions without hesitation either because you do not have strong feelings about being asked such questions or you want the job so much that you do not want to jeopardize your chances by possibly upsetting the interviewer.
- You may choose to not answer such questions by politely saying, "I do not choose to answer that question" or "I do not feel obligated to answer that question."
- You may choose not to answer such questions and scold the interviewer for asking. However, if you choose this option, the interview might be over.
- You may choose to ask the interviewer why he or she is asking the question or inquire into the connection between the question and the requirements of the job. In doing so, make sure your choice of words, tone of voice, and facial expressions are polite, positive, and professional.
- You may choose to respond to an interviewer's concern rather than answer the question directly. For example, instead of indicating how many children you have when asked, assure him or her that your obligations and activities in your personal life will not interfere with your job and professional responsibilities.

Being asked illegal and unethical questions is awkward, but it is a fact of life. The best thing you can do is anticipate such questions and decide in advance how you will be most comfortable responding.

Realistically during job interviews you should anticipate being asked one or more of the each of the types of interview questions discussed above. If you anticipate this, you won't be caught off guard during interviews which could easily happen if you assumed recruiters never ask illegal questions.

BEING ASKED ABOUT WEAKNESSES AND FAILURES

Now why do recruiters want to go and frustrate job candidates by asking about their weaknesses and failures? Why don't they just stick to topics about applicants' strengths and successes? Good interviewers will ask for information regarding your weaknesses and failures. They do so for the following reasons: (1) get a balanced picture of the job candidates—not only strengths and successes, (2) determine if job candidates are willing to be honest regarding those aspects of their lives, (3) decide what job candidates have learned from their failures, and (4) determine if job candidates are doing anything to overcome their weaknesses and reduce their instances of failure.

As you prepare for interviews, plan to be as honest and forthright about your weaknesses and failures as you are about your strengths and successes. You are not alone in having weaknesses and failures. We are all human enough to join you in those camps. However, you can impress recruiters by mentioning what you have done or are currently doing to overcome your weaknesses and reduce your instances of failure, and what you have learned from your failures.

DEVELOP QUESTIONS TO ASK RECRUITERS

Most interviewers expect job candidates to bring a list of questions to interviews. As you prepare for interviews, develop a list of questions. Keep in mind, however, that such lists may vary somewhat among different potential employers.

Develop a list of 10–12 questions. Developing a longer list is unrealistic because you will not have time to ask several questions. You may not even get the opportunity to ask all 10–12 questions, so prioritize them. This way you might at least get a chance to ask those most important to you. If you find yourself going through a series of on-site interviews, you might not get to ask one specific interviewer all your questions, but possibly you can spread them out over the series of interviews.

Be wise when developing your questions. Your questions, if carefully developed, can be persuasive. Develop questions that communicate that you have researched the organization and its general industry. Develop questions that communicate you understand the specific job you are considering and the potential employer's needs. Develop questions that communicate both clearly and strongly your interest in the organization and job. Generally speaking, questions about the job duties, company growth, and company goals are recommended; whereas, questions regarding pay and benefits are discouraged. The sample questions listed below are broken into good questions and poor questions.

Good Questions (they show your interest in the company)

- Last year, your company began marketing [name a product] in a new market. Are there plans to expand into other new markets in the near future?
- I'm aware of the following [specific responsibilities] associated with the job. Are there other responsibilities?
- If I'm hired, what contributions to the company would you like me to make during my first year? First five years?
- This sounds like a wonderful company. Please tell me more about why your employees are so happy working for you.

Poor Questions (they show interest in yourself, not in the company)

- How often can I expect a pay raise, and what is the typical percentage increase?
- Will the company pay tuition and fees for my MBA if I decide to go back to school?
- How many paid personal days and holidays will I receive? Will this number increase the longer I am with the company?
- How many weeks of vacation do I get, and how long do I need to wait before taking the first week of vacation?

As you can see from the examples above, you need to be careful regarding what questions make their way onto your list. Arriving at interviews with a list is admirable, while including good questions is critical.

Make sure your list of questions is visible to the interviewer. Write them down and make sure to set your list on your lap during the interview. The interviewer may not give you the opportunity to ask all your questions, or any of them for that matter, but he or she will be aware that you developed a list as expected.

This is a good time to mention a couple books that focus on questions to ask at interviews. The first is *101 Dynamite Questions to Ask at Your Job Interview* (Richard Fein) and the other is *201 Best Questions to Ask on Your Interview* (John Kador).

PERSUASIVE OPPORTUNITIES

Wise job candidates know the value of capitalizing on persuasive opportunities throughout interviews. Four key persuasive opportunities are discussed in the following section: reviewing your list of skills employers want in job candidates, reviewing your list of attributes employers want in job candidates, reviewing your list of merchandising qualities, and developing a list of success stories. Basically, if you have it and it is valued by potential employers, include it.

REVIEW YOUR LIST OF SKILLS EMPLOYERS WANT IN JOB CANDIDATES

There was a discussion in chapter 16 about the skills employers look for in job candidates and the persuasive potential of such awareness in the job search process. Just as you were encouraged to communicate these qualities in your cover letters and résumés, you are also encouraged to do so in your job interviews. The list of desired skills presented in chapter 16 is repeated below.

- Communication skills—especially listening, presentation, and writing skills
- Interpersonal skills (people skills)
- Social skills
- Teaming skills
- Analytical skills
- Decision-making skills
- Problem-solving skills
- Leadership skills
- Management skills
- Technology skills

Do not give up an opportunity to persuade potential employers that you are the right choice. Emphasize the desired skills you possess in your job interviews.

REVIEW YOUR LIST OF ATTRIBUTES EMPLOYERS WANT IN JOB CANDIDATES

A discussion in chapter 16 reviewed the attributes employers look for in candidates and the persuasive potential of such awareness in the search process. Just as you were encouraged to communicate these qualities in your cover letters and résumés, you are also encouraged to do so in your job interviews. The list of desired attributes presented in chapter 16 is repeated below. Recruiters look for job candidates who are:

- Polite
- Tactful
- Self-motivated
- Self-starters
- Flexible/adaptable
- Honest
- Ethical
- Open-minded
- Ambitious
- Willing to take risks
- Creative thinkers
- Receptive to business travel
- Open to other cultures

Do not give up an opportunity to persuade potential employers that you are the right choice. Emphasize the desired attributes you possess in your job interviews.

REVIEW YOUR LIST OF MERCHANDISING QUALITIES

Review your merchandising qualities (selling points) as you prepare for interviews. Your merchandising qualities are those qualities that make you an exceptional fit for a specific job and organization. Just as you were encouraged to mention these in your cover letters and résumés, you are also encouraged to do so in job interviews. Keep in mind that those qualities you choose to include will differ from employer to employer.

While preparing for job interviews, work your merchandising qualities into the questions you plan to ask recruiters. In addition, reflect on how you might work your merchandising qualities into your responses to recruiter's questions. By focusing the recruiter's attention on your merchandising qualities, you convince him or her that you are an exceptional fit for the job and organization.

DEVELOP A LIST OF SUCCESS STORIES

Each of us has success stories to tell. Whether they come from the workplace, school, or elsewhere, they can work to our advantage during job interviews. The most effective **success stories** are those that speak to times when we overcame obstacles and turned bad situations into successes. I am reminded of one of my former students who, despite several documented learning disabilities, worked hard and graduated from both college and law school. This young man certainly has several good success stories to draw from!

The trick is to develop a list of at least two or three success stories and then be prepared to share them during job interviews. Work your success stories into the questions you plan to ask recruiters. In addition, determine how you will be able to work your success stories

success stories
Examples of past successful experiences.

into your responses to recruiters' questions. Most recruiters look favorably on candidates who overcome adversity by turning it into success. Your challenge is to work such success stories into your interviews.

> ## SUMMARY: SECTION 3—
> ## PERSUASIVE OPPORTUNITIES
> - Review your list of skills that employers look for in job candidates.
> - Review your list of attributes that employers look for in job candidates.
> - Review your list of merchandising qualities (selling points) you can work into responses to recruiter questions and questions you will ask recruiters when you are given the opportunity to do so.
> - Develop a list of success stories you can share during interviews.

ADDITIONAL INTERVIEW PREPARATION SUGGESTIONS

As you have probably already concluded, preparing for job interviews is a time-consuming process. However, by putting in the time and effort necessary to prepare properly, you will enter interviews more confident and relaxed. This section contains useful interview preparation suggestions ranging from practicing responses to anticipated interview questions, determining your net worth, and preparing your references list to gathering materials to take to the interview, determining the route to the interview, and preparing yourself psychologically and physically.

PRACTICE

Practice your responses to anticipated interview questions either alone, before others, or before a video camera. However, try not to end up with responses that sound scripted. Use the same practice approach to asking the questions on your questions list. If available to you at your campus career center, conduct some mock interviews. Pay special attention to your nonverbal behaviors (e.g., eye contact, facial expressions, body position, posture, fidgeting). Your nonverbal actions play just as important a role as what you say.

DETERMINE YOUR BENEFITS WISH LIST

While you should avoid initiating a conversation regarding benefits during job interviews, you need to be prepared to discuss these issues when recruiters open the doors to such issues. If you are able to discuss benefits intelligently, you are more persuasive because you show you are prepared.

Do your homework ahead of time. Conduct the amount of research needed to determine not only what the typical benefits package is in the organization to which you are applying, but also the industry, regional, and/or local norms. If you have access to a campus career center, their staff can help you acquire such information.

Be ready to discuss and even make decisions regarding "cafeteria benefits packages." Under these systems, you will not receive all benefits offered by the company, but instead are allowed to choose a select number from a large list. This approach gives you a chance to customize your benefits package.

DETERMINE YOUR WORTH

You are strongly discouraged from initiating a conversation regarding salary during job interviews. However, you need to be prepared to discuss salary issues when recruiters bring up the topic. If you are able to discuss salary realistically and intelligently, you will be more persuasive than you would otherwise.

Here again, do your homework in advance of interviews. Conduct the amount of research needed to determine your current market value. This involves determining the typical salary range for a person with your training, qualifications, and experience levels. A good starting point to explore salaries is http://www.salary.com/. When determining specific ranges, however, remember these often change by industry and geographical location. In addition, you are advised to learn what specific range potential employers have in mind. If you have access to a campus career center, it can help you acquire information.

Once you learn the applicable salary range or ranges, remind yourself that it is unwise to announce the low-end figure when asked by an interviewer about your desired starting salary. At least, mention the midrange figure, but be able to justify your request. You may tie your salary request objectively into moving, living, or commuting expenses. If you decide to respond with the top-end figure, you may bid yourself out of consideration for the job. However, responding with the top-end figure gives interviewers some room to negotiate down, which places you in a cooperative light. The trick is knowing what your real bottom line is.

Salary negotiation is a broad and important topic worthy of extensive study. Such detailed attention is beyond the scope of this book, but there are several excellent resources available to you. For example, you might consider reading one of the following books about salary negotiation: *Five Minutes to a Higher Salary* (Lewis C. Lin), *What Color Is Your Parachute?* (Richard N. Bolles), and *Mastering Salary Negotiations* (Jayant Neogy).

Salary issues are important to all of us. However, when the salary issue is raised in job interviews, be knowledgeable regarding your market value and what the organization is willing to pay. Be careful not to undersell yourself, but at the same time, do not come across as unrealistic and greedy.

ANTICIPATE TESTING DURING THE INTERVIEWING PROCESS

Employers have been testing job candidates during the interview process for practically as long as job interviews have been conducted. They do so to test job candidates' abilities, skill levels, potential, knowledge level, etc., in a variety of areas. You will not be required to take every conceivable test during job interviews, but you are challenged to anticipate the specific types of exams potential employers may require you to take during the interviewing process and prepare accordingly. The following tests are examples of some that you might be required to take when applying for white-collar positions.

- Writing tests
- Presentations tests
- Applications software
- Handwriting tests
- Psychological tests
- Drug tests
- Personality tests

The test formats vary. For example, the multiple-choice format is often used for intelligence tests, whereas telephone, keyboarding, application software, and programming tests are typically hands-on tests at a computer. With analytical and math tests, you are often required to solve problems, and writing tests require you to do some writing. Interpersonal skills tests may find you participating in role-playing exercises. As for presentation tests, you may actually need to give a short, stand-up presentation.

PREPARE A LIST OF REFERENCES

While you are not required to do so, you are strongly encouraged to prepare a list of references to take to job interviews. You never know when you might be asked to provide such a list.

Your first task is to identify five or six references you would like to include on your references list. Secure each reference's permission before adding him or her to your list, however. Here is the suggested mix of references: three current or former supervisors/managers or fellow workers, one or two neighbors or friends, and a member of the clergy. Or, all of your references can be current or former supervisors/managers or fellow workers.

Next, type your list on a single piece of standard-size typing paper using a 12-point, legible font. Use the title "Job References for …" The title should be boldfaced and use a 14–16-point font. List the references right down the center of the paper. Be sure to include titles and employers for each, if applicable, plus addresses, phone numbers, and e-mail addresses. Then, make several copies to take along to each interview. If the recruiter does not ask for your references, near the end of the interview ask if he or she would like a copy. This makes you look prepared.

GATHER MATERIALS YOU SHOULD TAKE TO INTERVIEWS

As you prepare for interviews, gather the necessary materials to take along. What materials should you take? The following list provides the answer. Consider storing the items below in a professional-looking portfolio.

- Clear directions to the interview site
- Contact names and numbers at the interview site
- Some light reading material to fill time when waiting in the lobby or outer office
- A pad of paper
- Two or more pens or pencils (classy pens or pencils that are not chewed on)
- Name(s) and title(s) of interviewer(s)
- Business cards
- Information needed to fill out an application form (e.g., names, addresses, phone numbers, driver's license/number, social security number, military records)
- Samples of your writing or other work

What Are Employers Asking Your References? http://careerbuilder. ca/blog/2012/04/05/ what-areemployers-asking-your-references/

© *vribu/Shutterstock.com*

- Your list of questions to ask interviewer(s)
- Extra copies of your résumé—both traditional and electronic versions
- Copies of your grade transcripts
- Several copies of your references list
- A sampling of past letters of recommendation

This appears to be a long checklist of materials to take along, but keep in mind that they are all important and hold the potential to contribute positively to your interviews.

DETERMINE MODE OF TRANSPORTATION AND ROUTE TO YOUR INTERVIEW SITE AND WHEN TO LEAVE

This is so important. You do not want to arrive just in time or late for a job interview out of breath and flustered after running from the parking lot, parking garage, train station, or bus stop.

Making excuses for last-minute arrivals and showing up late for interviews does not cut it with most recruiters. Candidates are expected to not only arrive on time, but to also be composed and collected when the process begins. So what can you do to make sure you will be on time, composed, and collected? Here are some suggestions.

If you are going to drive to the interview:

- Before the day of the interview, map out your route and write down clear directions to the interview site.
- Before the day of the interview, drive the intended route if you must travel to an area unfamiliar to you. Drive the route during a weekday and the time of day you will be driving to the interview so you can better estimate your timing. If you drive the route on a Sunday afternoon when traffic is light, your timing will likely be way off on the day of the interview.
- Develop an alternate route to the interview site as a backup plan just in case unannounced construction or an accident interferes significantly with your main route to the interview.
- Even if you know how long it will take to travel your primary and secondary routes, it is still a good idea to leave early. Just how early? This depends on whether you will be traveling into a congested metropolitan area, how difficult it will be to find parking near your interview site, and whether you will need to navigate a maze of the elevators in a high-rise building to get to the interview site. It is always better to arrive early and kill time in your car or take a relaxing walk than to frantically rush into your interview.
- Have a relaxing drive. Seriously! You do not want to arrive stressed out.

If you are going to take a taxi, Uber vehicle, train, bus, or some combination thereof to the interview:

- If you are going to take a taxi, the evening before the interview reserve a taxi for the next day.
- If you are going to take a train or bus, the day before the interview write down the train or bus schedule, determine pickup and arrival locations, and transfers.
- Before the day of the interview, travel the route to the interview site so you can verify that the schedule meets your needs, and you are familiar with locations and transfers.

- Purchase train/bus passes or tickets you will need on the day of the interview and make sure you gather together appropriate change if that is what will be needed.
- Gather together credit cards and sufficient cash just in case there is an issue with your train(s) and/or bus(es), and you need to, in turn, take a taxi instead. Familiarize yourself with where you would be able to flag down a taxi near your bus stop(s) and/or train station(s).
- Public transportation is typically very reliable and sticks to schedule. However, it is still a good idea to take an earlier train or bus and give yourself some leeway.

If the thought of unforeseen traffic conditions or bus or train delays ruining your interview is a bit much to handle, here is a practical alternative. Instead of traveling to the interview, stay in a hotel near the interview site the night before. You will be able to get a bit more sleep and eliminate worries about unforeseen traffic problems and train or bus delays. You will arrive at your interview rested and less stressed.

PREPARE FOR GOOD PERSONAL HYGIENE AND APPEARANCE

Appropriate personal hygiene and appearance are very important to most recruiters, and both are within your control. A wealth of information on both topics is available to guide job candidates in the right direction. Unfortunately, some job candidates do not take time to research personal hygiene and appearance expectations, which leaves them open to less-than-favorable recruiter perceptions.

Personal Hygiene Expectations Martin Yate, employment communication expert, summed up personal hygiene considerations when he said, "It should go without saying that bad breath, dandruff, body odor, and dirty, unmanicured nails have the potential to undo all your efforts at putting across a good first impression."[3] None of us wants to be perceived as being slovenly, nor do any us want poor personal hygiene to ruin our chances of receiving a job offer; however, it happens. For that matter, one or a combination of the above examples can kill a positive interview outcome before the interviewer and candidate even enter the small-talk phase. Obviously, personal hygiene matters.

Smoking If you are a smoker, do not do so at job interviews. This refers to cigarettes, e-cigarettes, cigars, and pipes. Even the hint of smoke on you can turn off some recruiters. Store your interview clothing at a nonsmoking friend's home and do not smoke on your way to an interview.

It should go without saying that you should also avoid using chewing tobacco at job interviews.

Chewing Gum Chewing gum during an interview is distracting and looks unprofessional. It is best not to chew gum on your way to the interview site so you do not forget to dispose of it before meeting with the recruiter.

Appearance Expectations If you are unsure of your recruiter's appearance preferences, the general rule is that it is better to dress up and err on the side of formality than the opposite. Most business recruiters prefer that job candidates look neat, clean, and well-groomed and be dressed up. Despite the current casual dress trend in the U.S. workplace, most employers still expect a professional appearance. If you are not 100 percent certain about what professional appearance means, don't guess. Too much is at stake to do so. Figure 17-2 contains some helpful suggestions regarding professional appearance.

FIGURE 17–2: APPEARANCE SUGGESTIONS FOR WOMEN AND MEN

Appearance Suggestions for Women

- Moderate jewelry: earrings (one per ear), bracelets, necklaces, rings, and watches are acceptable
- Moderate makeup
- Moderate perfume if you choose to wear any (none is better)
- No visible tattoos
- No visible piercings in eyebrows, nose, and/or tongue
- Manicured nails
- Non-distracting hair style
- Natural hair color
- Dark-colored suit or pants suit
- Dress shoes with lower heels, polished
- Briefcase, portfolio, or purse of good-quality leather

© wavebreakmedia/Shutterstock.com

Appearance Suggestions for Men

- Moderate jewelry: rings and watches are acceptable; no earrings, bracelets, or necklaces
- No makeup
- Moderate cologne or aftershave if you choose to wear any (none is better)
- No visible tattoos
- No visible piercings in eyebrows, nose, and/or tongue
- Clean, well-trimmed fingernails
- Conservative hair style
- Natural hair color
- Conservative-style, dark-colored suit (not a sports coat and slacks)
- Dress shoes, polished
- Solid color shirt, preferably white
- Necktie, conservative pattern
- Socks same color as suit
- Briefcase or portfolio of good-quality leather

There are several good sources to learn about appropriate job interview appearance. For example, campus career centers typically offer a wealth of appearance advice. In addition, information regarding job interviewing appearance expectations can also be found in job search books and at related online sites.

As you might imagine, this business of getting dressed up for job interviews can get a bit expensive. If your budget is tight and you are getting started from scratch on putting together your interview wardrobe, there are practical cost-cutting measures. For example, you might be able to borrow some or all of your interview wardrobe from family members or friends. If that is not fruitful, consider purchasing the clothing at a thrift shop or a lower-cost clothing store. You can even cut cost on shoes by purchasing a pair of dress shoes at a discount shoe store such as *Payless Shoes*. Then, set these clothes and shoes aside for interviews only so they don't show wear.

If you are unfamiliar with the specifics of appropriate appearance for job interviews, do not wait any longer to educate yourself about recruiters' expectations. Candidate appearance is important to most business recruiters. Obviously, you do not want a recruiter to silently reject you before the interview begins because your appearance isn't in keeping with his or her expectations. This happens to job candidates every day, but does not have to happen to you!

PREPARE YOURSELF PSYCHOLOGICALLY AND PHYSICALLY

Obviously, you want to be at your best during interviews—alert, responsive, and on top of your game. You need to prepare both psychologically and physically. For example, relax the evening before an important interview (e.g., read a good book, exercise, go out to dinner or to a movie with friends, watch a favorite television show). Do not spend the evening rehearsing responses to sample questions over and over. Try to get a good night's sleep, but be careful not to oversleep. Sometimes when we sleep a greater number of hours than we are accustomed to, we wake up groggy the next day. The day of the interview, eat a good breakfast to fuel your body and mind. If you are scheduled for an early afternoon interview, eat an early, light lunch so you are not sleepy during your interview.

These suggestions are *really* important to your ability to influence recruiters positively. After all, if you are not alert and responsive during a job interview, why should a recruiter believe you would act differently on the job?

SUMMARY: SECTION 4—
ADDITIONAL INTERVIEW PREPARATION SUGGESTIONS

- Determine what you are looking for in the way of benefits and salary.
- Anticipate being required to participate in some on-site testing during the interview process.
- Prepare a list of references and other materials to take along to interviews.
- Determine your route to the interview and be realistic about the departure time.
- Be thorough in the attention you give to your personal hygiene and appearance.
- Prepare yourself psychologically and physically.

JOB INTERVIEWS: ON DECK

As recommended earlier in this chapter, you have arrived at your interview site early. If you have, you are off to a good start. Before you leave your car in the parking lot or parking garage to navigate your way into that office building, leave your smartphone or cell phone in your car. Recruiters do not appreciate job candidates' phones ringing during interviews. And apologizing for not turning them off does not cut it! Most people are irritated by individuals who allow their phones to ring in inappropriate settings, including job interviews, presentations, movie theaters, church services, weddings, and funerals.

Imagine now that you are waiting in the lobby or outer office area for the interviewer to either arrive or invite you into his or her office. You probably have a few minutes to kill—ideally around 15 minutes. Your waiting time might even be longer if the interviewer starts late, which is not uncommon. How will you fill this time, whether it is 15 minutes or longer? You could always stare at the ceiling tiles or count the number of leaves on the oversized plant in the lobby. Doing such things will only make you more nervous. You are better off relaxing. Here are some more productive suggestions.

- Greet and be nice to the receptionist if there is one. Recruiters often ask receptionists for their first impressions of job candidates.
- Make a trip to the restroom to freshen up.
- Throw away gum if you are chewing any.
- Locate a drinking fountain and get a drink of water.
- Do some light reading, possibly a paperback book or a magazine you brought along.

You should not kill time eating chips or candy bars; listening to music; playing computer games on your smartphone, tablet, or laptop; texting or e-mailing friends; or surfing the Internet. From a recruiter's perspective, doing such things does not portray you in a good light. Before the interview even starts, recruiters may already imagine you eating chips or candy bars in clients' lobbies, playing computer games in your office, e-mailing or texting friends, or surfing the Internet for nonjob purposes after being hired.

JOB INTERVIEWS: ON STAGE

Before discussing a number of interviewing suggestions, it is helpful to define the typical job interview phases. Most job interviews are approximately 45–60 minutes long and are broken into the four phases described below.

opening phase
The brief phase of the interview during which a good recruiter relaxes the candidate and shares the structure of the interview.

1. **Opening Phase:** In the opening phase, recruiters have two major goals in mind. One goal is to relax the job candidate, which is accomplished via a small-talk session typically lasting 2–5 minutes. This approach helps recruiters establish rapport with the candidates and increases candidates' willingness to share information openly throughout interviews. The other goal is to describe the structure of the interview. For example, the recruiter might say, "This interview will last for 45 minutes and end at 2 o'clock" or "Please hold your questions until I finish asking mine."

2. **Question-and-Answer Phase (recruiter questions):** During this phase recruiters hope to gather as much useful information as possible. This is typically the longest phase of the interview.

© Tom Wang/Shutterstock.com

closing phase
The phase of the interview when the recruiter clarifies outstanding issues and entertains unanswered questions.

3. **Question-and-Answer Phase (job candidate questions):** During this phase the tables are turned, and job candidates are allowed to ask questions of the interviewer. This phase is not typically as long as Phase 2. Some recruiters choose to intermingle Phases 2 and 3 by allowing job candidates to jump in with questions.

4. **Closing Phase:** The purpose of the closing phase is clarification. Beyond that goal, this phase provides both parties the opportunity to ask last-minute questions. The closing phase is a good time for job candidates to offer interviewers a copy of their list of references and for interviewers to tell job candidates when they will be contacted regarding hiring decisions.

Do not underestimate the influence of recruiters' first and last impressions of you on hiring decisions. Recruiters frequently form first impressions of job candidates before interviews begin. Furthermore, many have clear last impressions immediately after the interview. Recruiters' most common first and last impressions are presented in Figure 17-3.

FIGURE 17–3: FIRST AND LAST IMPRESSIONS

Characteristics That Most Influence Recruiters' First Impressions of Job Candidates

- Punctuality
- Appearance
- Handshake

If mishandled, any one of these could destroy a job candidate's hopes of a job offer before the interview even starts.

© Syda Productions/Shutterstock.com

What Recruiters Remember Most Immediately After Interviews

- Eye contact
- Facial expressions
- Appearance

If mishandled, any one of these could destroy a job candidate's hopes of a job offer. By the way, did you notice that *appearance* appears on both lists? Obviously, appearance is extremely important to recruiters.

INTERVIEWING SUGGESTIONS

Now you have moved to the start of the interview. The recruiter has invited you into his or her office. Here are a number of useful suggestions to help you from this point on. Before diving into the list of interviewing tips, consider taking out a few minutes and reading the article "5 Ways to Derail Your Interview." It contains some good basic reminders.

Know Your Recruiter's Name Use your recruiter's name during the greeting and intermittently throughout the interview. Doing so adds a degree of warmth to the interview and provides one more way to show the interviewer that you are prepared and take the interview opportunity seriously.

However, remember basic business etiquette by using your interviewer's title (e.g., Mr., Ms., Mrs., Dr.) as opposed to calling him or her by first name unless invited to do otherwise.

5 Ways to Derail Your Interview
http://www.cnn.com/2011/LIVING/05/30/derail.job.interview.cb/

For example, if your interviewer's name is Charlene Ward, and even if you know her marital status, you are advised to address her as Ms. Ward.

Eye Contact Establish eye contact from the outset. Doing so is not only expected, but is also a good way to communicate to the recruiter that you are confident.

Of course, you want to give the recruiter a normal amount of eye contact following the initial greeting on through the remainder of the interview. Exactly what is a normal amount of eye contact? In U.S. organizations this refers to the same amount of eye contact most of us give each other in our daily interactions in the workplace, in school, and out and about. It's a balance.

By positioning your body and head, you can improve not only your chances of providing good eye contact, but also your chances of showing interest. Square off your shoulders with the recruiter's, make sure your chin is up (not resting on your chest), and face him or her.

When job candidates give less eye contact than expected, recruiters are often left believing they are either not confident, are unfamiliar with standard interpersonal behavior, are uninterested or unprepared, or are providing false statements. In contrast, job candidates are advised not to give too much eye contact. By all means, do not stare. Doing so will creep out your interviewer, which will likely result in an early end to the interview and a rejection letter in your mailbox.

Smile When the recruiter greets you, be sure to smile. Doing so immediately communicates to the interviewer that you are positive and enthusiastic. Besides, smiling will help calm you.

While it is good advice to smile periodically throughout interviews, do not wear a smile during the entire interview. Doing so would be interpreted as bizarre behavior.

© kentoh/Shutterstock.com

Handshake Be prepared to shake hands with the recruiter before sitting down. Allow the interviewer to offer his or her hand first. You are in the recruiter's environment, so you are advised to let him or her take the lead. However, if you instinctively offer your hand before the recruiter offers his or hers, you have not committed an unforgiveable breach of etiquette.

If you are nervous going into the interview, and most of us are, determine if the hand you will offer is sweaty. If so, wipe it off inside your pants or skirt pocket before shaking hands with your interviewer. Most people do not like to grasp a clammy hand. The same is true of recruiters.

In the United States the recommended handshake can best be described as a firm grip and two or three pumps. Avoid using an overly firm (bone-crusher) grip. Interviews are not arm wrestling competitions, so back off and forgo physically hurting your interviewer. In contrast, avoid a limp grip. Doing so quickly communicates to interviewers that you either do not know what is proper protocol or you are not confident. Some male job candidates offer a less-than-firm grip to female recruiters out of fear of hurting them. Be consistent. Use a firm grip with female recruiters as well as with male recruiters. The total distance yours and your recruiter's hands should move up and down should be approximately one foot. That means six inches upward and six downward. Do not allow either your nervousness or enthusiasm to result in raising and lowering your hand a greater distance. Doing so would likely be perceived as being unprofessional.

FIGURE 17-4: WORLDWIDE HANDSHAKING CUSTOMS

United States	firm, solid grip, two to three pumps
Germany	firm grip, one pump
France	light grip and a quick shake
Japan	limp grip
Australia	firm grip
Latin America	light-to-moderate grasp, repeated frequently
Middle East	gentle and limp, light shaking throughout the greeting
Asia	delicate grip and brief shaking
Sweden	firm grip, eyes meet
Belgium	quick, light pressure
Russia	firm grip

Source: Barbara Pachter and Margorie Brody. Complete Business Etiquette Handbook. (Paramus, NJ: Prentice Hall, 1995), 285.

Sitting The general rule is to let your recruiter take the lead on this matter. Remain standing until the recruiter invites you to sit down. If the recruiter does not extend the invitation, wait until he or she sits down, then do the same.

In advance of some interviews, a receptionist might escort you into an interviewer's office or a conference room where the interview will be conducted. In such situations, go ahead and take a seat. However, when the recruiter enters the room, stand up and greet him or her. Then, follow the suggestions above regarding when to sit back down.

Your sitting posture is important to keep in mind. You are encouraged to sit upright and to not slump your shoulders. Crossing your legs at the knee compromises your ability to sit upright. Typically when we cross our legs at knee level, we tend to slide down slightly in our chairs, resulting in an overly relaxed, slouching appearance. In addition, lean forward at your waist slightly (approximately 3–4 inches). Doing so contributes to the perception that you are interested and listening intently.

Avoid crossing your arms. Many communication partners perceive this as a closed or defensive posture. You do not want a recruiter to form either impression.

© racom/Shutterstock.com

Once you sit down, remember to set your list of questions where they are visible to the recruiter. Recruiters want to know you have brought along a list of questions even if they do not give you a chance to ask them.

Beverage Offer You may be offered water, coffee, tea, or a soft drink. Accept if you like or decline politely if that is your desire. It is probably a good idea to at least accept a glass or bottle of water. You will be doing most of the talking during the interview, and your throat will probably get dry. This is even more likely to happen if you are going through a series of interviews during a day-long on-site visit.

Facial Expressions Essentially, you should wear a pleasant, warm, and friendly expression throughout the majority of the interview. In addition, smile intermittently when appropriate as suggested earlier.

A confused facial expression is acceptable if you have trouble understanding a question. However, if this happens frequently, the interviewer may form the impression that you are a poor listener. You may also find yourself projecting a confused expression when struggling to come up with a response to a question. This is expected occasionally, especially if asked a tough or tricky question. However, doing so frequently may give the impression that you did not prepare for the interview as thoroughly as you should have.

Be Enthusiastic Enthusiasm is a positive force that works to your advantage in job interviews. You want to communicate to an interviewer that you are genuinely excited about working for the organization. Enthusiasm throughout the interview demonstrates both your energy level and desire.

While enthusiastic job candidates are perceived as positive, be careful not to overdo it. Do not come across as unrealistically overconfident or cocky. These are turnoffs for most interviewers.

Be Well-Spoken Whether it's during the small-talk session of an interview or while responding to interviewers' questions, speak clearly. Vague and poorly-delivered responses increase your chances of receiving a rejection letter instead of a job offer.

Your responses to interviewers' questions should be concise as well as clear. Time is limited in job interviews, so do not frustrate interviewers with long-winded responses.

Control your speaking quality. You want recruiters to perceive you as a person who will speak properly and intelligently if hired. Just as one misspelled word or typo on a résumé can sabotage your job search, so can careless word choice and poor speaking patterns. Furthermore, be articulate. Avoid using verbal fillers such as *um* and *ah*. Replace verbal fillers with pauses. Do not pepper sentences with wasted words and phrases such as *ok, like,* and *you know* that leave recruiters with the impression that you are inarticulate and unprofessional.

Do not forget these reminders and suggestions when speaking to recruiters at job fairs and networking events as well as during telephone conversations. No matter the job search setting, your goal is to be a clear, articulate, and pleasant speaker. Sounds simple enough, but doing so can be challenging due to our speech habits and nervousness.

Avoid Distracting Nervous Mannerisms Some of us play out our nervous energy in counterproductive ways we are unaware of. This often happens in job interviews. You typically invest a lot of time and effort to get to the interview stage of the process and naturally want to do a good job. If you are like most, you will be nervous. However, you do not want that nervousness to result in a display of distracting mannerisms that threaten your chances of receiving a job offer.

You need to be aware of your unique distracting mannerisms, then work at eliminating or controlling them. For example, if you know you play with paper clips unconsciously, leave them at home. You might discover that you play with your necktie, in which case you should use a tie tack or tie pin and button your suit coat to keep it out of reach. If you play with your hair unknowingly, tie it back, and if you play with your necklace either don't wear one or wear a smaller one that is not easily accessible. For distracting mannerisms that are not as easily minimized like finger tapping (drumming), consider writing a reminder on your notepad so you will be conscious of this action each time you glance down.

Avoid Criticizing Even though you may have reason to criticize a current or former employer or coworker, doing so is not in your best interest. Interviewers often view job candidates who do that as having a negative personality, and they are not in any rush to bring negative people into their companies.

Think Before Answering It is not a crime to pause before responding to a question, even during stress interviews. Interviewers have as one of their main goals to gather useful information. If you need to think about your response before you answer, then do so. In this way, your interviewer will ultimately gather the information he or she needs. The interviewer may see you as a thoughtful person who does not speak without first thinking.

If you either did not hear a question clearly or need to buy a few more seconds to think through your response, ask the interviewer to repeat the question. Be careful not to do this often. Otherwise, the interviewer might believe you are inattentive or a poor listener. Keep in mind also that a pattern of lengthy and numerous pauses and requests to repeat or restate questions may leave a recruiter believing you entered the interview inadequately prepared.

© Pressmaster/Shutterstock.com

Respond Honestly Fight the natural urge to exaggerate and embellish. It is understandable that you want to sound good during interviews to persuade recruiters to make a job offer. However, in your quest to sound good, be careful not to exaggerate or tell lies.

Be as objective and honest in your responses as humanly possible. When in doubt about the validity of a response you are about to give, ask yourself if you will be able to fully validate and support it if asked to. If your answer is no, you need to rethink your response.

Honest responses are important to recruiters. Employers invest a lot of money in recruiting new employees. In turn, recruiters want to hire people who they believe are a good fit for the job opening and their company. Exaggerated or blatantly dishonest responses undermine recruiters' efforts. In addition, they may also undermine job candidates' goals of receiving job offers. In fact, it is not uncommon for managers to fire an employee if the manager finds the employee exaggerated or lied on his or her cover letter or résumé or during their interview(s).

Focus on Persuading the Recruiter Your ability to persuade recruiters is at the heart of your interviewing goals. Specifically, keep in mind the suggestion to prepare a list of your merchandising skills and personal attributes, success stories, and qualities that employers want in job candidates. This is not only about methodically responding to questions commonly asked during job interviews. You can and should take some control of your destiny during job interviews.

Focus on What You Can Do for the Employer Recruiters really want to hear what you are able to do for them, not what you want them to do for you. One obvious way you can do this involves integrating your merchandising qualities into as many of your responses and questions as possible. Another is to communicate those skills and personal attributes you have that are typically desired by employers. This is really all about communicating how you are able to help meet employers' needs. Of course, this implies you are familiar with an employer's needs as was discussed in detail in chapter 16.

Share Your Knowledge of the Job, Company, and Industry Many job candidates do not bother to learn much, if anything, about the job, company, or industry. They simply do not do the research, yet expect that they will somehow be able to discuss these matters intelligently during interviews.

Recruiters are impressed by candidates who have done their homework. Doing so shows a level of commitment to the search process and to the company. Share such knowledge whenever feasible in your responses to questions and in questions you ask interviewers. Also, work in some of the technical jargon and buzz words unique to the job, company, and industry.

Ask Questions Good interviewers invite questions during the question-and-answer phase or set aside time afterward for candidate questions. Asking questions provides one more opportunity to show you are prepared. Ask insightful questions and be careful not to waste everyone's time asking a question for which information was shared previously in the interview.

Ask Questions about Benefits and Salary at the Appropriate Time Do not ask questions about benefits and salary before the interviewer initiates the conversation. This is a tough one. Each of us is naturally curious about benefits and salary. However, they traditionally are sacred topics that are not discussed until interviewers choose to do so. Benefits and salary matters are rarely discussed during screening interviews. They are more often first raised later in selection interviews, even at the very end after interviewers have decided to make a job offer. This is especially true of salary.

© iQoncept/Shutterstock.com

Once the recruiter opens up a conversation about either benefits or salary, speak intelligently about each, keeping in mind suggestions made earlier regarding typical benefit packages, cafeteria benefits packages, salary ranges, and salary negotiation. Try not to come across as greedy and overly needy. This is not a setting in which you are encouraged to put on a poker face, pound your fist on your recruiter's desk, or stomp out of his or her office if you do not hear the figures you expected. Discussing and negotiating benefits and salary during job interviews is a subtle, refined process. Choose your words wisely and monitor your tone and facial expressions carefully so as not to work against yourself.

Know How to Conduct Yourself during Interviews over Cocktails If you find yourself participating in an interview in a social setting such as a restaurant, do not feel you have to drink alcoholic beverages because others are. You are within the guidelines of standard business etiquette if you order a soft drink, coffee, tea, or water instead.

Generally speaking, the best advice in these situations is not to order an alcoholic beverage. If you anticipate having an alcoholic beverage during the interview, however, make sure to eat in advance to offset the alcohol effects to some degree. Stick to only one drink, and drink it slowly so you do not feel pressured to order another. Let's be realistic about this. You are not entering into interview settings with the purpose of getting some free drinks like some do at open bar wedding receptions. You have a serious task before you and need to be in control to perform properly. With this in mind, seriously consider avoiding alcoholic beverages entirely during job interviews.

Know How to Conduct Yourself during Dinner Interviews Do not be surprised if some of your interviews are conducted over dinner or lunch. Such interviews are often conducted at upscale restaurants, which can be flattering because doing so suggests you have successfully made it past the initial screening interview and someone obviously sees potential in you. This all sounds great, but here are some important considerations to keep in mind about dinner and lunch interviews.

- When ordering, take your lead from the recruiter regarding price range.
- If the interviewer invites you to order first, order something in the middle of the price range.
- Order a meal that can be eaten easily. For example, pork chops with a baked potato and steamed vegetables would be a good choice. However, ribs, spaghetti, soup, crab legs, and oversized sandwiches can be a struggle. Slurping your soup or wearing your food on your blouse or shirt will obviously not impress recruiters. If you know ahead of time which restaurant you will meet at, look up the menu online so you are familiar with it.
- Do not order a large meal. You will be doing a lot of talking and you do not want to finish your meal well after your interviewer has finished his or hers.
- Do not ask for a to-go box if you do not finish your meal.
- If you have a soft drink or iced tea, do not chew on the ice.
- Decide in advance of lunch or dinner interviews whether you will order an alcoholic beverage if the recruiter does and invites you to do so. Keep in mind the guidelines regarding alcoholic beverages presented in the previous section.

In addition, avoid the "table manners sins" listed in Figure 17-5, and review the section on etiquette for business dining in chapter 2.

> ## FIGURE 17–5: THE 10 MOST COMMON TABLE MANNERS SINS AT BUSINESS MEALS
>
> 1. Chewing with your mouth open or speaking with food in your mouth
> 2. Putting used cutlery back on the table
> 3. Holding the knife like you are holding a dagger and the fork like you are bowing a cello
> 4. Ordering indecisively and finishing the meal well before or after everyone else
> 5. Using a cell phone during the meal
> 6. Putting keys, gloves, purse, or similar objects on the table
> 7. Picking or poking at your teeth
> 8. Flapping the napkin and putting it on the table before the end of the meal
> 9. Slouching, squirming, or tilting in your chair
> 10. Leaving lipstick smears
>
> *Source: Mary Mitchell with John Corr.* The Complete Idiot's Guide to Business Etiquette. *(Indianapolis, IN: Alpha Books, 2000), 167–69.*

One more reminder: Do not smoke during dinner or lunch interviews. Even if the recruiter lights up, which is very unlikely, it does not mean he or she wants to hire a smoker. Most employers today would rather not hire people who smoke because of concerns such as increased health insurance premiums, increased illnesses resulting in absenteeism, lower productivity resulting from health issues, and smoking work breaks that extend beyond regular work breaks for nonsmokers.

There is so much more to learn about conducting yourself properly during dinner and lunch interviews. Before jumping into the interviewing process, visit your campus career center. They typically have a wealth of related information.

End Interviews Effectively As your interview winds down, keep in mind that there is still much to do and little time to do it in. You have to stay on your toes and know exactly what is still on your list to accomplish. Here is a list of typical end-of-interview activities.

- Ask for clarification if needed. For example, you may need to inquire about a question you were asked previously.
- Ask if you will be put through a battery of tests and when.
- Offer the interviewer a copy of your résumé, transcripts, and list of references. Doing so often helps him or her and also shows you are prepared on yet another level.
- Express your interest in the job and in working for the company.
- If your interviewer has not already mentioned it, ask approximately when a decision will be made regarding the next round of interviews or the hiring decision.
- Smile, thank the interviewer for taking the time to meet with you, and then shake his or her hand firmly and exit.

As a follow-up to the previous suggestions, you should find the information in Figure 17-6 to be of interest.

FIGURE 17-6: WHAT IS MOST INFLUENTIAL IN AN INTERVIEW

- Your personality: how you present yourself during the interview
- Your experience
- The qualifications you show for the job you are interviewing for
- Your background and references
- The enthusiasm you show toward the company and the job
- Your educational and technical background
- Your growth potential
- Your compatibility (e.g., your ability to get along with coworkers)
- Your intelligence and capacity to learn
- How hard a worker you appear to be

Source: Robert Half. The Robert Half Way to Get Hired in Today's Job Market. *(New York: Bantam Books, 1983).*

SUMMARY: SECTION 6— JOB INTERVIEWS: ON STAGE

- The four interviewing phases include opening, question-and-answer (recruiter questions), question-and-answer (job candidate's questions), and closing.
- Areas to be aware of during job interviews include knowing the recruiter's name, making eye contact, smiling, shaking hands, sitting, and being offered a beverage.
- Control your facial expressions, show enthusiasm, be a good communicator, avoid nervous mannerisms, and avoid criticizing.
- Think before you answer questions, respond honestly, persuade the interviewer, communicate what you can do for the employer, share knowledge, and ask questions.
- Wait for the interviewer to take the lead on benefits and salary issues.
- Know how to end interviews effectively.

STEP 7: DEVELOPING EFFECTIVE FOLLOW-UP CORRESPONDENCE

Step 7 of the job search process follows the interview. This step involves developing and sending one or more forms of follow-up correspondence to those who interviewed you. For example, you should send a thank-you note to each person who interviewed you. In addition, a job offer may result in your sending either an acceptance letter or a letter declining the job offer.

Before discussing follow-up correspondence in detail, this is a time to remind ourselves that there are actually several things we should do following the job interview, which include thank-you notes, sending references, continuing to learn more about the company, and more. For a more extensive list of things you should do following job interviews, consider reading the article "10 Things to do after a Job Interview."

THANK-YOU NOTES

According to a Robert Half International survey, "91 percent of managers believe it's helpful for job candidates to show their appreciation after an interview."4 However, many U.S. job candidates do not express their appreciation either in writing or orally following interviews which compromises their odds of receiving job offers. Given how little time and effort it takes to express one's gratitude, it seems most foolish not to do so.

© karen roach/Shutterstock.com

You have decided that you will express your thanks following job interviews. That's a wise choice! So, how will you do this? Will you place a phone call, send a handwritten note, type your message, or send an e-mail or text message? Handwritten notes, phone calls, and e-mail messages are the more widely preferred methods. The least preferred of the choices is text messages. My personal preference is the handwritten **thank-you note**. Handwritten notes provide that personal touch that many recruiters seem to appreciate. While e-mail thank-you messages are acceptable, keep in mind that e-mail is often subjected to filtering systems that may remove your message before your intended receiver gets a chance to read it. Placing a phone call has a major shortcoming in that the odds of connecting with a recruiter on the first call are rare. Thus, an inefficient game of telephone tag may ensue. In such situations, you are not advised to simply leave a voicemail message.

No matter which method you use, keep your thank-you message short, and adhere strictly to the rules of grammar, punctuation, capitalization, number usage, and abbreviations. In addition, double check your spelling. Here are the basic elements of a good thank-you note.

- Thank the recruiter for meeting with you.
- Mention how much you enjoyed meeting with him or her.
- Thank him or her for sharing information about the position and company.
- Mention an example of specific information you enjoyed learning.
- Thank him or her for considering you for the job.
- Mention that you want the job.

Use the following suggestions regarding developing and distributing thank-you notes.

- Make sure your handwriting is legible.
- Send handwritten thank-you messages on thank-you cards. These cards usually come in a box of a dozen or so, have the words *Thank You* or *Thanks* on the outside, and are blank on the inside.
- Do your best to get your thank-you notes in recruiters' hands within 24 hours following interviews. You want your thank-you note to arrive quickly while you and your name are fresh in your interviewer's mind. In fact, consider arriving at interviews

thank-you note
A brief, handwritten note from the candidate to the recruiter following a job interview.

with your thank-you note envelope(s) pre-addressed and stamped. Then, immediately following the interview, you can write your thank-you note in your car and drop it in the first mailbox you see as you leave the interview site. The 24-hour suggestion is practical advice for the other "thank-you" methods as well.

Figure 17-7 is an example of a fairly well-written thank-you note.

FIGURE 17–7: SAMPLE THANK-YOU NOTE

4722 Riley, Apt. 23
College Park, MD 20740
(301) 555-4326
swilk18@gmail.com

April 24, 201_

Dear Mr. Garret,

Thank you for meeting with me this morning. It was a pleasure visiting with you.

Thank you for sharing so much interesting information about William Garret & Co., P.C. and the staff position in the tax department. I especially enjoyed learning about your firm's markets outside of the United States.

I am excited about the prospect of joining the William Garret & Co., P.C. team and look forward to hearing from you soon.

Sincerely,

Shondra Wilkins

In addition to sending thank-you notes following job interviews, consider sending them when others do favors or nice things for you. Doing so leaves a very favorable impression with most people and, in part, will help you grow strong professional relationships. A good start would be to purchase a couple of boxes of thank-you notes and books of postage stamps. Then, keep them handy.

JOB ACCEPTANCE LETTERS

Job acceptance letters are brief and keyboarded on standard 8½x11-inch typing paper using a 12-point type size and a legible font such as Arial or Times New Roman. Like thank-you notes, job acceptance letters should be mailed. Faxing or sending them as attachments to e-mail messages are discouraged.

© iQoncept/Shutterstock.com

- State the purpose of your letter.
- State the specific position you were offered.
- State the geographic location or office (e.g., Denver office) where you will be working.
- Mention how excited you are about working for the company.
- Thank the person to whom you are sending the job acceptance letter for his or her vote of confidence in you.

- Request details regarding starting date and time, etc., if they are not included in your job offer letter. If they are included in your offer letter, restate them in your acceptance letter so your contact person knows you are clear regarding your next move (e.g., It is my understanding that I am to report to Elgie Baker, Room 1403A, on Monday, March 12 at 8:30 a.m.).
- Thank the contact person a second time for his or her vote of confidence.
- Mention again how excited you are about this opportunity.

LETTERS DECLINING JOB OFFERS

These letters should be brief and keyboarded on standard 8½x11-inch typing paper using a 12-point type size and a legible font such as Arial or Times New Roman. Like all job-related correspondence, letters declining job offers should be mailed. Faxing or sending them as attachments to e-mail messages is discouraged. Recommended contents for letters declining job offers are listed here.

- State the purpose of your letter.
- State the specific position you were offered.
- State the geographic location or office (e.g., Denver office) where they intended to have you work.
- Explain briefly, politely, and tactfully why you are not accepting the job offer.
- Thank the contact person for his or her vote of confidence in you.
- Thank the contact person for the time and effort he or she devoted to considering you for the job.

Figure 17-8 contains a sample letter declining a job offer.

FIGURE 17–8: SAMPLE LETTER DECLINING A JOB OFFER

Dear _____,

I am writing to let you know that I have decided not to accept your kind job offer of the payroll position in the Birmingham office of DL Industries. While I believe the opportunity would have been beneficial for both of us, the untimely death of one of my close family members requires me to change my work plans.

Please accept my gratitude for your vote of confidence and the time and effort you devoted to considering me for the position. I wish you and DL Industries the best.

Sincerely,

Too often, job candidates who choose not to accept job offers do not take the time to send a letter declining the offer. Doing so is discourteous and leaves recruiters waiting and wondering. Sending such letters is proper procedure and a courteous gesture. You want to stay in recruiters' best graces. While you may not choose to accept a current job offer, you never know when in the future you will want the same recruiter or company to once again view you favorably for a job opening.

Sending follow-up correspondence after a job interview is strongly encouraged. Many recruiters view such correspondence as an expectation as well as a courtesy. Sending follow-up correspondence is often that extra effort that secures a job offer whereas failure to do so will often eliminate you from consideration. It does not take all that much time to do this the right way!

CHECKING BACK WITH RECRUITERS

Unless a recruiter has given you a specific date on which he or she will contact you about a hiring decision, it is appropriate for you to contact him or her inquiring about the status of the hiring decision. This is also true in situations when the contact date he or she gave you has come and gone with no contact.

Most recruiters do not mind if you contact them about the status of a hiring decision. In fact, it communicates a level of interest in the job and company that others often fail to communicate. However, in your zeal to become gainfully employed, do not be a pest. Your cause is not helped if interviewers perceive you as being a letter or telephone stalker. Some candidates are so out of touch with job search protocol that they contact recruiters daily, and sometimes more than once daily, nagging them about their hiring decision. Some even attach their résumé file to each nagging e-mail message. Do such actions sound like they will endear senders to recruiters? You know the answer. Checking back once a week is reasonable.

When checking back with interviewers following interviews, follow these suggestions.

- Either call or send a keyboarded inquiry.
- Do not e-mail, text, or tweet your inquiry. E-mail can get lost to filtering systems, text messages are considered to be too informal, and tweets are simply too short.
- Keep your message brief (e.g., briefly state the position in question, when you interviewed, and your ongoing interest in the position and company).
- Be polite.
- Use good grammar.

As stated previously, checking back with recruiters can be a good thing if done properly; being a pest will sabotage your job search efforts.

REASONS FOR REJECTION AFTER A JOB INTERVIEW

If you are like most, a job offer will not follow each of your interviews. Do not take it personally. You are simply more likely to receive a greater number of rejections than job offers over the course of your working years. There is a lot of competition out there for the same job opportunities you find attractive. Do your best to put a positive spin on employment rejections by accepting that they are typical byproducts of the job search process, and learn from them. You will likely receive some employment rejections via social media. Apparently there is no safe haven! If you do, there are four suggested ways to handle them that are discussed in the article "4 Ways to Handle Employer Rejection on Social Media."

You can take steps to decrease the number of rejections you receive. One way to do so is to adhere to the interviewing suggestions presented in this chapter. You can also acquire lists of reasons why job candidates are rejected following interviews. You will find such lists at Internet sites, in employment books, and at your campus career center. Common

4 Ways to Handle Employer Rejection on Social Media
http://articles.
chicagotribune.com/2012-09-17/classified/chi-how-to-handle-employer-rejection-on-social-media

examples range from arriving late, inappropriate appearance, inadequate skills, poor manners, and communicating too casually to insufficient eye contact, dishonest responses, lack of enthusiasm, slouching, and scuffed shoes.

Remind yourself that misuse of electronic communication devices such as smartphones can lead to disaster in job interviews. You might find it interesting that there are numerous cases of candidates who answered phone calls, sent or read text messages, or tweeted during job interviews. Sounds unbelievable, but it's true. Some candidates do such things out of habit. Their phone rings, and they automatically answer it. These are autopilot responses that damage their prospects. Then, there are those job candidates who are either unaware of or do not respect expected interview protocols. Practical advice to job candidates regarding this matter is to leave all electronic devices in your car or at home. That way they cannot work against you.

FIGURE 17–9: LANDING YOUR FIRST PROFESSIONAL JOB

James Citrin, a corporate headhunter at Spencer Stuart, is the author of the book *The Career Playbook*. The central focus of the book is helping millennials land and keep jobs. For example, Mr. Citrin encourages job hunters to acquire some work experience; build their confidence (e.g., practice interviewing); use social sites like LinkedIn to network and build relationships; and develop technical, problem-solving, communication, and analytical skills. You should find Mr. Citrin's book to be a valuable resource.

Source: James F. Peltz, "Tips on Landing Your First Job," The Dallas Morning News, July 19, 2015, 2D.

JOB RESIGNATION LETTERS

Now, let's flip the situation. Assume you were successful in landing a job and went to work for the employer, but eventually you decided to resign. Possibly a better job came along, or you decided to move to a different geographic location, change careers, or simply retire. We have our reasons.

Resignation letters should be brief and keyboarded on standard 8½x11-inch typing paper using a 12-point type size and a legible font such as Arial or Times New Roman. Like all job-related correspondence, ideally resignation letters should be mailed. Faxing or sending them as attachments to e-mail messages is discouraged. Recommended contents for job resignation letters are listed here.

- State clearly that you are resigning.
- Give clear indication of the last date you will be working taking into account that many organizations require such notice a specific number of days or weeks before the actual end date.
- Mention how much you enjoyed your fellow employees.
- Express your gratitude for the growth opportunities you were given.
- Wish the best for the organization.

Figure 17-10 contains a sample resignation letter.

FIGURE 17–10: SAMPLE RESIGNATION LETTER

Dear _____,

This letter is to inform you of my resignation from Pine Crest Corporation effective Friday, October 12, 20___.

While this was not an easy decision to make, it is for the best. I enjoy the managers and staff I worked with and appreciate the opportunities for growth that Pine Crest provided me.

I wish you and Pine Crest Corporation all the best.

Sincerely,

Here's one closing suggestion regarding resignation letters. Have you ever heard the expression "don't burn bridges"? Essentially, this expression refers to not compromising or destroying relationships. This is a good expression to keep in mind when writing resignation letters, especially if you are leaving on bad terms and/or have bad feelings about your soon-to-be previous employer. You just don't know when you will need their assistance in the future. So, don't write condescending and/or accusatory resignation letters that will very likely close the door on future assistance!

SUMMARY: SECTION 7— FOLLOW-UP CORRESPONDENCE

- Develop effective thank-you notes and mail them within 24 hours of the interview.
- Be prepared to develop effective job acceptance letters, job rejection letters, and job resignation letters.
- Check back with recruiters following interviews about the status of job decisions, but do not be a pest.
- Know the typical reasons candidates do not receive job offers following interviews.
- Wait for the interviewer to take the lead on benefits and salary issues.
- Know how to end interviews effectively.

MANAGING YOUR CAREER

Now that you have succeeded in the job search process, what can you do to increase your chances of achieving the career success you've dreamed about? You should already have some handle on how you define your career success goals. After all, Step 1 of the job search process had you reflecting on your career choice. In addition, you were encouraged in Step 5 to include both short-term and long-term career goals in your career objective in your résumé.

If your vision of career success is still hazy, spend some serious time reflecting on where you want to go with your career. Careers are like cross-country road trips. We all know the value of mapping out a long-distance road trip before setting out across country and not merely relying on a GPS to get us there. By doing so, we are more likely to arrive at our final destination and on time. Managing your career is like that. Increase your chances of realizing your career goals based on your preferred timetable by mapping out your career path. Even then, mapping out your career path does not necessarily provide you a guarantee that you will reach your career goals. Life events, workplace trends, responses to changing economic conditions, and global events (e.g., divorce, death of a loved one, relocated spouse, corporate downsizing, lengthy layoffs, voluntarily changing jobs) can knock us off of our career paths. However, if your chosen career and career path are important to you, pick yourself up and get back on the path.

Before going farther, this is a good place to talk about poor work habits—habits that can cost any of us our jobs and even our careers. No matter your level of training and education, we can all be tripped up by careless work habits.

8 Things New Employees Should Never Do http://money.usnews. com/money/blogs/ outside-voices- careers/2014/08/18/ 8-things-new-employees- should-never-do

---

FIGURE 17–11: THE 10 WORST WORK HABITS

1. Procrastination
2. Being a sloppy e-mailer (e.g., incomplete, poorly written)
3. Confusing informal with disrespectful (not showing respect for authority)
4. Taking advantage of leeway (e.g., dress codes, arrival and departure times)
5. Refusing to mingle (important for building camaraderie)
6. Always running late (becomes a trust issue)
7. Being rigid (being inflexible with others and with work assignments)
8. Acting as the resident contrarian
9. Badmouthing the company (e.g., in the workplace and on the Internet)
10. Office politicking (some cannot be avoided, but do not make it your mission)

Source: Anthony Balderrama. "The 10 Worst Work Habits." Retrieved from careerbuilder.com, June 3, 2009

In addition to avoiding the poor work habits mentioned in Figure 17-11, avoid doing other things that can be job-threatening such as complaining about your boss or work to others in person, on the phone, and on social media, and pushing the envelope on business expenses.

Figure 17-12 contains several recommended career management suggestions. With the exception of the first suggestion, they are not listed in any particular order. The first one on the list (choose a career …), however, is clearly the most important. Wise people know that life is far too short to spend even a single minute of it in a career they do not enjoy!

© Rafal Olechowski/Shutterstock.com

FIGURE 17–12: RECOMMENDED CAREER MANAGEMENT SUGGESTIONS

- Choose a career and work that you enjoy, at which you can excel, and to which you will remain committed.
- Be realistic about the rate at which job promotions will likely occur. For example, Millennials often indicate that they expect job promotions will occur often. This is not necessarily the norm.
- Keep in mind that skills such as empathizing, collaborating, creating, leading, and building relationships are becoming increasingly valued![5]
- Anticipate working at minimum to age 75 (even more reason to take the first suggestion seriously!).
- Over the years, be careful not to develop a pattern of changing employers with a relatively high degree of frequency. Such a pattern will eventually eliminate job opportunities.
- Do not let inappropriate appearance be your downfall. Even if your employer allows predominately casual dress, know which situations you are expected to dress up for (e.g., visiting a client's office, giving a presentation). Know what is meant by casual dress. For example, flip flops, tank tops, and blue jeans with holes in them are not acceptable!
- Keep your résumé current. (U.S. businesspeople change jobs, employers, and careers frequently.)
- Be an effective communicator in all settings and with all communication partners.
- Remain visible. (Volunteer for extra projects, attend company charity efforts and social events.)
- Get a mentor.
- Learn your company's power and political structures.
- Do not simply support your boss, make him or her look good.
- Belong to and have active roles in work-related professional associations.
- Network and nurture your networking relationships.
- Be accountable and dependable.
- Go the extra mile without being told to. (Then, be humble about it.)
- Learn how to communicate and interact effectively with people from other cultures.
- Learn how to communicate and interact effectively with people with difficult personality quirks. (Don't burn bridges!)
- Develop and practice excellent people (interpersonal) skills.
- Avoid reduced productivity resulting from being electronically connected too frequently (e.g., 24/7, during evenings, on weekends, on vacation).
- Avoid being connected to work 24/7 to avoid job/career burnout concerns. Strike a balance between work and your personal life. This is important for your health and emotional well-being.
- Understand that most managers do not want employees texting, tweeting, taking and placing phone calls, e-mailing and browsing the Internet during meetings, presentations, and training sessions.

FIGURE 17–12: RECOMMENDED CAREER MANAGEMENT SUGGESTIONS

- Avoid making arriving at work late a habit and, if you do arrive late, offer a sincere apology and give an honest explanation.
- Avoid using communication technology for personal reasons in the workplace (e.g., e-mailing friends, downloading music) with the exception of during designated breaks. Doing so can lead to job loss.
- Never stop learning.
- Embrace new technologies as they appear in the workplace. (Do not make yourself obsolete prematurely.)
- Learn all you can about how to manage people and organizations effectively.
- Be willing to travel on business when asked.
- Be willing to relocate geographically when asked.
- Be open to making horizontal, not only upward, career moves to enhance your career goals.
- Be willing to take risks—preferably calculated risks.
- Be willing to make decisions.
- Review your career periodically to see if it remains in alignment with your career goals and timetable.
- Be flexible. (Do not panic if you get knocked off of your career path and timetable. Brush yourself off, get back on the path, and move forward.)
- Avoid creating a job history that notes a pattern of switching employers frequently. Initially this may not be an issue, but eventually can exclude you from job consideration for obvious reasons.
- Take a time management workshop or read up on the topic. Doing so will benefit you at work as well as in your personal life.
- Read up on stress management or take a stress management workshop. Unmanaged stress is a silent killer when left unchecked. Unmanaged stress destroys jobs, careers, relationships, one's health, and even takes lives.
- Make time to enjoy some hobbies and interests outside of the workplace. Doing so will help you keep a balance between work and all of life's other demands, which will reduce some of your stress.

Numerous websites contain a wealth of career management information. A small sampling includes www.careers.org, www.truecareers.com, www.iccweb.com, www.quint-careers.com, www.careerpathsonline.net, www.assessment.com, www.careerbuilder.com, imdiversity.com, www.beyond.com, wfcresources.com, and careers.wsj.com.

The career advice shared in Figure 17-13 is directed toward college seniors and recent college grads. The information is intended to improve your experience as you launch your career.

FIGURE 17–13: SIX TIPS FOR SUCCESS FOR COLLEGE SENIORS AND RECENT GRADS

1. **Cut the expense fat** (e.g., gym memberships, expensive cell-phone plans, etc.). By doing so, you will be able to accept lower-paying jobs with greater career growth potential when they present themselves.

2. **Monitor your online image.** Essentially, you do not want your social media presence to compromise your employment opportunities. Determine what's out there, be honest, be careful about what you post in the future, and use free tools to monitor your online presence. Recruiters are scanning job applicants' social media profiles.

3. **Go beyond the textbooks.** Pick up work experience in the field you are preparing for before you graduate by doing one or more internships or co-ops.

4. **Be honest; have integrity.** Practice being the best possible person you can be, don't lie, say what you will do, and then do what you say.

5. **Show emotional intelligence.** Manage your emotions. Learn to reduce stress quickly.

6. **Help out wherever possible.** Go above and beyond whenever you can. No one ever got promoted or built a successful career by doing the bare minimum.

Source: From "New College Grads: 6 Tips for Success" by Sonia Acosta. Copyright © 2012 by Careerbuilder. Reprinted by permission.

The Critical First Year on the Job
http://www.nxtbook.com/nxtbooks/nace/JobChoices2012_science/index.php?startid=46

Professionalism: An Essential Career Skill
http://advice.careerbuilder.com/posts/professionalism-an-essential-career-skill

The information in the article "The Critical First Year on the Job" expands on the tips presented in Figure 17-13. This article offers suggestions ranging from learning the culture to becoming a savvy subordinate.

An overarching consideration to keep in mind as you enter the professional workplace with a host of career goals in tow is *professionalism*. Professionalism is difficult to define, but much like is said about obscenity, you know it when you see it. This is so with professionalism. Possibly the best way to understand what professionalism is, is to become acquainted with the core components of professionalism (e.g., accountability, humility). The article "Professionalism: An Essential Career Skill" contains the core components of professionalism.

Needless-to-say, if you are going to call yourself a professional and reap the rewards of being one, then conduct yourself as one. Doing so will increase your odds of achieving your career goals, gain the respect of others, and give you a strong sense of pride.

In closing, here's wishing you a successful career or careers! If you are like most, you will change careers two or more times during your post-college working years. Whether you change employers within your chosen career path or you change careers, you will certainly revisit all or some of the steps of the job search process several times during your working years. You should find the information shared in chapters 16 and 17 to be helpful for many years to come.

SUMMARY: SECTION 8— MANAGING YOUR CAREER

- Receiving a job offer is wonderful, but what you do after that is what determines if you achieve your career goals.
- The most important career management suggestion is: Choose a career and work that you enjoy, at which you can excel, and to which you will remain committed.
- Be aware of the common negative work habits that cost people their jobs and careers.
- Plan on two or more long careers.
- Understand that organizations are political in nature. You want to act accordingly.
- Be a team player, be flexible, and never stop learning and growing.
- Be willing to take risks and make decisions—step up to the plate.

Notes

1. R. D. Lock. *Job Search: Career Planning Guide, Book 2*, 5th ed. (Belmont, CA: Thomson Brooks/Cole, 2005), 205.

2. Paul Michael. "How to Answer 23 of the Most Common Interview Questions." *Wise Bread*. Retrieved from http://www.wisebread.com/how-to-answer-23-of-the-most-common-interview-questions, October 4, 2007.

3. Martin Yate. *Knock 'Em Dead*. (Holbrook, MA: Adams Media Corporation, 2002), 96.

4. Melissa Gushwa. "6 tips for acing the post-interview thank you." *Robert Half International*, http://www.linkedin.com/pulse/6-tips-for-acing-the-post-interview-than-you-melissa-gushwa September 12, 2012.

5. Geoff Colvin, "Humans Are Underrated." *Fortune*, (August 1, 2015): 100-113.

GLOSSARY

The key words that follow are bolded in the text within each chapter. In addition, they are presented in the chapter margins.

CHAPTER 1

COMMUNICATING IN ORGANIZATIONS

audience Refers to both senders and receivers.

audience analysis Refers to both encoding and decoding.

chronemics The use of time.

communication The lifeblood of all organizations involving constant exchanges of information through traditional and electronic communication media.

control function Communication initiated to control the behaviors of organization members as a means of realizing organizational goals.

diagonal communication Messages and information among people in different departments and at different levels of the organizational hierarchy.

downward communication Messages and information sent from a source higher in the organization to someone lower in the organization.

effective communication Occurs when receiver understands a message as the sender intends it to be understood and receiver then acts on the message as desired.

efficient communication Communication achieved with a minimum of wasted time and resources.

emotive (motivational) function Communication that influences organization members' feelings, emotions, and behaviors, thus increasing acceptance of and commitment to organizational goals.

environment The use of the physical setting.

formal communication Communication sanctioned by organizations and intended to meet organizational goals and objectives.

horizontal communication Messages and information among people and work groups on the same level of the organizational hierarchy.

informal communication Unofficial communication occurring outside of official organizational channels that may or may not address organizational concerns.

information function Communication initiated to gather, analyze, summarize, organize, and disperse information needed for decision making and for accomplishing organizational objectives and tasks.

kinesics The use of body language.

open communication environments Communication environments characterized by frequent communication among employees no matter their job titles and status, with trust, respect, and empathy being key components.

organizational communication All communication that takes place in organizations with both internal and external stakeholders.

paralanguage The use of voice.

proxemics The use of space.

tone Refers to the sender's attitude toward the receiver and the message subject.

upward communication Messages and information sent from a source lower in the organization to someone higher in the organization.

CHAPTER 2

COMMUNICATING APPROPRIATELY: BUSINESS ETIQUETTE

backstabber Someone who will turn on coworkers if it is to his or her benefit.

bigot Someone who makes demeaning remarks about people of a different ethnicity.

blamer Someone who goes behind another's back to assign blame to him or her when he or she is not present.

business etiquette Sets of proposed rules guiding how we interact with each other in the business place.

dining etiquette Guidelines for conducting ourselves during business meals.

introductions How people greet each other in the business place.

networking Building a network of professional contacts for business purposes.

sycophant Someone who flatters anyone who can advance his or her career.

tantrum thrower Someone who erupts into fits of rage for seemingly no reason.

tattletale Someone who willingly divulges something that should be held in confidence to another.

telephone etiquette Guidelines for placing and answering telephone calls in the business place.

victim Someone who is a pessimist and a chronic complainer.

CHAPTER 3
INTERCULTURAL COMMUNICATION

accent The prominence given in speech to a particular sound.

comfort zone The amount of personal space businesspeople prefer to maintain between themselves and their communication partners.

culture A complex of language, customs, behavior, and arts that express the identity of a people.

dialect A regional form of a language.

ethnocentric approach Multinational organizations that assign parent country nationals to all key management positions at both the top- and mid-management levels.

global approach Multinational organizations that make all management position assignments based on who is best qualified for the position, regardless of whether they are a parent country national, a host country national, or other.

high-context cultures Societies that derive meaning primarily from nonverbal and situational cues.

interpreters People who serve as oral translators between people speaking different languages.

low-context cultures Societies that derive meaning primarily from spoken and written words.

monochromatic time A preference for doing one thing at a time because time is limited, precise, segmented, and schedule driven.

multinational organization Company that produces and sells products and/or services in two or more countries.

nonverbal messages Messages communicated without words.

polycentric approach Multinational organizations that assign parent country nationals to top-level management positions and assign host country or regional country nationals to midlevel management positions and below.

polychromic time A preference for doing more than one thing at a time because time is flexible and multidimensional.

regiocentric approach Multinational organizations that assign parent country nationals to top-level management positions and assign host country or regional country nationals to midlevel management positions and below.

translators People who translate written documents and messages from one language to another.

CHAPTER 4
COMMUNICATION TECHNOLOGIES

assistive technologies Electronic devices enabling people with physical disabilities to communicate more easily and effectively.

e-books Books transmitted digitally and read on computers and e-readers.

e-business A broader term for e-commerce that implies servicing customers, collaborating with business partners, and conducting electronic transactions within an organization as well as addressing buying and selling transactions.

e-commerce (electronic commerce) The transactions involved in buying and selling products, services, and information over the Internet.

e-readers Electronic tablets designed for reading digitally transmitted e-books.

extranet A network linking the intranets of business partners via the Internet to create a virtually private network.

holoconferences Telepresence-based videoconferences in which screen images are replaced with 3-dimensional images of participants who are not physically present.

hyperlinks Links to other web pages.

information overload A situation in which people routinely receive more data and messages than they can effectively read, respond to, and act on.

information richness Refers to how robust a communication medium is.

Internet A self-regulated network connecting millions of computer networks around the globe.

Internet phones Devices delivering voice communications over IP networks such as the Internet.

interpersonal disconnection A potential problem directly related to the popularity of e-mail whereby users engage in fewer face-to-face and telephone conversations.

intranet A company-wide computer network serving as a LAN (local area network) and/or WAN (wide area network) developed with Internet technology.

netbook Small laptop whose main functions are to access e-mail, browse the Web, and use web-based applications.

plagiarism The passing off as one's own the writings and ideas of others.

polyphasic activity Doing more than one thing at a time (multitasking).

smartboards Large, interactive, electronic screens containing practical applications for business meetings and presentations.

smartphones Mobile phones offering advanced capabilities.

tablet Relatively small touch pads computers with capabilities ranging from Internet access to standard PC functions.

telecommuter An employee who performs some portion of his or her work away from the office while linked to the office electronically.

world phones Cell phones with global roaming capabilities.

World Wide Web (the Web) A collection of standards and protocols linking massive amounts of information on the Internet, thus enabling user access.

CHAPTER 5
SOCIAL MEDIA

blogosphere The universe of blogs.

emoticons Word substitutes such as smiley faces and frowning faces.

Facebook The most popular online social networking service and website.

Google+ An online social networking and identity service.

hedonometer A computerized sensor that surveys the Web to measure the collective happiness of millions of bloggers.

Instagram An online mobile social networking service that supports photo- and video-sharing.

LinkedIn An online business-oriented social networking service.

netiquette Rules about the proper and polite way to communicate with other people when using the Internet.

Pinterest An online social curation and social networking service.

social media Collective of online communication channels dedicated to community-based input, interaction, content sharing, and collaboration.

social networking The process of communicating with others via social media.

Tumblr An online microblogging platform and social networking website.

Twitter An online social networking and microblogging service.

CHAPTER 6
WRITING ELECTRONICALLY

electronic writing Messages developed and transmitted via electronic communication technologies such as e-mail, instant messaging, text messaging, and websites.

e-mail A method of exchanging digital messages from one author to one or more recipients.

e-mailhead E-mail letterhead.

e-policies Guidelines for using electronic communication.

e-tone Refers to the miscommunication that occurs when the writer has one tone of voice when writing the e-mail, but the recipient reads it in a totally different tone.

flame A hostile, blunt, rude, insensitive, or obscene e-mail.

instant messaging (IM) Exchanging text messages in real time between two or more people logged into a particular instant messaging service.

netiquette Guidelines for acceptable behavior when using electronic communication via email, instant messaging, text messaging, chat rooms, and discussion forums.

phishing The act of sending an e-mail to a user falsely claiming to be an established legitimate enterprise in an attempt to scam the user into surrendering private information that will be used for identity theft.

presence management Being able to determine if others are online and available.

shouting Using all CAPITAL LETTERS in an e-mail.

spamming Posting junk e-mail or unsolicited posts to a large number of e-mail addresses.

text message A short message that is sent electronically to a cell phone or other device.

website A set of interconnected Web pages starting with a homepage.

CHAPTER 7

PLANNING & DRAFTING BUSINESS DOCUMENTS

boilerplate language Text used again and again in similar situations.

clustering Establishing the relationships among the parts of your message.

direct method When organizing a document, state the purpose of the message—your main idea—at the beginning.

document modeling The process whereby workplace writers use documents or parts of documents already written for a similar situation as a template for their own writing.

doublespeak Language that appears to say something but really does not.

drafting The first pass at writing a document.

freewriting Putting your ideas on paper or computer screen without immediate concern for grammar, spelling, and other matters.

gatekeeper People who route and re-route your documents.

indirect method When organizing a document, begin the message with the evidence or explanation before presenting the purpose or main idea.

model document An existing document written for a similar situation.

planning The prewriting activity; typically includes defining your purpose, analyzing your audience, organizing your ideas, and choosing the right medium.

primary audience The readers for whom you develop your document.

secondary audience The readers who will be affected by your message or who will implement your decision or the decision of the primary audience.

sentence outline Uses complete sentences with correct punctuation to organize the outline.

slang Specialized language created and used by a particular person or group.

three-stage writing process The planning, drafting, and revising of a message or document.

topic outline Uses words or phrases for all outline ideas with no punctuation after the ideas.

unbiased language Words that do not reinforce a prejudice.

watchdog audience External critics not directly affected by a message (e.g., an advertisement), but who have substantial political, social, or economic power over an industry.

writer's block Describes the situation when a writer has difficulty getting started writing.

you-attitude Writing from your audience's point of view.

CHAPTER 8

REVISING BUSINESS DOCUMENTS

abstract words Language that is often unclear and subject to differing interpretations.

active voice A sentence in which the subject performs the action; opposite of passive voice.

clichés Overused, worn-out words or expressions.

dependent clause An incomplete sentence.

document cycling Involves sending a document to a fellow employee who makes suggestions and then passes the document on to another fellow employee who follows the same process.

jargon (buzzwords) Words peculiar to a particular profession that do not necessarily make sense to others outside of that profession.

justified text Text that is aligned along a vertical margin. Usually this means text is aligned along both the left and right margins.

layout The arrangement of text on a page.

parallel structure Two or more sentences are worded such that they have similar grammatical structures.

passive voice A sentence in which the subject or agent is acted upon; opposite of active voice.

plain English Writing in a style that readers can easily understand.

proofreading A final review of a document to catch oversights in need of correction such as misspellings.

readability A reader's ability to read and understand a document.

reader-based prose Writing that answers the reader's questions and/or emphasizes information the reader needs or expects to find.

redundancies Words that repeat the same idea unnecessarily such as a large giant.

revising Making written changes and/or improvements to a draft copy of a document.

sans serif typeface Font having no extenders on the ends of the letters.

serif typeface Font with tiny extenders on the ends of the letters.

superfluous words Unnecessary words in a sentence.

technical jargon Terms that allow experts within a discipline to speak and write to one another in a technical shorthand; not necessarily understood by non-experts.

typography Visual features of the text.

white space Areas in documents that do not contain text, numbers, figures, tables, graphs, and/or images.

writer-based prose Writing that focuses on the writer's thinking processes and needs rather than on the reader's questions or needs.

CHAPTER 9
BUSINESS LETTERS & MEMOS

attention line In the address block, drawing attention to a specific person or position.

block letter style Format for a business letter in which all lines, with the exception of the letterhead, begin at the left margin.

business letter A formal document typically sent to external communication partners.

business memo Informal document used to exchange information among people within an organization.

complimentary closing The letter's closing (e.g., Sincerely).

direct strategy Letter-writing style used for positive or neutral news in which the main idea is presented at the beginning of the letter.

indirect strategy Letter-writing style used for negative news in which the main idea is presented after the reasons building to the bad news have been presented.

informal/colorful style Language characterized by personal, conversational tone; active voice; strong verbs; colorful adjectives and adverbs; parallel structure; short sentences; everyday, concrete, and precise words.

modern business style Language characterized by confident, conversational, courteous, and sincere tone; active voice; strong verbs; parallel structure; short sentences; everyday, concrete, and precise words.

modified block style Format for a business letter in which the date, complimentary closing, written signature, and keyboarded name start at the horizontal center point and the first line of each paragraph is indented one-half inch.

passive/impersonal style Language characterized by official, bureaucratic tone; passive voice; excessive nominalization; convoluted sentence structure; superfluous, outdated, and redundant language; business and legal jargon; and abstract words.

persuasive strategy Letter-writing style used for persuasive letters in which the request is made after the reason(s) have been presented.

salutation The letter's greeting (e.g., Dear _____).

subject line Brief statement that specifies the letter's subject.

CHAPTER 10
BUSINESS REPORTS

analytical report A document identifying an issue or problem, presenting the relevant information, and interpreting that information.

business report A business document containing information designed to assist others in making an informed decision.

completion report Report proposing a solution to a problem based on report recommendations.

conclusions Logical inferences based on key report findings.

EndNote Bibliographic management system software.

executive summary A section of a document providing a summary of a report's essential facts and recommendations. Also known as a *synopsis*.

financial reports Reports addressing financial matters.

formal reports Informational or analytical reports employing formal language.

GoAnimate Software that enables a creator to develop short, animated videos and visual aids.

informal reports Short, informational reports employing conversational language.

informational report A document presenting facts, observations, and/or experiences only.

key findings What the report's data reveal.

letter of transmittal Brief letter that transmits a report to its reader(s) by stating who requested the report, when it was requested, the key findings, and words of appreciation for being asked to develop the report.

long reports Reports of 10 or more pages.

Microsoft Publisher Desktop publishing software that supports page layout and design.

mindmaps (e.g., Mindomo) Diagramming software for organizing projects visually.

non-periodic report Special-project report developed as needed.

OneNote Electronic three-ring binder software with tabs for data organization and storage.

periodic report Routine report.

persuasive reports A document intended to move the reader(s) to a desired action.

Prezi Cloud-based presentation software program for exploring and sharing ideas on a virtual canvas.

proposal Type of business report in which an offer from a seller to a prospective buyer is made.

Qualtrics Powerful software for designing, developing, and administering surveys and questionnaires.

recommendations Confident statements of proposed actions based on a report's conclusions.

RefWorks Web-based references management software package.

report preview Brief text laying out the topics presented in the report body in the same order that they appear in the report, followed by a discussion of why each topic is included.

report summary Section of a report containing the key findings, conclusions, and recommendations.

sales report Report addressing sales figures and trends.

short reports Reports of 1–9 pages; typically presenting routine matters.

statement of problem Text that identifies a report's specific concern(s).

statement of purpose Text that identifies a report's main objective.

talking caption headings Headings that identify the specific topic of discussion in a report; headings are typically longer than topic caption headings.

topic caption headings Headings that identify the topic of discussion in a report; typically 1–4 words long.

Wordle Visually appealing word clouds.

CHAPTER 11

DEVELOPING BUSINESS PRESENTATIONS

Apache Open Office Impress A presentation program analogous to Microsoft PowerPoint and Apple Keynote. Can export presentations to Adobe Flash (SWF) files, allowing them to be played on any computer with a Flash player installed. Impress lacks ready-made presentation designs but this can be overcome by downloading free templates online.

bar charts Graphs that show numerical comparisons.

Corel Presentations Presentation software similar to Microsoft PowerPoint.

document cameras They magnify images of two-and three-dimensional objects, documents, photographs, etc.

guidance reminders Reminders that speakers include in their presentation notes.

KISS Principle Keep It Short and Simple, which reminds speakers to design and develop visual aids that are short and simple.

line charts Graphs that show trends.

NCast system Technology for recording a presentation that can then be downloaded.

pie charts Graphs that show comparisons of parts of a whole.

PowerPoint A popular presentation software package.

presentation anxiety A tense, emotional state resulting from one's attitude and feelings about speaking in front of a group. Also known as *glossophobia*.

the hook pertains to the words you speak and visuals you display at the very beginning of your presentation that are intended to capture your audience's attention.

Toastmasters Well-respected organization that helps members improve their speaking abilities.

CHAPTER 12

DELIVERING BUSINESS PRESENTATIONS

first impression An audience's initial reaction to a speaker; may occur prior to the start of the presentation.

junk words Words and phrases such as *ok*, *like*, and *you know* that serve no purpose; speakers often include them while searching for their next words or switching to their next topic or point. Same as *verbal fillers*.

Murphy's Law If something can go wrong, it will; thus, speakers should plan accordingly.

podcast An audio file, usually in MP3 format, that can be delivered to a computer through an RSS feed, like the text entry of a blog.

pointers Devices that allow speakers to point to portions of visual aids to focus audience attention.

Q&A session Discussion following a business presentation in which the audience asks questions of speakers, and speakers respond to audience questions.

verbal fillers Sounds, words, and phrases that serve no purpose; speakers often include them while searching for their next words or switching to their next topic or point. Same as *junk words*.

webcast Audio or video broadcast over the Internet, either downloaded or streamed live.

CHAPTER 13

LISTENING

accepting Interpreting the meaning of a message as the speaker intended it to be interpreted.

active listener Someone who gives the speaker his or her undivided attention; listens for content, emotions, and nonverbal cues; and hears his or her speaker out before evaluating the soundness of a message.

casual listener Someone who listens for pleasure, recreation, amusement, or relaxation.

critical listener Someone who focuses on both understanding and evaluating (analyzing) a message.

focusing Limiting one's attention to the stimuli.

hearing The reception of sound through sensory channels.

interpreting Decoding and assigning meaning to what is heard.

listening The accurate perception of a message being communicated through a combination of words, emotions, and nonverbal cues.

marginal listener A superficial listener who hears sounds and words, but rarely absorbs their meaning and intent.

message content listener Someone who focuses his or her energies on listening mainly for message content.

non-listener Someone who makes no attempt to listen; can often be recognized by his or her blank stare and/or nervous mannerisms.

process-style listener A detail-oriented listener who likes to discuss issues in detail and often interrupts speakers to do so.

results-style listener Someone who is interested in hearing the bottom line or result of a message.

storing Placing all or part of a speaker's message in our mind (our memory).

selective listening Occurs when a person hears what he or she wants to hear.

CHAPTER 14

COMMUNICATING IN BUSINESS TEAMS

affinity groups Groups composed of individuals who meet regularly to exchange information, ideas, opinions, and experiences on a variety of issues in a safe and supportive atmosphere, resulting in personal and professional growth.

boards of directors or boards of trustees Top-level organizational groups in corporations.

cohesiveness The degree to which members are committed to a team and its goals.

conflict A condition of opposition and discord.

formal teams Teams created by management to accomplish certain organizational goals.

Google Drive Software that allows writing teams to create and edit documents online while collaborating in real time.

groupthink The tendency of highly cohesive groups and teams to value consensus at the price of decision-making quality.

independent collaboration Independent writers who each draft an entire report independently and simultaneously; then they compare the versions.

maintenance roles Those actions and behaviors that express the social and emotional needs of team members.

norms Behaviors to which team members are expected to adhere.

parallel collaboration Dividing the writing task into subtasks, so that all participants write their part of the document at the same time and send their drafts to each group member for comments.

problem-solving teams Teams that focus on specific issues in their areas of responsibility, develop potential solutions, and often are empowered to take action within defined limits.

quality circles or quality control circles Small teams of employees who strive to solve quality- and productivity-related problems.

reciprocal collaboration Collaborative writers working together to create a common document, using online collaboration tools or software that allows several collaborators to simultaneously modify a central document from their own computers.

sequential collaboration Dividing the writing task among the participants so that the output from one writer is passed to the next writer who writes a new draft incorporating his or her changes, who then passes it to the next writer who writes a new draft again, incorporating feedback from all the group members.

SharePoint An online site that aids writing teams with content and document management.

single writer strategy The best writer on the team writes the entire document.

skunkworks Teams formed to develop products or solve complex problems.

task forces or cross-functional teams Teams comprising individuals from different departments and work areas who are brought together to identify and solve mutual problems.

task roles Those actions and behaviors related to productivity and concerned with accomplishing the team's task.

team A small number of people with complementary competencies (abilities, skills, knowledge) who are committed to common performance goals and working relationships for which they hold themselves mutually accountable.

transnational teams Work groups composed of multinational members whose activities span multiple countries.

virtual teams Team members in different locations who collaborate through information technologies.

virtual writing teams Writing groups that complete all or portions of their work virtually using support tools ranging from wikis and SharePoint to Google Drive and blogs.

wikis A website that allows participating users to add, remove, and edit the content of a document quickly and easily.

work units or functional teams Teams composed of members who work together daily on a cluster of ongoing and interdependent tasks.

writing teams Two or more people who work together to produce a written document.

CHAPTER 15
COMMUNICATING IN BUSINESS MEETINGS

business meeting A gathering during which a purposeful exchange or transaction occurs among two or more people with a common interest, purpose, or problem.

conference calls Phone conversations involving three or more people.

electronic meeting systems Software that provides meeting participants with a way to communicate simultaneously and sometimes anonymously via computers during face-to-face meetings, videoconferences, and web conferences.

GoToMeeting Remote meeting software that enables the user to meet with other computer users, customers, clients, or colleagues via the Internet in real time.

meeting agenda A document that serves to guide a meeting.

Skype Software that allows users to communicate with others by voice, video, and instant messaging over the Internet.

telepresence systems (holoconferences) Videoconferences in which screen images are replaced with three-dimensional images of participants who are not physically present.

videoconferences Virtual meetings between two or more participants in two or more geographical locations during which they hear each other and view each other on screens or monitors.

videoconferencing A videoconference involving two or more participants in two or more geographical locations viewing each other on screens or monitors.

web conferences Meetings conducted over the Web.

CHAPTER 16
JOB SEARCH: PRE-INTERVIEW STEPS

chronological résumé A type of résumé in which the focus is on work and experience.

cover letter A letter paired with a résumé for the purpose of convincing a recruiter to grant you a job interview.

cross-functional information Information about areas outside of your major areas of training and experience that have some relationship to the job for which you are applying.

functional résumé A type of résumé that emphasizes functional experience, focusing on transferable skills and accomplishments.

good fit Implies that you know what you want to do for a livelihood, you are right for it, and it is right for you.

job search process The seven steps you are encouraged to take when seeking professional employment.

key words A list of 10–20 words or phrases that focus on skills, accomplishments, and qualities especially relevant to a potential employer that you should include in a scannable résumé.

merchandising qualities Those qualities that make you an "exceptional fit" for a job or an organization.

reader-centered tone Refers to developing a tone in a letter that gives the reader the impression that he or she is "center stage."

résumé An individual marketing tool, whether paired with a cover letter or not, that's purpose is to convince a recruiter to grant you a job interview.

scannable résumé A résumé that can be scanned into a résumé database clearly, accurately, and completely.

CHAPTER 17

JOB SEARCH: INTERVIEWS & BEYOND

behavioral questions Recruiters' questions designed to use a candidate's past performances and behaviors in similar situations as predictors of a candidate's future performance and behavior.

closed-ended questions Recruiter questions that result, by design, in short, limited responses.

closing phase The phase of the interview when the recruiter clarifies outstanding issues and entertains unanswered questions.

computer interviews Typically screening interviews that involve candidates sitting at a computer keying in responses to a set of questions.

group interviews One recruiter or a panel of recruiters in one session interviewing two or more job candidates simultaneously.

illegal questions Questions that interviewers are legally prohibited from asking unless the questions fit the guidelines of bona fide occupational qualifications.

on-campus interviews Relatively short screening interviews held on college campuses.

one-on-one interviews An interview of a job candidate by an individual recruiter.

online interviews Computer interviews conducted over the Internet.

on-site interviews Selection interviews held at employers' work sites.

open-ended questions Recruiter questions that require more than short, limited responses.

opening phase The brief phase of the interview during which a good recruiter relaxes the candidate and shares the structure of the interview.

panel interviews An individual candidate interviewed by two or more recruiters. Also known as team or board interviews.

question-and-answer phase The phase of the interview during which recruiters ask questions and may invite the candidate to ask some questions.

screening interviews Short interviews during which the recruiter's goal is to weed out unacceptable job applicants.

selection interviews Longer interviews where the goal is to select a job candidate for hiring consideration.

stress interviews Interviews in which recruiters attempt to determine how well job candidates handle pressure.

structured interviews Interviews in which recruiters ask predetermined questions, a practice that provides consistency when interviewing two or more candidates for the same position.

success stories Examples of past successful experiences.

phone interviews One-on-one, panel, or group interviews conducted over the telephone.

thank-you note A brief, handwritten note from the candidate to the recruiter following a job interview.

unstructured interviews Interviews in which recruiters have no set agenda for questions.

unusual (odd) questions Recruiter questions that appear to have no relationship to the position for which the candidate is interviewing.

video online interviews Online interviews with a video component.

videoconferencing interviews Screening interviews typically conducted using videoconferencing.

videotaped interviews Interviews in which recruiters typically send advance guidelines and questions to a candidate who responds in a professional studio setting and then sends the video to prospective employers.

INDEX

C

Camtasia Studio, 368
Capital letters, 269
Career choice, making, 545–49
Career management, 635–40
    suggestions for, 637–38
    ten worst work habits, 636
    tips for success, 639
Casual listener, 463
Cell phones, 127–29, 460
Chronemics, 6, 91
Chronological résumé, 574–76
Clarity, 19
Clichés, 85, 279
Client, 7
Clustering, 227
Cohesiveness, 484, 485
Collaborative writing, pros and cons, 505–6
Comfort zone, 92
Communication effectiveness
    impact of
        location, 10–11
        timing, 11
        writing tool, 13
    obstacles and challenges, 10
Communication in organizations
    affect on
        customers and clients, 8
        economies, 8–9
        employees, 8
        investors and suppliers, 8
        organizations, 7
        societies, 9
    assertive style for, 13, 14
    audience analysis, 11
    with businesspeople from other
        cultures, 16
    categories of, 6
    choice of best medium for, 13
    diagonal, 26–27
    downward, 23–24
    effective. *See* Communication
        effectiveness
    evaluation of
        effective communication, 19
        efficient communication, 20
    formal, 23
    horizontal, 25–26
    informal, 21–22
    networks, 23
    quality of, 7–9
    upward, 24–25
Communication medium, 135
Communication purpose worksheet, 227
Communication skills, 10
    intercultural, 16
    team, 15
Communications protocols, 118
Communication technologies
    circumstances for avoiding use of, 113
    developments in, 16
        keeping up with, 17, 111–14
        past, 114–18
    fax machine, 115
    health and safety threats, 139–40
    Internet, 117, 118–24
    job security and career threats, 139
    keeping up with, 111–14
    personal computer, 117
    predictions, 143–48
    printing press, 115
    telegraph, 115
    telephone, 116
    typewriter, 116
    wireless. *See* Wireless communication
        technology
Communicators
    assertive, 14
    congenial, 11–12
    ethical, 12
    ethical responsibilities of, 13
Company letterhead, 300
Company's culture, basic rules
    addressing others, 40
    dealing with difficult bosses, 47–48
    interacting with
        peers, 40–43
        subordinates, 43–44
        supervisor, 45
    relationship with the boss, 45–46
    to work, 43
Complex sentence, 278
Compound sentence, 278

K

L

M